NORBERT SZÁMVÉBER

LAST PANZER BATTLES IN HUNGARY

SPRING 1945

© PeKo Publishing Kft.

PUBLISHED BY
PeKo Publishing Kft.
8360 Keszthely, Bessenyei György utca 37., Hungary
Email: infp@pekobooks.com
www.pekobooks.com

AUTHOR
Norbert Számvéber

TRANSLATION
Blanka Gálné Bíró

EDITOR
Tom Cockle

PHOTOS
Central Archives of the Ministry of Defence of the Russian Federation

FIRST PUBLISHED
2020

Printed in Hungary

Gyomai Kner Nyomda Zrt.
www.gyomaikner.hu

ISBN 978-615-6602-27-5

All Rights Reserved!
No parts of this publication may be reproduced, or transmitted in any form or by any means, electronic or mechanical, including photocopying, recording or by any information storage and retrieval system, without permission from the Publisher in writing.

TABLE OF CONTENTS

FOREWORD 6

CHAPTER 1 9

    BEFORE THE NEW GERMAN ATTACK

CHAPTER 2 37

    OPERATION "FRÜHLINGSERWACHEN", 6 – 15 MARCH 1945

CHAPTER 3 147

    THE HUNGARIAN SECTION OF THE VIENNA OFFENSIVE

TABLES 393

PHOTOGRAPHS 425

MAPS AND ORGANISATIONAL CHARTS 437

FOREWORD

The Author's work, Páncélosok a Tiszántúlon has been published almost one and a half decades ago, in 2002 for the first time; this work was mainly concerned with the history of the armoured battle on the Great Hungarian Plain region in October 1944. Even then, the Author's firmly set purpose was to dedicate detailed publications for the armoured fighting combat in Hungary during 1944 – 1945, separately for each major operation or for the geographical areas the battles were fought in. With the present work, the Author's intention has been realized. Although in the future the Author is planning to revise editions of previously published works, complemented by the newest results of research in the field, the Dear Reader is now able to follow the combat actions of armoured fighting vehicles deployed in Hungary from August 1944 to April 1945 (with the exception of the north-eastern corner of the country, which is still the Author's debt; however, considering the significance of the combat actions in the mentioned area, these would most probably rather take up an article in a military periodical than a separate monograph).

The Author's close friends might have heard a number of times that the Author would never research the Operation "Frühlingserwachen" that has taken place in March 1945. The reason for this was that according to the Author's supposition, this operation has been a mere mud-pie tracking resembling First World War infantry operations and only supported by armoured fighting vehicles in a heavily restrained manner, thus, it was not a full-scale armoured operation as such. The Author still partly retains this assumption, however he has decided on the detailed research and publication of the topic for two reasons. On one hand, during the operations, on various locations heavy tactical-level armoured fighting vehicle combat actions were carried out, and on the other hand, without the detailed knowledge of these combat actions it would not be possible to completely understand the armoured warfare of the Soviet offensive against Vienna in the second half of March 1945.

The heavy combat – in which, similarly to the entirety of the warfare in Hungary in general, the armoured fighting vehicles have played a decisive role – has rendered a large number of villages in the Transdanubia to piles of rubble, and the arable lands were riddled with the dangerous memories of warfare which required great deal of effort to be completely removed. Luckily, on a small scale, peaceful everyday life has also profited somewhat from these events: the first coin dies of the newly issued Forint in 1946 have been manufactured from the excellent quality steel shafts of the destroyed German armoured fighting vehicles.

As before, in the earlier publications, the Author did not aim to research and introduce the full and complete history of the operations, but to offer a detailed description of the deployed armoured fighting vehicles, based on the widest range of sources available.

The history of the combat actions in the Transdanubia during March 1945 is far from being an abandoned piece of history. During the 1970s and 1980s, the late historian

Csaba Veress D. was the first to take extreme efforts to uncover the details of the combat actions in the Transdanubia (A Dunántúl hadi krónikája, Budapest, 1984) and in the area around Lake Balaton (A balatoni csata, Veszprém, 1976). Unfortunately the reference literature and notes are not the most reliable; at certain parts they are simply inaccurate, thus the Author had to refrain from using these works as sources, even despite they possess a wealth of information. The historian in his two-volume book published in the early 2000s (Magyarország hadikrónikája vol. I-II., Budapest, 2003) also mentions the current topic, however, unfortunately the work has been published without a notes and references section, therefore it is not possible to consider it as a scientific literary work. On the other hand, the contemporary international and national scientific results are almost completely missing from these works; therefore they rather seem to be the publication of a research process completed years before.

International literature – with the exception of (on many occasions, slightly biased) Russian military history publications, which are continuously arriving from the beginning of the 2000s – either almost completely neglect this topic, or keep repeating incorrect, at times directly false statements. It can be regarded as an exception that in 2007, Krisztián Ungváry has, in German, published a detailed summary of the combat actions in the Transdanubia during March 1945 in volume 8 of the German series on the Second World War (Das Deutsche Reich und der Zweite Weltkrieg. Band 8. Munich, 2007, pp. 926-955.). However, he has not researched Russian archive sources, and the text in its content does not exceed his monograph published two years earlier (A magyar honvédség a második világháborúban, Budapest, 2005).

If many others have already researched and published works about the topic of the combat history of March 1945 in the Transdanubia, why should the Author do it all over again? On one hand, it is necessary because the previous works have not concentrated on the combat history of the armoured fighting vehicles, therefore these works necessarily could not be very detailed, and on the other hand, because the newly surfaced Russian sources from archives and scientific literature, as well as the newly published German memoires created a possibility for the most detailed research on the topic that was ever possible.

The Author has commenced his research in this field already at the end of the 1990s, although the Author assumed at that time that he was not going to publish research results. His efforts have been, from the beginnings, continuously supported by many, including Péter Barnaky, Gábor Horváth, Péter Kocsis, Péter dr. Lippai, András Palásthy, László Schmidt, István Tóth, Tibor Vikár and István Zicherman. There were also many who are sadly no longer with us (József dr. Borus, Lajos Keresztes and Nándor Szabó). In various ways, these people have all contributed invaluably to making this present work possible to be published. The Author is greatly indebted to all of them!

The Author's family has again stood with him in a wonderful and the most patient manner during his working on this publication. The Author is extremely thankful for their patience and for their keeping up of the "heartland".

January 2017, Budapest,
The Author

CHAPTER 1

BEFORE THE NEW GERMAN ATTACK

*Operational situation in the Transdanubian region
in the middle of February 1945*

On 15 February 1945 the battles ended in the Transdanubia that were part of the large-scale German-Hungarian "Konrad" Operations aimed at relieving the encircled Budapest, as well as those that were executed as Part of the Soviet counter attack initiated on 27 January 1945.

The 3rd Ukrainian Front was unable to restore the frontline of 1 January 1945 by the end of February. The German troops held the recaptured section of the *Margarethen-Stellung* between Székesfehérvár and Lake Balaton, which protruded into the Mezőföld like a "balcony". This Székesfehérvár "balcony" served later as the starting point for the last great German offensive of the Second World War, Operation *"Frühlingserwachen"*.

It should not be discounted that the units of the 3rd Ukrainian Front fighting in the Transdanubia had not been able to gain even a meter of ground toward the west in one and a half months, compared to the frontline secured at the end of December 1944. Although it did not possess considerable strategic importance, it is a fact nevertheless, that the series of counterattacks launched by the Germans in January 1945 had even slightly pushed the Soviet troops back toward the east.

In January 1945, the Soviets had prevented the relief of German and Hungarian defenders in the encircled Budapest, and, as the result of heavy fighting, they finally captured the Hungarian capital in the middle of February. This has to be seen rather as a major political, and not military success; since the 3rd Ukrainian Front had gained firm ground in the Transdanubia in December 1944, then took an active part in the encirclement of Budapest from the west, Budapest could not have had any strategic importance left for the Germans, except, of course, Hitler's unrealistic plans and orders.

The clash of the superior power of the Soviet tactical reserves and the strategic superiority of the German armoured units in the last phase of the combat operations around Budapest, resulted in a stalemate situation in the Transdanubia: in the course of the fighting in the Transdanubia during January – February 1945, the Germans had weakened the units of the 3rd Ukrainian Front to such an extent that they were, without considerable replenishment and rest, suitable only for defensive tasks. According to the author's opinion, this meant a short interval of respite in this late period of the war for the German side that were in strategic defence and who were trying to save as much time as possible. In this regard, the respite may be considered a minor preventive success. Furthermore, this had happened when the Soviet troops pushing in the direction of Berlin were only 65 km away from the capital of the *Third Reich* in their bridgeheads at the Oder.

In the meantime, in the most complete secrecy, the transport of the units of the *SS-Panzer-Divisions* of *6. Panzerarmee* from the western front to Hungary commenced; and with these units the Germans had a chance again to take the tactical initiative in the Transdanubia.

Assault plans of the German Heeresgruppe Süd

In February 1945 on the western Hungarian theatre of war, the German high command had been preparing a large-scale assault against the Soviet 3rd Ukrainian Front that occupied the area to the west of Budapest and the eastern regions of the Transdanubia. The main objective of this was to secure the raw material resources, predominantly mineral oil, bauxite and manganese, the food provisions and the staging area in the Austrian military industrial regions and the approaches to Vienna, and to counter any attempts of the Soviets to push further westwards. Apart from this, the German high command had also anticipated that due to this attack, the Soviets would initiate the transfer of major forces from the direction of Berlin.

Adolf Hitler certainly wanted to save time. He wished to achieve this within the framework of such a large-scale offensive that would see the German-Hungarian troops eliminate the large Soviet bridgehead secured on the western bank of the Danube, push forward between the area east of Lake Velence and the mouth of the Dráva River toward the line of the Danube, and occupy bridgeheads on the eastern bank of the river at Dunapentele, Dunaföldvár and Baja. The tactical plan, the first draft of which had already been issued on 28 January 1945 as Operation *"Süd"* (Operation South), finally was codenamed *"Frühlingserwachen"* (Spring Awakening).

During the repulse of the counterattack of the 3rd Ukrainian Front initiated on 27 January 1945, *Heeresgruppe Süd* had finalized the plans of Operation *"Süd"* (Operation South) on orders of the Chief of the General Staff of the *Heer* (*Chef des Generalstabes des Heeres*), *Generaloberst* Heinz Guderian.

The heart of this plan was that the German *6. Armee* would launch an attack toward the south from its positions south of Székesfehérvár, jointly with the units of *IV. SS-Panzerkorps* and *Korpsgruppe "Breith"* (*III. Panzerkorps* and the Hungarian II Army Corps). At the same time, *2. Panzerarmee* would initiate Operation *"Eisbrecher"* from the area of Nagybajom toward the east, joined by the attack of four infantry divisions of *Oberbefehlshaber Südost* (OB Southeast) in a north-north-east direction, following the crossing of the Dráva River. With these three converging attacks, the Germans hoped to eliminate the bridgehead of the 3rd Ukrainian Front that occupied the ground west of the Danube, between Lake Balaton and the Dráva River. At the same time, the attack plan included the occupation of the line between the Danube and the mouth of the Dráva River.

According to *Heeresgruppe Süd*, there were three conditions necessary for the successful implementation of the attack:

- After the Soviet forces pushing north from the direction of Dunaföldvár are destroyed, Operation *"Konrad 3"* is to be renewed and the Soviet forces between the Vértes Mountains and the Danube, west of Budapest will be entirely eliminated.
- North of the Danube, on the frontline of the German *8. Armee* the situation will be secured to ensure this section will not need considerable relocation of forces later.
- The armoured divisions of the *Heeresgruppe* are to be replenished both in terms of personnel and equipment, and two to three newer infantry divisions need to be directed there.

The *Stab* of *Heeresgruppe Süd* stated in their telegram to *Oberbefehlshaber Südost* that *"Operation Süd"* could only be launched after German troops have successfully broken through towards Budapest. Therefore, the date of the planned operation had not yet been determined by the end of January 1945.[1]

The frontline of the German *8. Armee* stretching north of the Danube was to be strengthened by carrying out an attack. This latter had become Operation *"Südwind"* ("Southern Wind"), in which *1. SS* and *12. SS-Panzer-Divisions/I. SS-Panzerkorps/6. Panzerarmee* would be deployed. This operation was successfully accomplished between 17 – 24 February 1945, as it had eliminated the Soviet bridgehead west of the Garam River and contributed to the strengthening of the positions of the German *8. Armee* that was covering in the Komárom–Pozsony–Vienna direction. Considering its consequences, it was also increasingly disadvantageous to the chances of the new German attack planned in the Transdanubia. *SS-Obersturmbannführer* Georg Maier, the First Staff Officer (Ia) of *6. Panzerarmee* in this period, deemed the launching of the Operation *"Südwind"* detrimental based on the following aspects:

- in favour of an event of local significance, part of the reserves intended for the large-scale attack have been deployed way before this was due, furthermore, these units needed to be relocated to the Transdanubia in a time-consuming series of unit movements that required considerable fuel supply;
- as many of the soldiers of *I. SS-Panzerkorps/6. Panzerarmee* had been captured during Operation *"Südwind"*, their interrogation by the Soviets revealed the undercover relocation of the *SS-Panzer-Divisions* to Hungary and therefore the opportunity of a strategic surprise was lost;
- because of the untimely deployment, the training and retraining process of the fresh soldiers of the *SS*-units was considerably delayed;
- the battle casualties and material losses suffered by *I. SS-Panzerkorps* between 17 – 24 February 1945 were only partially replenished by the time of the launch of the planned attack at the beginning of March.[2]

---

[1] HM HIM Hadtörténelmi Levéltár (Budapest) microfilm archives, Kriegstagebuch Ia der Heeresgruppe Süd, Kriegstagebuch vom 28. 1. 1945 (roll no. 628., image no. 7212559-7212568.).
[2] Maier, Georg: *Drama zwischen Budapest und Wien. Der Endkampf der 6. Panzerarmee 1945.* Osnabrück, 1985. pp. 160-164.

During Operation *"Südwind" Heeresgruppe Süd* had already started to develop the plans for the attack in the Transdanubia. At first, *Generalmajor* Heinz Gaedcke, Chief of Staff of both the German *6. Armee* and *Armeegruppe "Balck"* at the same time, devised a plan; this was *"Lösung C1"* (Solution C1), the heart of which was the following:

- in the first phase the two *SS-Panzerkorps* of *6. Panzerarmee* with four divisions are to attack west of the Sárvíz, and to reach the Dombóvár–Komló–Szekszárd sector via the Siófok–Enying–Káloz line; upon arrival, they establish contact with *2. Panzer-Division* attacking from the east;
- one day later in the second phase *III. Panzerkorps/Armeegruppe "Balck"* with three armoured and three infantry divisions are to attack east of the Sárvíz, between Aba and Seregélyes toward the east and northeast, in order to reach the Adony–Kisvelence line and seal off the area between Lake Velence and the Danube, this way covering their left flank in the face of the Soviet troops concentrated west of Budapest;
- in the third phase, two armoured divisions of *III. Panzerkorps* are to be deployed between the Sárvíz and the Danube towards the west in the direction of Szekszárd, to cover the left flank of *6. Panzerarmee*, then with the two infantry divisions drawn forward behind them, they are to occupy the west bank of the Danube and counter the Soviet attempts to cross the river from the east bank.

This version would employ *IV. SS-Panzerkorps* in defence to be able to intervene and repel the attacks of the Soviet troops concentrated west of Budapest. The only advantage of this plan was that according to German reconnaissance, the concentrated attack of *6. Panzerarmee* would be able to target a weaker Soviet defence west of the Sárvíz than east of there. Due to the multiple relocation and regrouping actions necessary, these manoeuvres were time-consuming and until the complete success of phase 3, the left flank of *6. Panzerarmee* would be continuously exposed to Soviet attacks along the Sárvíz.

Generalleutnant Helmuth von Grolman, *Generalstabschef* of *Heeresgruppe Süd*, had altered the above plan with the name *"Lösung C2"* in that the Germans would launch the main assault east of the Sárvíz and between the Danube with five armoured divisions, where the terrain was more favourable for armour. The advantage of this version would have been that the Germans could reach Dunaföldvár and Paks earlier, thus eliminating the danger of a Soviet counterattack coming from the east.

The *Stab* of *6. Panzerarmee* did not favour any of the versions, because they were rightfully aware of the possibility that the *SS-Panzer-Divisions* attacking southwards would be prone to be ambushed by a westward thrust of the Soviet forces concentrated west of Budapest and north of Lake Velence, thus cutting them off from the reserves and the retreat routes as well. The *Stab* of *6. Panzerarmee* did not deem plausible that *IV. SS-Panzerkorps* in itself would be able to ward off a larger scale Soviet attack. Therefore in the first phase of the attack, the aim was to eliminate this threatening Soviet grouping, so that the Germans could turn south afterwards.

Therefore, the *Generalstabschef* of *6. Panzerarmee*, *Generalmajor der Waffen-SS* Fritz Krämer, developed a plan, which was named *"Lösung A"*. According to this, two armoured groups would launch a pincer-type attack towards the northeast along Lake Velence, while north of Zsámbék an infantry group would thrust east-southeast, and these two forces would together eliminate the Soviet forces concentrated west of Budapest. After this, the units would be regrouped and, simultaneously with the attack of *2. Panzerarmee,* they would be launched southwards to eliminate the Soviet bridgehead in the vicinity of Pécs in the eastern part of the Transdanubia.

This version was not favoured by the *Stab* of *Heeresgruppe Süd*, as this would have taken too much time and by the time the first phase would have been accomplished, the worn out units would not have been able to carry out the thrust southwards.

During the planning phase, which was called characteristically a "paper battle"[3] by *SS-Obersturmbannführer* Maier, *Generaloberst* Guderian suggested to the *Heeresgruppe* that *I. Kavallerie-Korps* would be deployed in subordination to *2. Panzerarmee*.

Then *Generalleutnant* von Grolman devised another plan, which was named *"Lösung B"*. According to this, one of the groups of *Armeegruppe "Balck"* would attack south-southeast from the Bicske sector, while the other group of *6. Panzerarmee* would attack south of the lake towards the area between Lake Velence and the Danube. The task of the German groups would be, in the first phase, to eliminate the Soviet forces in the Lake Velence–eastern outskirts of Székesfehérvár–Bicske sector, and to establish a defensive line in the Ercsi–Baracska–Bicske area. This would have been the prerequisite for the second phase, that is, the concentrated attack to the south of the five German armoured divisions. According to this version, after the elimination of the Soviet forces concentrated west of Budapest, *IV. SS-Panzerkorps* would serve as a mobile reserve behind the line. The disadvantage of this proposition was that the main forces would only be able to launch a delayed attack together with the forces of *2. Panzerarmee* and *Oberbefehlshaber Südost* in the Danube–Dráva–Balaton triangle and probably would be weakened during the accomplishment of the first phase.

Generalmajor Krämer deemed this version to be much more preferable, and he also supplemented it with, that in the first phase, the four *SS-Panzer-Divisions* of *6. Panzerarmee* would need to attack eastwards, north and south of Lake Velence, and then the northern group would turn south between the eastern end of the lake and the Danube. However, as *Armeegruppe "Balck"* had already experienced the terrain north of the lake to be unfavourable for armoured fighting vehicles, *Heeresgruppe Süd* dismissed Krämer's suggestions.

The versions of the plan were handed in to the commander in chief (*Oberbefehlshaber*) of *Heeresgruppe Süd*, *General der Infanterie* Otto Wöhler. He also had the opinion that the elimination of the Soviet forces east of Lake Velence and west of Budapest would be an essential prerequisite for the successful offensive to the south, in which the main course of attack should be executed by *6. Panzerarmee*. Therefore he favoured *"Lösung B"*, the first phase of which would have started on 5 March 1945 and the second phase subsequently on 14 March.[4]

On 22 February 1945, *Heeresgruppe Süd* sent the four versions of the plan to *Generaloberst* Guderian, together with the accompanying maps. The following day, the *Heeresgruppe* communicated via telegram to the *Oberbefehlshaber Südost* (*Generalfeldmarschall* Maximilian

---

3   See Maier, Georg: *Drama zwischen Budapest und Wien. Der Endkampf der 6. Panzerarmee 1945.* Osnabrück, 1985. p. 165.
4   NARA, T311, R162, F7213779.

von Weichs), that the planned attack would be launched on 5 March 1945, on the condition that Operation *"Südwind"* along the Garam was finished by 24 February 1945. In case the German *Oberkommando des Heeres (OKH)* had ordered the execution of a version which would be initiated with the elimination of the Soviet forces west of Budapest, the joint attack towards the south would have been delayed a further 8 to 9 days.[5]

Hitler wanted to discuss the plan in person with *General der Infanterie* Wöhler and *Generalfeldmarschall* von Weichs; therefore they needed to present themselves in person at the headquarters of the Führer on 25 February 1945.[6] Apart from them, naturally *SS-Oberstgruppenführer* Sepp Dietrich, *Kommandeur* of *6. Panzerarmee* was also present.[7]

On 25 February 1945 during the usual evening briefing, Hitler finalized his decision: *Heeresgruppe Süd* was to execute plan *"Lösung C2"*, that is, the suggestion of *Armeegruppe "Balck"* amended by *Generalleutnant* Grolman.

At 2245 hours, the *Generalleutnant* had already received Hitler's order for the execution of the plan, the launch of which was still set for 5 March 1945. At 2350 hours, *Generalleutnant* Grolman informed *6. Panzerarmee*.[8] This version however, had not reckoned with the assault against the Soviet forces concentrated west of Budapest, therefore the Germans unknowingly acted in favour of the attack plan of the Soviets.[9]

According to the orders received, *Heeresgruppe Süd* had, by 28 February, developed the detailed plan of Operation *"Frühlingserwachen"* from *"Lösung C2"*.

According to the plan handed in to the *Operationsabteilung* of the *Generalstab* of the *Oberkommando des Heeres* on the same day, *6. Panzerarmee* would launch the main assault in the direction of Dunapentele, Dunaföldvár and Szekszárd in order to split the defence of the 3rd Ukrainian Front in half. The right flank of the *Panzerarmee* in the staging area between Lake Balaton and Lake Velence was secured by *I. Kavallerie-Korps* with *3.* and *4. Kavallerie-Divisions*.

In the middle, in order to effect the successful crossing of the Sió Canal in the area of Simontornya, *1. SS-* and *12. SS-Panzer-Division*s, in subordination to *I. SS-Panzerkorps*, launched an attack west of the Sárvíz Canal. The left flank was to be covered by *2 SS-* and *9. SS-Panzer-Divisions/II. SS-Panzerkorps*, and *44. Reichsgrenadier-Division/II. SS-Panzerkorps*. The forward thrust of these divisions was planned to face Dunapentele and Dunaföldvár, where the Germans were to occupy bridgeheads on the eastern bank of the Danube. Afterwards, *44. Reichsgrenadier-Division* was to build out defensive positions between Dunaföldvár and Rácalmás.

The *6. Panzerarmee* was reinforced with *Volks-Artillerie-Korps 403*, one pioneer battalion, one bridging battalion and four military bridging columns. According to the original plan, the Hungarian 25th Infantry Division was to be deployed by *6. Panzerarmee* along the western bank of the Danube, between Foktő and Dunaföldvár. If the initial attack was successful, the German *23. Panzer-Division* would have been deployed by *Heeresgruppe Süd* either behind *I. Kavallerie-Korps*, or to secure the left flank of *II. SS-Panzerkorps*.

---

5   NARA, T311, R162, F7213815.
6   Maier, Georg: *Drama zwischen Budapest und Wien. Der Endkampf der 6. Panzerarmee 1945*. Osnabrück, 1985. pp. 165-170.
7   NARA, T311, R162, F7213851.
8   NARA, T311, R162, F7213843.
9   Maier, Georg: *Drama zwischen Budapest und Wien. Der Endkampf der 6. Panzerarmee 1945*. Osnabrück, 1985. p. 171.

South of Lake Velence, *III. Panzerkorps/ 6. Armee* of *General der Panzertruppe* Balck, with *1.* and *3 Panzer*, as well as *356. Infanterie-Divisions* and *schwere Panzer-Abteilung 509* was to attack eastwards, in the direction of the Váli-víz, in order to cover the left flank of *6. Panzerarmee* between Lake Velence and the Danube, in the Iváncsa east–Aggszentpéter–Kápolnásnyék area. The other divisions of *Armeegruppe "Balck"*, including the forces of *IV.SS-Panzerkorps* – remained in defence between Lake Velence and the Danube. The armoured combat group of the *6.Panzer-Division* was standing behind the *IV. SS-Panzerkorps* in reserve, in direct subordination to *6. Armee.*

Between Lake Balaton and the Dráva River, *LXVIII. Armeekorps/2. Panzerarmee* commanded by *General der Artillerie* Maximilian de Angelis, with its *13. Waffen-Gebirgs-Division der SS, 71. Infanterie-Division, 1. Volks-Gebirgs-Division, 16. SS-Panzergrenadier-Division, Sturmgeschütz-Brigade 191, Sturmartillerie-Brigade 261, 1222. Panzerjäger-Kompanie* and two armoured trains, and *XXII. Gebirgskorps* with *118. Jäger-Division, Panzergrenadier-Brigade 92 (mot.)* and with one armoured train were preparing in the Nagybajom area from the Kutas–Nagyatád sector to execute Operation *"Eisbrecher"* (Ice-breaker), that is, to thrust towards Kaposvár and Szekszárd. The *2. Panzerarmee* was to cooperate with *LXXXXI. Armeekorps z.b.V.* of the German *Heeresgruppe "E"* under *Generaloberst* Alexander Löhr, in combat south of the Dráva River, within its ranks *Festungs-Brigade 967, 104. Jäger*, and *297. Infanterie-Divisions, Division "Fischer"* consisting of *SS-Polizei-Regiments 5* and *18*, and *11. Luftwaffe-Feld-Division* in order to destroy the Soviet-Bulgarian forces situated between Szaporca and Babócsa. *LXXXXI. Armeekorps z.b.V.* was to attack as part of Operation *"Waldteufel"* (Forest Devil) towards Mohács, after crossing the Dráva River in the area of Donji Miholjac (Alsó-Miholjác) and Valpovo (Valpó).[10]

Operation *"Frühlingserwachen"* was to be launched at 0400 hours on the morning of 6 March 1945, following a short artillery barrage.

The main task of *Luftflotte 4* of the German *Luftwaffe* was to cover the attacking forces, especially the units of *6. Panzerarmee* with fighter aircraft against the Soviet combat aircraft depending on the availability of fuel, and to provide fighter aircraft support against anti-tank locations and bridges Additionally, they were to carry out intensive air reconnaissance over the Soviet troops concentrated west of Budapest and on the frontline of the German *8. Armee*, in order to be able to expose the preparations for launching an attack as soon as possible.[11]

Heeresgruppe Süd was informed by *Generaloberst* Guderian on 26 February 1945, that in order to carry out Operation *"Frühlingserwachen"*, the daily allowance of 400 m³ Otto-fuel[12] would be increased to 500 m³, but the other German army groups would also be allocated portions of the Hungarian fuel production.[13]

The total number of German troops assigned to the task of carrying out Operation *"Frühlingserwachen"*, in absence of detailed documents in this regard, can only be estimated.

---

10   For the introduced plan, as well as the combat orders communicated to the troops, see NARA, T311, R162, F7213875-7213877, F7214343-7214344, F7214346-7214348, F7214350-7214353.
11   NARA, T311, R162, F7214360.
12   This amount of fuel was not sufficient even in February 1945, as the fuel usage of the *Heeresgruppe* exceeded this amount by 2000 m³ per month. See NARA, T311, R162, F7214337.
13   NARA, T311, R162, F7214337-7214338.

On the other hand the author agrees with the former first general staff officer of *6. Panzerarmee* in that the total number of personnel the German troops deployed in the Transdanubia within Operation *"Frühlingserwachen"* did not exceed 220,000 soldiers, not including the Hungarian 25th Infantry Division. Of this, approximately 125,000 men belonged to the three corps of *6. Panzerarmee*; 45,000 men in *III. Panzerkorps*, and 50,000 men in *2. Panzerarmee*.[14]

The strength of *Heeresgruppe Süd* on 25 February 1945, without the four *SS-Panzer-Divisions*/*6. Panzerarmee*, besides, the corps and army HQ units, was 387,903. Of this, the combat-strength was 114,886 soldiers.[15]

According to Soviet data, *Heeresgruppe Süd*, in order to execute the main attack of Operation *"Frühlingserwachen"* between Lake Balaton and Lake Velence, had concentrated 147,000 soldiers, 807 tanks and assault guns, and a further 3200 guns and mortars. The German *Luftflotte 4* had approximately 850 German and Hungarian aircraft.[16] According to German archive sources, the forces assigned to carry out the attack within *6. Panzerarmee* had 433 combat-ready armoured fighting vehicles, *III. Panzerkorps* had 153 and *2. Panzerarmee* had 70, for a total of 656 combat-ready armoured fighting vehicles.[17]

Defence plan of the 3rd Ukrainian Front

On 17 February 1945, four days after the complete occupation of Budapest, the Headquarters of the Main Command of the Armed Forces of the USSR (Stavka) ordered the commanders of the 2nd and 3rd Ukrainian Fronts in combat in Hungary to prepare for another offensive in the direction of Vienna, Bratislava (Pozsony) and Brno. The launch of the offensive was set for 15 March 1945. In the meantime however, during the German attack against the bridgehead on the Garam River, Soviet reconnaissance discovered the presence of two *SS-Panzer-Divisions* of the German *6. Panzerarmee*, and also noticed significant forces concentrated in the Transdanubia.[18]

By 20 February 1945, the Soviets clarified the possible objectives that might have been assigned to the German groups. On that day, the commander of the 3rd Ukrainian Front, Marshal Tolbukhin, ordered that the units of the Front are to contain and eliminate the attacking forces at the previously prepared defence lines; then, in order to be able to completely destroy the German shock group and to extend the scope of success in the direction of Vienna, the units of the Front are to launch an attack. The defences were to be built up until 3 March 1945.[19]

---

14   See Maier, Georg: *Drama zwischen Budapest und Wien. Der Endkampf der 6. Panzerarmee 1945*. Osnabrück, 1985. p. 203.
15   NARA, T311, R162, F7214404.
16   *A Nagy Honvédő Háború története, 1941–1945*. vol. 5., Budapest, 1967. p. 162.
17   The Appendix contains the detailed armoured fighting vehicle strength of *6. Panzerarmee, Armeegruppe "Balck"* and *2. Panzerarmee* on 5 March 1945. In the case of *III. Panzerkorps*, the combat strength of *6. Panzer-Division*, subordinated subsequently, was not included in the calculations.
18   Malakhov, M. M.: A Balatontól Bécsig (excerpt). In: *Fejezetek hazánk felszabadításának történetéből*. Budapest, 1960. p. 110.
19   Malakhov, M. M.: A Balatontól Bécsig (excerpt). In: *Fejezetek hazánk felszabadításának történetéből*. Budapest, 1960. p. 117.

with a howitzer, a light artillery, a mortar and an anti-tank artillery brigade, plus a mortar and a self-propelled artillery regiment.[24]

In the first echelon of the 135th Rifle Corps between Alsótarnóca and Enying, the defence was held by two rifle divisions on a 16 km wide front, and in the second echelon one rifle division was placed. The battle line of the divisions was based on two echelons, however the rifle regiments, because of their two battalion-based organization were only able to create one-echeloned battle lines.[25]

The 104th Rifle Corps was prepared for defence between Enying and Lake Balaton in a 8 km defensive line. In the first echelon, one rifle division was placed and two rifle divisions were positioned in the second echelon. The rifle division in defence in the first echelon created its own battle line in two echelons.

The 26th Army had been preparing three defensive belts since 11 February 1945. On the right flank of the army and in the middle, the main defensive belt consisted of two positions. The first position was divided into two and occasionally three combat trenches. The second position, which equally consisted of two combat trenches, was situated approximately 2.5 – 3 km behind the front line of the main defensive belt. The depth of this position was approximately 1.5 – 2 km. There were fortifications built up between the two positions, which could also be used as connecting trenches. On the left flank of the army, in the sector of the 104th Rifle Corps, the main defensive belt consisted of three, not completely built up positions. The first position consisted of two continuous and one non-continuous combat trenches. The second position, 2.5 km behind the front line of the main defensive belt, consisted of only one non-continuous combat trench. There was a distance of 1.5 – 2 km between the first and the second positions. The third position was built up at a distance of 6 – 6.5 km from the front line of the main defensive belt from a continuous and two non-continuous combat trenches.

The second defensive belt was 3-5 km deep and consisted of two interconnected combat trenches, approximately 8–12 km from the front line of the main defensive belt. The majority of the settlements in the area of the defensive belt were prepared for all around defence.

The third defensive belt was built up on the right flank and in the middle of the army, on the Kisvelence–Perkáta–Dunapentele line, 15 – 25 km deep behind the front line of the main defensive belt. On the left flank of the army, this defensive belt was built out at a distance of 6 – 8 km from the front line of the second defensive belt, in the sector of Siófok 3 km south of Ságvár–Magyarkeszi–Pincehely. The army defensive belt had a depth of 3 to 4 km, and consisted of one and occasionally two combat trenches and fortifications.[26]

The 35th Guards and 37th Rifle Corps/27th Army under Lieutenant-General S. G. Trofimenko, occupied the position of the army defensive belt behind the 26th Army between Lake Velence and Dunapentele. The 33rd Rifle Corps was concentrated on the eastern bank of the Danube, in the sector of Kiskunlacháza.

The reinforcement of the defences between Lake Velence and Lake Balaton was planned so that case it was necessary, the forces of the 27th Army could be drawn forward to the

---

24 Malakhov, M. M.: A Balatontól Bécsig (excerpt). In: *Fejezetek hazánk felszabadításának történetéből*. Budapest, 1960. pp. 118-119.
25 Malakhov, M. M.: A Balatontól Bécsig (excerpt). In: *Fejezetek hazánk felszabadításának történetéből*. Budapest, 1960. p. 119.
26 Malakhov, M. M.: A Balatontól Bécsig (excerpt). In: *Fejezetek hazánk felszabadításának történetéből*. Budapest, 1960. p. 125.

main defensive belt of the 26th Army. One anti-tank artillery brigade, three anti-tank artillery regiments and two howitzer artillery regiments were planned to be relocated from the Front's reserves with a total of 302 guns, and from the frontline sections not targeted, into the section of the 26th Army.[27]

The 57th Army under Lieutenant-General M. N. Sarokhin, was defending the Zamárdi–Balatonkeresztúr–Ötvöskónyi–Kadarkút section. The main forces of the army were concentrated on a 60 km front between Balatonkeresztúr and Ötvöskónyi.

This front was occupied by the 6th Guards and the 64th Rifle Corps. The southern shore of Lake Balaton was defended by the 252nd Special (Amphibious) Car Battalion, as well as the 3rd and 53rd Motorcycle Regiment, with five and six T–34/85 tanks respectively. The 32nd Guards Mechanized Brigade was in army reserve in the Osztopán sector. The 57th Army later also received the 104th Guards Rifle Division. The anti-tank region of the army was situated in the Kaposvár sector, and was created from an anti-tank artillery regiment. The 864th Self-Propelled Artillery Regiment was also positioned here, with the army's mobile obstacle detachment.

In the defensive sector of the 57th Army, a main defensive line, a second and an army defensive belt were built up. Each of these was sectioned in two to three positions, and those consisted of one to two combat trenches. The tactical depth of the defence of the army was 10 – 15 km.[28]

The artillery of the 57th Army employed the so called "Groza" artillery coordination system, in which the units had previously agreed on the target areas and targets, plus the objectives assigned to the units taking part. Based on this, the commanders of the rifle units were able to call for effective fire support using code words: in the important directions as many as 100 guns and mortars could release fire at the same time on the same frontline kilometre.[29]

Left of the Soviet 57th Army up to the Dráva River, between Ötvöskónyi and Barcs the 8th, 10th and 12th Infantry Divisions/3rd Corps of the Bulgarian 1st Army under Lieutenant-General V. Stoychev, were positioned. Along the Dráva River, from Barcs to Torjánc, the 3rd, 11th and 16th Infantry Divisions/4th Corps of the army were positioned, as well as the 1st Independent Tank Battalion equipped with 22 German manufactured Panzer IVs and three armoured reconnaissance cars, two anti-tank artillery battalions and one independent anti-aircraft artillery regiment. Although at that time the Bulgarian 1st Independent Tank Battalion was subordinated to the 4th Corps, the unit that was stationed at Nagypeterd, east of Szigetvár, could only be deployed upon confirmation of the army commander.[30]

In the reserve of the 3rd Ukrainian Front, the following troops were concentrated: in the Lovasberény sector the 23rd Tank Corps, north of Dunaföldvár the 1st Guards Mechanized Corps, plus, on the right flank of the 26th Army, in the second defensive belt, in the Szolgaegyház–Nagylak sector, the 18th Tank Corps. The 5th Guards Cavalry Corps

---

27   Malakhov, M. M.: A Balatontól Bécsig (excerpt). In: *Fejezetek hazánk felszabadításának történetéből*. Budapest, 1960. p. 123.
28   Malakhov, M. M.: A Balatontól Bécsig (excerpt). In: *Fejezetek hazánk felszabadításának történetéből*. Budapest, 1960. p. 126.
29   Malakhov, M. M.: A Balatontól Bécsig (excerpt). In: *Fejezetek hazánk felszabadításának történetéből*. Budapest, 1960. p. 128.
30   Matev, Kaloyan: *The Armoured Forces of the Bulgarian Army 1936–45*. Solihull, 2015. p. 294.

was concentrated between Sáregres and Pincehely, the 84th Rifle Division in the sector of Dunaföldvár, and the 208th Self-Propelled Artillery Brigade was stationed in the area north of Dunapentele within the defensive section of the front. A further six artillery brigades and three mortar regiments had also been stationed there.

The defence of the Soviet 3rd Ukrainian Front was prepared and built up basically according to the requirements of the tactical regulations of 1943 still in effect, however, supplemented with the lessons learnt from the armoured battle at Kursk. At the same time, the defence system at Lake Balaton was also different from that of Kursk, mainly due to the fact that far less time had been left for preparing the defences, there were less forces available and also the number of echelons installed in-depth were fewer, compared to Kursk.[31] The Soviet units had mainly built up a network of earthworks based combat trenches and firing positions for the infantry, the artillery, the tanks and the self-propelled guns, and minefields had also been laid. In contrast to the Kursk preparations, there were no barbed wire obstacles, anti-tank obstacles, small earth-wooden fortifications or other fortification elements built up at Lake Balaton. The staff commander of the 4th Guards Army for example, had suggested on 27 February that the 38 *"knocked out immobile enemy tanks should be used as immobile firing positions"* on the army's frontline but it is unknown how much of the preparation work had taken place by 10 March 1945.[32]

The staff of the Front learned the lessons from the significant Soviet losses of the armoured battles around Székesfehérvár during January – February 1945. Marshal Tolbukhin therefore ordered that the defensive battle for retaining the occupied positions should be fought without carrying out front and army level counterattacks and that tactical level counterattacks should also be carried out only in special cases.[33]

The two tank and one mechanized corps of the Front remained in direct subordination to the front commander, and these units could be used for reinforcing the defence of the 26th and 27th Armies, without the subordination of them to the latter.[34] With this solution, it could be avoided that the army commanders would deploy the otherwise poorly replenished tank and mechanized (larger military unit) forces on a tactical level to restore the original situation, at the same time exposing them to the negative consequences of meeting the German armoured fighting vehicles in battle.

The defence system was mainly prepared for repelling the mass offensive of armoured groups, therefore, mainly in tactical depth, significant fortification and obstacle works had been constructed. On each frontline kilometre approximately 700-750 anti-tank and 600-690 anti-personnel mines were laid, but in the direction of the main line of attack, in front of the front line of the 26th Army, there were 2700 anti-tank and 2900 anti-personnel mines laid.[35]

---

31   Malakhov, M. M.: A Balatontól Bécsig (excerpt). In: *Fejezetek hazánk felszabadításának történetéből*. Budapest, 1960. p. 124.
32   Isaev, Aleksei–Kolomiets, Maksim: *Tomb of the Panzerwaffe. The Defeat of the 6th SS Panzer Army in Hungary 1945*. Solihull, 2014. p. 120.
33   Malakhov, M. M.: A Balatontól Bécsig (excerpt). In: *Fejezetek hazánk felszabadításának történetéből*. Budapest, 1960. p. 117.
34   Malakhov, M. M.: Magyarország felszabadításának befejezése. In: *Magyarország felszabadítása*. Budapest, 1975. p. 297.
35   Malakhov, M. M.: A Balatontól Bécsig (excerpt). In: *Fejezetek hazánk felszabadításának történetéből*. Budapest, 1960. p. 126.

The anti-tank defence system was based on immobile anti-tank positions, fortifications and sectors, plus manoeuvring anti-tank artillery reserves and mobile obstacle detachments. Apart from the anti-tank guns, the field and anti-aircraft guns, the tanks and the self-propelled guns were also included in the anti-tank fire system. These latter engaged the German armoured fighting vehicles typically immobile, from ambush positions employing direct fire.

In the section of the 4th Guards Army, there were 32 anti-tank regions, and in the section of the 26th Army 34; in total 66 anti-tank regions had been prepared. Seventy percent of them were placed into the tactical depth of the defence. The first such regions were placed approximately 500-800 m from the frontline of the Soviet main line of defence and they were echeloned 30-35 km in depth of the defence.[36]

An anti-tank region usually consisted of 8 to 16 guns of an anti-tank artillery battalion or artillery regiment, and 8 to 16 anti-tank rifles, which were reinforced at certain locations with armoured fighting vehicles, anti-aircraft guns, and engineering subunits equipped with mines. On rare occasions, in order to seal off the most important directions, the anti-tank region could also have been organized from the forces of an anti-tank artillery brigade (three regiments). The commander of the established region became the commander of the artillery unit or the larger military unit stationed in the region.[37]

The anti-tank artillery reserve of the 4th Guards Army consisted of three anti-tank artillery regiments with 48 guns, and the anti-tank artillery reserve of the 26th Army consisted of two anti-tank artillery regiments with 34 guns.[38]

The anti-tank positions of the rifle companies, each of 3 to 5 anti-tank guns, one to two tanks or self-propelled guns, an anti-tank rifle platoon and a mortar platoon, were grouped into twos or threes to form an anti-tank fortification at the battalions in defence in the main course of the attack. The rifle units were also organized as anti-tank groups too, and were equipped with anti-tank rifles, anti-tank hand grenades and mines.

On the frontline of the 4th Guards Army and the 26th Army, the average tactical density of the anti-tank artillery reached 18 guns per frontline kilometer.[39]

The Soviets prepared only one anti-tank region in the direction of Dinnyés–Kisvelence. There were two regions prepared in the Seregélyes–Adony direction, each consisting of 20 to 25 guns in the Seregélyes sector, and seven lesser regions in the depth of the defence. In the Székesfehérvár–Cece direction, behind the frontline, three anti-tank regions were built up, each consisting of 15 to 20 guns, and a further two were placed into the depths of the defence. The Soviets had extensively used the guns in ambush positions as deception; these opened fire only in close proximity, and they also employed dummy guns, which were used to mislead German target reconnaissance.[40]

On 6 March 1945, the 3rd Ukrainian Front had 185 artillery and mortar regiments, including the artillery regiments of the divisions. The strength of the army and front

---

[36] Isaev, Aleksei–Kolomiets, Maksim: *Tomb of the Panzerwaffe. The Defeat of the 6th SS Panzer Army in Hungary 1945*. Solihull, 2014. p. 130.
[37] Isaev, Aleksei–Kolomiets, Maksim: *Tomb of the Panzerwaffe. The Defeat of the 6th SS Panzer Army in Hungary 1945*. Solihull, 2014. p. 119.
[38] Malakhov, M. M.: A Balatontól Bécsig (excerpt). In: *Fejezetek hazánk felszabadításának történetéből*. Budapest, 1960. p. 131.
[39] Malakhov, M. M.: Magyarország felszabadításának befejezése. In: *Magyarország felszabadítása*. Budapest, 1975. p. 297.
[40] Isaev, Aleksei–Kolomiets, Maksim: *Tomb of the Panzerwaffe. The Defeat of the 6th SS Panzer Army in Hungary 1945*. Solihull, 2014. p. 130.

HQ artillery units were replenished to only 57-65 percent considering mortars, 57 and 76 mm guns.[41]

At the beginning of March 1945, despite considerable efforts of the supply units, the units of the 3rd Ukrainian Front suffered a serious lack of certain ammunition types. Among these were ammunition for the 57 mm anti-tank and the 122 mm field gun, and the 122 mm field howitzer. This may be explained by the fact that these types of ammunition had been used in large quantities during the siege of Budapest, and supply was not able to keep pace with the requirements.[42]

At the 3rd Ukrainian Front, from rifle regiments to army level, mobile obstacle detachments were placed in readiness, the size of which ranged from the engineering squad having 150 mines with one to two engineering battalions laying 3500-7000 mines:

- regiment mobile obstacle detachment (squad): with 50 anti-tank and 100 anti-infantry mines, 1 - 1.5 km from the frontline of defence with two horse-drawn vehicles;
- division mobile obstacle detachment (platoon): with 300 anti-tank and 200 anti-infantry mines, and 200 kg explosives, 3 – 5 km from the frontline of defence with one to two trucks;
- corps mobile obstacle detachment (company): with 500 anti-tank and 200 anti-infantry mines, and 500 kg explosives, 3 – 5 km from the frontline of defence with two to four trucks;
- army mobile obstacle detachment (one to two battalions): with 1500 – 3000 anti-tank and 2000 – 4000 anti-infantry mines, and 2000 – 3000 kg explosives with five trucks in the line of the command post of the commander of the army.[43]

Until 5 March 1945, 68 mobile obstacle detachments were formed within the ranks of the 3rd Ukrainian Front, with 73 vehicles, among them captured German armoured personnel carriers, 164 horse-drawn vehicles, 30,000 anti-tank mines and 9,000 anti-personnel mines, plus 8200 kg of explosives.[44]

At the end of February 1945, upon orders from the 3rd Ukrainian Front, committees had been monitoring the defence preparations and a number of deficiencies had been revealed. For example certain basic artillery units were not prepared for all around firing. At certain rifle division locations the anti-tank guns had been positioned in a line instead of echeloned battle orders. At a number of larger military units, cooperation between the rifle infantry and the artillery was insufficiently organized. The commanders of certain rifle units were not familiar with the code words with which they could request concentrated artillery fire support. In a number of rifle divisions, only two to three tanks had been assigned to serve as anti-tank artillery reserve, moreover, there were divisions that entirely lacked

---

41　Isaev, Aleksei–Kolomiets, Maksim: *Tomb of the Panzerwaffe. The Defeat of the 6th SS Panzer Army in Hungary 1945*. Solihull, 2014. p. 128. Detailed data regarding the armament of the artillery units of the 3rd Ukrainian Front as of 6 March 1945 are contained in Appendix.
42　Malakhov, M. M.: Magyarország felszabadításának befejezése. In: *Magyarország felszabadítása*. Budapest, 1975. p. 298.
43　Malakhov, M. M.: A Balatontól Bécsig (excerpt). In: *Fejezetek hazánk felszabadításának történetéből*. Budapest, 1960. p. 132.
44　Isaev, Aleksei–Kolomiets, Maksim: *Tomb of the Panzerwaffe. The Defeat of the 6th SS Panzer Army in Hungary 1945*. Solihull, 2014. p. 132.

such reserves. A general deficiency was that the units had not completed their defensive engineering works on time.[45]

During the organization between the land forces and the 17th Air Army, it was deemed sufficient that officers with radio equipment were assigned to the armies of the Front.

During this time, the Soviet 17th Air Army was carrying out continuous air reconnaissance and combat missions against the uncovered targets, mainly of tactical importance. There were no combat missions carried out against targets of considerable, operational importance, for example, the armoured groupings of the gathering German forces – because *"the Germans had masterfully disguised the concentration areas of their main strike groups"*.[46]

Despite this, on 3 March 1945 the Germans realized that Soviet air reconnaissance had discovered the German armoured concentration areas east of Veszprém and south of Székesfehérvár. Because of this, *Generalleutnant* Grolman had again pointed out the importance of strictly observing the camouflaging rules ordered for the armoured units.[47]

The German armoured units in the Transdanubia

During the fighting in January - February 1945 the armoured divisions of *Heeresgruppe Süd* had also become exhausted. Therefore, at the beginning of March 1945, the divisions would not have been able to carry out the planned offensive in the Transdanubia by themselves even despite the considerable amount of personnel replacements and the allocation of a large number of armoured fighting vehicles. Therefore, a regrouping of *6. Panzerarmee* was essential to be carried out.

The *6. Panzerarmee*, prior to being ordered to *Heeresgruppe Süd*, had received a 6000 replacements, upon direct orders from Hitler. Of this, 3000 men were reassigned from the *Kriegsmarine*, and another 3000 from the *Luftwaffe* and the *Reichs Arbeitsdienst* into the *Waffen-SS*. Of these, 4600 men were assigned to the combat forces, but 1400 men were still waiting for retraining and assignment on 24 March 1945. During March, the German *6. Panzerarmee* received a further four battalions, with 2000-3000 men, including the 1400 men not assigned earlier. According to data from 24 March 1945, a further 2190 police personnel had also been assigned to the German *6. Panzerarmee*, with whom the younger soldiers serving in the supply units of the *SS-Panzer-Divisions* were to be replaced so that the latter could be deployed in the frontline.[48]

The *6. Panzerarmee* with the four *SS-Panzer-Divisions* and the other corps and army HQ units consisted of 81,400 men in Hungary as of 1 March 1945; however, the number of battle casualties and the sick in the past 8 weeks, plus the missing in action of the past 4 weeks were not included the above number, that is, for example some of the casualties of the battle at the Garam.[49]

---

45 Malakhov, M. M.: A Balatontól Bécsig (excerpt). In: *Fejezetek hazánk felszabadításának történetéből*. Budapest, 1960. p. 136.
46 Malakhov, M. M.: A Balatontól Bécsig (excerpt). In: *Fejezetek hazánk felszabadításának történetéből*. Budapest, 1960. p. 130.
47 NARA, T311, R162, F7214363.
48 NARA, T311, R163, F7215058.
49 NARA, T311, R163, F7214948.

On 21 February, *6. Panzerarmee* requested that *Heeresgruppe Süd* allocate 200 m³ fuel for them, which was necessary to carry out the most essential training elements of the recently arrived soldiers such as rifle practice, basic training for vehicle drivers and practice.⁵⁰ This was also a sign that the *SS-Panzer-Divisions* did not have such a high combat value that might have been expected from the values in the strength reports.

It is especially characteristic how Georg Jestadt, a soldier serving in *SS-Panzer-Nachrichten-Abteilung 12*, who had previously served in *1. (Panther) Kompanie/SS-Panzer-Regiment 12*, and met up with his former comrades in Dég, after the launch of the attack, recalled:

"In the centre of Dég, I was walking past a Panther-platoon when I noticed some of my former comrades among them. We had been together in Normandy and later in the Ardennes with a radio operator and a gunner who, in the meantime, was promoted to the rank of Rottenführer and became a tank commander. They told me that the strength of the original Panther-Abteilung was significantly reduced, the old comrades were either wounded, dead or missing, and the few who were sent back from the hospitals, were not assigned any tanks in the company.

'We have more crews than tanks!', the Rottenführer said. 'The surplus armoured soldiers are waiting for their deployment somewhere at the supply column, which most probably will not happen anyway, and they will land in the end at an infantry company so that the Grenadiers can be replenished from their ranks',, they both told me. So I did not have any hopes to get back to the armoured regiment.

'Where are you now?', they asked me. 'In the Nachrichten-Abteilung' (signal battalion) I said.'Okay, Kamerad, stay where you are! With us you would not have any chance to be assigned to the tank crew. See? We are here with the remaining nine combat-ready tanks and this would be the Abteilung? This is hardly half a company! If the Panzerjägers[51] *and the few armoured personnel carrier-platoons were not with us, we would be the fifth column and not an armoured regiment of a division!'*

The two comrades who were decorated with Iron Cross IInd Class and Silver Panzer Badge were venting all their disappointment.

'The first three tanks were earlier in the 1ˢᵗ company, the next four in the 2ⁿᵈ company; the last two tanks belonged in the past to the former 4ᵗʰ company. This is a rag-tag group! On top of all this, we only receive half of the ammunition allocation, and the fuel tanks were only filled up to half of their capacity. And with all this, we should be the core of an armoured division, the strongest Abteilung in the armoured regiment, on whom they can count? They are talking gibberish!' I've heard enough."[52]

During assembly after the march of *6 Panzerarmee*, on 4 March 1945 in the Pér sector, two German armoured fighting vehicles collided and a German soldier was crushed to death.[53]

---

50 NARA, T311, R162, F7213758.
51 The *schwere Panzerjäger-Abteilung 560* of the *Heer* was subordinated to the *SS-Panzer-Regiment 12*, practically as a second *Panzer-Abteilung*.
52 Jestadt, Georg: *Ohne Siege und Hurra. Erlebnisse eines jungen Soldaten 1939–1945*. Norderstedt, 2005. p. 396.
53 Written statement of priest József Vincze based on the Historia Domus of Pér. Published in the monthly magazine Lapozgató, of Mezőörs.

A special unit was to be set up within the *SS-Jagdverbände* in *6. Panzerarmee*[54], equipped with approximately 20 captured Soviet T–34/85s, IS–2s and M4A2 tanks, which would have been used for deployment behind the Soviet frontline in reconnaissance and ambush. However the unit lacked the essential, trained tank crews and for a long time did not have the tanks either.[55] At the beginning of March 1945, in the units of the German *Heer* in combat in Hungary, for example, in *1. Panzer-Division*, volunteers were to be recruited who spoke Russian or Baltic languages to fill the gunner, loader and radio operator positions, but with very little luck. In the end, due to the lack of volunteers the unit was unable to be organized.[56]

On 1 March 1945, *1. SS-Panzer-Division*[57] moved from the southern sector of Érsekújvár to the Veszprém–Zirc sector. The unit had 18,871 men at that time. The wheeled vehicles were driven along the Komárom–Győr–Románd–Zirc–Veszprém road. The tracked vehicles were transported by train, but this was delayed due to the shortage of special train carriages designed for armoured fighting vehicles. When the frozen ground began to thaw, the terrain became virtually inaccessible everywhere apart from the built up roads.[58]

During the night of 4/5 March 1945, the combat groups of *1. SS-Panzer-Division* occupied their attack positions southeast of Polgárdi. According to records, on 3 March 1945 the *LSSAH* possessed four combat-ready Tiger B[59], 26 Panthers, 14 Panzer IV, 15 *Jagdpanzers* and assault guns, plus 21 7.5 cm heavy anti-tank guns. The infantry consisted of three battalions with a combat strength of more than 400 men, one battalion with more than 300 men and three battalions with more than 200 men[60]. This totalled at least 2100 *Panzergrenadiers* in seven battalions. The artillery consisted of four light and three heavy batteries, plus two medium and one heavy multiple rocket launcher batteries. The combat strength of *1. SS-Panzer-Division* was at 72%, and it was deemed to be suitable for limited scope attacks.[61]

The full strength of *12. SS-Panzer-Division*[62] on 1 March 1945, was 17,423 men.[63] On 3 March, 1945, the combat-ready armoured strength of *12. SS-Panzer-Division* consisted of nine Panther, 12 Panzer IV tanks, and 13 Panzer IV/70 *Jagdpanzers*. Of the vehicles in *schwere Panzerjäger-Abteilung 560*, six *Jagdpanthers* and eight Panzer IV/70 *Jagdpanzers* were

---

54 The special units of the *Waffen-SS* had been reorganized during October-November in 1944. According to certain sources, *3. Kompanie* of the *Jagdverband "Mitte"* (battalion-sized special unit) was intended to be a T–34 tank company. In December 1944 *SS-Obersturmführer* Walter Girg was intended to be appointed as the unit's commander. The plan was named *"Plattensee"* as the *Kompanie* was intended to be sent to Hungary. At that time, a similar unit was already in combat in Hungary, namely the so-called "Jaguar" armoured detachment, which was however not part of the *Waffen-SS*.
55 Berger, Hagen: *In Hitlers Auftrag hinter den feindlichen Linien.* Walter Girg. H. n. 2014. pp. 136-141.
56 Stoves, Rolf: Persönliches Kriegstagebuch Pz.Rgt. 1 (typewritten manuscript, copy owned by the author), entries on 1 and 2 March, 1945. This is only true for the action *"Plattensee"*. In February 1945 at last, the *Waffen-SS* has deployed a special unit containing a few T-34 tanks in West Prussia. See Berger, Hagen: *In Hitlers Auftrag hinter den feindlichen Linien.* Walter Girg. H. n. 2014. p. 149.
57 The Table of Organization and Equipment (TOE) for the *1.SS-Panzer-Division* as of 1 March 1945 is contained in the Appendix.
58 Tiemann, Ralf: *Die Leibstandarte.* Band IV/2. Osnabrück, 1987. p. 258.
59 Schneider, Wolfgang: *Tiger im Kampf.* Band II. Uelzen, 2001. p. 279.
60 The infantry combat strength (*Kampfstärke*) means the number of soldiers who are deployed to fight infantry combat in the first lines and the crew of those heavy armament which support the infantry soldiers directly from the frontline.
61 Tieke, Wilhelm: *Von Plattensee bis Österreich. Heeresgruppe Süd 1945.* Gummersbach, without year of publication, p. 17.
62 The Table of Organization and Equipment (TOE) for the *12.SS-Panzer-Division* as of 1 March 1945 is contained in the Appendix.
63 Maier, Georg: *Drama zwischen Budapest und Wien. Der Endkampf der 6. Panzerarmee 1945.* Osnabrück, 1985. p. 558.

in combat-ready condition. The *SS-Panzergrenadiers* had a combat strength of approximately 1700 men in one strong, one medium strength and five average battalions. The artillery of the *Division* consisted of six light and one heavy batteries, and four multiple rocket launcher batteries. The combat strength of the *Division* was at 50%, and it was deemed to be suitable for limited scope attacks as well.[64]

The assigned section of attack for the *Division* lay south of Kisláng in an east-west direction. There were no paved roads in the sector, which considerably increased the difficulties of movement. The *12. SS-Panzer-Division*, positioned on the left flank of *I. SS-Panzerkorps*, together with the other division, was to establish a bridgehead on the Sió Canal as the first step and, in order to achieve this, the following attack plan was prepared:

- *SS-Panzergrenadier-Regiment 25*, reinforced with *1. Kompanie/SS-Panzer-Pionier-Bataillon 12*, breaches the Soviet positions at Ecsipuszta, and as a short-term objective occupies Feketepuszta 5 km southeast of there;
- *SS-Panzergrenadier-Regiment 26,* without its *III. Bataillon*, reinforced with *2. Kompanie/ SS-Panzer-Pionier-Bataillon 12*, breaches the Soviet frontline south of Kisláng and as the next objective, occupies Ödönpuszta 3 km southeast of there;
- the armoured combat group with the tanks of *Panzer-Regiment 12*, the *Jagdpanzers* of *schwere Panzerjäger-Abteilung 560* and with the armoured personnel carriers of *III. / SS-Panzergrenadier-Regiment 26*[65] stands in readiness north of Ecsipuszta, so that after the *Panzergrenadiers* breach the Soviet positions, they can thrust forward in depth to reach the Sió Canal;
- *SS-Artillerie-Regiment 12*, *SS-Werfer-Abteilung 12* and the 8.8 cm guns of *SS-Panzer-Flak-Abteilung 12* will, following a short artillery barrage, support the combat of the *Panzergrenadier-Regiments*;
- the *Jagdpanzers* of *SS-Panzerjäger-Abteilung 12* are to follow the *Panzergrenadiers* and overwhelm the Soviet tanks, anti-tank guns and defensive fortifications;
- The *3. Kompanie/SS-Panzer-Pionier-Bataillon 12* prepares to support the crossing of the Sió Canal, and *4. Kompanie* is to remain in reserve to be deployed against armoured fighting vehicles and air targets;
- *SS-Panzer-Aufklärungs-Abteilung 12* stands in readiness for the *Divisionskommandeur*;
- *SS-Panzer-Nachrichten-Abteilung 12* is to build up the radio and wired signalling system (however there had been a radio silence ordered until the launch of the planned attack).[66]

Most likely the forces of *1. SS-Panzer-Division* were planned to be deployed in similar groupings and with similar objectives assigned, only the sectors were different.

The *2. SS-Panzer-Division*[67], in subordination to *II. SS-Panzerkorps,* was transported to Hungary between 8 and 13 February 1945. Its units were still to be replenished and

---

64   Meyer, Hubert: *Kriegsgeschichte der 12. SS-Panzerdivision „Hitlerjugend".* Band II. Osnabrück, 1987. 2nd edition, p. 494.
65   The *schwere* (heavy-weapons) *Kompanie* of *III. (Bataillon)/SS-Panzergrenadier-Regiment 26* had five 7.5 cm anti-tank guns as well that were already mounted on an armoured personnel carrier. These should not be mistaken for the armoured personnel carriers equipped with 7.5 cm L/24 tank guns.
66   Meyer, Hubert: *Kriegsgeschichte der 12. SS-Panzerdivision „Hitlerjugend".* Band II. Osnabrück, 1987. 2nd edition, pp. 495-496.
67   The Table of Organization and Equipment (TOE) for the *2. SS-Panzer-Division* as of 1 March 1945 is contained in the Appendix.

mostly possessed untrained reserves.[68] In order to maintain security, *2. SS-Panzer-Division* also received a codename: "*Ausbildungsgruppe Nord*" ("Training Group North"). Similarly to other units of *6. Panzerarmee,* the codenames were distributed up to *Bataillon*-level; these codenames included the commander's surname as well (*SS-Obersturmbannführer* Otto Weidinger's *SS-Panzergrenadier-Regiment 4* was codenamed "*Otto Nord*"). Because of the camouflaged movements, the soldiers were only be able to train in squads, and had to remove all tactical *SS*-vehicle markings and Ärmelstreifen (armbands).

The *Division* was notified that approximately four weeks would be available for completing training and replenishment. This was not considered to be a long time, as the units were all worn out following the battles in the Ardennes, and it also took considerable time to acquire the equipment, which was arriving with significant lags between shipments.[69]

On 29 January 1945, the command of the *Division* was taken over by *Generalleutnant der Waffen-SS, SS-Gruppenführer* Werner Ostendorff. The new commander had a hard time finding the *Divisionsstab* amongst the different codenames.[70]

On 2 March 1945, the *Division* was placed in combat readiness, although there were still two weeks of training ahead of them. Because of this, *I. (Bataillon)/SS-Panzergrenadier-Regiment 4* and *II. (Bataillon)/SS-Panzergrenadier-Regiment 3* had to be left behind, as the training of these had not been completed, and their vehicle strength was also not in combat-ready condition yet. Therefore the *Division* commenced the new attack with only two-thirds of its *Panzergrenadier* strength.[71]

In the morning of 3 March 1945, the units of *2. SS-Panzer-Division* commenced their march from the area of Csorna west on the route of Győr–Románd–Várpalota to occupy their assigned attack positions. The freshly fallen snow combined with thawing at the same time, resulted in the roads being in deplorable condition. The units, who were constantly battling with mud however, reached the area of Várpalota and Románd by the evening.[72]

The *Division* had a strength of 19,542 men, according to records as of 3 March 1945, six combat-ready Panthers, 24 Panzer IV tanks, 23 StuG. III assault guns, nine Jagdpanthers and 16 Panzer IV/70 *Jagdpanzers*, plus 23 7.5 cm anti-tank guns. Its infantry consisted of five strong *Panzergrenadier-Bataillons* and a medium strength field reserve battalion. One of its battalions was still not present due to replenishment. The combat strength of the *Panzergrenadiers* was minimal at around 2300 men. The artillery of the *Division*, together with the subordinated reinforcements consisted of 16 light and seven heavy howitzer batteries and one gun battery. The combat strength of the unit was only at 40%, however, despite this they were deemed to be suitable for limited scope attacks.[73]

---

[68] Weidinger, Otto: *Division Das Reich. Der Weg der 2. SS-Panzer-Division „Das Reich"*. Band V: 1943-1945. Osnabrück, without year of publication, pp. 434-435.

[69] Weidinger, Otto: *Division Das Reich. Der Weg der 2. SS-Panzer-Division „Das Reich"*. Band V: 1943-1945. Osnabrück, without year of publication, pp. 435-436.

[70] Weidinger, Otto: *Division Das Reich. Der Weg der 2. SS-Panzer-Division „Das Reich"*. Band V: 1943-1945. Osnabrück, without year of publication, p. 437.

[71] Weidinger, Otto: *Division Das Reich. Der Weg der 2. SS-Panzer-Division „Das Reich"*. Band V: 1943-1945. Osnabrück, without year of publication, p. 438.

[72] Weidinger, Otto: *Division Das Reich. Der Weg der 2. SS-Panzer-Division „Das Reich"*. Band V: 1943-1945. Osnabrück, without year of publication, p. 439.

[73] Tieke, Wilhelm: *Von Plattensee bis Österreich. Heeresgruppe Süd 1945*. Gummersbach, without year of publication, p. 18.

On 4 March 1945, it had become evident for the command of the *Division* that due to the muddy and overcrowded roads the units would not be able to occupy their points of departure before the appointed time.

The next day, on 5 March 1945 at 0300 hours *2. SS-Panzer-Division* continued its march to arrive at Bolondváritanya near Aba via Csetény and Székesfehérvár. As they had to leave their vehicles far behind the frontline because of "camouflage reasons", the troops marched nearly 20 km in full gear until they reached their area of departure.

According to the plans, during the attack of the following day, *SS-Panzergrenadier-Regiment 3* would lead the *Division* to break through the Soviet lines with an infantry attack, and afterwards make preparations for the possibility of launching the armoured combat group into combat. This latter consisted of *SS-Sturmbannführer* Dieter Kesten's *II. (Abteilung)/SS-Panzer-Regiment 2*, the armoured personnel carriers of *SS-Sturmbannführer* Heinz Werner's *III. (gepanzert) (Bataillon)/SS-Panzergrenadier-Regiment 4* and

II. (Bataillon)/SS-Panzergrenadier-Regiment 4. The armoured combat group was ordered to continue pushing the attack and to commence the pursuit of the Soviets as soon as the breakthrough was achieved.[74]

However, the chances for success were not high. A significant number of units had still not occupied their assigned positions. For example, the units of *SS-Panzergrenadier-Regiment 3* were still approximately 10 km from where they should have been, and they were marching on foot, which significantly exhausted the troops. As the units of *SS-Panzergrenadier-Regiment 4* had even farther to march, it seemed impossible for the *Panzergrenadiers* of the *Division* to prepare for the attack in time.[75]

The first transports of *9. SS-Panzer-Division*[76] set off for Hungary on 9 February 1945. The trains were travelling on the Regensburg–Passau–Linz–St. Pölten–Vienna–Wiener Neustadt–Sopron route, and arrived at Győr on 12 February 1945 where they unloaded. The *Stab/SS-Panzer-Regiment 9* and its Panthers unloaded in Komárom, and *II. (Abteilung)/SS-Panzer-Regiment 9* in Győr. *SS-Panzer-Aufklärungs-Abteilung 9* for example, only arrived at Ács on 1 March 1945 and marched forward to Győr.[77]

Units of *SS-Panzer-Artillerie-Regiment 9* (at least two batteries) remained in Győr, and were waiting for their guns and prime movers there. These batteries were not in combat together with the *Division* but were attached to *2. SS-Panzer-Division* later during the withdrawal.[78]

The *Panzer-Division,* arriving as a unit of *II. SS-Panzerkorps/6. Panzerarmee* was codenamed "*SS-Ausbildungsgruppe Süd*" ("Southern Training Group").[79]

---

74 Weidinger, Otto: *Division Das Reich. Der Weg der 2. SS-Panzer-Division „Das Reich".* Band V: 1943-1945. Osnabrück, without year of publication, p. 440.
75 Weidinger, Otto: *Division Das Reich. Der Weg der 2. SS-Panzer-Division „Das Reich".* Band V: 1943-1945. Osnabrück, without year of publication, p. 441.
76 The Table of Organization and Equipment (TOE) for the *9. SS-Panzer-Division* as of 1 March 1945 is contained in the Appendix.
77 Fürbringer, Herbert: *9. SS-Panzer-Division.* Heimdal, without year of publication, [1984] pp. 507-508.
78 Tieke, Wilhelm: *Im Feuersturm letzter Kriegsjahre. II. SS-Panzerkorps mit 9. und 10. SS-Division „Hohenstaufen" und „Frundsberg".* Osnabrück, without year of publication, [1975] p. 492.
79 Fürbringer, Herbert: *9. SS-Panzer-Division.* Heimdal, without year of publication, [1984] p. 506.

On 3 March 1945, the *Division* had a strength of 17,229 men and the combat-ready armoured strength was 24 Panther and 19 Panzer IV tanks, 16 StuG. III assault guns, 17 Panzer IV/70 and 10 Jagdpanther *Jagdpanzers*, plus four Flak-Panzer IV anti-aircraft armoured fighting vehicles. The combat strength of the *Panzergrenadiers* was approximately 2200 men in three strong, two medium strength and two average battalions. The 15 usable combat-ready 7.5 cm anti-tank guns of the *Division* were still at *SS-Panzer-Feldersatz-Bataillon 9*, because the necessary prime movers were missing. *SS-Panzer-Artillerie-Regiment 9* had only three light and two heavy combat-ready batteries. The combat strength of the heavy armament of the *Panzer-Division*, suitable for attack in a limited capacity, was 80 percent, while other units were at 60 percent.[80]

On 4 March 1945, the units of *9. SS-Panzer-Division* (without the armoured units) were marched from the area of Kisbér and Mór towards the planned attack positions at Falubattyán.[81] The mud-clogged and overcrowded roads considerably hindered the march forward of the SS-units, because the same route was also being used by *44. Reichsgrenadier-Division* subordinated to *II. SS-Panzerkorps* coming from the direction of Komárom, plus *3. and 4. Kavallerie-Divisions/I. Kavallerie-Korps* as well.[82]

On 5 March 1945 around 1300 hours, *9. SS-Panzer-Division* was given orders to launch an attack toward the southeast on the next day, at 0400 hours, under *II. SS-Panzerkorps*. According to their orders, the units of the armoured corps were to establish bridgeheads at first on the Danube at Dunapentele and Dunaföldvár, and afterwards were to turn south and thrust forward between the river and the Nádor Canal to Tolna. However, the units of the *Division* at the time of receiving the orders were at least a day's march from their attack positions. The *Kommandeurs* of *2. SS-* and *9. SS-Panzer-Divisions*, and the *Stab* of *II. SS-Panzerkorps* requested a postponement for the launch of the attack by one day, but permission for this was denied.[83]

The real combat force of the four *SS-Panzer-Divisions* of *6. Panzerarmee* was considerably beyond that of the divisions sent into combat in the Ardennes in December 1944, not to mention the SS-units fighting in Normandy during the summer of 1944. Prior to their deployment in Hungary, neither of these four divisions were fully replenished with tanks, therefore all four of them employed also *Jagdpanzers*, assault guns or heavy tanks of a formerly independent *Panzer-Abteilung* in order to have at least two combat-ready *Panzer-Abteilung*. In the author's opinion however, the most significant deficiency of the armoured SS units, was the insufficient general and specialized training of the personnel transferred from the *Kriegsmarine* and the *Luftwaffe* and their lack of combat experience. Although the SS-divisions were able to count on the combat skills of their ever-decreasing number of veterans, the number of veterans was constantly diminishing compared to the fresh soldiers.

---

80   Fürbringer, Herbert: *9. SS-Panzer-Division*. Heimdal, without year of publication, [1984] p. 508.
81   Tieke, Wilhelm: *Im Feuersturm letzter Kriegsjahre. II. SS-Panzerkorps mit 9. und 10. SS-Division „Hohenstaufen" und „Frundsberg"*. Osnabrück, without year of publication, [1975] p. 493.
82   Fürbringer, Herbert: *9. SS-Panzer-Division*. Heimdal, without year of publication, [1984] p. 508.
83   Tieke, Wilhelm: *Im Feuersturm letzter Kriegsjahre. II. SS-Panzerkorps mit 9. und 10. SS-Division „Hohenstaufen" und „Frundsberg"*. Osnabrück, without year of publication, [1975] pp. 495-496.

The German *3.* and *4. Kavallerie-Divisions/I. Kavallerie-Korps* had, besides their two *Reiter-Regiments* respectively, one *schwere Kavallerie-Abteilung* and a *Panzerjäger-Abteilung* each, in which they were able to deploy light tanks, assault guns, assault howitzers, *Jagdpanzers*, armoured personnel carriers, plus self-propelled and towed anti-aircraft guns.[84]

Between the period from the end of the battle for Budapest in the middle of February 1945 and the launch of Operation *"Frühlingserwachen"*, *1., 3., 6.* and *23. Panzer-Divisions*, plus the *3. SS-* and *5. SS-Panzer-Divisions* of *Armeegruppe "Balck"*, had been allocated a few troop replacements, but no new armoured fighting vehicles were issued. The replenishment however would have been highly due for these divisions, because by the evening of 27 January 1945, altogether 344 Panzer IV and StuG. III, 56 Jagdpanzer IV, 206 Panthers, 53 Tiger E or Tiger B, and 797 armoured personnel carriers were missing from their strength, based on the standard TOE. The *Heeresgruppe* asked for, as an immediate relief, 115 Panzer IV and assault guns, 20 Jagdpanzer IV *Jagdpanzers*, 70 Panthers, 18 Tigers and 200 armoured personnel carriers, but almost none of their requirements were met[85]

The *1. Panzer-Division* did not have either a *Flak-Abteilung* or a *Panzerjäger-Abteilung*, because the former was under reorganization in Bratislava, and the latter was still in Germany. The remaining Marder II and Marder III tank destroyers, equipped with 7.5 cm guns, were distributed between the *Divisionsbegleitkompanie, 9. Kompanie/Panzergrenadier-Regiment 1* and *4. Kompanie/Panzer-Aufklärungs-Abteilung 1*. The four Nashorn heavy tank destroyers (with 8.8 cm gun) were assigned to the *Stabsbatterie* of *I. (Abteilung)/Panzer-Artillerie-Regiment 73*. A few Panzer IV tanks from *Panzer-Regiment 1* were placed into *Panzer-Artillerie-Regiment 73.* as armoured artillery observation fighting vehicles.[86]

At the beginning of March 1945, the German *2. Panzerarmee* did not possess any armoured divisions. The units in its command were equipped only with assault guns, assault howitzers and *Jagdpanzers* but no tanks.

At the beginning of March 1945, among the troops assigned to carry out Operation *"Frühlingserwachen"*, apart from *44. Reichsgrenadier-Division*, there were only second grade (suitable for attack in a limited capacity) and third grade (compatible for defence without limitations) divisions.[87] Thus the attack plan to be carried out significantly exceeded the capabilities of the units assigned for this task.

The German armoured divisions, regardless of being *Heer* or *Waffen-SS* units, were fighting along unified tactical and command principles, despite the fact that the *SS-Panzer-Divisions* had six *Panzergrenadier-Bataillons* instead of four.

The main combat force of the armoured division was the armoured combat group, which generally consisted an armoured regiment, the *Panzergrenadier- Bataillon* reinforced

---

84 The Tables of Organization and Equipment (TOEs) for the *3.* and *4. Kavallerie-Divisions* as of 1 March 1945 are contained in the Appendix. At the end of November 1944 the *General der Infanterie* assigned to the German *Chef des Generalstabes des Heeres* suggested that further such cavalry units should be created in Hungary from the personnel who attended the cavalry training of the *SA*, because their combat strength equalled to that of the *Panzergrenadier-Divisions*, but for one replenishment they have only required 40 m³ fuel.

85 HM HIM Hadtörténelmi Levéltár (Budapest) microfilm archives, Kriegstagebuch Ia der Heeresgruppe Süd, Kriegstagebuch vom 28. 1. 1945 (roll no. 628., image no. 7212559- 7212568.).

86 The Tables of Organization and Equipment (TOEs) for the armoured divisions of *Armeegruppe "Balck"* as of 1 March 1945 are contained in the Appendix. The TOEs of *3. SS-* and *5. SS-Panzer-Divisions* included there are from 1 January 1945, but in their cases, no significant organizational changes have been effected until 1 March 1945.

87 Maier, Georg: *Drama zwischen Budapest und Wien. Der Endkampf der 6. Panzerarmee 1945*. Osnabrück, 1985. p. 199.

with self-propelled infantry guns and equipped with armoured personnel carriers, plus, self-propelled howitzers of the self-propelled *Artillerie-Abteilung* of the armoured artillery regiment and the company of the armoured pioneer battalion equipped with armoured personnel carriers.

The two *Panzergrenadier-Regiments*, one of them without its subordinated armoured personnel carrier battalions, usually formed separate combat groups, reinforced with one towed *Artillerie-Abteilung*, one motorized armoured pioneer company and an assault gun or *Jagdpanzer-Kompanie* of the *Panzerjäger-Abteilung* respectively. The *Panzer-Aufklärungs-Abteilung*, apart from its tactical reconnaissance duties, carried out in small size armoured reconnaissance groups, usually belonged to the reserve of the *Divisionskommandeur*. The 8.8 cm anti-aircraft guns of the *Flak-Abteilungen* of the divisions were usually employed in carrying out field artillery tasks as well. The units had a large number of 2 cm and 3.7 cm towed or self-propelled anti-aircraft guns, which were also used effectively against live and lightly armoured targets as "super-heavy machine guns", besides fulfilling their role as anti-aircraft weapons. In the spring of 1945 in Hungary, the *Panzergrenadier-Kompanie* of *1. SS-Panzer-Division* were given, besides their usual armament, 10 to 14 MG151/15 15 mm heavy machine guns or MG151/20 20 mm automatic cannons which were mounted against ground targets.[88]

Among the German armoured divisions assigned to take part in Operation *"Frühlingserwachen"*, there were no two of the same organizational type. As their order of battle was different on many points than the authorized tables of organization and equipment, and simply lacked some units or sub-units, not all of the divisions were able to form all of the above mentioned types of armoured combat groups.

The *9. SS-Panzer-Division* is a striking example, which did not have either a *Panzergrenadier-Bataillon* equipped with armoured personnel carriers, or a *Panzerjäger-Abteilung*. To counter this, an armoured personnel carrier group was formed within *SS-Panzer-Regiment 9* with 20 armoured personnel carriers, which were fighting together with the tanks, assault guns and *Jagdpanzers*. Their 15 Panzer IV/70 *Jagdpanzers* were concentrated in *9. Kompanie* of the *Panzer-Regiment* instead of the *Panzerjäger-Abteilung* and *5.* and *6. Kompanie* also received 8 of these as well as the *Regimentsstab*. The Jagdpanther *Jagdpanzers* were assigned to *4. Kompanie/I. (Abteilung)/SS-Panzer-Regiment 9* equipped with Panther tanks.[89]

In the *Panzer-Regiments* of the *1. SS-* and *12. SS-Panzer-Divisions,* the second *Panzer-Abteilung* was supplemented by permanently subordinating units formerly fighting independently, and the remaining Panzer IV and Panther tanks were grouped together into a mixed *Panzer-Abteilung*.

In the *Panzerjäger-Abteilung* of *2. SS-Panzer-Division*, StuG. III assault guns were fighting instead of Panzer IV/70 *Jagdpanzers*, however, in *7. Kompanie/SS-Panzer-Regiment 2,* there were another 21 Panzer IV/70. The Jagdpanthers of the *Division* formed the *8 Kompanie* of the *Panzer-Regiment*.

The *23. Panzer-Division* also did not have a *Panzergrenadier-Bataillon* equipped with armoured personnel carriers, therefore in most cases the *Panzer-Aufklärungs-Abteilung*

---

88 See the Table of Organization and Equipment (TOE) for the *1. SS-Panzer-Division* as of 1 March 1945 in the Appendix!
89 See the Table of Organization and Equipment (TOE) for *9. SS-Panzer-Division* as of 1 March 1945 in the Appendix!

was assigned to the armoured combat group. The *3. Panzer-Division* had only three *Panzergrenadier-Bataillons* instead of four.

From the autumn of 1944 the German armoured divisions, based on their experiences gained on the Eastern Front, employed the following combat methods and tactics of improvised counterattacks and pre-planned counter strikes against the Soviet units:

> "1. Immediate counterattacks following an enemy incursion are always successful. The enemy does not have time to establish defence and draw its heavy weapons forward (building out Pakfronts[90] and artillery positions).
> 2. Local reserves (tanks, assault guns and armoured personnel carriers together with the infantry) behind the main frontline [91] are to be placed in such a manner that attacks could be launched in any direction at anytime.
> 3. Counterattacks are to be launched even in case the support provided by artillery or heavy weapons is not immediately available. Surprise counts for a lot!
> 4. Counterattacks at night with tanks, assault guns and mounted infantry are almost always successful, because the enemy is not prepared for attacks of this kind and their infantry is confused. The mounted infantry at the same time protects the tanks from the tank destroyer units.
> 5. Infantry shall not be mounted on tanks during the day but they have to fight on foot. Otherwise they are going to suffer heavy losses because all of the fire of the enemy weapons are going to be concentrated on the tanks.
> 6. Enough time is to be given for the troops to prepare for the planned counterattack, because they are fighting an enemy who had all the necessary time to build up its fully established defences, and it is not uncommon to see 30-40 anti-tank guns in one anti-tank region.
> 7. When launching a pre-planned counterattack, it is useful to break through enemy infantry lines with their own infantry and pioneers even before dawn. The mine obstacles and obstacles are to be cleared by these. This way the armoured fighting vehicles may advance.
>
> The most important task of the armoured fighting vehicles is to break into the depths of the enemy and reach the set assault objectives; but not the least the destruction of remaining anti-tank guns on the battlefield. This task is to be accomplished by the supporting infantry.
> 8. Surprise is everything in the case of such counterattacks (encryption of all preparations, careful radio usage, reconnaissance and observation, advance only by night, radio broadcast encryption!)."[92]

In the Second World War, the German combat philosophy was the so-called task-oriented command and control (in German, *Auftragstaktik*). The essence of this was that

---

90 Frontline of anti-tank guns, German terminology for the Soviet anti-tank region.
91 In German, *Hauptkampflinie* (in short, *HKL*). The contemporary Hungarian military language named this as main line of defence. In practice, this was built up from the fire systems of the different units, the resistance nests sectioned in depth and width, and the fortifications. The side towards the enemy was named the flange line. See: *Magyarország a második világháborúban. Lexikon A–Zs.* Chief editor: Péter Sipos. Editor: István Ravasz. Budapest, 1997. p. 117.
92 See Nehring, Walther K.: *Die Geschichte der deutschen Panzerwaffe 1916-1945*. Augsburg, 1995. Appendix p. 40.

the superior in discussion with the subordinates, only outlined the major elements of the task to be carried out for his subordinates (tactical or operational aim and due date for carrying out different tasks); the subordinates developed plans and then carried out the actual sub-tasks and tasks independently, considering and conforming to the ever-changing actual situation. The most important tool of this task-oriented command and control was the radio receiver, and an essential personal requirement was the perfectly trained and combat-hardened officer and non-commissioned officer staff.[93]

Tank- and mechanized forces of the 3rd Ukrainian Front

At the beginning of March 1945, the tank and mechanized forces of the 3rd Ukrainian Front had a significantly decreased in combat value as a result of the heavy fighting in January and February 1945. In January 1945, the Front suffered the total loss of 802 tanks and self-propelled guns, and 163 in February.[94]

Of the 398 operational armoured fighting vehicles of the Front on 6 March 1945, only 193 were tanks. Of the 205 operational self-propelled guns, 95 were of the lightly armoured SU–76M type.[95]

The SU–76M self-propelled gun was not very popular among the Soviet troops. Aleksandr V. Rogachev, who took part in combat in Hungary as the commander of a 45 mm anti-tank gun battery of the 9th Guards Mechanized Corps, had almost been assigned to a self-propelled artillery regiment equipped with them in 1943. He remembered as follows:

> *"We have seen with our own eyes the shocking performance of the SU–76 at Kursk. Its ZiS–2 gun was not effective at all, its armour was thin and it did not have armour on the top that could have defended the crew from mortar fire. They burnt out easily... So they were given the nickname "Gorky candles". With a 45 mm you can find shelter on the ground, but if a SU–76 was hit, then you did not have a chance to get out of it alive."*[96]

The Soviet troops fighting in the Transdanubia at the beginning of March 1945, almost exclusively used the T–34/85 version equipped with 85 mm guns. According to sources, only one unit was an exception to this, the 249th Independent Tank Regiment, which was completely equipped with T-34s equipped with 76 mm guns.[97] Apart from this, the 18th

---

[93] For detailed analysis of the German command and control during Operation *"Frühlingserwachen"*, see: Lieutenant Colonel Péter Lippai: *A küldetésorientált katonai vezetésszemlélet lehetőségei és korlátai one hadtörténelmi példán keresztül bemutatva ("Tavaszi ébredés, 1945 március 6-1945. március 15.).* Doctoral thesis. Zrínyi Miklós Nemzetvédelmi Egyetem. Budapest, 2009.

[94] Central Archives of the Russian Defence Ministry (Podolsk), f. 243, op. 2900, gy. 1979, li. 69. The Appendix contains a detailed description of units and armoured fighting vehicle types. The German units had 322 irrecoverable losses of armoured fighting vehicles in the Transdanubia between 1 January – 15 February 1945, that is, the Soviet troops suffered three times the number of armoured losses during the Operations *"Konrad"* than the Germans.

[95] Isaev, Aleksei–Kolomiets, Maksim: *Tomb of the Panzerwaffe. The Defeat of the 6th SS Panzer Army in Hungary 1945.* Solihull, 2014. p. 138. The Appendix contains the armoured fighting vehicle strength of the tank and mechanized units of the 3rd Ukrainian Front on the evening of 5 March 1945.

[96] Quoted in Drabkin, Artem: *Panzer Killers. Anti-tank Warfare on the Eastern Front.* Barnsley, 2013. p. 201. The armoured fighting vehicle was also called the not quite flattering name "suka" (bitch) by the Soviet soldiers.

[97] Isaev, Aleksei–Kolomiets, Maksim: *Tomb of the Panzerwaffe. The Defeat of the 6th SS Panzer Army in Hungary 1945.* Solihull, 2014. p. 137.

Tank Corps and the 1201st Self-Propelled Artillery Regiment most likely had the same armoured fighting vehicles, though in lesser numbers.[98]

In the middle of February 1945, the 3rd Ukrainian Front received the freshly created 208th Self-Propelled Artillery Brigade which consisted of three self-propelled artillery regiments, with 21 SU–100 self-propelled guns in each, a reconnaissance company, an anti-aircraft machine gun company and repair and supply units. Each of the self-propelled artillery regiments consisted of a staff battery with one SU–100, four batteries with five SU–100s in each, one submachine-gun company, one engineering platoon, besides repair and supply units. The Brigade was concentrated in the Iváncsa–Adony–Pusztaszabolcs area after 18 February 1945.

In order to ease the shortage of armoured fighting vehicles, the Soviets used captured German armoured fighting vehicles as well. On 1 March 1945, the Soviet 3rd Mobile Tank Repairing Workshop had finished repairing 20 German armoured fighting vehicles, which were probably captured in Budapest. The crews had to be supplied by the 22nd Tank Training Regiment. The crews had been retrained at Budafok to be able to handle these armoured fighting vehicles and also to be able to correctly use them in service.[99]

The tank and mechanized forces of the 3rd Ukrainian Front assigned to the defence, were ordered to open fire at the approaching German armoured fighting vehicles from their ambush positions: the tanks from a 600-800 meter distance, the medium and heavy SU–85, SU–100, ISU–122 and ISU–152 self-propelled guns from 1000-1300 meters, and the light SU–76 self-propelled guns from 200-500 meters.[100]

The general Soviet command and control theory was order-controlled. The superiors both in defence and in attack situations, provided mostly written orders to their subordinates which were previously planned in detail, considering the suggestions of the subordinates. These subordinates were not able to deviate in any measure from the written orders, not even if the situation changed in the meantime. In the case of the latter, a new order came from above after the circumstances were reported. This considerably slowed down and complicated the control of the units. The only exceptions to the above were the night, forest and close quarters combat situations, plus the combat actions of the advance troops, where individual thinking and the initiative abilities of the commanders provided more freedom.

On the upper (corps, army and front) levels of the Soviet command and control, the soldiers were mostly highly trained and exceptionally skilful by the year 1945. Many of them earned the respect and recognition of the German high command too. At the time, the Germans commended many Soviet subunit-commanders as well. The middle levels of the Soviet command staff, mainly the divisional, brigade, regimental and battalion commanders however, mostly performed poorly, because the inflexibility of order-based command and control methods bound their hands and they were almost more afraid of their own superiors or the possible negative consequences of their decisions than of the enemy weapons.

---

98 Unfortunately the Soviet archival and literary sources rarely distinguish between different T-34 versions. Therefore, apart from the above mentioned few units, the T-34 tank in the text mostly means the T–34/85 type.
99 Central Archives of the Russian Defence Ministry (Podolsk), f. 243, op. 2928, gy. 131, li. 215.
100 M. Svirin – O. Baronov – M. Kolomiets – D. Nedogonov: *Boj u ozera Balaton*. Moscow, 1999. p. 50.

The main tool of the Soviet command was the wired field signalling system, which was considerably vulnerable to artillery fire, and its establishment or preparation during an attack was very time consuming. Command via radio system was negatively affected by the fact that the system almost always lacked the necessary amount of reliably working radios, armoured command vehicles and motorcycles that could have been used for contact and communication purposes. At the same time, even at the end of the war, a large number of Soviet tanks and self-propelled guns had only radio receivers and as the transmitter was missing, the device was only able to facilitate one-way communication.

Armoured fighting vehicle actions in the Transdanubia between 16 February – 5 March 1945

On 16 February 1945, in the sector of the 25th Honvéd Infantry Division, the 3rd Battery of the Hungarian 20th Assault Artillery Battalion [101], equipped with Jagdpanzer 38(t) *Jagdpanzers*, carried out a limited attack from the sector of Lepsény southeast in the direction of the Sió Canal. The commander of the 3rd Battery, 1st Lieutenant Taszíló Kárpáthy, remembers as follows:

> *"[…] our attack surprised the Soviet troops in their positions[102], the anti-tank weapons started firing only when the [Hungarian] assault guns were already at the first line. Breaking through this, despite the armoured fighting vehicles joining the combat in the meantime, we approached the Sió within a 1 – 1.5 km distance[103]. In the meantime, the 4th battery was also firing its high-explosive shells, with an exceptionally good result. The result of our attack in numbers: three knocked-out tanks, four destroyed multiple rocket launchers, three anti-tank guns rendered unserviceable. […]*
> *I have to mention the tactics here that were different from the German method, where, in case of an attack, two platoons thrust forward in attack, and the third one provided fire coverage. In the first 1000-1500 meters, we have raced with full throttle in one single line, while our mounted machine guns and the guns – the latter with very little accuracy of course, with delayed high-explosive shells – were firing. Here, mainly the morale effect was important. This method has proven as effective later on as well… […]*
> *We carried out a similar attack on 26 February, with similar success. Learning from our attack on 16 February, their tanks launched their attack earlier, but practically, this was ineffective. On this occasion we knocked out three tanks, and a number of anti-tank guns.*

---

101 In the middle of February 1945 the Hungarian 16th Assault Artillery Battalion had been withdrawn from the frontline. Its complete Jagdpanzer 38(t) *Jagdpanzer* strength was reassigned to the Hungarian 20th Assault Artillery Battalion. Five *Jagdpanzers* that needed repairs were transported by train from Veszprém to Csorna where they were sent to a German repair workshop unit. See BAMA, RH 2 Ost 5385 and 5433, and HM HIM Hadtörténelmi Levéltár (Budapest), Rohamtüzér-gyűjtemény, 13/2. collection, *A debreceni 16. rohamtüzérosztály története*. p. 18.

102 In this sector, the Soviet 74th Rifle Division was in defence, to which the 1897th Self-Propelled Artillery Regiment was subordinated with SU–76M self-propelled guns, plus the 3rd Battalion/35th Guards Mortar Regiment with multiple rocket launchers. See Central Archives of the Russian Defence Ministry (Podolsk), f. 1027, op. 1, gy. 14, li. 15.

103 Knowing the contemporary frontline this is hardly possible, therefore this is most probably an error and should be interpreted as the assault pushed forward one – one and a half km towards the Sió-canal.

During our retreat, one of the assault guns was submerged so deeply in the loose mud on the roads that it was immobilized. We tried to pull it out with two other guns, but with no success. At last, after the darkness set in, with heavy fire coverage, we managed to yank out the submerged assault gun with two Hansa-Lloyd movers."[104]

At 2100 hours on 17 February 1945, the Soviet 151st Rifle Division had, without artillery preparation, supported by six T-34/85 tanks of the 39th Tank Brigade/23rd Tank Division[105], launched an attack with a force of two battalions to occupy Dinnyés and as a result had taken control of the village around 2300 hours. The units of *5. SS-Panzer-Division* were only able to stop and contain the attack on the eastern outskirts of the train station west of the town.[106]

On 19 February 1945, at 2000 hours the units of the 151st Rifle Division, with artillery support and three T-34/85 tanks of the 39th Tank Brigade occupied the train station at Dinnyés. The three Soviet tanks occupied a defence position on the western edge of the train station, and another three did the same on the western outskirts of Dinnyés.[107] German counterattacks aimed at reoccupying the important road junction failed.[108]

In the afternoon of 25 February 1945, the Soviet 5th Guards Airborne Division launched an attack south and west of Zámoly, with a regiment-size force, artillery support and a few armoured fighting vehicles[109], against the protruding frontline salient of the German *3. SS-Panzer-Division*. The attack however collapsed at the German frontline in the crossfire of German artillery and heavy infantry weapons.

On 26 February 1945, east of Székesfehérvár, a lucky shot of one of the 15 cm heavy infantry guns of *5. SS-Panzer-Division* knocked out a Soviet tank.[110] This was most likely one of the T–34/85 tanks of the 3rd Tank Brigade/23rd Tank Corps, which was defending in the Kisfalud sector together with three other armoured fighting vehicles since 15 February 1945, in subordination to the 69th Guards Rifle Division.[111]

The Soviets launched an attack between the shore of Lake Balaton and the Siófok–Lepsény road, as well as east of the road itself, with a brigade-size force in each direction, in the sector of the Hungarian 3rd Army. East of the road the Soviet troops managed to occupy Alsótekeres situated 3 km west of Balatonbozsok.[112]

On the night of 26/27 February 1945, the armoured personnel carriers of the armoured combat group of the German *3. Panzer-Division* reoccupied Alsótekeres, then during the daytime completely cleared the frontline section between Lake Balaton and Balatonbozsok of any Soviet forces.[113]

---

104 Tasziló Kárpáthy: *A magyar királyi honvéd 20. rohamtüzérosztály története.* In: HM HIM Hadtörténelmi Levéltár (Budapest), Rohamtüzér-gyűjtemény, 14/7. collection. pp. 15-16.
105 Central Archives of the Russian Defence Ministry (Podolsk), f. 243, op. 2900, gy. 1782, li. 61.
106 NARA, T311, R162, F7214046 and F7214049.
107 Central Archives of the Russian Defence Ministry (Podolsk), f. 243, op. 2900, gy. 1782, li. 63.
108 NARA, T311, R162, F7214061.
109 The armoured fighting vehicles were most probably the 5th Guards Airborne Division's own SU–76M self-propelled guns.
110 NARA, T311, R162, F7214097.
111 Central Archives of the Russian Defence Ministry (Podolsk), f. 243, op. 2900, gy. 1782, li. 58 and 68.
112 NARA, T311, R162, F7214096.
113 NARA, T311, R162, F7214100.

On 28 February 1945 *,Heeresgruppe Süd*, while planning the new attack, asked the *OKH* not to take *I. (Abteilung)/Panzer-Regiment 24* from their subordination as had been ordered. The unit at that time had 33 operational Panther tanks, which were very important considering the upcoming new German attack. According to the original orders, this unit would have been taken over by a German armoured division, however according to the assessment of the *Korpsstab,* this hastened reassignment would greatly hinder the combat value of the armoured fighting vehicles. At last, the *OKH* approved that the *Panzer-Abteilung* would remain in its position for the time being.[114]

On the same day, *Eisenbahn-Panzerzug 64* was stationed in Nagykanizsa subordinated to *LXVIII. Armeekorps*, *Eisenbahn-Panzerzug 78* in Balatonberény in subordination to the *118. Jäger-Division* and *Eisenbahn-Panzerzug 79* in Bélavár in subordination to *13. Waffen-Gebirgs-Division der SS "Handschar".*[115]

At the end of February 1945, the German *5. Kompanie/Panzer-Regiment 1/1. Panzer-Division* held a demonstration practice in the sector of Falubattyán for the *Divisionskommandeur* on the subject "attack of a reinforced tank company with mounted *Panzergrenadiers*". As soon as the Panther tanks left the hard surfaced roads, they travelled approximately 20 meters before they sunk on the muddy fields and were immobilized. A detailed report of the experienced results was prepared for the *Stab/ III. Panzerkorps.*[116]

---

114 NARA, T311, R162, F7213694 and F7213696.
115 NARA, T311, R162, F7214107.
116 Stoves, O. G. Rolf: *1. Panzer-Division 1935–1945. Chronik einer der drei Stamm-Division der deutschen Panzerwaffe.* Bad Nauheim, 1961. p. 744.

CHAPTER 2

OPERATION *"FRÜHLINGSERWACHEN"*, 6 – 15 MARCH 1945

6 March 1945, Tuesday

(**WEATHER:** highest daytime temperature 0 Celsius, low cloud base, occasional snowing, impaired visibility. The condition of the unpaved roads was significantly worsened due to the snow and the warm weather, and these were mostly turned into seas of mud.)

South of the Dráva River *297. Infanterie-Division/ LXXXXI. Armeekorps z.b.V. / Heeresgruppe "E"* occupied a bridgehead by surprise on the river in the sector of Donji Miholjac (Alsómiholjác) opposite the Bulgarian 11th and 3rd Infantry Divisions, whereas *11. Luftwaffe-Feld-Division* occupied a bridgehead at Valpovo, 22 km southeast of Donji Miholjac opposite the Yugoslavian 16th and 51st Partisan Divisions. According to their orders, the *Divisions* were to thrust forward from the bridgeheads approximately 15-20 km northwards and occupy the hills in that direction. Following the joining of the bridgeheads and drawing forward the swiftly moving cavalry forces and the Cossack cavalry, the task was to close off the crossing points at Kiskőszeg and Mohács behind the Soviet troops.[117]

Units of *297. Infanterie-Division* successfully established a sufficiently deep bridgehead with the occupation of Drávaszabolcs, however a fatal supply mistake had put all their efforts at risk. The pioneer-units assigned to carry out the crossing were supplied with completely unusable fuel for their motorboats, therefore they had to carry out the complete manoeuvre by sheer manual power. Due to this, the crossing of *104. Jäger-Division* with their heavy armament (among these, the armoured fighting vehicles) to the northern bank suffered major delays. The completion of the military bridge was further hindered by attacks from Soviet combat aircraft.[118]

There were only a limited number of armoured fighting vehicles subordinated to *LXXXXI. Armeekorps z.b.V.*: approximately nine Marder II tank destroyers of *Panzerjäger-*

---

[117] Hnilicka, Karl: *Das Ende auf dem Balkan 1944/45 – Die militärische Räumung Jugoslaviens durch die deutsche Wehrmacht.* Musterschmidt – Göttingen, 1970. p. 124.
[118] Hnilicka, Karl: *Das Ende auf dem Balkan 1944/45 – Die militärische Räumung Jugoslaviens durch die deutsche Wehrmacht.* Musterschmidt – Göttingen, 1970. p. 124.

Abteilung/297. Infanterie-Division[119], the armoured reconnaissance group of *104. Jäger-Division* with five Panzer II light tanks and three armoured personnel carriers[120], five StuG. III assault guns of *1. Batterie/Sturmgeschütz-Brigade 191*, plus 16 Italian-manufactured M15/42 light tanks[121] of *Panzer-Abteilung 202*. Most likely *11. Luftwaffe-Feld-Division* also had a few German StuG. IIIs and Italian L40 assault guns.[122]

The attack was launched at 0400 hours in the sector of the German *2. Panzerarmee* following a short artillery barrage. The *71. Infanterie-Division/LXVIII. Armeekorps*[123] from the northern area of Kutas, breached the defences of the strongly resisting Soviet troops along the Jákó–Nagybajom road, occupied the southern and middle sectors of Jákó (the northern parts of the village remained in Soviet hands at that time), then established a covering defence on the Kutas southern edge – Jákó southern edge general line. During the battles around this sector, the Germans, according to their own reports, knocked out three Soviet T-34 tanks.[124] One of the soldiers of

II. (Bataillon)/Grenadier-Regiment 194 described the fighting in the southern parts of Jákó in the following way:

"As it was expected, the Russians have tried to reoccupy the lost southern parts of Jákó with a counterattack. Again the appointed kombat[125] *is the one whose superior calmness lets the enemy, dispersed on the plain, come closer, then overcomes them with infantry weapons and the two assault guns that have reached us in the meantime. However, we have not yet won over the Russians. Tanks are rolling out from the northern parts of Jákó down the main road of the village. Radio operators and signal crews hastily put down their devices and grab their Panzerfausts. A platoon equipped with hand-held anti-tank rocket launchers*[126] *is thrusting forward from house to house. The dauntless spirit wins over the steel: the platoon leader of the tank destroyer unit, Leutnant Springe, destroys one of the monsters with a Panzerfaust. The other T-34 turns back."*[127]

On that day in the north-western sector of Jákó, in coordination with the Soviet 113th Rifle Division, the 1201st Self-Propelled Artillery Regiment was in combat, which during the previous evening had 14 operational T-34 tanks in reserve of the commander of the 57th Army. On that day, the Regiment reported to have knocked out four German

---

119 See NARA, T78, R621, F000609.
120 See NARA, T78, R529, F000889.
121 Hnilicka, Karl: *Das Ende auf dem Balkan 1944/45 – Die militärische Räumung Jugoslaviens durch die deutsche Wehrmacht.* Musterschmidt – Göttingen, 1970. p. 123.
122 On 15 March 1945, the *11. Luftwaffe-Felddivision* had two-two German StuG. III and Italian L40 assault guns under repair. See NARA, T78, R624, F000524.
123 According to data as of 3 March 1945, 10 combat-ready assault guns of the *Sturmartillerie-Brigade 261* and seven Jagdpanzer 38(t) *Jagdpanzer*s of the *1222. Panzerjäger-Kompanie* were subordinated to the German *71. Infanteriedivision*. See NARA, T311, R162, F7214410.
124 NARA, T311, R162, F7214159.
125 The appointed *Bataillonskommandeur* was *Hauptmann* Siemsen.
126 In the original: *Ofenrohrzug*, that is "stovepipe" section. This was a common denomination for the 8.8 cm *Raketenpanzerbüchse* handheld anti-tank rocket launcher among the soldiers.
127 *Die 71. Infanterie-Division im Zweiten Weltkrieg 1939–1945. Gefechts- und Erlebnisberichte aus den Kämpfen der „Glückhaften Division" von Verdun bis Stalingrad, von Monte Cassino bis zum Plattensee.* Arbeitsgemeinschaft „Das Kleeblatt" (Hrsg.). Hildesheim, 1973. p. 412.

armoured fighting vehicles, and that they had lost only one tank of their own.[128] The 1201st Self-Propelled Artillery Regiment together with the forces of the 113th Rifle Division launched a successful counterattack from the south towards Jákó and pushed the Germans back 1 – 1.5 km.[129]

From the direction of Kaposmérő, the 864th Self-Propelled Artillery Regiment was directed to this sector as well, which at that time had 21 operational SU–76 self-propelled guns and one operational T-34 tank.[130]

The *II. (Bataillon)/Grenadier-Regiment 211*, attacking on the left flank of the German *71. Infanterie-Division,* reported at 1535 hours that its thrust forward was halted at Szabótanya, 1.5 km south-southeast of Nagybajom; Szabótanya was significantly reinforced and violently defended by the Soviets. For the support of the *Grenadiers* the Jagdpanzer 38(t) *Jagdpanzers* of *1222. Panzerjäger-Kompanie* were sent into combat. In coordination with the armoured fighting vehicles, the *Bataillon* occupied the farmstead, however it had suffered significant losses.[131]

The *16. SS-Panzergrenadier-Division*[132] launched an attack from the middle sector of Nagybajom towards the east, however the attack was halted by the resistance of the Soviet units and the mine obstacles they laid.

The *SS-Panzergrenadier-Division* was attacking from Nagybajom along the Nagybajom–Kaposvár road, with the point of the main effort on the left. The first objective of the *Division* was to break through the field fortifications of the Soviets directly east from Nagybajom.

SS-Panzergrenadier-Regiment 35, reinforced with *1. Kompanie/SS-Panzer-Regiment 16*, was assigned the task to breach the first defence line of the 113th Rifle Division and contain the Soviets until *SS-Panzergrenadier-Regiment 36*, thrusting forward with two other armoured companies, arrived. The latter was to break into the second defence line of the Soviet rifle division and reach the western edges of Pálmajor. *SS-Panzer-Aufklärungs-Abteilung 16* was tasked with thrusting forward through the broken Soviet defence lines until reaching Kaposfő with the StuG. III assault guns of *SS-Panzer-Abteilung 16*, and establish covering positions.[133]

The *SS-Panzergrenadier-Regiment*s however, could not be supported by the assault guns because they were bogged down in the mud even before reaching the Soviet mine obstacles. The frontal attack had been stopped around 0900 hours by the minefields, the muddy ground and the Soviets (especially their snipers) defending themselves in well-established positions. Around noon the Germans aborted any further attempts.

---

128 Central Archives of the Russian Defence Ministry (Podolsk), f. 243, op. 2928, gy. 131, li. 224.
129 M. Svirin – O. Baronov – M. Kolomiets – D. Nedogonov: *Boj u ozera Balaton*. Moscow, 1999. p. 56.
130 Central Archives of the Russian Defence Ministry (Podolsk), f. 243, op. 2928, gy. 131, li. 224.
131 *Die 71. Infanterie-Division im Zweiten Weltkrieg 1939–1945. Gefechts- und Erlebnisberichte aus den Kämpfen der „Glückhaften Division" von Verdun bis Stalingrad, von Monte Cassino bis zum Plattensee.* Arbeitsgemeinschaft „Das Kleeblatt" (Hrsg.). Hildesheim, 1973. p. 411.
132 According to data as of 3 March 1945, the German *16. SS-Panzergrenadier-Division,* besides their own 13 combat-ready assault guns, also received nine combat-ready assault guns of the *Sturmartillerie-Brigade 261*. See NARA, T311, R162, F7214410.
133 Puntigam, Josef Paul: *Vom Plattensee bis zur Mur. Die Kämpfe 1945 im Dreiländereck*. Feldbach, without year of publication, [1993], p. 38.

The *III. (Bataillon)/SS-Panzergrenadier-Regiment 36*, with ten assault guns of *Sturmartillerie-Brigade 261*, launched a containing attack at 1510 hours south of Nagybajom, but the attempt was stopped before reaching the Nagybajom–Kutas road.[134]

SS-Obersturmführer Otto-Heinz Rex, appointed *Kompaniechef* of 3. *Kompanie/SS-Panzer-Abteilung 16*, remembered this day as follows:

"After the units on our left and right had set off as early as 0400 hours, our division launched an attack from Nagybajom at 0600 hours in the direction of Kaposvár, in a two km wide sector. The Panzer-Abteilung (2. and 3. Kompanies) with the mounted III. (Bataillon)/SS-Panzergrenadier-Regiment 36, thrust through SS-Panzergrenadier-Regiment 35 as soon as the mine obstacles east of Nagybajom were cleared up.
The plan of the attack was the following: the 3. Kompanie diverts in a north-eastern direction, attacks the Nagybajom–Kaposvár road from the left, and thrusts forward 4 km west of Kaposfő. The 2. Kompanie was to attack along the Nagybajom–Kaposvár road. But everything happened completely differently.
The report came from the frontline at 0730 hours that the attack was going on as planned. At 1000 hours, the Panzer-Abteilung with the mounted III. (Bataillon)/SS-Panzergrenadier-Regiment 36, drew forward to Nagybajom and they were to occupy positions there on a secondary road. Our planned attack was aborted, as the whole assault was halted with heavy losses at the neighbouring unit and at us. In the afternoon the Panzer-Abteilung attacked south-east of Nagybajom toward the Nagybajom – Kaposvár road with II. and III. (Bataillons)/SS-Panzergrenadier-Regiment 36: the 2. Kompanie in inverted wedge formation and 3. Kompanie behind them, echeloned to the left. We received heavy fire from an anti-tank block position (concentrated fire of 8 anti-tank guns). In the second combat-trench system, we found built in flamethrowers, infantry and mines. The ground was wet and soggy and was very heavy. The armoured fighting vehicles were bogged down as soon as after just two manoeuvres. The marshy patches and a creek, which directly crossed our path of attack, caused further difficulties. Around 1600 hours, the division commander came to the combat position. He ordered 3. Kompanie to thrust forward to the road, regardless of what conditions they might find there. There were mine obstacles laid on the road. Regrouping 3. Kompanie into a column so that they can cross the bridge at the creek and clear the mine field. Untersturmführer Mück has fallen while he was driving his armoured fighting vehicle in the opening through the mine field, as it ran over a mine and was blown up, thus blocking the way. […] A snowstorm began. Harassing fire of the enemy artillery, and the Soviet snipers were also active. Almost all of the deployed armoured fighting vehicles were sunken on the difficult terrain. The pioneer platoon, the motorcycle reconnaissance platoon, parts of the infantry escort platoon, the armoured fighting vehicle crews and everyone who was alive and able to move, were building the embankment and working on freeing the armoured fighting vehicles, but most importantly, carried tree trunks from a distance of 800 meters. We have been working through the whole night."[135]

---

134 Puntigam, Josef Paul: *Vom Plattensee bis zur Mur. Die Kämpfe 1945 im Dreiländereck.* Feldbach, without year of publication, [1993], pp. 38-39.
135 Puntigam, Josef Paul: *Vom Plattensee bis zur Mur. Die Kämpfe 1945 im Dreiländereck.* Feldbach, without year of publication, [1993], pp. 47-48.

Units of the *SS-Division* were drawn forward south of Nagybajom, behind the left flank of *71. Infanterie-Division*. These forces crossed the Jákó-Nagybajom road 1.5 km south-southeast of Nagybajom, in order to turn northeast and attack the Soviet troops defending the area of Nagybajom.

1. Volks-Gebirgs-Division[136] also met with significant Soviet resistance northwest of Nagybajom, where they succeeded in occupying two farmstead groups (most likely Kismezőtanya), then during the morning they established defences.

In the early morning hours, *118. Jäger-Division/XXII. Gebirgskorps*[137] started off from the area southeast of Szenyér and thrust forward 2 km toward the east in the forest southeast of Mesztegnyő. The German unit, facing Soviet resistance, did not make any further territorial gains on the difficult terrain during rest of the day.[138]

The mobile obstacle detachments of the Soviet 57th Army laid 1350 anti-tank mines and 300 anti-infantry mines on that day south of Nagybajom. By dawn on the next day, they laid a further 3260 anti-tank mines and 1050 anti-infantry mines. The mobile obstacle detachments cooperated with the artillery and covered their firing positions with mine obstacles. With this, they forced the German armoured fighting vehicles to manoeuvre into the effective firing range of the anti-tank guns, exposing their vulnerable sides of thinner armour to concentrated, direct artillery fire.[139]

The units of the German *6. Panzerarmee* also launched their attack at 0400 hours, except for *II. SS-Panzerkorps*, which were only able to commence their manoeuvres towards the Soviet positions at 1830 hours.

The German *4. Kavallerie-Division/I. Kavallerie-Korps*, probably supported with the Jagdpanzer 38(t) *Jagdpanzers* of the Hungarian 1st Battery/20th Assault Artillery Battalion, unexpectedly occupied Alsótekeres, 3 km northeast of Point 139, and the hills south and southeast of there. The forces of the Soviet 93rd Rifle Division however, launched counterattacks from the area west of Enying, which were, according to the Germans, partly supported by armoured fighting vehicles[140]. The Soviets managed to throw the Germans back to their points of departure, although they suffered significant losses.

The forces of *3. Kavallerie-Division*[141] had to cross an extensive Soviet minefield, then, in the morning hours, opposite the Soviet 74th Rifle Division, they managed to occupy the hills east of Enying and northwest of Hill 162 (Ágoston Hill).

The *II.(Abteilung)/Reiter-Regiment 31* attacked towards Attilapuszta, however the Soviets managed to flank them therefore the attack had been halted. At this point, via a courier they requested the help of the Jagdpanzer 38(t) *Jagdpanzers* of the Hungarian 20th Assault

---

136 According to data as of 3 March 1945, 12 combat-ready assault guns of *Sturmartillerie-Brigade 261* were also subordinated to the German *1. Volks-Gebirgs-Division*. See NARA, T311, R162, F7214410.
137 According to data as of 3 March 1945, the German *118. Jäger-Division* possessed seven combat-ready assault guns. See NARA, T311, R162, F7214411.
138 NARA, T311, R162, F7214160.
139 Malakhov, M. M.: A Balatontól Bécsig (excerpt). In: *Fejezetek hazánk felszabadításának történetéből*. Budapest, 1960. pp. 160-161.
140 According to the available sources, the Soviets did not possess armoured fighting vehicles here.
141 The tracked fighting vehicles of *Panzerjäger-Abteilung 69* and *schwere Kavallerie-Abteilung 3/3. Kavallerie-Division*, and *I.* and *III. Abteilungs/Artillerie-Regiment 869* were transported by train to follow the *Division* from Tata towards Veszprém, but they did not arrive until the launch of the assault. See Witte, Hans Joachim – Offermann, Peter: *Die Boeselagerschen Reiter. Das Kavallerie-Regiment Mitte und die aus ihm hervorgegangene 3. Kavallerie-Brigade/Division*. München, 1998. pp. 373. and 381.

Artillery Battalion[142] (18 *Jagdpanzers* according to Soviet sources[143]). *Leutnant* Bose[144], serving here, remembers:

"We did not need to go forward too much when two guns were drawn forward beside their commander and opened fire immediately. I stepped down from the sidecar of the motorcycle and stood right next to the commander's gun, to observe the battle. The gunners were firing excellently and after a few rounds, the Russians started to spring up, first one by one, then in groups, fled the flat terrain and hid in a depression. The Major[145] commenced pushing forward and the Hungarians occupied the area with an energetic thrust. Then the cavalry – with Rittmeister Gollert-Hansen at the front[146] – dashed through the open flat area and occupied the farmstead. The Abteilung commander thanked the Hungarians for the excellent support, then they were drawn back with their Hetzers." [147]

Although the *II. (Abteilung)/Reiter-Regiment 31* occupied Attilapuszta at dawn at 0445 hours with Hungarian support, the Soviet 360th Rifle Regiment launched a counterattack and at 0510 hours the Germans were forced out of the group of houses.[148] The Hungarian *Jagdpanzers* were called again. The arrival of 12 Jagdpanzer 38(t)[149], together with the German *II. (Abteilung)/Reiter-Regiment 31*, partly in close combat, again reoccupied Attilapuszta around 0600 hours, then set off in the direction of Hill 162 (Ágoston Hill). Of the Hungarian *Jagdpanzers*, six secured Attilapuszta: three from the south, and three from the west[150].

The commander of the 3rd Battery of the Hungarian 20th Assault Artillery Battalion, 1st Lieutenant Tasziló Kárpáthy remembered the day as follows:

"Under my command, the 2nd and the 3rd batteries, plus the anti-tank battery[151] of the 20th Assault Artillery Battalion also took part [in the attack]. Looking back on that assault, my guardian angel, who was quite ambitious anyway, needed to be extremely watchful then, because during the whole battle there were misfortunes heaping on top of each other. When

---

142 At that time, the Hungarian 20th Assault Artillery Battalion was stationed at Rikimajor, southeast of Lepsény. See Bose, Georg: „*Ob's stürmt, oder schneit…*"! *Mit meinem Sturmgeschütz im Einsatz*. Erinnerungen Teil 2. Selbstverlag Bose, Einhausen, 2005. p. 249

143 Central Archives of the Russian Defence Ministry (Podolsk), f. 1214, op. 1, gy. 51, li 1.

144 In the absence of its own armoured fighting vehicles the armoured support of *3. Kavallerie-Division* was assigned to the Hungarian 2nd and 3rd Batteries/20th Assault Artillery Battalion. One of the officers of *Panzerjäger-Abteilung 69*, *Leutnant* Georg Bose was sent to the Hungarian unit as the liaison officer of *Reiter-Regiment 31*. See Bose, Georg: „*Ob's stürmt, oder schneit…*"! *Mit meinem Sturmgeschütz im Einsatz*. Erinnerungen Teil 2. Selbstverlag Bose, Einhausen, 2005. p. 249.

145 The commander of the Hungarian 20th Assault Artillery Battalion was Major József Henkey-Hőnig.

146 *Rittmeister* Hans-Detlef Gollert-Hansen was the *Abteilungskommandeur* of the German *II. (Abteilung)/Reiter-Regiment 31*.

147 Bose, Georg: „*Ob's stürmt, oder schneit…*"! *Mit meinem Sturmgeschütz im Einsatz*. Erinnerungen Teil 2. Selbstverlag Bose, Einhausen, 2005. p. 249.

148 Witte, Hans Joachim – Offermann, Peter: *Die Boeselagerschen Reiter. Das Kavallerie-Regiment Mitte und die aus ihm hervorgegangene 3. Kavallerie-Brigade/Division*. München, 1998. pp. 382-383.

149 According to the war log of the 3rd Ukrainian Front, Attilapuszta was occupied on that day by the Germans with a support of 12 armoured fighting vehicles.

150 Bose, Georg: „*Ob's stürmt, oder schneit…*"! *Mit meinem Sturmgeschütz im Einsatz*. Erinnerungen Teil 2. Selbstverlag Bose, Einhausen, 2005. p. 252.

151 According to data as of 5 March 1945, the Hungarian 20th Assault Artillery Battalion possessed a total of 36 Jagdpanzer 38(t) *Jagdpanzers*; of these, 22 were in combat-ready condition. All six 7.5 cm towed anti-tank guns of the 4th (Anti-Tank) Battery were combat-ready. See BAMA, RH 2 Ost 5455.

the 3rd *battery was marching in a column to occupy our attack positions, a mine exploded right under the assault gun moving at the head of the column. Luckily it only damaged the tracks. I changed into the next assault gun, which had the disadvantage of having only the 10 W radio like the other assault guns instead of the 30 W radio, and its effective range was considerably shorter. After occupying our attack positions, both batteries*[152] *launched the attack. After breaching the infantry positions, we met multiple rocket-launcher fire much heavier than usual, and a shell exploded right over the casing of my assault gun, slamming the open [escape hatch-] cover on my head. Luckily the power of the blow was decreased by the double arc of the headphones on my head, but even so, I was knocked unconscious for a few seconds."*[153]

The Soviet 109th Rifle Regiment however, launched a number of counterattacks from the sector of Ágoston Hill in the north-eastern direction, which were, according to the Germans, partly supported by armoured fighting vehicles as well[154]. These attempts were repulsed by the German-Hungarian troops. However, the attack of *3. Kavallerie-Division* aimed at the farmstead at Hill 162, which was transformed into a defensive strongpoint, was not successful. The German-Hungarian attack was halted.[155] According to the 74th Rifle Division, they had knocked out three armoured fighting vehicles on this day. The losses of the Division had been 25 dead, 69 wounded and one 76 mm divisional cannon.[156]

The *Ordonnanz* of *II. (Abteilung)/Reiter-Regiment 31, Leutnant* Jürgens was sent back to the command post of the *Regiment* to report to the *Regimentskommandeur*. The officer returned again to the frontline with a few Jagdpanzer 38(t) *Jagdpanzers* of the Hungarian 20th Assault Artillery Battalion into the frontline:

"The commander of the regiment and his staff went on foot along the road where the attack of the 6th [Schwadron] had been executed. I was following them with five Hetzers. I was sitting on the first, on the backside, behind the gunner's turret[157] *and 20 meters in front of the command post,* [158] *we ran over a mine. The crew were wounded and unable to fight, the Hetzer a total loss. I was thrown off it instantly. The tactical briefing was held right then…"*

The Soviet multiple rocket-launchers hit the location of the tactical briefing during a barrage. The *Kommandeur* of *Reiter-Regiment 31, Oberstleutnant* Wasmond von dem Knesebeck and *Kommandeur* of *II. (Abteilung)/Reiter-Regiment 31, Rittmeister* Gollert-Hansen and one other officer were killed instantly, and many were wounded. The dead were transported back on a Hungarian *Jagdpanzer*.[159]

---

152 This concerns the 2nd and 3rd Batteries equipped with *Jagdpanzers*.
153 Tasziló Kárpáthy: *A magyar királyi honvéd 20. rohamtüzérosztály története*. In: HM HIM Hadtörténelmi Levéltár (Budapest), Rohamtüzér-gyűjtemény, 14/7. collection. pp. 18-19.
154 The Soviet troops did not have armoured fighting vehicles here either.
155 NARA, T311, R162, F7214160.
156 Central Archives of the Russian Defence Ministry (Podolsk), f. 1214, op. 1, gy. 51, li 1.
157 There was no hatch on the Jagdpanzer 38(t) *Jagdpanzers*. Most probably the officer had his place behind the armoured shield of the machine gun.
158 Command post of *II. (Abteilung)/Reiter-Regiment 31* in the Attilapuszta sector.
159 Witte, Hans Joachim – Offermann, Peter: *Die Boeselagerschen Reiter. Das Kavallerie-Regiment Mitte und die aus ihm hervorgegangene 3. Kavallerie-Brigade/Division*. München, 1998. p. 384.

The attack of *12. SS-Panzer-Division/I. SS-Panzerkorps* launched from the sector of Kisláng towards the south, had been halted due to the extremely difficult terrain 1 km north of Feketepuszta, and on the hills south of Kisláng.

The Soviets were defending themselves in well-built and deeply sectioned positions, therefore the *SS-Panzergrenadiers* were stopped after taking the first few fortifications. The *II. (Bataillon)/SS-Panzergrenadier-Regiment 26* was forced to abort its attack as early as 0445 hours, 500 meters from Ödönpuszta. The reconnaissance of the *Bataillon* discovered five Soviet trenches behind each other. The heavy fire of the Soviet artillery inflicted serious damage to the *SS*-troops, which had been stranded outside the occupied Soviet positions. The ground was frozen which prevented the soldiers from digging themselves in. The low-altitude attacks of Soviet combat aircraft further slowed down the German advance.

The *II. (Bataillon)/SS-Panzergrenadier-Regiment 26* with the fire support of *SS-Werfer-Abteilung 12,* launched a new attack against Ödönpuszta around 1600 hours, however the attempt collapsed while suffering heavy losses from the fire of the Soviet multiple rocket launchers and mortars. Only one and a half hours later could *5. Kompanie/SS-Panzergrenadier-Regiment 26* breach the Soviet positions after which the Soviets abandoned their front line.

The *I. (Bataillon)/SS-Panzergrenadier-Regiment 26* had not been any more successful either. Supported by two Panzer IV/70 *Jagdpanzers 2. Kompanie* succeeded in throwing the Soviets out of their positions at around 1330 hours, who then retreated to Ödönpuszta, leaving their heavy weapons behind.

SS-Sturmbannführer Erich Kostenbader, *Kommandeur* of *SS-Panzergrenadier-Regiment 26* cancelled any further attacks of the unit due to the heavy losses they had suffered; the attack was to be continued the following day with armoured fighting vehicle support.

SS-Panzergrenadier-Regiment 25 was also involved in heavy combat and almost could not move forward at all. Therefore the armoured personnel carriers of the *III. (gepanzert) (Bataillon)/SS-Panzergrenadier-Regiment 26* were sent in to attack; these occupied Péterszállás but north of Feketepuszta Soviet fire halted them. The tanks in the sector of the division were not able to be deployed due to the unfavourable terrain conditions.[160]

The units of the *1. SS-Panzer-Division* had to cross an extensive minefield, after which the *Panzergrenadiers* who had been fighting almost without heavy weapons support, occupied Hill 149 west of Lobbmajor and the vine covered hills southwest of Soponya in heavy combat. Afterwards they pushed into the northern and south-western sides of Soponya. The armoured combat group, launching an attack northeast of Kisláng, was able to cover 2 km towards the southeast despite facing extremely difficult terrain conditions.[161]

The *Panzergruppe* of *SS-Sturmbannführer* Poetschke, launched its attack from the area northeast of Kisláng and managed to get into the rear of the Soviet 68th Guards Rifle Division. However, after covering 2 km the *SS-Panzers* were bogged down in the mud west of Hill 149. The minefield laid down by the Soviets disabled a number of German tanks and armoured personnel carriers, and a number of armoured fighting vehicles sunk in the

---

160 Meyer, Hubert: *Kriegsgeschichte der 12. SS-Panzerdivision „Hitlerjugend".* Band II. Osnabrück, 1987. 2nd edition, p. 496.
161 NARA, T311, R162, F7214161.

muddy terrain. The situation the Germans faced was worsened by the lack of ammunition, and their own artillery was almost unable to properly support them.[162]

The combat group of *SS-Panzergrenadier-Regiment 1* commenced its attack eastwards a short while later. The two company-size forces of Panzer IV/70 *Jagdpanzers* of *SS-Panzerjäger-Abteilung 1* supported the *SS-Panzergrenadiers,* who breached the positions of the Soviets in close combat, and in the evening reached the western edge of Soponya. Two of their battalions had flanked the houses and advanced into the village, however the southern part remained in the hands of the Soviets. By then, most of the *Jagdpanzers* had already been bogged down in the mud, and the German infantry had to fight without their effective support.[163]

On the north-western part of Káloz, the 72nd Independent Self-Propelled Artillery Battalion/68th Guards Rifle Division was holding positions, with two SU–76 M self-propelled guns, but until that time they had not been engaged in combat with the Germans.[164]

In contrast, the 1965th and 1966th Anti-Tank Artillery Regiments were engaged in heavy combat in the area of Káloz. The latter Regiment on that day reported to have knocked out 11 German armoured fighting vehicles, without any losses to themselves.[165]

The Soviet 26th Army, in defence between Lake Balaton and the Malom Canal, detected 60 attacking German tanks, 20 assault guns and *Jagdpanzers,* plus 60 armoured personnel carriers, altogether 157 German armoured fighting vehicles, along their complete frontline in the main offensive direction of the *I. SS-Panzerkorps.*[166] At about 1655 hours, 19 *Fw 190* ground attack aircraft of the German *Luftwaffe* began carrying out air strikes in the section of the German *I. SS-Panzerkorps* in the sector of Pálmajor and Külmajor, south-southeast of Kisláng.[167]

The attack of *II. SS-Panzerkorps* was launched through the frontline of *23. Panzer-Division*, which was kept, for the time being, in the reserve of *6. Armee.* The *SS*-units however, established contact with the forces of *Panzergrenadier-Regiments 128* and *126* in position there only after the artillery preparations were completed.

The weary soldiers of *SS-Panzergrenadier-Regiment 3/2. SS-Panzer-Division* only arrived at dawn in their attack position, when exactly at 0430 hours the corps artillery of *II. SS-Panzerkorps,* which was already in position, launched a short artillery barrage. The infantry of the *Division* did not launch their attack however, as *SS-Panzergrenadier-Regiment 3* was not present in its full strength.

SS-Panzer-Artillerie-Regiment 2 was also still en route, but its batteries had been ordered into firing positions along the march route in order to be able to join the artillery barrage. Naturally, the scarce ammunition supplies were quickly expended, and thus, although the

---

162 Tiemann, Ralf: *Die Leibstandarte*. Band IV/2. Osnabrück, 1987. p. 262. In subordination to *I. SS-Panzerkorps,* besides the artillery regiments and the multiple rocket launcher *Artillerie-Abteilungs, schwere SS-Artillerie-Abteilung 501* was also in combat there with eight 21 cm mortars and three 17 cm guns, as well as *SS-Vielfachwerfer-Batterie 522*. The latter had six double-row launch frames which all fired 8 cm wing-stabilized rockets; these were fitted on French-manufactured Somua half-track armoured fighting vehicles. See NARA, T78, R530, F000135.
163 Tiemann, Ralf: *Die Leibstandarte*. Band IV/2. Osnabrück, 1987. p. 263.
164 Central Archives of the Russian Defence Ministry (Podolsk), f. 243, op. 2928, gy. 131, li. 223.
165 Isaev, Aleksei–Kolomiets, Maksim: *Tomb of the Panzerwaffe. The Defeat of the 6th SS Panzer Army in Hungary 1945.* Solihull, 2014. p. 144.
166 War log of the 3rd Ukrainian Front from March 1945. Copy owned by the author. 6 March 1945, p. 5.
167 Central Archives of the Russian Defence Ministry (Podolsk), f. 440, op. 8311, gy. 98, li. 72/2.

Soviets had by this way been informed of the launch of the attack, they had not even seen any German infantry in the section of the *Division*. Due to this, the German *Division* completely lost the advantage of tactical surprise.[168]

SS-Panzergrenadier-Regiment 4 was yet in the sector of Úrhida on that day, and while its *Abteilung* arrived at Bolondváritanya on the following day, Soviet ground attack aircraft inflicted heavy losses on them on the open terrain without any cover. The main reason for the delay was that the Germans were moving two corps on one single road between Lake Velence and Lake Balaton.

During the late afternoon, *SS-Panzergrenadier-Regiment 3* was ordered to launch an attack towards the southeast, in the direction of the hills east of the Sárkeresztúr–Aba road. In the targeted sector the units of the 30th Rifle Corps/26th Army were waiting for the German attack in well built defensive positions. Due to lack of time, *2. SS-Panzer-Division* was not able to carry out either reconnaissance or terrain inspection.

The *Panzergrenadiers* of *9. SS-Panzer-Division* crossed the German main frontline around 0800 hours in the morning. Soviet ground attack aircraft were constantly attacking despite poor visibility conditions and the Soviet artillery and rocket launcher fire was also uninterrupted. This combination caused serious losses to the *Panzergrenadiers*. To tackle this situation, *23. Panzer-Division* sent forward a few of its tanks and *Jagdpanzers*, which knocked out the identified Soviet guns and mortars. However this did not help considerably and the attack of *9. SS-Panzer-Division* was halted. The *SS-Panzergrenadiers* suffered so many wounded that the *Sanitätsdienst* of *23. Panzer-Division* was also called in to assist in their care.[169]

At 1515 hours the *SS-Panzergrenadier* assault groups of the *II. SS-Panzerkorps* renewed their attack with artillery support, however they were bogged down once again in the heavy artillery fire of the Soviets. The majority of the *2. SS-Panzer-Division* arrived late, and their attack could only be launched at 1830 hours.[170]

Units of the Soviet 1st Guards Mechanized Corps, the 1st Guards Mechanized Brigade, the 18th Guards Tank Regiment with 15 M4A2 tanks, the 1821st Self-Propelled Artillery Regiment with five SU–100 self-propelled guns, and a company of the 54th Independent Guards Engineer Battalion, were establishing defensive positions on that day and positioned their armoured fighting vehicles in ambush positions in a sector about 1 km south of Sárkeresztúr–Jakabszállás–Heinrichmajor–Felsőtöbörzsök. The units, in addition to the infantry and artillery firing positions, assigned 64 firing positions for the M4A2 tanks, and a further 14 for the SU–100 self-propelled guns.[171]

On the frontline of *Armeegruppe "Balck"*, *1. Panzer-Division* and *356. Infanterie-Division* of *III. Panzerkorps*[172] , similarly to the other German groups, launched their attack at 0400 hours to prevent contact of the Soviet 155th Rifle Division/26th Army and the 1st

---

168   Weidinger, Otto: *Division Das Reich. Der Weg der 2. SS-Panzer-Division „Das Reich"*. Band V: 1943-1945. Osnabrück, without year of publication, p. 441.
169   Rebentisch, Ernst: *Zum Kaukasus und zu den Tauern. Die Geschichte der 23. Panzer-Division 1941–1945*. Esslingen, 1963. p. 484.
170   NARA, T311, R162, F7214161.
171   Central Archives of the Russian Defence Ministry (Podolsk), f. 243, op. 2928, gy. 131, li. 224.
172   The two *Divisions* were concentrated into a division-group (*Divisionsgruppe*) under command of *Generalmajor* Eberhard Thunert, *Kommandeur* of *1. Panzer-Division*.

Guards Fortified Region/4th Guards Army [173], in order to establish a bridgehead in the sector of Seregélyes. Due to the difficulties of the terrain and the lack of sufficient roads *3. Panzer-Division* remained in reserve.

Kampfgruppe "Ritz", the reinforced *Panzergrenadier-Regiment 1* of *1. Panzer-Division*, comprising the right flank assault group of the Germans did not succeed in attacking Pálinkaházpuszta southwest of Seregélyes, because of Soviet resistance and the cover fire from the section of the troops on the right prevented them carrying out the task. Due to a direct artillery hit on the command post of *Panzergrenadier-Regiment 1*, the *Regimentskommandeur*, *Major* Ritz was wounded together with a number of his staff.[174]

Panzergruppe "Elias"/1. Panzer-Division with the majority of the divisions Panther tanks remained for the time being in division reserve near Börgönd.[175]

The assault group in combat on the left flank, *Kampfgruppe "Bradel"* of *1. Panzer-Division* and *356. Infanterie-Division*, with 15 armoured fighting vehicles and 1500 infantry according to German records, had, after a short but heavy engagement, occupied the middle and northern parts of Seregélyes around 0815 hours in the morning[176], then with a swift thrust forward, occupied the only slightly damaged road bridge on the eastern edge of the village. The mansion house and the park on the north-eastern edge of the village were also occupied by the Germans. The German forces moving forward in a northern direction took Szerecsenypuszta also. The Germans detected 20 armoured fighting vehicles and infantry rifle troops arriving on 30 trucks from the direction of Perkáta, which they engaged 3 km east of Seregélyes with concentrated artillery fire.[177]

According to the original plan, *Kampfgruppe "Bradel"* was to be supported by the Tiger B heavy tanks of *3. Kompanie/schwere Panzer-Abteilung 509* southeast of Belsőbáránd, and the majority of the independent armoured force was to advance in the second echelon via Pálinkaházapuszta to the bridge at the eastern part of Seregélyes. The Tiger B heavy tanks of *3. Kompanie*, while moving into their attack positions, were bogged down and could not launch their attack.[178] The other two companies reached their attack positions, although with great effort only, and commenced moving forward, however they were

---

173 The 1st Guards Fortified Region was in defence of an approximately 10 km wide frontline. According to data as of 4 March 1945, its strength contained the following elements: 740 soldiers, 30 45 mm anti-tank guns and five 76 mm divisional guns, as well as 32 82 mm and 10 120 mm mortars. See Central Archives of the Russian Defence Ministry (Podolsk), f. 381, op. 8378, gy. 516, li. 20. However, the 24th Anti-Tank Artillery Brigade was also assigned to the same sector, which established a number of anti-tank regions from its 57 and 76 mm guns. Between 6-9 March, the Artillery Battalion reported to have knocked out 39 German armoured fighting vehicles and armoured personnel carriers, with losing 16 of their own guns. See Isaev, Aleksei–Kolomiets, Maksim: *Tomb of the Panzerwaffe. The Defeat of the 6th SS Panzer Army in Hungary 1945.* Solihull, 2014. p. 152.

174 Stoves, O. G. Rolf: *1. Panzer-Division 1935–1945. Chronik einer der drei Stamm-Division der deutschen Panzerwaffe.* Bad Nauheim, 1961. p. 748.

175 Stoves, Rolf: Persönliches Kriegstagebuch Pz.Rgt. 1 (typewritten manuscript, a copy owned by the author), entry on 6 March 1945. The armoured combat group of *1. Panzer-Division* consisted of the following units: the reinforced *1. Panzer-Kompanie/Panzer-Regiment 1* (*Oberleutnant* Hutter) and the armoured personnel carriers of *10. Panzer-Pionier-Kompanie/Panzergrenadier-Regiment 113* (*Oberleutnant* Fink). See Stoves, O. G. Rolf: *1. Panzer-Division 1935–1945. Chronik einer der drei Stamm-Division der deutschen Panzerwaffe.* Bad Nauheim, 1961. p. 747. According to the Tables of Organization and Equipment (TOE) of *1. Panzer-Division*, pioneer-armoured personnel carriers were exclusively found in the *Abteilungstabs* of *Panzer-Regiment 1*. The company was most probably equipped with armoured personnel carriers given over by *I. (Bataillon)/Panzergrenadier-Regiment 113*.

176 War log of the 3rd Ukrainian Front from March 1945. Copy owned by the author. 6 March 194., p. 3.

177 NARA, T311, R162, F7214161.

178 *History of the schwere Panzer-Abteilung 509* (typewritten manuscript). Copy owned by the author. p. 53.

targeted by the direct fire of the ISU-122 armoured fighting vehicles dug in on the hills surrounding Seregélyes.[179] The Tiger Bs knocked out four of these within a short time. The Panthers of *Panzer-Regiment 1* also opened fire on the Soviet heavy armoured fighting vehicles from 2000 meters, but they were not able to inflict any major damage on them. At that time, the *Kommandeur* of *schwere Panzer-Abteilung 509, Hauptmann* dr. König sent two Tiger Bs as reinforcement, which reported to have knocked out two ISU-122s. However, *schwere Panzer-Abteilung 509* was not able to continue the attack because they had to wait until the railroad bridge northwest of Seregélyes was repaired, to enable the heavy tanks to cross Háromág Creek.[180]

The German heavy tanks were engaged most likely by some of the arriving reinforced Soviet 18th Tank Corps. The 181st Tank Brigade with 15 tanks gathered at Felsőcikola around 1200 hours, the 170th Tank Brigade and the 1438th Self-Propelled Artillery Regiment with nine tanks and 12 SU–76Ms between Sándormajor and Point 116 (1.5 km east of Seregélyes), the 110th Tank Brigade and the 363th Guards Heavy Self-Propelled Artillery Regiment with 33 tanks, 16 ISU–122s and five ISU–152s south of Seregélyes, as far as Hill 159 (Csillag).[181] It was probably the heavy self-propelled guns of the latter unit that opened fire on the heavy Tiger Bs of *schwere Panzer-Abteilung 509*.

The Soviet armoured fighting vehicles were ordered to launch an attack against Seregélyes at 1700 hours in cooperation with one of the regiments of the 155th Rifle Division, and to reoccupy the village in cooperation with the 1st Guards Fortified Region. The 32nd Motorized Rifle Brigade, less one battalion, was still stationed in Felsőszolgaegyháza at that time. Also, 20 new T-34/85 tanks had arrived for the 110th Tank Brigade.[182]

According to archival sources, the assault order against Seregélyes was cancelled, so the forces of the 18th Tank Corps were left to strengthen the defences of the rifle units afterwards.[183] At the same time, a source recorded that parts of the 155th Rifle Division and the 110th Tank Brigade had indeed carried out the attack, but as their actions were not properly coordinated, and with too few operational armoured fighting vehicles available, the attempt failed in the end.[184]

The 208th Self-Propelled Artillery Brigade also was subordinated to the 18th Tank Corps, with its total of 63 operational SU–100 and three SU–76M self-propelled guns, plus two T-34 tanks[185]. The 1068th and 1922nd Self-Propelled Artillery Regiments of the Brigade were assembled at 1400 hours in the area of Pusztaszabolcs, and the 1016th Self-Propelled Artillery Regiment established a firing position between Felsőszolgaegyház and Szolgaegyház.[186]

---

179 In the *History of the schwere Panzer-Abteilung 509* IS–2 tanks are mentioned. However this is a mistake, because at that time, only the ISU-122 self-propelled guns of the 18th Tank Corps were in combat.
180 *History of the schwere Panzer-Abteilung 509* (typewritten manuscript). Copy owned by the author. pp. 53-54.
181 War log of the 18th Tank Corps from March 1945. Copy owned by the author. p. 5.
182 Central Archives of the Russian Defence Ministry (Podolsk), f. 243, op. 2928, gy. 131, li. 224.
183 Central Archives of the Russian Defence Ministry (Podolsk), f. 243, op. 2928, gy. 131, li. 226.
184 M. Svirin – O. Baronov – M. Kolomiets – D. Nedogonov: *Boj u ozera Balaton*. Moscow, 1999. p. 56.
185 The armoured fighting vehicle strength of the 208th Self-Propelled Artillery Brigade consisted of 63 SU–100s and three SU–76M self-propelled guns, three T–34/85 tanks, three BA–64 armoured cars, 10 M3A1 wheeled armoured transport vehicles and 10 M15A1 half-track self-propelled anti-aircraft guns. The latter were equipped with one 37 mm automatic cannon and two 12.7 mm heavy machine guns. See the summarized report of the 208th Self-Propelled Artillery Brigade of the period between 6 March and 6 April 1945. Copy owned by the author. p. 1. The 207th and the 209th Self-Propelled Artillery Brigade also had 10-10 such half-track self-propelled anti-aircraft armoured fighting vehicles.
186 Central Archives of the Russian Defence Ministry (Podolsk), f. 243, op. 2928, gy. 131, li. 224.

The Soviet 1202nd Self-Propelled Artillery Regiment, with its 14 SU–76M self-propelled guns, established firing positions 2 km southeast of Seregélyes at Point 108 upon orders from the 26th Army, then opened fire on the Germans at 1600 hours.[187]

According to Soviet opinion, the Germans were only able to occupy Seregélyes because contact between the 30th Rifle Corps and the 1st Guards Fortified Region was not organized properly. When the forces of the 1st Guards Fortified Region were pushed back by the Germans, the right flank of the 30th Rifle Corps was left defenceless. In order to bridge the gap, the corps commander deployed his own reserve troops, the 104th Guards Rifle Regiment/36th Guards Rifle Division on the night of 6/7 March 1945.[188]

In the evening report of *Armeegruppe "Balck"* concerns were voiced because they were still not able to direct a sufficient number of armoured fighting vehicles and heavy armament to Seregélyes due to the wet and muddy roads. In order to solve this problem, they planned to remove the railroad tracks from the embankment between Falubattyán and Seregélyes, and repair the railroad bridge northwest of Seregélyes to make the whole route accessible for armoured fighting vehicles and heavy armament.[189]

The ground attack aircraft of the Soviet air force were mostly active south of Lake Velence. The Germans detected about 70 Il–2 ground attack aircraft and 20 fighter-bombers with fighter support over *III. Panzerkorps*.[190] Due to more favourable weather conditions during the afternoon, the *Luftwaffe* was able to support the German troops between Lake Balaton and the Nádor Canal with approximately 45 ground attack and fighter aircraft missions.[191]

The war log of the German *Heeresgruppe Süd* recorded the following comments on that day in connection with the deployment of the armoured fighting vehicles:

"The weather is extremely unfavourable for attacking with armoured fighting vehicles. Although the roads and the terrain have somewhat dried up because of the windy weather of the last few days, repeated snowing and mild weather caused mud to form on the roads again. As the enemy has closed off the very few hard-surface roads with anti-tank block positions and mine obstacles, the wet and muddy terrain made it impossible to flank these positions and for the armoured fighting vehicles to fan out effectively, our armoured strength of considerable force was not able to be effectively deployed anywhere. Due to the restraints on ammunition usage, which had to be observed as early as during the artillery preparations because the supplies sent were insufficient for any longer attack, the full force of the first blow was to be endured by the infantry."[192]

An order from the *Generalinspekteur der Panzertruppe* issued on 27 February 1945, announced by the German *Heeresgruppe* that day, directed the *Kompanies/Panzerjäger-Abteilung* of the infantry, *Jäger* (light infantry) and mountain divisions equipped with

---

187 Central Archives of the Russian Defence Ministry (Podolsk), f. 243, op. 2928, gy. 178, li. 66.
188 Malakhov, M. M.: A Balatontól Bécsig (excerpt). In: *Fejezetek hazánk felszabadításának történetéből*. Budapest, 1960. p. 141.
189 NARA, T311, R162, F7214173.
190 BAMA, RH 2/1995 Blatt 125.
191 NARA, T311, R163, F7215263.
192 NARA, T311, R162, F7214164.

Jagdpanzers or assault guns were to be renamed as *Jagdpanzer-Kompanies* instead of *Panzerjäger-Kompanies*, keeping the numbering of the original units.[193]

7 March 1945, Wednesday

(**WEATHER**: highest daytime temperature 4 Celsius, cloudy skies, mild snowing. The unpaved roads and the open terrain was considerably sodden.)

On the front of *2. Panzerarmee* the fortified position established by *71. Infanterie-Division/ LXVIII.Armeekorps* between Kutas and Jákó was assaulted by Soviet-Bulgarian forces with company and battalion-size units, but the Germans repulsed them. *Grenadier-Regiments 191* and *211* of the *Division* were engaged in heavy combat from 1100 hours, clearing the northern part of Jákó and occupying the Jákó–Nagybajom railway station. Afterwards, with the support of the artillery and the Jagdpanzer 38(t) *Jagdpanzers* of the *1222. Jagdpanzer-Kompanie*[194], they occupied Jajgatópuszta and Point 176 north-northeast from there by 1600 hours. During these battles, the Germans had, according to their own reports, knocked out four T-34 tanks[195], most likely from the 1201st Self-Propelled Artillery Regiment.

On the same day, the German *Eisenbahn-Panzerzug 64* and *79* were subordinated to *71. Infanterie-Division*. The armoured trains, supplemented by *Eisenbahn-Panzerzug 78*, were patrolling mainly on the southwestern edge of Lake Balaton and Somogyszob, and between Gyékényes and Vízvár.[196]

During the night of 6/7 March 1945, the *Division* regrouped the majority of its forces in the area south of Nagybajom, where *71. Infanterie-Division* won a small amount of ground towards the east. *SS-Panzergrenadier-Regiment 36*, *Panzer-Abteilung 16* and *SS-Panzer-Aufklärungs-Abteilung 16* at the back of the *Infanterie-Division* were preparing for another attack. *SS-Panzergrenadier-Regiment 35* was gathering west of Nagybajom with the units dead and wounded soldiers.[197]

The *I. (Bataillon)/Panzergrenadier-Regiment 36/16. SS-Panzergrenadier-Division*, supported by *1. Kompanie/SS-Panzer-Abteilung 16* and *Sturmartillerie-Brigade 261,* renewed its attack at 0430 hours from the area south-southeast of Nagybajom, and in intense combat, they occupied Balázskapuszta 3 km north of Jákó. After this, *III. (Bataillon)/Panzergrenadier-Regiment 36* moved forward to the eastern outskirts of Juhászlaktanya 2 km southeast of Nagybajom, where they repulsed a Soviet battalion-size counterattack.[198]

---

193   NARA, T311, R162, F7214407.
194   *Die 71. Infanterie-Division im Zweiten Weltkrieg 1939–1945. Gefechts- und Erlebnisberichte aus den Kämpfen der „Glückhaften Division" von Verdun bis Stalingrad, von Monte Cassino bis zum Plattensee. Arbeitsgemeinschaft „Das Kleeblatt" (Hrsg.).* Hildesheim, 1973. p. 413.
195   NARA, T311, R162, F7214178. According to the report, the Germans knocked out another two tanks in the sector the day before.
196   Sawodny, Wolfgang: *Deutsche Panzerzüge*. Eggolsheim, without year of publication, p. 140.
197   Puntigam, Josef Paul: *Vom Plattensee bis zur Mur. Die Kämpfe 1945 im Dreiländereck*. Feldbach, without year of publication, [1993], pp. 48-49., furthermore Tieke p. 22.
198   Puntigam, Josef Paul: *Vom Plattensee bis zur Mur. Die Kämpfe 1945 im Dreiländereck*. Feldbach, without year of publication, [1993], pp. 53-54.

Around 1800 hours, the Soviets launched an attack against Balázskapuszta with 30 armoured fighting vehicles[199] and mounted rifle infantry.[200] According to their own reports, the Germans knocked out three armoured fighting vehicles[201] and repulsed the attack. In the area of Balázskapuszta one of the batteries of the 864th Self-Propelled Artillery Regiment lost one SU-76M self-propelled gun that was burnt out, leaving them with 20 operational SU–76Ms and one operational T–34.[202]

The Soviet 1201st Self-Propelled Artillery Regiment in combat between Jákó and Balázskapuszta reported on that day to have knocked out two German armoured fighting vehicles and two guns. Their own losses amounted to 10 knocked out T–34s, of which two had been burnt out, and one of the remaining tanks had been captured by the Germans. By that evening the Regiment only had three remaining operational tanks.[203]

The German *1. Volks-Gebirgs-Division* repulsed a number of Soviet attacks of company strength northwest of Nagybajom.

The *118. Jäger-Division/XXII. Gebirgskorps* with one of its *Jäger-Regiments* had taken over the northern front of *1 Volks-Gebirgs-Division* during the night of 6/7 March 1945. The German *Jägers* repulsed a company-strength attack on the left flank of the unit.

In the section of *Kampfgruppe "Steyrer"*, the defenders repulsed a company-sized attack west of Mesztegnyő. During the late afternoon, southeast of Keszthely, the Soviets approached the German-Hungarian positions with a battalion-size force.[204] During this time, *Eisenbahn-Panzerzug 78* was subordinated to the *Kampfgruppe*.

Southeast of Kéthely, during the evening, the forces of the *Kampfgruppe* repulsed four battalion size attacks, and eliminated one penetration.[205]

On the front of the German *6. Panzerarmee, 4. Kavallerie-Division/I. Kavallerie-Korps* was not engaged in any significant action on that day, nevertheless it regrouped its forces in order to continue the attack. The main elements were the Jagdpanzer IV *Jagdpanzers*, the light tanks, armoured personnel carriers, and towed 2 cm and self-propelled 3.7 cm anti-tank guns of *schwere Kavallerie-Abteilung 4,* which were subordinated to *3. Kavallerie-Division*[206]; and with these, they attempted to deploy the armoured forces of the *Kavallerie-Armeekorps* in concentration.

At 0130 hours, *3. Kavallerie-Division* continued its attack, then, in the early morning hours, after heavy close quarters combat, occupied the farmstead at Hill 162 (Ágoston Hill) and repulsed a Soviet company sized counterattack. The German cavalry forces would have continued their attack southwards with support from assault guns, however the attempt was soon halted again on a Soviet minefield.[207]

---

199   These approximately 30 Soviet armoured fighting vehicles were most likely the combined strength of the 1201st and the 864th Self-Propelled Artillery Regiments.
200   NARA, T311, R162, F7214178.
201   The Soviets had certainly towed two of the knocked out armoured fighting vehicles away. See BAMA, RH 2/1995 Blatt 43.
202   Central Archives of the Russian Defence Ministry (Podolsk), f. 243, op. 2928, gy. 131, li. 226.
203   Central Archives of the Russian Defence Ministry (Podolsk), f. 243, op. 2928, gy. 131, li. 226. The regiment lost these 10 tanks most likely during the fighting on 6 and 7 March 1945, and not only on 7 March, however the summarized report on losses may have suffered delays.
204   NARA, T311, R162, F7214179.
205   NARA, T311, R162, F7214192.
206   NARA, T311, R163, F7215274. The assault guns of *Panzerjäger-Abteilung 70* most likely remained in the subordination of *4. Kavallerie-Division*.
207   NARA, T311, R162, F7214179.

In the sector of *I. SS-Panzerkorps*, *12. SS-Panzer-Division* occupied Ödönpuszta and Pálmajor 2 km southwest from there. Further German advances however had again been bogged down on the Feketepuszta north to Aranyospuszta general line by the perfectly prepared and heavily defended Soviet positions. The Germans here planned to renew their attack following a regrouping.[208]

SS-Panzergrenadier-Regiment 25 renewed its attack against Feketepuszta, but hadn't gained any ground and its advance was soon halted.

The *II. (Bataillon)/SS-Panzergrenadier-Regiment 26*, launched an attack at 0440 hours toward Ödönpuszta, supported by *2. Kompanie/SS-Panzer-Pionier-Regiment 12*, one *SS-Panzer-Kompanie* and units of the armoured personnel carrier (APC) battalion. The area was occupied soon after 0500 hours.

The *I. (Bataillon)/SS-Panzergrenadier-Regiment 26* continued its attack and occupied Pálmajor. The *II. (Bataillon)/SS-Panzergrenadier-Regiment 26* advanced with the tanks and armoured personnel carriers and reached the northern outskirts of Aranyospuszta. However, the Germans were halted here once more, and *SS-Panzergrenadier-Regiment 26* was forced to repel counterattacks directed against its right flank. This task was carried out with the support of tanks and the *Grille* self-propelled heavy infantry guns.[209]

The armoured combat group of *1. SS-Panzer-Division*, after advancing eastwards the previous evening, approached to within 1 km Káloz from the west.[210] During the attack, one of the armoured personnel carriers equipped with a 7.5 cm short-barrelled tank gun from *12. Kompanie/III. (Bataillon)/SS-Panzergrenadier-Regiment 2*, was knocked out by the Soviets.[211]

During the night of 6/7 March 1945, *SS-Brigadeführer Kumm* regrouped his forces. As *III. (Bataillon)/SS-Panzergrenadier-Regiment 1* remained in the northern sector of Soponya, the regrouped forces for the main effort of the *Division* were gathered in the sector of Ödönpuszta. This reinforced combat group consisted of the armoured combat group of *SS-Obersturmbannführer* Joachim Peiper and units of the two *SS-Panzergrenadier-Regiments*. They launched their attack early in the morning. They bypassed Káloz, then turned eastwards and reached the Káloz–Simontornya road. The combat group of *SS-Panzergrenadier-Regiment 2* sealed the road from the south, and the armoured group ambushed the rear of the Soviet forces defending Káloz from the south and at around 1200 hours, a group of Panzer IV tanks[212] breached the village. The Germans occupied Káloz following a short, but intensive engagement.[213]

Káloz was secured by *II. (Bataillon)/SS-Panzergrenadier-Regiment 1*. The combat group turned northwards with the remaining forces of *SS-Panzergrenadier-Regiment 1* to occupy

---

208   NARA, T311, R162, F7214179.
209   Meyer, Hubert: *Kriegsgeschichte der 12. SS-Panzerdivision „Hitlerjugend"*. Band II. Osnabrück, 1987. 2nd edition. p. 497.
210   NARA, T311, R163, F7215267.
211   *Mit goldener Nahkampfspange. Werner Kindler – Ein Panzergrenadier der Leibstandarte.* H.n., 2010. p. 268. The top sergeant of *12.* (heavy weapons) *Kompanie*, *SS-Oberscharführer* Eduard Funk died on the same day in Polgárdi, when one of the Sd.Kfz. 251/21 three-barrelled 2 cm automatic cannons of the *Kompanie* accidentally fired a round and he was hit.
212   Tiemann, Ralf: *Chronik der 7. Panzerkompanie. An vorderster Front in der 1. SS-Panzerdivision „Leibstandarte SS Adolf Hitler"*. Selent, 2015. p. 246. According to the book the Panzer IV tanks had already breached Káloz on 6 March 1945, however according to the division's history written by the same author, this only happened one day later.
213   Tiemann, Ralf: *Die Leibstandarte*. Band IV/2. Osnabrück, 1987. p. 265.

Soponya. The Soviets defending the southern sector of the village were encircled and eliminated in close combat by the forces of the *kampfgruppe* together with *III. (Bataillon)/SS-Panzergrenadier-Regiment 1* advancing from the north-northeast by the evening. Some of the defending Soviet forces were able to break out of the encirclement through the Sárvíz Canal towards the east.[214]

Two SU–76M self-propelled guns of the 72nd Guards Independent Self-Propelled Artillery Battalion/68th Guards Rifle Division, reported to have knocked out eight armoured fighting vehicles on the western edge of Káloz, but the Germans in turn, knocked out both Soviet fighting vehicles, which were burnt out. The Soviet unit, which now remained without any armoured fighting vehicles, retreated to Sárkeresztúr.[215]

The forces of the *SS-Division* were attacking from the east, cutting through the Káloz–Simontornya road and then, turning northwards, took Káloz in heavy close quarters combat, and managed to hold the village despite a number of Soviet counterattacks that were launched from the north. Subsequently, the *SS*-units attacked northwards from Káloz and occupied Belmajor, then pushed into the southern part of Soponya and into the park of surrounding the mansion house situated there. Clearing and securing the village and the area east of Lobbmajor was still going on during the evening hours.[216]

At 1245 hours, the German *Luftwaffe* carried out an airstrike with 19 Fw 190 ground attack aircraft targeting the area of Káloz and the vehicle traffic moving on the road leading from Sárbogárd to Sárkeresztúr.[217]

At Káloz, the Soviet rifle infantry left the 1965th Anti-Tank Artillery Regiment/43rd Anti-Tank Artillery Brigade alone in the morning hours and retreated. Twenty German armoured fighting vehicles assaulted the 57 mm ZIS-2 anti-tank guns of the 6th Battery. The tanks advanced at a speed of approximately 30 km/h with fire support from multiple rocket-launchers. Due to the rainy weather and unfavourable visibility conditions, the Soviets guns could only open fire from a short distance, 100 to 200 meters. Near the houses of the village, the Soviets reported to have knocked out six armoured fighting vehicles, a Tiger B among them. The battery was also firing sub-caliber size shells at the German armoured fighting vehicles. A small armoured group of the German forces thrust into the northern part of Káloz with six tanks, but there the 3rd Battery/1965th Anti-Tank Artillery Regiment knocked out another three armoured fighting vehicles[218]. The other German tanks advancing southwards were disabled by the 4th Battery. Following this, the Germans ambushed the firing positions of the batteries with *Panzergrenadier* assault groups, an effort also supported by *Jagdpanzer* fire from a distance. The Soviet 1965th and 1966th Anti-Tank Artillery Regiments had been engaged in battle with the German infantry for hours. By the evening, the 1965th Anti-Tank Artillery Regiment was saved by the support of the retreating Soviet rifle infantry, but its sister regiment was kept under heavy fire by the Germans on three sides, and it was soon encircled.

---

214 Tiemann, Ralf: *Die Leibstandarte*. Band IV/2. Osnabrück, 1987. p. 266.
215 Central Archives of the Russian Defence Ministry (Podolsk), f. 243, op. 2928, gy. 131, li. 226.
216 NARA, T311, R162, F7214179. The Germans understood when interrogating the prisoners that during the night of 6/7 March, the Soviets reinforced the Soponya sector with another three battalions.
217 Central Archives of the Russian Defence Ministry (Podolsk), f. 440, op. 8311, gy. 98, li. 72/2.
218 One of these was certainly a Flak-Panzer IV anti-aircraft armoured fighting vehicle.

The 1966th Anti-Tank Artillery Regiment had lost all its guns, however its personnel managed to break out of the encirclement and they reached their own forces. According to the daily strength report of the 43rd Anti-Tank Artillery Brigade, they knocked out 44 German tanks and five armoured personnel carriers, but lost 32 guns, of which 17 were 57 mm. Of its three regiments, only the 1964th Anti-Tank Artillery Regiment was able to continue fighting at Sárszentágota, the other two regiments having been drawn back for replenishment.[219]

In order to reinforce the defence of the Soviet 26th Army, on the same day the 22nd Independent Tank Regiment was formed out of the 22nd Training Tank Regiment, which, at 2200 hours in the night commenced its 115 km march towards the Sió Canal. The Regiment at that time had 13 T-34 tanks, one KV–1S heavy tank, four SU–76M and one SU–85 self-propelled guns. The armoured fighting vehicles were to establish ambush positions in the Dég–Point 152–Lajoskomárom area.[220]

During the afternoon, the units of *II. SS-Panzerkorps* advanced 6 km into the defences of the Soviet units in heavy combat, with the support of their own ground attack aircraft.

At 1230 hours, 16 Fw 190 and Me 109 aircraft of the German *Luftwaffe* assaulted the Soviet tank and artillery positions, and the guns of the Soviet 981st Anti-Tank Artillery Regiment in the area of Sárosd. Altogether, the Germans dropped 260 5-25 kg bombs. At 1735 hours, 12 Me 109 and 13 Fw 190 aircraft attacked Cece and Sárbogárd, dropping another 16 50 and 100 kg bombs.[221]

The *44. Reichsgrenadier-Division* occupied the farmsteads 4 km northeast of Aba.

At 0500 hours, in the section of *2. SS-Panzer-Division, SS-Panzergrenadier-Regiment 3*, following orders received the day before, launched an attack with the support of a few armoured fighting vehicles. The assault of the *Panzergrenadiers* was not preceded by artillery fire. Furthermore, they launched the attack at the same spot where they would have the day before, and the Soviets were already waiting for them. The situation of the *SS-Panzergrenadiers* was worsened by the fact that the supporting armoured fighting vehicles were bogged down in the mud on the right flank of the *Regiment*. The Germans reached the Aba–Sárosd road and occupied the hill dominating the area (Hill 140), but their further advance had lost its momentum in the absence of armoured support. The attack of *2. SS-Panzer-Division* advanced as far as Hill 159 (Csillag), 4 km west of Sárosd by the end of the day. The command post of *SS-Panzergrenadier-Regiment 3* was established in a formerly occupied Soviet pillbox.[222] In two days, the *Division* had lost 18 killed and 84 wounded soldiers.[223]

The left flank combat group of *9. SS-Panzer-Division* occupied Pálinkaházpuszta 1 km southeast of Seregélyes, where they established contact with the forces of *III. Panzerkorps*. The right-flank combat group of the *Division* that was advancing at a better pace, joined

---

219 M. Svirin – O. Baronov – M. Kolomiets – D. Nedogonov: *Boj u ozera Balaton*. Moscow, 1999. pp. 56-57.
220 Central Archives of the Russian Defence Ministry (Podolsk), f. 243, op. 2928, gy. 131, li. 226.
221 Central Archives of the Russian Defence Ministry (Podolsk), f. 440, op. 8311, gy. 98, li. 72/2.
222 Tieke, Wilhelm: *Von Plattensee bis Österreich. Heeresgruppe Süd 1945*. Gummersbach, without year of publication, p. 24., furthermore Weidinger, Otto: *Division Das Reich. Der Weg der 2. SS-Panzer-Division „Das Reich"*. Band V: 1943-1945. Osnabrück, without year of publication, p. 443.
223 BAMA, RH-19, V/62 Kriegstagebuch der Heeresgruppe Süd Anlageband, Tägliche Verluste u. Pz. Ausfälle zur Vorlage beim Führer vom 10. 3. 1945.

the forces of *2. SS-Panzer-Division*. By the evening, the *SS*-units attacking in the middle sector were able to advance up to Point 153, 5 km northwest of Sárosd.[224]

The weight of combat was almost exclusively borne by the *SS-Panzergrenadiers*, as the deployment of the heavy armament and the armoured fighting vehicles was rendered practically impossible by the wet and muddy roads. Only one company of *SS-Panzer-Regiment 9,* commanded by *SS-Obersturmbannführer* Telkamp, was able to support the infantry because the single paved road in the sector of the *Division* was unable to accommodate any more armoured fighting vehicles.[225]

Three batteries of *SS-Panzer-Flak-Abteilung 9* established firing positions at the airfield near Székesfehérvár.[226]

The Soviets launched a number of counterattacks in the sector of *II. SS-Panzerkorps*, which were also supported by a few, armoured fighting vehicles.[227] These were mainly the armoured fighting vehicles of the 110th Tank Brigade and the 363rd Guards Heavy Self-Propelled Artillery Regiment of the 18th Tank Corps, which reported on that day to have knocked out eight German armoured fighting vehicles on the Seregélyes south – Point 140– Hill 159 (Csillag) section. Their own losses consisted of two knocked out T–34/85s and three ISU–122s, of which, one was burnt out.[228] One of the tank companies of the 110th Tank Brigade and an ISU–122 Battery were ordered to the north-eastern edge of Aba and to Point 112 there, in order to cover the left flank of the Corps as well as reinforcing the defence of the rifle infantry.[229] The forces of the 18th Tank Corps in combat here were attacked by 75 German aircraft, of which the Soviets reported to have shot down one Fw 190 ground attack aircraft.[230]

The 1st Battalion/104th Guard Rifle Regiment, deployed on the night of 6/7 March 1945 from the reserves of the Soviet 30th Rifle Corps and, established defensive positions on Hill 159 (Csillag)–Szőlőhegy–Sárkeresztúr north train station section. They had two dug-in tanks, likely from the 110th Tank Brigade.[231]

The 1068th and 1922nd Self-Propelled Artillery Regiments/208th Self-Propelled Artillery Brigade on that day were subordinated to the 26th Army and at 1530 hours marched on the Dunapentele–Dunaföldvár–Cece route to the sector of Cece.[232]

The units of the Soviet 1st Guards Mechanized Corps continued to build up their defences in the area of Sárkeresztúr. The following ambush positions were established by the 18th Guards Tank Regiment with the 1821st Self-Propelled Artillery Regiment and the two companies of the 1st Battalion/1st Guards Mechanized Brigade, plus one engineer company:

---

224 NARA, T311, R162, F7214180.
225 Tieke, Wilhelm: *Im Feuersturm letzter Kriegsjahre. II. SS-Panzerkorps mit 9. und 10. SS-Division „Hohenstaufen" und „Frundsberg".* Osnabrück, without year of publication, [1975] p. 498.
226 Fürbringer, Herbert: *9. SS-Panzer-Division.* Heimdal, without year of publication, [1984] p. 508.
227 NARA, T311, R162, F7214178.
228 Central Archives of the Russian Defence Ministry (Podolsk), f. 243, op. 2928, gy. 131, li. 227.
229 Central Archives of the Russian Defence Ministry (Podolsk), f. 243, op. 2928, gy. 131, li. 226.
230 War log of the 18th Tank Corps for March 1945. Copy owned by the author. pp. 6. and 8.
231 Malakhov, M. M.: A Balatontól Bécsig (excerpt). In: *Fejezetek hazánk felszabadításának történetéből.* Budapest, 1960. p. 142.
232 Central Archives of the Russian Defence Ministry (Podolsk), f. 243, op. 2928, gy. 131, li. 227.

- on the eastern and western edges of Sárkeresztúr: three M4A2s and one SU–100;
- 900 m southeast of Jakabszállás: three M4A2s and one SU–100;
- north-western slope of Point 143 (southeast of Heinrichmajor) six M4A2s and two SU–100s;
- 2 km northeast of Felsőtöbörzsök: three M4A2s and one SU–100.

These Soviet forces, besides establishing defences, were conducting reconnaissance on the Sárkeresztúr–Soponya road in order to gain information on the movements of the Germans.[233]

The commander of the Soviet 26th Army ordered the 21st Rifle Division in his reserve into the subordination of the 30th Rifle Corps. The units of the Division occupied the second defensive belt between Középkörtvélyes and Alsótöbörzsök.[234]

The *1. Panzer-Division* and *356. Infanterie-Division/III. Panzerkorps* of *Armeegruppe "Balck"* occupied the southern part of Seregélyes (except the cemetery) on the evening of 6 March 1945, then reached Point 108 located 800 meters north of Szerecsenypuszta. During the day, the German troops had not continued combat action here, but were preoccupied with the engineering works necessary for drawing forward the armoured fighting vehicles and the heavy armament of *3. Panzer-Division* and *schwere Panzer-Abteilung 509*. The commander of the *Armeegruppe*, *General der Panzertruppe* Balck, assumed that with the improvement of the weather, his troops would have a better chance for a completely successful assault.[235]

During the day, via the repaired railroad bridge, *schwere Panzer-Abteilung 509* marched to Seregélyes and established covering positions on the edge of the village.[236]

Panzergrenadier-Regiment 113/1. Panzer-Division had on that day cleared the southern part of Seregélyes, and repulsed an attack of six Soviet armoured fighting vehicles from the direction of Sárosd; then, in the evening, tried to occupy the cemetery southeast of Seregélyes. During the night of 7/8 March 1945, the Germans repaired the Seregélyes road bridge, which had been secured by the Panthers of *3. Kompanie/Panzer-Regiment 1*.[237]

The commander of the anti-tank rifle platoon of the Soviet 436th Rifle Regiment/155th Rifle Division, 2nd Lieutenant Ivan G. Kiselyev had blown up one of the two German armoured fighting vehicles that breached the defences, with two anti-tank mines. The officer himself had also died and was awarded the Hero of the Soviet Union posthumously.[238]

During the morning, northeast of Seregélyes, *356. Infanterie-Division* repulsed a Soviet battalion-size attack that was supported by a few armoured fighting vehicles, one of which the Germans knocked out. During the afternoon the German *Grenadiers* occupied the small wooded area 2 km northeast of Seregélyes.[239]

---

233 Central Archives of the Russian Defence Ministry (Podolsk), f. 243, op. 2928, gy. 131, li. 226.
234 Malakhov, M. M.: A Balatontól Bécsig (excerpt). In: *Fejezetek hazánk felszabadításának történetéből*. Budapest, 1960. p. 142.
235 NARA, T311, R162, F7214178.
236 *History of the schwere Panzer-Abteilung 509* (typewritten manuscript). Copy owned by the author. p. 54.
237 Stoves, Rolf: Persönliches Kriegstagebuch Pz.Rgt. 1 (typewritten manuscript, a copy owned by the author), entry on 7 March 1945.
238 HM HIM Hadtörténelmi Levéltár (Budapest), Szovjetunió Hőse kitüntetések gyűjteménye (*Collection of Hero of the Soviet Union awards*), 586.
239 NARA, T311, R162, F7214188.

By 6/7 March 1945, the two German *Divisions* lost altogether 649 men and 49 armoured fighting vehicles. However the tanks and assault guns were disabled only temporarily, due to mechanical reasons, mostly because of the strain they were subjected to advancing on the muddy roads.[240] At the same time the Germans in the area of Seregélyes during the first two days of the assault, reported 38 known and 80 presumed Soviet dead, six knocked out armoured fighting vehicles[241], 19 anti-tank and artillery guns, 13 machine guns and seven mortars, plus two aircraft shot down.[242]

The anti-tank positions and regions fighting in the defensive belt of the Soviet 30th Rifle Corps stopped the assault of the German armoured fighting vehicles and provided time for the units of the 18th Tank Corps to regroup in the south-eastern sector of Seregélyes. These forces then sealed off the gap between the right flank of the 30th Rifle Corps and the defeated units of the 1st Guards Fortified Region. On the first two days of the German attack, the commander of the 3rd Ukrainian Front regrouped three anti-tank artillery regiments from the section of the 4th Guards Army to the front south of Lake Velence.[243]

The forces of the Soviet 18th Tank Corps assigned to Seregélyes were not only employed in reinforcing the defences of the rifle forces, but also for reinstating the weakened morale and will to fight. 1st Lieutenant Vasily P. Brjukhov, one of the company commanders of the 170th Tank Brigade remembers the events as such:

"By the end of the second day of the enemy advance, they managed to drive a wedge 4 km wide into our defence lines, and our troops had fled. The kombrig ordered a combat discipline unit to be established to be able to stop the fleeing soldiers and take over command. Colonel Chunihin arrived at our observation position where Captain Klaustyn was appointed to the role. The kombat ordered me to establish a machine gun unit from the reserve tank crews, the machine gun rifle units and the radio operators."[244]

The Soviet 1016th Self-Propelled Artillery Regiment of the 208th Self-Propelled Artillery Brigade was still in combat in the sector of the 18th Tank Corps and occupied firing positions 3 km east of Seregélyes.[245] This latter regiment was placed battery by battery 400-500 meters apart from the battle line of the tanks of the 18th Tank Corps. For the SU–100 armoured fighting vehicles all around firing positions were prepared, 6 meters wide and one meter deep, which were all interconnected. The soldiers of the machine gun company of the regiment established defensive positions 50 – 75 meters from the assault guns, to be able to secure the armoured fighting vehicles against the German tank destroyer infantry troops equipped with *Panzerfausts* and handheld anti-tank rocket launchers. Three of the four batteries of the regiment were deployed in

---

240 NARA, T311, R163, F7215284.
241 The German troops reported one of these tanks north of Seregélyes, and five south of the village. See BAMA, RH 2/1995 Blatt 42. The latter were most likely the armoured fighting vehicles of the 110th Tank Brigade and the 363rd Guards Heavy Self-Propelled Artillery Regiment arriving from Sárosd.
242 NARA, T311, R163, F7215285.
243 Malakhov, M. M.: A Balatontól Bécsig (excerpt). In: *Fejezetek hazánk felszabadításának történetéből*. Budapest, 1960. p. 144.
244 Bryukhov, Vasiliy: *Red Army Tank Commander. At War in a T–34 on the Eastern Front*. Barnsley, 2013. p. 167.
245 Central Archives of the Russian Defence Ministry (Podolsk), f. 243, op. 2928, gy. 178, li. 67/2.

the first echelon and the fourth was deployed in the second echelon, 500-700 meters deeper. The SU–100 self-propelled guns usually opened fire from 1000 meters aiming at the German heavy tanks. It had been revealed quickly that the SU–100 armoured fighting vehicles would also need machine guns capable of all around firing, which these vehicles did not have.[246]

On that day, *III. Panzerkorps* received some major reinforcements: *schwere Panzer-Abteilung 509*, *Sturmpanzer-Abteilung 219*[247], and *Flammpanzer-Kompanie 351* were subordinated to *1. Panzer-Division*;

356. Infanterie-Division received *Sturmartillerie-Brigade 303*, and *3. Panzer-Division* received *I. (Abteilung)/Panzer-Regiment 24*. The *3. Kompanie/Panzer-Regiment 6/3. Panzer-Division* returned from Germany with ten new Panther tanks, which were equipped with night vision devices.[248]

The corps artillery had also been significantly reinforced by subordinating *Artillerie-Brigade 959* plus *Volks-Werfer Brigades 17* and *19* as well. The Hungarian 3rd Army, as part of *Armeegruppe "Balck"*, was given command of the German *Sturmartillerie-Brigade 239*, which was sent to Bánhida.[249]

Assigned to the Soviet 23rd Tank Corps, the 366th Guards Heavy Self-Propelled Artillery Regiment that was stationed at Lovasberény received 15 captured German armoured fighting vehicles, two Panther tanks and 13 self-propelled guns and assault guns[250], from the 3rd Mobile Tank Workshop. Of these, five SU–150s (*Hummel*), one SU–105 (*Wespe*) and two SU–75s (StuG. III or StuG. IV) had already arrived on that day.[251]

On the same day, it became evident to the Germans that they would be able to deploy major armoured forces exclusively on hard-surface roads in the present weather circumstances. These roads were running from Enying, Káloz, Sárkeresztúr and Sárosd toward the southeast, and from Seregélyes, Perkáta, Dunapentele and Dinnyés toward the northeast. In the current situation, any bypassing manoeuvres could be executed exclusively by the infantry. Therefore, the Germans were forced to attack the rear of those villages that the Soviets had built up as defensive fortifications exclusively with infantry, in order to make it possible for the armoured forces to pass through. The local success of *1. SS-Panzer-Division* at occupying Káloz and Soponya served this purpose.[252]

German radio reconnaissance had uncovered from intercepted radio transmissions and

---

246 Central Archives of the Russian Defence Ministry (Podolsk), f. 339, op. 5179, gy. 69, li. 233-235. The commander of the tanks and mechanized troops of the 27th Army ordered after 12 March 1945 that the SU–100 self-propelled guns of the 207th, 208th and 209th Self-Propelled Artillery Brigades are to be equipped with light machine guns because these vehicles were being employed as tanks increasingly often. See M. Svirin – O. Baronov – M. Kolomiets – D. Nedogonov: *Boj u ozera Balaton*. Moscow, 1999. p. 64.
247 All 20 Sturmpanzer IVs were concentrated in *2. Kompanie/Sturmpanzer-Abteilung 219*, of which nine were combat-ready on 6 March 1945. The *1.* and *3. Kompanies* had already been transported away from Hungary in January 1945. The *3. Kompanie* had returned to Hungary on 23 March 1945 equipped with Sturmpanzer IV armoured fighting vehicles, but was employed north of the Danube. See Bertram, Ludwig: Sturmpanzerabteilung 219. In: *Der Sturmartillerist*. Heft 101. 1991. p. 2338.
248 NARA, T78, R621, F000738.
249 NARA, T311, R163, F7215274.
250 Of these, seven 15 cm *Hummel*s and two 10.5 cm *Wespe*s were self-propelled howitzers, and four were StuG. III and StuG. IV assault guns. See Central Archives of the Russian Defence Ministry (Podolsk), f. 243, op. 2928, gy. 131, li. 228. These German armoured fighting vehicles received an overpainting of red stars, and their wheels were painted black so that they could be easily distinguished from the enemy armoured fighting vehicles during combat.
251 Central Archives of the Russian Defence Ministry (Podolsk), f. 243, op. 2928, gy. 131, li. 225.
252 NARA, T311, R162, F7214182-7214183.

aerial observations of the *Luftwaffe,* that the Soviet 18th Tank Corps had been ordered to the vicinity of the frontline east of the Nádor Canal.[253]

8 March 1945, Thursday

(**WEATHER**: highest daytime temperature under 0 Celsius, varying cloud density, mild snowfall at different locations. The condition of the roads was slightly improving due to the frost at dawn, but was deteriorating again during the day.)

On the frontline near the Dráva River, the forces of *LXXXXI. Armeekorps z.b.V.* tried to break through from the Donji Miholjac and Valpovo bridgeheads, but met significant resistance.[254]

The Bulgarian 1st Independent Tank Battalion/1st Army at Drávaszabolcs prepared for a counterattack against the northern parts of the village. The Bulgarian Panzer IV tanks had to start off when their own assaulting infantry reached the northern edge of the village.[255]

During the day, on the front of *2. Panzerarmee, 16. SS-Panzergrenadier-Division* had only advanced one km from Balázskapuszta toward the northeast, although in heavy combat.[256]

The *I. (Bataillon)/SS-Panzergrenadier-Regiment 36* went on the defence at Balázskapuszta and repulsed three Soviet attacks of battalion strength by the morning, which were supported by 30 tanks. The Germans immobilized three T-34s here, and one was captured.

SS-Panzergrenadier-Regiment 36, SS-Panzer-Abteilung 16 and *SS-Panzer-Aufklärungs-Abteilung 16* prepared for a new attack in the sector of Balázskapuszta, in order to occupy the Juhászlak-farmstead and Points 175 and 179.

The assault was launched at 1010 hours and during heavy combat,

III. (Bataillon)/SS-Panzergrenadier-Regiment 36 occupied the Mészáros hill and the Juhászlak farmstead, then, by the evening, approached the Nagybajom–Kaposvár road at Point 174 within 400 meters, where the unit went on the defence. The *Kompaniechef* of *3. Kompanie/SS-Panzer-Abteilung 16, Obersturmführer* Rex noted the following in his diary:

"At 1030 hours we start off again. The 1. Panzer-Kompanie takes over the fire support in the direction of the vineyard [Mészáros Hill – the author]. This has to be taken over by assault guns to be able to follow 1. Kompanie. But a different thing happens. We receive heavy anti-tank fire. My assault gun is set on fire due to the hits we receive. Other armoured fighting vehicles also sustain anti-tank and artillery fire hits. Luckily there is no total loss. The assault guns are forced to take up positions behind a slope. [...]

In the evening, we get to know that most of the assault guns were sunk in the muddy swamp. The ground freezes, and thaws again. At 1900 hours briefing at Balázskapuszta at the command post of I. (Bataillon)/SS-Panzergrenadier-Regiment 36. The order to attack: I. (Bataillon)/SS-

---

253　NARA, T311, R162, F7214184.
254　Hnlicka, Karl: *Das Ende auf dem Balkan 1944/45 – Die militärische Räumung Jugoslaviens durch die deutsche Wehrmacht.* Musterschmidt – Göttingen, 1970. p. 124.
255　Matev, Kaloyan: *The Armoured Forces of the Bulgarian Army 1936–45.* Solihull, 2015. p. 307.
256　NARA, T311, R162, F7214191-7214192.

Panzergrenadier-Regiment 36, Panzer-Aufklärungs-Abteilung 16 and SS-Panzer-Abteilung 16 launch the attack. Task: to capture and secure Point 174; the 3. Panzer-Kompanie with the mounted I.(Bataillon)/SS-Panzergrenadier-Regiment 36 as vanguard battalion breaks through. A report arrives from Hauptsturmführer Lehmann's III.Bataillon that the Wendland company captured Point 174 and with this, the Nagybajom–Kaposvár road is in the hands of the unit. New order: I. (Bataillon)/SS-Panzergrenadier-Regiment 36 secures Balázskapuszta. The Panzer-Abteilung secures and hurriedly withdraws the assault guns."[257]

One of the officers of *SS-Panzergrenadier-Regiment 36* remembered that day as follows:

"Our armoured fighting vehicles sustained losses right from the beginning. Those that were not engulfed in flames or immobilized, turned to the north to try to get closer to the enemy via a deeper valley, and also not to be knocked out one by one out in the open field. As far as we could tell, in the depression many of the assault guns have sunken in the mud. Soon we have left behind the first armoured fighting vehicle."[258]

During the night, the Soviets had taken back Point 174 and hurled back *III. (Bataillon)/SS-Panzergrenadier-Regiment 36* to the Juhászlak farmstead.[259]

The Soviet 113rd Rifle Division was supported by the 864th Self-Propelled Artillery Regiment with 19 SU–76M self-propelled guns and one T–34 tank 1.5 km west of the Kiskorpád railway station. during these battles the self-propelled guns repelled four German attacks, losing two knocked out SU–76Ms.[260]

The Soviet 1201st Self-Propelled Artillery Regiment with its two remaining operational T–34 tanks was in defence 1.5 km south of the Kiskorpád railway station. In the Kiskorpád area, in reserve to the commander of the 57th Army, stood the 52nd Tank Regiment with 19 T–34 tanks, three motorized rifle battalions and a mortar battery, all from the ranks of the 32nd Independent Guards Mechanized Brigade.[261]

During the afternoon, the German 71. *Infanterie-Division* advanced along the Jákó–Szomajom railroad, centred on the southern side and 1.5 km northeast of the railway station of Jákó, and in heavy combat in the forest, thrust into the first combat trench of the third defensive position of the Soviets. During the evening however, the Soviet counterattacks repelled the Germans to the area between the second and the third defensive positions.[262]

Interestingly, according to the diary of the commander of the tank and mechanized forces of the Soviet 3rd Ukrainian Front, the Germans had deployed approximately 60 tanks and 50 assault guns in the direction of Jákó–Kaposvár.[263] However, according to German sources, there were no tanks in the ranks of *2. Panzerarmee* at that time.

257 Puntigam, Josef Paul: *Vom Plattensee bis zur Mur. Die Kämpfe 1945 im Dreiländereck*. Feldbach, without year of publication, [1993], p. 62.
258 Puntigam, Josef Paul: *Vom Plattensee bis zur Mur. Die Kämpfe 1945 im Dreiländereck*. Feldbach, without year of publication, [1993], p. 56.
259 Puntigam, Josef Paul: *Vom Plattensee bis zur Mur. Die Kämpfe 1945 im Dreiländereck*. Feldbach, without year of publication, [1993], pp. 54-62.
260 Central Archives of the Russian Defence Ministry (Podolsk), f. 243, op. 2928, gy. 131, li. 228.
261 Central Archives of the Russian Defence Ministry (Podolsk), f. 243, op. 2928, gy. 131, li. 228.
262 NARA, T311, R162, F7214191-7214192.
263 Central Archives of the Russian Defence Ministry (Podolsk), f. 243, op. 2928, gy. 131, li. 228.

In heavy combat, *1. Volks-Gebirgs-Division* reached the western edge of Szabótanya 1.5 km southeast from Nagybajom.[264]

On the front of *118. Jäger-Division/XXII. Gebirgskorps,* apart from the artillery harassing fire, there were no major battles carried out.[265]

Between 6 and 8 March 1945, *2. Panzerarmee* lost 2200 men. According to the units' own reports, they captured 125 Soviet soldiers, disarmed 5580 mines and knocked out 14 Soviet tanks and assault guns.[266]

On the front of *I. Kavallerie-Korps/6. Panzerarmee, 4. Kavallerie-Division*[267] had not been involved in significant combat on that day either. On that day, the 25th Honvéd Infantry Regiment/Hungarian 25th Infantry Division was subordinated to the German *Division*.

The renewed attack of *3. Kavallerie-Division*[268] from the farmstead near Hill 162 around noon was not successful, as the assault guns had been bogged down on the Soviet mine obstacles in the first minutes.[269] Following another regrouping, the German unit renewed its attack at 2100 hours towards Mezőkomárom. By that time, the *Pioniere* opened a corridor in the Soviet minefield by clearing another 850 mines.[270]

The *12. SS-Panzer-Division/I. SS-Panzerkorps*[271] with *SS-Panzergrenadier-Regiment 25*, supported by tanks and armored personnel carriers, occupied Pinkócpuszta around 1930 hours, then advanced towards the Enying–Dég road, which they cut through 1 km west of Ősztelek. The armoured combat group of the *Division,* advanced from the sector of Pinkócpuszta to the northeastern outskirts of Dég, where the German armoured fighting vehicles were again stopped by Soviet mine obstacles. The armoured combat group spent the night 3 km west of Dég.

The other armoured combat group of *12. SS-Panzer-Division* had occupied Kishörcsökpuszta and Aranyospuszta 2 km southwest of there during a night fight.[272]

At 0515 hours, *SS-Panzergrenadier-Regiment 26* launched an attack again. One of the supporting *Jagdpanzers* was soon disabled. By the evening, the *Regiment* had approached Dég from the northeast to within 4 km. The Soviet positions established on the northern edge of the village were targeted by the *Grille* self-propelled heavy infantry guns. During one of the combat missions of the Soviet ground attack aircraft, the *Regimentskommandeur, SS-Sturmbannführer* Kostenbader was fatally injured. The command of the *Regiment* was taken over by *SS-Obersturmbannführer* Erich Braun.

---

264 NARA, T311, R162, F7214192.
265 NARA, T311, R162, F7214192.
266 NARA, T311, R163, F7215302.
267 On the same day, *4. Kavallerie-Division* had four combat-ready Panzer II and Luchs light tanks, nine assault guns and *Jagdpanzers*, plus eight armoured personnel carriers. See NARA, T311, R162, F7214562.
268 On that day, *3. Kavallerie-Division* had 12 combat-ready assault guns and *Jagdpanzers*, plus four armoured personnel carriers. A further two light tanks of *4. Kavallerie-Division* were also subordinated to them. See NARA, T311, R162, F7214562.
269 NARA, T311, R163, F7215276.
270 NARA, T311, R162, F7214192.
271 The combat-ready armoured fighting vehicle strength of *12. SS-Panzer-Division* on that day consisted of 18 Panzer IV and Panther tanks, two Panzer IV/70 (V) *Jagdpanzers*, plus 116 armoured personnel carriers. The subordinated *schwere Panzerjäger-Abteilung 560* had six combat-ready Panzer IV/70 (V) and four Jagdpanther *Jagdpanzers*, plus one combat-ready armoured personnel carrier. See NARA, T311, R162, F7214561-7214562.
272 NARA, T311, R162, F7214192.

At the contact point of the two *SS-Panzergrenadier-Regiments*, at a road junction 2 km east of Pinkócpuszta, the road towards Dég was secured by the the Soviets and reinforced with anti-tank guns. For the elimination of this position, a separate armoured combat group for night combat was deployed, which was commanded by *SS-Hauptsturmführer* Hans Siegel. The unit consisted of two companies of *schwere Panzerjäger-Abteilung 560*, a few Panzer IV tanks and anti-aircraft armoured fighting vehicles, and the units of *SS-Panzer-Aufklärungs-Abteilung 12*, altogether approximately 40 armoured combat vehicles. Following the elimination the Soviet fortification, the armoured combat group of Siegel was to advance to Antalmajor in order to be able to support the attack against Dég on the following day.

The armoured combat group started off around midnight. The armoured fighting vehicles attacked in a wide assault wedge, firing tracer shells and surprised the Soviet position at the crossroad, which was eliminated without any German losses. Afterwards, the German armoured fighting vehicles commanded by Siegel, advanced in the darkness without firing; of these vehicles, only 9 and a few armoured personnel carriers reached Antalmajor at around 0500 hours on 9 March 1945 with the others lagging behind.[273]

On that day, the *Division* lost 21 killed including two officers, 106 wounded including six officers, and eight missing in action, altogether 135 men. 38 tanks, 29 *Jagdpanzers*, plus 77 armoured personnel carriers and armoured cars were under repair. The *schwere Panzerjäger-Abteilung 560* subordinated to the *Division*, had 10 Panzer IV/70 *Jagdpanzers* and 18 Jagdpanthers that needed repairs.[274]

The *1. SS-Panzer-Division* on the same day renewed its attack late in the afternoon. The combat group of *SS-Panzergrenadier-Regiment 2* deployed on the right flank, attacking toward the south from Káloz and in the evening, occupied Nagyhörcsökpuszta. The armoured group joined them by the evening, after they breached a Soviet anti-tank region in the sector of Pusztaegred with the loss of a Panzer IV, then they continued their attack toward the road between Igar and Cece. Here however, the German armoured fighting vehicles ran into another Soviet anti-tank region and their attack was halted.[275]

The battalions of *SS-Panzergrenadier-Regiment 1* were preoccupied with clearing Soponya and Káloz on that day.[276] During the fighting that day, the *Division* lost 57 killed including 1 officer, 263 wounded including three officers, and one missing in action, altogether 321 men.

On that day, the *Division* had 23 combat-ready tanks, seven *Jagdpanzers*, plus 133 armoured fighting vehicles and armoured cars. Another 41 tanks, 15 assault guns and 49 armoured fighting vehicles and armoured cars were under repair. *1. SS-Panzer-Division* did not sustain any total armour losses during the first three days of combat.[277]

---

273 Meyer, Hubert: *Kriegsgeschichte der 12. SS-Panzerdivision „Hitlerjugend"*. Band II. Osnabrück, 1987. 2nd edition. pp. 497-498.
274 BAMA, RH-19, V/62 Kriegstagebuch der Heeresgruppe Süd Anlageband, Tägliche Verluste u. Pz. Ausfälle zur Vorlage beim Führer vom 10. 3. 1945.
275 Tiemann, Ralf: *Chronik der 7. Panzerkompanie. An vorderster Front in der 1. SS-Panzerdivision „Leibstandarte SS Adolf Hitler"*. Selent, 2015. p. 246.
276 Tiemann, Ralf: *Die Leibstandarte*. Band IV/2. Osnabrück, 1987. p. 268.
277 BAMA, RH-19, V/62 Kriegstagebuch der Heeresgruppe Süd Anlageband, Tägliche Verluste u. Pz. Ausfälle zur Vorlage beim Führer vom 10. 3. 1945.

The forces of *1. SS-Panzer-Division*[278] cleared Soponya in heavy close quarters combat, then an armoured combat group approached to within 3 km of Dég from the east-northeast, and in the evening hours occupied Point 134, 1.5 km northeast of the village. The other combat group of the unit occupied Nagyhörcsökpuszta around 2100 hours, then continued its attack towards the south.[279]

The two armoured combat groups of *I. SS-Panzerkorps* took part in combat action that night, then attacked towards Dég, on converging lines. At the same time, the Germans succeeded in clearing the Soponya–Káloz road for their own armoured fighting vehicles.[280]

In the sector of the Soviet 236th Rifle Division/26th Army, the 1068th Self-Propelled Artillery Regiment/208th Self-Propelled Artillery Brigade, deployed as reinforcements, were engaged in combat around 1500 hours with the German combat groups, attacking with 24 and 15 armoured fighting vehicles,[281] in the Nagyhörcsökpuszta–Antalmajor–Dég sector and repelled five German attacks by 1800 hours. During this time, the Regiment reported to have knocked out five German tanks, one *Jagdpanzer* and four armoured personnel carriers. They lost three SU-100 self-propelled guns, two of which were burnt out. The 1922nd Self-Propelled Artillery Regiment, as the anti-tank artillery reserve of the 26th Army, was gathered in the sector of Sáregres.[282] West of the Malom Canal, the 233rd and 236th Rifle Divisions were also supported by the 1008th and 1245th Anti-Tank Artillery Regiments of the 49th Anti-Tank Artillery Brigade.[283]

According to one Russian researcher, the 1068th Self-Propelled Artillery Regiment/208th Self-Propelled Artillery Brigade marching in column, was surprised by an assault of the advancing German armour, and as the Brigade commander had not coordinated his actions with the Rifle Divisions waiting for the SU–100 self-propelled guns, the Regiment lost 14 of their 21 guns, then retreated to Sáregres. However, these events have not been confirmed by Soviet archival sources uncovered by the author.[284]

On the same day, another armoured unit of the 26th Army arrived. After a delay of 11 hours, from around 0400 hours in the morning, the 22nd Independent Tank Regiment created ambush positions at the northern edge of the forest northwest of Dég, at Szúnyogpuszta, on the Hill 159, north of Lajoskomárom, and on the northwestern edge of Lajoskomárom. At that time, the Regiment had 13 operational T–34 tanks, one KV–1 heavy tank and four SU–85s, however on that day, the armoured fighting vehicles were not engaged in combat.[285]

---

278 On the same day, *1. SS-Panzer-Division* had 23 combat-ready Panzer IV and Panther tanks, seven Panzer IV/70 (V) *Jagdpanzers* and 133 armoured personnel carriers. The subordinated *schwere Panzer-Abteilung 501* had 31 combat-ready Tiger B and Flakpanzer IV armoured fighting vehicles, plus nine armoured personnel carriers. See NARA, T311, R162, F7214561-7214562.
279 NARA, T311, R162, F7214192.
280 NARA, T311, R162, F7214195-7214196.
281 Summarized report of the 208th Self-Propelled Artillery Brigade of the period between 6 March – 6 April 1945. Copy owned by the author. p. 5.
282 Central Archives of the Russian Defence Ministry (Podolsk), f. 243, op. 2928, gy. 131, li. 228. According to the summarized report of the 208th Self-Propelled Artillery Brigade the 1068th Self-Propelled Artillery Regiment reported on 8 March to have knocked out 23 tanks, six *Jagdpanzers* and two armoured personnel carriers. This data is not verified by German sources.
283 Isaev, Aleksei–Kolomiets, Maksim: *Tomb of the Panzerwaffe. The Defeat of the 6th SS Panzer Army in Hungary 1945.* Solihull, 2014. p. 153.
284 Isaev, Aleksei–Kolomiets, Maksim: *Tomb of the Panzerwaffe. The Defeat of the 6th SS Panzer Army in Hungary 1945.* Solihull, 2014. p. 153.
285 Central Archives of the Russian Defence Ministry (Podolsk), f. 243, op. 2928, gy. 131, li. 228.

Around midnight on 7 March 1945, *44. Reichsgrenadier-Division/II. SS-Panzerkorps*[286] occupied Point 141 3.5 km northeast of Sárkeresztúr, then, during the day, launched its attack 6 km southwest of Sárosd towards the southwest and reached a line of hills 3 km north-northeast of Sárkeresztúr. In the meantime, the Germans repulsed a Soviet attack of two battalions in strength, which was also supported by armoured fighting vehicles. During this action the Germans reported to have knocked out seven Soviet armoured fighting vehicles.[287]

The attack of *2. SS-* and *9. SS-Panzer-Divisions*[288] had not advanced very far, as Soviet troops were covering them with fire from the hills 4 km west of Sárosd.

Beginning at 1410 hours, for 40 minutes, 24 German Fw 190 ground attack aircraft raided the Soviet artillery positions in the area of Sárosd.[289] Although the German ground attack aircraft of *Luftflotte 4* were also supporting the SS-troops, they were not able to breach the Soviet defence system that was deeply echeloned, and also strengthened by a number of reinforced strongpoints and dug in armoured fighting vehicles.

After this, the forces of the two *SS-Panzer-Divisions* were regrouped, and at 1915 hours, renewed their attack towards the eastern perimeter of Sárkeresztúr.[290]

This time, in heavy combat, *2. SS-Panzer-Division* managed to reach Points 105 and 141, 3 to 4 km east of Aba. During the fighting on 7 and 8 March 1945, four tanks and one assault gun of the *Division* were destroyed and 35 tanks, 27 assault guns and *Jagdpanzers*, and 149 armoured personnel carriers and armoured cars were under repair.[291]

Around 2200 hours, *9. SS-Panzer-Division* occupied the Soviet positions 3.5 km west of Sárosd in the area of Hill 159 (Csillag), but not the hill itself, and occupied Csillagmajor and Szárnyasmajor 3 km northwest of Sárosd[292] with 20-25 armoured fighting vehicles and *Panzergrenadier*-infantry in regiment strength[293].

On that day, the *Division* lost 29 killed, 84 wounded including five officers and two missing in action, altogether 115 men. The *Division* had 43 combat-ready tanks, 27 assault guns and *Jagdpanzers*, plus 139 armoured personnel carriers and armoured reconnaissance cars. Another 28 tanks, 20 assault guns and *Jagdpanzers*, 69 armoured personnel carriers and armoured cars were under repair.[294]

In the defence sector of the 1st Guards Mechanized Corps, the Germans launched an attack at 0100 hours with a battalion-size force aiming at the concealed positions of the 18th Guards Tank Regiment and the 1821st Self-Propelled Artillery Regiment. Guards Lieutenant Colonel Ivan U. Leshenko, the commander of the Regiment did not want to

---

286 The *44. Reichsgrenadier-Division* had six Jagdpanzer 38(t) *Jagdpanzers* in combat-ready condition on that day. See NARA, T311, R162, F7214562.
287 NARA, T311, R162, F7214193.
288 On that day, *2. SS-Panzer-Division* had 26 combat-ready tanks, plus 22 assault guns and *Jagdpanzers*, as well as 75 armoured personnel carriers. The *9. SS-Panzer-Division* had 43 tanks, 27 assault guns and *Jagdpanzers*, plus 139 armoured personnel carriers in combat-ready condition. See NARA, T311, R162, F7214561.
289 Central Archives of the Russian Defence Ministry (Podolsk), f. 440, op. 8311, gy. 98, li. 72/2.
290 NARA, T311, R162, F7214193.
291 BAMA, RH-19, V/62 Kriegstagebuch der Heeresgruppe Süd Anlageband, Tägliche Verluste u. Pz. Ausfälle zur Vorlage beim Führer vom 10. 3. 1945.
292 NARA, T311, R163, F7215287.
293 Central Archives of the Russian Defence Ministry (Podolsk), f. 243, op. 2928, gy. 131, li. 231.
294 BAMA, RH-19, V/62 Kriegstagebuch der Heeresgruppe Süd Anlageband, Tägliche Verluste u. Pz. Ausfälle zur Vorlage beim Führer vom 10. 3. 1945.

expose the positions of his armoured troops, and so repelled the infantry attack solely with armoured transport vehicles and the fire of the hull machine guns of the T-34 recovery tanks. The Germans repeated the attack at 0800 hours and reached the area of Heinrichmajor by 0930 hours. The Soviets used the same method with the armoured transport vehicles and fire of the hull machine guns of T-34 recovery tanks, and again repelled the attack during which the Soviets captured 25 prisoners.[295]

The 11th Guards Motorcycle Battalion of the Corps arrived at Sárszentágota. The 1st Guards Mechanized Corps had on that evening, 48 operational M4A2s, three T–34 tanks and 17 SU–100 self-propelled guns.[296]

Between Point 140 northeast of Sárosd and Hill 159 (Csillag), west of Sárosd, the 110th Tank Brigade/18th Tank Corps and the 363rd Guards Heavy Self-Propelled Artillery Regiment/18th Tank Corps repulsed nine German attacks on that day from the north and northwest. During these actions, the Soviet armoured fighting vehicles reported to have knocked out 24 German tanks while their own losses amounted to six knocked out T-34 tanks of which, five were burnt out, and five ISU-122s of which, two burnt out.[297] By the evening, in the 110th Tank Brigade, 27 tanks remained operational and nine ISU-122 were operational in the 363rd Guards Heavy Self-Propelled Artillery Regiment. The forces of the Corps were attacked on that day in the area of Seregélyes and Sárosd by 50 German aircraft, flying in successive waves, in formations of 15 to 30 aircraft.[298]

The 1016th Self-Propelled Artillery Regiment/208th Self-Propelled Artillery Brigade had been in combat on the northern edge of Sárosd together with the forces of the 18th Tank Corps on that day.[299] During the fighting for Hill 159, the Regiment reported to have knocked out three heavy German tanks, most likely Panthers, and their own losses amounted to two burnt out ISU-100s.[300]

Until 0600 hours in the morning, the 1202nd Self-Propelled Artillery Regiment was engaged in combat with the Germans in firing positions 1.5 km south of Seregélyes; then, upon orders from the 26th Army, the unit relocated to the north-western edge of Sárosd after 0800 hours. The regiment lost a burnt out SU-76m, leaving 13 remaining operational self-propelled guns.[301]

On the front of *III. Panzerkorps/Armeegruppe "Balck"*, *Panzergrenadier-Regiment 113/1. Panzer-Division* launched an attack southwards from Seregélyes, occupied the cemetery southeast of the village, which pushed the frontline outwards 1 km. East of Seregélyes, *Panzergrenadier-Regiment 1* and *Panzer-Aufklärungs-Abteilung 1/1. Panzer-Division* advanced towards the east, while two battalions of *356. Infanterie-Division* advanced towards the northeast. With this, the Germans extended the bridgehead at Seregélyes 2 km toward the east and 1.5 km toward the northeast.

---

295   Central Archives of the Russian Defence Ministry (Podolsk), f. 243, op. 2928, gy. 131, li. 229.
296   Central Archives of the Russian Defence Ministry (Podolsk), f. 243, op. 2928, gy. 178, li. 68/2.
297   Central Archives of the Russian Defence Ministry (Podolsk), f. 243, op. 2928, gy. 131, li. 229.
298   War log of the 18th Tank Corps for March 1945. Copy owned by the author. 8. o.
299   Central Archives of the Russian Defence Ministry (Podolsk), f. 243, op. 2928, gy. 131, li. 228.
300   Summarized report of the 208th Self-Propelled Artillery Brigade of the period between 6 March – 6 April 1945. Copy owned by the author. p. 5. The report mentions knocked out Tiger tanks, however their presence is not verified by German sources.
301   Central Archives of the Russian Defence Ministry (Podolsk), f. 243, op. 2928, gy. 131, li. 228.

The *1. Panzer-Division* in the bridgehead deployed smaller groups of 5 to 8 Panthers and armoured pioneers mounted on armoured personnel carriers in order to support the *Panzergrenadiers* and the *Grenadiers*. Part of the *Division*'s armour repair workshop were drawn forward from Hajmáskér to the airfield of Börgönd.[302]

On that day, near Sándormajor, the 170th Tank Brigade and the 1438th Self-Propelled Artillery Regiment/18th Tank Corps repelled three German attacks from the direction of Seregélyes, and reported to have knocked out a German armoured fighting vehicle. At the same time, their own losses were two knocked out T–34s, one of which burnt out, and three SU–76Ms. The 181st Tank Brigade was in reserve to the commander of the Corps, at the north-western edge of Felsőszolgaegyháza.[303] On that day, 14 new T-34/85 tanks arrived for the Corps at the train station of Ócsa.[304]

An officer of the 170th Tank Brigade, 1st Lieutenant Brjukhov remembered the events as follows:

"The commander[305] of the SU-100 self-propelled gun battalion [correctly: regiment – the author] assigned to the brigade yesterday, was repeatedly asking the kombrig to confirm permission for opening fire for their long-range 100 mm cannons. Chunihin was watching the movements of the enemy suspiciously, and answered every time: "Hold on!" Our tanks had also not fired yet. The kombrig signalled to open fire only when the enemy was within 500 meters. At once, every tank, self-propelled gun and anti-tank gun started to roll out fire and also our aircraft were flying past. An extremely heavy and lethal battle commenced.
The German tanks held to their combat methodology and by exploiting the inconsistencies in the ground, were searching for contact points or otherwise weak sections of our positions, as they were swirling around and slowly creeping toward our lines. By noon, we repelled the first enemy attack successfully. The enemy lost two tanks and three armoured transport vehicles; they retreated and continued firing from a covered position. In the second half of the day, the Germans attacked from Seregélyes with a battalion-size force and the support of eight tanks, but we also repelled this attack."[306]

The restoration of the railroad bridge northwest of Seregélyes was considerably hindered by the constant harassment of Soviet fighter, ground-attack and bomber aircraft, and it was expected not to be ready until around 0400 hours on 9 March 1945.[307]

General der Panzertruppe Balck and *General der Infanterie* Wöhler were discussing the deployment of *III. Panzerkorps* on the following day. The incoming *3. Panzer-Division* was to attack from the area of Seregélyes towards the east, south of Hill 145 (Öreg Hill)

---

302 Stoves, Rolf: Persönliches Kriegstagebuch Pz.Rgt. 1 (typewritten manuscript, a copy owned by the author), entry on 8 March 1945.
303 Central Archives of the Russian Defence Ministry (Podolsk), f. 243, op. 2928, gy. 131, li. 229.
304 Central Archives of the Russian Defence Ministry (Podolsk), f. 243, op. 2928, gy. 178, li. 68/2.
305 This most likely refers to the commander of the 1016th Self-Propelled Artillery Regiment/208th Self-Propelled Artillery Brigade, Lieutenant Colonel (later Colonel) Pavel Viktorovich Makacyuba.
306 Bryukhov, Vasiliy: *Red Army Tank Commander. At War in a T–34 on the Eastern Front*. Barnsley, 2013. pp. 169-170.
307 NARA, T311, R162, F7214193.

dominating the area; the *1. Panzer-Division* was to attack northwards from Seregélyes, towards Dinnyés, then along the southern shore of Lake Velence towards Kápolnásnyék; and *356. Infanterie-Division* was to attack between *1.* and *3. Panzer-Divisions*.[308]

Luftflotte 4 flew 230 missions on that day to support the German *6. Panzerarmee*, and in 70 night missions performed by ground attack aircraft, it had attacked the Soviet unit movements in progress east of the Nádor Canal. Nagybajom was hit twice by Soviet air attack; the village was attacked by 16 bombers and five to six ground attack aircraft. Székesfehérvár was also bombed twice on that day by the Soviets. The Germans counted 150 IL-2 ground attack aircraft, 100 A-20 Boston bombers and 110 fighter aircraft over *III. Panzerkorps* and *IV. SS-Panzerkorps* positions, that were assaulting the German frontlines, waterway crossings, supply lines and villages beyond the frontlines with bombs and machine guns.[309] The front of *6. Panzerarmee* was raided by a large number of Soviet bombers, mainly in the sector of *II. SS-Panzerkorps* where the Germans had counted 52 A-20 Bostons[310]. On that day, not only Soviet but also American lend-lease aircraft were fighting over the Transdanubia, bombing Komárom. The Germans reported to have shot down 14 Soviet and American planes.[311]

The reconnaissance of the German *Heeresgruppe* identified the Soviet 18th Tank Corps in the area of Sárosd, which they presumed were equipped with approximately 60 to 150 armoured fighting vehicles.[312] German reconnaissance assumed that the Soviets had not yet drawn into combat the forces of the 1st Guards and 2nd Guards Mechanized Corps, and the 23rd Tank Corps. The Germans also assumed that the Soviets were building up a new defensive line behind the Sió Canal, centred around Simontornya, where the forces of the 5th Guards Cavalry Corps were to be drawn forward. German reconnaissance had searched in vain for the Soviet 7th Mechanized Corps since the beginning of February 1945.[313]

The *Heeresgruppe* concentrated the Hungarian 25th Infantry Division and the German *23. Panzer-Division*[314] behind the attacking groups of German *6. Panzerarmee* behind the line separating *I. Kavallerie* and *I. SS-Panzerkorps* and behind *44. Reichsgrenadier-Division* respectively, to be prepared in case the Soviet defences were breached.[315]

On that day, *6. Panzer-Division* was directly subordinated to *Heeresgruppe Süd*, and was assembled in the area of Mór–Isztimér–Fehérvárcsurgó.[316]

---

308   NARA, T311, R162, F7214206.
309   BAMA, RH 2/1995 Blatt 137.
310   BAMA, RH 2/1995 Blatt 138.
311   NARA, T311, R162, F7214195, furthermore NARA, T311, R163, F7215281.
312   NARA, T311, R162, F7214206.
313   NARA, T311, R162, F7214196-7214197. The reason for this is that on 2 March 1945 the 3rd Ukrainian Front handed over the 7th Mechanized Corps (mostly personnel, without significant amounts of armament or armoured fighting vehicles) to the 2nd Ukrainian Front, then it was assigned to the sector of Bucharest and Ploesti. See the war log of the 3rd Ukrainian Front from March 1945. Copy owned by the author. 2 March 1945, pp. 7-8.
314   According to data as of 1 March 1945, *23. Panzer-Division* was suitable for attack in a limited capacity. The fact is characteristic that of the 36 existing Panther tanks of *Panzer-Regiment 23* only 16 were combat-ready, and of the 20 under repair, 17 were waiting for new engines. The low quality fuel caused further engine-related malfunctions. See BAMA, RH 10/159 Blatt 113. On 8 March the *Division* had 25 combat-ready tanks, 22 assault guns and *Jagdpanzers*, and 82 armoured personnel carriers. See NARA, T311, R162, F7214561.
315   NARA, T311, R162, F7214197.
316   NARA, T311, R163, F7215283.

The *23. Panzer-Division* at the same time was regrouped in the area of Pápa–Celldömölk–Jánosháza–Devecser, and in connection with this, the results of the terrain reconnaissance were to be reported to the *Heeresgruppe* by 14 March 1945.[317]

9 March 1945, Friday

(**WEATHER**: night frost, during the day the highest daytime temperature is slightly over 0 Celsius, varied cloud density, windy, occasional billowing of snow. The driveability of the unpaved roads was slightly improved.)

Along the Dráva River, the Panzer IV tanks of the 1ˢᵗ Independent Tank Battalion/Bulgarian 1ˢᵗ Army were supporting the Bulgarian infantry at Szödöny, 1 km northeast of Drávacsehi. When the Tank Battalion reached its assigned point of departure, the infantry to be supported had not arrived yet. The Bulgarian tanks launched their attack against the cluster of houses without infantry support, but the German anti-tank guns knocked out a Panzer IV and the attack failed. On that day, the Battalion also launched an attack against Drávaszabolcs, and the Germans knocked out one of the Panzer IVs with a *Panzerfaust*.[318]

On the front of *LXVIII. Armeekorps/2. Panzerarmee*, *16. SS-Panzergrenadier-Division* and the forces of *1. Volks-Gebirgs-Division* reached the Nagybajom–Kaposvár road 4 km southeast of Nagybajom during the evening of 8 March 1945. However the Soviet troops repulsed the Germans early on the night of 8/9 March 1945 with counterattacks supported by armoured fighting vehicles.[319]

SS-Panzergrenadier-Regiment 36/16. SS-Panzergrenadier-Division was in defence on the Juhászlak-farmstead–Mészáros Hill–Balázskapuszta line. Here the Germans were slightly pushed back by the Soviets and *SS-Panzer-Abteilung 16* tried to tow away their assault guns that were knocked out or bogged down the previous day. During the day, the *SS-Panzergrenadiers* were replaced by the forces of *118. Jäger-Division*.[320]

In the sector, northwest of Kiskorpád, the Soviet 864ᵗʰ Self-Propelled Artillery Regiment was fighting with 17 SU–76M self-propelled guns and one T–34 tank. On 8 and 9 March 1945 the Regiment lost four knocked out self-propelled guns, two of which had been burnt out, probably on 9 March 1945.[321]

The *71. Infanterie-Division* was only able to push forward at two of its strongpoints east of the southern area of Jákó, a little towards the east.

The German *3. Kavallerie-Division/I. Kavallerie-Korps/6. Panzerarmee* during its forceful attack in the morning, cut through the Enying – Dég road with its left flank, and in the meantime captured significant amounts of Soviet heavy armament and prisoners of

---

317   NARA, T311, R162, F7214451.
318   Matev, Kaloyan: *The Armoured Forces of the Bulgarian Army 1936–45*. Solihull, 2015. p. 307.
319   NARA, T311, R162, F7214211.
320   Puntigam, Josef Paul: *Vom Plattensee bis zur Mur. Die Kämpfe 1945 im Dreiländereck*. Feldbach, without year of publication, [1993], p. 64.
321   Central Archives of the Russian Defence Ministry (Podolsk), f. 243, op. 2928, gy. 178, li. 69.

war.[322] *Reiter-Regiment 31* set off from Ágostonpuszta and occupied Hill 162 (Ágoston Hill) and Óhódospuszta, where the Germans cut through the road. Exploiting this achievement, an armoured combat group was formed from the assault guns and *Jagdpanzers* of *Panzerjäger-Abteilung 69*, with armoured personnel carriers and anti-aircraft guns of *schwere Kavallerie-Abteilung 3*, under the *Kommandeur* of *Panzerjäger-Abteilung 69*, *Hauptmann* von Falkenhausen. The armoured combat group was thrown into combat from the direction of Óhódospuszta towards Mezőkomárom to occupy the bridges there. However, the attack of the armoured combat group was halted, following which the unit established firing positions on the hills around Óhódospuszta.[323]

The right flank of the corps, most likely *4. Kavallerie-Division*, breached the south-eastern part of Enying again around 1530 hours, and during the afternoon *3. Kavallerie-Division* again set off towards the north-western outskirts of Mezőkomárom.[324]

The 22nd Independent Tank Regiment of the Soviet 26th Army with 13 T–34 tanks and two self-propelled guns had been in heavy combat throughout the whole day with the German troops in the Szúnyogpuszta–Lajoskomárom area.[325]

The commander of the 3rd Battery of the Hungarian 20th Assault Artillery Battalion supporting *3. Kavallerie-Division*, 1st Lieutenant Tasziló Kárpáthy, remembered the events as follows:

> *"We had been engaged in heavy combat with the appearing T-34s during which my [assault gun's] right driving gear was hit, after which the vehicle was at first immobilized, but since the oil duct was also on fire, and was spreading on the inside of the assault gun, we were forced to leave the vehicle. As we later saw, the fire spread to the fuel tank and the ammunition inside the gun was blown up. After leaving our vehicle, we were considerably anxious, until the assault guns that were sent to our aid came for us."*[326]

The plan was to deploy the Hungarian 25th Infantry Division against the Soviet units still in combat between Enying and Siófok; the Hungarian unit, together with the Hungarian 153rd Machine-Towed Multiple Rocket-Launcher Artillery Battalion[327] was subordinated to *I. Kavallerie-Korps*.[328]

By the morning, the forces of *12. SS-Panzer-Division/I. SS-Panzerkorps* occupied the bend in the road 3 km southwest of Pinkócpuszta and closed off the Enying–Dég road. After the *SS*-troops occupied Ősztelek, they launched an attack against the western edge of Dég.[329]

---

322 NARA, T311, R162, F7214211.
323 Quoted by Witte, Hans Joachim – Offermann, Peter: *Die Boeselagerschen Reiter. Das Kavallerie-Regiment Mitte und die aus ihm hervorgegangene 3. Kavallerie-Brigade/Division*. München, 1998. p. 388.
324 NARA, T311, R162, F7214220.
325 Central Archives of the Russian Defence Ministry (Podolsk), f. 243, op. 2928, gy. 131, li. 230
326 Tasziló Kárpáthy: *A magyar királyi honvéd 20. rohamtüzérosztály története*. In: HM HIM Hadtörténelmi Levéltár (Budapest), Rohamtüzér-gyűjtemény, 14/7. collection. pp. 18-19.
327 The Hungarian artillery unit was placed in direct subordination to the German *6. Panzerarmee* on that evening, but they were planned to be deployed in the sector of *I. Kavallerie-Korps* in order to support the 25th Honvéd Infantry Division. See NARA, T311, R162, F7214468.
328 NARA, T311, R162, F7214215.
329 NARA, T311, R163, F7215287.

Under cover of the morning mist, the units of the two *SS-Panzergrenadier-Regiment*s and *Panzer-Kampfgruppe "Siegel"* launched an attack against Dég. The commander of the latter unit watched from a Jagdpanther while his armoured combat vehicles carried out a frontal attack against the village, while its anti-aircraft armoured vehicles bypassed towards the northwest, launching their own attack. In Dég, the Germans ran into approximately 12 Soviet SU–100 self-propelled guns, and knocked out a number of them. One of the Soviet self-propelled guns was knocked out from behind by a German anti-aircraft armoured fighting vehicle; the shell, most likely 3.7 cm, was fired from 50 meters and penetrated through the engine compartment. The surprised SU-100 armoured fighting vehicles left Dég in a south and south-eastern direction, and retreated. They crossed the creek southeast of the village by driving two SU-100s into the creek next to the bridge and the remaining vehicles drove to the other side over top of them.[330]

The units of the two *SS-Panzergrenadier-Regiments,* attacking with the armoured fighting vehicles cleared Dég while the armoured combat group continued its attack southwards. The tanks of one of the armoured companies equipped with Panthers was bogged down and sank, and they were finally towed away in the evening.[331] By the evening, *SS-Panzergrenadier-Regiment 25* and *III. (gepanzert) (Bataillon)/SS-Panzergrenadier-Regiment 26* advanced to the north-western outskirts of Mezőszilas. The *II. (Bataillon)/SS-Panzergrenadier-Regiment 26*, equipped with Panzer IV/70 *Jagdpanzers,* also stood north of Mezőszilas by the evening, as well as the *I. (Bataillon)/SS-Panzergrenadier-Regiment 26.*[332]

After clearing further Soviet mine obstacles, the *Division* continued fighting 4 km south-southwest of Dég on extremely muddy terrain, and with its units tried to occupy Mezőszilas, which was achieved by *SS-Panzergrenadier-Regiment 26* at around 2100 hours.[333]

From the early morning hours, the Soviet 1068th Self-Propelled Artillery Regiment/208th Self-Propelled Artillery Brigade was engaged in heavy combat with 30 armoured fighting vehicles and 20 armoured personnel carriers northeast of Dég, in the sector of Antalmajor and Hunyorosmajor. During more than 4 hours of action the Soviet rifle infantry retreated, abandoning their SU–100s. The Soviet self-propelled guns reported to have knocked out six Tiger tanks, two *Jagdpanzers* and 11 armoured personnel carriers. On that day, five of the seven knocked out SU-100s of the 1068th Self-Propelled Artillery Regiment were burnt out. From the crews, 12 men including four officers, were killed and 15 were wounded.[334] Following orders of the 26th Army, the Regiment retreated to the northern edge of Mezőszilas until 1600 hours. During the action on 8 and 9 March 1945, the Regiment lost eight burnt out SU-100s, and another three of the knocked out self-propelled guns needed medium-extent repairs.[335]

---

330 Meyer, Hubert: *Kriegsgeschichte der 12. SS-Panzerdivision „Hitlerjugend".* Band II. Osnabrück, 1987. 2nd edition. p. 499.
331 In 1998, in written response to the questionnaire of the author, *SS-Hauptsturmführer* Hans Siegel mentioned that towing away the sunken armoured fighting vehicles southeast of Dég caused considerable loss of time that in his opinion that was why they were not able to occupy the sector of Simontornya in time on the southern bank of the Sió Canal.
332 Meyer, Hubert: *Kriegsgeschichte der 12. SS-Panzerdivision „Hitlerjugend".* Band II. Osnabrück, 1987. 2nd edition. pp. 498-499.
333 NARA, T311, R162, F7214211.
334 Summarized report of the 208th Self-Propelled Artillery Brigade of the period between 6 March – 6 April 1945. Copy owned by the author. p. 6.
335 Central Archives of the Russian Defence Ministry (Podolsk), f. 243, op. 2928, gy. 178, li. 69.

The 1922nd Self-Propelled Artillery Regiment of the Brigade was engaged in combat with the Germans, who were equipped with 10 tanks and 10 armoured personnel carriers, throughout the day at Mezőszilas and in the sector of Hill 162 (Galancsér) and from this location, they reported to have knocked out six German tanks, two assault guns and 33 armoured personnel carriers. When, during the early afternoon, the Soviet rifle infantry retreated from this area, the SU–100s were only covered by an engineer pioneer platoon and the Regiment's own submachine gun platoon. The commander of the Brigade sent an M3A1 armoured transport vehicle platoon and one of the M15A1 platoons of the self-propelled anti-aircraft company as reinforcement. The 37 mm automatic cannons and the 12.7 mm machine guns perfectly covered the self-propelled guns, which did not have their own machine guns. The armoured fighting vehicles of the Regiment in this way were able to repel the German attack and reported to have knocked out five tanks and two armoured fighting vehicles with their own loss of two burnt out SU–100s.[336] The commander of the 26th Army had also withdrawn the 1922nd Self-Propelled Artillery Regiment, which established defensive positions around 1800 hours on the northern outskirts of Sáregres.[337]

In the morning, *1. SS-Panzer-Division* continued its attack on both of its flanks. From the sector of Nagyhörcsökpuszta, *Panzergruppe "Peiper"* and units of *SS-Panzergrenadier-Regiment 2* on the right flank, launched their attack towards Simontornya, while on the left flank, *SS-Panzergrenadier-Regiment 1,* with *SS-Panzer-Aufklärungs-Abteilung 1* and *SS-Panzerjäger-Abteilung 1* together, launched their attack towards Sáregres.

The armoured group could, despite the unfavourable condition of the roads and the minefields, fight as they did earlier on the Eastern Front. During the fighting at Normandy and in the Ardennes, Allied air superiority prevented armoured attacks being carried out during the daytime. At the front, the Tiger B, Panthers and the Panzer IV tanks were rolling in wide or inverted tank wedges. Behind them, in open formation, the anti-aircraft armoured fighting vehicles were following, equipped with 2 or 3.7 cm anti-aircraft guns, which, during close quarters combat, were to support the *Panzergrenadiers*. A few Panther tanks were there as well, which engaged the Soviet armoured fighting vehicles as they appeared. Behind the tanks, the *Panzergrenadier-Bataillon*, equipped with armoured personnel carriers, also fanned out.[338]

The troops on the right flank reached the hills around Jánosházamajor, but here the Soviet anti-tank blocking positions and artillery fire from the southern bank of the Sió Canal stopped them.

The troops in combat on the left flank, advanced on the Nagyhörcsökpuszta–Sáregres route and ran into a solid Soviet defence at Huszárpuszta and Fáncspuszta. Following their success in breaking the resistance there, they continued their march, but a Soviet anti-tank blocking position in front of Sáregres halted their progress. In the late afternoon both flanks renewed their attacks. On the right flank, the units succeeded in advancing up to the hills

---

336   Summarized report of the 208th Self-Propelled Artillery Brigade of the period between 6 March – 6 April 1945. Copy owned by the author. p. 7.
337   Central Archives of the Russian Defence Ministry (Podolsk), f. 243, op. 2928, gy. 131, li. 230th
338   Agte, Patrick: *Jochen Peiper. Kommandeur Panzerregiment Leibstandarte*. Berg am Starnberger See, 1998. p. 351.

west of Simontornya, and on the left flank, to Sáregres. For the night, the division went into defence on the same line.[339]

The *1. SS-Panzer-Division* attacked through Huszárpuszta and reached the northern outskirts of Simontornya, where it ran into an extensive Soviet anti-tank region, but could still keep the traffic hubs of the village under fire with special attention on the crossing over the Sió Canal. On the road from Huszárpuszta towards Simontornya, on Hill 157, one Panzer IV tank of *SS-Panzer-Regiment 1*, which was keeping the Simontornya–Cece road under fire, was knocked out at 0630 hours in the morning after three hits from one of the 37 mm automatic cannons of the 1st Battery/1084th Anti-Aircraft Artillery Regiment. However, the commander of the Battery and one of his officers were killed in the engagement with the German armoured fighting vehicle.[340]

West of Huszárpuszta and at Fancspuszta the Soviet forces were continuously in combat. Fancspuszta was finally occupied by the Germans in the evening, and detected a large number of artillery positions and anti-tank strongpoints on the eastern bank of the Nádor Canal.[341]

The Soviets created an extremely strong anti-tank region between Simontornya and Cece, under the commander of the 49th Anti-Tank Artillery Brigade, which possessed more than 100 field, anti-aircraft and self-propelled guns with the following units:

- 1008th Anti-Tank Artillery Regiment/49th Anti-Tank Artillery Brigade
- 1249th Anti-Tank Artillery Regiment/49th Anti-Tank Artillery Brigade;
- 117th Independent Anti-Tank Artillery Regiment;
- 1953th Self-Propelled Artillery Regiment/209th Self-Propelled Artillery Brigade;
- a battalion of the 407th Light Artillery Regiment;
- 1089th Anti-Aircraft Artillery Regiment;
- 268th Guards Anti-Aircraft Artillery Regiment;
- 227th Independent Anti-Aircraft Artillery Battalion;
- a battalion equipped with captured German 8.8 cm anti-aircraft guns.[342]

Five T-34/85 tanks of the 71st Tank Regiment/5th Guards Cavalry Corps were fighting in the sector of Hill 157 (Igar), 4 km north of Simontornya.[343]

The forces of *I. Kavallerie-Korps* and *I. SS-Panzerkorps* were to occupy bridgeheads on the Sió Canal as soon as possible, the former in the sector of Mezőkomárom, the latter at Ozora and Simontornya, to prevent the Soviets from establishing defences on the southern bank. At the same time, they had to provide support to the bogged down *II. SS-Panzerkorps* by attacking the flanks of the Soviet forces fighting in the Aba–Sárkeresztúr–Sárosd triangle through the Nádor Canal.[344]

---

339 Tiemann, Ralf: *Die Leibstandarte*. Band IV/2. Osnabrück, 1987. p. 270.
340 Central Archives of the Russian Defence Ministry (Podolsk), f. 440, op. 8311, gy. 98, li. 76.
341 NARA, T311, R162, F7214211.
342 Isaev, Aleksei–Kolomiets, Maksim: *Tomb of the Panzerwaffe. The Defeat of the 6th SS Panzer Army in Hungary 1945*. Solihull, 2014. p. 153.
343 Central Archives of the Russian Defence Ministry (Podolsk), f. 243, op. 2928, gy. 131, li. 231.
344 NARA, T311, R162, F7214214.

To achieve this, *23. Panzer-Division*, subordinated to *II. SS-Panzerkorps* on that day, was to be deployed, and was then to advance along the western bank of the Malom Canal, then cross the Nádor Canal at Sáregres and attack the rear the Soviet troops fighting between Sárkeresztúr and Sárosd, thus severing their supply lines as well.[345] However, the *Stab* of *6. Panzerarmee* later determined that the *Division* would not likely to succeed here, therefore they would instead be deployed via Cece towards Dunaföldvár. If they would have received immediate orders to execute the plan, according to the command of the German *6. Panzerarmee*, a *Panzergrenadier*-regiment of *23. Panzer-Division*, reinforced by armoured fighting vehicles, could have set off as early as 1600 hours on the same day.[346] Apart from the above, the *Stab* of *6. Panzerarmee* also advised that a combat group of regimental strength of *II. SS-Panzerkorps* should be drawn towards the west via the Sárvíz, then from there the unit should again cross the two canals in the sector of Káloz and attack in the rear the Soviet troops fighting at Sárkeresztúr.[347]

At 0500 in the morning, the divisional artillery executed a short but effective barrage in the sector of *2. SS-Panzer-Division/II. SS-Panzerkorps*. The *SS-Panzergrenadier*s launched their attack in the direction of Points 149 and 153, beside Hill 159 (Csillag) which were occupied successfully. The *II. (Bataillon)/SS-Panzergrenadier-Regiment 4* secured the left flank of *SS-Panzergrenadier-Regiment 3*.

In the morning, the armoured combat group also went on the attack. Their target was Hill 159 (Csillag). In the meantime, *SS-Panzergrenadier-Regiment 3* remained in the occupied Soviet positions and prepared to secure the right flank of the *Division*, as towards their right-hand neighbour, *I. SS-Panzerkorps*, the frontline was not continuous.

SS-Obersturmbannführer Weidinger had extreme difficulty in leading the attack of the armoured combat group, as there was an apparent lack of necessary radios. What is more, the *SS-Panzers* had problems with the Soviet's anti-tank guns as they rolled through Hill 159. The heavy fire destroyed three German tanks in quick succession. The armoured fighting vehicles could not continue their advance, and the attack was halted. The full weight of the battle on that day was carried by the armoured combat vehicles and the armoured personnel carriers of *III. Bataillon/SS-Panzergrenadier-Regiment 4*.

Later in the morning, *SS-Gruppenführer* Ostendorff arrived at the combined command post of the *Panzergrenadier-Regiments*, to discuss the further course of attack. *SS-Panzergrenadier-Regiment 3* was ordered to launch an assault in order to help their right side neighbour, *44. Reichsgrenadier-Division*, over almost untrackable terrain. The *Regimentskommandeur*, *SS-Obersturmbannführer* Wisliceny did not agree with this, which led to a violent argument with the *Divisionskommandeur*.

On the road back, Ostendorff's VW-Kübelwagen was directly hit by artillery and the *Divisionskommandeur* was severely wounded.[348] The officer escorting him died. The command of the *Division* was temporarily assigned to the commander of *SS-Panzer-Artillerie-Regiment 2*, *SS-Standartenführer* Kreutz.

---

[345] NARA, T311, R162, F7214215.
[346] NARA, T311, R162, F7214219.
[347] NARA, T311, R162, F7214220.
[348] Ostendorff died on 1 May 1945 in a military hospital near Bad Aussee. On 6 May he posthumously received the Oak Leaves for his Knight's Cross of the Iron Cross (*Ritterkreuz des Eisernen Kreuzes mit Eichenlaub*).

Around noon the Soviets launched a counterattack, but this was repulsed by the Germans. Then the armoured combat group launched an assault among the withdrawing Soviets and breached their main line of defence. The newly gained territory was held by the *SS-Panzers* and armoured personnel carriers to serve as the starting point of the new attack, intended for the next day.[349]

Early in the morning on the front of *9. SS-Panzer-Division*, the Soviets had reoccupied Csillagmajor 3 km west of Sárosd with the support of the 110th Tank Brigade. Around noon the Germans repulsed another Soviet attack that was supported by armoured fighting vehicles west of Sárosd, then, following the withdrawing Soviets, they breached their defences.

Around 1600 another German attack was launched towards the northwestern outskirts of Sárosd, and was gaining ground very slowly. The 110th Tank Brigade and the 363rd Guards Heavy Self-Propelled Artillery Regiment of the 18th Tank Corps, plus the 2nd and 3rd Battalions/32nd Motorized Rifle Brigade reinforced with the 292nd Mortar Regiment repulsed nine German attacks with 10 to 30 German armoured fighting vehicles in each assault, on the Seregélyes south 1.5 km–Point 149-Seregélyes south-southwest 3.5 km–Szárnyasmajor–Jakabszállás section. Units of the Corps reported to have knocked out 12 German tanks and eight armoured personnel carriers; their own losses included five knocked out T–34/85 tanks, two of which were burnt out.

In the evening, the 18th Tank Corps had 59 operational T–34 tanks, six ISU–152, seven ISU–122 and nine SU–76M self-propelled guns together with the reinforced 170th Tank Brigade in combat east of Seregélyes.[350] For the Corps, another 16 T–34/85 tanks arrived by rail at Ócsa.[351] The positions of the 18th Tank Corps were again attacked by approximately 100 German aircraft in formations of 16-20 planes.[352]

From 1130 hours, 17 Fw 190 ground attack aircraft of the German *Luftwaffe* raided the area of Sárkeresztúr, Sárosd and Nagyhantos, dropping 40 bombs. After 1430 hours, another 12 German aircraft targeted the Soviet troops fighting on the northern and northwestern edge of Sárosd.[353]

The SU-100 armoured fighting vehicles of the Soviet 1016th Self-Propelled Artillery Regiment/208th Self-Propelled Artillery Brigade were in combat continuously throughout the day with the Germans on the northwestern edge of Sárosd.[354]

Soon after, the vicar at Sárosd mentioned in his report of the events the fate of the village as well:

"In the meantime, the armoured battle that commenced on 6 March was raging at the first houses of the village, approximately 1.5 km from the church. At Sárosd, there were two Russian divisions in the village, an infantry and an armoured division. Approximately 300 tanks were seen in the village, which were firing at the opposing Germans from the first houses of

---

349 Weidinger, Otto: *Division Das Reich. Der Weg der 2. SS-Panzer-Division „Das Reich".* Band V: 1943-1945. Osnabrück, without year of publication, p. 445.
350 Central Archives of the Russian Defence Ministry (Podolsk), f. 243, op. 2928, gy. 131, li. 231.
351 Central Archives of the Russian Defence Ministry (Podolsk), f. 243, op. 2928, gy. 178, li. 69/2.
352 War log of the 18th Tank Corps for March 1945. Copy owned by the author. p. 11.
353 Central Archives of the Russian Defence Ministry (Podolsk), f. 440, op. 8311, gy. 98, li. 72/2.
354 Central Archives of the Russian Defence Ministry (Podolsk), f. 243, op. 2928, gy. 131, li. 230th

the village. My village was razed and destroyed beyond measure. 60 percent of the homes were unfit to live in, and I have not seen any building that would not have the marks of destruction. This terrible tank battle lasted until 23 March. The evicted villagers started to slowly come back to their village only after that."[355]

After darkness descended at around 1900 hours, the forces of *9. SS-Panzer-Division* reoccupied Csillagmajor against heavy Soviet resistance. In the sector of the Soviet 155th Rifle Division, the 1964th Anti-Tank Artillery Regiment was also deployed. The German armoured fighting vehicles formed around the farmstead in a half circle, then set fire to the buildings with tracer shells fired from machine guns. This made the situation of the crews of the guns and tanks in defence there extremely difficult, because they were blinded by the flames, and at the same time, their outlines were clearly visible to the Germans. The Soviet artillery crews were only able to target anything based on the muzzle flashes, but the German response was much more accurate. According to the Soviets, some of the German armoured fighting vehicle crews had night vision devices.[356] In this critical situation, one of the batteries of the 1964th Anti-Tank Artillery Regiment was shifted towards the flanks of the German armoured fighting vehicles. From a distance of approximately 50 meters, the anti-tank guns knocked out three German armoured fighting vehicles, and managed to slow down the attackers for just enough time to let the Soviets retreat in order from the area. In the meantime, the commander of the 27th Army deployed the 363rd Guards Heavy Self-Propelled Artillery Regiment, which advanced from the Point 159 (Csillag) towards the east-southeast 1 – 1.5 km and stopped the German advance with fire from his vehicles. The moment was exploited by the commander of the 1964th Anti-Tank Artillery Regiment to withdraw its own batteries that were used to cover the retreat. The batteries of the anti-tank artillery regiment reported that during the night, they had knocked out 10 German tanks and armoured fighting vehicles and lost eight anti-tank guns.[357]

During this action, the Germans reported the capture of four T-70s and two T-34s.[358] The relief of *23. Panzer-Division* with one of the regimental groups of *44. Reichsgrenadier-Division* was planned to take place during the night of 9/10 March 1945.[359]

On the front of *III. Panzerkorps/Armeegruppe "Balck" Panzergrenadier-Regiment 113/1. Panzer-Division*, reinforced by armoured pioneers, towed anti-tank guns, and their own *Hummel* self-propelled howitzers, together with *I. (Bataillon)/Grenadier-Regiment 871/356. Infanterie-Division*, and supported by Panther tanks of *1.* and *4. Kompanies/Panzer-Regiment 1*, launched an attack from the northern outskirts of Seregélyes toward the north. Using the bridges repaired by the army HQ pioneer units, units of *schwere Panzer-Abteilung 509* also arrived at the German bridgehead with Tiger B heavy tanks.

---

355   *Inter arma. Források a székesfehérvári egyházmegye történetéből II.* Edited by, introduction written by, notes added by, and indices added by Gergely Mózessy. Székesfehérvár, 2004. p. 233.
356   This is not verified by any German archival data or scientific literature source. At the same time, this is not even probable because in that case the German armoured fighting vehicles would not burn the nearby houses: the intensive light of the fire would have decreased the usability of the night vision devices.
357   Isaev, Aleksei–Kolomiets, Maksim: *Tomb of the Panzerwaffe. The Defeat of the 6th SS Panzer Army in Hungary 1945.* Solihull, 2014.p. 155.
358   BAMA, RH 2/1995 Blatt 57.
359   NARA, T311, R162, F7214212.

Despite heavy resistance from the Soviets, the Germans occupied Felsőszerecseny and Point 128 3.5 km south-southeast of Dinnyés using armoured personnel carriers of *I. (Bataillon)/ Panzergrenadier-Regiment 113*, Panthers of *1 .Kompanie/Panzer-Regiment 1* and a few Tiger B heavy tanks from *schwere Panzer-Abteilung 509*. Until then, the Soviets had been able to direct their artillery fire and their aircraft attacks against the sector of the railroad bridge situated northwest of Seregélyes that was repaired that afternoon..

One of the companies of *Panzergrenadier-Regiment 113*, securing the area east of Felsőszerecseny, was reinforced with a few *Marder* tank destroyers, one 8.8 cm anti-aircraft artillery unit and Panther tanks, in order to cover the rear of the *Regiment* from the direction of Dinnyés.[360]

The advance of the German *3. Panzer-Division* could only begin on that day, after the completion of the railroad bridge. The first units of the *Division* arrived at the bridgehead around 1815 hours. However the German assault, launched from Seregélyes from the east, advanced very little, due to heavy resistance from the Soviet units.[361] Here, *Panzergrenadier-Regiment 1/1. Panzer-Division* tried to occupy Hill 145 (Öreg Hill), but Soviet forces repulsed the attack, inflicting heavy losses. The *Divisionskommandeur*, *Generalmajor* Thunert, who always commanded his forces from the front line from his command armoured personnel carrier – was lightly wounded. During his three days of absence to recuperate, the *Division* was commanded by the 1st general staff officer (Ia) *Oberst i.G.* Krantz..[362]

Armeegruppe "Balck" planned that very early in the morning on the next day, an attack by the complete *III. Panzerkorps* would be launched.[363]

At the same time, *General der Panzertruppe* Balck also advised that *3. SS-* and *5. SS-Panzer-Divisions/IV. SS-Panzerkorps*, the armoured combat group of the Hungarian 2nd Honvéd Armoured Division and, if possible, *6. Panzer-Division* were to launch an attack from the northern outskirts of Székesfehérvár with the goal of capturing the Velence–Lovasberény sector, to contain the Soviet troops west and southwest of Budapest, and to prevent their regrouping.[364]

The German *Luftflotte 4* commenced air support of the troops starting around noon, after the weather conditions had improved considerably. In 330 missions they reported to have shot down 19 Soviet planes.[365]

The forces of the 3rd Ukrainian Front were close to exhaustion, as almost all of their reserves were thrown into combat in the first four days of the German attack, including the units of the 27th Army. Facing this situation, Marshal Tolbukhin requested from the High Command Headquarters to allow them to deploy the fully replenished 9th Guards Army, which had just been subordinated at 0000 hours, to reinforce the defense. The response was negative. Stalin and the Soviet high command forbade the 9th Guards Army to be used

---

[360] Stoves, Rolf: *Persönliches Kriegstagebuch Pz.Rgt. 1* (typewritten manuscript, a copy owned by the author), entry from 9 March 1945.
[361] NARA, T311, R162, F7214212.
[362] Stoves, O. G. Rolf: *1. Panzer-Division 1935–1945. Chronik einer der drei Stamm-Division der deutschen Panzerwaffe.* Bad Nauheim, 1961. pp. 749-750.
[363] NARA, T311, R162, F7214223.
[364] NARA, T311, R162, F7214223.
[365] NARA, T311, R163, F7215291.

to stop the German attack, which in their opinion was already losing its momentum; the unit was placed in reserve for the assault against Vienna.[366]

Therefore the 3rd Ukrainian Front used the last of its own resources, and the 2nd Ukrainian Front also offered help. Marshal Tolbukhin sent off the significantly worn and exhausted 23rd Tank Corps from his own reserves[367] from the area of Lovasberény towards Dunaföldvár. The 366th Guards Heavy Self-Propelled Artillery Regiment was released from subordination to the Corps, but remained in place and with 15 captured German armoured fighting vehicles, and was stationed 1.5 km southwest of Lovasberény.[368]

On the same day further armoured reinforcements arrived in the Transdanubia from the 2nd Ukrainian Front. The 207th Self-Propelled Artillery Brigade, with 60 operational SU–100s, three SU–57 self-propelled guns, and two T–34/85 tanks, was assembled in the Ercsi sector after marching 160km during the night. After this, it was ordered to the sector of Hercegfalva (today Mezőfalva). The 209th Self-Propelled Artillery Brigade with 57 operational SU–100s, three SU–57 self-propelled guns, and two T–34/85 tanks[369] marched 150 km from Pilisszentiván to Cece, where it was assigned to the 26th Army. The Brigade established defences at 1600 hours on the Ozora–Simontornya–Sáregres line.[370]

10 March 1945, Saturday

(**WEATHER**: highest daytime temperature over 0 Celsius, generally closed cloud base, snowing and raining. The condition of the roads were worsened because they were soaked and muddy.)

The *LXXXXI. Armeekorps z.b.V.* fighting along the Dráva River, still occupied the bridgehead at Valpovo. Northwest of there, in the bridgehead established at Donji Miholjac, the Soviet-Bulgarian forces occupied Matty and Gordisa, then launched an attack southwards along the road and railroad to Harkány, with armoured support.

The Bulgarian 1st Independent Tank Battalion was subordinated to the Soviet 133rd Rifle Corps, under Major General Pavel Artyushenko, that had just arrived.

The Soviet–Bulgarian units advancing through Drávaszabolcs approached to within 1.5 km of the ferry point of the Germans from the north. The Germans then stopped the advance and pushed the Soviet-Bulgarian troops back to the northern edge of Drávaszabolcs with a counterattack.

---

[366] Malakhov, M. M.: A Balatontól Bécsig (excerpt). In: *Fejezetek hazánk felszabadításának történetéből.* Budapest, 1960. p. 149.

[367] The forces of the 23rd Tank Corps consisted only of the following units at that time: 3rd Tank Brigade, the 1443rd Self-Propelled Artillery Regiment and one of the battalions of the 56th Motorized Rifle Brigade. The 39th and 135th Tank Brigade and the majority of the 56th Motorized Rifle Brigade were assembled in the sector of Soroksár for reorganization and replenishment. At that time, the Corps had 21 operational 21 T–34/85 tanks, one IS–2 heavy tank, and eight ISU–122 self-propelled guns. They received another three IS–2 heavy tanks and four ISU–152 self-propelled guns from the strength of the 366th Guards Heavy Self-Propelled Artillery Regiment. Of this, see Central Archives of the Russian Defence Ministry (Podolsk), f. 243, op. 2928, gy. 178, li. 69/2.

[368] Central Archives of the Russian Defence Ministry (Podolsk), f. 243, op. 2928, gy. 131, li. 230th

[369] Apart from these, the 207th and 209th Self-Propelled Artillery Brigade each had 10 American manufactured M3A1 wheeled armoured transport vehicles and 10 M15A1 half-track self-propelled anti-aircraft automatic cannons.

[370] Central Archives of the Russian Defence Ministry (Podolsk), f. 243, op. 2928, gy. 131, li. 231 and 232.

During the close quarters combat raging in Drávaszabolcs, the Bulgarian 1st Independent Tank Battalion lost a number of Panzer IV tanks against the German *Grenadiers* wielding *Panzerfausts* and handheld anti-tank rocket launchers.[371]

The line of the bridgehead there ran on a line from Donji Miholjac east 6 km from the Dráva River, to the southwestern edge of Gordisa, to the east and central part of Drávaszabolcs, to the northern edge of Drávapalkonya, the northeastern side of Drávacsehi back to the Drava River 4 km northwest of Donji Miholjac.[372]

On the front of *2. Panzerarmee*, after being reorganized the day before, *16. SS-Panzergrenadier-Division/LXVIII. Armeekorps*[373] together with units of *71. Infanterie-Division*[374], launched an attack in the morning at 1030 hours from the Kutas–Jákó sector toward the south with the goal of finding a weak spot in the frontline of the Bulgarian 12th Infantry Division.

On the left flank of *16. SS-Panzergrenadier-Division, SS-Panzergrenadier-Regiment 35*, reinforced by assault guns, was advancing while on the right flank, *SS-Panzergrenadier-Regiment 36* was doing the same. The attack was also supported by the Focke-Wulf Fw 190 aircraft of the German *Schlachtgeschwader 10*.[375] The *Kompaniechef* of *3. Kompanie/SS-Panzer-Abteilung 16, SS-Obersturmführer* Rex remembers it the following way:

"Kisbajom was held by Bulgarian troops (units of the Bulgarian 1st Army) in well prepared positions. SS-Panzergrenadier-Regiment 35 and the Panzer-Abteilung attacked at 1030 hours. The task of Kampfgruppe Rex [3. Panzer-Kompanie – the author] was to occupy and secure Kisbajom and, in the direction of Szabás, the two bridges west of Kisbajom. Kampfgruppe Geiger [2. Panzer-Kompanie – the author] was to push through Kampfgruppe Rex once at the bridge, and together they were to advance over the embankment towards Szabás. The forward artillery observer travelled with 3. Panzer-Kompanie as the commander of one of the armoured fighting vehicles. [...]

At 1030 hours the time had come. There was extremely heavy preventive fire from mortars, rocket launchers and artillery. We detected an anti-tank blocking position on the edge of the village and at the edge of the forest north-west of there, partly camouflaged as haystacks and well equipped with heavy machine guns. The enemy trench system had two interconnected trenches with, machine gun, sniper and anti-tank rifle firing positions and dug-in bunkers. Mine obstacles had been placed between the two trench systems. The attack of II. (Bataillon)/SS-Panzergrenadier-Regiment 35 was halted by the defensive fire of the

---

371 Matev, Kaloyan: *The Armoured Forces of the Bulgarian Army 1936–45*. Solihull, 2015. p. 307.
372 NARA, T311, R162, F7214226-7214227.
373 On that day, *16. SS-Panzergrenadier-Division* had 19 combat-ready assault guns and 20 7.5 cm anti-tank guns. The combat strength of the Panzergrenadiers was approximately 1300 persons together with the SS-Panzer-Pionier-Abteilung 16, in one strong, three average and three weak battalions. The artillery consisted of six light and thee heavy batteries, and two 8.8 cm anti-aircraft gun batteries. The Division was suitable for attack in a limited capacity; the mobility was 79 percent. See NARA, T311, R162, F7214524. On the same day, 10 new StuG.III assault guns arrived for SS-Panzer-Abteilung 16. See NARA, T78, R621, F000751.
374 On that day, *1171. Jagdpanzer-Kompanie/71. Infanterie-Division* received 10 Jagdpanzer 38(t) *Jagdpanzers*. See NARA, T78, R621, F000779. However, the *Jagdpanzers* had not yet arrived in Hungary for some time. The *1222. Jagdpanzer-Kompanie*, in subordination to the *Division* had also received 10 new Jagdpanzer 38(t) *Jagdpanzers* between 6 and 20 March,but not from the central allotment. These arrived by 21 March.
375 Puntigam, Josef Paul: *Vom Plattensee bis zur Mur. Die Kämpfe 1945 im Dreiländereck*. Feldbach, without year of publication, [1993], pp. 67. and 314.

Bulgarians, until Kampfgruppe Rex attacked them in the direction of Kisbajom, ignoring the dangers of the mine obstacles and breaking the deadlock. Suddenly,, 100-200 m in front of the first trench, hundreds of Bulgarians left their positions in the direction of the forest west of Kisbajom. The enemy suffered terrible losses, because all of the armoured fighting vehicles were firing high-explosive shells and heavy, utterly destructive machine gun fire. The commanders were firing with submachine guns, throwing hand grenades and using rifle grenade launchers. The mine obstacles were detected between the two trench systems and we either overcame or bypassed them. Our losses on the mine obstacles were one armoured fighting vehicle destroyed, three dead (among them the forward artillery observer, Obersturmführer Rosen), one armoured fighting vehicle is immobilized, one dead at the escape (Oberscharführer Keune, owner of the Close Combat Clasp), and two armoured fighting vehicles sunk. The bridges west of Kisbajom were reached without any further resistance and we defused the explosives. We did not continue the attack towards Szabás because there is no infantry support available for crossing through the forest and the armoured group only had two combat-ready vehicles left."[376]

One of the soldiers of *SS-Panzergrenadier-Regiment 35* saw this attack as follows:

*"[…] Left of us, on the open field, the assault guns of our division, with mounted infantry were coming, under command of Hauptsturmführer Knobelspies.
The attack begins! The assault guns are blazing fire from all barrels, the Grenadiers jumped off them and ran for cover behind or on the sides of the assault guns. From the rear, a horse-drawn artillery battery of the land army was approaching at breakneck speed, turned in, prepared its armament and then proceeded to fire at the Bulgarian positions from all of the barrels. Not even a film could depict this scene better! The attack of the assault guns was going on finely, the artillery of the land army and the assault guns were firing from all of their barrels. During their ceaseless firing, two assault guns hit mines and their tracks were damaged. They could still support the attack of the Grenadiers, and the Bulgarians started to run away – they were fleeing in groups."*[377]

SS-Panzergrenadier-Regiment 36 was supported by *Panzergruppes "Knobelspies"* and *"Reinhardt"* of *SS-Panzer-Abteilung 16* west of the Nagybajom–Kutas–Szabás road. The assault gun of the *Abteilungskommandeur* hit a mine at the beginning of the attack. The *SS*-units occupied the northern part of Szabás. During this action two more *SS*-assault guns were disabled, as their taper gear was broken.[378]

Until darkness set in, the Germans, despite the heavy initial resistance and a number of Soviet and Bulgarian counterattacks, reached the Beleg southeast 2.5 km–Szabás–Kisbajom

---

376 Puntigam, Josef Paul: *Vom Plattensee bis zur Mur. Die Kämpfe 1945 im Dreiländereck*. Feldbach, without year of publication, [1993], pp. 74-75.

377 Puntigam, Josef Paul: *Vom Plattensee bis zur Mur. Die Kämpfe 1945 im Dreiländereck*. Feldbach, without year of publication, [1993], p. 68.

378 Breakage of the taper gear due to fragility happened so often to the StuG. III assault guns of *SS-Panzer-Abteilung 16* during March 1945, that the troops started suspecting sabotage during the manufacturing process. See Puntigam, Josef Paul: *Vom Plattensee bis zur Mur. Die Kämpfe 1945 im Dreiländereck*. Feldbach, without year of publication, [1993], p. 23.

south 2 km–Kisbajom east 2 km creek estuary–Jákó south line. On the southern edge of Szabás and in the Móric Forest south of Kisbajom the Soviets continued to fight.[379]

After darkness descended, the Soviets penetrated into part of the village held by the Germans, where both sides suffered considerable losses. Here the assault guns of *SS-Panzer-Abteilung 16* could only be deployed in a limited capability.[380]

The defence of the 299th Soviet Rifle Division on the north-western edge of Csököly was supported by the units of the 864th Self-Propelled Artillery Regiment. In the fighting around this area, one Soviet SU–76M was burnt out.[381]

3 km southeast of Nagybajom, probably in the vicinity of Juhászlaktanya, the Soviets launched heavy attacks against the frontlines of *1. Volks-Gebirgs-Division* with two regiments of infantry, with the support of tanks and self-propelled guns of the 864th Self-Propelled Artillery Regiment[382] and the 249th Tank Regiment[383]. The Germans repelled these attempts.[384]

The Soviet 57th Army mostly used large caliber guns against the German armoured fighting vehicles, but the Germans also suffered serious losses from the 57 and 76 mm guns, because the latter were firing at them from an angle. The Soviets, in order to direct the German armoured fighting vehicles into the firing range of the guns of the anti-tank artillery, established mine fields in the expected routes of the Germans, and built dummy firing positions to draw the attention of the Germans from the more important targets.[385]

Afterwards, the main forces of the German *2. Panzerarmee* were to continue their attack toward Mike, in order to reach the rear of the Soviet defences and eliminate the artillery positions. For the time being, they abandoned the idea of continuing the advance eastwards and establishing contact with

I. Kavallerie-Korps.[386] The Chief of Staff of the German *Heer*, *Generaloberst* Guderian, together with Hitler, held the latter to be of primary importance for *2. Panzerarmee*.[387]

During the night of 9/10 March 1945, in the sector of *6. Panzerarmee*, *4. Kavallerie-Division/I. Kavallerie-Korps*[388] launched an attack from the north towards Enying, but the Soviets repulsed the attempt. In a night battle, *3. Kavallerie-Division*[389] occupied Pusztaszentmihályfa 5 km northeast of Ádánd, and Hill 159 2 km north of Lajoskomárom. Reconnaissance carried out by the Germans by the following morning had established that along the southern bank of the Sió Canal and along the Mezőkomárom–Dég road, there were

---

379 NARA, T311, R162, F7214227.
380 Puntigam, Josef Paul: *Vom Plattensee bis zur Mur. Die Kämpfe 1945 im Dreiländereck*. Feldbach, without year of publication, [1993], p. 85.
381 Central Archives of the Russian Defence Ministry (Podolsk), f. 243, op. 2928, gy. 131, li. 233.
382 In the evening the 864th Self-Propelled Artillery Regiment had 16 operational SU–76M armoured fighting vehicles and one T–34 tank.
383 On that day, the 249th Tank Regiment was not deployed, but was assembling at Kiskorpád with their 10 operational T–34 tanks, so that they could reinforce the defence of the 64th Rifle Corps. Therefore the tanks of the unit could only provide fire support. See Central Archives of the Russian Defence Ministry (Podolsk), f. 243, op. 2928, gy. 178, li. 70.
384 NARA, T311, R162, F7214227.
385 Malakhov, M. M.: Magyarország felszabadításának befejezése. In: *Magyarország felszabadítása*. Budapest, 1975. p. 302.
386 NARA, T311, R162, F7214232.
387 NARA, T311, R162, F7214234.
388 *4. Kavallerie-Division* had two combat-ready Panzer II or Luchs light tanks and four assault guns on that day. See NARA, T311, R162, F7214525.
389 On that day, the *3. Kavallerie-Division* had three assault guns, two assault howitzers and two Jagdpanzer IV *Jagdpanzers* in combat-ready condition. See NARA, T311, R162, F7214526.

extensive positions occupied by the Soviets, protected with a number of anti-tank guns.[390]

The Soviet 22nd Independent Tank Regiment[391] also fought at Mezőkomárom on the same day, and engaged the forces of *3. Kavallerie-Division* from ambush positions with two to four armoured fighting vehicles.

The *Kommandeur* of *3. Kavallerie-Division*, *Generalmajor* Peter von der Groeben, disclosed at the situational briefing held at Tisztavízpuszta that he was to occupy Mezőkomárom and Szabadhídvég, and the bridges connecting the two villages on the Sió Canal the next day in a surprise attack, supported by seven assault guns and *Jagdpanzers* of *Panzerjäger-Abteilung 69*. *Leutnant* Bose, an officer of the *Panzerjäger-Abteilung* advised that five armoured fighting vehicles and the majority of the cavalry should launch a diversion attack before dawn. As soon as this contained the Soviets, the two other armoured companies and a cavalry company should set off from the northern end of Mezőkomárom, occupy one of the bridges in a surprise attack, and establish a bridgehead on the southern bank of the Sió Canal. The *Kommandeur* of *3. Kavallerie-Division* accepted the suggestion and timed the attack for the morning on the next day, when a company-size force of self-propelled anti-aircraft guns were to arrive[392]. If the plan succeeded, the *Divisionskommandeur* promised he would recommend *Leutnant* Bose for the Oak Leaves of the Knight's Cross of the Iron Cross (*Ritterkreuz des Eisernen Kreuzes mit Eichenlaub*).[393]

The *4. Kavallerie-Division/I. Kavallerie-Korps,* together with the units of the Hungarian 25th Infantry Division[394], after the heavy close quarters combat experienced during the whole day, occupied Enying and Hill 165 west of the village. The bridge at Enying fell into possession of the German-Hungarian troops undamaged. The units of the cavalry corps continued their attack in the south-eastern direction.[395] The Hungarian forces had the task to eliminate the Soviet forces that were stuck in the Balaton–Sió Canal–Enying triangle with an attack in the direction of Siófok.[396] The occupation of the villages of Lajoskomárom and Mezőkomárom that were still held by the Soviets, was not deemed as important to the Germans as was the soonest possible breakthrough to the banks of the Sió Canal.[397]

The Hungarian I and III Battalions of the 14th Honvéd Infantry Regiment were ordered to Lepsény by railroad from the area northwest of Lake Balaton, but at this time they were still under the commanded of *Heeresgruppe Süd*.[398]

The main forces of *I. SS-Panzerkorps* closed up on the line of the Sió Canal on a wide front, but the Soviets still held bridgeheads in the areas of Ozora, Simontornya and Sáregres. The Soviets on the northern bank of the canal, had the strongest defences in the hills

---

390 NARA, T311, R163, F7215295.
391 In the morning of that day, the 22nd Independent Tank Regiment had 11 operational T–34 tanks, four SU–76M and SU–85 self-propelled guns. See Central Archives of the Russian Defence Ministry (Podolsk), f. 243, op. 2928, gy. 178, li. 70.
392 The *schwere Kavallerie-Abteilung 3* only had towed anti-aircraft guns. These most likely had been the self-propelled 3.7 cm anti-aircraft automatic cannons of *schwere Kavallerie-Abteilung 4/4. Kavallerie-Division*. The *schwere Kavallerie-Abteilung 4* was subordinated to *3. Kavallerie-Division* on 7 March and were probably assigned to *Panzer-Kampfgruppe "Falkenhausen"*.
393 Bose, Georg: „Ob's stürmt, oder schneit…"! Mit meinem Sturmgeschütz im Einsatz. Erinnerungen Teil 2. Selbstverlag Bose, Einhausen, 2005. pp. 259-260.
394 The nine Jagdpanzer 38(t) *Jagdpanzers* of the 20th Assault Artillery Battalion were subordinated to the Hungarian 25th Honvéd Infantry Division. See NARA, T311, R162, F7214525.
395 NARA, T311, R162, F7214227.
396 NARA, T311, R162, F7214230th
397 NARA, T311, R162, F7214234.
398 NARA, T311, R162, F7214477.

surrounding Simontornya and at Ozora, and their counterattacks against Jánosházamajor were aimed at keeping the Cece–Simontornya road open. These attempts however had been repulsed by the forces of *1. SS-Panzer-Division*.

SS-Panzergrenadier-Regiment 26/12. SS-Panzer-Division[399] advanced from the area of Mezőszilas on the night of 9/10 March 1945 to the northern sector of Igar. The fact that the right flank of the *Division* was uncovered, considerably hindered the attack of *SS-Panzergrenadier-Regiment 25*.

The strength of the *Division* was 11,299 men, of which, the combat strength was 5173. The *Panzergrenadiers* had five weak and one medium battalions with approximately 700 combat soldiers. The divisional artillery consisted of six light and one heavy batteries and three batteries of multiple rocket launchers. There were no available towing vehicles for 25 of the guns. The *Division* was only suitable for attack in a limited capacity and their combat strength was at 50%.[400]

1. SS-Panzer-Division[401] continued its attack against the Soviet positions established between Simontornya and Sáregres. The Soviets had been strongly defending these two of their bridgeheads on the Sió Canal through a series of tank and infantry counterattacks, as they were moving the majority of their supplies on the Cece–Simontornya road.[402] The *Kompaniechef* of *3. Kompanie/SS-Panzer-Regiment 1.*, *SS-Obersturmführer* Werner Sternebeck, remembered the combat actions on 9 and 10 March 1945:

> *"During these two days, we had to repel infantry and tank assaults as well. This in turn greatly hinders our manoeuvrability. According to the terrain inspection and the reconnaissance data, Simontornya is situated in a depression in the ground, therefore a camouflaged approach to the village is not possible. Furthermore, the village was prepared for defence with significant anti-tank and anti-aircraft block positions.*
> *We have to cross an approximately 500-700 meter long, southwards slanting, open field in order to reach the village: on the foreground slopes it is impossible to stop and fire at short intervals.*
> *We have tried a number of times to approach Simontornya from the north-east and the north-west via the roads in the depression, but in vain, because as soon as the first tank arrives from any of the shallow roads, it will be knocked out instantly. This has happened to me too."*[403]

On that day, the *Division* had 12 heavy anti-tank guns. The combat strength of the infantry in six weak and two medium battalions was at least 1000 men. The artillery consisted of three light and one heavy howitzer battery, one gun battery, and two medium

---

[399] *12. SS-Panzer-Division* possessed six Panzer IV and nine Panther tanks, plus six Panzer IV/70 (V) *Jagdpanzers*, and *schwere Panzerjäger-Abteilung 560* had four combat-ready Jagdpanthers besides one Panzer IV/70 (V) *Jagdpanzer*.. See NARA, T311, R162, F7214526.

[400] Meyer, Hubert: *Kriegsgeschichte der 12. SS-Panzerdivision „Hitlerjugend"*. Band II. Osnabrück, 1987. 2nd edition. p. 499.

[401] On that day, *1. SS-Panzer-Division* had 12 Panzer IV, 11 Panther and four TigerB tanks in combat-ready condition (the latter in *schwere SS-Panzer-Abteilung 501*).

[402] Tiemann, Ralf: *Die Leibstandarte*. Band IV/2. Osnabrück, 1987. pp. 272-273.

[403] Quoted by Tiemann, Ralf: *Chronik der 7. Panzerkompanie. An vorderster Front in der 1. SS-Panzerdivision „Leibstandarte SS Adolf Hitler"*. Selent, 2015. p. 248.

multiple rocket launcher batteries. For three of the 21 cm multiple rocket launchers, there were no appropriate prime movers available. The mobility of the *Division* was at 70%, but it was only suitable for attack in a limited capacity. Its strength was 12,461 and of this, 4288 soldiers were ready for service.[404]

The Soviet 1068th Self-Propelled Artillery Regiment/208th Self-Propelled Artillery Brigade established firing positions on the northern edge of Ozora. Two batteries of the 1922nd Self-Propelled Artillery Regiment were also engaged in combat here.[405] At 0800 hours in the morning, in the defensive section of the 1068th Self-Propelled Artillery Regiment, two Tiger Bs, three Panthers and six Panzer IV tanks, plus 12 armoured personnel carriers attacked from the direction of Tüskésmajor towards Ozora. Three German tanks broke into Ozora, but they were destroyed by the SU-100 self-propelled guns of the Regiment. Around 1100 hours, another two SU-100s arrived from the southern bank of the Sió Canal and occupied firing positions on the north-eastern edge of Ozora. They reported to have knocked out another two German tanks and two armoured personnel vehicles.[406]

The 3rd and 4th Batteries/1922nd Self-Propelled Artillery Regiment were engaged in battle at Tótipuszta with the German armoured column (according to Soviet data, 40 armoured fighting vehicles and 16 armoured personnel carriers) approaching from Harasztbogárdpuszta, 500 m north of Ozora. The 4th Battery was held by the Germans frontally, while the 3rd Battery was bypassed to get around to their flanks. The Soviet SU–100 self-propelled guns reported to have destroyed eight tanks and two anti-tank guns, while during the pursuit of the retreating column, they reported to have knocked out another four heavy tanks and five armoured personnel carriers.[407]

The 1951st Self-Propelled Artillery Regiment/209th Self-Propelled Artillery Brigade was fighting with 20 operational SU–100s between Sáregres and Jánosházamajor, and the 1953rd Self-Propelled Artillery Regiment with 18 SU–100s was engaged in combat on the northern and north-western edges of Simontornya. The 1952nd Self-Propelled Artillery Regiment established firing positions on the northern and north-western edges of Ozora for its 20 SU–100 self-propelled guns. All three Regiments were assigned a platoon of M15A1 half-track self-propelled anti-aircraft guns, from the brigade's own self-propelled anti-aircraft company. The 209th Self-Propelled Artillery Brigade was supported by the 2nd Battalion/12th Engineering Assault Brigade, which provided engineer support, covered the SU-100 movements and in case it was necessary, could quickly lay minefields in any direction from which an armoured assault could be expected.[408] The Brigade lost four burnt out SU-100s that day in a short engagement with the Germans.[409]

---

[404] BAMA, RH-19, V/62 Kriegstagebuch der Heeresgruppe Süd Anlageband, Tägliche Verluste u. Pz. Ausfälle zur Vorlage beim Führer vom 10. 3. 1945.
[405] Central Archives of the Russian Defence Ministry (Podolsk), f. 243, op. 2928, gy. 131, li. 233.
[406] Summarized report of the 208th Self-Propelled Artillery Brigade of the period between 6 March – 6 April 1945. Copy owned by the author. pp. 7-8.
[407] Summarized report of the 208th Self-Propelled Artillery Brigade of the period between 6 March – 6 April 1945. Copy owned by the author. p. 9.
[408] Combat report of the 209th Self-Propelled Artillery Brigade of the period between 10 March – 30 April 1945. Copy owned by the author. p. 2.
[409] Central Archives of the Russian Defence Ministry (Podolsk), f. 243, op. 2928, gy. 131, li. 233.

The German *23. Panzer-Division*[410] was given the task of occupying Sáregres. The *Regimentskommandeur* of the *Panzer-Regiment 23*, *Oberstleutnant* Prinz Max zu Waldeck und Pyrmont, organized a *Kampfgruppe* from units of the *Panzer-Regiment* and the armoured personnel carriers of *Panzer-Aufklärungs-Abteilung 23*. A few of the tanks remained in reserve under command of *Hauptmann* Gerhard Fischer.

Panzergrenadier-Regiment 126 and the *Kampfgruppe* launched their attack from Fáncs, 2.5 km northwest of Sáregres, at 1125 hours while 2 km north of Sáregres, the Soviets had established a number of firing positions for their anti-tank guns and armoured fighting vehicles. The Germans occupied the small hill in 10 minutes with a dashing assault, throwing back the Soviet troops behind the railway station and to the edge of Sáregres. The German tanks engaged the edge of the village in fire, where they knocked out a number of anti-tank guns and infantry fortifications. Afterwards, *Panzergrenadier-Regiments 126* and *128*, were able to close up. In a fight that lasted 1.5 hours, *Panzer-Regiment 23* reported to have knocked out seven Soviet armoured fighting vehicles and seven anti-tank guns without any losses of their own.

The German *Panzergrenadiers* launched an attack at 1415 hours against Sáregres. The German armoured fighting vehicles and armoured personnel carriers bypassed to the right, then launched the attack from the northwest. The Soviet troops had been fighting with superhuman bravery. Although the Germans knocked out another armoured fighting vehicle and two anti-tank guns, their attack was ultimately a failure, as they were not able to breach the Soviet anti-tank region established on the long sloping stretch of ground. The Germans established defensive positions on the ground they had taken so far. The hill north of Sáregres was secured by one of the tank groups with the *2. and 3. Kompanies/ Panzer-Aufklärungs-Abteilung 23*.[411]

On the same day, three SU-100 batteries of the 1922nd Self-Propelled Artillery Regiment, plus the 71st Tank Regiment/5th Guards Cavalry Corps with five T–34/85 tanks, and the 1896th Self-Propelled Artillery Regiment with six SU–76M armoured fighting vehicles were in combat at Sáregres.[412] The latter unit lost a burnt out self-propelled gun during the day.[413]

The commander of the Soviet 26th Army reinforced the Cece–Simontornya sector, with two anti-tank artillery regiments besides the units of the 209th Self-Propelled Artillery Brigade, the 71st Tank Regiment and the 1896th Self-Propelled Artillery Regiment.[414]

While the main forces of *23. Panzer-Division* were attacking Sáregres, the Jagdpanzer IV *Jagdpanzers* of *Panzerjäger-Abteilung 128*, at the request of *1. SS-Panzer-Division*, were sent to a farmstead, Zichyángyád, southeast of Dég, where according to hearsay, wounded German soldiers were captured by the Soviets. The arriving *Jagdpanzers* found nobody at the scene, but one of the armoured groups of *12. SS-Panzer-Division* mistook them for

---

410 The combat-ready armoured fighting vehicle strength of *23. Panzer-Division* consisted of on that day 11 Panther and six Panzer IV tanks, two StuG. III assault guns, 11 Jagdpanzer IVs and four Panzer IV/70 *Jagdpanzers*. See NARA, T311, R162, F7214526.
411 Rebentisch, Ernst: *Zum Kaukasus und zu den Tauern. Die Geschichte der 23. Panzer-Division 1941–1945*. Esslingen, 1963. pp. 486-487.
412 Central Archives of the Russian Defence Ministry (Podolsk), f. 243, op. 2928, gy. 178, li. 70., and f. 243, op. 2928, gy. 131, li. 234.
413 Central Archives of the Russian Defence Ministry (Podolsk), f. 243, op. 2928, gy. 131, li. 236.
414 Malakhov, M. M.: Magyarország felszabadításának befejezése. In: *Magyarország felszabadítása*. Budapest, 1975. p. 307.

the enemy and destroyed three Jagdpanzer IVs.[415] The *SS-Panzers* probably mixed them up with the Soviet SU–100 self-propelled guns, which were frequent in the area.

The concentration of *23. Panzer-Division* on the Káloz–Sáregres road was considerably slowed down by the fire of the Soviet field and anti-tank artillery.[416] During the day, *Volks-Artillerie-Korps 403* was drawn forward in the sector of *I. SS-Panzerkorps* in order to help assist in the preparation of the German occupation of the bridgehead on the southern bank of the Sió Canal with its considerable firepower.

The *44. Reichsgrenadier-Division/II. SS-Panzerkorps*[417] and *2. SS-Panzer-Division* had, after extremely heavy fighting, occupied Szőlőhegy northeast of Sárkeresztúr, then reached the Sárkeresztúr–Sárosd road. Afterwards, the units of *2. SS-Panzer-Division* occupied the road junction 2 km southwest of Sárosd, which was held despite numerous Soviet counterattacks.

With six armoured fighting vehicles the Soviets launched an attack in the direction of the hill, probably Point 141, 4 km west of Jakabszállás, temporarily breaching the defences of *2. SS-Panzer-Division* but in the end they were repelled. The Germans launched an attack again and ran into the attack positions of a Soviet tank unit, probably the 110th Tank Brigade.[418] This Soviet tank unit was pushed back toward the east after knocking out two of its armoured fighting vehicles, then after breaching the Soviet positions, the units of *2. SS-Panzer-Division*[419] reached the hills 3 km east of Sárkeresztúr and the sector west-southwest of Jakabszállás.[420] On that day, the strength of the *Division* was 9259 men, of which 3893 soldiers were fit for service. The three medium and two medium strength battalions of the *Panzergrenadiers* meant there was approximately 1200 combat ready men. The divisional artillery consisted of six light and three heavy artillery batteries. The unit was only capable of limited attacks, with a strength of 60 %.[421]

During the fighting around Sárkeresztúr, a soldier of the submachine gun battalion of the 110th Tank Brigade was conspicuous with his outstanding combat performance, Vasily R. Gorodetsky held his position in the face of the German infantry attack, although he himself was wounded. He was awarded the title Hero of the Soviet Union for his actions.[422]

The *SS-Kampfgruppe* of *SS-Panzer-Aufklärungs-Abteilung 2,* reinforced with pioneers and heavy armament, set off from the area of Káloz towards the northeast, advancing along the road leading to Sárkeresztúr towards Point 102, 2 km southwest of Sárkeresztúr.

The Soviet 1st Guards Mechanized Brigade/1st Guards Mechanized Corps held nine defensive strongpoints, of which four also had armoured fighting vehicles:

---

415 Rebentisch, Ernst: *Zum Kaukasus und zu den Tauern. Die Geschichte der 23. Panzer-Division 1941–1945.* Esslingen, 1963. p. 487.
416 NARA, T311, R162, F7214228.
417 On that day, *44. Reichsgrenadier-Division* had three combat-ready Jagdpanzer 38(t) *Jagdpanzers* and two *Marder* III tank destroyers. See NARA, T311, R162, F7214526.
418 NARA, T311, R162, F7214228.
419 Accoring to the relevant data for the day, *2. SS-Panzer-Division*'s combat-ready armoured fighting vehicle strength consisted of the following: two Panthers and eight Panzer IVs, 12 StuG. III assault guns, seven Panzer IV/70 (V) and nine Jagdpanther *Jagdpanzers*. See NARA, T311, R162, F7214527.
420 NARA, T311, R163, F7215305.
421 Tieke, Wilhelm: *Von Plattensee bis Österreich. Heeresgruppe Süd 1945.* Gummersbach, without year of publication, p. 32.
422 See HM HIM Hadtörténelmi Levéltár (Budapest), Szovjetunió Hőse kitüntetések gyűjteménye (*Collection of Hero of the Soviet Union awards*), 605.

- at Sárkeresztúr nine M4A2 tanks, three SU–100 self-propelled guns and a motorized rifle company;
- at Heinrichmajor six M4A2 tanks, two SU–100 self-propelled guns and a motorized rifle company;
- at the railway station of Sárszentágota five M4A2 tanks, two SU–100 self-propelled guns and a motorized rifle platoon;
- at Felsőtöbörzsök five M4A2 tanks, two SU–100 self-propelled guns and a motorized rifle platoon.

The 3rd Guards Mechanized Brigade of the Corps had positioned its forces into 5 defensive strongpoints:

- at Sármellékipuszta six M4A2 tanks, four SU–100 self-propelled guns and a motorized rifle company;
- at Point 103, 1.5 km southwest of Rétszilas, four M4A2 tanks and a motorized rifle company;
- at Cece six M4A2 tanks, four SU–100 self-propelled guns and a motorized rifle battalion;
- at Sárszentmiklós five M4A2 tanks;
- at Vancsaytanya, 1 km east of Cece, three M4A2 tanks.[423]

According to certain Russian sources, west of Sárszentágota the Soviets deployed two self-propelled artillery battalions that did not have any unit numbers, from the reserves of the 27th Army, which were equipped with captured German armoured fighting vehicles. One of these units was equipped with eight 15 cm *Hummel* self-propelled howitzers (named SU–150), and the other was equipped with six self-propelled 8.8 cm anti-aircraft guns (named SU–88). The Soviets quickly lost all of their armoured fighting vehicles in the firestorm from the German armoured fighting vehicles.[424]

During the whole day, in the western outskirts of Sárosd, *9. SS-Panzer-Division*[425] had repelled assaults of battalion-size forces, supported by the armoured fighting vehicles of the 110th Tank Brigade/18th Tank Corps and 363rd Guards Heavy Self-Propelled Artillery Regiment/18th Tank Corps.[426]

On that day, *9. SS-Panzer-Division*'s strength was 9739 men, of these, 5010 were ready for service. The *Panzergrenadiers* had three strong and four weak battalions with

---

423 Central Archives of the Russian Defence Ministry (Podolsk), f. 381, op. 8378, gy. 516, li. 79.
424 Kolomiets, Maksim–Mosansky, Ilja: *Trofei v Krasznoj Armii 1941–45*. Moscow, 1999. p. 53. According to the Russian authors, the armoured fighting vehicles designated as SU–88s were *Nashorn* tank destroyers, however, based on the surviving German archival sources these could not have been captured between October 1944 and March 1945, from the strength of *Heeresgruppe Süd*. It is probable that these are the same as the lost *Nashorns* of the German *schwere Panzerjäger-Abteilung 93* that were destroyed during the period of August – September 1944 in Romania, then they retreated to the northern part of Transylvania. These *Nashorns* then might have been repaired by the Soviets. If they were, on the other hand, not *Nashorns*, then they might have been self-propelled 8.8 cm anti-aircraft guns mounted on a VOMAG-manufactured wheeled bus chassis that belonged to the German *I. (self-propelled) (Abteilung)/Flak-Regiment 40*, a unit which suffered considerable losses in the sector of Budapest.
425 On that day, *9. SS-Panzer-Division* had 17 combat-ready Panther tanks, 15 StuG. III assault guns, seven Panzer IV/70 (V) and six Jagdpanther *Jagdpanzers*, plus nine Flakpanzer IV anti-aircraft armoured fighting vehicles. See NARA, T311, R162, F7214527.
426 NARA, T311, R162, F7214228.

approximately 1600 soldiers. They had fifteen 7.5 cm anti-tank guns in the *Panzer-Feldersatz-Bataillon* while *SS-Panzer-Artillerie-Regiment 9,* had three light and one heavy batteries, plus three of their howitzer and one of their gun batteries were under replenishment. The mobility of the *Division* was at 65% however, the unit was suitable exclusively for defensive tasks.[427]

The 181st Tank Brigade, upon orders from the commander of the 18th Tank Corps, marched from Felsőszolgaegyháza to the western outskirts of Sárosd, in order to establish defensive positions in the sector of Zsigmondmajor, Heinrichmajor and Külsőpüspökmajor, but the unit was relocated on the same day to the sector of Zichyújfalu, east of Seregélyes.[428]

The Soviet 1202th Self-Propelled Artillery Regiment, in firing positions on the northern edge of Sárosd with 13 operational SU–76Ms had, on the previous day (9 March), been reassigned from the 26th Army to the 27th Army. On that day, the Regiment reported to have knocked out three guns and six machine guns, with no losses of their own.[429]

The 1016th Self-Propelled Artillery Regiment/208th Self-Propelled Artillery Brigade, equipped with SU–100 self-propelled guns, was also defending the sector of Sárosd against the Germans attacking from the direction of Hill 159 (Csillag).[430]

The forces of *6. Panzerarmee* had, between 6 and 10 March 1945, defused approximately 15,000 Soviet and German mines used by the Soviets.[431]

Around 0700 hours in the morning, on the front of *Armeegruppe "Balck", 3. Panzer-Division/III. Panzerkorps* and units of *356. Infanterie-Division* launched a general assault along the Seregélyes–Pusztaszabolcs railroad in an eastern direction with the aim of capturing the significant Hill 145 (Öreg Hill) however, Soviet troops bitterly defended the area and the Germans were only able to achieve minor territorial gains.[432]

Reinforced by the 26 combat-ready Tiger B heavy tanks of *schwere Panzer-Abteilung 509*[433], *1. Panzer-Division*[434] set off from the northern outskirts of Szerecsenypuszta towards the north and northeast, and despite difficulties with the terrain, resistance from the 4th Guards Rifle Division, the 170th Tank Brigade/18th Tank Corps and the 1438th Self-Propelled Artillery Regiment/18th Tank Corps[435], occupied Agárdpuszta, Dinnyés and the railway station of the latter. After, the Germans were forced to travel over roads

---

427 Fürbringer, Herbert: *9. SS-Panzer-Division*. Heimdal, without year of publication, [1984] p. 510.
428 War log of the 18th Tank Corps for March 1945. Copy owned by the author. pp. 13-14.
429 Central Archives of the Russian Defence Ministry (Podolsk), f. 243, op. 2928, gy. 131, li. 232.
430 Central Archives of the Russian Defence Ministry (Podolsk), f. 243, op. 2928, gy. 131, li. 233.
431 NARA, T311, R163, F7215297.
432 NARA, T311, R162, F7214228.
433 *History of the schwere Panzer-Abteilung 509* (typewritten manuscript). Copy owned by the author. p. 54. The Tiger B heavy tanks were stranded in Seregélyes from 7 to 10 March due to the muddy terrain.
434 On that day, the German *1. Panzer-Division* reported as combat-ready only four Panther and two Panzer IV tanks. See NARA, T311, R162, F7214528. Contradicting the former, the diaries of a few officers of *Panzer-Regiment 1* contain entries based on which on this day, altogether 20 Panther tanks of *1.* and *4. Kompanies/Panzer-Regiment 1* and approximately 25-30 armoured personnel carriers of the regimental armoured pioneer companies were attacking in the direction of Dinnyés. See Stoves, Rolf: Persönliches Kriegstagebuch Pz.Rgt. 1 (typewritten manuscript, a copy owned by the author), entry from 10 March 1945.
1. Panzer-Division most likely kept a double register of their combat-ready armoured fighting vehicles, which was overlooked by officers formerly serving in *1. Panzer-Division*) on corps and army level as well.
435 The forces of the 18th Tank Corps deployed on the Seregélyes–Sárosd–Aba line on that morning had altogether 74 operational T–34 and T–34/85 tanks, plus seven ISU–122, six ISU–152 and two SU–76M self-propelled guns, as well as the 21 SU–100 armoured fighting vehicles of the subordinated 1016th Self-Propelled Artillery Regiment.

ruined by the Soviets and cross blown up bridges on more than one occasion on their way to Kápolnásnyék, but they managed to capture Gárdony on the same day.[436] During the fighting southwest of Dinnyés, the Germans overran an anti-tank region of 10 guns and reported to have knocked out a number of T–34/85 tanks.[437]

The German *3. Panzer-Division*[438] launched its attack in the morning at 0900 hours, following a single barrage that its *Panzer-Artillerie-Regiment 75* fired on the opposing Soviet forces. The German forces launching the attack were soon overwhelmed by waves of Soviet ground attack aircraft and bombers. The Germans suffered significant losses in the first hour.

The *3. Kompanie/Panzergrenadier-Regiment 3* lost all of its armoured personnel carriers in a short time and the armoured personnel carrier of the commander of *II. (Bataillon)/Panzergrenadier-Regiment 3* received a direct hit, which seriously wounded the *Bataillonskommandeur, Hautpmann* Seifert. The attack of *3. Panzer-Division* was halted, and the situation could not be turned around, not even with the arrival of *Kampfgruppe "Bradel"* from *1. Panzer-Division*. The muddy ground and the Soviet airstrikes made it considerably difficult not only to carry out attack manoeuvres but supply operations as well. *Kampfgruppe "Medicus"*, led by the *Kommandeur* of *Panzerjäger-Abteilung* of the *Division*, could not be deployed at all on that day.[439]

1st Lieutenant Brjukhov, commander of the Soviet 1st Tank Battalion/170th Tank Brigade, remembers the days combat as follows:

"In the morning of 10 March the Germans, following a 1.5 hour artillery barrage, launched an attack against us from the area of Point 128 and from Szerecseny[puszta] toward Point.126 [Káló Hill – the author] and toward Korcsma[440] from the railway station of Seregélyes. Heavy fighting commenced on the section defended by the 2nd Tank Battalion, which lasted for four hours. The enemy – after losing two tanks, three armoured transport vehicles, and few dozen soldiers – was stopped at last and proceeded to reinforce the positions they reached so far. We had lost only one tank in the engagement. Our battalion with the submachine gunners and the two batteries of the 1438th Self-Propelled Artillery Regiment repelled the attacks from Seregélyes toward Korcsma, while the enemy lost one tank and one armoured transport vehicle."[441]

In the afternoon of that day, the Soviet 181th Tank Brigade arrived at the railway station of Zichyújfalu, then established defensive positions between Zichyújfalu and Györgymajor.[442]

The 18th Tank Corps suffered the total loss of four burnt out T–34/85 tanks and one knocked out SU–76M in combat during the day.[443] Together with these, between 6 and

---

436 NARA, T311, R162, F7214228.
437 BAMA, RH 2/1995 Blatt 152.
438 *3. Panzer-Division* had on that day 37 combat-ready Panthers and 11 Panzer IV tanks, three assault guns, plus 16 Jagdpanzer IV and Panzer IV/70 *Jagdpanzers*. See NARA, T311, R162, F7214528.
439 *Geschichte der 3. Panzer-Division. Herausgegeben vom Traditionsverband der Division.* Berlin, 1967. p. 466.
440 On the maps used by the Soviets, the building standing on the northern edge of Hill 145 (Öreghegy).
441 Bryukhov, Vasiliy: *Red Army Tank Commander. At War in a T–34 on the Eastern Front.* Barnsley, 2013. pp. 170-171.
442 Central Archives of the Russian Defence Ministry (Podolsk), f. 243, op. 2928, gy. 131, li. 234.
443 War log of the 18th Tank Corps for March 1945. Copy owned by the author. p. 14.

10 March 1945, the Corps was forced to remove 11 T–34/85s, three ISU–122s and one SU–76M from its combat strength.[444]

On the basis of the modest success of *1. Panzer-Division,* the plan was formulated that after reaching the eastern side of Lake Velence, an armoured assault should be launched via Pusztaszabolcs towards Adony, which would threaten the rear of the Soviet troops defending in the area of Sárosd and Seregélyes. It would then be able to seal off the area between the Danube and Lake Velence, eliminating the Soviet position at Seregélyes from the rear. In order to be able to carry out this plan, later in the evening *Armeegruppe "Balck"* was assigned *6. Panzer-Division* that was, until then, in reserve in the Mór area[445]. With this, the *Armeegruppe* planned to form a significant armoured group northeast of Seregélyes. They did not exclude the possibility of subordinating *2. SS-Panzer-Division* to *III. Panzerkorps* in case of success, or it would be deployed as subordinated to *I. SS-Panzerkorps* through the Malom and Nádor Canals eastwards, in the direction of the Danube.[446] However, with the regrouping of *6. Panzer-Division,* the frontline between Székesfehérvár and the Danube would be left without any significant assigned armoured reserves. This was justified by *General der Infanterie* Wöhler to *Generaloberst* Guderian in their late night briefing with the fact that the Soviets were not that strong on that frontline section anyway.[447]

The Soviets had also been expecting something similar to happen, therefore they directed the freshly arrived 912th Self-Propelled Artillery Regiment/207th Self-Propelled Artillery Brigade/27th Army against the German armoured forces that might possibly break through in the direction of Ercsi and the unit was directed from Hercegfalva (today Mezőfalva) to Kisvelence.[448] The 1004th and 1011th Self-Propelled Artillery Regiments of the Brigade established defensive positions in the sector of Hercegfalva together with the 56th Engineering Battalion, in order to be able to stop the German armoured fighting vehicles coming from the northwest and the west attacking toward Dunapentele and Dunaföldvár.[449]

The Soviet 23rd Tank Corps received orders from the 27th Army at 1900 hours to establish a defensive line with its forces ready for action[450] in the Kisvelence–Tutyimajor–Tükröspuszta–Szabolcspuszta area by the next morning. The units had to be brought forward on the Dunapentele–Adony route.

The 3rd Ukrainian Front received a considerable number of armoured replacements on the same day. 21 SU–76Ms arrived at Baja and 29 at Szekszárd. Of these, nine were given to the 1896th Self-Propelled Artillery Regiment, 21 to the 1891st Self-Propelled Artillery Regiment, seven were given to the 1202nd Self-Propelled Artillery Regiment, and nine were given to the 18th Tank Corps. Of the 20 M4A2s, 10 were given to the 18th Guards- and 20th Guards Tank Regiments/1st Guards Mechanized Corps respectively. 20 new T–34/85s

---

444 Central Archives of the Russian Defence Ministry (Podolsk), f. 243, op. 2928, gy. 178, li. 71/2.
445 On that day, *6. Panzer-Division* had 37 combat-ready Panther and 14 Panzer IV tanks, plus 12 Jagdpanzer IV *Jagdpanzers*. See NARA, T311, R162, F7214528.
446 NARA, T311, R162, F7214232.
447 NARA, T311, R162, F7214241.
448 Central Archives of the Russian Defence Ministry (Podolsk), f. 243, op. 2928, gy. 131, li. 232.
449 War log of the 207th Self-Propelled Artillery Brigade, 10 March 1945. Copy owned by the author.
450 At that time, the 23rd Tank Corps possessed the 3rd Tank Brigade, the 1443rd Self-Propelled Artillery Regiment, one battalion, one artillery battalion and mortar battery of the 56th Motorized Rifle Brigade, as well as Corps' own artillery units. Its operational armoured fighting vehicle strength consisted of 41 T–34/85 tanks, four IS–2 havy tanks, plus eight ISU–122 and two ISU–152 self-propelled guns.

were assigned to the 23rd Tank Corps. The 25 SU–76M self-propelled guns unloaded at Ócsa were used to replenish the independent self-propelled artillery battalions of the rifle divisions within the 4th Guards Army.[451]

German reconnaissance on that day identified the presence of the Soviet 27th Army between Lake Velence and the Sárvíz River, and detected that Soviet armoured fighting vehicles were crossing the Danube at Ercsi, but they were not able to determine the units themselves.[452]

During the first five days of Operation *"Frühlingserwachen"*, the German troops breached the main and the second defensive belts of the Soviet 3rd Ukrainian Front. At the same time, the assaulting forces were not able to divide the Soviet units into two and they had not reached the Danube either, as in January 1945. To achieve this, they would have to break through the defensive belt of the Front, and the defensive area around.[453]

11 March 1945, Sunday

(**WEATHER**: highest daytime temperature 4 Celsius, stormy and cloudy sky during the night, during the day the sky is partially cloudy. The road conditions are still unfavourable, but the winds are continuously drying them up.)

In the Donji Miholjac bridgehead along the Dráva River frontline, the attack of the German *104. Jäger-Division* reached the southern edge of Matty, but was not able to recapture the village. The Germans, in heavy combat, penetrated into the northern part of Drávaszabolcs, then the counterattack of the Soviet–Bulgarian forces temporarily pushed them from the village. During the evening hours however, the Germans launched another attack and recaptured the whole village of Drávaszabolcs.[454] The Soviet–Bulgarian forces however, strengthened by armoured support, kept continuously attacking the German frontline between Kendergyár and Dázsong.[455]

The forces of the Soviet 84th Rifle Division, supported by the Panzer IV tanks of the Bulgarian 1st Independent Tank Battalion were finally able to occupy the railway station at Drávaszabolcs.[456]

The Soviet 53rd Motorcycle Regiment/57th Army was relocated from the area of Andocs to Pélmonostor with 10 T–34/85 tanks, to the area northeast of the German bridgehead at Valpovo.[457]

In order to exploit the successes of the previous day on the frontline of *2. Panzerarmee*, *Kampfgruppe "Bötcher"/LXVIII. Armeekorps*, together with the Hungarian "Bakony" Regiment, followed the Soviet troops fighting delaying battles in the Nagyatád–Beleg

---

451 Central Archives of the Russian Defence Ministry (Podolsk), f. 243, op. 2928, gy. 131, li. 234.
452 NARA, T311, R162, F7214231.
453 Malakhov, M. M.: Magyarország felszabadításának befejezése. In: *Magyarország felszabadítása*. Budapest, 1975. p. 308.
454 NARA, T311, R162, F7214244-7214245.
455 BAMA, RH 2/1995 Blatt 156.
456 Matev, Kaloyan: *The Armoured Forces of the Bulgarian Army 1936–45*. Solihull, 2015. p. 307.
457 Central Archives of the Russian Defence Ministry (Podolsk), f. 243, op. 2928, gy. 131, li. 236.

sector, and reached the line of the creek between the northern edge of Henész directly east of Nagyatád and the farmstead, most likely Bélaházapuszta, 2.5 km southwest of Szabás. *Kampfgruppe "Rudno"*[458] cleared the southern part of Szabás in close quarters combat that raged through the whole day, and drove out a Soviet unit west of the village.[459]

On the night of 10/11 March 1945, *16 SS-Panzergrenadier-Division* south of Kisbajom, cleared the northern and western parts of Szabás, then moved from the small forested area south of Kisbajom, and supported by the six StuG. III assault guns of *SS-Panzer-Abteilung 16*,[460] occupied Prépostpuszta 1.5 km southeast of Szabás. The Soviets however launched a regiment-size counterattack with armoured support, and recaptured the farmstead. Further attacks of the *SS*-units were unsuccessful here.[461]

At 0700 hours in the morning *II. (Bataillon)/SS-Panzergrenadier-Regiment 35* and units of *SS-Panzergrenadier-Regiment 36*, together with the assault guns of *SS-Panzer-Abteilung 16*, prepared to continue their advance towards Nagykorpád. The Soviets launched an artillery barrage on the German units, and they aborted the attack.

SS-Panzer-Abteilung 16 lost a StuG. III assault gun as irrecoverable during the fighting in the Kisbajom and Szabás area on 10 and 11 March 1945, another four required extensive repairs due to problems with the taper gear, tracks and drive sprockets and another four were sunk in on the muddy ground.[462]

At 1300 hours, a *Grenadier-Regiment* of *71. Infanterie-Division* started to relieve the units of *16. SS-Panzergrenadier-Division*, which was then reassembled in the area west of Marcali for a new assault.[463]

On the night of 10/11 March 1945, *71. Infanterie-Division* repulsed a small Soviet armoured assault south of Kisbajom, then, during the day, launched an attack from the southern outskirts of Kisbajom in the direction of the Falusi forest 3 km east of Nagykorpád; however this later attack proved unsuccessful. The Germans detected a Soviet division had arrived as reinforcements for the Bulgarian troops. The Germans repulsed a Soviet attack against Jákó.[464] In this region the 864th Self-Propelled Artillery Regiment was the only active Soviet unit with armoured fighting vehicles this day in the direction of Csököly. During the attack one SU–76M self-propelled gun was burnt out. The Regiment had 18 remaining operational armoured fighting vehicles.[465]

The *1. Volks-Gebirgs-Division* was constantly engaged in combat on that day, and repelled continuous Soviet attacks 4 km southeast of Nagybajom.[466] The Soviet rifle troops were supported here by 10 T-34 tanks of the 249th Tank Regiment.[467]

---

458 The combat group was organized from *Sturmbrigade "Rudno"*, *Gebirgs-Pionier-Abteilung 44* and *Pionier-Bataillon 41*.
459 NARA, T311, R162, F7214245.
460 Puntigam, Josef Paul: *Vom Plattensee bis zur Mur. Die Kämpfe 1945 im Dreiländereck.* Feldbach, without year of publication, [1993], p. 85.
461 NARA, T311, R162, F7214245.
462 Puntigam, Josef Paul: *Vom Plattensee bis zur Mur. Die Kämpfe 1945 im Dreiländereck.* Feldbach, without year of publication, [1993], p. 85.
463 Puntigam, Josef Paul: *Vom Plattensee bis zur Mur. Die Kämpfe 1945 im Dreiländereck.* Feldbach, without year of publication, [1993], 77. and p. 319.
464 NARA, T311, R162, F7214245.
465 Central Archives of the Russian Defence Ministry (Podolsk), f. 243, op. 2928, gy. 131, li. 236.
466 NARA, T311, R162, F7214245.
467 Central Archives of the Russian Defence Ministry (Podolsk), f. 243, op. 2928, gy. 131, li. 235. The 249th Tank Regiment received on that day a (most likely repaired) T–34 tank from the 1201st Self-Propelled Artillery Regiment.

The *2. Panzerarmee* was ordered to cancel their assault toward the south and to reassemble its forces in order to be able to continue the attack from north of Nagybajom toward the east. The attack was to begin on 13 March 1945, and establish contact with *I. Kavallerie-Korps*.[468]

During the night of 10/11 March 1945, the German *4. Kavallerie-Division/I. Kavallerie-Korps/6. Panzerarmee,* together with units of the Hungarian 25th Infantry Division, occupied Hill 163, 4 km west of Enying and Hill 157, 3 km southwest of there during a night raid.

At 0600 hours, in the defensive sector of the Soviet 93rd Rifle Division, the 25th Honvéd Infantry Division advanced from Gamásza, via Point 119 directly south of Sós Lake, towards Siófok on the road with two infantry companies and two armoured fighting vehicles, most likely the two Jagdpanzer 38(t) *Jagdpanzers* of the Hungarian 20th Assault Artillery Battalion. However at Balatonszabadi-fürdőtelep, in the area of the Zsófia Children's Sanitarium, one of the T-34 tanks of the 22nd Independent Tank Regiment, commanded by Junior Lieutenant Kortyanovych, lay waiting in an ambush position hidden by a tree behind the positions of the rifle infantry, among the houses on the north-eastern edge of the sanitarium. The Hungarian armoured fighting vehicles were advancing at a speed of 15 km/h with a 40 meter gap between them. The Soviet tank crew saw them at a distance of 1700 meters. When the Hungarians were only about 400-450 meters from the ambush position, the T-34 opened fire. The first Hungarian armoured fighting vehicle burst into flames and the second one inaccurately returned fire. Some of the Hungarian infantry retreated, and sought cover behind the burning armoured fighting vehicle. The other vehicle approached the T-34 to within 350 meters, but then was destroyed its tracks with two well-placed hits. The vehicle stopped, the crew escaped and retreated with the infantry around 0645 hours, in a flurry of Soviet rifle fire.

Two hours later, at 0845 hours another three Hungarian *Jagdpanzers* arrived at the Point 119 with an infantry company, then proceeded towards the knocked out armoured fighting vehicles at a speed of 12-15 km/h. The vehicle at the head was supported by fire from the two other vehicles behind, then they closed up on it as well. High-explosive shells were raining down on the position of the Soviet rifle troops while the supporting Hungarian infantry were spraying them with rifle and submachine gun fire. When the Hungarian armoured fighting vehicles were 300-350 meters away from the T–34, it opened fire again. The Hungarian armoured fighting vehicle on the left caught fire, and the one on the right stopped firing and turned. The T-34 knocked out the escaping vehicle with its fourth shot. The third *Jagdpanzer* then retreated. Approximately 20 dead Hungarian soldiers were left at the scene.[469]

During the night, *3. Kavallerie-Division* established a bridgehead 1.5 km north of Pusztaszentmihályfa on the western bank of Csíkgát Creek, and advancing southwest from there in the morning, reached the northern bank of the Sió Canal.[470]

---

468   NARA, T311, R162, F7214251.
469   Central Archives of the Russian Defence Ministry (Podolsk), f. 440, op. 8311, gy. 98, li. 99-102.
470   NARA, T311, R163, F7215305.

In the morning, the *Kommandeur* of *3. Kavallerie-Division* launched the assault against Mezőkomárom, but not following the advice given by the now absent *Leutnant* Bose[471]. At around 0800 hours the four self-propelled 2 cm anti-aircraft guns arrived as expected, and were sent into an attack against Mezőkomárom, together with the assault guns in broad daylight instead of under cover of darkness. The Soviet machine gun fire mowed down the crews of the anti-aircraft guns in their open vehicles and the attack collapsed.[472]

During the day, the German-Hungarian forces followed the retreating Soviet forces towards the Sió Canal on a wide front while maintaining contact with their rearguard. With its right flank, *I. Kavallerie-Korps* arrived at Lake Balaton south-eastern shore–Siófok northeast 3 km–Balatonszabadi north 2 km–Enying southwest 3.5 km sector, and with its left flank to the Sió Canal, between the location 3 km southeast from Siómaros and the mouth of the Csíkgát Creek coming from the direction of Enying.

On the southern bank of the Sió Canal the German-Hungarian troops observed considerable Soviet forces, supported with a number of anti-tank guns and armoured fighting vehicles. The Germans proceeded to assign the sectors for crossing.[473] At the same time, the northern bank of the Sió Canal was reached by some units of *3. Kavallerie-Division*.[474]

Three SU-100 batteries of the Soviet 1952nd Self-Propelled Artillery Regiment/20th Self-Propelled Artillery Brigade, established firing positions south of the Sió Canal on the northern edge of Szabadhídvég, and one battery positioned itself at Felsőnyék.[475] North of the canal, at Mezőkomárom, the Soviet 22nd Independent Tank Regiment was in combat with 15 operational tanks and self-propelled guns.[476]

The resistance of the Soviet troops had been increasing in the bridgeheads at Ozora, Simontornya and northwest of Cece.

On the night of 10/11 March 1945, *SS-Panzergrenadier-Regiment 26* occupied Igar. South of the village the Soviets were strongly defending their bridgehead at Simontornya. The *II. (Bataillon)/SS-Panzergrenadier-Regiment 26* defended Igar against the Soviet counterattacks, however *I. (Bataillon)/SS-Panzergrenadier-Regiment 26* deployed to the right of there and repulsed the Soviets.

During the day, *SS-Panzergrenadier-Regiment 26*, without it's *III. Bataillon*, was subordinated to *1. SS-Panzer-Division*. The *Regiment*, with the support of six *Jagdpanzers* of *SS-Panzerjäger-Abteilung 12* and the forces of *1. SS-Panzer-Division*, occupied the fork in the road 1.5 km south of Igar and a hill 2 km north of Simontornya. The *Regiment* remained in subordination due to the planned attack by *1. SS-Panzer-Division* against Simontornya and the establishment of a bridgehead on the following day.

The task for *SS-Panzergrenadier-Regiment 25* on that day was to establish a bridgehead at Ozora on the Sió Canal. In order to achieve this, two armoured personnel carrier

---

471 The armoured fighting vehicle of *Leutnant* Bose was damaged due to a Soviet artillery hit en route to the point of departure, and it had to be brought back to the rear for repair.
472 Bose, Georg: „*Ob's stürmt, oder schneit…"! Mit meinem Sturmgeschütz im Einsatz*. Erinnerungen Teil 2. Selbstverlag Bose, Einhausen, 2005. p. 261.
473 NARA, T311, R162, F7214246.
474 NARA, T311, R162, F7214255.
475 Central Archives of the Russian Defence Ministry (Podolsk), f. 243, op. 2928, gy. 131, li. 235.
476 Of these, 10 were T–34 tanks, three SU–76Ms and one SU–85 self-propelled gun, plus one KV–1S heavy tank. See Central Archives of the Russian Defence Ministry (Podolsk), f. 243, op. 2928, gy. 178, li. 71.

companies and the entire remaining combat-ready armoured strength of six Panzer IV and nine Panther tanks, as well as four Jagdpanthers and one Panzer IV/70 *Jagdpanzer*, were subordinated to them. Preparations were delayed, because the *Jagdpanzers* had not yet been refuelled and ammunition replenished. The armoured personnel carriers waiting on the open plains were successfully camouflaged, however the *Jagdpanzers* suffered losses from raiding Soviet ground attack aircraft.

At last, during the morning, following an artillery barrage, the assault was launched. The first echelon consisted of the armoured fighting vehicles. In battle formation, every two tanks or *Jagdpanzers* were followed by one or two armoured personnel carriers.

The attack of *12. SS-Panzer-Division* approached Ozora to within 800 meters from the northwest, but further advance was soon halted by Soviet resistance when the Germans had approached within 400 meters of the canal. By that time the 1st Battery/1952nd Self-Propelled Artillery Regiment/209th Self-Propelled Artillery Brigade had been relocated from Felsőnyék to Ozora. The SU–100 self-propelled guns established ambush positions in the village southeast of the bridge over the Sió Canal and from this location, three of the approaching armoured fighting vehicles of *12. SS-Panzer-Division* were knocked out.[477] The fourth Panzer IV tank was already on the bridge when it was hit and immobilised with a thrown track, completely blocking the bridge. They tried to tow it away under cover of artificial smoke, but this was prevented by the Soviet anti-tank and self-propelled guns. The German armoured personnel carriers retreated at the first shots to a road depression, where the crew of the knocked out vehicles had also gathered. *SS-Sturmmann* Heinz Müller of *4. Kompanie/SS-Panzer-Regiment 12* remembered these events as follows:

"The first Soviet shots had knocked out the first three tanks. The attack was impossible to carry out any further. Company commander Peitsch was with me in the tank; we drove forward to take over coverage of the retreating armoured personnel carriers. A haystack was standing halfway between the road depression and the bushes that offered coverage. There lay the dead commander of the company commander's detachment. We laid him on the engine compartment and then we went back. A Panther might also have been knocked out, from those that were covering us. When we arrived to safety, we assessed the situation and it turned out that we had been hit four times by anti-tank gun shells."[478]

The *III. (Bataillon)/SS-Panzergrenadier-Regiment 26* established positions on the northern bank of the canal, then when *SS-Panzergrenadier-Regiment 25* arrived they set up holding positions. After these steps were taken, the German attack launched that day in order to occupy the bridge and establish a bridgehead ended in failure.[479]

From 2 km northwest of the Középbogárd–Kulapuszta area, reconnaissance was carried out to the west and southwest, and 2 km east of Kulapuszta a crossing of the canal was

---

[477] Central Archives of the Russian Defence Ministry (Podolsk), f. 440, op. 8311, gy. 98, li. 87.
[478] Quoted by Meyer, Hubert: *Kriegsgeschichte der 12. SS-Panzerdivision „Hitlerjugend"*. Band II. Osnabrück, 1987. 2nd edition. p. 500.
[479] Meyer, Hubert: *Kriegsgeschichte der 12. SS-Panzerdivision „Hitlerjugend"*. Band II. Osnabrück, 1987. 2nd edition. p. 500.

considered.[480] *SS-Panzergrenadier-Regiment 26* was subordinated on the same day to *1. SS-Panzer-Division*.

In heavy fighting, *1. SS-Panzer-Division* managed to occupy the fork in the road 1.5 km south of Igar and the hill 2 km southeast of the village, Point 138, then to reach the narrow-gauge railroad line west of Simontornya.[481] The 3rd Battery/Soviet 227th Independent Anti-Aircraft Artillery Battalion, fighting 1 km east of Simontornya with its 85 mm guns, reported to have knocked out seven German tanks and two *Jagdpanzers* from a distance of 200 to 400 meters.[482]

Beginning at 1355 hours, the German *Luftwaffe* carried out a mission lasting approximately twenty minutes, targeting the area of Ozora with 10 Fw 190 ground attack aircraft and the area of Simontornya with another 16 Fw 190s. At Simontornya the German planes dropped at least 60 bombs.[483]

The attack of *23. Panzer-Division* was halted on the frontline between the western edge of Sáregres and the hill 2 km west of there, Point 144. The Germans collected their forces and in the late afternoon launched another attack, which resulted in a raging battle extending into the evening hours.[484]

The first assault was launched at 0500 hours by *Panzergruppe "Fischer"/Panzer-Regiment 25* against Sáregres from the northwest which was repelled by the Soviets. Then *Panzergruppe "zu Waldeck und Pyrmont"* joined in from the north, together with the armoured personnel carriers of *Panzer-Aufklärungs-Abteilung 23*, but this, also proved to be fruitless. The defenders of the Soviet anti-tank region firmly resisted any assault attempts, strengthened by the continuous support of the Soviet ground attack aircraft.

At 1100 hours, the *Panzergrenadier-Regiments* of *23. Panzer-Division* tried again, but the Soviets repulsed their attempts.

Around noon, *Panzer-Regiment 23* with *2.* and *3. Kompanie/Panzer-Aufklärungs-Abteilung 23* received orders to occupy Point 113 2 km southwest of Sáregres. At 1615 hours, *Panzergruppe "Fischer"* set off from the Határ Valley 3 km west of Sáregres, occupied Point 144 east from there, but the attack was halted just in front of Point 133. During this action Soviet armoured fighting vehicles and anti-tank guns destroyed three German Panther tanks.[485]

The Soviet 1951st Self-Propelled Artillery Regiment/209th Self-Propelled Artillery Brigade was engaged in combat on the northern edge of Sáregres and on Point 122 southwest of there while the 1953rd Self-Propelled Artillery Regiment was in combat on the northern section of Simontornya. The SU-100 self-propelled guns of the 2nd Battery of the latter Regiment, held off an attack of 14 tanks from *1. SS-Panzer-Division*, from their firing position on the eastern shore of the lake west of the railway station of Simontornya, and at a distance of 1500 meters destroyed three,, including two Panthers.[486]

---

480 NARA, T311, R162, F7214246.
481 NARA, T311, R162, F7214246.
482 Central Archives of the Russian Defence Ministry (Podolsk), f. 440, op. 8311, gy. 98, li. 77.
483 Central Archives of the Russian Defence Ministry (Podolsk), f. 440, op. 8311, gy. 98, li. 72.
484 NARA, T311, R162, F7214246.
485 Rebentisch, Ernst: *Zum Kaukasus und zu den Tauern. Die Geschichte der 23. Panzer-Division 1941–1945*. Esslingen, 1963. p. 487.
486 Central Archives of the Russian Defence Ministry (Podolsk), f. 440, op. 8311, gy. 98, li. 86.

On that day, the 209th Self-Propelled Artillery Brigade lost five knocked out SU–100s of which, four burnt out. In the evening, a total of 56 SU–100s, three SU–76Ms and two T–34s were operational.[487]

Five T–34/85 tanks of the Soviet 71st Tank Regiment/5th Guards Cavalry Corps and seven SU-76M self-propelled guns of the 1896th Self-Propelled Artillery Regiment were in combat 2 km northwest of Sáregres.[488]

That evening, the *Stab* of *Heeresgruppe Süd* asked the *Stab* of 6. *Panzerarmee* why 23. *Panzer-Division* wasn't already occupied with the canal crossing planned to take place north of Sáregres. The German 6. *Panzerarmee* replied that Sáregres needed to be occupied first because the Soviets had established a strong tank and artillery group there, which would keep the whole area under covering fire.[489] Because of the forced attack against Sáregres, the *Kommandeur* of 23. *Panzer-Division*, *Generalmajor* von Radowitz and *SS-Obersgruppenführer* Dietrich, had a considerably tense relationship.[490]

On that day, from the Soviet 26th Army, the 1068th and 1922nd Self-Propelled Artillery Regiments/208th Self-Propelled Artillery Brigade were drawn back into reserve and the units assembled at Dunaföldvár. The 1016th Self-Propelled Artillery Regiment was still fighting in subordination to the 18th Tank Corps at Sárosd.[491] The 208th Self-Propelled Artillery Brigade had lost 15 SU-100s deemed as irrecoverable from 6 to 11 March 1945.[492]

The Soviet 36th Guards Rifle Division was defending Sárkeresztúr quite strongly in the sector of *II. SS-Panzerkorps*. In order to occupy the village, *SS-Sturmbannführer* Krag's *SS-Panzer-Aufklärungs-Abteilung 2* was relocated from the sector of *II. SS-Panzerkorps* to that of *I. SS-Panzerkorps*. The armoured cars and armoured personnel carriers marched via Soponya in the direction of Káloz. The reinforced *Aufklärungs-Abteilung* crossed the Nádor Canal 2 km northeast of Káloz and launched an attack against Sárkeresztúr from the southwest. The Germans were unable to properly organize coordinated fire due to the difficult terrain , so they retreated in the face of heavy Soviet resistance to the western bank of the Malom Canal. The *3. Kompanie* of the *Abteilung* in the meantime occupied a bridge arching over the canal and established a small bridgehead on the eastern bank. Meanwhile, *1. Panzerspähwagen-Kompanie mounted in half-tracks,* carried out reconnaissance and set up holding positions around Káloz.[493]

The majority of 2. *SS-Panzer-Division* continued their attack between Aba and Sárosd in a southeast direction. Around 0900 hours, the armoured combat group launched an attack again. *SS-Panzergrenadier-Regiment 3* secured the right flank, and carried out limited objective attacks.

Supported by German ground attack aircraft, 2. *SS-Panzer-Division* succeeded in renewing their attack. *SS-Obersturmbannführer* Weidinger led the actions of the armoured

---

487 Central Archives of the Russian Defence Ministry (Podolsk), f. 243, op. 2928, gy. 131, li. 235.
488 Central Archives of the Russian Defence Ministry (Podolsk), f. 243, op. 2928, gy. 131, li. 236.
489 NARA, T311, R162, F7214254.
490 Rebentisch, Ernst: *Zum Kaukasus und zu den Tauern. Die Geschichte der 23. Panzer-Division 1941–1945*. Esslingen, 1963. p. 487.
491 Central Archives of the Russian Defence Ministry (Podolsk), f. 243, op. 2928, gy. 131, li. 235.
492 Central Archives of the Russian Defence Ministry (Podolsk), f. 243, op. 2928, gy. 178, li. 71.
493 Weidinger, Otto: *Division Das Reich. Der Weg der 2. SS-Panzer-Division „Das Reich"*. Band V: 1943-1945. Osnabrück, without year of publication, pp. 445-446.

combat group from his command armoured personnel carrier. The Panzer IV tanks, Panzer IV/70 (V) and the Jagdpanther *Jagdpanzers* of *II. (Abteilung)/SS-Panzer-Regiment 2*, with the armoured personnel carriers of *III. (Bataillon)/SS-Panzergrenadier-Regiment 4* were supported by the *Hummel* self-propelled howitzers of

3. *Batterie/I. (Abteilung)/SS-Panzer-Artillerie-Regiment 2* and the infantry of *II. (Bataillon)/ SS-Panzergrenadier-Regiment 4*. The attack unfolded successfully and during the course of the morning the Germans occupied Hill 159 (Csillag). *SS-Obersturmbannführer* Stückler, the divisional Ia, was lightly wounded during the fighting.

SS-Panzer-Flak-Abteilung 2 was covering the movements of the *Division* and shot down a Soviet reconnaissance aircraft.

The armoured combat group of *2. SS-Panzer-Division* continued its attack to the south from east of Sárkeresztúr and advanced to Heinrichmajor. During the fighting the *SS*-units reported to have knocked out six Soviet tanks, including two with *Panzerfausts* and three with anti-tank guns[494], but a few German armoured fighting vehicles and armoured personnel carriers were also damaged. The *II.* and *III. (Bataillons)/SS-Panzergrenadier-Regiment 4* suffered particularly heavy losses.[495] *SS-Hauptsturmführer* Hartmut Braun, *Kommandeur* of *SS-Panzerjäger-Abteilung 2*, who were supporting the *SS-Panzergrenadiers* with StuG. III assault guns, was killed in the sector of Külsőpüspökmajor. One of the Panzer IV tank commanders of *II. (Abteilung)/SS-Panzer-Regiment 2* remembers the events:

"I rendered two anti-tank guns unusable early in the first attack. After this, we ourselves were hit on the turret, which impacted with an enormous blow inside – but the armour held up from the attack. Otherwise, we were saying "Good night, Marie", and that "Somebody just rang the bell". Another hit impacted on the tracks, so we were unable to manoeuvre. We had to get out and try to insert a new track pin. Then we received another hit, and the vehicle caught fire – this was the end! Thank God all of the crew managed to get out and we took cover. The other two tanks of the Abteilung were also disabled, but with them, there were dead and wounded as well. The remainder of the Abteilung, approximately 25 armoured fighting vehicles, established perimeter defences and were engaged in combat on three sides against the Soviet tanks, which were in a favourable, elevated position. I was again without an armoured fighting vehicle and I was assigned to the commander with a special task, so I was able to follow the course of the battle.

The command post of the Abteilung was established in a horse stall [most probably within the area of Heinrichmajor – the author], which had however aroused suspicion in the Soviets and they locked the building under fire. This was horrible because the armour piercing shells breached the two opposing walls in one single crack and were flying above our heads; it was overwhelming. We had to dig ourselves in within the stall although the impacts were fairly high. The commander led the battle from this command post, as much as it was possible. Our armoured fighting vehicles inflicted hits upon the enemy, but we also suffered losses. This

---

[494] NARA, T311, R162, F7214246. The Soviet 18th Tank Corps have irrecoverably lost on that day five T–34/85 tanks. See Central Archives of the Russian Defence Ministry (Podolsk), f. 243, op. 2928, gy. 131, li. 238.
[495] Weidinger, Otto: *Division Das Reich. Der Weg der 2. SS-Panzer-Division „Das Reich"*. Band V: 1943-1945. Osnabrück, without year of publication, p. 447. The author dates these events to 12 March, although the war log of the *Heeresgruppe Süd* mentions 11 March.

was going on until the night, then of course all went silent. But in the early morning hours the fire fight resumed; and our armoured fighting vehicles were still not able to cope with the Soviets who had occupied far better positions."[496]

The Soviets defending Sárkeresztúr successfully resisted the attacks of the units of *44. Reichsgrenadier-Division* and *2. SS-Panzer-Division*.

The Soviet 1st Guards Mechanized Corps, according to the orders received from the Staff of the 3rd Ukrainian Front, had to establish and build up defences southeast of Sárkeresztúr along the Tóthmajor–Szilfamajor–Gardamajor–Sármellékipuszta–Cece line with the 3rd Guards Mechanized Brigade and the SU-100 self-propelled guns of the 382nd Guards Self-Propelled Artillery Regiment. The 1st Guards Mechanized Brigade and the 1821st Self-Propelled Artillery Regiment were still in defence in the sector of Jakabszállás, Heinrichmajor, Sárkeresztúr, Sárszentágota and Alsótöbörzsök.[497] The Corps lost two burnt out M4A2 tanks northwest of Heinrichmajor.[498]

From then on, the German *44. Reichsgrenadier-Division*, together with the units of *2. SS-Panzer-Division*, were to occupy Aba and Sárkeresztúr, as the Soviets would have been able to hold the south facing German forces under fire from these villages. The *9. SS-Panzer-Division* was to cover the stretched left flank of *2. SS-Panzer-Division* against the Soviet attacks anticipated from Sárosd.[499] *Grenadier-Regiment 132/44. Reichsgrenadier-Division* was subordinated to *2. SS-Panzer-Division*.[500]

The 110th Tank Brigade/18th Tank Corps and the 363rd Guards Heavy Self-Propelled Artillery Regiment/18th Tank Corps, together with two battalions of the 32nd Motorized Rifle Brigade and the SU-100 self-propelled guns of the 1016th Self-Propelled Artillery Regiment repelled nine smaller scale German attacks on that day. Afterwards, at 1700 hours, from the direction of Hill 159, 20 German tanks and six armoured personnel carriers together with a regiment-sized *Panzergrenadier* unit, attacked toward the south, and in heavy combat, reached Külsőpüspökmajor and Heinrichmajor.[501] The 110th Tank Brigade lost five knocked out T–34/85 tanks, two of which burned out, during this action.[502]

According to the report of *6. Panzerarmee*, the Soviet troops on its frontline between 6 and 11 March 1945, lost 1077 dead, 140 prisoners of war, 34 knocked out tanks and self-propelled guns, 36 artillery guns, 109 anti-tank guns, 55 anti-tank rifles, 15 mortars, 105 machine guns, and eight aircraft, shot down by land forces. They also defused 20,917 mines.[503]

---

496 Written memories of N. N. Copy owned by the author. pp. 51-52.
497 Central Archives of the Russian Defence Ministry (Podolsk), f. 243, op. 2928, gy. 131, li. 236. On that day, the 1st Guards Mechanized Corps had 67 operational M4A2 tanks and 17 SU–100 self-propelled guns.
498 Central Archives of the Russian Defence Ministry (Podolsk), f. 243, op. 2928, gy. 131, li. 238.
499 NARA, T311, R162, F7214256.
500 Tieke, Wilhelm: *Von Plattensee bis Österreich. Heeresgruppe Süd 1945*. Gummersbach, without year of publication, p. 34.
501 War log of the 18th Tank Corps for March 1945. Copy owned by the author. p. 15.
502 War log of the 18th Tank Corps for March 1945. Copy owned by the author. p. 16.
503 NARA, T311, R163, F7215314.

On the front of *III. Panzerkorps/Armeegruppe "Balck"*, *3. Panzer-Division*, without its *Panzergrenadier-Regiment 394*[504], launched an attack from the north-eastern outskirts of Szerecsenypuszta towards the southeast and advanced 2 km in heavy combat. The Soviet 170th Tank Brigade and the 1438th Self-Propelled Artillery Brigade in defence there, lost three burnt out T–34/85s and one SU–76M. The Germans wanted to occupy Sándormajor, which lay 2 km northwest of the essentially important Hill 145 (Öreg Hill). The combat raged on into the evening hours.

Panzer-Aufklärungs-Abteilung 1/1. Panzer-Division overcame significant Soviet resistance and occupied Csiribmajor, Pálmajor and Gárdonymajor. *Panzergrenadier-Regiment 1* launched an attack from the direction of Agárdpuszta, and *Panzergrenadier-Regiment 113* launched their attack from the direction of Gárdony towards the northeast. *Panzergrenadier-Regiment 1* advanced approximately 2.5 km in heavy fighting, however the attack of *Panzergrenadier-Regiment 113* towards Kisvelence and the road fork northeast of there was unsuccessful. This resulted despite the support of 10 Panther tanks of *1. Kompanie/Panzer-Regiment 1*[505] and the Tiger B heavy tanks of *schwere Panzer-Abteilung 509*[506], due to strong resistance from the Soviet troops and gunfire coming from Velence.[507] This was a failure, because according to *Armeegruppe "Balck"*, it would have been imperative to first occupy the road intersection directly south of the mansion house at Kápolnásnyék.[508]

The armoured combat groups of the two *Panzer-Divisions* deployed in combat were able to slowly advance due to the soggy terrain and the increasing resistance from the Soviet side.[509]

The Germans planned to deploy *6. Panzer-Division* that was moving from Mór southeast in the direction of Falubattyán, towards Szolgaegyháza to occupy the railroad-road intersection 2 km northeast of there and Pusztaszabolcs, in order to reach the Danube past Adony.[510] At that time, the *Kommandeur* of *6. Armee*, *General der Panzertruppe* Balck, was in command of the armoured combat group of the *Division* advancing towards Seregélyes with 20 tanks of *Panzer-Regiment 11* and the armoured personnel carriers of *II. (Bataillon)/Panzergrenadier-Regiment 114*.[511] The Hungarian I and III Battalions of the 14th Infantry Regiment arrived on that day at Lepsény.[512]

After 0800 hours, the forces of the Soviet 23rd Tank Corps established defensive positions on the Tivadarmajor to the western edge of the railway station at Pusztaszabolcs line. The 1443rd Self-Propelled Artillery Regiment established firing positions on Iváncsa. The artillery of the Corps occupied their firing positions in the sector of Kápolnásnyék.[513]

---

504   *Panzergrenadier-Regiment 394* was subordinated on that day to *356. Infanterie-Division* and remained in defence.
505   Stoves, Rolf: Persönliches Kriegstagebuch Pz.Rgt. 1 (typewritten manuscript, a copy owned by the author), entry from 11 March 1945. In the repair workshop of *Panzer-Regiment 1* at Hajmáskér there were at least 20-25 such damaged tanks – mostly Panthers – waiting which could have been repaired within 36 hours of the arrival of the promised spare parts.
506   History of the *schwere Panzer-Abteilung 509* (typewritten manuscript). Copy owned by the author. p. 54. In the manuscript, due to a typing error, the description of the combat actions between 11-13 March slipped by one day.
507   NARA, T311, R162, F7214247.
508   NARA, T311, R162, F7214257.
509   NARA, T311, R162, F7214257.
510   NARA, T311, R162, F7214251.
511   BAMA, N 106/4, diary of *General der Panzertruppe* Hermann Breith, 11 March 1945.
512   NARA, T311, R163, F7215312.
513   Central Archives of the Russian Defence Ministry (Podolsk), f. 243, op. 2928, gy. 131, li. 236. The operational units of the 23rd Tank Corps had on that day 41 operational T–34/85 tanks, four IS–2 heavy tanks, eight ISU–122 and two ISU–152 self-propelled guns. The 135th Tank Brigade was stationed at Soroksár for the time being, as they did not have armoured fighting vehicles.

The 207th Self-Propelled Artillery Brigade[514] was subordinated to the 23rd Tank Corps. After 1100 hours, the 1004th Self-Propelled Artillery Regiment established firing positions in the sector of Kápolnásnyék, the 912nd Self-Propelled Artillery Regiment in the sector of Kisvelence, and the 1011th Self-Propelled Artillery Regiment in the sector of Tutyimajor and Tükröspuszta.[515] The 1004th Self-Propelled Artillery Regiment remained in the Brigade commander's reserve in the Kápolnásnyék sector, with the task of repelling a German armoured attack anticipated from the direction of Gárdony and presumably aimed towards Martonvásár.[516]

Another three anti-tank artillery regiments were relocated to the sector of the 35th Guards Rifle Corps/27th Army in defence directly south of Lake Velence.[517]

The ground attack aircraft of the Soviet Air Force were primarily attacking the units at the head of the German *6. Panzerarmee* in the sector of Igar and Simontornya.[518]

The German *Luftflotte 4* also concentrated its missions in the sector of Simontornya, where they targeted Soviet artillery, anti-tank and anti-aircraft positions, vehicle traffic and the Soviet aircraft active there. On that day, the airmen reported to have shot down 14 Soviet planes.[519]

German reconnaissance had correctly anticipated the 5th Guards Cavalry Corps would be present along the Sió Canal, but they knew nothing about the 18th Tank Corps identified around Sárosd. According to radio reconnaissance data the Germans detected the supply lines of the Cavalry-Mechanized Group "Pliev" fighting in Upper Hungary (Felvidék), to be around Érd, and realizing the connection between this news and that of the Soviet armoured fighting vehicles crossing at Ercsi the day before, came to the conclusion that the Soviets may, after the replenishment of their swiftly moving forces, create a group for an operational counteroffensive in the Budapest sector.[520]

Indeed, on that day Stalin stated to the Staff of the 3rd Ukrainian Front, that in order to be able to prepare the offensive against Vienna with the main forces of the 4th Guards and the 9th Guards Army, he ordered the replenishment of the 1st Guards Mechanized Corps, the 18th and 23rd Tank Corps, and the 5th Guards Cavalry Corps with 100 M4A2s, 280 T–34/85 tanks, 70 SU–100s, 30 ISU–122s, 20 ISU–152s, 30 SU–85s and 100 SU–76M self-propelled guns, a total of 630 armoured fighting vehicles.[521] Of the above, 100 M4A2s, 199 T–34/85s and 150 SU–76Ms had already arrived in March 1945.[522] The 207th and

---

514 On that day, the 207th Self-Propelled Artillery Brigade had 62 operational SU–100, three SU–57 and two T–34 armoured fighting vehicles. See Central Archives of the Russian Defence Ministry (Podolsk), f. 243, op. 2928, gy. 131, li. 236.
515 Central Archives of the Russian Defence Ministry (Podolsk), f. 243, op. 2928, gy. 131, li. 238.
516 War log of the 207th Self-Propelled Artillery Brigade, 11 March 1945. Copy owned by the author.
517 Malakhov, M. M.: Magyarország felszabadításának befejezése. In: *Magyarország felszabadítása*. Budapest, 1975. p. 309.
518 NARA, T311, R162, F7214248.
519 NARA, T311, R162, F7214249th
520 NARA, T311, R162, F7214250.
521 War log of the 3rd Ukrainian Front from March 1945. Copy owned by the author. 11 March 1945., Stalin's additions to the Directive nr. 11038, issued on 9 March 1945, by the Headquarters of the Main Command of the Armed Forces of the USSR (Stavka), p. 2.
522 Central Archives of the Russian Defence Ministry (Podolsk), f. 243, op. 2928, gy. 131, li. 296. The 100 M4A2 tanks were given to the 1st Guards Mechanized Corps. The 18th Tank Corps received 122 T–34/85s and 15 SU–76Ms. The 23rd Tank Corps received 48 T–34/85s, and the 53rd Motorized Regiment received 10 T–34/85s. The 5th Guards Cavalry Corps were given 19 T–34/85 tanks and 13 SU–76M self-propelled guns. The six independent self-propelled artillery battalions of the 4th Guards Army received 46 SU–76Ms. As replenishment, the 1891st and 1201st Self-Propelled Artillery Regiments each received 21, the 1202nd Self-Propelled Artillery Regiment received seven, the 72nd Guards Independent Self-Propelled Artillery Battalion received 10, the 432nd Guards Independent Self-Propelled Artillery Battalion received five, and the 122. Guards Independent Self-Propelled Artillery Battalion received 12 SU–76Ms.

209th Self-Propelled Artillery Brigades of the 3rd Ukrainian Front received, after 6 March 1945, 126 SU–100s instead of 70, and six T–34s, six SU–57s and three SU–76Ms. Together with these, the forces of the Front had indeed received 590 tanks and self-propelled guns as replenishment or reinforcement, not counting the units of the 6th Guards Tank Army subordinated to them in the second half of March.

12 March 1945, Monday

(**WEATHER**: highest daytime temperature over 0 Celsius, generally cloudy sky, occasional raining. The quality of the roads is still extremely unfavourable, the unpaved roads and the open terrain is hardly driveable even for the tracked vehicles.)

On the Dráva River frontline, the Soviet 122nd Rifle Division/133rd Rifle Corps with the Panzer IV tanks of the Bulgarian 1st Independent Tank Battalion, continued to engage the German bridgehead at Drávaszabolcs. In the attack, all of the Bulgarian tanks were disabled either due to German fire or mechanical problems.[523] Therefore, the Battalion was withdrawn from the frontline by the Bulgarian 1st Army, and was put into reserve in the sector of Pécs. During their deployment in March 1945, in five days of combat, the Panzer IV tanks had fired 586 high-explosive shells.[524] This means that if we count the standard German ammunition allowance of 87 shells per vehicle, the 22 Panzer IV tanks, on average, only used around 30% of one ammunition replenishment during these actions.[525]

The Soviet 1891st Self-Propelled Artillery Regiment, with 21 operational SU–76Ms, was gathering in the Pécs sector in subordination to the 133rd Rifle Corps, to be deployed against the German bridgehead at Drávaszabolcs[526], most likely to replace the disabled Bulgarian tanks.

On the front of *2. Panzerarmee* on the night of 11/12 March 1945, the Germans ambushed and occupied the Soviet combat trenches running from Nagyatád towards the east. *Kampfgruppe "Rudno"* straightened its frontlines during a night raid between Szabás and Nagykorpád. During this fighting, the 864th Self-Propelled Artillery Regiment, in support of the Soviet 299th Rifle Division, lost four burnt out SU-76Ms on the Móric Forest–southern edge of Szabás sector.[527]

---

523 In Hungary, the Bulgarian 1st Independent Tank Battalion irrecoverably lost eight of their 22 Panzer IV tanks; the others survived the war and were transported back to Bulgaria. See Matev, Kaloyan: *The Armoured Forces of the Bulgarian Army 1936–45*. Solihull, 2015. p. 292.
524 Matev, Kaloyan: *The Armoured Forces of the Bulgarian Army 1936–45*. Solihull, 2015. p. 307.
525 Naturally it can easily be imagined that there was not sufficient ammunition supplies available. However, in this case it is interesting that according to the Bulgarian author researching the topic, the tanks were almost continuously in combat for the five days and they had been replenished with ammunition and fuel three or four times a day. Due to the fact that this replenishment was carried out as per regulations, 3 km from the frontline, on one occasion only 1 km from there, German artillery hit one of the Bulgarian Panzer IVs that arrived for replenishment. See Matev, Kaloyan: *The Armoured Forces of the Bulgarian Army 1936–45*. Solihull, 2015. p. 307.
526 Central Archives of the Russian Defence Ministry (Podolsk), f. 243, op. 2928, gy. 131, li. 237.
527 Central Archives of the Russian Defence Ministry (Podolsk), f. 243, op. 2928, gy. 131, li. 237.

During the night, *1. Volks-Gebirgs-Division* repelled a Soviet attack of two battalion strength, 4 km southeast of Nagybajom. During the day, German regrouping manoeuvres were continued.[528]

The *16. SS-Panzergrenadier-Division* and *1. Volks-Gebirgs-Division* were subordinated to *XXII. Gebirgskorps*. The former assembled in the sector of Marcali, and the latter in the western and south-western outskirts of Kéthely to be able to take part in the coming assault operation.[529]

The *2. Panzerarmee* considered deploying *Panzergrenadier-Brigade 92 (mot.)*, reinforced by armoured fighting vehicles, in order to establish contact with *I. Kavallerie-Korps/6. Panzerarmee* on the road at the shore leading south of Lake Balaton.[530]

On that day, around noon, a German armoured train at the railway station of Somogyszob was attacked in a low-altitude raid carried out by Soviet aircraft.[531]

On the right flank of *I Kavallerie-Korps/6. Panzerarmee*, the advance of the Hungarian 25th Infantry Division during the day did not result in any appreciable gains. The Soviets launched an attack of battalion strength against the Hill 157 (Kustyán Hill) 4 km southwest of Enying, but the Hungarian troops repulsed this and disabled a Soviet armoured fighting vehicle with a *Panzerfaust*.[532]

An armoured group with six tanks of the Soviet 22nd Independent Tank Regiment fought in this region, at Balatonszabadi. The armoured fighting vehicles of the unit were also active in smaller armoured groupings of 2 to 5 vehicles around Lajoskomárom, Mezőkomárom and Ádánd.[533]

According to certain sources, on that day the Soviets deployed in the Enying sector, a tank battalion that had no unit number attached, and was equipped with captured German armoured fighting vehicles. The strength of this unit consisted of four "*heavy tanks*" most likely Panthers, seven "*medium tanks*", most likely Panzer IVs and two assault guns, either StuG. IIIs or StuG. IVs. The makeshift unit was moving directly towards the German-Hungarian troops, when, by mistake, Soviet Il–2 ground attack aircraft attacked them. As a result of the air raid, two armoured fighting vehicles burnt out, and five were immobilized in the soft and muddy terrain.[534]

In the evening *I. Kavallerie-Korps* was given the I and III Battalions/14th Infantry Regiment/20th Honvéd Infantry Division, to clear Mezőkomárom and Lajoskomárom, from the area of which the Soviets would be able to threaten the German forces in combat along the Sió Canal.[535]

On the right flank of *I. Kavallerie-Korps*, on the road running on the southern shore of Lake Balaton, the Germans were planning a new attack with units reinforced by the Jagdpanzer 38(t) *Jagdpanzers* of the Hungarian 20th Assault Artillery Battalion and tanks

---

528 NARA, T311, R162, F7214261.
529 NARA, T311, R163, F7215322.
530 NARA, T311, R162, F7214268.
531 BAMA, RH 2/1995 Blatt 56.
532 NARA, T311, R162, F7214262.
533 Central Archives of the Russian Defence Ministry (Podolsk), f. 243, op. 2928, gy. 131, li. 237., furthermore f. 243, op. 2928, gy. 178, li. 72.
534 Kolomiets, Maksim–Mosansky, Ilja: *Trofei v Karasznoj Armii 1941–45*. Moscow, 1999. pp. 53-54.
535 NARA, T311, R162, F7214268.

that returned to the troops after having been repaired[536], in order to establish contact with the *2. Panzerarmee* as soon as possible.[537]

On the night of 11/12 March 1945, *4. Kavallerie-Division* and the units of the *3. Kavallerie-Division* crossed the Sió Canal on a 3 km wide front west of the mouth of Csíkgát Creek running into the canal, and established a 3 km wide and in average, 2 km deep bridgehead, which was held despite Soviet counterattacks with six armoured fighting vehicles. During these engagements the Germans knocked out a Soviet tank.[538] The *II. (Abteilung)/Reiter-Regiment 32* managed to capture Hill 146 (Kavicsos Hill) 3 km northwest of Szabadhídvég. Via the pontoon bridge built by the pioneers, the assault guns and *Jagdpanzers* of *Panzerjäger-Abteilung 69* were also able to cross into the bridgehead, and proceeded to provide rifle and machine gun fire to the *Kavallerie* fighting as infantry.[539] The *Schwadron-Chef* of *6. Schwadron* of the *Abteilung*, *Leutnant* Bohle, remembered this day as follows:

"...the enemy displayed heavy resistance with armoured fighting vehicles and artillery. Our own assault guns, which established positions on the hills behind our backs, supported the assault and knocked out five armoured fighting vehicles[540]. When we breached the Soviet positions, the Soviet armoured fighting vehicles tried to run us down, but our assault guns either knocked them out or forced them to retreat. The Russian tanks set off frantically towards us. Our assault guns took care of the remainder, forcing us to seek cover from the heavy firing. The Soviets retreated."[541]

The *Schwadron-Chef* of *3. Schwadron/Reiter-Regiment 32*, *Leutnant* Bode, directed the artillery fire on his own positions in the chaos of combat, but the Germans suffered hardly any losses because they had been hiding in foxholes to seek protection from the armoured fighting vehicles. According to the recollections of the officer:

"On that day, we repelled four Soviet tank assaults from 15 T-34s with the fire directed on our own lines by the forward artillery observer. During the fighting Leutnant Dette was killed when he jumped out of a foxhole to hunt down one of the T-34s with a Panzerfaust, but the other armoured fighting vehicle standing by had shot him with its machine gun. Thank you for that, Dette!"[542]

---

536 As the German *I. Kavallerie-Korps* had its own tanks only in the form of the Panzer II and Luchs light tanks of the *4. Kavallerie-Division*, the author does not deem impossible that they wanted to deploy one more time the captured German armoured fighting vehicles that were deployed at Enying by the Soviets and that fell victim to "friendly fire".

537 NARA, T311, R162, F7214268.

538 NARA, T311, R162, F7214262.

539 Bose, Georg: „*Ob's stürmt, oder schneit...*"! *Mit meinem Sturmgeschütz im Einsatz*. Erinnerungen Teil 2. Selbstverlag Bose, Einhausen, 2005. p. 264.

540 The units of the Soviet 22nd Independent Tank Regiment and the 209th Self-Propelled Artillery Brigade were in combat in the sector of Ádánd and Szabadhídvég. Unfortunately these two units were deployed in different sectors and their armoured fighting vehicles losses on that day are not clearly distinguishable per sector.

541 Idézi Witte, Hans Joachim – Offermann, Peter: *Die Boeselagerschen Reiter. Das Kavallerie-Regiment Mitte und die aus ihm hervorgegangene 3. Kavallerie-Brigade/Division*. München, 1998. p. 392.

542 Idézi Witte, Hans Joachim – Offermann, Peter: *Die Boeselagerschen Reiter. Das Kavallerie-Regiment Mitte und die aus ihm hervorgegangene 3. Kavallerie-Brigade/Division*. München, 1998. p. 393. *Leutnant* Erich Horst Dette was killed on 13 March 1945, according to the registers of the Volksbund Deutsche Kriegsgräberfürsorge e. V (German War Graves Commission).

Around 3.5 km north-east of Ádánd, the Germans eliminated the remaining Soviet bridgehead on the northern bank. The two German *Kavallerie-Divisions* were to attack again from the southern bank of the Sió Canal towards the general direction of Iregszemcse.[543]

The *12. SS-Panzer-Division/I. SS-Panzerkorps* had tried a number of times, though unsuccessfully, to cross the Sió Canal east of Kulapuszta.[544]

At 0430 hours, *SS-Panzergrenadier-Regiment 25* launched a new attack at Ozora to occupy a bridgehead on the southern bank of the Sió Canal, however several attempts failed, with the units suffering heavy losses.

The *I. and II. (Bataillon)/SS-Panzergrenadier-Regiment 26* subordinated to *1. SS-Panzer-Division* with the support of the Panzer IV/70 *Jagdpanzers* of *SS-Panzerjäger-Abteilung 12*, the *Regiment*'s own heavy armament and the German artillery, launched an attack west of Simontornya. The attack of *SS-Panzergrenadier-Regiment 26* and *SS-Panzer-Aufklärungs-Abteilung 1*, timed at 0430 hours failed on the first time. In the afternoon, directly west of Simontornya at the railroad bridge, they were able to complete the crossing, where the *SS-Panzer-Pioniere* deployed assault boats and small boats. However the Soviets blew the bridge up. *SS-Untersturmführer* Hans-Jürgen Ross, *Kompaniechef* of *2. Kompanie/SS-Panzergrenadier-Regiment 26* saw the beginning of the attack:

"The 2. Kompanie/SS-Panzergrenadier-Regiment 26 is advancing widely fanned out, in the coverage of the Panzerjägers. The 1. and 3. Kompanies take over securing on the flanks. 250 meters from the enemy positions we receive heavy anti-tank gun fire. The Panzerjägers make a hasty smoke shield and retreat to the safety of the houses in Igar. The Panzergrenadiers continue the attack."[545]

The *II. (Bataillon)/SS-Panzergrenadier-Regiment 26* reached the canal at 1430 hours, on the front of *I. (Bataillon)/SS-Panzergrenadier-Regiment 26*, but heavy Soviet artillery and mortar fire prevented them from crossing to the southern bank until as late as 1830 hours. After both *Bataillons* crossed over, they established a bridgehead approximately 300 meters wide and 100 meters deep. During the night the Soviets initiated a number of unsuccessful assaults against the small bridgehead of the Germans. *Panzer-Aufklärungs-Abteilung/1. SS-Panzer-Division* also used this crossing point.[546]

By continuing fighting into the night, the Germans succeeded in occupying the hills running south of the canal with an assault, and thus creating a bridgehead of 2 km width and 1.5 km deep.[547]

During the night of 11/12 March 1945, units of *SS-Panzer-Regiment 1* and *SS-Panzergrenadier-Regiment 1* of *1. SS-Panzer-Division* broke into the area of Simontornya and during the day occupied the village, except for its eastern side. On the east and in the factory site, heavy close quarters fighting raged on into the evening, in which the Soviets

---

543 NARA, T311, R162, F7214268.
544 NARA, T311, R162, F7214262.
545 Meyer, Hubert: *Kriegsgeschichte der 12. SS-Panzerdivision „Hitlerjugend"*. Band II. Osnabrück, 1987. 2nd edition. p. 501.
546 Meyer, Hubert: *Kriegsgeschichte der 12. SS-Panzerdivision „Hitlerjugend"*. Band II. Osnabrück, 1987. 2nd edition. p. 501.
547 NARA, T311, R162, F7214262.

strongly resisted and attempted a number of counterattacks. In the assault and the ensuing close quarters combat, the *SS-Panzergruppe* lost five tanks, but at last they succeeded in occupying Simontornya. In *SS-Obersturmführer* Sternebeck's own words:

> *"Attack against Simontornya. Starting off from behind the slope, we ride like madmen through the open and sloping field, and without short stoppages for firing, we reach the western edge of the village. From here, we continue our advance towards the east and the south through the village. The close quarters combat is short and violent, then Simontornya is clearly in our hands. During the attack we have lost three tanks in the open field, and further two in the village. The enemy is not able to withdraw its anti-tank and anti-aircraft block positions, therefore they are either destroyed or captured."*[548]

Shortly after, the heavy weapons of *1. SS-Panzer-Division* appeared and were positioned around the village.[549] North and northeast of Simontornya, the Germans had reached the railroad.[550]

During the evening, *SS-Panzer-Regiment 1* celebrated with *SS-Sturmbannführer* Poetschke, who had that day been awarded the Oak Leaves to his Knight's Cross of the Iron Cross, (*Ritterkreuz des Eisernen Kreuzes mit Eichenlaub*) for his actions during the elimination of the Garam bridgehead. *SS-Brigadeführer* Kumm was also present at the celebration, whom the usually reserved and stern *SS-Obersturmbannführer* Peiper, had beaten in a tricky drinking contest. The *Divisionskommandeur* fell into a deep sleep, and as a joke, he was transported back to his own command post on a Panther tank.[551]

Based on the interrogation of captured soldiers, the Germans identified the units in combat around Simontornya as the Soviet 1953rd Self-Propelled Artillery Regiment/209th Self-Propelled Artillery Brigade plus two other regiments of the Brigade as well.[552]

In fact, one of the batteries of the 1953rd Self-Propelled Artillery Regiment/209th Self-Propelled Artillery Brigade was in combat at Sáregres, one battery was at the southern edge of Simontornya and two batteries were on Hill 220, 1 km south of Simontornya. Two batteries of the 1951st Self-Propelled Artillery Regiment were in firing position on the northern edge of Sáregres and two others at the southern edge of Simontornya. The 1952nd Self-Propelled Artillery Regiment was deployed in a dispersed manner along the Sió Canal with eight SU–100s on the southern edge of Simontornya, seven at Ozora, two at Felsőnyék, and four at Ádánd. On that day, the SU-100 self-propelled guns of the 6th Battery/1952nd Self-Propelled Artillery Regiment in combat at Ozora[553] reported

---

[548] Idézi Tiemann, Ralf: *Chronik der 7. Panzerkompanie. An vorderster Front in der 1. SS-Panzerdivision „Leibstandarte SS Adolf Hitler"*. Selent, 2015. pp. 249-250.
[549] Tiemann, Ralf: *Die Leibstandarte*. Band IV/2. Osnabrück, 1987. pp. 277-279.
[550] NARA, T311, R162, F7214262.
[551] Westemeier, Jens: *Joachim Peiper (1915–1976). SS-Standartenführer. Eine Biographie*. Osnabrück, 1996. p. 104. Peiper and Kumm had already fought together at Kharkov in 1943, as *Bataillonskommandeur*s.
[552] BAMA, RH 2/1995 Blatt 57.
[553] Within the 209th Self-Propelled Artillery Brigade the batteries were most likely progressively numbered. Therefore the 1st to 4th Batteries were placed in the 1951st Self-Propelled Artillery Regiment, the 5th to 8th Batteries were placed into the 1952nd Regiment, and the 9th to 12th Batteries were in the 1953rd Regiment. For this, see the combat report of the 209th Self-Propelled Artillery Brigade of the period between 10 March – 30 April 1945. Copy owned by the author. p. 3.

to have knocked out three Panzer IV tanks.[554] Between 7 and 12 March 1945, the 209th Self-Propelled Artillery Brigade suffered eight total losses of SU-100s.[555]

Panzergrenadier-Regiments 126 and *128/23. Panzer-Division* and the two tank destroyer companies of *Panzerjäger-Abteilung 28*, launched an attack at 1600 hours against the Soviet bridgehead at Sáregres, but the attempt failed, also giving an opportunity for the Soviets to reoccupy Jánosházamajor with a counterattack. At the same time, *Panzergruppe "Fischer"* with 17 armoured fighting vehicles, launched a new attack from the Határ Valley. Although heavy fire was inflicted on them from Simontornya and Point 133, they managed to reach the Simontornya–Cece road by the evening and the road-railroad intersection 2 km south-west of Sáregres. However the railroad embankment there proved to be an effective obstacle against armoured fighting vehicles. The German armour was engaged by fire from the Soviet anti-tank guns and armoured fighting vehicles from the direction of Sáregres and Alsómajor. At dusk, the Soviets continued to keep the Germans under fire by the light of illumination rockets. Contact with the barbed wire defences set off the delayed-action release of illumination shells shot into the air, turning the German tanks into living targets.[556]

The *Panzergrenadiers* of *23. Panzer-Division* and the Jagdpanzer IV *Jagdpanzers* of *Panzerjäger-Abteilung 128* in the meantime reoccupied Jánosházamajor and Point 133 east of there.[557]

Between Cece and Point 122 south of Sáregres, the units of the Soviet 5th Guards Cavalry Corps were supported by five T-34/85 tanks of the 71st Tank Regiment and 18 SU-76Ms of the 1896th Self-Propelled Artillery Regiment.[558] On that day, the 71st Tank Regiment lost three burnt out T–34/85s.[559]

The *44. Reichsgrenadier-Division/ II. SS-Panzerkorps* and the units of *2. SS-Panzer-Division* launched an attack at 0600 hours, then broke into Aba from the north and east. After they occupied the village, in the evening hours they continued their advance towards Sárkeresztúr, however violent resistance from the Soviet troops considerably slowed their progress.[560] During the fighting, the Germans reported to have knocked out one Soviet self-propelled gun and captured five T–34 tanks.[561] The *Kompaniechef* of *1. Kompanie/Panzerjäger-Abteilung 46/44. Reichsgrenadier-Division*, *Leutnant* Josef Glatz, winner of the Knight's Cross of the Iron Cross, was seriously wounded while fighting in a captured T-34 tank.[562]

The Soviets relocated the 1202nd Self-Propelled Artillery Regiment with 20 operational SU–76M self-propelled guns, from Sárosd for the defence of Sárkeresztúr. The unit occupied firing positions on the western edge of the village, but were not engaged in further combat on that day.[563]

---

554 Combat report of the 209th Self-Propelled Artillery Brigade of the period between 10 March – 30 April 1945.. Copy owned by the author. p. 3.
555 Central Archives of the Russian Defence Ministry (Podolsk), f. 243, op. 2928, gy. 131, li. 237.
556 Rebentisch, Ernst: *Zum Kaukasus und zu den Tauern. Die Geschichte der 23. Panzer-Division 1941–1945*. Esslingen, 1963. p. 487.
557 NARA, T311, R162, F7214262.
558 Central Archives of the Russian Defence Ministry (Podolsk), f. 243, op. 2928, gy. 131, li. 238.
559 Central Archives of the Russian Defence Ministry (Podolsk), f. 243, op. 2928, gy. 178., li. 75.
560 NARA, T311, R162, F7214263.
561 BAMA, RH 2/1995 Blatt 56. The Soviet 18th Tank Corps lost on that day four T-34s as irrecoverable losses. See Central Archives of the Russian Defence Ministry (Podolsk), f. 243, op. 2928, gy. 131, li. 241.
562 Agis, Hermann: *Das Ende am Plattensee. Die Hoch- und Deutschmeister (44. I.D.) im Endkampf*. Nürnberg, 2006. p. 426.
563 Central Archives of the Russian Defence Ministry (Podolsk), f. 243, op. 2928, gy. 131, li. 237.

Sárkeresztúr was also attacked by the reinforced *SS-Panzer-Aufklärungs-Abteilung 2* from west of the bridgehead established northeast of Káloz. The German group advanced considerably well and reached the western edge of Szentimremajor, and approached Sárkeresztúr itself from the west to within 800 meters. The *2.* and *3. Kompanies/SS-Panzer-Aufklärungs-Abteilung 2* launched a new attack along the Káloz–Sárkeresztúr road, but this attempt also failed. A few hundred meters in front of Sárkeresztúr, the attack was halted. During the night, *2. Kompanie/SS-Panzer-Aufklärungs-Abteilung 2* repulsed a powerful Soviet attack. During the day, *Grenadier-Regiment 132* was reassigned and subordinated to *44. Reichsgrenadier-Division*.[564]

On the next day, a new *Kommandeur* was appointed to *2. SS-Panzer-Division*, *SS-Standartenführer* Rudolf Lehmann, former chief of staff of *I. SS-Panzerkorps*, took over command from the seriously wounded Ostendorff. At the same time, *SS-Obersturmbannführer* Albert Stückler became the chief of staff of *I. SS-Panzerkorps* and *SS-Sturmbannführer* Ralf Tiemann became general staff officer (Ia) of *2. SS-Panzer-Division* to replace him.[565]

The armoured combat group of *2. SS-Panzer-Division* repulsed the units of the Soviet 1st Guards Mechanized Brigade and occupied Heinrichmajor[566], following which they also held off a number of Soviet assault attempts from the south, supported by armoured fighting vehicles, mostly directed at the Germans fighting east of the farmstead.[567] The Soviets lost three M4A2 tanks here.[568] *SS-Hauptscharführer* Emil Seibold, *Zugführer* of *8. (Jagdpanther)-Kompanie/II. (Abteilung)/SS-Panzer-Regiment 2* knocked out his 65th enemy armoured fighting vehicle on that day, for which he was awarded the Knight's Cross of the Iron Cross.[569]

The armoured combat group of the *Division* had advanced the farthest south-east of all the units of *II. SS-Panzerkorps*. In the narrow corridor towards Heinrichmajor, it was only possible to move supplies during the night. As the stretched flanks of the combat group were unable to be adequately defended by *II. (Bataillon)/SS-Panzergrenadier-Regiment 4*, the Soviets immediately launched a series of counterattacks. The Soviet assault was becoming so fierce that the Germans were forced to go on the defence.

The *Flak-Abteilung* of the *Division* was constantly engaged in combat defending against Soviet ground attack aircraft. In their experience, the covering fire of the 8.8 cm guns was an efficient measure against them.[570]

In the front of *9. SS-Panzer-Division*, increased reconnaissance and raiding actions were performed on the Soviet side and there were no large scale attacks launched.[571]

---

564 Tieke, Wilhelm: *Von Plattensee bis Österreich. Heeresgruppe Süd 1945*. Gummersbach, without year of publication, p. 35., furthermore Weidinger, Otto: *Division Das Reich. Der Weg der 2. SS-Panzer-Division „Das Reich"*. Band V: 1943-1945. Osnabrück, without year of publication, p. 450.
565 Weidinger, Otto: *Division Das Reich. Der Weg der 2. SS-Panzer-Division „Das Reich"*. Band V: 1943-1945. Osnabrück, without year of publication, p. 447.
566 Central Archives of the Russian Defence Ministry (Podolsk), f. 243, op. 2928, gy. 131, li. 238.
567 NARA, T311, R162, F7214263.
568 Central Archives of the Russian Defence Ministry (Podolsk), f. 243, op. 2928, gy. 178, li. 74/2.
569 Weidinger, Otto: *Division Das Reich. Der Weg der 2. SS-Panzer-Division „Das Reich"*. Band V: 1943-1945. Osnabrück, without year of publication, p. 447.
570 Weidinger, Otto: *Division Das Reich. Der Weg der 2. SS-Panzer-Division „Das Reich"*. Band V: 1943-1945. Osnabrück, without year of publication, p. 452.
571 NARA, T311, R162, F7214263.

After 1200 hours, the Soviet 27th Army ordered the 1922nd Self-Propelled Artillery Regiment/208th Self-Propelled Artillery Brigade from the sector of Dunaföldvár to the area between Szilfamajor and Nagylók, 6 km south of Sárosd,[572] in case the Germans continued their attack from Heinrichmajor toward the south-southeast.

The *3. Panzer-Division/III. Panzerkorps/Armeegruppe "Balck"*, was ordered to launch an attack with one combat group, toward Ferencmajor from the eastern outskirts of Felsőszerecseny, and with another, towards Zichyújfalu, then to cut off and seal the Seregélyes–Perkáta road near Felsőszolgaegyháza.[573]

The *I. (Bataillon)/Panzergrenadier-Regiment 3/3. Panzer-Division* under the command of *Major* Schulze, launched an attack together with the Panther tanks of *2. Kompanie/Panzer-Regiment 6*, commanded by *Oberleutnant* Albert Blaich, to occupy Júliamajor, 5 km northeast of Seregélyes. The German tanks and armoured personnel carriers, despite heavy anti-tank fire, were successful, however they had to retreat for the night.[574]

At 0845 hours, the *Division* with one of its combat groups had indeed launched an attack from Csiribmajor towards the southeast, but it was only able to approach to within 800 meters of Zichyúfalu from the northwest.[575] *Panzergrenadier-Regiment 394* returned into the subordination of the *Division* on that day.[576]

The objective of the arriving *6. Panzer-Division* was to attack from Csiribmajor with two combat groups, and advance via Tivadarmajor, Pálmajor and Tükröspuszta towards Pusztaszabolcs.[577] The third combat group, on the right flank, advanced from the northeastern outskirts of Csiribmajor toward the southeast, but they only covered 2 km and reached Gulyaakol.[578]

In the morning, *I. (Abteilung)/Panzer-Regiment 24* from *3. Panzer-Division*, was subordinated to *6. Panzer-Division*.[579] The Panthers, originally 33 combat-ready vehicles, marched through the whole night, through the railroad embankment northwest of Seregélyes, sometimes only at a walking pace, and arrived at the southern edge of Gárdony at 0700 hours the next morning. The *2.* and *3. Schwadron/I. Abteilung*[580] were cooperating with the combat group on the left flank of *6. Panzer-Division*, while *1.* and *4. Schwadron/I. Abteilung* were cooperating with the combat group in the middle. The independent *Panzer-Abteilung* took part in the attack against Tivadarmajor with 27 Panther tanks.[581]

The *6. Panzer-Division*, not waiting for the combat group on their right-flank to close up, launched its attack at 0845 hours. The armoured column advanced on a wet and slippery road. At the head was *1. Schwadron/I. (Abteilung)/Panzer-Regiment 24*, with

---

572 Central Archives of the Russian Defence Ministry (Podolsk), f. 243, op. 2928, gy. 178, li. 72/2.
573 NARA, T311, R162, F7214271.
574 *Geschichte der 3. Panzer-Division. Herausgegeben vom Traditionsverband der Division.* Berlin, 1967. p. 466.
575 NARA, T311, R162, F7214263.
576 NARA, T311, R163, F7215323.
577 NARA, T311, R162, F7214271.
578 NARA, T311, R162, F7214263.
579 NARA, T311, R163, F7215323.
580 The German *Panzer-Regiment 24* was organized from *Reiter-Regiment 2*, therefore, out of respect for their own traditions they continued to use cavalry insignia, unit names and ranks.
581 Senger und Etterlin, von F.M. jr.: *Die 24. Panzer-Division vormals 1. Kavallerie-Division 1939–1945.* Neckargemünd, 1962. p. 309.

4. Schwadron marching behind.. Soviet ground attack aircraft appeared in the cloudy sky, then proceeded to attack the nearby roads and villages with their bombs and machine-guns. Soon the Soviet artillery also engaged the armoured fighting vehicles. After advancing 5 km, the Panther tanks at the head of the column reached a small rectangular forest northwest of Tivadarmajor. A number of the shells fired from Soviet mortars and heavy field guns exploded above the trees preventing the tank commanders inspecting the surroundings from their tank turrets because of constantly falling splinters. When the Germans glimpsed the buildings of Tivadarmajor, *1. Schwadron* left the road and tried to fan out towards the left. Soon explosive impacts were shaking the Panthers as they had run into a minefield. As Soviet tanks and anti-tank guns arrived from Tivadarmajor, they opened fire at the Germans and the Panthers returned the fire. The commander of *I. (Abteilung)/Panzer-Regiment 24*, *Rittmeister* Gert-Axel Weidemann sent *4. Schwadron* left of the *1. Schwadron*, to provide fire support for the latter, and the pioneer-platoon of *I. Abteilung* proceeded to open a corridor through the minefield, under constant Soviet artillery fire.[582]

Meanwhile, *3. Schwadron* under *Leutnant* Neumeyer, swung too far to the right and lost contact with the combat group *on the left flank* of *6. Panzer-Division*. From one of the hills, Soviet anti-tank guns opened fire at them and a number of Panthers were hit. The commander of one of the tanks, who arrived as a replacement from the *Kriegsmarine*, reported via radio that he was *"hit on the middle of the ship's hull!"* The attack of *3. Schwadron* was held up.[583]

In the centre combat group, the pioneers defused 27 mines. Tivadarmajor was to be occupied by *1.* and *4. Schwadron* in order to be able to flank the Soviet troops which impeded the advance of *3. Schwadron*. The *1. Schwadron*, with fire support from *4. Schwadron*, pushed forward through the cleared corridor in the minefield but then more mine blasts could be heard. The Germans were suspicious that remote controlled detonating devices were being employed by the Soviets. *Rittmeister* Weidemann decided to order a Panther platoon to fan out over a larger area, with the other armoured fighting vehicles providing fire support, to be able to cover the approximately 800 meters to Tivadarmajor. His audacity paid off when the Panther tanks, all lined up and rapidly fired high-explosive shells into the buildings of Tivadarmajor, which were then engulfed in flame and smoke. *Oberleutnant* Wolter successfully reached Tivadarmajor with five Panthers under cover of this fire, broke into the Soviet positions and reported to have destroyed 10 anti-tank guns in the process. The other Panthers were able to follow and close up as they followed in their tracks. The arriving *Panzergrenadiers* and armoured troops, riding on the tanks with fire support from the Panthers, eliminated the pockets of resistance one by one. At dusk, Tivadarmajor was in German hands.[584]

Exploiting this success, the combat group on the left flank of *6. Panzer-Division* started off towards Tükröspuszta with *2.* and *3. Schwadron/I. (Abteilung)/Panzer-Regiment 24*, but the Soviet defence stopped them. The Panthers used up all their ammunition, and

---

[582] Weidemann, Gert-Axel: *Unser Regiment. Reiter-Regiment 2 – Panzer-Regiment 24*. Groß-Umstadt, 1982. pp. 274-275.
[583] Weidemann, Gert-Axel: *Unser Regiment. Reiter-Regiment 2 – Panzer-Regiment 24*. Groß-Umstadt, 1982. p. 275.
[584] Weidemann, Gert-Axel: *Unser Regiment. Reiter-Regiment 2 – Panzer-Regiment 24*. Groß-Umstadt, 1982. pp. 275-276.

the attack had to be called off in the evening. The tanks of *I. (Abteilung)/Panzer-Regiment 24* returned back to Tivadarmajor where they replenished their fuel and ammunition.[585]

The Soviet 181st Tank Brigade/18th Tank Corps, reinforced by one of the battalions of the 452nd Light Artillery Regiment, was in defensive positions between Tivadarmajor and Zichyújfalu. The Brigade reported that they had knocked out 17 German armoured fighting vehicles on that day, against their own losses of four knocked out T–34/85s, three of which burnt out, and six knocked out 76 mm divisional guns. The 170th Tank Brigade and the 1438th Self-Propelled Artillery Regiment, in combat in the sector of Sándormajor and Hill 145 (Öreghegy), reported to have knocked out two armoured personnel carriers, and losing one burnt out T–34/85 and one burnt out SU–76M.[586]

An officer of the 170th Tank Brigade, 1st Lieutenant Brjukhov remembered the events as follows:

"It seemed that the Germans have understood at last, that they will not be able to achieve any significant gains with tanks or assault guns employed in small groups, and therefore on the night of 11 March, they brought approximately three infantry regiments and 50 tanks in the sector of Belmajor and Szerecseny[puszta], to be able to launch their attack the following day after an artillery barrage and aircraft raid. The enemy has thrown all of their divisions into combat.
There were very few tanks left in our brigade.[587] They were stretched out on a very wide frontline, with big gaps between them, which were defended by the submachine gunners who had retreated from the first lines, plus subunits from the first strongpoint with self-propelled and anti-tank guns. Therefore losing even just one tank could have resulted a gaping hole in our defence, through which the enemy could have achieved a deep penetration into our lines. The kombrig had a handful of self-propelled guns left in his reserves, which were to close off the gaps if necessary. The defensive positions were our saviours, which were perfectly prepared, according to the engineering troops. Our tanks were deeply dug into the ground, and were also camouflaged with only the turrets above ground. When advancing, it was very difficult to hit them. The infantry had an excellently established combat trench and connection trench system prepared."[588]

The German *Kampfgruppe "Bradel"* of *1. Panzer-Division* and its *Panzer-Regiment 1* had, on the night of 11/12 March 1945, repulsed a smaller scale Soviet attack southeast of Gárdony. Afterwards, the *Division*, reinforced by *schwere Panzer-Abteilung 509*, was ordered to set off from the sector of Agárd and Gárdony and occupy Hill 184 southwest of Tutyimajor and Point 176 west of Sikítótanya together with the farm houses, then keep the Kisvelence–Pusztaszabolcs road under fire.[589]

---

585 Weidemann, Gert-Axel: *Unser Regiment. Reiter-Regiment 2 – Panzer-Regiment 24*. Groß-Umstadt, 1982. p. 276.
586 War log of the 18th Tank Corps for March 1945. Copy owned by the author. pp. 17-18.
587 On that morning, the 170th Tank Brigade had 16 operational T–34/85 tanks, and the 1438th Self-Propelled Artillery Regiment had 10 operational SU–76Ms.
588 Bryukhov, Vasiliy: *Red Army Tank Commander. At War in a T–34 on the Eastern Front*. Barnsley, 2013. p. 171.
589 NARA, T311, R162, F7214272.

The German *Kampfgruppe "Bradel"*, consisting of the majority of *Panzergrenadier-Regiment 113*, supported by 12 Panther tanks, attacked eastwards, in the direction of Tükröspuszta. The majority of *schwere Panzer-Abteilung 509* also supported this *Kampfgruppe*. *Kampfgruppe "Neumann"* of *Panzer-Regiment 1* with 10 Panthers, three 2 cm self-propelled anti-aircraft guns, a few pioneer-armoured personnel carriers and the four Tiger B heavy tanks of *schwere Panzer-Abteilung 509*, advanced from Agárd in a south-southeast direction. The *I. (Bataillon)/Panzergrenadier-Regiment 113* with its armoured personnel carriers followed *Kampfgruppe "Neumann"*.[590]

At 0630 hours in the morning, the Germans launched an attack from the southern outskirts of Gárdony, from Pálmajor and Csiribmajor to the east with, according to Soviet sources, approximately 60 armoured fighting vehicles and a regiment-size force of *Panzergrenadier*-infantry[591], then, after extremely heavy fighting, occupied their objectives by 1000 hours.

Two batteries of the Soviet 912th Self-Propelled Artillery Regiment/207th Self-Propelled Artillery Brigade, opened fire on the Germans from the area south of Belső Hajdútanya, and two batteries of the 1011th Self-Propelled Artillery Regiment opened fire from the north-western slopes of Hill 184 with its dug-in SU-100s. Faced with this resistance, the Germans modified their course of attack, and advanced towards Hill 184 and Tutyimajor and the left flank of the 1011th Self-Propelled Artillery Regiment. The commander of the 1011th Self-Propelled Artillery Regiment deployed his own reserves, and as a result the German armoured fighting vehicles were not able to get past them in the direction of Tanyák and Szarvastanya.[592]

The 1011th Self-Propelled Artillery Regiment was practically destroyed in this action in one single hour.[593] Directly northwest of Tükröspuszta at Point 163, it lost four SU-100s and at Hill 184 in front of Tutyimajor it lost another 14 burnt out SU–100s. West of Belső Hajdútanya the Germans knocked out three more SU-100s of the 912th Self-Propelled Artillery Regiment.[594]

Sergeant Ivan G. Vihrov, gun commander of the 5th Battery/1030th Artillery Regiment/78th Rifle Division, found himself face to face with 16-18 Tiger B heavy tanks and a battalion of German infantry advancing while he was defending Hill 184. He left his position and approached to within 200-300 meters. He then knocked out four German heavy tanks and two assault guns with his gun. After his gunner was wounded, the Sergeant took his place and knocked out two more Tiger Bs and two assault guns. For his deeds he was later awarded the Hero of the Soviet Union.[595]

---

590 Stoves, Rolf: Persönliches Kriegstagebuch Pz.Rgt. 1 (typewritten manuscript, a copy owned by the author), entry from 12 March 1945. The seriously damaged Panther tanks that were towed to the repair workshop at Börgönd were transported by train to Hajmáskér, because the fuel had to be spared as much as possible. According to the division's history however, by that evening only five Panther tanks and two command tanks were in combat-ready condition. See Stoves, O. G. Rolf: *1. Panzer-Division 1935–1945. Chronik einer der drei Stamm-Division der deutschen Panzerwaffe*. Bad Nauheim, 1961. p. 752. In this case, the cause of the difference is most probably the double register of the *1. Panzer-Division*.
591 War log of the 207th Self-Propelled Artillery Brigade, 12 March 1945. Copy owned by the author.
592 War log of the 207th Self-Propelled Artillery Brigade, 12 March 1945. Copy owned by the author.
593 Central Archives of the Russian Defence Ministry (Podolsk), f. 243, op. 2900, gy. 1570, li. 67.
594 War log of the 207th Self-Propelled Artillery Brigade, 12 March 1945. Copy owned by the author.
595 See HM HIM Hadtörténelmi Levéltár (Budapest), Szovjetunió Hőse kitüntetések gyűjteménye (*Collection of Hero of the Soviet Union awards*), 618.

The Germans reported knocking out 20 Soviet self-propelled guns in this engagement, while they themselves, according to their own data, lost nine armoured fighting vehicles.[596] The Germans also acquired the radio message documents of the commander of the Soviet 1011th Self-Propelled Artillery Regiment/207th Self-Propelled Artillery Brigade.[597]

According to the history of *schwere Panzer-Abteilung 509*, this was *"the hardest engagement the unit experienced in its whole existence"*:

"While the extremely brave pioneers, despite their losses, opened corridors in the minefields, the 16 Königstigers of schwere Panzer-Abteilung 509 were fighting a bitter battle with the heavy Soviet tank destroyers. The fight was raging and at last the Königstigers pushed their way through the enemy mine field, while 122 mm armoured shells[598] were constantly raining on them. One tank after the other dropped out of combat with heavy damage. Three Königstigers were hit so badly that they had to be written off as a total loss.[599] But one Jagdpanzer after the other were enflamed by our hits. In the end, only two Königstigers were crawling forward, slowly, painfully, but unstoppably towards the elevated position, into the middle of the position of the Soviet tank destroyers, the command tank of Hauptmann dr. König and another from the 2nd company. There were 24 smoldering ruins of ISU-122 type Jagdpanzers left there.[600] We reached our objective. The two Königstigers immediately opened fire from their elevated position on the Kápolnásnyék–Iváncsa[601] road running deep below, and knocked out two guns from a 76.2 mm anti-tank battery.

After the Grenadiers closed up to the elevated position, and had taken that over, the commander of the Abteilung left his tank and the escort tank there to hold the position, and he himself in an armoured personnel carrier visited the command post of the combat group, then the 1. Panzer-Division. There, Hauptmann dr. König was congratulated on the success achieved, which would have been impossible without the deployment of the Königstigers. But the commander of the Abteilung was not happy, despite the commendations and the success. He was thinking about the huge losses."[602]

During the fighting around Belső Hajdútanya, a Guards Sergeant gun commander of the Soviet 315th Guards Anti-Tank Artillery Regiment, Mikhail S. Chursin, earned himself recognition when he knocked out four Tiger B heavy tanks out of nine with his gun, although he himself was killed during the engagement. He was posthumously awarded the Hero of the Soviet Union.[603]

---

596 NARA, T311, R162, F7214263. According to the Germans the majority of the armoured fighting vehicles were repairable within a short time frame.
597 BAMA, RH 2/1998 Blatt 40.
598 The Germans believed that they were facing ISU–122 self-propelled guns.
599 The three Tiger B heavy tanks that were damaged beyond repair, had only been deleted from the unit strength after 21 March 1945.
600 The Soviet units have lost on that day 21 knocked out SU–100s in the encounter, of which, 19 burnt out)
601 Correctly this is the road leading from Kápolnásnyék towards Pusztaszabolcs.
602 *History of the schwere Panzer-Abteilung 509* (typewritten manuscript). Copy owned by the author. p. 55.
603 HM HIM Hadtörténelmi Levéltár (Budapest), Szovjetunió Hőse kitüntetések gyűjteménye (*Collection of Hero of the Soviet Union awards*), 556-557. The commander of the 315th Guards Anti-Tank Artillery Regiment, Guards Lieutenant Colonel Grigory A. Czeh was also awarded the Hero of the Soviet Union after his regiment reported to have knocked out 12 German armoured fighting vehicles during the defensive actions of 8 – 15 March 1945. See HM HIM Hadtörténelmi Levéltár (Budapest), Szovjetunió Hőse kitüntetések gyűjteménye (*Collection of Hero of the Soviet Union awards*), 559-560.

After the German armoured fighting vehicles had pushed back units of the Soviet 78th Rifle Division and inflicted serious losses on the 207th Self-Propelled Artillery Brigade, the 3rd Tank Brigade/23rd Tank Corps and the 1443rd Self-Propelled Artillery Regiment/23rd Tank Corps engaged them in combat.

The Soviet tanks and self-propelled guns were hiding in ambush positions and opened fire at a distance of 400-600 meters, reporting to have knocked out 19 German tanks. Their own losses consisted of two burnt out T–34/85s. Two tank commanders, Junior Lieutenants Kotov and Dmitriev earned recognition during this combat, when they reported to have knocked out nine German tanks.[604] A tank commander of the 3rd Tank Battalion/3rd Tank Brigade, Junior Lieutenant Stepan G. Cuprenkov achieved an even more astonishing feat:

"In the morning of 12 March, the enemy launched an attack of approximately 50 heavy tanks and large numbers of infantry against our positions. They exploited their superiority in numbers, the enemy was wedged into the lines of our infantry. Letting the enemy come very close, comrade Cuprenkov knocked out three German heavy tanks at extremely close range, and 40 infantry soldiers. [...]
Two hours later the enemy again attempted an attack with 70 tanks and large numbers of infantry. Firing from an ambush position, comrade Cuprenkov again set a German heavy tank on fire... killing approximately 30 soldiers and officers. The super heavy [Tiger B – the author] tanks, getting past the battle line of the infantry, got in the rear of our tanks. Feeling the very low efficiency of the frontal firing, comrade Cuprenkov left the ambush position with full speed and ambushed the German tanks in the rear. He pushed after them and set fire to two "Königstigers" type super heavy tanks... [...]"[605]

Apart from this, the 1501st Anti-Tank Artillery Regiment reported to have knocked out another three German heavy tanks from its firing position at Szilfástanya, east of Tutyimajor.[606]

On that day, *III. Panzerkorps*, received *Volks-Werfer-Brigade 19*, and *1. Panzer-Division* received *Artillerie-Brigade 959*.[607]

The fuel shortage situation at *Heeresgruppe Süd* was worsening. Between 6 and 12 March 1945, the units had used up 609 m³ of fuel per day. Due to Allied air raids against the oil refineries around Komárom, during the same time period, they were only able to manufacture 322 m³ fuel per day, which was 731 m³ less than what was required. In these circumstances, the units were forced to decrease their fuel consumption by 1/6, but according to their calculations, even with these measures they only had provisions to last until approximately the end of March.[608]

---

[604] War log of the 23rd Tank Corps for March 1945. Copy owned by the author. p. 6.
[605] HM HIM Hadtörténelmi Levéltár (Budapest), Szovjetunió Hőse kitüntetések gyűjteménye (*Collection of Hero of the Soviet Union awards*), 563.
[606] Central Archives of the Russian Defence Ministry (Podolsk), f. 3418, op. 1, gy. 81, li. 16.
[607] NARA, T311, R163, F7215323.
[608] NARA, T311, R162, F7214548.

13 March, 1945, Tuesday

(**WEATHER**: highest daytime temperature around 6 Celsius, partly clouded, partly clear sky, and visibility conditions are favourable. The condition of the roads is still poor, but they have already started to dry up.)

On the Dráva line, the Soviet 1891st Self-Propelled Artillery Regiment lost one SU-76M self-propelled gun in combat against the German bridgehead at Drávaszabolcs.[609]

The Germans continued to reassemble along the frontline of *2. Panzerarmee* and there were no major engagements in this sector on that day.[610] During the time period between 6 – 13 March 1945, the *Panzerarmee* lost four assault guns, 51 submachine guns, 38 machine guns, 51 anti-tank guns, three 8 cm mortars, one 10.5 cm field howitzer and one mountain gun.[611]

The Soviet 1201st Self-Propelled Artillery Regiment, with 20 SU–76Ms and one T–34 tank, established firing positions in the sector of Csököly, in the defensive system of the 299th Rifle Division/64th Rifle Corps. At the same time, the 864th Self-Propelled Artillery Regiment marched into the sector of Kadarkút with 16 operational SU–76M self-propelled guns.[612]

According to the morning report of *6. Panzerarmee*, on the right flank of the German *I. Kavallerie-Korps/6. Panzerarmee*, the Hungarian 25th Infantry Division, reinforced by the Jagdpanzer 38(t) *Jagdpanzers* of the 20th Assault Artillery Battalion, broke into the eastern section of Siófok during the morning. This however, later turned out to be incorrect. The Hungarian Division had not even commenced its assault against the city, the main reason for which, was the failure and significant losses among the Hungarian *Jagdpanzers*. The Germans ordered an inquiry into the incident.[613] During the morning, the Hungarian units held up Soviet attacks of one to two company strength, meanwhile holding their positions most of the time.[614]

The *3.* and *4. Kavallerie-Divisions* strongly resisted, the Soviet attacks, partially supported by armoured fighting vehicles, against the German occupied bridgehead east of Ádánd. The Soviets advanced as far as the German bridge created over the Sió Canal, but the light tanks, armoured personnel carriers and automatic cannons of *schwere Kavallerie-Abteilung 4/4. Kavallerie-Division* under *Major* Hacke, and the soldiers of *I. (Abteilung)/Reiter-Regiment 5* under *Rittmeister* Epping, eliminated this incursion and held the area of the bridgehead.[615] In the fighting around the bridge, the assault guns and *Jagdpanzers* of *Panzerjäger-Abteilung 69* were also deployed, which kept the German cavalry from falling back. Supported by these armoured fighting vehicles, they at last

---

609 Central Archives of the Russian Defence Ministry (Podolsk), f. 243, op. 2928, gy. 178, li. 74/2.
610 NARA, T311, R162, F7214275.
611 NARA, T311, R162, F7214553-7214554.
612 Central Archives of the Russian Defence Ministry (Podolsk), f. 243, op. 2928, gy. 131, li. 240.
613 NARA, T311, R162, F7214281-7214282. Unfortunately no record of the result of the investigation has been found as yet. It is not impossible that the Hungarians were referring to the armoured fighting vehicle losses of the 20th Assault Artillery Battalion on 11 March 1945, which were inflicted on them east of Balatonszabadi-fürdőtelep, that is in the outskirts of Siófok.
614 NARA, T311, R162, F7214275.
615 NARA, T311, R163, F7215372.

pushed the Soviets out of the area of the bridgehead with a counterattack, and reoccupied their former positions again.[616]

At dawn, 2 km northwest of Szabadhídvég, *3. Kavallerie-Division* set off against Hill 146[617] Their units were encircled there, forcing them to break out and return to the bridgehead.

Units of the Hungarian 14th Honvéd Infantry Regiment had taken Lajoskomárom without a fight, however Mezőkomárom was still in Soviet hands.[618]

The Soviet 22nd Independent Tank Regiment was supporting the forces of the 66th Guards Rifle Division with about four T–34 tanks and two SU–76M self-propelled guns at the north-western and eastern edge of Mezőkomárom, five T–34s and one KV–1S heavy tank in the area of Hill 146 (Kavicsos Hill) 3 km northwest of Szabadhídvég, and three T–34s on the northern edge of Balatonszabadi. The Germans knocked out the KV–1S heavy tank during the engagement that day, but it was not burnt out.[619]

Of the 21 operational armoured fighting vehicles of the Soviet 1952nd Self-Propelled Artillery Regiment/209th Self-Propelled Artillery Brigade, four SU-100s were used at Szabadhídvég, two at Felsőnyék, two at Ozora, four at Tolnanémedi, and five at Sárszentlőrinc to support the rifle forces. Five SU-100s of the 1953rd Self-Propelled Artillery Regiment were in combat 1 km south of Simontornya, four on the southern side of Cece, and two in the sector of Sáregres. The Regiment on that day lost two knocked out SU-100s, one of which burnt out.[620] As opposed to this, the 209th Self-Propelled Artillery Brigade reported to have knocked out four German Tiger Bs, four Panthers and three Panzer IV tanks.[621]

On the front of *I. SS-Panzerkorps* the Soviet attacks had temporarily narrowed down the bridgehead in the sector of Simontornya, held by *SS-Panzergrenadier-Regiment 26* and *SS-Panzer-Aufklärungs-Abteilung 1*. After this, the Germans attacked again, and reoccupied the lost hill, most likely Point 125, from the Soviet forces who were also supported by armoured fighting vehicles. Following this, they extended the frontline of the bridgehead towards the southeast up to the southern edge of the cemetery at Simontornya.

SS-Panzergrenadier-Regiment 26, which had been subordinated to *12. SS-Panzer-Division* on that day, received orders to occupy Hill 220, 2 km south of Simontornya.

The attack commenced at 0625 hours. The armoured fighting vehicles and the armoured personnel carriers equipped with three-barrelled 2 cm automatic cannons (Sd.Kfz.251/21) provided effective fire support from the northern bank of the Sió Canal. By 1200 hours, *II. (Bataillon)/SS-Panzergrenadier-Regiment 26* reached the objective. At the time, forces of *1. SS-Panzergrenadier-Regiment/1. SS-Panzer-Division* were also assaulting the same target east of the *Bataillon*. During the day, the Soviets tried multiple times to launch counterattacks in order to reoccupy the hill with the support of rifle units, armoured fighting vehicles and

---

616 Witte, Hans Joachim – Offermann, Peter: *Die Boeselagerschen Reiter. Das Kavallerie-Regiment Mitte und die aus ihm hervorgegangene 3. Kavallerie-Brigade/Division*. München, 1998. p. 395.
617 Not to be mistaken with the Kaviicsos Hill of similar height!
618 NARA, T311, R162, F7214276.
619 Central Archives of the Russian Defence Ministry (Podolsk), f. 243, op. 2928, gy. 131, li. 240.
620 Central Archives of the Russian Defence Ministry (Podolsk), f. 243, op. 2928, gy. 131, li. 239.
621 Central Archives of the Russian Defence Ministry (Podolsk), f. 243, op. 2928, gy. 131, li. 240. The 1951st and 1953rd Self-Propelled Artillery Regiments/209th Self-Propelled Artillery Brigade had reported to have knocked out altogether 29 German tanks, two assault guns and six armoured personnel carriers between 10-13 March 1945. See the combat report of the 209th Self-Propelled Artillery Brigade of the period between 10 March – 30 April. Copy owned by the author. p. 3.

self-propelled anti-aircraft guns[622]. During the night, on one occasion they breached the fortified positions of *II.(Bataillon)/SS-Panzergrenadier-Regiment 26*, but they were driven out. The *Divisionsbegleitkompanie* was also subordinated to *SS-Panzergrenadier-Regiment 26*.[623]

The *Division*, in the first eight days of the German offensive, from 6 to 13 March 1945, lost 148 killed including five officers, 656 wounded including 19 officers and 153 missing in action, altogether 957 men. The strength of the units was at 12,295 men, 4594 of which were combat ready. Of the armoured fighting vehicles, 15 tanks, 18 *Jagdpanzers*[624], and 117 armoured personnel carriers and armoured cars were in combat-ready condition. Another 39 tanks, 49 *Jagdpanzers*, 77 armoured personnel carriers and armoured cars were being repaired at the same time. During the previous eight days, five tanks and two *Jagdpanzers* of the *Division* were destroyed in combat.[625]

The *1. SS-Panzer-Division* was fighting to widen the bridgehead established the previous day. *SS-Panzergrenadier-Regiment 1* and units of *SS-Panzergrenadier-Regiment 26* started off with the support of the *Division's* artillery, heavy infantry weapons, and anti-aircraft guns and after bitter fighting, occupied Hill 220 south of Simontornya.

In defence of the bridgehead, *Panzer-Pionier-Bataillon 1* with the help from *12. SS-Panzer-Division* on the right flank, under constant Soviet artillery fire, started to construct a military bridge over the Sió Canal, which was approximately 30 meters wide and 4.5 meters deep. The work was progressing slowly due to constant fire from the Soviet troops, and then in the evening, the completed bridge collapsed under the weight of a German armoured fighting vehicle. Due to this, only two of the Panzer IV/70 *Jagdpanzers* assigned to support the *SS-Panzergrenadiers* on the other side in the bridgehead, were able to cross to the southern bank, which in turn provided effective fire support and disabled two Soviet self-propelled guns. After the bridge had been repaired, four more *SS-Jagdpanzers* arrived, most likely from *SS-Panzerjäger-Abteilung 12*.

In the first eight days of the offensive from 6 to 13 March, the *Division* lost 211 men killed including six officers, 1075 wounded including 16 officers and 149 missing in action including one officer, a total of 1435 men. The strength of *1. SS-Panzer-Division* was 12,075 men, however, of this, only 3492 men were combat-ready. Of its 86 tanks, 28 were combat-ready, and of 22 assault guns and *Jagdpanzers*, 12 were combat-ready. All the others were under repair. From 6 to 13 March 1945, the *Division* had lost 12 tanks and one *Jagdpanzer*. Of their 198 armoured personnel carriers and armoured cars, 152 were combat-ready.[626]

Two German attacks against the Soviet bridgehead at Cece failed despite support from *Luftwaffe* ground attack aircraft.[627]

At 0200 hours, *23. Panzer-Division* launched an assault southeast of the road-railroad intersection 2 km northeast of Simontornya, however the attack failed. *Panzergrenadier-*

---

622 These were most likely the SU–100 armoured fighting vehicles and M15A1 self-propelled anti-aircraft automatic cannons of the Soviet 1953rd Self-Propelled Artillery Regiment/209th Self-Propelled Artillery Brigade.
623 Meyer, Hubert: *Kriegsgeschichte der 12. SS-Panzerdivision „Hitlerjugend"*. Band II. Osnabrück, 1987. 2nd edition. p. 502.
624 Together with the vehicle of the *schwere Panzerjäger-Abteilung 560*.
625 BAMA, RH-19, V/62 Kriegstagebuch der Heeresgruppe Süd Anlageband, Führermeldung vom 15. 3. 1945.
626 BAMA, RH-19, V/62, Kriegstagebuch der Heeresgruppe Süd Anlageband, Führermeldung vom 15. 3. 1945.
627 NARA, T311, R162, F7214276.

Regiment 126 and *128* had, at 0830 hours, launched another attack against Sáregres, but the German assault troops did not advance, despite the artillery supporting them. At 1535 hours, *2. Kompanie/ Panzergrenadier-Regiment 128* reached the northern edge of the village, but they were soon pushed back.

At 1335 hours, twelve German Fw 190 ground attack aircraft launched an air raid against Sáregres and Cece followed by a raid launched against Cece at 1500 hours.[628] Following the air raids, the *Panzergrenadiers* attacked again, but this renewed attempt was also halted at 1630 hours. Afterwards, the *Panzergrenadiers* attempted the assault once again supported by *Panzer-Aufklärungs-Abteilung 23,* with its armoured personnel carriers and the assault units of *Panzer-Pionier-Bataillon 51*. At 1735 hours, *I. (Bataillon)/Panzergrenadier-Regiment 128,* broke into the northern part of Sáregres, and the armoured personnel carriers fought their way into the cemetery. Around 1900 hours, part of the *Division* with the support of ground attack aircraft, advanced into the middle of the village, and a lengthy engagement ensued.[629] At last, the Germans managed to completely occupy all of Sáregres.

In the meantime, at 1930 hours, *2. Kompanie/Panzergrenadier-Regiment 128* had broken into the Egresi mill, but the fire of the Soviet armoured fighting vehicles and machine guns stopped them 100 meters short of the two road bridges east of their position. The *Kompanie* was relieved by *I. (Bataillon)/Panzergrenadier-Regiment 128*. During the night, the *Panzergrenadiers* of *23. Panzer-Division* went into defensive positions around Sáregres with their frontline facing to the east.

During the day, the armoured group of *23. Panzer-Division* was in combat in the sector of the road-railroad intersection 2 km northeast of Simontornya and 3 km southwest of Sáregres. In the afternoon, the German armoured fighting vehicles reported having destroyed one T–34/85 tank and three self-propelled guns, but no progress was made in the south-eastern direction. The German armoured group seriously lacked ammunition and was constantly harassed by the Soviet ground attack aircraft. One of the Panther tanks had been destroyed by a direct hit of an aerial bomb. After darkness had set in, *Panzergruppe "Fischer"* launched a new attack along the Simontornya–Cece road eastwards, running down the Soviet defence and successfully clearing Alsómajor. During the engagements on that day, the armoured group reported to have knocked out one T–34/85, six self-propelled guns, two transport vehicles, seven anti-tank guns, one anti-aircraft gun, 10 anti-tank rifles, eight machine guns and one light machine gun, besides capturing an SU–76M.[630]

The Soviet 1951st Self-Propelled Artillery Regiment/209th Self-Propelled Artillery Brigade was also fighting around Sáregres with 15 SU-100s, together with the 71st Tank Regiment/5th Guards Cavalry Corps and its 1896th Self-Propelled Artillery Regiment.[631]

---

[628] Central Archives of the Russian Defence Ministry (Podolsk), f. 440, op. 8311, gy. 98, li. 72. After the failure of the German attack, at 1700 hours another air raid had been carried out against Cece. In this sector the Germans released approximately 100 bombs on that day, according to Soviet sources.

[629] NARA, T311, R162, F7214276, furthermore Rebentisch, Ernst: *Zum Kaukasus und zu den Tauern. Die Geschichte der 23. Panzer-Division 1941–1945.* Esslingen, 1963. p. 488.

[630] Rebentisch, Ernst: *Zum Kaukasus und zu den Tauern. Die Geschichte der 23. Panzer-Division 1941–1945.* Esslingen, 1963. p. 489.

[631] Central Archives of the Russian Defence Ministry (Podolsk), f. 243, op. 2928, gy. 131, li. 239.

On the night of 12/13 March 1945, in the sector of *II. SS-Panzerkorps,* the Germans attempted to establish a bridgehead south of Aba on the Nádor Canal. The road bridge was blown up by the Soviets.[632]

On the right flank of the *Division*, west of Sárkeresztúr, the Soviets launched an attack with armoured fighting vehicles and a company-sized force, but the Germans held them back. There were Soviet attacks as well launched from the south and southwest against the bridgehead of the reinforced *SS-Panzer-Aufklärungs-Abteilung 2* northeast of Káloz, however these also were unsuccessful.[633]

The *44. Reichsgrenadier-Division* launched an attack against Sárkeresztúr, but the Soviet troops strongly defended their positions, and in the unfavourable terrain conditions the Germans were unable to advance. Soviet counterattacks had even pushed them back from their earlier positions.[634]

The armoured combat group of *2. SS-Panzer-Division,* in combat at Heinrichmajor,[635] was attacked four times by battalion-strength Soviet forces from the south and southeast, which were also supported by 10 M4A2 tanks. At 1000 hours, units of the 1st Guards Mechanized Brigade occupied Heinrichmajor, however the Germans reoccupied it at 1300 hours deploying 15-20 armoured fighting vehicles and a regiment of *Panzergrenadier*. During these engagements, the Soviets lost four M4A2 tanks and one SU–100 self-propelled gun.[636] According to Soviet sources, the German losses consisted of six knocked out tanks and six other tanks that ran on landmines, plus nine knocked out armoured personnel carriers and five that ran on landmines.[637]

Heinrichmajor was being defended as a forward position and was visited by *SS-Obersturmbannführer* Weidinger, *Kommandeur* of *SS-Panzergrenadier-Regiment 4*, to familiarize himself with the situation. Although abandoning the untenable positions was requested a number of times by the *Division*, all requests were denied by *II. SS-Panzerkorps*. The losses of the defenders increased day by day. According to German observations, the Soviets had towed away their damaged armoured fighting vehicles during the night.

In the first eight days of combat during the offensive from 6 to 13 March, *2. SS-Panzer-Division* lost 132 killed, 675 wounded and 174 missing in action, altogether 1005 men. The strength of the *Division* was 9143 men, of which 3344 were combat-ready. Of its 51 available tanks, only 11 were combat-ready, while of its 56 assault guns and *Jagdpanzers*, only 17 were combat-ready. Of its 223 armoured personnel carriers and armoured cars, only 133 were in combat-ready condition. The *Division* had lost between 6 – 13 March 1945, four destroyed tanks, plus five assault guns and *Jagdpanzers*.[638]

---

632 NARA, T311, R163, F7215325.
633 NARA, T311, R162, F7214276.
634 NARA, T311, R162, F7214276.
635 The armoured combat group in defence here was fighting in a corridor hardly three km wide. The Soviet tracer rounds were crossing over the Germans' heads during the night.
636 Central Archives of the Russian Defence Ministry (Podolsk), f. 243, op. 2928, gy. 178, li. 77.
637 Central Archives of the Russian Defence Ministry (Podolsk), f. 243, op. 2928, gy. 131, li. 241.
638 BAMA, RH-19, V/62 Kriegstagebuch der Heeresgruppe Süd Anlageband, Führermeldung vom 15. 3. 1945.

At the same time, the Soviets tried three times to get their battalion and regiment-size attacks through from the west and east towards Külsőpüspökmajor, 4 km south-southwest of Sárosd, in order to close off and encircle the German armoured combat group. Units of *2. SS-Panzer-Division* repulsed and stopped these attacks, and knocked out four T–34/85 tanks, two of which were disabled in close combat, with *Panzerfausts*.[639] The Soviet 110th Tank Brigade lost on that day, one burnt out T–34/85 and one which was destroyed by a mine.[640]

On the front of *9. SS-Panzer-Division,* heavy fighting continued, although these battles were only of local importance, and did not in any way alter the frontline.

The *Division* lost, between 6 and 13 March 1945, 153 killed including 11 officers, 536 wounded including 25 officers and 105 missing in action, altogether 794 men. On that day, the strength of the troops was 8029 men, of which, 4320 were combat-ready. In the fighting between 7 – 13 March 1945, *SS-Panzer-Regiment 9* only lost four tanks that were irrecoverable. Of its 56 remaining tanks, 23 were combat-ready. The *Division* had 57 *Jagdpanzers* and assault guns, and of these, 27 were combat-ready. Of the 224 armoured personnel carriers and armoured cars, 151 were combat-ready.[641]

Two batteries of the 1016th Self-Propelled Artillery Regiment/208th Self-Propelled Artillery Brigade, fighting in subordination to the 18th Tank Corps was in combat at Szárnyasmajor, one battery was at Jakabszállás, and one other battery was marching en route to Zichyújfalu at 1800 hours. The 110th Tank Brigade and the 363rd Guards Heavy Self-Propelled Artillery Regiment, plus two battalions of the 32nd Motorized Rifle Brigade of the Corps, were in defence in the area of Seregélyes south 1.5 km to Point 140–Szárnyasmajor–Csillagmajor–Jakabszállás.[642]

German reconnaissance had, until then, identified 60 Soviet tanks and self-propelled guns along the frontline of *II. SS-Panzerkorps*.[643]

The forces of the Soviet 1202nd Self-Propelled Artillery Regiment were split on that day, with two batteries remaining on the western edge of Sárosd in firing positions, and another two batteries establishing defences at Nagyhantos. The Regiment had 18 operational SU–76M self-propelled guns.[644]

In the front of *III. Panzerkorps/Armeegruppe "Balck", I. (Bataillon)/Panzergrenadier-Regiment 3/3. Panzer-Division,* occupied Júliamajor at 1300 hours on the same day with a surprise attack, aided by artillery support. The armoured personnel carriers of *2. Kompanie* under command of *Leutnant* von Heydebreck, charged out of the forest north of the farmstead, surprised the Soviets and occupied the farmstead. The attack was followed shortly after by *Oberstleutnant* Martin Weymann, *Kommandeur* of *Panzergrenadier-Regiment 3,* together with the *Bataillonskommandeur.* Suddenly, *Oberstleutnant* Weymann collapsed after being shot in the head, most likely by a Soviet sniper who had noticed him. His armoured personnel carrier transported him back from the frontline at once, but the

---

639 NARA, T311, R162, F7214276.
640 War log of the 18th Tank Corps for March 1945. Copy owned by the author. p. 20.
641 BAMA, RH-19, V/62 Kriegstagebuch der Heeresgruppe Süd Anlageband, Führermeldung vom 15. 3. 1945.
642 Central Archives of the Russian Defence Ministry (Podolsk), f. 243, op. 2928, gy. 131, li. 241.
643 NARA, T311, R162, F7214286.
644 Central Archives of the Russian Defence Ministry (Podolsk), f. 243, op. 2928, gy. 131, li. 239.

medics of the *Division* were not able to help. From there, he was taken to a brain surgeon at the *SS*-hospital at Hajmáskér and then to Szombathely where he died. The command of *Panzergrenadier-Regiment 3* was taken over by *Major* Schulze, and *Hauptmann* Treppe took over the command of *I. (Bataillon)/Panzergrenadier-Regiment 3* from the *Major*.[645]

The *3. Panzer-Division* left behind a holding force in the sector of Júliamajor, then after regrouping, launched an attack toward the southeast with two other combat groups. *Panzer-Aufklärungs-Abteilung 3*, reinforced by armoured fighting vehicles, occupied Mihálymajor on the right flank, 4 km northeast of Seregélyes after heavy fighting, knocking out three Soviet tanks, while on the left flank *Panzergrenadier-Regiment 3*, also reinforced by armoured fighting vehicles, attempted to take Ferencmajor.[646]

The right-flank and centre combat group of *6. Panzer-Division* occupied the heavily reinforced and strongly defended villages of Gulyaakol and Csongrád,[647] 5 km northest of Pusztaszabolcs. During this action the Germans reported to have knocked out three Soviet tanks. Further attempts to continue the attack were unsuccessful due to the increasingly strong resistance of the Soviets. The Germans reassembled their forces so they could push through the open field towards the east.

The *1.* and *4. Schwadrons/I. (Abteilung)/Panzer-Regiment 24*, subordinated to *6. Panzer-Division,* attacked with 14 combat-ready Panther tanks from Tivadarmajor towards the east, in the direction of Csongrád and then Nádormajor. The *3. Schwadron* repeated its attack against Tüköspuszta on the previous day. Csongrád was occupied by the Germans after a short engagement, and they reported to have destroyed a large number of anti-tank guns. The Soviet artillery and mortars opened fire at the Germans again, and the bombers of the 17th Air Army also appeared in the sky. Past Csongrád, pushing towards Nádormajor, the Panthers again ran into a minefield. When the armoured fighting vehicles tried to bypass towards the south, fire from tanks and anti-tank guns greeted them from the hills south of Nádormajor. They encountered a swamp-ridden section of terrain stretching at right angles to the direction of the German attack. resulting in the failure of the attack.

The *1.* and *4. Schwadrons* received an order to detour and circle towards the north across the frontline of the combat group on the left flank of *6. Panzer-Division*. At that time, the Panthers were engaged in fire by Soviet armoured fighting vehicles and reported to have knocked out seven partially dug in T–34/85s.[648] The Panthers advanced further towards the east, but another minefield stopped them in their tracks. The commanders of *1.* and *3. Schwadrons* were wounded by mortar fire.[649]

The combat group on the left flank of *6. Panzer-Division,* with the support of the armoured fighting vehicles of *3. Schwadron/Panzer-Regiment 24* occupied Tüköspuszta, 6 km nortwest of Pusztaszabolcs, after heavy fighting.[650] However the attackers became exhausted and ground to a halt. The *I. (Abteilung)/Panzer-Regiment 24* was withdrawn from

---

645 *Geschichte der 3. Panzer-Division. Herausgegeben vom Traditionsverband der Division.* Berlin, 1967. pp. 466-467.
646 NARA, T311, R162, F7214277.
647 The Germans had identified parts of the Soviet 163rd Rifle Division in the sector of the farmstead called Csongrád, and with this, it became evident to them that the Soviet 27th Army stood in their way between the Sárvíz and Lake Velence.
648 Senger und Etterlin, von F.M. jr.: *Die 24. Panzer-Division vormals 1. Kavallerie-Division 1939–1945.* Neckargemünd, 1962. p. 309.
649 Weidemann, Gert-Axel: *Unser Regiment. Reiter-Regiment 2 – Panzer-Regiment 24.* Groß-Umstadt, 1982. p. 276.
650 NARA, T311, R162, F7214277.

the frontline on the night of 13/14 March 1945, and the damaged Panthers were towed back.[651] During the extremely heavy fighting of 12 and 13 March 1945, the unit had only suffered one Panther as a total loss, however the unit now only had three combat-ready tanks for the next day, and all the other vehicles were in need of repairs.

North of Tükröspuszta, the 3rd Tank Brigade/23rd Tank Corps reported to have knocked out 14 German armoured fighting vehicles, including two Tiger Bs[652] and 11 armoured personnel carriers. Of these, seven tanks were knocked out by the tank of Lieutenant Duvinin. Junior Lieutenant Cuprenkov, who had fought heroically the day before, also knocked out one German tank, however his own tank was also hit during the engagement. Following a brief period of fighting in the already burning vehicle, the crew abandoned the vehicle. The Junior Lieutenant, for his deeds in combat the day before and on that day, was awarded the decoration Hero of the Soviet Union.[653]

The Soviet 3rd Tank Brigade lost five knocked out T–34/85 tanks, four of which were burnt out, while fighting in the sector of Szarvastanya and Nándormajor. Of the armoured fighting vehicles of the 1443rd Self-Propelled Artillery Regiment also deployed at Tükröspuszta, the Germans knocked out two ISU–122s, one of which burnt out).[654]

The Soviet 181st Tank Brigade/18th Tank Corps was defending between Mihálymajor, Point 124 northwest of Zichyújfalu, Zichyújfalu and Hippolitpuszta, then the Germans pushed them back to Györgymajor. Three tanks from the Brigade were hit and burnt out at Gulyaakol, and a another five at Györgymajor.[655] The 170th Tank Brigade and the 1443rd Self-Propelled Artillery Regiment with the 1st Battalion/32nd Motorized Rifle Brigade was holding the frontline from Seregélyes to Sándormajor.[656] Their losses amounted to three burnt out tanks and one burnt out SU–76M.

The attack of *Panzergrenadier-Regiment 1/1. Panzer-Division* towards Tükröspuszta on the night of 12/13 March 1945 was unsuccessful. An instrumental cause of this was the fact that one of the mobile obstacle detachments of the Soviet 35th Guards Rifle Corps planted at least 200 anti-tank mines in the Belső Hajdútanya sector during the night. A number of the German armoured fighting vehicles ran onto this field and became disabled. The immobilized armoured fighting vehicles were kept under fire by the Soviet artillery.[657]

On the night of 12/13 March 1945, a short time after midnight, *Hauptmann* dr. König, *Kommandeur* of *schwere Panzer-Abteilung 509* went to the command post of *1. Panzer-Division* in Seregélyes and asked that their Tiger Bs be drawn back from the frontline because of needed maintenance. Permission was denied by the First Staff Officer (Ia) of *1.*

---

651 Weidemann, Gert-Axel: *Unser Regiment. Reiter-Regiment 2 – Panzer-Regiment 24*. Groß-Umstadt, 1982. p. 276.
652 The *schwere Panzer-Abteilung 509* had not been engaged in combat for the remainder of the day. However it is not impossible that the Tiger B heavy tanks had been targeted again which had been disabled the day before in the vicinity of Hill 184 northwest of Tükröspuszta, and the recovery of which started on that day.
653 HM HIM Hadtörténelmi Levéltár (Budapest), Szovjetunió Hőse kitüntetések gyűjteménye (*Collection of Hero of the Soviet Union awards*), 563-564.
654 Central Archives of the Russian Defence Ministry (Podolsk), f. 243, op. 2928, gy. 178, li. 76/2, furthermore war log of the 23rd Tank Corps for March 1945. Copy owned by the author. pp. 7-8.
655 War log of the 18th Tank Corps for March 1945. Copy owned by the author. p. 19. The 181st Tank Brigade lost on that day nine burnt out tanks and by the evening it had 11 operational T–34/85s.
656 Central Archives of the Russian Defence Ministry (Podolsk), f. 243, op. 2928, gy. 131, li. 230. On that day, the 18th Tank Corps possessed 63 operational T–34 tanks, 11 of their own ISU–122s, six ISU–152s and 18 SU–76M self-propelled guns, plus19 subordinated SU–100 armoured fighting vehicles.
657 Malakhov, M. M.: A Balatontól Bécsig (excerpt). In: *Fejezetek hazánk felszabadításának történetéből*. Budapest, 1960. p. 154.

Panzer-Division, Oberst i.G. Krantz. *Hauptmann* dr. König however, received permission to submit his request directly to the *Stab* of *III. Panzerkorps*. The *Kommandeur, General der Panzertruppen* Breith, listened to the report of *Hauptmann* dr. König, and after some discussions with his chief of staff, he granted permission for the withdrawal of *schwere Panzer-Abteilung 509*. The disabled, knocked out or damaged heavy tanks were then towed into Seregélyes where their repair and maintenance was begun.[658]

Units of the German *1. Panzer-Division*[659] with 17 Panther tanks of *Panzer-Regiment 1*, a few pioneer-armoured personnel carriers and one of the companies of *II. (Bataillon)/Panzergrenadier-Regiment 113* mounted on tanks, advanced in the afternoon to the southwestern outskirts of Kisvelence and turned back a number of Soviet counterattacks 3 km southeast of Gárdony. Gárdony, cleared by *10. Panzer-Pionier-Kompanie/Panzergrenadier-Regiment 113*[660] was targeted by a heavy barrage from the Soviet artillery in the direction of Velence and Kápolnásnyék.[661]

After darkness had set in, the majority of *II. (Bataillon)/Panzergrenadier-Regiment 113*, reinforced by *Marder* tank destroyers and towed anti-tank guns, held off strong Soviet attacks south of Gárdony and southeast of Agárdpuszta. Toward *3. Panzer-Division*, only armoured personnel carriers and *Flakpanzer IV* self-propelled four-barrelled 2 cm anti-aircraft guns maintained contact.[662]

The troops of the German *356. Infanterie-Division* remained in defence but its strength was depleted. The *Division* reported a mere 400-450 soldiers as combat-ready for that day.[663]

On the same day, the Soviet 27th Army ordered the 1068th Self-Propelled Artillery Regiment/208th Self-Propelled Artillery Brigade into defence in the sector of Szabolcspuszta and Pusztaszabolcs to the west.[664] The Regiments of the 207th Self-Propelled Artillery Brigade, though having suffered serious losses the previous day, were in defence on the Kisvelence, Hajdúpuszta and Szarvaspuszta line with 40 operational SU–100s, three SU–57s (American lend-lease T48 57mm GMC) and two T–34 armoured fighting vehicles.[665] Two batteries of the 1004th Self-Propelled Artillery Regiment occupied defence positions at Györgymajor and Kolompos as ordered by the Staff of the 23rd Tank Corps. The Brigade lost another burnt out SU–100 on that day.[666]

The German *III. Panzerkorps* reported on that day to have destroyed 20 armoured fighting vehicles and 12 anti-tank guns, in addition to capturing one armoured fighting

---

[658] *History of the schwere Panzer-Abteilung 509* (typewritten manuscript). Copy owned by the author. p. 55.
[659] On that day, *Panzer-Regiment 1/1. Panzer-Division* reported 27 combat-ready Panthers and one Panzer III command tank. The *Regiment* had two captured T–34/85 tanks, however they had kept their existence hidden. See Stoves, Rolf: Persönliches Kriegstagebuch Pz.Rgt. 1 (typewritten manuscript, a copy owned by the author), entry from 13 March 1945.
[660] Stoves, Rolf: Persönliches Kriegstagebuch Pz.Rgt. 1 (typewritten manuscript, a copy owned by the author), entry from 13 March 1945.
[661] NARA, T311, R162, F7214277.
[662] Stoves, Rolf: Persönliches Kriegstagebuch Pz.Rgt. 1 (typewritten manuscript, a copy owned by the author), entry from 13 March 1945.
[663] NARA, T311, R162, F7214284.
[664] Central Archives of the Russian Defence Ministry (Podolsk), f. 243, op. 2928, gy. 131, li. 239.
[665] Central Archives of the Russian Defence Ministry (Podolsk), f. 243, op. 2928, gy. 131, li. 240. On 12 March 1945 the 207th Self-Propelled Artillery Brigade lost 21 knocked out SU–100s, of which 19 were burnt out. With this, the 1011th Self-Propelled Artillery Regiment was practically destroyed in one single hour.
[666] Central Archives of the Russian Defence Ministry (Podolsk), f. 243, op. 2928, gy. 178, li. 76/2. Interestingly, the 207th Self-Propelled Artillery Brigade had not noted down any losses in their war log for 13 March 1945.

vehicle and 49 prisoners.[667] *General der Panzertruppe* Hermann Breith, *Kommandeur* of the armoured corps, clearly stated in his daily situational report that further German attacks were meaningless, as the German objectives were already well known to the Soviets and the terrain east of the Sárvíz prevented armoured forces fanning out beyond the roads, and it was not possible to deploy concentrated armoured forces.[668]

On 6 March 1945, *III. Panzerkorps* had 153 combat-ready tanks, assault guns and *Jagdpanzers*, but by 13 March only 63 remained combat-ready.[669] Between 6 - 13 March 1945, the armoured corps lost 346 killed, 1485 wounded, 224 missing in action and 163 suffering various illnesses.[670] Of its armoured strength, one Panzer IV and six Panther tanks, as well as four armoured personnel carriers were total losses.[671]

Overall, the performance of *III. Panzerkorps* fell very short of what the Germans had expected.[672] On the next day, the forces of the *3.* and *6. Panzer-Divisions* were to start off in a western direction to cut through the Seregélyes–Perkáta road east of Hill 145 (Öreg Hill), considered a hard nut to crack in itself, and if the plans had worked as prepared, they would have coordinated with *2. SS-* and *9. SS-Panzer-Divisions* to push southeast toward Sárosd.[673]

On the front of *IV. SS-Panzerkorps*, German reconnaissance detected major unit movements on the Lovasberény–Székesfehérvár road. In the southern and northern outskirts of Zámoly they again detected unit movements and saw that approximately 700 soldiers were advancing towards the frontline[674] At that time, the Germans assumed that these troops had arrived as replacements or that they had arrived to carry out small-scale relief attacks.[675]

On that day, the Soviet 9th Guards Army was subordinated to the 3rd Ukrainian Front, with 20-25 operational SU–76Ms of the 1513rd, 1523rd and 1524rd Self-Propelled Artillery Regiments. The regiments, in order, were assembling in the Lovasberény, Csákvár and Kajászószentpéter sector.[676]

From noon on that day, the German *Luftflotte 4.* supported the German-Hungarian troops flying 280 missions, mostly with ground attack aircraft in the Simontornya sector, and with fighters between Sárkeresztúr and Lake Velence. According to unconfirmed reports the pilots destroyed one tank, caused 10 major explosions at Simontornya and shot down 12 Soviet planes in aerial combat.[677]

At the German *Heeresgruppe Süd,* it was admitted that resistance of Soviet troops had increased significantly and their counterattacks had become more organized. The Germans assumed that they only had one chance now to break through, provided they could concentrate their armoured forces and form one single main thrust, as long as

---

667 NARA, T311, R163, F7215341.
668 NARA, T311, R162, F7214566-7214567.
669 NARA, T311, R162, F7214566-7214567.
670 NARA, T311, R163, F7214879.
671 NARA, T311, R163, F7214880.
672 NARA, T311, R162, F7214283.
673 NARA, T311, R162, F7214285.
674 NARA, T311, R162, F7214277.
675 NARA, T311, R162, F7214285.
676 Central Archives of the Russian Defence Ministry (Podolsk), f. 243, op. 2928, gy. 131, li. 239.
677 NARA, T311, R162, F7214279.

it was possible to advance across the poor ground conditions. The most advantageous direction at that time seemed to be the route between the Sárvíz and Lake Velence towards the Danube[678]

14 March 1945, Wednesday

(**WEATHER**: highest daytime temperature 13 Celsius, sunny and warm weather, cloudy in places. The roads are drying up; the terrain is increasingly passable by armoured fightng vehicles.)

On that day, *Heeresgruppe "E"* ordered the forces of *LXXXI. Armeekorps z.b.V.* to gradually abandon the Donji Miholjac and the Valpovo bridgeheads, leaving rearguards behind, and to retreat to the southern bank of the Dráva River.[679]

After 1400 hours the Soviet 1891st Self-Propelled Artillery Regiment supporting the Bulgarian 6th Infantry Division 2 km north of Drávaszabolcs in the direction of Drávacsehi, lost two burnt out SU–76Ms.[680]

On the front of *2. Panzerarmee, 16. SS-Panzergrenadier-Division/XXII. Gebirgskorps* launched its attack at 0900 hours from the sector of Marcali against the Soviet 6th Guards Rifle Corps along the road leading towards Libickozma. At first, the Germans again had to push through a Soviet minefield. The majority of the *SS*-troops approached the south side of Csömend from the west to within 1.5 km.[681]

The units of *16. SS-Panzergrenadier-Division,* advancing along the Marcali–Boronka road were bogged down in the mud and among the Soviet minefields. Two of the three combat-ready StuG. IIIs of *Panzergruppe "Rex"* of the *3. Kompanie/SS-Panzer-Abteilung 16,* were disabled when they ran on mines in a field previously reported to be cleared. These damaged armoured fighting vehicles were then only able to provide fire support for the attack. *Panzergruppe "Burger"* of *1. Kompanie/SS-Panzer-Abteilung 16* and *Panzergruppe "Geiger"* of *2. Kompanie* supported the *Panzergrenadiers*.[682]

The Soviets had blown the two bridges over the Sári Canal east of Marcali. After the *SS-Division* partially reassembled south of Marcali, the German attack was renewed at 1400 hours. The *I.* and *II. (Bataillons)/SS-Panzergrenadier-Regiment 36, SS-Panzer-Abteilung 16, SS-Panzer-Aufklärungs-Abteilung 16,* plus *II. (Bataillon)/SS-Panzergrenadier-Regiment 35* and the assault guns of two batteries of *Sturmartillerie-Brigade 261* were advancing towards Boronka. However the Germans had again bogged down south of the village. Only *I. (Bataillon)/SS-Panzergrenadier-Regiment 36* with nine assault guns of *Sturmartillerie-Brigade*

---

678 NARA, T311, R162, F7214280.
679 This was carried out by the troops between 15-20 March 1945. See Hnilicka, Karl: *Das Ende auf dem Balkan 1944/45 – Die militärische Räumung Jugoslaviens durch die deutsche Wehrmacht.* Musterschmidt – Göttingen, 1970. p. 125.
680 Central Archives of the Russian Defence Ministry (Podolsk), f. 243, op. 2928, gy. 131, li. 243. According to other sources, the 1891st Self-Propelled Artillery Regiment lost one armoured fighting vehicle as irrecoverable on 13 March, and another one on 14 March. See Central Archives of the Russian Defence Ministry (Podolsk), f. 243, op. 2928, gy. 178, li. 76/2 and 79.
681 NARA, T311, R162, F7214288.
682 Puntigam, Josef Paul: *Vom Plattensee bis zur Mur. Die Kämpfe 1945 im Dreiländereck.* Feldbach, without year of publication, [1993], p. 101.

261 managed to break into the village and establish a bridgehead at the canal. During the night however, the Soviet 61st Guards Rifle Division reoccupied Boronka. The advance of the *SS-Panzergrenadier-Division* was standing 1 km west of Csömend, and their forces were once again reassembled for the offensive planned for the next day.[683]

On that day, the command of the Soviet 57th Army ordered the 1255th Anti-Tank Artillery Regiment and the 47th Gun Artillery Regiment to Nikla, then in the afternoon two batteries of the 42nd Guards Corps Artillery Regiment also arrived, the latter with 122 mm A-19 guns. The next morning, the 20th Guards Rifle Division with the 46th Guards Artillery Regiment was also directed here, along with the 104th Rifle Division and the 290th Gun Artillery Regiment from the Front's reserve.[684]

On the right flank of *1. Volks-Gebirgs-Division,* starting from the sector of Kéthely, the assaulting combat group was bogged down in front of the Soviet fortified position. The other combat group launched an attack from the Sári Forest, 1 km east of the railway station of Kéthely, crossed the Öv Canal, then broke through the Soviet positions behind it and approached the northern edge of Somogyszentpál 1.5 km from the west.[685]

On the same day, *2. Panzerarmee* was able to achieve a salient of only 4 km into the defences of the Soviet 57th Army.[686]

On the night of 13/14 March 1945, on the right flank of *I. Kavallerie-Korps/6. Panzerarmee,* the forces of the Hungarian 25th Infantry Division outflanked the fortified positions of the Soviets in the sector of Hill 137 (Pusztatorony) and Hill 133 (Öreg Hill) and occupied Felsőmajor, 2 km north of Balatonszabadi. During the day, the Hungarian troops attacked in the direction of Balatonszabadi-fürdőtelep 4 km northwest of Siófok and towards the vineyards 3 km northwest of there, but they made very little progress in the face of heavy Soviet resistance. Felsőmajor, occupied by Hungarian troops the previous evening, fell back into Soviet hands.[687]

The *3.* and *4. Kavallerie-Division* held back eight Soviet attacks against the bridgehead east of Ádánd during the night and following day. The Soviets had attacked with regimental size forces, supported by armoured fighting vehicles. From the sector of Szabadhídvég, 15 Soviet armoured fighting vehicles supporting a battalion of rifle infantry, launched an attack, which the Germans were only able to repel in close combat. The cavalry forces claimed to have knocked out five Soviet tanks and to have immobilized one other tank, according to unconfirmed reports.[688] The *Kommandeur* of *I. (Abteilung)/Reiter-Regiment 5, Rittmeister* Epping, destroyed three of these tanks with his troops using *Panzerfausts*. The *Rittmeister* was wounded during the attack.[689]

Two assault guns of *Panzerjäger-Abteilung 69* took part in the fighting in the afternoon as well under the command of *Leutnants* Bose and Pelz. The two assault guns were not more than five meters away from each other in firing position. For *Leutnant* Pelz, this was

---

683 Puntigam, Josef Paul: *Vom Plattensee bis zur Mur. Die Kämpfe 1945 im Dreiländereck.* Feldbach, without year of publication, [1993], p. 88.
684 M. Svirin – O. Baronov – M. Kolomiets – D. Nedogonov: *Boj u ozera Balaton.* Moscow, 1999. p. 69.
685 NARA, T311, R162, F7214289.
686 NARA, T311, R162, F7214288.
687 NARA, T311, R162, F7214289.
688 NARA, T311, R162, F7214289.
689 NARA, T311, R163, F7215372.

his first combat mission. The Soviets were advancing from the direction of Szabadhídvég with two T–34/85 tanks, most likely from the 22nd Independent Tank Regiment. *Leutnant* Bose advised to let them get closer. Bose's loader, NCO Tietz, followed the movement of the two tanks closely, even behind a dried out small patch of forest. When the Soviet armoured fighting vehicles closed up to 800 meters from the two assault guns, *Leutnant* Bose told Pelz to take the one on the right and he would take the one on the left himself. The armour-piercing shell of Bose's assault gun hit the right side T–34/85 on the turret ring, which detonated in a matter of seconds and the turret flew off the tank. Leutnant Pelz also fired, but after his hit, there was no explosion or smoke. Despite this, he shouted over to his comrade happily that he knocked the Soviet out. *Leutnant* Bose saw through his binoculars that the Soviet tank had only been damaged on its left side tracks, and the turret was turned towards the Germans. The tank opened fire and at that moment, Bose's gunner knocked out the second tank too, and fire lashed out of the tank's escape hatch. *Leutnant* Pelz' assault gun was also hit by the Soviets but to their good fortune, only with a phosphorus smoke grenade.[690] The assault gun drew back to its starting position where the fire on the outside of the armour was quickly put out by the crew. *Leutnant* Pelz was literally baptised in fire.[691]

In the area, the Soviet 22nd Independent Tank Regiment's three T–34 tanks and two SU–76M self-propelled guns, were engaged in combat on the north-western and eastern edge of Mezőkomárom. Four T–34s, one SU–76M and one SU–85 self-propelled gun were in combat in the sector of Hill 146 (Kavicsos Hill) 3 km northwest of Szabadhídvég, and three T34s were engaged in combat in the sector of the Zsófia children's sanitarium, 3 km northeast of Siófok.[692]

The I and II Battalions/Hungarian 14th Honvéd Infantry Regiment were subordinated to *3. Kavallerie-Division*.[693]

In the line of *I. SS-Panzerkorps,* the Soviets transferred forces to hold the northern bank of the Sió Canal at Belsősári, but *SS-Panzergrenadier-Regiment 25* completely sealed this attempt off. The majority of the tanks and *Jagdpanzers* of *12. SS-Panzer-Division*, including the heavy armament were stranded on the northern bank because the military bridge was again damaged. The bridge over the Sió Canal was badly damaged by Soviet artillery and mortar fire and the Germans had begun to build an emergency bridge north of there.[694]

Although the Soviets launched a number of counterattacks that day, *SS-Panzergrenadier-Regiment 1* and units of *SS-Panzergrenadier-Regiment 26* managed to extend the Simontornya bridgehead to Point 115, 2 km southeast of the village. However there was still fighting going on around the Point. West of there, the pressure of the Soviet units pushed the Germans back to the northern edge of Hill 220 (Mósi Hill).[695]

---

690 During the Second World War, smoke grenades were not standard equipment on the T–34/85 tanks, however they were standard on the T–34 and SU–76M armoured fighting vehicles. Thus most likely a third Soviet armoured fighting vehicle which went unnoticed by the Germans had hit the assault gun.
691 Bose, Georg: „Ob's stürmt, oder schneit…"! Mit meinem Sturmgeschütz im Einsatz. Erinnerungen Teil 2. Selbstverlag Bose, Einhausen, 2005. p. 269.
692 Central Archives of the Russian Defence Ministry (Podolsk), f. 243, op. 2928, gy. 178, li. 76.
693 NARA, T311, R163, F7215340.
694 Meyer, Hubert: *Kriegsgeschichte der 12. SS-Panzerdivision „Hitlerjugend"*. Band II. Osnabrück, 1987. 2nd edition. p. 502.
695 NARA, T311, R162, F7214289.

The forces of *SS-Panzer-Regiment 1* were withdrawn from Simontornya on that day and were assembled in the area of Dég.

SS-Panzergrenadier-Regiment 2 with the *Jagdpanzers* of *SS-Panzerjäger-Abteilung 1* and the forces of *23. Panzer-Division* launched an assault from Sáregres against the Soviet occupied bridgehead on the Sió Canal and pushed the Soviets back to the opposite bank, in the direction of Cece.

SS-Unterscharführer Hans Baumann, driver of one of the Panzer IV/70 (V) *Jagdpanzers* of *SS-Panzerjäger-Abteilung 12* remembered the combat around the Simontornya bridgehead:

"When we stumbled upon the Soviets, they attacked us with Sherman tanks[696]. I noticed the gun of Untersturmführer Probst the crew to which Harry also belonged. Suddenly the escape hatch was blown off into the air – they were hit. Three persons clambered out. I was not able to discern who had climbed out therefore I did not know anything about the fate of Harry thereafter. [...]
Our deployment was continued. At a row of shrubs, Untersturmführer Rehn[697], our gunner and I climbed out to inspect the surroundings. Through an opening on the shrubbery we noticed a T-34 at a distance of approximately 300 meters. We slowly and silently rolled towards this opening, and turned the vehicle to the correct position. The gun barrel was just over the small hill right in front of the opening and the first shot was already a hit. What we did not see earlier was behind the first there was another, this time a well concealed T-34. We got that also. With that we now achieved three victories[698] with Untersturmführer Rehn on this day. Afterwards we were attacking alongside the infantry. We were standing on a hill. The Soviets were attacking with a large number of T-34s. We were firing at a distance of 1000 meters. Here the hit only depends on pure luck. We received heavy fire from a big farmstead because approximately 20 T-34s[699] were gathered there with mounted escort infantry. As I was counting them and got to the number 20, I felt a small push in my shoulder. Then I noticed my armpit was hit, but I was still holding myself together. Three or four of us with our armoured fighting vehicles, withdrew at full speed because in the meantime we were cut off. Everybody was gathered on the hill. We waited until nightfall when the order for retreat reached us. It was a very slow process at the dim moonlight. We were fantasizing about enemy hiding everywhere. We were constantly waiting for the enemy to open fire at us. Fritz Eckstein,[700] who had the Knight's Cross, was also there. When we arrived in the narrow valley, we stumbled upon Soviets. One of the Untersturmführers knocked out a T–34 and we did not have any armour-piercing shells anymore. I saw the armoured fighting vehicles

---

[696] In the sector of Simontornya, the nearest M4A2 Sherman tanks were at that time stationed at Cece, four of which were in the 3rd Guards Mechanized Brigade/1st Guards Mechanized Corps. It is likely that these were also deployed against the *SS*-troops that crossed the Sió Canal, but the Germans had met in the Simontornya sector mainly the four T–34/85 tanks of the Soviet 71st Tank Regiment/5th Guards Cavalry Corps and the 18 SU–76M self-propelled guns of the 1896th Self-Propelled Artillery Regiment. See Central Archives of the Russian Defence Ministry (Podolsk), f. 243, op. 2928, gy. 131, li. 241 and 244.

[697] *SS-Untersturmführer* Rehn was the commander of Baumann's Panzer IV/70 (V) *Jagdpanzer*.

[698] The *Jagdpanzer* had already knocked out a Soviet armoured fighting vehicle that day along the Sió Canal. See Baumann, Hans: *Mein Einsatz als Panzerjäger*. Wanzleben, 2014. p. 38.

[699] Most likely these were not only T–34 tanks, but also SU–76M self-propelled guns with the soldiers of the 5th Guards Cavalry Corps.

[700] *SS-Rottenführer* Fritz Eckstein served as a gunner of a Jagdpanzer IV *Jagdpanzer* and knocked out 26 Allied armoured fighting vehicles in Normandy, for which he was awarded the German Knight's Cross of the Iron Cross on 18 November 1944.

standing there and for the sake of safety we fired three high-explosive shells, of which at least one detonated on the turret of one of the T-34s. The mounted infantry flew off in the air. And then we were hit from the front. The transverse gearbox was damaged. The order came to abandon the vehicle. We were lucky, we found very good coverage in a drainage ditch against infantry weapons. After that we continued our retreat, and reached a very steep slope. I ran away later when our armoured fighting vehicle was badly burning. It was highly probable that the remaining high-explosive shells would explode."[701]

The 71st Tank Regiment supporting the units of the Soviet 5th Guards Cavalry Corps, by the evening on that day, had only two operational T–34/85 tanks, which were engaged in combat with the Germans together with the 1896th Self-Propelled Artillery Regiment 2 km south of Simontornya. The 71st Tank Regiment reported to have lost two burnt out T–34/85s.[702] The 1896th Self-Propelled Artillery Regiment, on that day lost three burnt out SU–76Ms and only had 18 operational armoured fighting vehicles left.[703]

Following three days of heavy fighting, the forces of the German *23. Panzer-Division* cleared the sector of Sáregres and with this eliminated the Soviet bridgehead west of Cece.[704] The command of *Panzer-Regiment 23* was taken over by *Major i. G.* Jahns from *Oberstleutnant* zu Waldeck und Pyrmont, who was placed in commander reserve.[705]

Five Fw 190 ground attack planes of the German *Luftwaffe* completed a mission at 1017 hours in the sector of Cece.[706]

Of the 13 operational S-100s of the 1951st Self-Propelled Artillery Regiment/209th Self-Propelled Artillery Brigade, three were in firing positions on the western edge of Cece and 10 were at Csordakút, 3 km south-east of Cece. Of the 12 SU-100s of the 1953rd Self-Propelled Artillery Regiment, five were in action on the south-western edge of Cece, and five were situated 3 km southeast of Simontornya. The 1952nd Self-Propelled Artillery Regiment had 21 operational SU–100s, four of which were positioned 2 km southeast of Simontornya, two southwest of there, two were at Tolnanémedi, two at the northern edge of Ozora, two on the northern edge of Felsőnyék, one 4 km northwest of Szabadhídvég, and five at Pincehely in the reserve of the regiment commander. In the fighting that day, the Brigade lost three burnt out SU-100s and one SU-57.[707]

On the front of *II. SS-Panzerkorps*, the bridgehead held by the reinforced *SS-Panzer-Aufklärungs-Abteilung 2* northeast of Káloz, was attacked by the Soviets on the night of 13/14 March 1945. The Germans succeeded in holding their bridgehead position although it was narrowed down to 500 meters. During the day, *SS-Panzer-Aufklärungs-Abteilung 2* again launched an attack from the bridgehead established at Káloz in the direction of Sárkeresztúr. Following some initial German success, the Soviets deployed fresh reserves

---

701 Baumann, Hans: *Mein Einsatz als Panzerjäger*. Wanzleben, 2014. pp. 39-40.
702 Central Archives of the Russian Defence Ministry (Podolsk), f. 243, op. 2928, gy. 178, li. 80.
703 Central Archives of the Russian Defence Ministry (Podolsk), f. 243, op. 2928, gy. 131, li. 244.
704 NARA, T311, R162, F7214289.
705 Rebentisch, Ernst: *Zum Kaukasus und zu den Tauern. Die Geschichte der 23. Panzer-Division 1941–1945*. Esslingen, 1963. p. 489.
706 Central Archives of the Russian Defence Ministry (Podolsk), f. 440, op. 8311, gy. 98, li. 72.
707 Central Archives of the Russian Defence Ministry (Podolsk), f. 243, op. 2928, gy. 131, li. 242. The SU–57 was burnt out most likely due to the air raid by German ground attack aircraft.

and with the support of 10-20 armoured fighting vehicles, launched counterattacks and pushed them back.[708]

At 0400 hours, *44. Reichsgrenadier-Division* and *SS-Panzergrenadier-Regiment 3/2. SS-Panzer-Division* set off, then broke through the northern, north-eastern and eastern areas of Sárkeresztúr. However, following the arrival of their reinforcements, the Soviets launched assaults supported by 10-20 armoured fighting vehicles of the 1st Guards Mechanized Brigade and pushed the Germans back beyond the Kiscsatorna Canal, and to the western edge of the vineyards directly east of Sárkeresztúr. West of Sárosd, likely in the sector of Szőlőhegy southwest of Csillagmajor, the Germans eliminated two Soviet assembly areas during the day and knocked out two tanks.[709]

At 1300 hours, the 1st Guards Mechanized Brigade launched an attack from Sárkeresztúr towards Külsőpüspökmajor, but this was unsuccessful. During the late afternoon, the Soviets launched a new attack from the area of Sárkeresztúr, with the armoured support of the 1st Guards Mechanized Brigade against Point 104, 1 km northeast of the village, but the Germans stopped this attempt as well.[710]

Eight Soviet armoured fighting vehicles took part in the fighting around Heinrichmajor on that day with two M4A2 tanks and three SU–100s of the 1st Guards Mechanized Corps east of the farmstead, and three ISU-122s southeast of there, probably belonging to the 18th Tank Corps, that were reassigned here.

The forces of the 1st Guards Mechanized Corps reported to have knocked out three German armoured fighting vehicles and 10 armoured personnel carriers during the fighting that day. Their own losses amounted to three knocked out M4A2 tanks, one of which burnt out, and one burnt out armoured transport vehicle.[711]

On that day, *SS-Obersturmbannführer* Weidinger, *Kommandeur* of *SS-Panzergrenadier-Regiment 4* received a report informing him that

I. (Bataillon)/SS-Panzergrenadier-Regiment 4, earlier left behind, was moving up towards the *Regiment* and at the moment was stationed at Városlőd.[712]

On the night of 13/14 March 1945, the Germans detected the noise of Soviet tanks in the vicinity of Csillagmajor, 2.5 km west of Sárosd.[713] During the day, some units of *9. SS-Panzer-Division* reached and eliminated two Soviet defensive positions and reported to have knocked out two tanks.[714]

The *3. Panzer-Division/III. Panzerkorps/Armeegruppe "Balck"*, attacking from the northeast, succeeded in taking Mihálymajor and Ferencmajor the previous evening, then, during the day, occupied Sándormajor and Point 126 in extremely heavy combat. During the fighting, the Germans reported to have knocked out seven Soviet tanks and one self-propelled gun.

---

708   Tieke, Wilhelm: *Von Plattensee bis Österreich. Heeresgruppe Süd 1945*. Gummersbach, without year of publication, pp. 38-39.
709   NARA, T311, R162, F7214290.
710   NARA, T311, R163, F7215343.
711   Central Archives of the Russian Defence Ministry (Podolsk), f. 243, op. 2928, gy. 131, li. 243.
712   Weidinger, Otto: *Division Das Reich. Der Weg der 2. SS-Panzer-Division „Das Reich"*. Band V: 1943-1945. Osnabrück, without year of publication, p. 454.
713   NARA, T311, R163, F7215334.
714   Tieke, Wilhelm: *Von Plattensee bis Österreich. Heeresgruppe Süd 1945*. Gummersbach, without year of publication, p. 39. The Soviet sources do not verify the destruction of the two armoured fighting vehicles.

The Soviet 170th Tank Brigade and the 1438th Self-Propelled Artillery Regiment/18th Tank Corps, with the 1st Battalion/32nd Motorized Rifle Brigade, held off five German attacks, which had been launched with battalion and regiment-size *Panzergrenadier* forces supported by 15-20 armoured fighting vehicles and 10-40 armoured personnel carriers. Total Soviet losses amounted to four burnt out T–34/85s and five SU–76Ms.[715]

1st Lieutenant Vasily P. Brjukhov, squadron commander of the 1st Battalion of the 17th Tank Brigade, remembered the events as such:

"The kombrig urgently demanded from the liaison officer of the air force that our ground attack aircraft should provide essential coverage for the brigade. The Major of the air force called the central command post to beg them to send at least some aircraft to our defensive sector. At last – to our great joy – the Ilyushins [Il–2 ground attack aircrafts – the author] arrived over us. Red tracer shells were fired up from the observation post of the brigade towards the enemy positions – this was the prearranged plan, with which we could point out targets for the aircraft. But the Ilyushins suddenly started to circle round and started to bomb our own positions! I could not contain myself. I jumped out on the edge of the trench and was running along, shaking my fist towards the sky and cursing the air force. Luckily the bomb explosions were not too close to me, but others were not this lucky as there were large numbers of dead and wounded among the submachine gunners, the infantry of the strongpoints and the artillery crews. 1st Lieutenant Talizin's squadron command tank was destroyed by a direct hit and driver Sergeant Aleksei Obirin, gunner Sergeant Arutyunian and loader Mikhail Kachaikin, who had survived so much already during the war, lost their lives.

The liaison officer of the air force was shouting in the radio, desperately trying to redirect the Ilyushins to the enemy positions, but the pilots were flagrantly disregarding either his signals or his pleas. At last, when they dropped all their bombs, they left and went back to their airfield, and we were shouting curses after them.

The enemy exploited the friendly fire of the planes and pressed the attack against Point 126 and occupied Sándormajor. The brigade had to retreat for the first time during the course of the defensive operation, and we were now establishing new positions along the railroad line north of Korcsma. The enemy, after losing eight tanks, 16 armoured personnel carriers, and approximately 100 soldiers, had stopped at last and reinforced its positions. In comparison, our Brigade lost four tanks, one SU-100, and a few dozen submachine gunners and riflemen. The 2nd Battalion only had 4 remaining tanks from the original 10, which had arrived five days earlier. Our battalion had five [tanks – the author] left, and only one SU-100 in the self-propelled artillery regiment[716]. All of the anti-tank guns were lost. In the submachine gun companies each had 20 soldiers, and in the mortar company only two mortars were left in operational condition."[717]

---

715   Central Archives of the Russian Defence Ministry (Podolsk), f. 243, op. 2928, gy. 131, li. 243.
716   The Soviet officer was thinking most likely of the only remaining operational armoured fighting vehicle of the battery of the 1016th Self-Propelled Artillery Regiment assigned to the 170th Tank Brigade, and not of the whole strength of the regiment.
717   Bryukhov, Vasiliy: *Red Army Tank Commander. At War in a T–34 on the Eastern Front*. Barnsley, 2013. pp. 174-175.

In the sector of Zichyújfalu, the Soviets received reinforcements as 12 tanks were approaching with mounted rifle infantry from the southeast.[718]

Among the arriving reinforcements was the Soviet 1016th Self-Propelled Artillery Regiment/208th Self-Propelled Artillery Brigade with 17 operational SU–100 self-propelled guns, two batteries of which established firing positions at Hippolitpuszta and the railway station of Zichyújfalu, and one battery at the sector of Hill 145 (Öreghegy), with another battery at Felsőszolgaegyháza. The eight SU-100s of the 1068th Self-Propelled Artillery Regiment were also en route to the troops and were also to be deployed in the sector of Hill 145 for defence. The 1922nd Self-Propelled Artillery Regiment was in position 4 km southwest of Hercegfalva. On that morning, the Brigade had 43 operational SU–100s, three SU–76Ms and two T–34 armoured fighting vehicles, but the units were not engaged in combat.[719]

The German *6. Panzer-Division* did not launch any attacks on that day. The only fighting was in defence, opposing Soviet attacks of company strength south and north of Csongrád and against Tükröspuszta.[720]

The Soviet 23rd Tank Corps was further reinforcing its defensive system. The 3rd Tank Brigade with the 1443rd Self-Propelled Artillery Regiment and the 1501st Anti-Tank Artillery Regiment were in position at Szilfástanya with six 76 mm divisional guns, at the eastern edge of Tükröspuszta with one ISU–122 battery, at Nádormajor with an ISU–122 battery and one T–34/85 tank platoon, with four ISU-152s, seven T–34/85s and three IS–2s between Szabolcspuszta and the railway station of Pusztaszabolcs. Between Kolompos and Alsóbesnyő another 20 T–34/85s were held in corps reserve.[721]

The *3. Panzer-Division/III. Panzerkorps* wanted, with one last attempt, to encircle and occupy Hill 145 (Öreghegy), east of Seregélyes, from the northeast because this was the centre of the local Soviet defence. On all other frontline sections, the units of the *Panzerkorps* were in defence.[722]

The defensive positions held by *Kampfgruppe "Bradel"/1. Panzer-Division,* southwest of Kisvelence and east of Agárdpuszta, were assaulted three times by Soviets penal units supported by artillery and ground attack aircraft. The last attempt was almost successful in breaching the fortified positions but five Panther tanks of *Panzer-Regiment 1* and a few armoured pioneer squads in armoured personnel carriers were able to repel them.[723]

At Agárdpuszta, the armoured personnel carriers of *10. Kompanie/Panzer-Pionier-Regiment 113* and the flamethrower tanks of *351. Flammpanzer-Kompanie* outflanked and attacked the Soviets and pushed them back toward the east.[724]

---

718 NARA, T311, R162, F7214290.
719 Central Archives of the Russian Defence Ministry (Podolsk), f. 243, op. 2928, gy. 178, li. 76.
720 NARA, T311, R162, F7214290.
721 Central Archives of the Russian Defence Ministry (Podolsk), f. 243, op. 2900, gy. 1782, li. 291.
722 NARA, T311, R162, F7214296.
723 Stoves, Rolf: Persönliches Kriegstagebuch Pz.Rgt. 1 (typewritten manuscript, a copy owned by the author), entry from 14 March 1945.
724 Stoves, O. G. Rolf: *1. Panzer-Division 1935–1945. Chronik einer der drei Stamm-Division der deutschen Panzerwaffe*. Bad Nauheim, 1961. p. 751.

Panzer-Aufklärungs-Abteilung 1 which had been in the reserve of *III. Panzerkorps*, was reinforced with six Panther tanks and was drawn forward from Börgönd to Dinnyés where it was given the task of securing the position.[725]

The ground-attack and fighter aircraft of *Luftflotte 4* were supporting their troops mainly south of Lake Velence and the pilots reported to have shot 25 Soviet planes. The Soviet Air Force was most active over the area between the Sárvíz and Lake Velence and American bomber formations were attacking Komárom and Érsekújvár, inflicting heavy damage on the oil refineries and the railroad system.[726]

By the ninth day of the operation, it seemed certain by the German *Heeresgruppe* that the Soviets were preparing for an operational level offensive in the sector of Székesfehérvár–Zámoly. According to the data obtained from German air reconnaissance, approximately 3000 vehicles were moving towards the area from the direction of Budapest. The Germans also correctly assumed the primary goal of the planned operation: to close and seal off, then destroy the armoured forces in combat between Lake Balaton and Lake Velence, and to capture the Mór corridor. German reconnaissance anticipated the launch of the attack for the next day, or the day after that at the latest.[727]

Due to this, the reserve of *IV. SS-Panzerkorps* was mobilized, as well as reinforcements from *Armeegruppe "Balck"* with two armoured battalions and artillery units[728]. The *Heeresgruppe* ordered *Panzergrenadier-Brigade 92 (mot.)/2. Panzerarmee* to occupy positions behind the Hungarian 1st Hussars Division/3rd Army, and the replenished *Sturmartillerie-Brigade 325/8. Armee* to Mór. However, the *Panzergrenadier* unit could not be scheduled to arrive any earlier than four days.[729] The defence of the Mór corridor was reinforced by *General der Panzertruppe* Balck with six companies of 8.8 cm anti-tank guns of *Festungs-Pak-Verband IX* and with a heavy anti-aircraft artillery *Abteilung*, with 8.8 cm anti-aircraft guns.[730] The heavy anti-tank gun companies were concentrated in the Mór–Fehérvárcsurgó–Iszkaszentgyörgy–Sárszentmihály area.[731]

Because of the anticipated attack and possible breakthrough of the Soviet troops, behind the frontlines of *IV. SS-Panzerkorps* and the Hungarian 3rd Army, a fortified line of armour was to be set up and tank destroyer units were to be established. Other tank destroyer units were to be placed and readied in the sector of Zirc and Kisbér as well.[732]

Anticipating a Soviet attack in the sector of Székesfehérvár, the *Heeresgruppe* thought it possible that sooner or later the defence might need reinforcement by *I. SS-Panzerkorps*. Therefore, they wanted to decisively end the fighting between the Sárvíz and Lake Velence. To achieve this, the most appropriate way was a concentrated attack of the two *SS-Panzerkorps*

---

725 Stoves, Rolf: Persönliches Kriegstagebuch Pz.Rgt. 1 (typewritten manuscript, a copy owned by the author), entry from 14 March 1945.
726 NARA, T311, R162, F7214291.
727 NARA, T311, R162, F7214292.
728 The *Heeres-Artillerie-Brigade 959* was transferred from *III. Panzerkorps* to *IV. SS-Panzerkorps*. The Panther tanks of *I. (Abteilung)/Panzer-Regiment 24* had been directly subordinated by *Armeegruppe "Balck"*, but for the time being they had been deployed in the sector of *III. Panzerkorps*. The Tiger B heavy tanks of *schwere Panzer-Abteilung 509* were withdrawn from the frontline and were ordered to the sector of Seregélyes. See NARA, T311, R163, F7215340.
729 NARA, T311, R162, F7214293.
730 NARA, T311, R162, F7214297.
731 NARA, T311, R163, F7215340.
732 NARA, T311, R163, F7215341.

and *III. Panzerkorps* either towards Dunapentele or Dunaföldvár.[733] The request from the *Heeresgruppe* to reassemble *I. SS-Panzerkorps* in the rear of *II. SS-Panzerkorps* and *III. Panzerkorps* was denied at 0220 hours on the next day by Hitler via the *Oberkommando des Heeres*. The *I. SS-Panzerkorps* was to attack further towards the south from Simontornya.[734]

15 March 1945, Thursday

(**WEATHER**: highest daytime temperature 9 Celsius, generally damp and the sky cloudy. The unpaved roads and the open terrain are continuing to dry up.)

On the front along the Dráva River, in the bridgehead of *LXXXXI. Armeekorps z.b.V.* at Donji Miholjac, the Soviet and Bulgarian troops again occupied Drávaszabolcs and broke into the area of Drávacsehi as well.[735] Of seven *Marder* II tank destroyers of the German *Panzerjäger-Abteilung/297. Infanterie-Division* fighting in the bridgehead, only four were in combat-ready condition.[736]

In the area of Drávapalkonya, the Soviet 1891st Self-Propelled Artillery Regiment lost two burnt out SU–76Ms. By the evening, the Regiment had 16 operational self-propelled guns.[737]

The *16. SS-Panzergrenadier-Division/XXII. Gebirgskorps/2. Panzerarmee*[738] occupied the forest east of Boronka and the village itself. The *SS-Panzergrenadiers* launched their attack from the south against Boronka at 0600 hours. Three hours later, the assault guns also joined them. The village was occupied by *II. (Bataillon)/SS-Panzergrenadier-Regiment 35*. *SS-Panzer-Aufklärungs-Abteilung 16* occupied the forest north of the Boronka–Nikla road, and with this, they were able to cover the area of Boronka from the east. The *Divisionsbegleitkompanie*, one of the companies of *SS-Panzer-Abteilung 16* and a Hungarian police battalion were trying to eliminate the Soviet positions between Marcali and Kisgomba from the south toward the north. The *SS-Panzergrenadiers* suffered heavy losses during the battle.

In the afternoon, the Soviets launched an attack along the road leading from Csömend to Boronka with 21 T–34 tanks of the 32nd Independent Guards Mechanized Brigade [739] and reoccupied the forest east of Boronka. Here approximately 15 soldiers of *I. (Bataillon)/SS-Panzergrenadier-Regiment 36* and three StuG. III assault guns of *Panzergruppe "Reinhardt"/SS-Panzer-Abteilung 16,* established perimeter defences. Four assault guns of *Panzergruppe "Böhmer"* of *1. Kompanie/SS-Panzer-Regiment 16* and 40 *Panzergrenadiers* from *SS-Panzergrenadier-Regiment 35,* tried in vain to relieve them. Of the four armoured fighting vehicles, three bogged down and were forced to engage the enemy in close combat. The encircled *SS*-unit broke out successfully at dawn the following day, and reached their own

---

733 According to the opinion of the staff of the German *6. Panzerarmee* this German assault could have been opened on 20 March 1945 at the earliest. See NARA, T311, R162, F7214299.
734 NARA, T311, R162, F7214294.
735 NARA, T311, R162, F7214303.
736 NARA, T78, R624, F000526.
737 Central Archives of the Russian Defence Ministry (Podolsk), f. 243, op. 2928, gy. 178, li. 82.
738 On that day, *SS-Panzer-Abteilung 16* and *Sturmartillerie-Abteilung 261* subordinated to the *Division* had 62 assault guns. Of these, 47 were combat-ready.
739 Central Archives of the Russian Defence Ministry (Podolsk), f. 243, op. 2928, gy. 131, li. 245.

positions at Boronka. However, the three immobilized armoured fighting vehicles had to be blown up at 0900 hours on 16 March 1945.[740]

At 1900 hours that evening, the Soviet 61st Guards Rifle Division launched another counterattack. The Germans knocked out two T–34 tanks and captured a third one, but the cemetery in the northern part of Boronka was in Soviet hands at the end.[741]

Combat was still raging on in the evening hours.[742] During the late evening, the Soviets broke into Boronka with tank support. The Germans pushed them back and out of the village in heavy close quarters combat during the night, and reached the eastern edge of the village again. They also reported knocking out a Soviet armoured fighting vehicle. However, the Soviets held their ground in the area of Boronka with three tanks and rifle infantry. The Soviets encircled a small *SS-Kampfgruppe* on the road leading to Csömend, southeast of Boronka, and another German attack was initiated for their relief.[743]

The Soviet 52nd Tank Regiment/32nd Independent Guards Mechanized Brigade lost two burnt out T-34s in the Boronka sector on that day.[744]

During the night of 14/15 March 1945, the German *1. Volks-Gebirgs-Division* fought off four attacks launched by less than battalion-size units, then in the morning cleared the sector 3 km northwest of Somogyszentpál. The Germans regrouped their forces, and at 2000 hours in the evening, launched an assault against the Soviet positions defending Somogyszentpál.[745]

The attacking divisions of *2. Panzerarmee* lost 3600 soldiers from a strength of 10,000 men, which comprised more than one third of their initial fighting strength between 6 – 15 March 1945.[746]

On the right flank of the German *I. Kavallerie-Korps/6. Panzerarmee* the Hungarian 25th Infantry Division launched an attack in the direction of the vineyard at Hill 133 (Öreghegy), 3 km northeast of Balatonszabadi (Öreghegy) but despite their initial success, the Soviets pushed the Hungarian troops back with a counterattack.[747]

During the night of 14/15 March 1945, *3.* and *4. Kavallerie-Divisions* further enlarged their own bridgehead in a night assault east of Ádánd on the southern bank of the Sió Canal. The *4. Kavallerie-Division* approached to within 500 meters of Pélpuszta from the north at 0400 hours.[748] The Soviets launched a battalion sized counterattack of rifle infantry supported by five armoured fighting vehicles, however this was repelled by the Germans and they reached the Szélesmajor–Szabadhídvég line 1.5 km northwest and 4 km west of Szabadhídvég. The Soviets kept the German bridgehead and the newly occupied frontline under fire during the whole day.[749]

---

740 Puntigam, Josef Paul: *Vom Plattensee bis zur Mur. Die Kämpfe 1945 im Dreiländereck.* Feldbach, without year of publication, [1993], p. 101.
741 Puntigam, Josef Paul: *Vom Plattensee bis zur Mur. Die Kämpfe 1945 im Dreiländereck.* Feldbach, without year of publication, [1993], pp.88-89.
742 NARA, T311, R162, F7214303.
743 NARA, T311, R163, F7215352.
744 Central Archives of the Russian Defence Ministry (Podolsk), f. 243, op. 2928, gy. 131, li. 248.
745 NARA, T311, R162, F7214304.
746 NARA, T311, R162, F7214308.
747 NARA, T311, R162, F7214304.
748 NARA, T311, R163, F7215343.
749 NARA, T311, R162, F7214304.

Units of the Hungarian 14th Honvéd Infantry Regiment launched an assault from the northeast and occupied the railway station at Mezőkomárom, then broke through the northern part of the village and eliminated the Soviet bridgehead. They defeated the Soviet troops in combat at Belsősári on the other bank of the Sió Canal and then closed up with their whole frontline on the northern bank of the canal.[750]

On the same day, the Soviet 22nd Independent Tank Regiment was in combat with four T–34s and one SU–76M at the northern edge of Szabadhídvég, three T–34 tanks and one SU–85 self-propelled gun 3 km northwest of Szabadhídvég, and with three T–34s in the sector of the Zsófia children's sanitarium 3 km northeast of Siófok.[751]

In the sector of *I. SS-Panzerkorps*, there was a fight raging in the sector of the German bridgehead south of Simontornya. In heavy combat, the Germans managed to slightly enlarge the area of their bridgehead toward the south and southeast.[752]

Between 0800 and 0900 hours that morning, the Soviets breached the positions of *SS-Panzergrenadier-Regiment 26/12. SS-Panzer-Division* which were lying 300 meters south of the Sió Canal, however the Germans soon pushed back these forces. German artillery kept the previously detected Soviet targets under harassing fire.[753]

On that day, the armoured strength of the *Division* consisted of 24 Panthers of which 9 were combat-ready and 23 Panzer IV tanks of which 10 were combat-ready. They also had 30 Panzer IV/70 *Jagdpanzers* of which 10 were combat-ready and eight Flak-Panzer IV anti-aircraft armoured fighting vehicles of which two were combat-ready. The *schwere Panzerjäger-Abteilung 560* had 13 Jagdpanthers with seven combat-ready and 20 Panzer IV/70 *Jagdpanzers with five combat-ready.*

SS-Panzergrenadier-Regiment 1/1. SS-Panzer-Division with the support of *II. (Abteilung)/SS-Panzer-Artillerie-Regiment 1,* managed to extend the bridgehead about 500 meters by noon, and to occupy Hill 133. At the same time, one of the assault units of the *Regiment* established contact 2 km east of Simontornya with the units of *SS-Panzergrenadier-Regiment 2* in combat south of Sáregres. *SS-Panzer-Aufklärungs-Abteilung 1* was in defence, subordinated to *2. SS-Panzer-Division* east of Káloz.

The Soviet 1896th Self-Propelled Artillery Regiment engaged in the area, lost two burnt out SU-76Ms 2.5 km south of Simontornya.[754]

The Germans moved forward a 17 cm long-range gun to the western outskirts of Sáregres, which kept the western and north-western edges of Dunaföldvár under harassing fire from the afternoon onwards.[755]

On the front of *II. SS-Panzerkorps,* the reinforced *SS-Panzer-Aufklärungs-Abteilung 2* managed to keep its bridgehead northeast of Káloz in the face of three, at least battalion-size Soviet attacks, effectively aided by four 21 cm howitzers.[756]

---

750 NARA, T311, R162, F7214304.
751 Central Archives of the Russian Defence Ministry (Podolsk), f. 243, op. 2928, gy. 178, li. 79.
752 NARA, T311, R162, F7214304.
753 Meyer, Hubert: *Kriegsgeschichte der 12. SS-Panzerdivision „Hitlerjugend"*. Band II. Osnabrück, 1987. 2nd edition. p. 503.
754 Central Archives of the Russian Defence Ministry (Podolsk), f. 243, op. 2928, gy. 178, li. 83.
755 NARA, T311, R163, F7215352.
756 NARA, T311, R162, F7214304.

The Germans also kept the bridgehead north of Sárkeresztúr, on the Kiscsatorna established the day before by *44. Reichsgrenadier-Division*, despite repeated assault attempts from the Soviets. The *Pionier-Bataillon* of the *Division*, under direct fire of the Soviets, constructed two 60 ton bridges on the Kiscsatorna Canal capable of handling Panther tanks..

In front of *2. SS-Panzer-Division* on the night of 14/15 March 1945, the Soviets breached the frontline east of Heinrichmajor, but the *SS*-units eliminated the incursion with a counterattack. Losses among the German defenders were constantly growing. Abandoning the forward position was again dismissed by the *II. SS-Panzerkorps*.

During the day, the attack of *SS-Panzergrenadier-Regiment 3* from the east against Sárkeresztúr breached the eastern part of the village through the railroad line, but Soviet resistance was consolidated and halted the German advance.[757]

The Soviet 1st Guards Mechanized Corps engaged in combat in the area that day, had 60 operational M4A2, three T–34/85 tanks and 13 SU–100 self-propelled guns. The 1st Guards Mechanized Brigade was defending five defensive strongpoints with 28 tanks and five self-propelled guns in the Heinrichmajor west 2 km – Point 104 northeast of Sárkeresztúr – Sárkeresztúr – Szentimremajor – Sárszentágota area. The 3rd Guards Mechanized Brigade with 23 tanks and eight SU–100 self-propelled guns of the 382nd Guard Self-Propelled Artillery Regiment was defending on the Zsigmondmajor, south of Jakabszállás – Point 141 east of Heinrichmajor – Point 143 southeast of Heinrichmajor – Szilfamajor line in three defensive strongpoints. A company of the 20th Guards Tank Regiment stood at Tóthmajor in reserve.[758]

The *3. Panzer-Division/III. Panzerkorps/Armeegruppe "Balck"* launched its attack in the morning at 0830 hours, from 5 km northeast of Seregélyes toward the south, through the Seregélyes–Pusztaszabolcs railroad line with the aim of occupying Hill 145 (Öreghegy).[759] However, the German attack failed in the face of the Soviet defence reinforced by the large number of anti-tank guns and the partially dug in armoured fighting vehicles of the 18th Tank Corps and the 208th Self-Propelled Artillery Brigade. The Soviets knocked out five of the German armoured fighting vehicles that were supporting the *Panzergrenadiers*, against the loss of one Soviet tank, which was reported to be knocked out by the Germans. Almost 40 percent of the armoured fighting vehicles of *3. Panzer-Division* had been disabled and after this, the *Division* went into defensive positions along the railroad line.[760]

The failed attack was carried out by *Panzergrenadier-Regiment 3* with the support of *I. (Abteilung)/Panzer-Regiment 6*. The open topped armoured personnel carriers had a hard time dealing with the accurate mortar fire of the Soviets. The Germans reached the railroad embankment north of Hill 145 (Öreghegy), however they were unable to break through the Soviet anti-tank defences in operation there. At that time, *Oberleutnant* Blaich came to the rescue with a few Panther tanks of *2. Kompanie/Panzer-Regiment 6*. The armoured

---

757 NARA, T311, R162, F7214305.
758 Central Archives of the Russian Defence Ministry (Podolsk), f. 243, op. 2928, gy. 131, li. 246.
759 Originally, *3. Panzer-Division* planned to open their attack against Hill 145 on the night of 14/15 March 1945. However dense fog during the night prevented the deployment of the Panther tanks equipped with night-vision devices (*"den Einsatz von Panzern mit Sondergerät"*). See NARA, T311, R162, F7214310. Only 10 Panthers of *3. Kompanie/Panzer-Regiment 6* had been equipped with such devices. However, after 15 March, these devices were removed from the Panthers and were sent to Vienna to avoid being captured by the Soviets.
760 NARA, T311, R162, F7214305.

fighting vehicles engaged the Soviet guns from an elevated point. The first Panther that tried to cross over the railroad embankment, was instantly knocked out by the Soviets. When a second one also tried to cross at the same spot, it was knocked out by one of the SU-100 self-propelled guns of the 208th Self-Propelled Artillery Brigade[761]. The SU–100 self-propelled guns were slowly rolling towards the railroad embankment, where the German *Panzergrenadiers* were lying almost defenceless. *Oberleutnant* Blaich started off in their direction with his remaining Panthers, which fired during a quick halt and thus destroyed one of the SU-100s. After this, the Soviet self-propelled guns disabled another Panther then knocked out the tank of *Oberleutnant* Blaich as well. The commander of *I. (Bataillon)/Panzergrenadier-Regiment 3*, *Hauptmann* Treppe, collected the surviving crew members of the knocked out command tank in his armoured personnel carrier, but the *Oberleutnant* was killed in action. Afterwards, *Hauptmann* Treppe ordered a retreat towards Júliamajor. It took hours for the German column to reach the small forest northeast of the farmstead where the command post was directly hit by Soviet artillery.[762]

The company commander of the 1st Battalion/170th Tank Brigade, 1st Lieutenant Brjukhov remembered the events as follows:

> *"In our sector they launched their attack somewhat later than was usual. After a short period of artillery fire, one infantry battalion was advancing from the direction of Sándormajor supported by seven tanks and eight armoured carrier vehicles; another infantry company and five tanks were attacking the 2nd Battalion from the small forest 1 km east of Sándormajor.*
> *The remaining soldiers of the worn out and tired brigade – dug in in crudely prepared positions – engaged the enemy in the last, decisive battle at Balaton. The enemy was attacking moderately, almost reluctantly. Their tanks were firing from a greater distance, although when the distance was decreased, the intensity intensified; the German artillery was keeping us under fire continuously. The tanks of Dzhigunskiy and Potolicin moved somewhat more forward than the others and they were the first to contact the enemy tanks. They managed to destroy one enemy vehicle, but in the return fire both crews died like heroes. Through the gap the enemy breached our positions, but the company commander, Smolyakov rushed forward without hesitation and destroyed one of the tanks. The remaining German tanks retreated, giving the opportunity to the battalion to continue fighting the enemy back. Smolyakov placed his tank in the middle of the front line, and closed off the route of the possible enemy attack, manoeuvring to the spot where he was most needed.*
> *In the sector of the 2nd Battalion heavy combat was raging. Sharkisyan fanned out his three remaining tanks on a wide area. He himself was in Jemelin's tank and made up the middle resistance nest with Dejev's tank on the right, and the tank of Burlaky on the left. He ordered them not to open fire without being ordered to do so. The enemy was slowly creeping forward, increasing their firing action. Our tanks were standing in*

---

761 According to the history of *3. Panzer-Division*, IS-2 tanks were in combat here as well, however Soviet archival sources exclude this. The Germans might have thought, due to the firepower of the SU-100 self-propelled guns of the 208th Self-Propelled Artillery Brigade stationed nearby, that they were facing heavy tanks.
762 *Geschichte der 3. Panzer-Division. Herausgegeben vom Traditionsverband der Division*. Berlin, 1967. p. 467.

silence, waiting for their time to come. Then, when the enemy came very close, the three tanks and the submachine gunners opened fire all at once, firing heavy and accurate fire. The enemy stopped and was trying to search for coverage, but they continued to fire. The tank of Lieutenant Burlaky was hit, although an enemy vehicle was also set on fire after being hit by Dejev and Sharkisyan. The submachine gunners of Sirolyev forced the enemy to retreat.

A calm period came on the battlefield. The kombrig received a report stating that there were four tanks remaining in the 1st Battalion, two in the 2nd Battalion; there were no more than 10 people in each trench. Our last self-propelled gun was destroyed in the defensive battle around Korcsma. Chunihin ordered that we must fight until the very end. For the last battle, Klaustyn was appointed deputy Chief of Staff of the brigade and I took over the battalion.

In the second half of the day the enemy launched a new attack. I was using old crosswise trenches, I lined up the tanks with a 250 meter space between them. The submachine gunners established defences in the middle, a short distance in front of the tanks. Again we let the enemy come closer so that we can engage them from close: all tanks were firing concentrated fire on the enemy armoured transport vehicles and tanks. Two of their vehicles stopped immediately, and the remaining Germans decided that they do not have any further chances, they stopped and started firing from where they were."[763]

Therefore, by the evening, six T–34/85s remained operational in the 170th Tank Brigade in defence in the Sándormajor sector, and 13 SU-100s in the 1438th Self-Propelled Artillery Regiment. The 181st Tank Brigade in defence at Györgymajor, had 12 operational armoured fighting vehicles.[764] On that day, the Corps irrecoverably lost one T–34/85 and three SU–76Ms.[765] Also, one SU-100 self-propelled gun of the 1068th Self-Propelled Artillery Regiment/208th Self-Propelled Artillery Brigade was burnt out during the fighting in the Sándormajor area.[766] The 1016th Self-Propelled Artillery Regiment reported to have knocked out five German tanks including one Tiger B, one assault gun and 13 armoured personnel carriers fighting east of Hill 145. The losses of the Regiment included three knocked out SU-100s, two of which were soon repaired by the repair-maintenance platoon.

The *1. Panzer-Division*'s 10 Panther tanks, four 2 cm self-propelled anti-aircraft guns and pioneer-armoured personnel carriers eliminated a number of penetrations of the Soviet rifle infantry between the south-eastern outskirts of Gárdony and Agárdpuszta on the front of *Panzergrenadier-Regiment 113*. During the night the damaged tanks were towed in column to Börgönd. *Panzer-Pionier-Bataillon 37*, reinforced by four Panthers, relieved *Panzer-Aufklärungs-Abteilung 1* in the holding positions at Dinnyés.[767]

The Soviet 23rd Tank Corps in defence on the Szarvastanya, 4.5 km southeast of Gárdony – Nándormajor – Pusztaszabolcs railway station –Kolompos – Alsóbesnyő sector

---

763 Bryukhov, Vasiliy: *Red Army Tank Commander. At War in a T–34 on the Eastern Front.* Barnsley, 2013. pp. 175-176.
764 Central Archives of the Russian Defence Ministry (Podolsk), f. 243, op. 2928, gy. 131, li. 246.
765 Central Archives of the Russian Defence Ministry (Podolsk), f. 243, op. 2928, gy. 178, li. 82.
766 Central Archives of the Russian Defence Ministry (Podolsk), f. 243, op. 2928, gy. 178, li. 82.
767 Stoves, Rolf: Persönliches Kriegstagebuch Pz.Rgt. 1 (typewritten manuscript, a copy owned by the author), entry from 15 March 1945.

was not engaged in any substantial combat action on that day, because the German troops opposing the Soviets were deploying only small reconnaissance units of 10-25 soldiers supported by two to five armoured fighting vehicles. At that time, the 3rd Tank Brigade had 31 operational T–34s and one IS–2 tank, the 1443rd Self-Propelled Artillery Regiment had eight ISU–122s and four ISU–152 self-propelled guns as well as three IS–2 tanks. The 207th Self-Propelled Artillery Brigade, subordinated to the Corps, had 40 operational SU–100s, three SU–57s and two T–34s.[768]

During the combat action of Operation *"Frühlingserwachen"* between 6 – 15 March 1945, German troops reported to have knocked out and captured the following amount of Soviet armoured fighting vehicles:

- *I. Kavallerie-Korps*: 12 tanks and self-propelled guns;
- *I. SS-Panzerkorps*: 63 tanks and self-propelled guns;
- *II. SS-Panzerkorps*: 41 tanks and self-propelled guns;
- *III. Panzerkorps*: 87 tanks and self-propelled guns;
- 203 armoured fighting vehicles in total.[769]

The *Festungs-Pak-Verband IX* was directly subordinated to *IV. SS-Panzerkorps*, and *Sturmartillerie-Brigade 325*[770] was directly subordinated to *Armeegruppe "Balck"*.[771]

German reconnaissance detected that a liaison officer from the Soviet 5th Ground Attack Aircraft Corps was assigned to the 2nd Guards Mechanized Corps. From this, the Germans concluded that the Mechanized Corps was to be deployed very soon. The reassembly of the 6th Guards Tank Army and the Cavalry Mechanized Group "Pliev" to the Transdanubia was not confirmed yet. Therefore, based on the vehicle movements detected on that day, the Germans assumed that the 23rd Tank Corps was to be located opposite *IV. SS-Panzerkorps* as well.[772]

That evening at 2130 hours, *Generaloberst* Guderian communicated to *General der Infanterie* Wöhler that at last, following the renewed arguments of the *Heeresgruppe*, Hitler, while insisting on keeping the German bridgehead east of Ádánd and at Simontornya, had allowed the reassembly of *I. SS-Panzerkorps* in order to organize a concentrated German attack to be launched east of the Sárvíz. As per the orders of the Führer, this was to be completed in three days.[773] However, soon it turned out that it was already too late.

The Soviet 366th Guards Heavy Self-Propelled Artillery Regiment/4th Guards Army was moved forward from Lovasberény to Csala, northeast of Székesfehérvár, with 14 operational captured German self-propelled howitzers and assault guns, two Panthers and one Panzer IV tank.[774]

---

768 Central Archives of the Russian Defence Ministry (Podolsk), f. 243, op. 2928, gy. 131, li. 246.
769 NARA, T311, R163, F7215169.
770 On that day, *Sturmgeschütz-Brigade 325* had 19 of the 23 StuG. III assault guns, and nine of the 11 StuH. 42 assault howitzers in combat-ready condition. See NARA, T78, R624, F000515.
771 NARA, T311, R163, F7215350.
772 NARA, T311, R162, F7214307.
773 NARA, T311, R162, F7214313.
774 Central Archives of the Russian Defence Ministry (Podolsk), f. 243, op. 2928, gy. 131, li. 244.

*Performance of the armoured fighting units during
the Operation "Frühlingserwachen"*

The armoured divisions of *Heeresgruppe Süd* were far from completing their tactical aims on 15 March 1945, but contrary to popular belief, the forces of *6. Panzerarmee* had not yet been ordered into defence.

During the 10 days of the operation, the Germans had breached the Soviet defences for a distance of 30 kms west of the Sárvíz, and 12 km south of Lake Velence. With the occupation of the bridgeheads on the southern bank of the Sió Canal, *I. SS-Panzerkorps* and *I. Kavallerie-Korps* completed their first task, although with considerable delay. However, they were unable to break out of the bridgeheads and continue the assault until the complete fulfillment of the operational aim. The Soviet troops had decisively stopped the German attack at their defensive lines.[775]

An officer of the 170th Tank Brigade, 1st Lieutenant Brjukhov remembered the attack of the German armoured fighting vehicles as follows:

"During the lengthy combat operations in Hungary, we have learnt a few things about the tactics of the enemy. After a short, but intensive artillery bombardment, Tiger tanks were moving forward in small groups. The assault guns were following them from 500-600 meters distance, to eliminate our anti-tank weapons. The flanks were secured by lighter type tanks and small units of mounted infantry. The heavy tanks avoided the frontal attack, they were rather seeking the contact points and the flanks trying to bypass the company and battalion strength defence strongpoints. The Germans have given up trying to neutralize the [Soviet – the author] artillery and infantry, and they tried everything to break as deeply into our defence lines as possible, assaulting us from the rear and occupying the most important positions in the depth of our defence."[776]

The Staff of the Soviet 26th Army summarized the experiences of the Self-Propelled Artillery Brigades equipped with SU–100 self-propelled guns regarding the combat actions of the German armoured fighting vehicles during Operation *"Frühlingserwachen"* as follows:

"At the beginning of the operations, the enemy tanks were deployed in large quantities. These were rolling in front of the infantry, 400-600 meters in between, in some cases more distance could be noticed. Counting on the dynamism of the attack and the weak anti-tank defence of the enemy, the tanks of the opposing forces disengaged from the infantry on a number of occasions, and bypassing our positions, tried to get in our rear to accomplish their objective. In case they met with organized anti-tank defence or effective firing system, and suffered significant losses in tanks, they were forced to adopt the system of infantry assaults, which were supported by smaller groups of tanks and self-propelled guns [assault guns and Jagdpanzers – the author]. This meant approximately 10-20 tanks at a time. The direction of the assault was chosen as the slopes of hills and the terrain sections without roads. In these cases, the

---

[775] Malakhov, M. M.: A Balatontól Bécsig (excerpt). In: *Fejezetek hazánk felszabadításának történetéből*. Budapest, 1960. p. 156.
[776] Bryukhov, Vasiliy: *Red Army Tank Commander. At War in a T–34 on the Eastern Front*. Barnsley, 2013. p. 169.

tanks were moving forward in a fanned out manner, among the battle lines of the infantry. There were two to three self-propelled guns [assault guns and Jagdpanzers – the author] on the flanks, and if there were no available self-propelled guns, then the flanks were covered by heavy tanks.

While the enemy was carrying out an assault on one of the sections, they tried to give the impression of a large-scale tank assault on an other section. In order to achieve this, they concentrated almost 20 tanks and 10-15 armoured unit transport vehicles [armoured personnel carriers – the author] on a considerably wide frontline section, which moved to an open, well-visible plain, and were demonstrating their presence to our infantry, trying to make an impression of great concentrated force and flanking manoeuvres. Because of the large distances (approximately 3 km) the [SU–100 – the author] self-propelled guns were not able to shoot, while the [Soviet – the author] infantry, which has not yet shed the "tank fear", retreated in the face of [German – the author] artillery and mortar fire. All the while the enemy submachine gunner [Panzergrenadier – the author] units infiltrated our trenches, where they moved forward slowly and cautiously.

If the enemy soldiers detected our self-propelled guns and initiated engagement, their tanks tried to move under cover, and only their turret were left exposed. All tank firepower was concentrated on the targets, trying to destroy the self-propelled guns with their concentrated intensive fire or force them to change their firing positions."[777]

The SU–100 self-propelled guns could engage the German heavy and medium tanks in effective fire from a distance of 1000-1300 meters, and the lighter armoured fighting vehicles from a distance of 1500 meters or more.[778]

According to Soviet opinions, the Germans, despite their "significant armoured superiority", were not able to achieve a breakthrough on any frontline sections of the 3rd Ukrainian Front. The manoeuvring pace of Soviet supplies was on many occasions quicker than the assault movement of the German armoured forces. During the defensive operations 45 Soviet artillery brigades, artillery regiments or independent artillery battalions carried out regrouping, partly within the corps or armies, and partly between armies and from the front's reserves.[779]

During the defensive operations between 6 – 15 March 1945, the number of self-propelled guns in the tank and mechanized forces of the 3rd Ukrainian Front exceeded 60 percent, that is, they played a crucial role in stopping the German offensive.[780] This is even truer for the SU–100 self-propelled guns. If the three Self-Propelled Artillery Brigades equipped with these, would not have been deployed, the German armoured fighting vehicles would have been able to push much deeper into the defences of the Soviet troops.

The defensive operations in March 1945 in the Transdanubia were compared many times to those of the Kursk tank battle in July 1943. Undoubtedly there are similarities,

---

[777] Central Archives of the Russian Defence Ministry (Podolsk), f. 440, op. 8311, gy. 98, li. 89. The author wished to express his gratitude towards István Zichermann for his invaluable help in translating the document.
[778] Central Archives of the Russian Defence Ministry (Podolsk), f. 243, op. 2900, gy. 1570, li. 183.
[779] Malakhov, M. M.: Magyarország felszabadításának befejezése. In: *Magyarország felszabadítása*. Budapest, 1975. p. 312.
[780] Isaev, Aleksei–Kolomiets, Maksim: *Tomb of the Panzerwaffe. The Defeat of the 6th SS Panzer Army in Hungary 1945*. Solihull, 2014. p. 138.

for example that the Soviets deliberately went into deeply echeloned defences in both cases, to stop the mass assault of the German armoured fighting vehicles, to absorb all their forces and to eliminate them.

However, the rates of the two offensives are different. In the Transdanubia, the width of the frontline and the depth of the defence, as well as the number of deployed forces and armoured fighting vehicles were much smaller than at Kursk. There was an important difference too: at Kursk, the Soviets launched army-level counterattacks during the defensive operations against the German armoured forces that had breached the Soviet defences, one of which resulted in the tank battle at Prokhorovka. In the Transdanubia, tank battles between larger armoured groups had not taken place, like the armoured battles in January – February 1945, partly because the Soviets tried to avoid launching their smaller number of armoured fighting vehicles in a counterattack. On the other hand, the wet and muddy terrain did not let the German armoured divisions fan out properly.

During the defensive operations in the Transdanubia, in the same way as in the summer of 1943 in the Kursk salient, the basis of the Soviet fire system was the mass deployment of divisional and anti-tank artillery. The weak spot of the Soviet anti-tank system in the Transdanubia proved to be the rifle infantry, which displayed a weak resistance to the German armoured fighting vehicles. In many cases, the rifle infantry had not even withstood the first assault of the German tanks and assault guns before retreating in a disorderly manner.[781]

According to the author's opinion, the "tank fear" experienced by the Soviet rifle infantry could be intensified by the fact that they did not have effective handheld anti-tank weapons which could be easily handled, like the *Panzerfaust* or the *Panzerschreck*. The effect of the incendiary bottles and the cumulative anti-tank handheld grenades were not comparable to the former, not to mention the, by then completely obsolete, 14.5 mm anti-tank rifle.[782]

The Soviet divisional, anti-tank and self-propelled artillery provided excellent performance during a defensive operation from a tactical point of view, as their guns often opened fire from a short distance on the German armoured fighting vehicles, luring them into a fire trap, then concentrating the fire of three to four batteries on them at once.[783]

During the defensive operations, the tank and mechanized forces of the 3rd Ukrainian Front were acting as ordered, mainly firing from a standing position in ambush, in previously prepared defensive sectors, on the flanks of the enemy's predetermined direction of movement. The forwarding of tanks and self-propelled guns into these defensive positions were covered by the concentrated fire of the artillery of the anti-tank regions.[784]

The Soviet decision, which placed the tanks and self-propelled guns in ambush positions and partially dug them in, instead of being used in carrying out counterattacks and

---

[781] M. Svirin – O. Baronov – M. Kolomiets – D. Nedogonov: *Boj u ozera Balaton*. Moscow, 1999. 71. o.
[782] Although anti-tank rifles proved to be effective during the war against the vehicle commanders peering out of the escape hatches, or when knocking out armoured cars and armoured personnel carriers, but they were not able to pierce the armour of tanks and assault guns in the spring of 1945 anymore.
[783] M. Svirin – O. Baronov – M. Kolomiets – D. Nedogonov: *Boj u ozera Balaton*. Moscow, 1999. p. 76.
[784] Malakhov, M. M.: A Balatontól Bécsig (excerpt). In: *Fejezetek hazánk felszabadításának történetéből*. Budapest, 1960. p. 144.

counteroffensives, proved to be the correct decision in the author's opinion. Besides avoiding the losses they might have suffered in a contact battle, the decision was also most likely made due to the fact that the muddy and damp terrain seriously decreased the manoeuvrability of the Soviet armoured fighting vehicles.

The tank and mechanized units were also employed as mobile anti-tank artillery reserves. They occupied firing positions prepared beforehand in the anticipated attack route of the Germans, and their own manoeuvres were coordinated with the artillery placed into covered firing positions and anti-tank regions.[785]

In the event the German armoured fighting vehicles were unsuccessful in breaching the Soviet anti-tank fire system during the day, then, on that night, the German infantry assault units would try to eliminate the crews of the Soviet anti-tank guns with handheld weapons. Because of this, the Soviets reinforced their anti-tank regions with mortars and provided lighting devices for the subunits in these positions.[786]

According to the 3rd Ukrainian Front's own data, the German troops had lost between 6 – 15 March 1945, approximately 45,000 dead and captured, approximately 500 tanks and assault guns, 500 armoured personnel carriers, more than 280 guns and mortars, more than 1300 cars and 50 aircraft.[787]

According to German archive data, the German units deployed in Operation *"Frühlingserwachen"* suffered the following losses in the period of 6 – 13 March 1945:

- *Heeresgruppe E*: 506 killed, 1798 wounded, 156 missing in action.
- *2. Panzerarmee*: 508 killed including 34 officers, 2897 wounded including 87 officers and 157 missing in action including one officer.
- *6. Panzerarmee*: 963 killed including 49 officers, 4328 wounded including 154 officers and, 628 missing in action including four officers.
- *III. Panzerkorps*: 474 killed including 12 officers, 2093 wounded including 64 officers and 310 missing in action.
- Total casualties: 2451 killed, 11,116 wounded and 1251 missing in action.[788]

It can clearly be seen from the above that the total combat losses of German troops between 6 – 13 March 1945, did not exceed 15,000 men. The number of killed and missing soldiers remained under 4,000. The losses incurred on the missing two days, 14 and 15 March, could not exceed another 41,000 killed and captured men. Due to the above statistics, the Soviet data should be considered to be highly exaggerated.

According to Soviet data, between 6 – 15 March 1945, 130 German tanks and assault guns had been destroyed in minefields established by the mobile obstacle units.[789] This data can be verified from reports and memories with the addition that the majority of these tanks and assault guns had not been destroyed, only immobilised.

---

785 Malakhov, M. M.: A Balatontól Bécsig (excerpt). In: *Fejezetek hazánk felszabadításának történetéből*. Budapest, 1960. p. 169.
786 Malakhov, M. M.: A Balatontól Bécsig (excerpt). In: *Fejezetek hazánk felszabadításának történetéből*. Budapest, 1960. pp. 150-151.
787 Malakhov, M. M.: A Balatontól Bécsig (excerpt). In: *Fejezetek hazánk felszabadításának történetéből*. Budapest, 1960. p. 162.
788 NARA, T311, R162, F7214563.
789 Malakhov, M. M.: A Balatontól Bécsig (excerpt). In: *Fejezetek hazánk felszabadításának történetéből*. Budapest, 1960. p. 164.

During the 10 days of defensive operations, the units of the 3rd Ukrainian Front reported to have knocked out the following German armoured fighting vehicles:

- the 4th Guards Army knocked out seven tanks and assault guns
- the 26th Army destroyed 186 tanks and assault guns and knocked out 136 more, plus destroyed 75 and knocked out 43 armoured personnel carriers.
- the 27th Army destroyed 104 and knocked out 162 tanks and assault guns, plus destroyed 41 and knocked out 54 armoured personnel carriers.
- the 57th Army destroyed 34 and knocked out 27 tanks and assault guns, and destroyed another four armoured personnel carriers.[790]

Based on this data, the Soviet forces should have knocked out 656 German armoured fighting vehicles and of these, 324 were destroyed during Operation *"Frühlingserwachen"*.[791]

According to German archival data, *6. Panzerarmee* had only lost 30 tanks and 11 assault guns and *Jagdpanzers*, a total of 41 armoured fighting vehicles between 6 – 15 March 1945.[792] Between 6 – 15 March 1945, in *III. Panzerkorps* a total of 11 tanks[793], and in *2. Panzerarmee* between 6 – 21 March 1945, another 16 assault guns and *Jagdpanzers* were destroyed.[794] This is 68 destroyed German armoured fighting vehicles during Operation *"Frühlingserwachen"*. We need to consider the Hungarian 20th Assault Artillery Battalion as well, where at least five *Jagdpanzers* had been destroyed.

This was not the complete number of total armoured losses of the German-Hungarian troops, as a large number of vehicles were disabled after they had been knocked out, ran on a mine or were immobilized by the muddy terrain.[795] However these were counted as repairable, and thus were not deducted from the armoured strength of the given unit.

According to certain sources, the Soviet anti-tank artillery crews received a cash "bonus" for each destroyed enemy armoured fighting vehicle, 500 rubles for the gun commander and 300 rubles for the gunner.[796] The tank crews also received the same prize, although in their case, eyewitness confirmation was required. This was probably a requirement of the artillery crews as well. For example, 1st Lieutenant Brjukhov, an officer of the 170th Tank Brigade, reported that throughout the war, he knocked out 28 German armoured fighting vehicles while having nine tanks knocked out from under him, but he only received the prize money for nine of his claims.[797] In the author's opinion, this could be one of the most important causes of the significantly larger number of knocked out German armoured fighting vehicles claimed by the Soviets.

---

790 Isaev, Aleksei–Kolomiets, Maksim: *Tomb of the Panzerwaffe. The Defeat of the 6th SS Panzer Army in Hungary 1945*. Solihull, 2014. p. 173.
791 Isaev, Aleksei–Kolomiets, Maksim: *Tomb of the Panzerwaffe. The Defeat of the 6th SS Panzer Army in Hungary 1945*. Solihull, 2014. p. 172.
792 Armoured fighting vehicle strength of *6. Panzerarmee* and the casualties as of 15 March 1945 are contained in the Appendix.
793 Of these, three Tiger B heavy tanks were only rated as irrecoverable after 15 March 1945, although they were knocked out on 12 March.
794 The armoured fighting vehicle strength as of 15 and 21 March 1945 of *Armeegruppe "Balck"* and *2. Panzer-Division* are contained in the Appendix.
795 For example, there were still 411 combat-ready German armoured fighting vehicles in the sector of *6. Panzerarmee* on 5 March, but only 266 on 15 March.
796 Drabkin, Artem: *Panzer Killers. Anti-tank Warfare on the Eastern Front*. Barnsley, 2013. p. 202.
797 Drabkin, Artem – Sheremet, Oleg: *T–34 in action. Soviet Tank Troops in WWII*. Mechanicsburg, 2008. p. 142.

According to contemporary Soviet analysis, between 6 to 15 March 1945, 80 percent of the armoured strength of *6. Panzerarmee* was destroyed by Soviet anti-tank artillery, tanks, self-propelled guns and aircraft.[798] This can't be an accurate statement, given the above listed facts.

One of the works, written by Russian authors and translated into English recently, has even incorporated the idea into its title, namely, that between 6 – 15 March 1945, the Transdanubia became the *"tomb of the Panzerwaffe"*. The authors estimate the losses of *6. Panzerarmee* during Operation *"Frühlingserwachen"* to be at least 250 destroyed tanks, assault guns and *Jagdpanzers*.[799] This does not even include the German-Hungarian armoured fighting vehicles destroyed or damaged by the Soviet air force as the authors did not investigate this subject.

During the defensive operations at Lake Balaton between 6 and 15 March 1945, the 3rd Ukrainian Front suffered 32,899 casualties, of which 8492 had been killed or went missing in action. The tank and mechanized forces of the Front at the same time lost 154 tanks and self propelled guns deemed as irrecoverable, based on their own reports.[800]

Naturally the Soviet troops also had many more armoured fighting vehicles that had been knocked out than destroyed. For example, the Soviet 18th Tank Corps lost the following number of armoured fighting vehicles during the defensive operations between 6 - 20 March 1945:

- gunfire knocked out 103 T–34 and T–34/85 tanks, of which 48 were damaged beyond repair;
- ran on mines: three T–34/85 tanks, of which one was damaged beyond repair;
- other reasons: another 30 tanks became temporarily disabled;
- gunfire knocked out 18 ISU–122 self-propelled guns, of which three were damaged beyond repair;
- other reasons: another four ISU–122 self-propelled guns became temporarily disabled;
- gunfire knocked out three ISU–152 self-propelled guns, of which one was damaged beyond repair;
- gunfire knocked out 26 SU–76M self-propelled guns, of which 14 were damaged beyond repair;
- other reasons: another two SU–76M self-propelled guns became temporarily disabled.[801]

---

798 Quoted by Isaev, Aleksei–Kolomiets, Maksim: *Tomb of the Panzerwaffe. The Defeat of the 6th SS Panzer Army in Hungary 1945.* Solihull, 2014. p. 172.
799 See Isaev, Aleksei–Kolomiets, Maksim: *Tomb of the Panzerwaffe. The Defeat of the 6th SS Panzer Army in Hungary 1945.* Solihull, 2014. p. 174. In that work, to prove the 250 irrecoverable German armoured fighting vehicle losses between 6-15 March 1945, the authors partly use photographs as evidence (see their argument on p. 174 of their work) that were taken evidently in January - February 1945, as the background is snowy. The reason for this is that these were photographed in the areas that remained in Soviet hands after the *"Konrad"* operations. The photographs assessing the captured vehicles taken after Operation *"Frühlingserwachen"* and the Vienna Offensive were taken in the second half of March 1945, and there is no snow in the background in these photographs. At the same time, the work, in more than the half of its entire length, 98 pages out of 184, despite its title, is preoccupied with the *"Konrad"* operations and the siege of Budapest which events have no connection with *6. Panzerarmee*.
800 The Appendix contains the detailed data of the irrecoverable armoured fighting vehicle losses of the 3rd Ukrainian Front between 6-15 March 1945.
801 Central Archives of the Russian Defence Ministry (Podolsk), f. 3415, op. 1, gy. 77, li. 139/2.

Interestingly, the 18th Tank Corps had not lost any armoured fighting vehicles due to enemy aircraft raids during the defensive operations, although their battle lines were attacked multiple times. As a comparison, between 2 January and 5 March 1945, the Corps lost 24 tanks and nine ISU–122 self-propelled guns due to enemy aircraft action, of which all but two tanks were burnt out.[802]

---

[802] Central Archives of the Russian Defence Ministry (Podolsk), f. 3415, op. 1, gy. 77, li. 139/2.

CHAPTER 3

THE HUNGARIAN SECTION OF THE VIENNA OFFENSIVE

*Plans for the Soviet offensive and combat strength
of the units dedicated to the cause*

The Headquarters of the Main Command of the Armed Forces of the USSR (Stavka) had planned the tasks to be carried out during the Vienna Offensive by the 3rd Ukrainian Front and the left flank of the 2nd Ukrainian Front, that is, the 46th Army, on 9 March 1945, still during the German offensive. The aim of the operation was to eliminate the German *Heeresgruppe Süd*, to occupy the whole territory of Hungary, advance in Slovakia and to occupy the Vienna sector. According to the tactical plan, the Soviet troops with three combined arms and one tank army, with support from two air armies, would break the German-Hungarian defence of *6. Armee* in the Székesfehérvár sector, then encircle and destroy *6. Panzerarmee* positioned between the Danube and Lake Balaton. Afterwards, the forces of the two fronts would develop their assault in the direction of Vienna and in Slovakia.

According to this, the 2nd Ukrainian Front was ordered to launch an attack on 17 or 18 March 1945 with the 46th Army, and together with the right flank of the 3rd Ukrainian Front, eliminate the German-Hungarian forces south of the Danube, and then proceed to advance in the general direction of Győr–Mosonmagyaróvár. The 3rd Ukrainian Front was to launch an attack on 16 March 1945 at the latest with its troops on the right-flank, and to expand their success in the general direction of Pápa–Sopron.

Marshal Malinovsky, the commander of the 2nd Ukrainian Front decided that he was going to launch an attack north of the Danube, from the Garam River toward Trenčín with the 40th, 53th (combined arms) Army, the 7th Guards Army, the 1st Guards Cavalry-Mechanized Group, and the Romanian 1st and 4th Armies.

However, the main course of attack was to be carried out by the 46th Army fanning out from the Danube to Csabdi, attacking in the direction of Győr, with 12 rifle divisions, 68 armoured fighting vehicles, and 2686 guns and mortars, in cooperation with the 2nd Guards Mechanized Corps which had 96 tanks and self-propelled guns. The 46th Army, with some of its units and the 2nd Guards Mechanized Corps, had to reach the western edge of Komárom, to close off the retreat route of the German-Hungarian troops southwest of Esztergom, and to eliminate these forces with the help of the Danube Flotilla with its 29 armoured gunboats, seven minelayer and 10 minesweeper vessels, 78 fighter aircraft and the 83rd Naval Infantry Brigade.

The 7th Guards Army and the troops on the left flank of the 53rd Army were to attack in the direction of Pozsony–Malacky–Brno, as soon as the 46th Army had achieved success. The breach was to be exploited by the forces of the 1st Guards Cavalry-Mechanized Group with a swift advance, to prevent the Germans occupying the defensive sectors on the right bank of the Nyitra, the Vág and the Morva Rivers. At the same time, the 40th Army, the majority of the 53rd Army and the Romanian 1st and 4th Armies were to launch an attack in the direction of the Low Tatras and Selmecbánya. Marshal Malinovsky assumed that his troops could cut off the retreat routes of the German troops in combat south of the Danube and swiftly occupy Vienna.

Before the offensive, the 2nd Ukrainian Front had 359,000 soldiers, 365 tanks and self-propelled guns[803], 7860 guns and mortars, and 637 aircraft of the 4th Air Army. Of these, 101,500 soldiers were deployed within the 46th Army and the 2nd Guards Mechanized Corps south of the Danube.[804]

Marshal Tolbukhin, the commander of the 3rd Ukrainian Front, planned that with the troops on the right-flank of his Front, he would deliver the main strike in the direction of Veszprém. The forces of the 9th Guards and the 4th Guards Army, numbering 18 rifle divisions, 197 tanks and self-propelled guns, and 3900 guns and mortars would breach the defences of the German-Hungarian troops, then would encircle them with a west-southwest facing attack, then afterwards, together with the 27th and 26th Armies attacking in the direction of Polgárdi, they would destroy *6. Panzerarmee* and units of *6. Armee* south and southwest of Székesfehérvár.

Following this, the 3rd Ukrainian Front with the main forces of the two guards armies, would deliver the main strike in the direction of Pápa and Sopron, and however, would also attack in the direction of Szombathely and Zalaegerszeg with their forces, in order to outflank the troops of *2. Panzerarmee* in defence between Lake Balaton and the Dráva River. The units on the left-flank of the Front, the Soviet 57th Army and the Bulgarian 1st Army were tasked with destroying the defences of *2. Panzerarmee* south of Lake Balaton, and to occupy the Nagykanizsa sector. The 5th Guards Cavalry Corps stood in reserve for the Front in the Siófok sector.

On 16 March 1945, the 3rd Ukrainian Front had 714 tanks and self-propelled guns, of which 681 were operational.[805] On the same day, the Front received the 6th Guards Tank Army from the 2nd Ukrainian Front, which had 425 tanks and self-propelled guns.

With this, the 3rd Ukrainian Front concentrated the following strength to carry out the offensive: 536,700 soldiers[806], 42 rifle, four airborne and three cavalry divisions, three tank and two mechanized corps, one independent mechanized brigade, three self-propelled artillery brigades, one fortified region, and one air army. Of the concentrated 1139 armoured fighting vehicles, 1104 were operational.

---

803 Without the strength of the 6th Guards Tank Army.
804 Krivoseev, G. F. (red.): *Velikaya Otechestvennaya bez grifa sekretnosti. Kniga poter*. Moscow, 2010. p. 168.
805 The Appendix contains the detailed data of the armoured fighting vehicle strength of the 3rd Ukrainian Front as of 16 March 1945.
806 Krivoseev, G. F. (red.): *Velikaya Otechestvennaya bez grifa sekretnosti. Kniga poter*. Moscow, 2010. p. 168.

Interestingly, among the operational armoured fighting vehicles of the 3rd Ukrainian Front, according to the comparison of data from 16 and 17 March 1945, there were 269 T–34s or T–34/85s, and 285 M4A2s besides 565 various types of self-propelled guns.[807] Based on this data, the number of the self-propelled guns in combat in the sector of the 3rd Ukrainian Front was almost the same as the number of tanks, and the number of the American-manufactured M4A2s was larger then both of the T-34 types.

The Soviet assault was based on the principles of "deep battle". Marshall M. N. Tukhachevsky (1897 – 1937), who fell victim to the Stalin-initiated purges, had a leading role in developing this theory. The core of the theory is as follows: to hold and contain the full depth of the enemy defence at once, followed by swiftly breaching the depths of the enemy's tactical defences in the chosen direction and the exploitation of the breach in depth. In order to ensure success, the forces were grouped in four echelons:

- the rifle corps of the *assault echelon* equipped with tanks and artillery had the task of breaking through the tactical depths of the enemy lines;
- the *success exploitation echelon*'s fast group consisting of tank, mechanized or cavalry corps was deployed after the breakthrough and would advance in the gap opened by the first echelon, widening it with its assault, while outflanking and encircling the enemy;
- the *air echelon* (air force and airborne troops) was used to hold and contain the depths of defence;
- the *reserve echelon* would be used to supplement the losses.[808]

Throughout 1944 and 1945, the Soviet high command was usually able to concentrate five to seven rifle battalions, 200-250 guns and mortars, 20-30 tanks and self-propelled guns, and two to four engineering pioneer companies for each kilometer of the breakthrough sector.[809]

As soon as the rifle infantry, supported by tanks and self-propelled guns, as well as artillery and ground attack aircraft, had broken through the tactical depth of the enemy lines, the tank and mechanized forces were to be thrown into combat. In case the infantry was not able to completely break through the enemy lines, the tank and mechanized corps were deployed to complete the breakthrough process, however in these cases the armoured losses were expected to rise significantly.

In the operational depth of the enemy defence, the tank armies and the swiftly moving corps, less frequently the rifle divisions having their own self-propelled guns, separated so-called advance troops from their strength. These chased the retreating enemy units in depths of 20-50 km, bypassed stronger enemy fortifications, occupied significant objectives, such as bridges, crossing points, railway stations, road intersections or villages, and kept these until the arrival of the main forces. In the case of corps, these advance troops were usually of brigade strength, 800-1200 men, and in case of tank armies either a tank brigade

---

[807] The number of other Soviet tank types did not exceed 15.
[808] *Magyarország a második világháborúban. Lexikon A-Zs.* Főszerkesztő: Sipos Péter. Szerkesztő: Ravasz István. Budapest, 1997. p. 311. It needs to be noted however that the tasks of the air echelon were usually carried out only by the air force, as from the end of 1942, the majority of the airborne troops were deployed as rifle forces out of necessity.
[809] Radzhievsky, A. I. (ed.): *Az ezred harcászata*. Budapest, 1979. p. 21.

or one of the corps was assigned to this task. The advance troops were also employed on a tactical level. In the case of a division or a brigade, this was mostly a reinforced battalion, and a reinforced company in the case of battalions.

Besides tanks and self-propelled guns, Soviet wartime industry was manufacturing armoured reconnaissance vehicles, although the latter were not produced in significant amounts. Armoured transport vehicles were not manufactured however, and due to this, the infantry of the tank and mechanized units were mostly transported by those trucks that were sent from the USA to the Soviet Union.[810] However these trucks were not able to follow the armoured fighting vehicles under heavy enemy fire or on difficult terrain, therefore the tanks needed to wait for the rifle troops from time to time. The wheeled and half-track armoured transport vehicles were assigned to the reconnaissance and ground forces anti-aircraft subunits of the tank and mechanized forces.

If rapid movement was essential, the infantry was mounted upon tanks as "airborne". This however prevented the tanks from firing accurately because they could not turn their turrets when the infantry was mounted. Moreover, enemy tank fire also inflicted heavy losses among the Soviet infantry.

If the attack was halted by an enemy fortification, the Soviets, as opposed to the German method, outflanked them and left only weak forces there to contain the enemy, then sought to encircle their fortification from every direction and eliminate it only after that.

Combat forces of the German-Hungarian troops in the sector assigned for the Soviet breakthrough

The forces of *IV. SS-Panzerkorps* had not taken part in Operation *"Frühlingserwachen"*, however from 16 March 1945, they played a crucial role in the defence of the rear of *6. Panzerarmee* advancing to the Sió Canal.

On 22 February 1945, *3. SS-Panzer-Division* was reassembled on the southern edges of the Vértes mountains. After the troops had taken over the sector of *4. Kavallerie-Division* which was relocated to Lake Balaton, the Royal Hungarian 2nd Armoured Division of *vitéz* Colonel Endre Zádor was also subordinated to *Divisionskommandeur SS-Brigadeführer* Becker, together with a few independent battalions. Thus a new *Divisionsgruppe "Totenkopf"* was created, which was attached on the north to the Hungarian 1st Hussars Division and on the south to *5. SS-Panzer-Division*.[811]

On 24 February 1945, the units of *3. SS-Panzer-Division* occupied their new positions, and established the centre of their defence around Zámoly.

On 3 March 1945, the strength of the *Division* was 12,801 men, of which, 5441 were ready for service.[812]

---

810 Soviet industry manufactured 314.676 trucks between 1941-1945, but the majority of these were not fit to be deployed on rough terrain. The Soviet Union received 376,617 trucks from the USA, and the majority of these were the 2.5 ton US6 Studebaker type that had excellent terrain-tracking capabilities. See Zaloga, Steven J. – Ness, Leland S.: *Red Army Handbook 1939–45*. Gloucestershire, 1998. p. 187.
811 Vopersal, Wolfgang: *Soldaten, Kämpfer, Kameraden. Marsch und Kämpfe der SS-Totenkopfdivision*. Band Vb. Bielefeld, 1991. p. 681.
812 Vopersal, Wolfgang: *Soldaten, Kämpfer, Kameraden. Marsch und Kämpfe der SS-Totenkopfdivision*. Band Vb. Bielefeld, 1991. p. 694.

On 5 March 1945, the *SS-Division* sent a liaison officer to the Hungarian 2nd Armoured Division, which reported the following:

"The Hungarians are very friendly. Their armament is good. They are all equipped with '44 type rapid fire guns [Sturmgewehr 44 assault rifle – the author]. They also have MG 42s and 8 cm mortars too. However their food supplies are miserable."[813]

On 8 March 1945, the command of *SS-Panzer-Regiment 3* was taken over by *SS-Sturmbannführer* Anton Berlin. The *I. (Abteilung)/SS-Panzer-Regiment 3* was commanded by *SS-Hauptsturmführer* dr. Alfons Martin, and *II. (Abteilung)/SS-Panzer-Regiment 3* was commanded by *SS-Hauptsturmführer* Kuno Leibl.[814]

On 10 March 1945, the combat-ready armoured strength of the *Division* consisted of 16 Panzer IVs, eight Panthers and seven Tiger E tanks, five Jagdpanzer IV *Jagdpanzers* and 12 StuG. III assault guns. One strong and six medium strength infantry battalions had a combined combat strength of 2200 men. The divisional artillery had five light and five heavy batteries. The *Division* was suitable for attack in a limited capacity and their mobility was rated as 80%.[815]

On that day, the four battalions and one worn out pioneer battalion of the Hungarian 2nd Armoured Division had a combat strength of no more than 1200 men. The 3rd Tank Regiment had 16 combat-ready Panzer IV tanks. The Division possessed two anti-tank guns and four 10.5 cm howitzer batteries. Based on its combat force however, it was only suitable for defence in a limited capacity.[816]

On 11 March 1945, the commander of the *schwere Panzer-Kompanie* equipped with Tiger E tanks was *SS-Obersturmführer* Wenke. *SS-Panzerjäger-Abteilung 3* was taken over by *SS-Obersturmführer* Ludwig Zeitz.[817]

On 14 March 1945, the reserves of the *Division* were as follows:

- *I. (Bataillon)/SS-Panzergrenadier-Regiment 6* at Sárkeresztes,
- *I. (Bataillon)/SS-Panzergrenadier-Regiment 5* at Magyaralmás,
- two companies of *II. (Bataillon)/SS-Panzergrenadier-Regiment 5*, two companies of *SS-Panzer-Aufklärungs-Abteilung 3*, the *Divisionsbegleitkompanie* and the majority of *SS-Panzerjäger-Abteilung 3* at Söréd,
- *III. (Bataillon)/SS-Panzergrenadier-Regiment 5* and two companies of *II. (Bataillon)/SS-Panzergrenadier-Regiment 5* at Bodajk,
- the units of *SS-Panzerjäger-Abteilung 3* were in readiness in Mór.[818]

---

813 Idézi Vopersal, Wolfgang: *Soldaten, Kämpfer, Kameraden. Marsch und Kämpfe der SS-Totenkopfdivision.* Band Vb. Bielefeld, 1991. i.m. p. 695. It needs to be noted that such modern equipment of the Hungarian 2nd Armoured Division is not mentioned anywhere else.
814 Vopersal, Wolfgang: *Soldaten, Kämpfer, Kameraden. Marsch und Kämpfe der SS-Totenkopfdivision.* Band Vb. Bielefeld, 1991. p. 700.
815 NARA, T311, R162, F7214529.
816 NARA, T311, R162, F7214529.
817 Vopersal, Wolfgang: *Soldaten, Kämpfer, Kameraden. Marsch und Kämpfe der SS-Totenkopfdivision.* Band Vb. Bielefeld, 1991. p. 704.
818 Tieke, Wilhelm: *Von Plattensee bis Österreich. Heeresgruppe Süd 1945.* Gummersbach, without year of publication, p. 40.

On 23 February 1945, *5. SS-Panzer-Division* had taken over the frontline section of *3. SS-Panzer-Division*, which stretched from the southern edge of Székesfehérvár to Moha. *SS-Panzergrenadier-Regiment 10 was* on the right flank of the new positions and the left flank was held by *SS-Panzergrenadier-Regiment 9*. The *II. (Abteilung)/SS-Panzer-Regiment 5* had also established positions on the left flank.[819] As *5. SS-Panzer-Division*, similar to the other units of *IV. SS-Panzerkorps*, had not taken part in Operation *"Frühlingserwachen"*, the period without any major enemy engagements lasted as late as 16 March 1945, the beginning of the Soviet "Vienna Offensive".

On 10 March 1945, *5. SS-Panzer-Division* had 13 combat-ready Panthers and four Panzer IV tanks, one StuG. IV assault gun and seven Jagdpanzer IV *Jagdpanzers*. The combat strength of the *Panzergrenadier* infantry was approximately 2100 men in two strong, three medium strength and two average battalions. *SS-Panzer-Artillerie-Regiment 5* had six light and four heavy batteries. The *Division* was only suitable for attack in a limited capacity, and its mobility was rated at only 46 percent.[820]

On 14 March 1945, *SS-Panzer-Aufklärungs-Abteilung 5* and *II. (Bataillon)/ SS-Panzergrenadier-Regiment 9* were at Csór, and the *Divisionsbegleitkompanie* was at Iszkaszentgyörgy as corps reserve. The *I. (Bataillon)/SS-Panzergrenadier-Regiment 24 "Danmark"*, subordinated to the *Division*, was positioned in the western part of Székesfehérvár.[821]

That meant that *IV. SS-Panzerkorps* soon had approximately 5500 combat-ready infantry and 98 combat-ready armoured fighting vehicles to face two complete Soviet Guards Armies, to which a Guards Tank Army was also attached from 19 March 1945.

16 March 1945, Friday

(**WEATHER**: the highest daytime temperature was 10 Celsius; foggy in the morning, but sunny during the day, locally damp spots. The condition of the roads improved considerably, however the open ground conditions were still not suitable for the armoured fighting vehicles.)

That evening in the Transdanubia, 1264 operational tanks and self-propelled guns of the 2nd and 3rd Ukrainian Fronts stood face to face with the approximately 635 combat-ready armoured fighting vehicles of *Heeresgruppe Süd*.[822]

On the frontline along the Dráva River, the Soviet–Bulgarian forces reoccupied Drávapalkonya.[823]

The Soviet 1891st Self-Propelled Artillery Regiment knocked out two guns, five mortars, four heavy and 14 light machine guns, and captured 62 enemy soldiers during

---

819 Klapdor, Ewald: *Mit dem Panzerregiment 5 Wiking im Osten*. Siek, 1981. p. 323.
820 Tieke, Wilhelm: *Von Plattensee bis Österreich. Heeresgruppe Süd 1945*. Gummersbach, without year of publication, p. 33.
821 Tieke, Wilhelm: *Von Plattensee bis Österreich. Heeresgruppe Süd 1945*. Gummersbach, without year of publication, p. 40.
822 The Appendix details the armoured fighting vehicles of the Soviet 2nd and 3rd Ukrainian Fronts and the German *Heeresgruppe Süd* stationed in the Transdanubia on 15 and 16 March 1945.
823 NARA, T311, R162, F7214588.

this action. Their own losses amounted to five SU–76M self-propelled guns between 13 – 16 March 1945.[824]

At the front of *2. Panzerarmee, 1. Volks-Gebirgs-Division/XXII. Gebirgskorps*, supported by eight assault guns of *Sturmgeschütz-Brigade 191*, advanced from Somogyszentpál towards Csömend and on the flanks, eliminated the significantly reinforced Soviet positions, then, after having turned back Soviet counterattacks, with two battalions and the support of 25 armoured fighting vehicles[825], they broke into the center of Csömend.[826] During this action the Germans reportedly knocked out 16 Soviet tanks and four self-propelled guns.[827] Of these, nine tanks and four self-propelled guns were knocked out by *Sturmgeschütz-Brigade 191* without incurring any losses of their own, and with this, they achieved their 501st knocked out armoured fighting vehicle since their establishment.[828]

At 1200 hours, *16. SS-Panzergrenadier-Division* exploited the success of *1. Volks-Gebirgs-Division*, and launched an attack along the road leading southwest from the direction of Boronka. The Soviets put up heavy resistance, however, despite this the SS-units reached the general line 2 km southwest of and 1 km northwest of Csömend by 1730 hours, then they proceeded to take Csömend itself.[829]

Along the front of *16. SS-Panzergrenadier-Division,* the remnants of *I. (Bataillon)/ SS-Panzergrenadier-Regiment 36* and *I. (Bataillon)/SS-Panzergrenadier-Regiment 36* were supported by *Panzergruppe "Reinhardt"/SS-Panzer-Abteilung 16* with four StuG. III assault guns. The *II. and III. (Bataillons)/SS-Panzergrenadier-Regiment 35* and *SS-Panzer-Aufklärungs-Abteilung 16* were supported by *Panzergruppe "Knobelspies"/ SS-Panzer-Abteilung 16* with the four assault guns. This grouping, together with *1. Kompanie/I.(Bataillon)/Volks-Gebirgsjäger-Regiment 98*, launched an attack at 1200 hours via Csömend against Nikla. The right flank of the assault troops attacking in the direction of Gyótapuszta, and was covered by two companies of *I. (Bataillon)/Volks-Gebirgsjäger-Regiment 98* and *Panzergruppe "Rex"* of *SS-Panzer-Abteilung 16*.[830]

The attack progressed slowly. In front of Csömend, the Germans ran into 30 anti-tank guns and 12 152 mm gun howitzers firing directly. During the evening, the Germans pushed into Csömend, but they were not able to occupy the village. By the evening, they had advanced up to the line running 2 km southwest and 1 km northwest of the village.[831]

SS-Hauptsturmführer Knobelspies, *Kommandeur* of *SS-Panzer-Abteilung 16* noted the following in his diary:

---

824 Central Archives of the Russian Defence Ministry (Podolsk), f. 243, op. 2928, gy. 131, li. 248.
825 In the sector the T-34 tanks of the 52nd Tank Regiment/32nd Independent Guards Mechanized Brigade and the SU–76M self-propelled guns of the 864th Self-Propelled Artillery Regiment were in combat; these units lost on that day 10 burnt out, and four knocked out, of which 2 were burnt out, self-propelled guns respectively. See Central Archives of the Russian Defence Ministry (Podolsk), f. 243, op. 2928, gy. 131, li. 248.
826 NARA, T311, R162, F7214589.
827 NARA, T311, R163, F7215372.
828 NARA, T311, R163, F7215398.
829 NARA, T311, R162, F7214589.
830 Puntigam, Josef Paul: *Vom Plattensee bis zur Mur. Die Kämpfe 1945 im Dreiländereck.* Feldbach, without year of publication, [1993], p. 101.
831 Puntigam, Josef Paul: *Vom Plattensee bis zur Mur. Die Kämpfe 1945 im Dreiländereck.* Feldbach, without year of publication, [1993], p. 93.

"Following the occupation of Boronka, around noon on 16 March, during preparations for the next attack against Nikla, information came from the division commander via radio that the enemy is working on lining up significant artillery and anti-tank forces in the clearing of the forest east of Boronka. According to the order, the Panzer-Abteilung was to attack with all available forces at once and destroy the enemy. There was no infantry available. The commander of the Panzer-Abteilung was to personally lead the assault. They demanded that an immediate report be sent confirming achievement. The available forces were concentrated. With the two assault guns just arrived from the repair workshops, we had seven vehicles, one reinforced infantry platoon and two pioneer squads with submachine guns and semi-automatic rifles. We were able to march out in half an hour.
[...]
I went on a reconnaissance mission forward with the infantry squads up until the point from where we could already see what the Soviets were up to. The infantry platoon fanned out in a wide section and took positions, and as much as possible, drew closer with the task of identifying the anti—tank guns and upon being ordered via radio, open fire at them. Reinhardt [Zugführer of 1. Panzer-Kompanie – the author] had chosen the forest road on the right with three vehicles, and I had the left road with four vehicles, and we agreed on advancing with as little noise as possible, then with a quick burst of speed push through [the forest – the author] and attack by surprise, at the same time when my group and the infantry platoon opened fire too. Unterscharführer Kelm was advancing at the head of my group. The first shot was heard, but from a Soviet anti-tank gun. Upon hearing this, the infantry machine gun fire immediately started without being ordered to on radio, thanks to the commitment of their commander. Unterscharführer Schmidt, the commander of the second tank, reported that Kelm's vehicle was hit.
Schmidt saw the escape hatch rim fly off Kelm's vehicle, and he immediately went into cover and knocked the anti-tank gun out. Our infantry and pioneers also joined in and the fire fight was raging with full force. Soon we could hear the guns of Reinhardt's group detonating like lashes, which, as we later found out, completely surprised the enemy. I sent Unterscharführer Ringel forward, who was the fourth vehicle behind me, to join the combat. I myself got out to see Unterscharführer Kelm. I jumped on his vehicle. The sight was horrible, the rim flying off completely beheaded Kelm. The crew was soaked in blood and thoroughly shocked. Together we pulled poor dead Kelm out and I sent the crew back. Kelm's assault gun had not suffered any other damage and was still mobile. Sepp Strunz, the driver of Schmidt's vehicle moved the vehicle a bit backwards, and a emergency driver later drove it back. We again joined the fight and opened fire with all barrels. Our machine guns stopped, we occupied the forest clearing and the enemy gave up after a short time. Luckily their guns were not yet ready to fire.
Approximately 30-40 Soviets, who had either made makeshift trenches behind the vehicles and the guns, or hidden, surrendered. Everybody else was either dead, wounded or ran away. Apart from the dead Kelm, we only had a few wounded soldiers, who were treated alongside the Russian wounded soldiers. A few of our assault guns were hit, however no major damage was done..
[...]

After the arrival of the commander of the division, the report was handed over and an inspection of the captured armament, equipment and vehicles was made. It seemed that the Soviets had sensed the danger because they were firing at us with artillery, Stalin-organs and heavy mortars. Luckily the heavily wounded were already brought away and our armoured fighting vehicles were fanned out on a wide front on the forest roads with wide gaps between them. The shells mostly hit the trees, and among the Soviet guns and vehicles. The Stalin-organ shells were jammed all too often and caused little damage. Our soldiers were covered within the armoured fighting vehicles and under them. The commander of the division, Schmidt, Strunz and I were hiding under one of the assault guns.
[…]
In the distance, approximately 1000 meters away, we noticed large numbers of horse-drawn vehicles. It must have been the reinforcements intended for the artillery and anti-tank positions. The commander of the division ordered the commander of the Abteilung to act accordingly. Out went the word to Reinhardt to commence with a number of assault guns and two four-barrelled anti-aircraft automatic cannons, and encircling them from behind, should surround their position with high-explosive shells then systematically destroy them. The commander of the division expressed his appreciation to the small combat group. It was not possible to send back the captured armament, therefore the pioneers destroyed them. The commander of the division could only promise weak infantry forces for securing the forest line. A platoon from I. (Bataillon)/Panzer-Regiment 36 with approximately 20 soldiers and all available members of the staff company, as well as three assault guns under command of Untersturmführer Böhmer, received a briefing regarding the task. The armoured group pulled back to Boronka, was to launch a counterattack during the night with infantry, pioneers and reconnaissance squads, as well as II. (Bataillon)/Panzer-Regiment 35 to counter the night assault of the Soviets. The units suffered heavy losses but they managed to reclaim the line and held it. Elsewhere Böhmer, in his reportedly very tight situation and in extreme anguish close to shock, had blown up three bogged down armoured fighting vehicles, even though these would have been needed for the attack against Nikla. During the night attack, [of the previous night – the author] Reinhardt and his platoon had excellently supported Sturmbannführer Gantzer's I. (Bataillon)/Panzer-Regiment 36. For this, Reinhardt was commended to receive the Knight's Cross of the Iron Cross and was introduced for promotion to Untersturmführer. He deserves this for real."[832]

The two German divisions, supported by assault guns, had, by 1915 hours, reached the eastern edge of Csömend, then advancing forward, they occupied the bridge on the Malom ditch just eastwards of the village.[833]

Around midnight, *Panzergruppe "Rex"* attacking in the direction of Gyótapuszta, was engaged in fire by Soviet armoured fighting vehicles from the Nagygyótai Forest. The commander's cupola and the armoured skirt (*Panzerschürze*) of the assault gun of the commander of the group had been destroyed. While trying to manoeuvre back, all but one

---

[832] Puntigam, Josef Paul: *Vom Plattensee bis zur Mur. Die Kämpfe 1945 im Dreiländereck.* Feldbach, without year of publication, [1993], pp. 97-100. *SS-Hauptscharführer* Reinhardt did not receive the Knight's Cross of the Iron Cross in the end.
[833] NARA, T311, R163, F7215362.

SS-assault gun had been bogged down in the previously occupied old Soviet trenches. After the still mobile StuG. III disabled the Soviet armoured fighting vehicles, the German attack reached Gyótapuszta. In the meantime the assault gun had been knocked out by the Soviets. During the difficult, but in the end successful attack, the assault guns of *Panzergruppe "Rex"* had knocked out two Soviet tanks, and significantly damaged another two.[834]

Kampfgruppe "Steyrer" closed up to the attack of *16. SS-Panzergrenadier-Division* and with *SS-Polizei-Regiment 6* as well as a Hungarian police battalion, reached the line between the southern edge of the forest northeast of Bize and the mill south of Bize.[835]

According to German data, on the front of *2. Panzerarmee* between 14 and 16 March 1945, 18 Soviet tanks and 14 self-propelled guns were either captured or knocked out.[836]

On the right flank of *I. Kavallerie-Korps/6. Panzerarmee* the Hungarian 25th Infantry Division repelled a number of regiment-sized Soviet counterattacks, which were also supported by two armoured fighting vehicles. Due to the Soviet pressure however, the Hungarian troops were forced to give up Hill 133 again (Öreghegy) 3 km northeast of Balatonszabadi.[837]

The bridgehead area of *4. Kavallerie-Division* was still calm. From the bridgehead of *3. Kavallerie-Division* south of the Sió Canal, vehicle traffic was detected from the direction of Szabadhídvég moving to the south. The Soviets had occupied a smaller bridgehead in the sector of Felsőnyék on the northern bank of the Sió Canal.[838]

The *12. SS-Panzer-Division/I. SS-Panzerkorps* directed forces for the elimination of the Soviet bridgehead created north of Ozora.[839]

Early in the morning, *SS-Panzergrenadier-Regiment 26* was relieved and drawn back. At *II. (Bataillon)/SS-Panzergrenadier-Regiment 26,* the transition was completed at 0910 hours. The *Bataillon* then marched to Igar where they received replacements of men and material. *SS-Panzergrenadier-Regiment 25* was to launch an attack against the Soviet bridgehead at Ozora in order to confuse the enemy. The divisional artillery had expended a considerable amount of ammunition during the day.[840]

In the bridgehead held by *1. SS-Panzer-Division* south of Simontornya, the German pioneers completed a temporary bridge on the same day. After the bridge had been repaired, *SS-Panzergrenadier-Regiment 1* with the support of the arriving heavy armament, was able to repel the Soviet attacks, which were supported by artillery fire.[841]

The forces of the Soviet 209th Self-Propelled Artillery Brigade were still in combat along the Sió Canal fanned out on a wide front. The 1951st Self-Propelled Artillery Regiment had eight SU–100s at the northern edge of Cece and six at Csordakút in firing position. Seven self-propelled guns of the 1953rd Self-Propelled Artillery Regiment were stationed 2 km southeast of Simontornya, and five were at Sárszentlőrinc. Six SU-100 self-propelled guns

---

[834] Puntigam, Josef Paul: *Vom Plattensee bis zur Mur. Die Kämpfe 1945 im Dreiländereck.* Feldbach, without year of publication, [1993], pp. 101-103.
[835] NARA, T311, R162, F7214606.
[836] NARA, T311, R163, F7215386.
[837] NARA, T311, R162, F7214589.
[838] NARA, T311, R162, F7214589.
[839] NARA, T311, R162, F7214589.
[840] Meyer, Hubert: *Kriegsgeschichte der 12. SS-Panzerdivision „Hitlerjugend".* Band II. Osnabrück, 1987. 2nd edition. p. 504.
[841] Tiemann, Ralf: *Die Leibstandarte.* Band IV/2. Osnabrück, 1987. p. 290.

of the 1952nd Self-Propelled Artillery Regiment were in firing position on the western and eastern slopes of Hill 220 located 2.5 km southwest of Simontornya, two SU–100s were at Tolnanémedi, five at Pincehely, two at Ozora, three at Felsőnyék, and two at Szabadhídvég.[842]

On the night of 15/16 March 1945, at 0100 hours, the German *23. Panzer-Division* attempted to cross the Sárvíz 2.5 km southeast and 2 km northwest of Örspuszta, together with the assault groups of *I. (Bataillon)/Panzergrenadier-Regiment 128*, also supported by *Artillerie* units. However, the attempt failed. At 0730 hours in the morning, the Germans managed to establish a small bridgehead east of Örspuszta with significant artillery support. The violent counterattacks of the Soviet troops forced them to retreat back to the western bank of the Malom Canal.[843] Afterwards, *I. (Bataillon)/Panzergrenadier-Regiment 128* marched to Ötvenkilencmajor.

During the night of 15/16 March 1945, on the front of *II. SS-Panzerkorps*, the Soviets launched an attack from the south and from the east with heavy artillery support against the German bridgehead held northeast of Káloz. However this was repulsed by the armoured personnel carriers of the reinforced *2. Kompanie/SS-Panzer-Aufklärungs-Abteilung 2*. Following the attack, the Germans counted 70 dead Soviet soldiers.[844] In the evening orders arrived for the reconnaissance units to abandon their positions on the bridge over the canal and both of their *SS-Panzer-Aufklärungs-Kompanies* were to reassemble north of Káloz.

On the night of 15/16 March 1945, a German combat group[845] broke into the eastern section of Sárkeresztúr where they held their positions in heavy close quarters combat.[846] The Soviet troops also launched an attack from the village in a north-eastern direction, but the Germans repelled that. At nightfall, the Germans detected vehicle traffic from Sárosd towards the southeast.[847]

The 110th Tank Brigade/18th Tank Corps, in action against the German armoured fighting vehicles west of Sárosd, lost two burnt out T–34/85s, while claiming to have knocked out one tank and one armoured personnel carrier.[848]

On the front of *III. Panzerkorps/Armeegruppe "Balck"*, the Soviets launched four attacks, of battalion strength each, against the left flank of *6. Panzer-Division* south of Kápolnásnyék, and against the positions of *1. Panzer-Division*. The Germans turned back most of these attacks, although the Soviets managed to enter the southern sector of Gárdony, where a German counterattack was initiated to eliminate the incursion.[849]

Along the front of *1. Panzer-Division, Kampfgruppe "Bradel"* composed of *Panzergrenadier-Regiment 113* with *I. (Abteilung)/Panzer-Artillerie-Regiment 73 (self propelled)*, a few Panzer IV tanks and assault guns, and some towed anti-tank guns, along with the 14 Panther tanks of *Panzer-Regiment 1* and two self-propelled 2 cm four-barrelled anti-aircraft guns held the section. Orders were received in which it was stated that the

---

842   Central Archives of the Russian Defence Ministry (Podolsk), f. 243, op. 2928, gy. 131, li. 248.
843   NARA, T311, R162, F7214589.
844   NARA, T311, R162, F7214589.
845   It is not yet known if these were the forces of *44. Reichsgrenadier-Division* or *SS-Panzergrenadier-Regiment 3/2. SS-Panzer-Division*.
846   NARA, T311, R163, F7215352.
847   NARA, T311, R162, F7214589.
848   War log of the 18th Tank Corps for March 1945. Copy owned by the author. p. 26.
849   NARA, T311, R162, F7214590.

damaged tracked vehicles were to be withdrawn from Seregélyes to Börgönd, and from Börgönd to Hajmáskér. In the area behind *III. Panzerkorps*, especially around Litér, Berhida and Hajmáskér, the activity of the Soviet air force had significantly increased. Therefore the armoured maintenance units were forced to camouflage the damaged armoured fighting vehicles, many of which needed to be left out in the open field. The *6. Kompanie/Panzer-Regiment 1* was reorganized as a *Grenadier-Kompanie* with machine guns removed from damaged tanks, carbines, submachine guns and *Panzerfausts*, and their infantry training began.[850]

East of Seregélyes, in the sector of Hill 145 (Öreghegy) and Mihálymajor the 170th Tank Brigade in defence with the 1438th and 1068th Self-Propelled Artillery Regiments had been engaged in a fire fight from their positions with the German tanks and artillery. The Soviets reported to have knocked out five tanks and four armoured personnel carriers while losing two burnt out T–34/85s.[851]

Between Székesfehérvár and the Vértes mountains, on the front of *IV. SS-Panzerkorps* and the Hungarian VIII Army Corps, at around 1238 hours on the same day, all hell broke loose as the Soviet 4th Guards and 9th Guards Army launched their attack.

The Soviets launched a massive artillery barrage, mostly with mortars and multiple rocket launchers supported by airstrikes, after which they launched battalion-size attacks against the two corps and the right flank of the German *96. Infanterie-Division.* Exploiting specific features of the terrain, the rifle units were attacking in groups of 500-1500 men, which were supported by smaller groups of about 60 armoured fighting vehicles.[852] The second echelon of the rifle units were approaching the German–Hungarian positions in marching order, as they were hoping for a swift breakthrough.[853]

The valiantly attacking Soviet rifle troops, supported by artillery and ground attack aircraft, however, suffered serious losses, then their attacks were halted and sealed off within the tactical depth of the German-Hungarian defences who had deployed their reserves.[854]

According to Soviet opinions, the two guards armies did not exploit the confused state of the defenders and had not advanced swiftly enough. Communication between the infantry and the artillery was not without problems, and was lost a number of times.[855]

Between Lake Velence and Sárkeresztes, the Soviets achieved minor, local incursions with the support of 10 armoured fighting vehicles, but these were eliminated by the Germans, mostly by counterattacks.

In the front of *5. SS-Panzer-Division,* the *SS-Panzergrenadiers,* who had been in combat for weeks now in reinforced defensive positions, repelled the assaults of the Soviet rifle troops with support from the armoured fighting vehicle of the *Division* firing high-explosive shells.[856]

Two Panzer IV tanks and a StuG.IV assault gun of *SS-Panzer-Regiment 5* stood in holding positions in the front of the outermost houses on the outskirts of the town. The

---

850 Stoves, Rolf: Persönliches Kriegstagebuch Pz.Rgt. 1 (typewritten manuscript, a copy owned by the author), entry from 16 March 1945.
851 War log of the 18th Tank Corps for March 1945. Copy owned by the author. p. 25.
852 NARA, T311, R162, F7214593.
853 NARA, T311, R162, F7214593.
854 NARA, T311, R162, F7214593.
855 Malakhov, M. M.: A Balatontól Bécsig (excerpt). In: *Fejezetek hazánk felszabadításának történetéből.* Budapest, 1960. p. 185.
856 Klapdor, Ewald: *Mit dem Panzerregiment 5 Wiking im Osten.* Siek, 1981. p. 332.

mortar and artillery fire were raising up so much dust that the German armoured fighting vehicles were not able to see the ground in front of them, so they retreated to safety at the edge of Székesfehérvár. The commander of the Panzer IV with turret number '201', *SS-Unterscharführer* Siegfried Melinkat positioned his tank among the houses, behind a road blockade, with the motor running. Another Panzer IV was positioned somewhat behind '201', in a way that there was no visual contact between the two tanks. The Soviets stopped their artillery fire and the rifle troops began their assault. The Soviet anti-tank guns were keeping the street under fire, where one of the shells directly hit the road block. One of the drive sprockets of the Panzer IV '201' was damaged and the vehicle was immobilized. *SS-Unterscharführer* Melinkat, over an open radio frequency and without coding his message, requested an immediate tow from his position. The commander of his combat group reminded him of the correct radio discipline which was met by the officer with cursing. The Soviet soldiers were approaching the immobile tank and were within 50-60 meters and the German supporting infantry had retreated after exchanging a few shots with the enemy. Because of the road block, it was not possible to use the main gun of the tank against such close targets, so there was nothing else left for the crew to do but to try and keep the Soviet soldiers at bay with submachine gun fire and handheld grenades. At last, the other Panzer IV arrived, which turned around and quickly put their tow cables on '201', which as it was towed backwards, kept the road blockade under machine gun fire. The two tanks successfully moved back from the front, escorted by the fire of the Soviet anti-tank guns, and finally arrived at the repair workshop of *SS-Panzer-Regiment 5*.[857]

The *I. (Bataillon)/SS-Panzergrenadier-Regiment 23*, stationed in Veszprém had been drawn forward in reserve to the area of Inota. The command post of *5. SS-Panzer-Division* was located at Iszkaszentgyörgy.[858]

The Rifle Divisions of the Soviet 4th Guards Army with their own self-propelled artillery battalions were engaged in combat in the following areas during the early hours of evening on that day:

- the 75th Guards Independent Self-Propelled Artillery Battalion/69th Guards Rifle Division with 10 SU–76M and one T–70 armoured fighting vehicle at Kisfalud with one battery and at Pákozd with two batteries;
- the 44th Guards Independent Self-Propelled Artillery Battalion/41st Guards Rifle Division with eight SU–76M, one T–70 armoured fighting vehicle and one captured German *Wespe* self-propelled howitzer at Csala;
- the 85th Guards Independent Self-Propelled Artillery Battalion/80th Guards Rifle Division with eight SU–76Ms and one T–70 armoured fighting vehicle, plus one captured German Panther tank 500 meters southwest of Máriamajor;
- the 13th Guards Independent Self-Propelled Artillery Battalion/5th Guards Airborne Division with 11 SU–76M self-propelled guns at Hill 171 with two batteries 1 km southeast of Gyulamajor and one battery east of Moha;

---

857 Fey, Will: *Armor Battles of the Waffen-SS, 1943–45*. Winnipeg, 1996. p. 259.
858 Tieke, Wilhelm: *Von Plattensee bis Österreich. Heeresgruppe Süd 1945*. Gummersbach, without year of publication, p. 45.

- the 8th Guards Independent Self-Propelled Artillery Battalion/7th Guards Airborne Division with 12 SU–76M self-propelled guns at the western edge of Pátka;
- the 69th Guards Independent Self-Propelled Artillery Battalion/62nd Guards Rifle Division with eight SU–76M self-propelled guns at the north-eastern edge of Pákozd.

The armoured fighting vehicles advanced with the battle line of the rifle troops and provided direct fire support to them.[859] During the fighting, only one single Soviet tank from the independent self-propelled artillery battalions was destroyed.[860]

The 366th Guards Heavy Self-Propelled Artillery Regiment/4th Guards Army with its captured German armoured fighting vehicles was in army reserve near Kisfalud.[861]

The commander of the 4th Guards Army ordered the forces attacking Székesfehérvár not to let themselves get engaged in a lengthy fight, but to encircle the city from the north and south, and push their assault in a southwest direction only. Furthermore, they were told to deploy only a certain amount of their forces to occupy Székesfehérvár, which should be completed by 18 March 1945.[862]

Along the front of the Hungarian 2nd Honvéd Armoured Division, on the left flank of *IV. SS-Panzerkorps* between Sárkeresztes and Gánt, the Soviets broke through the positions at Zámoly and Borbálapuszta on a wide front with four groups of at least battalion or regiment strength each, and following the Hungarian troops who were retreating in panic, pushed 4 km deep into the German-Hungarian defences.

The forces of the Soviet 9th Guards Army occupied Csákberény with armoured support, where on the streets three Hungarian tanks were fighting a delaying action. According to data from 15 March 1945, of the 24 available Hungarian Panzer IVs, 16 were in combat-ready condition, but neither of the two Hungarian Panthers were.

The command of the Hungarian 2nd Honvéd Armoured Division ordered the village to be reoccupied by the armoured force. However, the terrain was inadequate for the armoured fighting vehicles to negotiate, due to the thick undergrowth and there was not a sufficient amount of infantry support against the superiority of the Soviets. As a result, the Hungarian tank commanders reported one after the other via radio that their tanks had "broken down", in order to avoid taking part in combat.[863]

According to the observations of *1. Batterie/SS-Panzer-Flak-Abteilung 3* in combat at Söréd, the Soviets were targeting Felsőpuszta 1.5 km north of Magyaralmás with multiple rocket launchers and that a number of armoured fighting vehicles had been burnt out.[864] The Soviet armoured fighting vehicles were advancing on the road leading from Csákberény towards Söréd.[865]

---

859 Central Archives of the Russian Defence Ministry (Podolsk), f. 243, op. 2928, gy. 131, li. 247.
860 Central Archives of the Russian Defence Ministry (Podolsk), f. 243, op. 2928, gy. 178, li. 84.
861 Central Archives of the Russian Defence Ministry (Podolsk), f. 243, op. 2928, gy. 131, li. 247.
862 Malakhov, M. M.: A Balatontól Bécsig (excerpt). In: *Fejezetek hazánk felszabadításának történetéből*. Budapest, 1960. p. 187.
863 Norbert Számvéber: A hazáért mind halálig. Vitéz Tarczay Ervin páncélos százados. In: Regiment 2005/2.
864 A few days later German prisoners had seen the wrecks of four T–34/85s and one IS–2 heavy tank near the farmstead. See Vopersal, Wolfgang: *Soldaten, Kämpfer, Kameraden. Marsch und Kämpfe der SS-Totenkopfdivision*. Band Vb. Bielefeld, 1991. p. 720. These Soviet armoured fighting vehicles were knocked out during combat around the beginning of January 1945, but the Soviet rockets must have set them aflame them once again.
865 Stöber, Hans: *Die Flugabwehrverbände der Waffen-SS. Aufstellung, Gliederung, Luftverteidigung und Einsätze an den Fronten*. Preussisch Oldendorf, 1984. p. 556.

Between Söréd and Csókakő, the armoured personnel carriers of *SS-Panzer-Aufklärungs-Abteilung 3* were covering the frontline.[866]

The strongest Soviet attacks had fallen on the front of *Divisionsgruppe "Totenkopf"* and *3. SS-Panzer-Division* had sealed off a number of penetrations. The *Divisionskommandeur* deployed all of the reserves from his command post at Fehérvárcsurgó on the same day. Thus, *3. SS-Panzer-Division* held the frontline section that was assigned to them on the first day.[867]

The Panther tanks of *I. (Abteilung)/SS-Panzer-Regiment 3* were in combat in subordination to *I. (Bataillon)/SS-Panzergrenadier-Regiment 5* in the sector of Magyaralmás. Four tanks were in action east of Magyaralmás near the frontline with three Panthers north of Magyaralmás supporting the motorized rifle forces of the Hungarian 2nd Armoured Division, and one command Panther was stationed in Magyaralmás, at the outermost houses of the village. During the day, another two Panthers arrived from the repair workshop company at Söréd. The attack of the Soviet 98th Guards Rifle Division against Magyaralmás and Borbálamajor was introduced by a heavy preparatory artillery barrage, which inflicted casualties to *I. (Abteilung)/SS-Panzer-Regiment 3*. Around 1500 hours, five Panthers and two Panzer IV tanks, with *I. (Bataillon)/SS-Panzergrenadier-Regiment 5*, launched a counterattack against the 98th Guards Rifle Division. The *Panzergrenadiers* left their armoured personnel carriers in Magyaralmás and rode on the Panthers. When the counterattack was launched, one of the *SS-Panzergrenadiers* who hailed from Transylvania, was hit by a Soviet rifle bullet, fell off the vehicle and was crushed under its tracks. Four Panthers were attacking from Magyaralmás toward Borbálamajor and the fifth Panther was guarding their flank. The attempt was repulsed by the Soviets, while knocking out or immobilising all five of the Panthers. One of the vehicles was bogged down in the mud 1.5 km east of Magyaralmás, after its tracks were damaged by one of the 57 mm anti-tank guns of the Soviet 302th Guards Rifle Regiment near Hill 225. The crew abandoned the vehicle.[868]

Around 1600 hours, one of the *Panzergrenadier-Bataillons* of *3. SS-Panzer-Division* launched a new counterattack with the support of 15 armoured fighting vehicles against part of the 98th Guards Rifle Division directly east of Magyaralmás. Forty minutes later, Soviet multiple rocket launchers opened fire on the sector of the Catholic church and the main street of Magyaralmás, where a battalion-size force of German infantry and four Panther tanks were gathering.[869]

The three Panther tanks deployed north of Magyaralmás were also engaged in heavy artillery fire, which made visual contact between the armoured fighting vehicles extremely difficult. The Soviet rifle infantry attacked the armoured fighting vehicles with anti-tank mines, which in turn tried to keep the enemy tank destroyer teams at bay with machine gun fire. The turret of one of the Panthers became stuck due to the detonation of an anti-

---

[866] Vopersal, Wolfgang: *Soldaten, Kämpfer, Kameraden. Marsch und Kämpfe der SS-Totenkopfdivision*. Band Vb. Bielefeld, 1991. p. 724.
[867] Tieke, Wilhelm: *Von Plattensee bis Österreich. Heeresgruppe Süd 1945*. Gummersbach, without year of publication, p. 45.
[868] Vopersal, Wolfgang: *Soldaten, Kämpfer, Kameraden. Marsch und Kämpfe der SS-Totenkopfdivision*. Band Vb. Bielefeld, 1991. p. 719., and Wood, Ian Michael: *History of the Totenkopf's Panther-Abteilung*. Keszthely, 2015. p. 93.
[869] Wood, Ian Michael: *History of the Totenkopf's Panther-Abteilung*. Keszthely, 2015. p. 93.

tank mine. The three German armoured fighting vehicles retreated to Magyaralmás. The Germans noticed that while the Soviet infantry was valiantly attacking the Panthers, they did not engage the Tiger E heavy tanks of *SS-Panzer-Regiment 3*.[870]

Southeast of Sárkeresztes, at Point 166 on the Székesfehérvár–Zámoly road, the Soviet troops overran the forward positions of *SS-Panzergrenadier-Regiment 6*. The *Regimentskommandeur*, *SS-Obersturmbannführer* Franz Kleffner was killed when his command armoured personnel carrier was directly hit.

Sárkeresztes was defended by *I. (Bataillon)/SS-Panzergrenadier-Regiment 6* and the Panzer IV tanks of *5. Kompanie/SS-Panzer-Regiment 3*. The Soviet rifle infantry had overrun the positions of one of the battalions of the Hungarian 20th Honvéd Infantry Division and only the direct fire of the *Wespe* and *Hummel* self-propelled howitzers of *I. (Abteilung)/SS-Panzer-Artillerie-Regiment 3* was able to stop them. The Panzer IV tanks were supporting their own infantry with high-explosive shells.[871]

The incursion of the Soviet 4th Guards and 9th Guards Army was sealed off by the Germans on a line following the northern exit road from Székesfehérvár 4 km–Sárkeresztes northeast 3 km Borbálapuszta–Magyaralmás road east two km–Csákberény, and launched counterattacks.[872] During the fighting on that day,13 Soviet armoured fighting vehicles were reported to have been knocked out in the front of *IV. SS-Panzerkorps*.[873]

On the same day, north of Székesfehérvár the rifle forces of the Soviet 9th Guards Army were supported by the 1513th and 1523rd Self-Propelled Artillery Regiments. The 25 SU–76M self-propelled guns of the 1524th Self-Propelled Artillery Regiment were standing in army reserve at Ráckeresztúr. By the end of the day, the 1523rd Self-Propelled Artillery Regiment was fighting on the eastern slopes of Hill 231 (Tóhelydomb) 2.5 km southeast of Söréd and lost seven burnt out SU–76Ms.

The 1513th Self-Propelled Artillery Regiment was supporting the 303rd Guards Rifle Regiment/99th Guards Rifle Division and was engaged in combat 1.5 km east of Moha during the evening. They reported five burnt out SU-76Ms 6 km north of Székesfehérvár, in the eastern outskirts of Sárkeresztes while another three were waiting for the recovery vehicles. By the evening, the 1523rd Self-Propelled Artillery Regiment had 19 operational armoured fighting vehicles left, and the 1513th Self-Propelled Artillery Regiment had 16 operational armoured fighting vehicles.[874]

On the same day, the 3rd Ukrainian Front received several new armoured fighting

---

870 Wood, Ian Michael: *History of the Totenkopf's Panther-Abteilung*. Keszthely, 2015. pp. 93-94.
871 Vopersal, Wolfgang: *Soldaten, Kämpfer, Kameraden. Marsch und Kämpfe der SS-Totenkopfdivision*. Band Vb. Bielefeld, 1991. p. 717-718.
872 NARA, T311, R162, F7214590.
873 NARA, T311, R163, F7215361.
874 Central Archives of the Russian Defence Ministry (Podolsk), f. 243, op. 2928, gy. 131, li. 247. Interestingly, the 1513rd Self-Propelled Artillery Regiment's own evening report depicts a much heavier armoured fighting vehicle loss, 14 burnt out SU-76Ms and one in need of major repair and reports only 10 remaining operational self-propelled guns. See Central Archives of the Russian Defence Ministry (Podolsk), f. 911, op. 1, gy. 169, li. 227. What might be the reason for the difference? On that day, *IV. SS-Panzerkorps* reported knocking out only 13 Soviet armoured fighting vehicles, and this covers the combined armoured fighting vehicle losses of the 1513rd and 1523rd Self-Propelled Artillery Regiments, plus the 4th Guards Army on that day. Based on this, according to the author's opinion, it is probable that the 1513rd Self-Propelled Artillery Regiment was hit by the "friendly fire" of Soviet ground attack aircraft or artillery, and this caused the destruction of nine SU–76Ms. Unfortunately the regimental report does not contain a single reference to these events. Later, in summarizing of the losses of the 9th Guards Army, these nine destroyed self-propelled guns were not taken into account, which supports the author's assumption.

vehicles. Altogether, 51 SU–76Ms arrived, of which 21 were allocated to the independent self-propelled artillery battalions of the 4th Guards Army at Ócsa, 12 were sent from Siklós to the 122nd Independent Self-Propelled Artillery Battalion/84th Rifle Division, seven were sent from Szekszárd to the 72nd Guards Independent Self-Propelled Artillery Battalion/68th Guards Rifle Division, five were given to the 432nd Independent Self-Propelled Artillery Battalion/316th Rifle Division, and six were allocated to the 18th Tank Corps.[875]

The forces of the Front had not fully completed the tasks assigned for the first day of the offensive, but they managed to push into the defences of the German-Hungarian forces at a number of locations. Because of this, it became necessary for the Front to deploy the tank and larger mechanized units in order to be able to exploit the success achieved so far. However, these units were not yet available in combat-readiness at that time behind the 4th Guards and 9th Guards Armies. Therefore on that day, the Soviet high command ordered the 2nd Ukrainian Front to hand over the 6th Guards Tank Army to the 3rd Ukrainian Front.[876] As well, the rifle forces had not yet managed to break through the tactical depth of the German-Hungarian defences, therefore the new tank and mechanized forces to be deployed needed to complete this latter task as well.

On the frontline of the 2nd Ukrainian Front

The Soviets launched seven different attacks of battalion and regiment-size against the positions of the 1st Hussars Division/Hungarian VIII Army Corps. The attacking forces were wedged into the right flank of the Army Corps and the left flank of *IV. SS-Panzerkorps*. The Soviets had also breached the defences west of Pusztakápolna, on the Csákvár–Kecskéd road, west of Vérteskozma, and 4 km north of Vérteskozma. At these points, the German and Hungarian forces tried to eliminate the penetrations by deploying local reserves. Kőhányáspuszta and Várgesztes along the important mountain passes fell into Soviet hands, but southeast of Felsőgalla and Csabdi the assault attempts were repelled by the defenders.[877]

The German *Füsilier-Bataillon 96*, subordinated to the Hungarian 1st Hussars Division, was retreating while engaged in delaying actions from Majkpuszta towards Kecskéd. At the road junction 2 km southeast of Kecskéd, the *Bataillon* established contact with the assault gun-battery sent from *Panzergrenadier-Brigade 92 (mot.)* as reinforcement.[878] In the evening, the *Füsilier-Bataillon* established defences at Kecskéd together with the assault guns, a Hungarian 10.5 cm light field artillery battery and a cavalry battalion. After nightfall, Soviet troops launched an attack against the village with heavy artillery support. The German–Hungarian troops repelled the attack with the help of the assault guns, and eliminated a local incursion. Around midnight, the *Kommandeur* of *Panzergrenadier-Brigade 92 (mot.)*, *Oberst* Herbert Grosser, arrived at Kecskéd, then left three assault

---

[875] Central Archives of the Russian Defence Ministry (Podolsk), f. 243, op. 2928, gy. 131, li. 249th
[876] Malakhov, M. M.: A Balatontól Bécsig (excerpt). In: *Fejezetek hazánk felszabadításának történetéből*. Budapest, 1960. p. 186.
[877] NARA, T311, R162, F7214591.
[878] *Panzergrenadier-Brigade 92 (mot.)* did not have assault guns of their own. Most likely one of the batteries of *Sturmartillerie-Brigade 239* was sent to support *Füsilier-Bataillon 96*. At this time, *Sturmartillerie-Brigade 239* was directly subordinated to the Hungarian 3rd Army.

guns in the village and promised that a pioneer company would be sent there to blow up the bridge on Által Creek.[879]

On the front of the German *711. Infanterie-Division*, southwest of Kirva, the Soviets breached the defences with a battalion-size force, however the defenders launched a counterattack here as well.[880]

The rifle forces of the Soviet 46th Army were supported by three self-propelled artillery regiments in the most important lines of assault in order to break through the depths of the tactical defence of the German–Hungarian units.

On the same day, the armoured strength of the 991st Self-Propelled Artillery Regiment consisted of 18 operational SU–76M self-propelled guns and three captured Panther tanks[881]. The Regiment, in subordination to the 52nd Rifle Division/68th Rifle Corps, commenced assault operations in the sector of Csákvár. During the march to the point of departure via Zsámbék–Bicske–Vértesboglár–Csákvár, one SU–76M and the three Panther tanks became disabled due to mechanical problems. The commander of the Regiment, Lieutenant Colonel Vasily Ivanovich Gorgeyev, discussed the details of cooperation with the battalion commanders of the 429th Rifle Regiment. Every self-propelled artillery battery was reinforced with an engineer (pioneer) unit.

The 991st Self-Propelled Artillery Regiment was assigned to work together with the 429th Rifle Regiment and attack in the direction of Kőhányáspuszta–Oroszlány–Dad, occupy Oroszlány and then Dad. At 0400 hours, the SU–76M self-propelled guns occupied their positions on the south-western slopes of Kotló Hill. At 1400 hours, following a 30 minute artillery barrage, the penal company of the 52nd Rifle Division launched an attack in order to occupy Kőhányáspuszta. At 1500 hours, the 991st Self-Propelled Artillery Regiment also set out, and moved forward to the edge of the little forest northwest of Kőhányáspuszta together with the 2nd Battalion/429th Rifle Regiment.[882]

The 1505th Self-Propelled Artillery Regiment, waiting three km northeast of Csákvár, consisted of 16 operational SU–76Ms, five captured German assault guns and a *Wespe* self-propelled howitzer at the beginning of the attack. The armoured units were given the task to coordinate with the 431st Rifle Regiment/52nd Rifle Division and launch an attack in the Majkpuszta–Kőhányáspuszta–Oroszlány–Bokod railway station–Dad direction, then reach the road junction 2 km northwest of Majkpuszta, and cut through the Dad–Kömlőd road. The 1505th Self-Propelled Artillery Regiment set off at 1400 hours with the rifle units.[883]

The 1897th Self-Propelled Artillery Regiment was waiting for the launch of the attack 800 meters north of Újbarok with 21 operational SU–76M self-propelled guns. The Regiment was subordinated to the 180th Rifle Division and was to support the rifle forces, but in the end it was not deployed on that day.[884]

The Soviet 2nd Guards Mechanized Corps was gathered in the sector of Csákvár,

---

[879] Pohlman, Hartwig: *Geschichte der 96. Infanterie-Division, 1939–1945*. Bad Nauheim, 1959. p. 375.
[880] NARA, T311, R162, F7214591.
[881] The three Panther tanks were captured by the Soviets in Buda in February 1945, then they were allotted to the 991st Self-Propelled Artillery Regiment stationed in the sector of Mány on 20 February but needed repair. See Central Archives of the Russian Defence Ministry (Podolsk), f. 240, op. 2799, gy. 342, li. 183.
[882] Central Archives of the Russian Defence Ministry (Podolsk), f. 240, op. 2799, gy. 342, li. 109.
[883] Central Archives of the Russian Defence Ministry (Podolsk), f. 240, op. 2799, gy. 342, li. 112.
[884] Central Archives of the Russian Defence Ministry (Podolsk), f. 240, op. 2799, gy. 342, li. 115.

Gurdimajor and Móricmajor with orders to set off the following day from the Alsógalla–Oroszlány–Pusztavám sector and with infantry of the 68th and 75th Rifle Corps, to arrive at the Tata–Kocs line by the end of the first day of the assault, and to occupy the sector of Komárom and Ács by the end of the second day. One of the brigades of the Corps was to counter and stop the German-Hungarian troops retreating towards the west in the sector of Dunaalmás–Agostyán.[885]

The 112th Independent Self-Propelled Artillery Battalion/99th Rifle Division with three operational SU–76Ms and one T–70 tank was stationed on the southern edge of Tabajd.[886]

In the sector of the assault of the 46th Army, the Danube Flotilla was employed with 29 armoured gunboats amongst other craft.[887] Depending on different types, these were equipped with, apart from anti-aircraft heavy machine guns and possibly multiple rocket launcher mounts, two T-34 turrets on type 1124, and one on type 1125. These were also called "water tanks".[888]

The German *Luftflotte 4.* had supported the German troops flying approximately 300 missions in the sector of *2. Panzerarmee*, along the Sárvíz, and north of Székesfehérvár. The fighter and ground attack aircraft pilots reported to have shot down 28 Soviet aircraft, four of which were unconfirmed[889]. Apart from this, the German and Hungarian ground attack aircraft bombed the railway stations of Dombóvár and Sárszentmiklós too.[890]

The Soviet night bomber units targeted Veszprém during the evening hours, as well as the railway stations of Herend and Szentgál, the road between Ajka and Városlőd and the road traffic. Due to the air raid, the crude oil and fuel supplies stored at the railway station of Herend were blown up. 17 people were left dead and 30 were wounded in the blast.[891]

German reconnaissance assumed that the Soviet 2nd Guards Mechanized Corps and the 23rd Tank Corps, were deployed in the assault initiated north of Székesfehérvár, but without any significant replacements in terms of armoured fighting vehicles so far.[892]

West of the Vértes, the Germans concentrated *Panzergrenadier-Brigade 92 (mot.)*[893], *Sturmgeschütz-Brigade 325*, and *Panzer-Aufklärungs-Abteilung 1/1. Panzer-Division* in Nádasdladány, because they were anticipating a breakthrough of the Soviets via the passes in the mountains towards Komárom, exploiting the weak points in the defences of the Hungarian 1st Hussars Division[894]. Therefore, *Armeegruppe "Balck"* requested the withdrawal of *356. Infanterie-Division* from the Seregélyes bridgehead to move it west of the Vértes.

---

885 Central Archives of the Russian Defence Ministry (Podolsk), f. 240, op. 2799, gy. 357, li. 7.
886 Central Archives of the Russian Defence Ministry (Podolsk), f. 961, op. 1, gy. 340, li. 157.
887 Malakhov, M. M.: Magyarország felszabadításának befejezése. In: *Magyarország felszabadítása*. Budapest, 1975. p. 318.
888 See http://wio.ru/fleet/ww2armorb.htm (last retrieved: 27 September 2016.)
889 NARA, T311, R163, F7215358.
890 NARA, T311, R162, F7214592.
891 HM HIM Hadtörténelmi Levéltár (Budapest), m. kir. Honvéd Vezérkar Főnöke irata, Fővezérség napi helyzettájékoztatói, 1945. március 16-i és március 17-i jelentés. (*Daily situational reports of the High Command, reports from 16 and 17 March.*)
892 NARA, T311, R162, F7214593.
893 The vanguard units of the motorized units of the Brigade arrived at the Nagyigmánd sector on that day. According to Soviet reconnaissance data, the Brigade had five tanks as well. See Central Archives of the Russian Defence Ministry (Podolsk), f. 240, op. 2799, gy. 357, li. 7. Most likely however these were assault guns subordinated to the Brigade.
894 On that day, the Hungarian 1st Cavalry Division received the German *96. Infanterie-Division*'s *Füsilier-Bataillon 96*.

The German *Oberkommando des Heeres* gave permission for the regrouping of *Volks-Artillerie-Korps 403*, and all of the armoured reconnaissance battalions[895] into the sector west of the Vértes, however the decision to withdraw *356. Infanterie-Division* had to be made by Hitler.[896]

At the German *Heeresgruppe,* their own plan to concentrate the armoured assault east of the Sárvíz was still being considered. At 0730 hours that morning, the telegram from the Führer giving permission to launch a concentrated attack with *I. SS* and *II. SS-Panzerkorps* and *III. Panzerkorps* under command of the German *6. Panzerarmee.* At 2130 hours in the evening the German *6. Panzerarmee* sent the timetable for the regrouping action to the *Heeresgruppe.*[897] At 2305 hours that night *General der Infanterie* Wöhler discussed the attack plan with *Generaloberst* Guderian. The commander of *Heeresgruppe Süd* reported that he had issued orders to *6. Armee* and *6. Panzerarmee,* that the assault east of the Sárvíz was to be carried out regardless of the men or materials available, and to break through the Soviet defence at last. Guderian agreed and elaborated on the necessity of the armoured fighting vehicles arriving on the banks of the Danube in one night, because there was a precedent during Operation *"Konrad 3",* on the night of 18/19 January 1945.[898] However the Soviet attack launched on the same day around midday north of Székesfehérvár practically put an end to German expectations.

17 March 1945, Saturday

(**WEATHER**: highest daytime temperature 10 Celsius, sky mostly cloudy, local showers. The condition of the roads had worsened again due to rain.)

The 1891st Self-Propelled Artillery Regiment supporting the 122nd Rifle Division in combat along the Dráva line for the occupation of Drávacsehi, had that day, knocked out four mortars, two flamethrowers, and four machine guns. Their own losses amounted to one burnt out SU–76M, leaving the Regiment with 15 operational self-propelled guns.[899]

On the same day, the Bulgarian 1st Independent Tank Battalion/1st Army was provided with captured enemy armoured fighting vehicles from the 3rd Ukrainian Front to be able to replace the armoured losses they had suffered since the beginning of March:

- three StuG. III assault guns,
- two StuG. IV/Jagdpanzer IV/Panzer IV/70 *Jagdpanzers,*

---

895   On that day, *Panzer-Aufklärungs-Abteilungs 1, 3* and *6* were directly subordinated to *III. Panzerkorps,* but at that time, *Kampfgruppe "Streith"* was created under command of *Oberst* Streith, *Regimentskommandeur* of *Panzer-Regiment 1,* for the time being with the following units: *Panzer-Aufklärungs-Abteilungs 3* and *6,* and *schwere Panzer-Abteilung 509.* The following day, on 17 March 1945, this *Kampfgruppe* was to launch an attack against the Soviet troops that had crossed the railway line between Székesfehérvár and Lake Velence. See BAMA, N 106/4, Hermann Breith páncélos tábornok naplója, 1945. március 16. (Diary of *General der Panzertruppe* Breith, 16 March 1945.)
896   NARA, T311, R162, F7214594.
897   NARA, T311, R162, F7214596.
898   NARA, T311, R162, F7214598.
899   Central Archives of the Russian Defence Ministry (Podolsk), f. 243, op. 2928, gy. 131, li. 251.

- four Jagdpanzer 38(t) *Jagdpanzers*,
- one Hungarian Turán tank,
- two Italian Semovente L.40 da 47/32 self-propelled guns.[900]

The captured armoured fighting vehicles were transported by trains from the Budafok workshop of the 3rd mobile tank repair workshop.

On the front of the German *XXII. Gebirgskorps/2. Panzerarmee, 16. SS-Panzergrenadier-Division*[901] continued its assault together with the subordinated *Sturmbataillon "Rudno"* at 0400 hours from the south-western outskirts of Csömend towards the south and southeast. The Germans met little to no resistance, and reached the Csömend southwest three km (Gyótapuszta)–Csömend south 2.5 km road junction line.[902]

The Soviet motorized rifle battalions of the 32nd Independent Guards Mechanized Brigade and the 864th Self-Propelled Artillery Regiment, continued the defensive battle southwards, on the Bize–Üsztőpuszta–Szőkepuszta–Hill 146 (Nyírespuszta) line. The Self-Propelled Artillery Regiment supported the 1st Motorized Rifle Battalion/32nd Independent Guards Mechanized Brigade near Hill 146, but lost seven knocked out SU–76Ms of which five were burnt out, leaving them with nine remaining operational self-propelled guns. They reported to have eliminated two German assault guns, 15 cars, five mortars and 11 machine guns.[903]

On the night of 16/17 March 1945, *1. Volks-Gebirgs-Division* cleared Csömend, and at dawn launched an attack towards the east via the bridge occupied east of the village. However, the attempt was halted by the fire of eight T-34 tanks of the Soviet 20th Guards Rifle Division and the 52nd Tank Regiment[904], and the German mountain troops went over on the defence in the sector of Nikla.[905]

On the right flank of the German *I. Kavallerie-Korps/6. Panzerarmee,* the Hungarian 25th Infantry Division[906] with the subordinated Hungarian multiple rocket launchers, kept the unit concentration area, complete with armoured fighting vehicles, under fire in the area of Balatonszabadi.[907]

The units of *3. Kavallerie-Division* were withdrawn from the bridgehead occupied on the southern bank of the Sió Canal, as they were to assemble in the sector of Balatonaliga,

---

900 Matev, Kaloyan: *The Armoured Forces of the Bulgarian Army 1936–45*. Solihull, 2015. p. 325. There was an independent battery organized from the German assault guns and the *Jagdpanzers* within the tank battalion. A Hungarian Turán tank and two Italian self-propelled guns were assigned to a reconnaissance section of the reconnaissance company of the battalion. Originally, the Soviets wanted to reassign one Panther tank and two Hungarian Nimród self-propelled anti-aircraft guns but they had not yet arrived.

901 The strength of *16. SS-Panzergrenadier-Division* was 9966 men, of which 3432 were ready for service as infantry. *SS-Panzer-Abteilung 16* had 15 combat-ready assault guns, and 19 7.5 cm anti-tank guns. The combat strength of the *Panzergrenadiers* in one average and five weak battalions, together with *SS-Panzer-Aufklärungs-Abteilung 16*, was approximately 700 men. The *I. (Bataillon)/Volks-Gebirgsjäger-Regiment 98* was also subordinated to the *Division*. *SS-Artillerie-Regiment 16* had six light and three heavy batteries. The *SS-Division* was only capable for defence, and its mobility was 40 percent. See NARA, T311, R163, F7214975.

902 NARA, T311, R162, F7214606.

903 Central Archives of the Russian Defence Ministry (Podolsk), f. 243, op. 2928, gy. 131, li. 251.

904 Central Archives of the Russian Defence Ministry (Podolsk), f. 243, op. 2928, gy. 131, li. 251.

905 NARA, T311, R162, F7214606.

906 The 13 combat-ready Jagdpanzer 38(t) *Jagdpanzers* of the Hungarian 20th Assault Artillery Battalion were also in subordination to the Hungarian Division. See NARA, T311, R163, F7214975.

907 NARA, T311, R162, F7214606.

to be able to launch an attack against the concentrated Soviet forces in the sector of Siófok. The *4. Kavallerie-Division* however continued to successfully defend the bridgehead 2 km northwest of Szabadhídvég, in the sector of Hill 146, where the Soviets launched seven attacks, each of battalion or regimental strength, with significant artillery and multiple rocket launcher fire support, and six armoured fighting vehicles. The Soviet troops suffered heavy losses due to counter-fire from the German artillery and *Panzerjäger-Abteilung 70/4. Kavallerie-Division*[908]. The Soviet 22nd Independent Tank Regiment lost three destroyed T–34s during this action.[909] The German losses were also significant.[910]

During the evening following the engagement, the Soviet 22nd Independent Tank Regiment was in action with three T–34s and one SU–76M self-propelled gun at Szabadhídvég, and with three T–34s at the Zsófia children's sanitarium at Balatonszabadi-fürdőtelep.[911]

The *3. Kavallerie-Division*[912] pushed the Soviet forces to the southern bank of the Sió Canal in the northern outskirts of Felsőnyék, although the Soviets had also gained ground on the northern bank during the afternoon.[913]

The *12. SS-Panzer-Division/I. SS-Panzerkorps*[914] together with the forces of *SS-Panzergrenadier-Regiment 25*, eliminated the Soviet bridgehead north of Ozora, and blew up the bridge found there.[915]

Meanwhile the units of the *Division* had started regrouping. On that day, the strength of the *Division* was 12,128 men, of which 4780 were combat-ready. The combat strength of the *Panzergrenadiers* was approximately 1600 soldiers in one strong, three medium and three weak battalions. The artillery consisted of six light, and one heavy howitzer battery, one 10 cm gun battery and four multiple rocket launcher batteries. The *Division* was suitable for attack in a limited capacity and its mobility was 51 percent.[916]

On the front of *1. SS-Panzer-Division*,[917] the Soviets carried out two reconnaissance missions from the south against the Simontornya bridgehead held by the Germans, however the *SS*-troops drove them back. The Soviets had been keeping the bridgehead and the newly completed military bridge under fire throughout the day. When a German Panzer IV/70 (V) *Jagdpanzer* attempted to cross the bridge, it collapsed, probably because it had already been damaged by earlier artillery fire. The Germans immediately started to repair it.[918]

On that day, the relief of the *Division* and its relocation to the north began. While the *SS-Panzergrenadiers* were in defence during the whole day south of Simontornya, their

---

908 The *70. Panzerjäger-Abteilung 70/4. Kavallerie-Division* had only two combat-ready assault guns on that day. See NARA, T311, R163, F7214975.
909 Central Archives of the Russian Defence Ministry (Podolsk), f. 243, op. 2928, gy. 178, li. 84.
910 NARA, T311, R162, F7214606-7214607.
911 Central Archives of the Russian Defence Ministry (Podolsk), f. 243, op. 2928, gy. 131, li. 251.
912 On that day, *3. Kavallerie-Division* had five combat-ready assault guns and three Jagdpanzer IV *Jagdpanzers*. See NARA, T311, R163, F7214976.
913 NARA, T311, R162, F7214607.
914 On that day, *12. SS-Panzer-Division* had six combat-ready Panthers and 12 Panzer IV tanks, plus 12 Panzer IV/70 (V) *Jagdpanzers*. The *schwere Panzerjäger-Abteilung 560* in subordination to them had eight combat-ready Panzer IV/70 (V)s and three Jagdpanther *Jagdpanzers*. See NARA, T311, R163, F7215012.
915 NARA, T311, R162, F7214607.
916 NARA, T311, R163, F7215012.
917 Based on data of that day, *1. SS-Panzer-Division* had 14 combat-ready Panther and 14 Panzer IV tanks plus four Panzer IV/70 (V) *Jagdpanzers*. The subordinated *schwere SS-Panzer-Abteilung 501* had nine combat-ready Tiger B heavy tanks. See NARA, T311, R163, F7215012.
918 NARA, T311, R162, F7214607.

heavy armament was gradually withdrawn via the canal. However, as the military bridge collapsed again, the withdrawal had to be postponed until the next day.[919]

Of the 12,370 men of the *Division,* only 4215 were ready for service. The infantry consisted of a medium strength, four average and two weak battalions, with a combat strength of approximately 1300 soldiers. The divisional artillery had three light and three heavy howitzer batteries, a gun battery and two multiple rocket launchers. The mobility of the unit was 68 percent and it was held to be suitable for limited scope attacks.[920]

The *23. Panzer-Division*[921] proceeded to relieve *1. SS-Panzer-Division* in the Simontornya bridgehead. The combat-ready tanks of *Panzer-Regiment 23,* under command of *Oberleutnant* Quintel, were being moved toward Simontornya, however before reaching the village, they were met with heavy Soviet artillery attacks and continuous Soviet ground-attack air raids were carried out against them. During the day, *Panzergrenadier-Regiments 126* and *128* distributed the freshly arrived supplies among the companies, and on the night of 17/18 March 1945, they proceeded to relieve the *Panzergrenadiers* of *1. SS-Panzer-Division*. All three *Abteilung* of *Panzergrenadier-Regiment 128* established firing positions north of Simontornya.[922]

The Soviet 209th Self-Propelled Artillery Brigade, with its strength distributed among firing positions scattered along the southern bank of the Sió Canal, was not engaged in battle on that day. Its strength consisted of 46 operational SU–100s, two SU–57s and two T–34s.[923]

In the section of *II. SS-Panzerkorps, 44. Reichsgrenadier-Division*[924] launched an attack at 0445 hours against a reinforced Sárkeresztúr, defended by significant Soviet forces. The Germans reached the railroad line from the east with a battalion-size infantry unit and 10-12 armoured fighting vehicles, and their spearhead broke through the eastern part of the village. However, the forces of the Soviet 36th Guards Rifle Division, supported by the 1st Guards Mechanized Brigade and the 1821st Self-Propelled Artillery Regiment with 27 M4A2 tanks and five SU–100 self-propelled guns, launched a number of counterattacks and soon pushed them back to their point of departure.[925] During this action, Guards Lieutenant Lazariev, serving in the 18th Guards Tank Regiment, reported to have knocked out three German armoured fighting vehicles with his M4A2 tank.[926] On that day, during the course of the assault initiated by *44. Reichsgrenadier-Division*, based on German reports, two supporting Panther tanks from *2. SS-Panzer-Division* had been knocked out.[927]

---

919 Tiemann, Ralf: *Die Leibstandarte.* Band IV/2. Osnabrück, 1987. p. 294.
920 See NARA, T311, R163, F7215012.
921 On that day, *23. Panzer-Division* had seven combat-ready Panthers and seven Panzer IV tanks, two assault guns and nine Jagdpanzer IV *Jagdpanzers*. See NARA, T311, R163, F7214976.
922 Rebentisch, Ernst: *Zum Kaukasus und zu den Tauern. Die Geschichte der 23. Panzer-Division 1941–1945.* Esslingen, 1963. p. 491.
923 Central Archives of the Russian Defence Ministry (Podolsk), f. 243, op. 2928, gy. 131, li. 250.
924 Of the *44. Reichsgrenadier-Division*'s own Jagdpanzer 38(t) *Jagdpanzers*, only three were combat-ready on that day, however three Panther tanks and six StuG. III assault guns were combat-ready with the subordinated *2. SS-Panzer-Division.* Apart from these, eight Panthera and six Panzer IV tanks, six StuG. III assault guns, 13 Panzer IV/70 (V) and Jagdpanther *Jagdpanzers* were combat-ready with *2. SS-Panzer-Division.* The combat-ready armoured fighting vehicle strength of *9. SS-Panzer-Division* on that day consisted of 13 Panthers and 16 Panzer IV tanks, 11 assault guns, 10 Panzer IV/70 (V)s and eight Jagdpanther *Jagdpanzers.* See NARA, T311, R163, F7215012 and F7215013.
925 NARA, T311, R162, F7214607.
926 Summarized report of the 1st Guards Mechanized Corps of the combat actions during March – April 1945. Copy owned by the author. p. 11.
927 Agis, Hermann: *Das Ende am Plattensee. Die Hoch- und Deutschmeister (44. I.D.) im Endkampf.* Nürnberg, 2006. p. 175.

The armoured combat group of *2. SS-Panzer-Division* was still holding their forward positions around Heinrichmajor. The *III. (Bataillon)/SS-Panzergrenadier-Regiment 4*, supported by a few armoured fighting vehicles, was defending an almost completely destroyed house and its surroundings in continuous close combat.

The strength of the *Division* on that day was 11,633 men, of which 4575 were combat-ready. The infantry possessed four average and one medium strength battalion,with a combat strength of approximately 1100 soldiers. Two *Panzergrenadier* battalions were still stationed in the areas behind the frontline. The divisional artillery consisted of six light and three heavy batteries. The *Division* was suitable for attack in a limited capacity and its mobility was 60 percent.[928]

The Soviet 2nd Guards Mechanized Brigade with 27 M4A2s and 9th Guards Tank Brigade with 31 M4A2s of the 1st Guards Mechanized Corps, were assembling in the sector of Paks. Together with these, the Corps had on that day 118 operational M4A2s, three T–34/85s and 13 SU–100s.[929]

On the front of *9. SS-Panzer-Division,* combat actions of local significance were in progress. The strength of the *Division* was 10,820 men, of which 4614 were combat-ready. The combat strength of the *Panzergrenadier-Infanterie* in one medium strength, three strong and three weak battalions was approximately 1800 soldiers. Fifteen 7.5 cm anti-tanks guns, without their prime movers, were at the *Panzer-Feldreserve-Bataillon. SS-Panzer-Artillerie-Regiment 9* had four light and two heavy batteries, and two more were being replenished. The mobility of the *Division* was 65 percent, and was again found to be suitable for limited scope attacks.[930]

On the night of 16/17 March 1945, on the front of *III. Panzerkorps/Armeegruppe "Balck",* units of the German *1. Panzer-Division*[931] eliminated a Soviet penetration in the northeastern part of Gárdony.[932] In the second half of the day, after the evening had set in, the armoured *Kampfgruppe "Elias"/Panzer-Regiment 1* with 15 Panther tanks and the 20 armoured personnel carriers of the armoured pioneer companies, were covering the reoccupation of the front of *Panzergrenadier-Regiment 113*, following which, the unit was placed in defence between Agárdpuszta and the eastern outskirts of Seregélyes.[933]

Hajmáskér was raided by the Soviet air force at the same time the Panzer IV/70 *Jagdpanzers* of the *Panzerjäger-Abteilung/12. SS-Panzer-Division* were moving through the area. The repair workshop company of *Panzer-Regiment 1* working there suffered some losses.[934]

During the morning, the Soviets launched three containing attacks of company and battalion-size east of Seregélyes and northwest of Pusztaszabolcs, which were held off by the Germans.

---

928   Tieke, Wilhelm: *Von Plattensee bis Österreich. Heeresgruppe Süd 1945.* Gummersbach, without year of publication, p. 50.
929   Central Archives of the Russian Defence Ministry (Podolsk), f. 243, op. 2928, gy. 131, li. 252.
930   Tieke, Wilhelm: *Von Plattensee bis Österreich. Heeresgruppe Süd 1945.* Gummersbach, without year of publication, p. 50.
931   On that day, *1. Panzer-Division* had 14 combat-ready Panthers and one Panzer IV tank. See NARA, T311, R163, F7214976.
932   NARA, T311, R163, F7215363.
933   Stoves, Rolf: Persönliches Kriegstagebuch Pz.Rgt. 1 (typewritten manuscript, a copy owned by the author), entry from 17 March 1945
934   Stoves, Rolf: Persönliches Kriegstagebuch Pz.Rgt. 1 (typewritten manuscript, a copy owned by the author), entry from 17 March 1945

However in the afternoon, east of Seregélyes, four assaults from the south and southeast were launched against the positions of *3. Panzer-Division*[935], all with battalion strength and with the support of a few armoured fighting vehicles. The 181th Tank Brigade was supporting part of the 3rd Guards Airborne Division and at around 1600 hours, they occupied Mihálymajor and Ferencmajor. During this action, the Germans knocked out four T–34/85s of which, two were burnt out.

The 170th Tank Brigade escorted the forces of the 320th Rifle Division during their attack launched in the direction of Sándormajor, and lost one tank knocked out.[936] According to an officer of the Tank Brigade, 1st Lieutenant Brjukhov, they had hardly covered one km when the Germans stopped them, and by that time, the Brigade had already lost two tanks and a few dozen soldiers.[937]

In the Seregélyes sector, the Soviet troops were attacking with 20 armoured fighting vehicles, however the unit of *III. Panzerkorps*, with a short withdrawal, were able to hold up the attacks. During this combat action the Germans reported to have knocked out six Soviet tanks.[938]

At 1630 hours, the Germans launched a counterattack at Mihálymajor. The *3. Panzer-Division* reoccupied Mihálymajor and Ferencmajor with a regiment of *Panzergrenadier-Infanterie* and 15 armoured fighting vehicles. The 18th Tank Corps reported to have knocked out that day, three German tanks and four armoured personnel carriers while their own losses amounted to five knocked out T–34/85s, of which two were burnt out. Of those tanks that were not burnt out, two remained in Mihálymajor, in an area controlled by the Germans.[939]

Kampfgruppe "Streith"[940], consisting of *Panzer-Aufklärungs-Abteilung 3 and 6* plus *schwere Panzer-Abteilung 509*, did not succeed in their attempt that day to reoccupy the earlier German positions along the railroad line between Székesfehérvár and Lake Velence.[941] The *schwere Panzer-Abteilung 509* had 20 combat-ready Tiger B heavy tanks.[942]

Three km southeast of Székesfehérvár, at Point 134, the Soviet troops were supported by 21 SU–100 self-propelled guns of the 1004th Self-Propelled Artillery Regiment[943]/207th Self-Propelled Artillery Brigade, assigned from the 27th Army to the 4th Guards Army. The self-propelled guns were escorting the 204th Rifle Regiment/23rd Rifle Corps towards

---

935   On that day, *3. Panzer-Division* had 11 combat-ready Panthers and seven Panzer IV tanks, four Panzer IV/70 and Jagdpanzer IV *Jagdpanzers* plus one assault gun. See NARA, T311, R163, F7214976.
936   War log of the 18th Tank Corps for March 1945. Copy owned by the author. p. 27. The 181st Tank Brigade had eight, and the 170th Tank Brigade had three operational tanks; the 1438th Self-Propelled Artillery Regiment had nine remaining SU–76M self-propelled guns.
937   Bryukhov, Vasiliy: *Red Army Tank Commander. At War in a T–34 on the Eastern Front*. Barnsley, 2013. p. 178.
938   NARA, T311, R162, F7214608.
939   Central Archives of the Russian Defence Ministry (Podolsk), f. 243, op. 2928, gy. 131, li. 251.
940   The commander of the combat group became the *Kommandeur* of *Panzer-Regiment 1*, *Oberst* Egon Streith. He had originally been the commander of a Panther tank with turret number 956 from *Panzer-Regiment 1*, however, according to the diary of the 2nd radio operator and loader, *Obergefreiter* Erich Krüger, after his armoured fighting vehicle was knocked out and he was injured in the armoured battle on the Great Hungarian Plain on 7 October 1944, he had never sat in an armoured fighting vehicle again. See Krüger, Erich: Kriegstagebuch. Typewritten manuscript. Copy owned by the author. entry from 22 March 1945
941   BAMA, N 106/4, Diary of *General der Panzertruppe* Hermann Breith, 17 March 1945.
942   *History of the schwere Panzer-Abteilung 509* (typewritten manuscript). Copy owned by the author. p. 56.
943   The 1004th Self-Propelled Artillery Regiment arrived in the sector of Pákozd on 17 March 1945 at 0030 hours, and then continued their march towards Point 134.

Point 122 that dominated the railroad-road crossing 2 km southeast of there.[944] During the engagement with the German armoured fighting vehicles that were attacking from that direction, the Regiment reported to have destroyed four Tiger B and three Panther tanks. Their own losses were five knocked out self-propelled guns of which four were burnt out[945] and another three SU–100s were bogged down on the muddy terrain.[946]

Between Lake Velence and the Bicske–Bánhida railroad lines, the Soviet troops continued to attack with their rifle troops, which were also supported by armoured groups with no more than 20 armoured fighting vehicles in each case. The centres of these attacks were on the south-eastern and northern outskirts of Székesfehérvár, in the sector of Sárkeresztes and Söréd and along the Csákvár–Kecskéd and Vérteskozma–Környe roads.

The Soviet 1523rd Self-Propelled Artillery Regiment/9th Guards Army was in firing position with 19 SU–76Ms 2 km west of Csákberény and was keeping the German–Hungarian positions under fire. The 1513rd Self-Propelled Artillery Regiment was supporting the 98th Guards Rifle Division with 16 SU–76M self-propelled guns 6 km northwest of Székesfehérvár, in the western outskirts of Sárkeresztes and Belmajor.[947]

Between Sárkeresztes and Söréd the Soviet rifle forces, supported by armoured groups with no more than 10 armoured fighting vehicles, reached the Székesfehérvár–Söréd road on a wide front, despite heavy German defences in the area.

Sárkeresztes was defended by *I.* and *III. (Bataillons)/SS-Panzergrenadier-Regiment 6* with the Panzer IV tanks of *II. (Abteilung)/SS-Panzer-Regiment 3*, but units of the Soviet 98th Guards and 99th Guards Rifle Division outflanked and encircled the village, then occupied it with one concentrated assault. The German defenders broke out towards Moha.[948]

Early in the morning at Magyaralmás, five Panther tanks of 3. *SS-Panzer-Division* and a company of *I. (Bataillon)/SS-Panzergrenadier-Regiment 5* were assembling to carry out a counterattack against the 98th Guards Rifle Division that was assaulting the village. The Panthers attacked towards Borbálapuszta, against the right flank of the 296th Guards Rifle Regiment. The 2 cm self-propelled anti-aircraft guns of *14.(Flak) Kompanie/SS-Panzergrenadier-Regiment 5* were supporting them, but one of the guns was soon knocked out by the Soviets. The left flank of the 296th Guards Rifle Regiment was attacked by a force of approximately 20 German armoured fighting vehicles and one *Panzergrenadier-Bataillon*. Although the Panzer IV tanks of *II. (Abteilung)/SS-Panzer-Regiment 3* reached the edge of Borbálapuszta, the Panthers were pushed back to Magyaralmás.

Not long before 0700 hours in the morning, four Panther tanks and the units of *SS-Panzergrenadier-Regiment 5* were gathered on the eastern edges of Magyaralmás. Soviet artillery observers noticed them, and ordered a barrage from the multiple rocket launchers, which forced the Germans to withdraw. At the same time, two Panthers and two Panzer IVs were in firing positions on the eastern edge of Magyaralmás, and another two Panthers were inside the village itself. During the course of the morning, the German

---

944 War log of the 207th Self-Propelled Artillery Brigade, 17 March 1945. Copy owned by the author.
945 War log of the 207th Self-Propelled Artillery Brigade, 18 March 1945. Copy owned by the author.
946 Central Archives of the Russian Defence Ministry (Podolsk), f. 243, op. 2928, gy. 178, li. 86.
947 Central Archives of the Russian Defence Ministry (Podolsk), f. 243, op. 2928, gy. 178, li. 84.
948 Vopersal, Wolfgang: *Soldaten, Kämpfer, Kameraden. Marsch und Kämpfe der SS-Totenkopfdivision*. Band Vb. Bielefeld, 1991. p. 725.

tanks had successfully stopped the assault of the Soviet 98th Guards Rifle Division. The Soviets launched artillery barrages on the village with multiple rocket launchers a number of times. Around the church, four Panthers and two armoured personnel carriers were destroyed by the artillery fire. The command post of *I. (Abteilung)/SS-Panzer-Regiment 3* was directly hit, where the *Abteilungskommandeur,* SS-Hauptsturmführer dr. Alfons Martin, was killed.

On the Székesfehérvár–Mór road the *Divisionsbegleitkompanie* of *3. SS-Panzer-Division* was supported by one Panther tank together with one armoured personnel carrier mounting a 7.5 cm short-barrelled tank gun of *SS-Panzer-Aufklärungs-Abteilung 3*, together with a StuG. III assault gun of *SS-Panzerjäger-Abteilung 3*, while they were being pushed back from Söréd towards Magyaralmás. The Panther tank was firing high explosive shells at the Soviet rifle infantry attacking through an open field. At around noon, the Soviets managed to occupy the northern and middle parts of Magyaralmás.

The Panthers in combat in the village were retreating to Fehérvárcsurgó, where three tanks were soon attacked by Soviet Il–2 ground attack aircraft. The command of the remaining Panthers of *I. (Abteilung)/SS-Panzer-Regiment 3* was taken over by SS-Obersturmführer Lummitsch. Around 1600 hours, *I. (Bataillon)/SS-Panzergrenadier-Regiment 5,* abandoned the southern part of Magyaralmás and retreated, leaving 11 armoured personnel carriers behind. Around the village, the Soviets found the wrecks of 13 German armoured fighting vehicles and 13 armoured personnel carriers.[949]

The Tiger E tanks of *9. Kompanie/SS-Panzer-Regiment 3*, not including two in holding positions to the north, were standing in reserve at Magyaralmás and were making adjustments to their guns, using entrance doors as targets. Because of the Soviet attack, the Tigers were forced to retreat to Bodajk. En route, two of Tigers became bogged down in the mud. One of them was destroyed by the Germans with an 8.8 cm tank gun, and the other tank, with turret number 912, was successfully towed into Székesfehérvár.[950]

2.5 km southwest of Söréd, a gap appeared in the German frontline, and an attempt to close it was made by the armoured personnel carriers of *SS-Panzer-Aufklärungs-Abteilung 3* and StuG. III assault guns of *SS-Panzerjäger-Abteilung3*.[951]

The Soviet attack against Söréd, with approximately 1500 rifle troops was repelled by units of *3. SS-Panzer-Division* and the Hungarian 2nd Armoured Division. Captain Ervin Tarczay, an officer of the I Battalion/Hungarian 3rd Tank Regiment, returning from leave, joined the fighting on 17 March at Söréd. According to certain eyewitnesses, the Captain demanded a tank for himself, to execute the attack towards Csákberény that was ordered the day before. It is suspected that his motivation was to be awarded the Hungarian Officer's Gold Medal for Bravery (*Magyar Tiszti Arany Vitézségi Érem*).

Söréd, assaulted by the Soviet 332nd Guards Rifle Regiment/104th Guards Rifle Division, was not defended exclusively by the Hungarian armoured troops as the 2nd Honvéd Armoured Division was fighting in subordination to *3. SS-Panzer-Division/*

---

949   Wood, Ian Michael: *History of the Totenkopf's Panther-Abteilung.* Keszthely, 2015. pp. 96-97.
950   Schneider, Wolfgang: *Tiger der Division Totenkopf.* Uelzen, 2009. p. 253. The Tiger E that was towed into Székesfehérvár was later captured by the Soviets.
951   Vopersal, Wolfgang: *Soldaten, Kämpfer, Kameraden. Marsch und Kämpfe der SS-Totenkopfdivision.* Band Vb. Bielefeld, 1991. p. 726.

IV. SS-Panzerkorps. SS-Panzerjäger-Abteilung 3 was also stationed at Söréd under *SS-Sturmbannführer* Ludwig Zeitz. According to records from 15 March 1945, it had 13 StuG. III assault guns and three *Marder* tank destroyers in combat-ready condition plus its Jagdpanzer IV *Jagdpanzers* were in combat at Mór. Furthermore, the units of *SS-Panzer-Aufklärungs-Abteilung 3* were also there with armoured personnel carriers and at the last moment, the units of *I. (Bataillon)/SS-Panzergrenadier-Regiment 24* also arrived, commanded by *SS-Sturmbannführer* Hermann im Masche. Apart from this, *1. Batterie/ SS-Panzer-Flak-Abteilung 3* was also in combat at Söréd with 8.8 cm guns.

Captain Tarczay established firing positions with four Panzer IV tanks in Söréd among the houses that lined the road leading to Csákberény. Another three Hungarian Panzer IVs were waiting for the Soviet attack at the road crossing of Csókakő. Units of the Soviet 104th Guards Rifle Division launched furious infantry attacks, but suffered extreme losses from the fire of the Hungarian and German armoured fighting vehicles. Despite this, the Soviets had almost entirely encircled the village by the evening of 17 March 1945, and entrenched themselves within 300 meters of the houses. By that time, the ammunition of the Hungarian tanks and the German assault guns and tank destroyers was largely spent.[952]

At 1600 hours, *1. Batterie/SS-Panzer-Flak-Abteilung 3* was given orders to retreat to Bodajk. Their two 8.8 cm guns were to be placed in firing position at the railway station there. At the same time, the *Hummel* and *Wespe* self-propelled howitzers of *SS-Panzer-Artillerie-Regiment 3* raced past from Söréd towards Mór at high speed.[953]

The Soviets continued the attack and breached the frontline of 3. *SS-Panzer-Division* at multiple locations. By the evening the forces of the Red Army reached the Söréd–Sárkeresztes road and the latter village, and soon occupied Magyaralmás. North of Sárkeresztes, the Germans were still holding a few strongpoints in the evening. Part of the *Division* had successfully contained and stopped the Soviet attacks south of Csókakő and also 3.5 km east of Mór.[954]

SS-Panzer-Aufklärungs-Abteilung 3 sent out three heavy reconnaissance armoured cars toward the northwest from their command post at Csókakő in order to reconnoitre the 1 – 1.5 km wide gap in the frontline of the Hungarian 2nd Armoured Division. Two Hungarian Panzer IV tanks stood in firing position in the left bend of the road leading to Mór. As the 2 cm automatic cannons opened fire at the Soviet rifle infantry swarming out of the forest, they responded with anti-tank rifle fire. One of the 8.8 cm guns of *Festungs-Pak-Verband IX* was in firing position in the vicinity. Soviet artillery started to drop artillery fire on the area, so the German armoured cars returned to Csókakő around noon to replenish the ammunition in their vehicles.[955]

Soon a Soviet rifle assault was launched against Csókakő, which ended in heavy close quarters combat. One of the heavy armoured reconnaissance cars was knocked out. The

---

952 Norbert Számvéber: A hazáért mind halálig. Vitéz Tarczay Ervin páncélos százados. In: Regiment, issue 2005/2.
953 Stöber, Hans: *Die Flugabwehrverbände der Waffen-SS. Aufstellung, Gliederung, Luftverteidigung und Einsätze an den Fronten.* Preussisch Oldendorf, 1984. p. 557.
954 NARA, T311, R162, F7214608.
955 Vopersal, Wolfgang: *Soldaten, Kämpfer, Kameraden. Marsch und Kämpfe der SS-Totenkopfdivision.* Band Vb. Bielefeld, 1991. p. 729.

motorized rifle infantry of the Hungarian 2nd Armoured Division retreated in an orderly manner under cover of the Panzer IV tanks towards Mór.[956]

The remaining two German heavy armoured reconnaissance cars reached the two Hungarian Panzer IV tanks on the road leading to Mór around 1630 hours. According to one of the German armoured car commanders:

"I went to talk to the two tank commanders about how we could manage to keep this position. When I climbed up on the first tank, I saw that the crew was working at that very moment on how they could disable their vehicle. At the same moment we received strong fire from the Hungarian positions abandoned earlier. Csókakő is lost. The Russians were thrusting westwards from there. We set off for Mór on the valley road."[957]

Mór was defended by *III. (Bataillon)/SS-Panzergrenadier-Regiment 5/3. SS-Panzer-Division*, units of *SS-Panzer-Aufklärungs-Abteilung 3*, four Jagdpanzer IV *Jagdpanzers* of *1. Kompanie/SS-Panzerjäger-Abteilung 3* under *SS-Oberscharführer* Hans Mühlrath, and four Panzer IV tanks of the Hungarian 2nd Armoured Division. Although the Soviet troops managed to break into the village, the fire of the *SS-Jagdpanzers* and two heavy armoured reconnaissance cars repelled them again. *SS-Oberscharführer* Mühlrath suggested giving up Mór and establishing new defensive positions 5 km southwards along the railroad. However this was dismissed by his superiors, as Mór had to be held at all costs according to Hitler's.[958]

By the evening, the Soviets penetrated the frontline of *3. SS-Panzer-Division*, severing tactical contact with the *SS-Kampfgruppe*.[959]

The *5. SS-Panzer-Division* repelled an approximately division-size Soviet assault launched northeast and north of Székesfehérvár and inflicted heavy losses on the assaulting forces.[960]

However, *5. SS-Panzer-Division* did not have any reserves left to counter and eliminate one of the Soviet penetrations north of Székesfehérvár. Therefore reserve *Leutnant* Eugen Weyde (cover name Pankoff), commander of the "Jaguar" detachment of the German *Frontaufklärungstrupp 213*[961] dressed up as a Soviet Captain, took six captured Soviet T-34/85 tanks and 40 volunteers dressed as Soviet soldiers, either Germans speaking Russian or former Soviet prisoners of war, and assaulted the Soviet troops by surprise. The special German unit destroyed 15 light machine guns, 15 machine guns, eight anti-tank

---

956 Vopersal, Wolfgang: *Soldaten, Kämpfer, Kameraden. Marsch und Kämpfe der SS-Totenkopfdivision.* Band Vb. Bielefeld, 1991. p. 731.
957 Idézi Vopersal, Wolfgang: *Soldaten, Kämpfer, Kameraden. Marsch und Kämpfe der SS-Totenkopfdivision.* Band Vb. Bielefeld, 1991. pp. 731-732.
958 Mühlrath, Hans: Ungarn – Reise in die Vergangenheit.
959 Vopersal, Wolfgang: *Soldaten, Kämpfer, Kameraden. Marsch und Kämpfe der SS-Totenkopfdivision.* Band Vb. Bielefeld, 1991. p. 733.
960 NARA, T311, R162, F7214608.
961 These *Frontaufklärungstrupp*s were not only employed by the Germans in case of individual actions of special importance, but were continuously used for gathering data and to harass the enemy. At least one such *Frontaufklärungstrupp* was deployed in Hungary as well. This topic was mentioned in the work of Krisztián Ungváry in his work "Budapest ostroma" based on German archival sources.
In subordination to the German *Heeresgruppe Süd* in combat in Hungary *Frontaufklärungskompanie 206* was present. Within the strength of the latter was the *Frontaufklärungstrupp 213* deployed, which established *Beute-Panzerverband "Jaguar"* by 30 September 1944 still at *Heeresgruppe A*. The unit was equipped with captured Soviet tanks. The special unit was subordinated to *Heeresgruppe Süd* on 1 October 1944.

rifles and four anti-tank gun positions, knocked out a Soviet tank and killed more than 100 soldiers. Their own losses amounted to 24 dead and a knocked out captured Soviet tank. As a result of this ambush the Germans were able to reoccupy their former positions again.[962]

The Soviet Rifle Divisions of the 4th Guards Army in combat east and north of Székesfehérvár, with their self-propelled artillery battalions, equipped with 78 operational SU–76M self-propelled guns and five tanks, were active in the following sectors in the early evening hours on that day:

- the 75th Guards Independent Self-Propelled Artillery Battalion/69th Guards Rifle Division between the western shore of Lake Velence and Kisfalud;
- the 44th Guards Independent Self-Propelled Artillery Battalion/41st Guards Rifle Division 300 meters north of Kiskecskemét and on the northern edge of Székesfehérvár;
- the 85th Guards Independent Self-Propelled Artillery Battalion/80th Guards Rifle Division[963] at Polgármalom and 500 meters northeast of Point 115 north of Székesfehérvár;
- the 13th Guards Independent Self-Propelled Artillery Battalion/5th Guards Airborne Division was in combat between Polgármalom and Hill 153 (Gombócleső);
- the 8th Guards Independent Self-Propelled Artillery Battalion/7th Guards Airborne Division with 11 SU–76M self-propelled guns and one T–34 tank provided the reserve for the division commander at Máriamajor;
- the 69th Guards Independent Self-Propelled Artillery Battalion/62nd Guards Rifle Division with eight SU–76Ms and one T–34 tank was in the reserve for the division commander on the northern edge of Kisfalud.[964]

The 366th Guards Heavy Self-Propelled Artillery Regiment/4th Guards Army was engaged in combat with the German troops in the south-western outskirts of Székesfehérvár, with 13 operational German self-propelled howitzers and assault guns and two Panthers.[965]

The armoured fighting vehicles were pushing forward in the battle line of the rifle forces and provided direct fire support for them.[966] During these battles, only one Soviet tank was destroyed from the independent self-propelled artillery battalions.[967]

On the frontline of the 2nd Ukrainian Front

The right flank of the Hungarian 1st Hussars Division, without Soviet pressure, retreated and established new positions 4 km northeast of Pusztavám. On the Division's left flank, the Soviets had broken through in the area of Oroszlány on the Csákvár–Kecskéd as well

---

962 Bundesarchiv–Militärarchiv (Freiburg im Breisgau), RH 7/V 313. Introduction of reserve *Leutnant* Eugen Weyde for the decoration *Deutsches Kreuz in Gold*, 6 April 1945.
963 The 85th Guards Independent Sef-Propelled Artillery Battalion lost a T–34 tank on that day. See Central Archives of the Russian Defence Ministry (Podolsk), f. 243, op. 2928, gy. 131, li. 250. This was probably knocked out by *Beute-Panzerverband "Jaguar"*.
964 Central Archives of the Russian Defence Ministry (Podolsk), f. 243, op. 2928, gy. 131, li. 250.
965 Central Archives of the Russian Defence Ministry (Podolsk), f. 243, op. 2928, gy. 178, li. 84.
966 Central Archives of the Russian Defence Ministry (Podolsk), f. 243, op. 2928, gy. 131, li. 247.
967 Central Archives of the Russian Defence Ministry (Podolsk), f. 243, op. 2928, gy. 178, li. 84.

as on the Vérteskozma–Környe road with 13 armoured fighting vehicles, and the rifle infantry occupied Majkpuszta and Vértessomló.

At 0730 hours that morning, the Soviet 991st Self-Propelled Artillery Regiment launched an attack in the direction of Oroszlány with the 2nd Battalion/429th Rifle Regiment. The SU–76M self-propelled guns were moving forward within the battle line of the rifle forces and destroyed the firing positions of the German–Hungarian forces. At noon, the self-propelled guns and the 429th Rifle Regiment reached the edges of Oroszlány and then proceeded to occupy the town after a 1 hour engagement. The defenders retreated via Által Creek towards Bokod and Dad. The SU–76M self-propelled guns destroyed two mortar batteries, four guns and 18 firing positions, as well as capturing 52 enemy soldiers. Their own losses were one dead, 1st Lieutenant Petrenko, commander of the 2nd Battery, and two wounded.[968]

The 1505th Self-Propelled Artillery Battalion also took part in the battle for Oroszlány. Two of their SU–76M batteries reached the south-eastern edge of the town around 1200 hours, while another two batteries reached Point 259. The Soviet self-propelled artillery crews reported to have knocked out five anti-tank guns and eight fortifications, with their own losses amounting to three wounded. At 1300 hours the 1505th Self-Propelled Artillery Regiment supported the forces of the 223rd Rifle Division in their assault launched on Kecskéd.[969]

One of the regrouped battalions of the German *Panzergrenadier-Brigade 92 (mot.)*[970] had just reached the north-western outskirts of Vértessomló and launched a counterattack to regain the village. The Soviets had been attacking the industrial area around Felsőgalla from the south, although they had been repelled with counterattacks. At the same time, the salient southwest of the railroad-road junction 4.5 km southeast from Felsőgalla, was eliminated by the Soviets.[971]

The Soviet 1897th Self-Propelled Artillery Regiment/46th Army was supporting the forces of the 180th Rifle Division and on that day launched an attack from Újbarok towards Szár. The SU–76M self-propelled guns of the 2nd Battery of the Regiment together with the 86th Rifle Regiment reached the bridge 1 km northwest of the Szár railway station around 1400 hours. The self-propelled guns of the 1st and 4th Batteries were fighting with the 21st Rifle Regiment for the Szár railway station. The 3rd Battery, together with the 42nd Rifle Regiment, was in the reserve of the Division's commander. By the end of the day, the 1897th Self-Propelled Artillery Regiment, together with the 180th Rifle Division, were to have reached Hill 187 2 km south of Nagy Lake in the Tata–Vértesszőlős sector, but this was not accomplished.[972]

The Soviets launched battalion strength attacks west of Csabdi, north of Mány and northwest of Zsámbék, but all were pushed back by the defenders with counterattacks, however the German-Hungarian assault aimed at the restoration of the earlier frontline northwest of Kirva was not successful.[973]

---

968 Central Archives of the Russian Defence Ministry (Podolsk), f. 240, op. 2799, gy. 342, li. 109.
969 Central Archives of the Russian Defence Ministry (Podolsk), f. 240, op. 2799, gy. 342, li. 112.
970 The *Brigade* that was subordinated on that day to the Hungarian 3rd Army, had at that time two motorized *Panzergrenadier-Bataillon*s, one pioneer battalion, one artillery battalion and one 3.7 cm anti-aircraft gun company.
971 NARA, T311, R162, F7214608.
972 Central Archives of the Russian Defence Ministry (Podolsk), f. 240, op. 2799, gy. 342, li. 115.
973 NARA, T311, R162, F7214609.

On that day, the German *Sturmgeschütz-Brigade 325* arrived in the Mór sector from 8. *Armee*, where it was subordinated to the Hungarian 3rd Army, as well as *Panzer-Aufklärungs-Abteilung 1*, which was en route from Nádasdladány towards Pusztavám.[974]

The German *Luftflotte 4 had* been mainly supporting the defensive actions of *Armeegruppe "Balck"*, flying 180 missions. The pilots reported destroying two armoured fighting vehicles and to have shot down three Soviet planes.[975]

According to the incorrect assumptions of German reconnaissance, the 23rd Tank Corps was most likely deployed in the frontline of the Soviet 4th Guards Army, which was attacking towards the north-eastern edge of Lake Balaton with five to seven rifle divisions in a southwest direction.[976] The Germans supposed that the direction of the attack of the 10th Rifle Division/9th Guards Army would be Várpalota–Veszprém, with the 2nd Guards Mechanized Corps in its section. But this was also incorrect. The 9th Guards Army was to work in cooperation with the 46th Army and force a breakthrough in the Vértes mountains. They were still not entirely convinced of the presence of 6th Guards Tank Army and Cavalry-Mechanized Group "Pliev" in the Transdanubia, however they were certain that in the case of a breakthrough attempt, these armoured forces would also be deployed.[977]

The forces of the Soviet 6th Guards Tank Army transferred to the 3rd Ukrainian Front from the 2nd Ukrainian Front, were indeed assembling in the Transdanubia on the same day around 1700 hours. The 5th Guards Tank Corps was in the sector of Pátka and Zámoly with 9435 men, 111 operational T–34/85 tanks and 21 SU–76M self-propelled guns, 63 guns, 70 mortars and 233 machine guns, and the 9th Guards Mechanized Corps at Csákvár with 11, 717 men, 167 operational M4A2 tanks and 17 SU–76M self-propelled guns, 75 guns, 125 mortars and 364 machine guns[978]. The Army's 51th Guards Self-Propelled Artillery Brigade was also en route[979] with 60 SU–76M self-propelled guns and four T–70 light tanks, as well as its 4th Guards Motorcycle Regiment with 1137 men, seven Mk IX Valentine tanks, 13 guns and mortars, and its field and artillery units. The Army's 202nd Light Artillery Brigade had 48 76 mm ZiS–3 and 20 100 mm BS–3 towed guns.[980] The commander of the 6th Guards Tank Army, comprising 27,712 men, Colonel General Kravchenko, was also stationed in Csákvár with his staff.[981]

According to records from 16 March 1945, the following units in the 5th Guards Tank Corps were waiting for the launch of the attack:

- in the 20th Guards Tank Brigade: 49 operational tanks and 211 motorized rifles;
- in the 21st Guards Tank Brigade: 11 tanks and 254 motorized rifles;

---

[974] NARA, T311, R163, F7215370.
[975] NARA, T311, R162, F7214610.
[976] NARA, T311, R162, F7214610.
[977] NARA, T311, R162, F7214611.
[978] Central Archives of the Russian Defence Ministry (Podolsk), f. 339, op. 5179, gy. 87, li. 62.
[979] The 51st Guards Self-Propelled Artillery Brigade consisted of three self-propelled artillery battalions, with 20 SU–76M self-propelled guns and one T–70 light tank in each, and five-five self-propelled guns in four batteries. The 207th, 208th and 209th Self-Propelled Artillery Brigades, equipped with SU–100 armoured fighting vehicles, had three regiments each, however there were only four batteries in each regiments, with five SU–100 self-propelled guns.
[980] Central Archives of the Russian Defence Ministry (Podolsk), f. 339, op. 5179, gy. 106, li. 338. The shell of the latter gun was able to pierce 170 mm armour from a distance of 1000 metres, and 190 mm from a distance of 500 metres.
[981] Central Archives of the Russian Defence Ministry (Podolsk), f. 243, op. 2928, gy. 131, li. 249 and 250.

- in the 22nd Guards Tank Brigade: 51 tanks and 187 motorized rifles;
- in the 6th Guards Motorized Rifle Brigade: 1766 soldiers ready for service;
- in the 1458th Self-Propelled Artillery Regiment: 21 SU–76Ms;
- in the 15th Independent Guards Motorcycle Battalion: four tanks, 12 BA–64 armoured cars and 24 motorcycles;
- in the 4th Guards Signal Battalion: two tanks and 11 BA–64 armoured cars. [982]

In the case of the 9th Guards Mechanized Corps this data was as follows:

- in the 18th Guards Mechanized Brigade: 29 operational tanks and 400 motorized rifles;
- in the 30h Guards Mechanized Brigade: 34 tanks and 775 motorized rifles;
- in the 31st Guards Mechanized Brigade: 28 tanks and 553 motorized rifles;
- in the 46th Guards Tank Brigade: 65 tanks and 211 motorized rifles;
- in the 14th Guards Motorcycle Battalion: 10 tanks and 306 soldiers ready for service;
- corps HQ units with three tanks;
- in the subordinated 697th Self-Propelled Artillery Regiment: 17 SU–76Ms.[983]

The 3rd Ukrainian Front received 58 new M4A2 tanks in Szekszárd on the same day, which were immediately assigned to the 2nd Guards Mechanized Brigade and the 9th Guards Tank Brigades/1st Guards Mechanized Corps. The 39th Tank Brigade/23rd Tank Corps received 14 T–34/85s that arrived at Ócsa.[984]

Considering the operational situation, *Heeresgruppe Süd* requested the *Oberkommando des Heeres* (*OKH*) to allow the transfer of *356. Infanterie-Division* to the Mór sector, to be able to seal off any possible Soviet breakthrough west of the Vértes mountains, and *I. SS-Panzerkorps* at Falubattyán to shift to the south-western outskirts of Székesfehérvár, to enable the unit to launch counterattacks against the Soviet forces facing west from the sector of Várpalota.[985] The *II. SS-Panzerkorps* was to be concentrated behind *I. SS-Panzerkorps* and the *Heeresgruppe* had repeated its earlier request that *16. SS-Panzergrenadier-Division* from *2. Panzerarmee* should be placed in direct subordination to them as a central reserve.[986]

Armeegruppe "Balck" wanted to withdraw one armoured division from the Seregélyes northeast to Agárd line even at the expense of shortening the frontline of *III. Panzerkorps* in order to be able to cover their rear from the northeast.[987] Apart from the withdrawal of *16. SS-Panzergrenadier-Division*, Hitler approved all the requests on the next day around 0130. This practically meant the end of the planned new German armoured assault east of the Sárvíz, and with this, Operation *"Frühlingserwachen"* as well.

---

982   See the war log of the 5th Guards Tank Corps of March 1945. Copy owned by the author. p. 8.
983   War log of the 9th Guards Mechanized Corps from 3 March – 14 April 1945. Copy owned by the author. p. 6-7.
984   Central Archives of the Russian Defence Ministry (Podolsk), f. 243, op. 2928, gy. 131, li. 252.
985   NARA, T311, R162, F7214611-7214612. According to the initial understanding of *Armeegruppe "Balck"* one of the *SS-Panzer-Divisions* was to attack from Bodajk via Magyaralmás towards Zámoly, and the other from Mór towards Csákberény.
986   NARA, T311, R162, F7214619-7214620.
987   NARA, T311, R162, F7214616.

Between 6 – 17 March 1945 the Germans had, according to their reports, inflicted the following losses to the Soviet troops during Operation *"Frühlingserwachen"* and the first two days of the Vienna Offensive:

- 3282 counted and 1880 presumed (altogether 5162) dead;
- 237 knocked out tanks and self-propelled guns;
- 30 aircraft shot down by anti-aircraft units;
- 26 artillery guns;
- 11 anti-aircraft guns;
- 507 anti-tank guns;
- 96 mortars;
- 465 light machine guns and machine guns;
- 166 anti-tank rifles;
- 131 submachine guns.[988]

18 March 1945, Sunday

(**WEATHER**: highest daytime temperature 15 Celsius, partly clear, partly cloudy skies, and local showers. The roads are driveable, and the open terrain is partially driveable.)

On the Dráva line, one of the SU–76M self-propelled guns of the 1891st Self-Propelled Artillery Battalion supporting the Soviet 122nd Rifle Division, ran over a mine in the vicinity of Drávacsehi leaving the Regiment with 16 operational self-propelled guns.[989]

The 53rd Motorcycle Regiment with 10 T–34/85 tanks and 137 motorcycles, was preparing for an attack at the German bridgehead at Valpovo towards Torjánc in conjunction with the 84th Rifle Division.[990] The Soviet 122nd Independent Self-Propelled Artillery Battalion had 12 operational SU–76M self-propelled guns on that day.[991]

On the front of *2. Panzerarmee*, *16.SS-Panzergrenadier-Division/XXII. Gebirgskorps* together with *Sturmbrigade "Rudno"* had, after heavy fighting in the forest, reached the front the general line between the edge of the forest directly north of Mesztegnyő and the farmstead (Kopárpuszta) 2 km southwest of Libickozma. In the meantime, the German troops repelled a number of Soviet counterattacks, which were also supported by armoured fighting vehicles.

Panzergruppe "Reinhardt"/SS-Panzer-Abteilung 16, was to support *Sturmbrigade "Rudno"*, however all of the assault guns were disabled during the drive forward, with broken taper gears from crossing over fallen logs.[992]

---

988 NARA, T311, R163, F7215372.
989 Central Archives of the Russian Defence Ministry (Podolsk), f. 243, op. 2928, gy. 131, li. 254.
990 Central Archives of the Russian Defence Ministry (Podolsk), f. 243, op. 2928, gy. 131, li. 254.
991 Central Archives of the Russian Defence Ministry (Podolsk), f. 243, op. 2928, gy. 178, li. 86/2.
992 Puntigam, Josef Paul: *Vom Plattensee bis zur Mur. Die Kämpfe 1945 im Dreiländereck*. Feldbach, without year of publication, [1993], p. 103.

In the sector the Soviet 32nd Independent Guards Mechanized Brigade with seven T–34 tanks, the 864th Self-Propelled Artillery Regiment with nine SU–76Ms and one T-34 company of the 249th Independent Tank Regiment were in combat. The latter had, in subordination to the 32nd Independent Guards Mechanized Brigade, reported to have knocked out three German assault guns at Üsztőpuszta, with the loss of one knocked out T–34 tank.[993]

The forces of *1. Volks-Gebirgs-Division* drove back a Soviet attack against the southeastern part of Csömend.[994]

On the same day, *Grenadier-Regiment 191/71. Infanterie-Division, I. (Bataillon)/Gebirgsjäger-Regiment 98/1. Volks-Gebirgs-Division* and *Sturmbrigade "Rudno"* were subordinated to *16. SS-Panzergrenadier-Division*.[995]

In the front of the German *I. Kavallerie-Korps/6. Panzerarmee*, the Soviet troops launched a battalion-size assault against the positions of the 25th Honvéd Infantry Division in the sector of Hill 125 four km north of Balatonszabadi, however apart from a temporary incursion, the defenders drove off their attempt. At the same time, 5 km north-northeast of Balatonszabadi, among the vineyards on the western outskirts of Enying, a Soviet breakthrough had to be sealed off by the German *Reiter-Regiment 32, Panzerjäger-Abteilung 69* and *schwere Kavallerie-Abteilung 3*[996] of the *3. Kavallerie-Division*. Here the Germans immediately launched a counterattack from the north and the northeast.[997]

The *3. Kavallerie-Division* had taken over command on the frontline of the 25th Honvéd Infantry Division and at the same time, the 1st and 25th Honvéd Infantry Regiments, the 25th Honvéd Reconnaissance Battalion, and the 20th Assault Artillery Battalion, were subordinated to the 25th Honvéd Infantry Division and equipped with Jagdpanzer 38(t) *Jagdpanzers* and were also subordinated to the German unit.[998]

During the whole day, *4. Kavallerie-Division* repelled continuous battalion-size Soviet attacks initiated against the German bridgehead held east of Ádánd. The German military bridge damaged on the night of 17/18 March 1945 was repaired.[999]

The Soviet 22nd Independent Tank Regiment stood in defence with three T–34 tanks on the western edge of Szabadhídvég, and with three other T–34s near Balatonszabadifürdőtelep, near the Zsófia children's sanitarium.[1000]

The majority of *3. Kavallerie-Division* pushed the Soviet forces to the southern bank of the Sió Canal northeast of Felsőnyék. The retreating Soviets blew up the bridge found there.[1001]

Both *SS-Panzer-Divisions* of *I. SS-Panzerkorps* began to march to their new assembly area from the Simontornya bridgehead to the sector of Dég–Enying, although the majority

---

993 Central Archives of the Russian Defence Ministry (Podolsk), f. 243, op. 2928, gy. 131, li. 254.
994 NARA, T311, R162, F7214625. The *44. Gebirgs-Panzerjäger-Abteilung 44/1. Volks-Gebirgs-Division* received 10 Jagdpanzer 38(t) *Jagdpanzers* on that day. See NARA, T78, R621, F000779. However the *Jagdpanzers* had not yet arrived to Hungary.
995 NARA, T311, R163, F7215384.
996 Witte, Hans Joachim – Offermann, Peter: *Die Boeselagerschen Reiter. Das Kavallerie-Regiment Mitte und die aus ihm hervorgegangene 3. Kavallerie-Brigade/Division*. München, 1998. p. 407.
997 NARA, T311, R162, F7214626.
998 NARA, T311, R163, F7215384.
999 NARA, T311, R162, F7214626.
1000 Central Archives of the Russian Defence Ministry (Podolsk), f. 243, op. 2928, gy. 178, li. 86/2.
1001 NARA, T311, R162, F7214626.

of *1. SS-Panzer-Division* had set off only after dark, around 1730 hours.[1002] This had been completed by 1800 hours on the same day.

The *12. SS-Panzer-Division* were assembling 9 km northwest of Székesfehérvár, in the sector of Falubattyán. As the forces of *I. SS-Panzerkorps* were planned to carry out an attack from the Mór–Fehérvárcsurgó line against the Soviets attacking between Lake Velence and the Vértes mountains, in the evening, *12. SS-Panzer-Division* set off to march to the southern sector of Mór. The vehicle columns were moving slowly in the darkness.[1003]

As they no longer possessed any significance, *Heeresgruppe Süd* cancelled the use of codenames for the units of *6. Panzerarmee*.[1004] *SS-Panzer-Aufklärungs-Abteilung 1* was still subordinated to *2. SS-Panzer-Division*.[1005]

The *23. Panzer-Division*, subordinated to *I. Kavallerie-Korps* on the same day, took over the defence of the Simontornya bridgehead from the regrouped *I. SS-Panzerkorps*. The Germans repelled the battalion and regiment-size attacks launched during the morning against the bridgehead, and eliminated the temporary incursions with counterattacks. The Germans noticed that the Soviets had positioned reinforcements on the eastern side of the bridgehead.[1006]

At noon the Soviet troops launched a new attack with ground attack aircraft support and broke into the positions of *I. (Bataillon)/Panzergrenadier-Regiment 126* and *I. (Bataillon)/Panzergrenadier-Regiment 128*. The armoured group of *Panzer-Regiment 23* launched a counterattack towards Hill 220, 1.5 km southwest of Simonytornya, but this was unsuccessful. Afterwards, the German *Panzergrenadiers* were forced to move their frontline back towards the village. *Panzer-Pionier-Bataillon 51* placed mines in all possible directions of any attacks, mostly the spring mines (S-mines) that were especially effective against live troops. In the evening *Panzergruppe "Fischer"* of the *Division* with 19 armoured fighting vehicles of *Panzer-Regiment 23* and the armoured personnel carriers of *2. Kompanie/Panzer-Aufklärungs-Abteilung 23*, was ordered to Dég.[1007]

The Soviet 71st Tank Regiment with three T–34/85s and the 1896th Self-Propelled Artillery Regiment with 16 SU–76Ms of the 5th Guards Cavalry Corps, were in combat 2 km southwest of Simontornya. On that day, they reported to have knocked out eight German tanks, 11 armoured personnel carriers, eight mortars, eight guns and 25 machine gun nests.[1008]

On the front of *II. SS-Panzerkorps,* small Soviet combat forces had secretly crossed the Nádor and the Malom Canals towards the west, east of Káloz, and at two locations northeast of Nagyhörcsökpuszta. In the wooded area three km southeast of Káloz, the Germans detected the concentration of significant Soviet forces.[1009] The reinforced *SS-Kampfgruppe "Krag"* with *SS-Panzer-Aufklärungs-Abteilung 2* and *SS-Panzer-Aufklärungs-Abteilung 1* subordinated, was itself subordinated to *II. SS-Panzerkorps* on the same day.[1010]

1002 NARA, T311, R162, F7214626.
1003 Meyer, Hubert: *Kriegsgeschichte der 12. SS-Panzerdivision „Hitlerjugend"*. Band II. Osnabrück, 1987. 2nd edition. p. 505.
1004 BAMA, RH-19, V/63 Kriegstagebuch der Heeresgruppe Süd, Ia Nr. 3635/45 geh. vom 18. 3. 1945.
1005 Tiemann, Ralf: *Die Leibstandarte*. Band IV/2. Osnabrück, 1987. p. 296.
1006 NARA, T311, R162, F7214626.
1007 Rebentisch, Ernst: *Zum Kaukasus und zu den Tauern. Die Geschichte der 23. Panzer-Division 1941–1945*. Esslingen, 1963. p. 491.
1008 Central Archives of the Russian Defence Ministry (Podolsk), f. 243, op. 2928, gy. 131, li. 255.
1009 NARA, T311, R162, F7214626.
1010 NARA, T311, R163, F7215384.

The forces of *44. Reichsgrenadier-Division* repelled Soviet battalion-size attacks, supported by armoured fighting vehicles that were launched from the direction of the vineyards east of Sárkeresztúr and from the northern parts of the village, and knocked out two tanks.[1011]

The armoured combat group of *2. SS-Panzer-Division* repelled battalion-size attacks from the south and from the east in the sector of Heinrichmajor.[1012]

The *Kommandeur* of *III. (Bataillon)/SS-Panzergrenadier-Regiment 4* in combat at the farmstead, announced that the *Division* was going to knock out its 3000th enemy armoured fighting vehicle very soon. In the event this was achieved with a *Panzerfaust* or by an anti-tank gunner, this would earn the soldier 14 days leave, and eight days leave in case this was achieved by member of an armoured fighting vehicle or gun crew. An opportunity showed up soon, as the Soviets, following preparatory artillery fire, launched a new attack with the support of five tanks.[1013]. The gunner of one of the Panther-platoon commanders of *4. Kompanie/SS-Panzer-Regiment 2*, *SS-Oberscharführer* Ernst Barkmann, who was decorated with the Knight's Cross of the Iron Cross, was the swiftest and knocked out the 3000th enemy armoured fighting vehicle of the unit. Following the fire of the German armoured platoon, two of the five Soviet tanks were engulfed in flames, two were disabled and one retreated, covered in smoke.[1014]

The Soviet 1st Guards Mechanized Corps reported on that day to have lost six knocked out M4A2 tanks of which two were burnt out. The 9th Guards Tank Brigade had arrived from replenishment around 2030 hours and was assembling at Sárosd.[1015]

On the front of *9. SS-Panzer-Division*, west of Jakabszállás the Soviet 786th Rifle Regiment/155th Rifle Division and units of the reinforced 110th Tank Brigade with six T–34/85s, four ISU–122s and two ISU–152 armoured fighting vehicles, were attacking with a regiment-size force, and with a battalion-size force west of Sárosd. The attacks were repulsed by the Germans, inflicting heavy losses on the Soviets. However a new attack was launched west of Sárosd with a regiment-size force with armoured support, and this had broken through. The SS-troops repelled the Soviet forces in close combat, knocked out two of their tanks and reoccupied their former positions again.[1016]

Subsequently, however, Hill 159 (Csillag) west of Sárosd, fell into Soviet hands.[1017] The units of the 110th Tank Brigade and the 155th Rifle Division occupied the hill around at 1600 hours, and held it against the German counterattacks. The Soviets reported knocking out two tanks and four armoured personnel carriers here.[1018]

1011 NARA, T311, R162, F7214626.
1012 NARA, T311, R162, F7214626.
1013 Although the German source mentions T-34 tanks, these were in all probability the M4A2 tanks of the 20th Guards Tank Regiment/3rd Guards Mechanized Brigade stationed in the area of Heinrichmajor. It should be noted here that the German reports and recollections of the combat actions during March 1945 almost always mix up the T-34 variants with the M4A2 armoured fighting vehicles, the IS–2 heavy tanks with the ISU–122 and ISU–152 heavy self-propelled guns, and the latter with the SU–100 self-propelled guns. It also happened that the SU–100 self-propelled guns were deemed to be SU–85s which is perhaps the most easily justifiable mistake.
1014 Weidinger, Otto: *Division Das Reich. Der Weg der 2. SS-Panzer-Division „Das Reich"*. Band V: 1943-1945. Osnabrück, without year of publication, pp. 458-459.
1015 Central Archives of the Russian Defence Ministry (Podolsk), f. 243, op. 2928, gy. 131, li. 255.
1016 NARA, T311, R162, F7214627.
1017 NARA, T311, R163, F7215387.
1018 Central Archives of the Russian Defence Ministry (Podolsk), f. 243, op. 2928, gy. 131, li. 254.

By late afternoon orders arrived for *2. SS-Panzer-Division* to be withdrawn and gathered southwest of Székesfehérvár. The two *SS-Panzergrenadier-Regiments* were to withdraw their forces after darkness set in and gather at Nádasdladány. They were to set off during the night to be able to stop the rapidly progressing attack of the 46th Army.

The withdrawal of *SS-Panzergrenadier-Regiment 3* and *II. (Bataillon)/SS-Panzergrenadier-Regiment 4* was completed almost flawlessly. The Soviets attacking from Sárkeresztúr towards Aba were repulsed by the rearguard of *SS-Panzergrenadier-Regiment 3*.

The withdrawal of the armoured combat group from the sector of Heinrichmajor was a more difficult task, because the Soviets were in the vicinity and also the battalion command post was packed with severely wounded soldiers. At last, with the close cooperation of the whole unit, the wounded were saved. The retreat was covered by the Panther tank platoon of *SS-Oberscharführer* Barkmann. The damaged armoured fighting vehicles and armoured personnel carriers around the farmstead were able to be towed away by the maintenance units. The SS-vehicle columns heading for Székesfehérvár were attacked by artillery fire and air raids. The retreating Germans were targeted by Soviet ISU–122 and ISU–152 self-propelled guns as well, most likely from the reoccupied Hill 159.[1019]

On the front of *Armeegruppe "Balck"*, at Lake Balaton and along the southern shore of Lake Velence, there was relative calmness on that day.

On the front of *III. Panzerkorps*, during the evening of 17/18 March 1945, 5 km northeast of Seregélyes, the Germans eliminated a Soviet incursion when they knocked out eight of their armoured fighting vehicles including two with *Panzerfausts*.[1020]

Panzergrenadier-Regiment 113 (*Kampfgruppe "Bradel"*), reinforced with *I. (Abteilung)/Panzer-Regiment 1/1. Panzer-Division*, and *Panzergrenadier-Regiment 1* (*Kampfgruppe "Huppert"*) reinforced with towed anti-tank guns and *Marder* tank destroyers, had taken over the defence of the positions around Seregélyes replacing the withdrawn *356. Infanterie-Division* and *3. Panzer-Division* that was shifted westwards. *Gruppe "Koehler"*, consisting of *Panzer-Aufklärungs-Abteilung 1* reinforced by six Panthers and a few self-propelled 2 cm anti-aircraft guns, plus the motorized companies of *Panzer-Pionier-Bataillon 37* successfully halted the Soviet attack between the north-western outskirts of Dinnyés and the south-western outskirts of Pákozd, and the south-eastern edge of the vineyards of Székesfehérvár which had been launched shortly before midnight. Following this, part of the Hungarian *SS-Regiment "Ney"* sealed off the gap. With this accomplished, the endangered right flank of *5. SS-Panzer-Division* was covered.[1021]

The *I. (Abteilung)/Panzer-Regiment 24* had 11 combat-ready Panthers, which were subordinated to *1. Panzer-Division* under command of *Leutnant* Jonas. Acting on orders from *Kampfgruppe "Streith"*, the *Leutnant* went on a reconnaissance mission with three Panthers south of Székesfehérvár in order to be able to clear the actual positions of the Soviet troops. The Panthers advanced through the Soviet frontline to a depth of 2 km, but they

---

1019 Weidinger, Otto: *Division Das Reich. Der Weg der 2. SS-Panzer-Division „Das Reich"*. Band V: 1943-1945. Osnabrück, without year of publication, pp. 460-461. The German source in this case also mentions IS-2 heavy tanks, however these were not deployed in the area.
1020 NARA, T311, R163, F7215376.
1021 Stoves, Rolf: *Persönliches Kriegstagebuch Pz.Rgt. 1* (typewritten manuscript, a copy owned by the author), entry from 18 March 1945.

were not able to gather any valuable information from the mission. This was because the Soviets had simply ceased fire at the approach of the Panthers, so that the Panthers were not able to detect their positions and report their firing positions via radio.[1022]

During the day, the Soviets launched an attack against the German–Hungarian troops in defence along the Székesfehérvár–Seregélyes railroad four km southeast of Székesfehérvár.[1023]

The extremely heavy Soviet attack was still progressing on the front of *IV. SS-Panzerkorps* and the Hungarian 3rd Army. Between the northern shore of Lake Balaton and the Bicske–Bánhida railroad, the Soviets deployed large numbers of rifle infantry and armoured groups of approximately 20 armoured fighting vehicles in each, and were pushing forward on a wide front. The pressure was the heaviest between Székesfehérvár and the Vértes Mountains towards the west-southwest. At the same time, the Soviet troops were also attacking from the sector of Oroszlány and Vértessomló in a northwest direction. The rifle infantry suffered considerable losses from the return fire of the German–Hungarian defence. Among the German troops, *3. SS-Panzer-Division* had suffered particularly high losses.[1024]

The Soviet assaults launched against the northern and eastern edges of Székesfehérvár were repulsed by the forces of *5. SS-Panzer-Division,* partly by counterattacks.

The rifle troops, supported by armoured fighting vehicles and ground attack aircraft, launched their assault early in the morning. Nine Panther tanks of *SS-Panzer-Regiment 5* were waiting for the attackers in well concealed firing positions along the Székesfehérvár–Mór road. The Germans counted 50-60 Soviet armoured fighting vehicles taking part in the assault and the Panthers reported by nightfall they had knocked out 22 of them. Their own losses amounted to two tanks.[1025]

Despite the above, the Soviet armoured fighting vehicles reached on that same day the command post of the *Divisionskommandeur, SS-Standartenführer* Ullrich, which was set up at Iszkaszentgyörgy. The left flank of the *Division* had to be withdrawn to the northern edge of Székesfehérvár because that remained exposed after 3. *SS-Panzer-Division* was pushed back.

SS-Panzergrenadier-Regiment 9 tried to establish a fortified defensive position along the Székesfehérvár–Csór–Várpalota road and thus cover the *Division* from the north. The right flank was pushed back by the Soviets to the station at Székesfehérvár.[1026]

The Soviets were pushing forward from the sector of Sárkeresztes with significant rifle forces, supported by armoured fighting vehicles in a south-western and western direction. These were the forces of the Soviet 37th Guards Rifle Corps and the SU-76M self-propelled guns of the 1513rd Self-Propelled Artillery Regiment. In the battle line of the rifle forces, the advance troop of the 20th Guards Tank Brigade/5th Guards Tank Corps/6th Guards Tank

---

1022 Weidemann, Gert-Axel: *Unser Regiment. Reiter-Regiment 2 – Panzer-Regiment 24.* Groß-Umstadt, 1982. p. 277.
1023 NARA, T311, R162, F7214627.
1024 NARA, T311, R162, F7214627.
1025 Klapdor, Ewald: *Mit dem Panzerregiment 5 Wiking im Osten.* Siek, 1981. p. 332. In the morning hours the Panthers knocked out six Soviet armoured fighting vehicles in a short period of time, and around noon disabled seven from a distance of approximately 1400 meters and six more were heavily damaged. They lost only one Panther by 1600 hours. Around 1700 hours the Soviet armoured fighting vehicles on the left flank of the Panthers reached the Székesfehérvár–Mór road. The first three Soviet tanks were immediately knocked out. The *6. Kompanie/SS-Panzer-Regiment 5* contained the attackers, and *5. Kompanie* bypassed them and got in their rear. As the positions switched the Soviets knocked out another Panther.
1026 Klapdor, Ewald: *Mit dem Panzerregiment 5 Wiking im Osten.* Siek, 1981. p. 333.

Army was also deployed. The unit consisted of a tank battalion of the 20th Guards Tank Brigade, a submachine gun rifle company, a SU-76M battery of the 1458th Self-Propelled Artillery Regiment and a battalion of the 391st Guards Anti-Tank Artillery Regiment. By 1300 hours, the unit reached Sárkeresztes.[1027]

As soon as the attackers crossed the Székesfehérvár–Csór road 5 km northwest of Székesfehérvár heading in a southern direction, the Germans launched a counterattack from the town.[1028]

The Soviet 366th Guards Heavy Self-Propelled Artillery Regiment/4th Guards Army established firing positions east of Székesfehérvár and covered the roads leading out of town towards Csala and Kisfalud with six operational *Hummel* and a captured *Wespe* self-propelled howitzers, two captured German assault guns, a Panzer IV and a Panther tank. During the engagement, German artillery knocked out two of the captured German self-propelled howitzers, one of which burnt out, and three more were bogged down in the mud.[1029]

The independent self-propelled-artillery battalions of the 4th Guards Army were fighting with their own divisions on that day:

- the 75th Guards Independent Self-Propelled Artillery Battalion/69th Guards Rifle Division with 11 SU–76Ms between the western shore of Lake Velence and Kisfalud;
- the 44th Guards Independent Self-Propelled Artillery Battalion/41st Guards Rifle Division with 11 SU–76Ms 300 meters north of Kiskecskemét and at the northern edge of Székesfehérvár;
- the 85th Guards Independent Self-Propelled Artillery Battalion/80th Guards Rifle Division with 12 SU–76M between Points 115 and 118 northwest of Székesfehérvár;
- the 13th Guards Independent Self-Propelled Artillery Battalion/5th Guards Airborne Division with 11 SU–76Ms at Imremajor, northwest of Székesfehérvár;
- the 8th Guards Independent Self-Propelled Artillery Battalion/7th Guards Airborne Division with 12 SU–76Ms on Hill 153 (Gombócleső)–Gyulamajor–Városi vízműtelep (town waterworks)–Hóhérkút line;
- the 69th Guards Independent Self-Propelled Artillery Battalion/62nd Guards Rifle Division with 11 SU–76Ms on the northern edge of Kisfalud in reserve to the division commander.[1030]

The independent self-propelled-artillery battalions of the 4th Guards Army lost three burnt out SU–76Ms and one tank during the course of the day.[1031]

The Soviet 207th Self-Propelled Artillery Brigade was transferred from the 27th Army to the 4th Guards Army. The 1004th Self-Propelled Artillery Regiment with 16 operational SU–100 self-propelled guns was still in firing position at Point 134, 3 km southeast of Székesfehérvár, in order to prevent a German breakthrough towards the northwest, in the direction of the town. The SU–100 self-propelled guns were fighting in ambush

---

1027 Central Archives of the Russian Defence Ministry (Podolsk), f. 3403, op. 1, gy. 69, li. 308.
1028 NARA, T311, R162, F7214627.
1029 Central Archives of the Russian Defence Ministry (Podolsk), f. 243, op. 2928, gy. 178, li. 86.
1030 Central Archives of the Russian Defence Ministry (Podolsk), f. 243, op. 2928, gy. 131, li. 253.
1031 Central Archives of the Russian Defence Ministry (Podolsk), f. 243, op. 2928, gy. 178, li. 88/2.

positions, and reported to have knocked out five Tiger B heavy tanks and one armoured personnel carrier.[1032]

The 912th Self-Propelled Artillery Regiment was marching from the direction of Kisvelence towards Pákozd with 17 SU–100 self-propelled guns, and the 1011th Self-Propelled Artillery Regiment was still in firing positions southeast of Kisvelence, at Szilfástanya but without any operational armoured fighting vehicles.[1033]

The 1922nd Self-Propelled Artillery Regiment/208th Self-Propelled Artillery Brigade with 17 SU–100s had also been subordinated to the 4th Guards Army and was assembled in the sector of Kápolnásnyék.[1034]

In the morning, on the front of *3. SS-Panzer-Division*, the Soviets again assaulted the makeshift positions of the Germans. Mór was still defended by a mixed combat group of the division reinforced with anti-aircraft guns. There was heavy fighting going on in the town into the evening. However the forces of the division in defence west of Magyaralmás were thrown back by the Soviets. The soldiers of *SS-Brigadeführer* Becker were fighting a bitter battle west of Sárkeresztes as well. [1035]

The *III. (Bataillon)/SS-Panzergrenadier-Regiment 6* and the remaining Panzer IV tanks of *II. (Abteilung)/SS-Panzer-Regiment 3* in defence at Moha were forced to give up the village and retreat toward Inota after extremely heavy close quarters combat.[1036]

Soviet troops entered Iszkaszentgyörgy and the forested area northwest of there, after a number of failed attempts following heavy close quarters combat. The Soviets, attacking westwards from Magyaralmás, occupied Fehérvárcsurgó after heavy fighting. The village was defended by the soldiers of *I. (Abteilung)/SS-Panzer-Regiment 3* mostly fighting as infantry, the armoured personnel carriers of *I. (Bataillon)/SS-Panzergrenadier-Regiment 5* and the *Divisionsbegleitkompanie/3. SS-Panzer-Division*. According to the recollections of the local priest of the events in July 1945:

"As the German military command realized that they could not keep the frontline any longer, they ordered their soldiers to burn the village down. On 18 March around noon, the retreating army set off to do their devilish work, and they were spraying phosphorus from their tanks on our houses, while firing at our thatched roof houses with phosphorus shells[1037] from the church tower. Very soon the whole village was in flames. Trying to quench the fire was out of question, so out of 297 houses 208 burnt down, in many cases with the farm animals and, moreover, also with the old or sick residents inside."[1038]

1032 War log of the 207th Self-Propelled Artillery Brigade, 19 March 1945. Copy owned by the author.
1033 Central Archives of the Russian Defence Ministry (Podolsk), f. 243, op. 2928, gy. 131, li. 253.
1034 Central Archives of the Russian Defence Ministry (Podolsk), f. 243, op. 2928, gy. 131, li. 253.
1035 Tieke, Wilhelm: *Von Plattensee bis Österreich. Heeresgruppe Süd 1945.* Gummersbach, without year of publication, p. 52.
1036 Vopersal, Wolfgang: *Soldaten, Kämpfer, Kameraden. Marsch und Kämpfe der SS-Totenkopfdivision.* Band Vb. Bielefeld, 1991. p. 739.
1037 Although it is not impossible that the *Flammpanzer IIIs* of *Flammpanzer-Kompanie 351*, subordinated to the German *1. Panzer-Division* in combat farther from the village, were assigned to burn the village down, however it is much more probable that this task was assigned to the Sd.Kfz. 251/16 flamethrower armoured fighting vehicles of *SS-Panzergrenadier-Regiment 5/3. SS-Panzer-Division*, which were deployed in the regimental *(16.) Panzer-Pionier-Kompanie*. Most likely the Germans fired incendiary tracer rounds from the church tower into the houses. The cause of this behaviour is still unknown today. It can also be established that the destruction happened during the exceptionally heavy close quarters combat within the village and not as part of a targeted retaliation attack.
1038 *Inter arma. Források a székesfehérvári egyházmegye történetéből II.* Edited, introduction written, annotated and references compiled by Gergely Mózessy. Székesfehérvár, 2004. p. 149.

The SS-soldiers pushed out of Fehérvárcsurgó were retreating towards Guttamási during the afternoon.[1039] South of the village one of the Panthers of *I. (Abteilung)/SS-Panzer-Regiment 3* became bogged down in the mud along the road leading to Mór and it was only possible to free the vehicle after a complicated recovery mission. Another tank turned back from Magyaralmás and drove through Söréd to join the *Divisionsbegleitkompanie/3. SS-Panzer-Division.*[1040]

At dawn, Söréd was approached by three Soviet M4A2 tanks, which were knocked out by two *SS-Panzergrenadiers* with *Panzerfausts*, from a forward position covering their troops. As one of the soldiers remembered:

"Two tanks burnt out, and the third was immobilized. Around 0945 hours they completely cut us off and an armoured group with mounted Soviet cadets literally mowed us down."[1041]

The Hungarian and German armoured fighting vehicles defending Söréd were alarmed again at 0900 hours in the morning. This time the village was attacked not only by the Soviet 332nd Guards Rifle Regiment, but also units of the 30th Guards Mechanized Brigade/9th Guards Mechanized Corps with the 84th Guards Tank Regiment attached and with the support of 20 M4A2 armoured fighting vehicles. At first, only two Soviet tanks approached along the Fehérvári road from the east. Captain Tarczay was sitting in one of the three Hungarian Panzer IV tanks that set off against them. Around 1000 hours that morning, the Hungarian armoured fighting vehicles knocked out the two Soviet tanks, and also, according to their report, they destroyed two trucks, three horse-drawn mortars, a number of machine guns, many carts and approximately a company of Soviet rifle infantry troops..

Around 1345 hours, an order arrived from *SS-Sturmbannführer* Zeitz, *Kommandeur* of *SS-Panzerjäger-Abteilung 3,* directing the units to retreat to the church at Söréd. During the withdrawal, the tank of Captain Tarczay sunk in on the wet ground and it was immobilized. According to the statement of the gunner later, the tank was also knocked out by the Soviets. The armoured fighting vehicle that was abandoned by its crew, was soon surrounded by the Soviet rifle infantry.

Around 1600 hours, the Soviet troops launched a direct assault against the village. As it was witnessed by Hans Geißendörfer, one of the assault gun commanders of *3. Kompanie/SS-Panzerjäger-Abteilung 3*:

"They are attacking on all sides with infantry and very heavy tanks[1042]*. I am standing at the outbound road with one of the assault guns, and resist as much as I can. The courage and caution of my loader, Gerhard Haeger, has to be mentioned here. At Söréd, our comrades – as the ammunition is running very low – are fighting with spades, pitchforks and scythes. The*

[1039] Vopersal, Wolfgang: *Soldaten, Kämpfer, Kameraden. Marsch und Kämpfe der SS-Totenkopfdivision.* Band Vb. Bielefeld, 1991. p. 740.
[1040] Wood, Ian Michael: *History of the Totenkopf's Panther-Abteilung.* Keszthely, 2015. pp. 98-99.
[1041] Quoted by Vopersal, Wolfgang: *Soldaten, Kämpfer, Kameraden. Marsch und Kämpfe der SS-Totenkopfdivision.* Band Vb. Bielefeld, 1991. p. 727.
[1042] This is certainly an exaggeration, as Söréd was only assaulted by M4A2 tanks.

tanks of the Ivan, if they get too close, are sent up in the sky with Panzerfausts or magnetic anti-tank mines. The commander of our maintenance unit, SS-Unterscharführer Uhle, knocks out two heavy tanks with Panzerfausts in such a manner in a very short time. In the midst of all this hell, a courier comes to tell us that everything is over at Söréd and explains in which direction we should head with our assault gun. The Obersturmführer of the 'Danmark' battalion[1043] *orders that the wounded whom we cannot take with us, and who are not able to kill themselves, should be sent to the 'Great Army' by an Unterscharführer, who volunteers to remain with them, because nobody can expect any mercy from the Russians."*[1044]

In the meantime the Soviet rifle forces already reached the church. One of the still combat-ready Hungarian Panzer IV tanks, commanded by 1st Lieutenant István Korbuly, knocked out a Soviet armoured fighting vehicle from a distance of 300 meters. The assault guns and self-propelled anti-tank guns of *SS-Panzerjäger-Abteilung 3* tried to break out from the church towards Bodajk, but they were bogged down in the wet, soggy ground west of Söréd. The Germans blew up or knocked out the still combat-ready armoured fighting vehicles with *Panzerfausts*, and continued on foot towards Bodajk, where at last they reached their own lines. Captain Tarczay also saw it was impossible to go any further with tanks, and decided that the breakout should be attempted on foot.

The commander of *I. (Bataillon)/SS-Panzergrenadier-Regiment 24*, SS-Sturmbannführer Hermann im Masche, ordered the combined German–Hungarian breakout manoeuvre to be carried out with approximately 50 German and 15 Hungarian defenders at the front, which began after darkness had set in, northwest toward the road junction at Csókakő. The soldiers were moving in zigzag lines, running through the infantry and mortar fire showering them from every direction. *SS-Sturmbannführer* im Masche was killed, together with a number of his men. Captain Ervin Tarczay was wounded on his right knee, but as there were no bandages available, they could not dress his wounds. 1st Lieutenant István Korbuly and another soldier tried to carry him, but the severely wounded Captain collapsed. The others fled, and with a wide detour, at last reached Bodajk.[1045]

After this, Söréd was occupied by the Soviets following a concentrated attack, supported by 20 armoured fighting vehicles.[1046] The village was taken by the 30th Guards Mechanized Brigade/9th Guards Mechanized Corps. The 1st Motorized Rifle Battalion commanded by Guards Captain Ivan T. Goncharov, was reinforced with a company of M4A2 tanks and an artillery battery. Guards Captain Goncharov had stealthily led his unit to their point of departure, and launched a surprise attack. According to Soviet records, the Germans

---

1043 The parent regiment of *I. (Bataillon)/SS-Panzergrenadier-Regiment 24* was named "Danmark", as this was organized mostly from Danish volunteers. By the spring of 1945. mostly German soldiers were serving in the unit.
1044 Quoted by Vopersal, Wolfgang: *Soldaten, Kämpfer, Kameraden. Marsch und Kämpfe der SS-Totenkopfdivision.* Band Vb. Bielefeld, 1991. p. 742.
1045 Norbert Számvéber: A hazáért mind halálig. Vitéz Tarczay Ervin páncélos százados. In: Regiment issue 2005/2. Captain Ervin Tarczay, who was perhaps the best known Hungarian tank "ace", was last seen on 18 March 1945. Officially he was declared as missing, but based on the above events, he most likely bled out and died somewhere on the outskirts of Söréd. His death certificate was only issued on 14 September 1948 at Bodajk. According to the official casualties report, the Captain was buried in the southwestern sector of Söréd in the so-called "macskadűlői földek" part of the village. If this is correct, unfortunately there is no solid evidence on how his body could have been at the southwestern edge of the village given that he was seriously wounded northwest of Söréd.
1046 NARA, T311, R162, F7214627.

lost 21 tanks, assault guns and *Jagdpanzers*, and 35 armoured personnel carriers. Guards Captain Goncharov was later awarded with the Hero of the Soviet Union for his deed.[1047]

North of Söréd five *Hummel* self-propelled howitzers of *I. (Abteilung)/SS-Panzer-Artillerie-Regiment 3/3. SS-Panzer-Division*, were knocked out by the Soviets from an ambush position.[1048]

Around 1345 hours, Bodajk was approached from the direction of Söréd by eight Soviet M4A2 tanks, which were moving on the road. The Soviets opened fire on the 8.8 cm guns of *1. Batterie/SS-Panzer-Flak-Abteilung 3*. Luckily for the Germans, the tanks were not firing high-explosive shells but armour-piercing rounds with which they would have to achieve direct hits to succeed. The German 8.8 cm anti-aircraft guns were delayed joining the combat as their gun carriages were sunken in the wet and muddy ground. At last the German guns opened fire, but as they did not have enough armour-piercing rounds, they were also firing high-explosive shells with impact fuses at the Soviet armoured fighting vehicles. The engines of the M4A2 tanks roared as they switched to reverse. Two armoured fighting vehicles remained where they were, as their crew had abandoned them. In the bend of the road, a third M4A2 was also disabled. All three Soviet tanks were knocked out by one German 8.8 cm gun, named "Anton" by its crew. The Germans did not suffer any losses.[1049]

Around 1745 hours, the M4A2 tanks of the 30th Guards Mechanized Brigade advanced again on the road leading from Söréd to Bodajk. Again "Anton" opened fire at them and in three minutes, knocked out three armoured fighting vehicles without suffering any losses.[1050]

On the same day, the right flank of the 3rd Ukrainian Front, the forces of the 4th Guards- and 9th Guards Army widened the breach to 36 km and pushed forward.

According to Soviet opinions, the cause of the slow pace of the Soviet advance in the first few days was that the two guards armies had an insufficient number of tanks to support the infantry.[1051] This is true in the real sense of the word, as the two guards armies had, in the evening of 16 March 1945, only six operational tanks. At the same time, the 9th Guards Army had 74 operational self-propelled guns, and the 4th Guards Army had 111 operational self-propelled guns. On the 9th Guards Army's breach through the German lines, there were nine tanks and self-propelled guns fighting on each frontline kilometer, and there were 20 tanks and self-propelled guns on each frontline kilometer of the 4th Guards Army.[1052] That is, the rifle forces would have been supported by 191 armoured fighting vehicles at the beginning of the attack, compared to the 98 combat-ready tanks, assault guns, *Jagdpanzers* and tank destroyers of *IV. SS-Panzerkorps*.[1053]

1047 See HM HIM Hadtörténelmi Levéltár (Budapest), Szovjetunió Hőse kitüntetések gyűjteménye (*Collection of Hero of the Soviet Union awards*), 608.
1048 Wood, Ian Michael: *History of the Totenkopf's Panther-Abteilung*. Keszthely, 2015. p. 99.
1049 Stöber, Hans: *Die Flugabwehrverbände der Waffen-SS. Aufstellung, Gliederung, Luftverteidigung und Einsätze an den Fronten*. Preussisch Oldendorf, 1984. p. 559.
1050 Stöber, Hans: *Die Flugabwehrverbände der Waffen-SS. Aufstellung, Gliederung, Luftverteidigung und Einsätze an den Fronten*. Preussisch Oldendorf, 1984. p. 559.
1051 Malakhov, M. M.: A Balatontól Bécsig (excerpt). In: *Fejezetek hazánk felszabadításának történetéből*. Budapest, 1960. p. 187.
1052 Malakhov, M. M.: A Balatontól Bécsig (excerpt). In: *Fejezetek hazánk felszabadításának történetéből*. Budapest, 1960. pp. 179-180.
1053 Of the combat-ready armoured fighting vehicles of *IV. SS-Panzerkorps*, unfortunately there is no reliable source on the Hungarian manufactured armoured fighting vehicles of the Hungarian 2nd Armoured Division for that day.

The forces of the Soviet 6th Guards Tank Army were assembled throughout the day with the 46th Guards Tank Brigade/9th Guards Mechanized Corps assembled at Söréd at around 1800 hours, the 18th Guards and 31st Guards Mechanized Brigades at Felsőpuszta and the 30th Guards Mechanized Brigade in the sector of Hill 173, 3 km south of Söréd. The Corps had on that evening, 166 M4A2 tanks of which 162 were operational and 18 SU–76M self-propelled guns of which 17 were operational.[1054]

The Corps was reinforced with the 301st Light Artillery Regiment, the 391st Guards Anti-Tank Artillery Regiment, the 454th Guards Mortar Regiment, the 127th Guards Mortar (multiple rocket launcher) Artillery Battalion, the 392nd Anti-Aircraft Artillery Regiment, the 697th Self-Propelled Artillery Regiment with 17 SU–76Ms, the 364th Guards Heavy Self-Propelled Artillery Regiment and the 51st Guards Self-Propelled Artillery Brigade. The 51st Guards Self-Propelled Artillery Brigade directly subordinated to the 6th Guards Tank Army was gathered at Lovasberény with 60 operational SU–76M self-propelled guns. The 364th Guards Heavy Self-Propelled Artillery Regiment had 21 operational ISU–122s.[1055]

The 20th Guards and 22nd Guards Tank Brigade/5th Guards Tank Corps were waiting for deployment at Zámoly, and the 21st Guards Tank Brigade and the 6th Guards Motorized Rifle Brigade were waiting in the sector of Pátka to be deployed. The Corps had 120 T-34/85 tanks, of which 111 were operational; furthermore, of 21 SU–76Ms[1056], 17 were operational.

The Corps was reinforced by the 458th Mortar Regiment, the 15th Independent Guards Mortar (multiple rocket launcher) Artillery Battalion, the 388th and 697th Anti-Aircraft Artillery Regiments, the 1315th Light Artillery Regiment and the 26th Light Artillery Brigade.[1057]

The remnants of the Hungarian 2nd Honvéd Armoured Division were pushed back by the Soviets from the sector of Csókakő toward the west.[1058]

The forces of *IV. SS-Panzerkorps* were trying to establish a new frontline on the southwestern edge of the Iszkaszentgyörgy–Gúttamási–Bodajk line. Part of *3. SS-Panzer-Division*, with the help of anti-aircraft guns, were successfully defending the inner areas of Mór and the railway station against a number of Soviet infantry attacks launched from the southeast, east, north and northwest.[1059] Here the Jagdpanzer IV *Jagdpanzers* of *1. Kompanie/SS-Panzerjäger-Abteilung 3* reported to have knocked out seven T-34 tanks from the armoured fighting vehicles supporting the Soviet 106th Guards Rifle Division attacking from the north, in 20 minutes.[1060] At the entrance of Nagyveleg, one of the 7.5 cm anti-tank guns of *III. (Bataillon)/SS-Panzergrenadier-Regiment 5* knocked out four armoured fighting vehicles, T-34s according to German sources, before suffering a direct hit. In two hours of heavy combat the village had been taken by the Soviets.[1061]

1054 The SU–76M self-propelled guns were serving in the 697th Self-Propelled Artillery Regiment, which was earlier directly subordinated to the 6th Guards Tank Army.
1055 Central Archives of the Russian Defence Ministry (Podolsk), f. 243, op. 2928, gy. 131, li. 252.
1056 The SU–75M self-propelled guns belonged to the 1458th Self-Propelled Artillery Regiment.
1057 Central Archives of the Russian Defence Ministry (Podolsk), f. 243, op. 2928, gy. 131, li. 252.
1058 NARA, T311, R162, F7214628.
1059 NARA, T311, R162, F7214628. In the future, *SS-Panzer-Aufklärungs-Abteilung 1* and *12/SS-Panzer-Regiment 1* were also planned to be reassigned to here, however this had not happened.
1060 Mühlrath, Hans: Ungarn – Reise in die Vergangenheit.
1061 Vopersal, Wolfgang: *Soldaten, Kämpfer, Kameraden. Marsch und Kämpfe der SS-Totenkopfdivision*. Band Vb. Bielefeld, 1991. p. 744.

In the sector at that time there were no Soviet T–34 or T–34/85 tanks in combat, therefore it is probable that the Germans were engaged in combat with the SU-76M self-propelled guns of the 1523rd Self-Propelled Artillery Regiment/9th Guards Army. The Regiment lost three burnt out self-propelled guns on that day at Mór, but the possibility can not be entirely excluded that other armoured fighting vehicles were also knocked out as well. The Soviets captured Mór around 1830 hours, however there were encircled German pockets of active resistance still in the town.

The 1st Battery/1513rd Self-Propelled Artillery Regiment reached the edge of Moha at 1435 hours, where the SU-76M with tactical identification number 123 was hit and burnt out with one crew member killed. At the end of the day, the Regiment was acting in coordination with the 300th Guards Rifle Regiment within the battle line of the rifle forces 1.5 km west of Moha. Five of the SU-76Ms of the Regiment were destroyed on that day, while they in turn, knocked out a Jagdpanther *Jagdpanzer*[1062], two guns and three mortars, and captured, among others, three StuG. III assault guns, one Panzer IV tank and three armoured personnel carriers.[1063] The 1524th Self-Propelled Artillery Regiment was still stationed in Ráckeresztúr as army reserve, with 25 SU–76M self-propelled guns.[1064]

On the frontline of the 2nd Ukrainian Front

In the front of the Hungarian 3rd Army, the Soviets occupied Pusztavám and with a force the size of two regiments advanced into the forested area southeast of Csákvár. Bokod was defended by a smaller German combat group, but the Soviets captured this village as well. The Soviets were advancing towards the northwest and took Dad, in the north-western outskirts of which, the German–Hungarian troops tried to establish new makeshift positions facing the southeast.[1065]

The Soviet 991st Self-Propelled Artillery Regiment with the 429th Rifle Regiment/52nd Rifle Division were tasked with establishing a bridgehead on the western bank of Által Creek, then, carrying the attack on, occupying Bokod and Dad by the end of the day. The SU–76M self-propelled guns launched their attack with the rifles at 0700 hours against Bokod and by around 0900 hours they had entirely occupied the village.[1066]

Between the western outskirts of Dad and the south-eastern outskirts of Császár the German *Kampfgruppe "Wolf"*, created from *Sturmgeschütz-Brigade 325* and *Panzer-Aufklärungs-Abteilung 1*, was to establish a blocking position.[1067] The German armoured combat group was subordinated to the Hungarian 1st Hussars Division.[1068]

Around 1000 hours, part of *Kampfgruppe "Wolf"* launched a counterattack with nine assault guns of *Sturmgeschütz-Brigade 325* and outflanked the 3rd Battalion/429th Rifle

---

1062 The Jagdpanther *Jagdpanzer* was most likely from the ranks of *schwere Panzerjäger-Abteilung 560*, subordinated to *12. SS-Panzer-Division* which was en route to Mór.
1063 Central Archives of the Russian Defence Ministry (Podolsk), f. 911, op. 1, gy. 169, li. 234.
1064 Central Archives of the Russian Defence Ministry (Podolsk), f. 243, op. 2928, gy. 131, li. 253.
1065 NARA, T311, R162, F7214628.
1066 Central Archives of the Russian Defence Ministry (Podolsk), f. 240, op. 2799, gy. 342, li. 109.
1067 NARA, T311, R162, F7214635.
1068 NARA, T311, R163, F7215384.

Regiment marching from Bokod to Dad. The other two battalions of the Regiment were already in combat in the western sector of Dad. The 1st Battery/991st Self-Propelled Artillery Regiment thrust through the village, and established an ambush position on the southwestern edge of Dad. The 3rd Battery established firing positions on the southern slopes of Hill 215, 1 km southeast of Dad. The 2nd Battery was guarding the other two batteries from the south, 1.5 km west of Hill 215. Of the German assault guns, one was knocked out together with an armoured personnel carrier, upon which the other armoured fighting vehicles retreated towards the northwest. The 1st Battery/991st Self-Propelled Artillery Regiment at this point launched a counterattack and destroyed a further two German assault guns. The Germans retreated towards the west. Around 1400 hours the SU–76M self-propelled guns, together with the 429th Rifle Regiment, cleared Dad. The losses of the 991st Self-Propelled Artillery Regiment amounted to a burnt out SU–76M 1.5 km west of the Hill 215, and three of the crew were badly burnt.[1069]

The Soviets had been attacking with large rifle and armoured forces from the sector of Oroszlány–Majkpuszta and pushed the small number of defenders to the northern edge of Kecskéd, then continued their advance in the direction of Kömlőd. During this action, the defenders reported to have knocked out nine Soviet armoured fighting vehicles.[1070]

The Soviet 1505nd Self-Propelled Artillery Regiment/46th Army and the 223rd Rifle Division/1039th Rifle Regiment launched their attack at 0900 hours against Kecskéd, following a 30 minute artillery barrage. Around 800 meters east of the village, under German-Hungarian artillery fire from the direction of Point 189, 1 km northeast of Kecskéd, the Soviet rifles sought coverage by crouching on the ground. In the fight for Kecskéd on that day the 1505th Self-Propelled Artillery Regiment lost six knocked out SU–76Ms, four of which burnt out, plus four dead and four wounded men. The self-propelled guns of the Regiment established firing positions around 1300 hours at the edge of the forest east of the village.[1071]

The German *Füsilier-Bataillon 96*, in combat at Kecskéd together with a Hungarian Hussars battalion, turned back and retreated towards Környe at dawn, then established defensive positions 3 km west of there. The bridge on Által Creek was blown up by the pioneers of *Panzergrenadier-Brigade 92 (mot.)*.

Southeast of Környe, the part of *Panzergrenadier-Brigade 92 (mot.)* reinforced with assault guns,[1072] repelled the Soviet attacks, and contained them at the expense of minor ground losses. The Soviet troops were attacking in the direction of the Felsőgalla industrial site, but their advance was halted by counterattacks 3 km southwest of Alsógalla, three km south of Felsőgalla on the south-eastern edge of the latter village.[1073]

The Soviet 1897th Self-Propelled Artillery Regiment/46th Army was fighting with one of its batteries that day together with the 21th Rifle Regiment/180th Rifle Division, 1km northwest of the railway station at Szár, and with one of its batteries supported the 86th Rifle Regiment along the road leading to Felsőgalla. The SU–76M battery was in the

---

[1069] Central Archives of the Russian Defence Ministry (Podolsk), f. 240, op. 2799, gy. 342, li. 109-110.
[1070] NARA, T311, R162, F7214628.
[1071] Central Archives of the Russian Defence Ministry (Podolsk), f. 240, op. 2799, gy. 342, li. 112.
[1072] *Panzergrenadier-Brigade 92 (mot.)* was most likely supported by the armoured fighting vehicles of *Sturmartillerie-Brigade 239*.
[1073] NARA, T311, R162, F7214628.

reserve of the commander of the 21s Rifle Regiment, and one belonged to the 42nd Rifle Regiment. The 1897th Self-Propelled Artillery Regiment was tasked with supporting the 21st and 86th Rifle Regiments with one battery each, and to occupy Felsőgalla by the end of the day. However, the Soviets were not able to cope with the fire from the assault guns and infantry positions, not even with the support of the SU–76Ms. The self-propelled guns claimed to have knocked out one gun and three machine guns. Their own losses consisted of two wounded soldiers.[1074]

On the front of *96.* and *711. Infanterie-Divisions,* the Soviets launched battalion-size containing attacks, which were repulsed by the Germans, partly by counterattacks.[1075]

The Soviet 2nd Guards Mechanized Corps was drawn forward around 2200 hours that night to Dad and its units prepared for deployment.[1076]

The forces of the German *Luftflotte 4.* mainly supported the battles of *Armeegruppe "Balck",* flying 300 fighter and ground attack air missions, during which they raided vehicle columns, villages and artillery positions.[1077]

German reconnaissance had not detected any other high level Soviet units that were being deployed in the Transdanubia. However, the Germans expected that the Soviets would most likely be deploying swift moving units drawn forward from behind their lines via the Vértes Mountains and in the direction of Lake Balaton for the anticipated assault.[1078]

The frontline south of Lake Velence had to be drawn back to the Káloz east–Aba east–Seregélyes bridgehead–Agárdpuszta north-eastern edge line on the night of 18/19 March 1945 and again to the Seregélyes bridgehead – Dinnyés line during the following night. This was due to the departure of the regrouped German forces including ‚*I. SS-Panzerkorps, 356. Infanterie-Division*[1079] and *6. Panzer-Division*[1080]. Parallel to this, *2. SS-Panzer-Division* and *6 .Panzer-Division* had to be withdrawn on the night of 18/19 March, and the *Stab/II. SS-Panzerkorps* and *9. SS-Panzer-Division* on the night of 19/20 March 1945. According to the plan, *II. SS-Panzerkorps* with its two *SS-Panzer-Divisions* were to gather in the south-western outskirts of Székesfehérvár, to support and replenish the planned counterattack of *I. SS-Panzerkorps.*[1081]

On the same morning, *General der Panzertruppe* Balck expressly warned the *Heeresgruppe* not to execute the planned counterattack, as there were many creeks flowing through in the path of the assault, and in his opinion, it was probable that the forward attack of the German armoured troops would quickly grind to a halt. Instead of this, he advised that *I. SS-Panzerkorps* should instead attack from the northern outskirts of Bicske toward the south in the direction of the northern shore of Lake Velence, and opposite to this attack, another assault should be launched from the Seregélyes bridgehead toward the northwest.[1082]

1074 Central Archives of the Russian Defence Ministry (Podolsk), f. 240, op. 2799, gy. 342, li. 115.
1075 NARA, T311, R162, F7214628.
1076 Central Archives of the Russian Defence Ministry (Podolsk), f. 240, op. 2799, gy. 357, li. 10.
1077 NARA, T311, R162, F7214628.
1078 NARA, T311, R162, F7214628.
1079 According to data as of 17 March 1945, the *356. Infanterie-Division* had eight combat-ready Jagdpanzer 38(t) *Jagdpanzers*. See NARA, T311, R163, F7214976.
1080 According to data as of 17 March 1945, the *6. Panzer-Division* had 25 combat-ready Panthers and eight Panzer IV tanks plus 10 Jagdpanzer IV *Jagdpanzers*. See NARA, T311, R163, F7214976.
1081 NARA, T311, R162, F7214631.
1082 NARA, T311, R162, F7214634.

Because of the unified command and control of the planned counterattack on 19 March 1945, at 1400 hours the German *6. Panzerarmee* took over command between the south-western edge of Lake Velence and the Danube, and the same was done on the Balaton–Sárvíz–Lake Velence front by *6. Armee*. The *Stab/XXXXIII. Armeekorps*, arriving from *8. Armee*, took over command of the German frontline to be established west of the Vértes Mountains. Subsequently, the Stab of the Hungarian 3rd Army was in command of the German–Hungarian forces in combat in the Vértes Mountains and the sector of Esztergom.[1083]

As the Germans were especially concerned that the Soviets would quickly reach the sector of Komárom west of the Vértes, *6. Panzer-Division*,[1084] assigned to *III. Panzerkorps*, was planned to be sent to the south-eastern outskirts of Kisbér[1085], to be able to cover the roads leading to Komárom, which were especially important in terms of transport and supplies. The arrival of the *Panzer-Division* and *356. Infanterie-Division* on the Kisbér–Nagyigmánd line was to be protected by the 7.5 cm and 8.8 cm guns of *Panzerjäger-Abteilung 662* rerouted to Tata-Tóváros.[1086]

The workshop company of *Panzer-Regiment 11/6. Panzer-Division* was working at Nagyigmánd. Its commander, *Oberleutnant* Müller, ordered the repaired tanks taken off the railroad cars, sent out reconnaissance patrols, and as the combat commander of the village, prepared for its defence with as few as 75 men. The *Oberleutnant* sent five repaired tanks and 20 men as reinforcements to Csép, 6 km south of the village, where until then only 70 German soldiers were stationed. With their help, they succeeded in repelling two battalion-size Soviet attacks against Csép on the night of 18/19 March 1945. The Soviets assaulting Nagyigmánd were held by the fire of the repaired tanks and Jagdpanzer IV *Jagdpanzers* that were at the workshop.[1087]

Along with this, the German *8. Armee* was ordered to send the combat-ready units of *Panzerkorps "Feldherrnhalle"*, still under reorganization, (initially the *I. (Bataillon)/Panzergrenadier-Regiment 66*) to Komárom, where they were deployed in defence of the bridgehead established south of the town and to cover the guns of *II. (Abteilung)/Flak-Regiment 241*.[1088] The first unit to arrive was *I. (Bataillon)/Panzergrenadier-Regiment 66*.

Because of the Soviet forces pushing forward northwest of Székesfehérvár, *Heeresgruppe Süd* was concerned that the forces of *I. Kavallerie-Korps* in combat along the Sió Canal might be cut off from the main forces. Therefore they requested *Oberkommando der Wehrmacht*, to give permission that the units of the cavalry corps could retreat to their points of departure occupied before the launch of Operation *"Frühlingserwachen"*. This request was granted by Hitler via the OKH at dawn the next morning.[1089] Afterwards, the troops had to defend the eastern edge of the Lake Balaton–Balatonbozsok–Kisláng–Nagyláng–Aba line. At the same time, the *Stab/6. Panzerarmee* signalled that the withdrawal should be halted for two

---

1083   NARA, T311, R162, F7214631.
1084   Instead of *6. Panzer-Division* the regimental combat group of *1. SS-Panzer-Division* in reserve was to cover the rear of *III. Panzerkorps* from the north-northwest.
1085   The reinforced *Panzergrenadier-Regiment 4/6. Panzer-Division* set off for Kisbér on that day.
1086   NARA, T311, R162, F7214957.
1087   Paul, Wolfgang: *Brennpunkte. Die Geschichte der 6. Panzerdivision (1. leichte) 1937–1945*. Krefeld, 1977. pp. 449-450.
1088   NARA, T311, R162, F7214632, furthermore T311, R162, F7214636.
1089   NARA, T311, R162, F7214632.

days in order to avoid traffic jams on the few roads available in the narrowing terrain at Székesfehérvár, and also to leave enough time for the damaged armoured fighting vehicles and the other materials to be salvaged and transported to the rear.[1090]

The *Heeresgruppe* asked the *OKH* to suspend the codenames for the *SS-Panzertruppen*, the order prohibiting the use of their real names and along with this, the retention of the *SS*-pay books because this caused considerable confusion and difficulty especially in the transport of the wounded soldiers. The OKH approved this and from 0000 hours on 19 March 1945, suspended all orders in connection with codenames.[1091]

19 March 1945, Monday

(**WEATHER**: highest daytime temperature 8 Celsius, clear sky, and good visibility conditions. The roads and the open terrain were continually drying up.)

The 1891st Self-Propelled Artillery Regiment that was in combat against the Drávaszabolcs bridgehead that was eliminated on the same day, was assembling in the Drávacsehi sector that afternoon with 16 SU–76M self-propelled guns.[1092]

The units of the 84th Rifle Division attacking the German bridgehead at Valpovo with the support of the 53rd Motorcycle Regiment, were in combat southeast of Torjánc, in the vicinity of Zsidópuszta. The Germans knocked out six T-34/85s of the tank company of the Motorcycle Regiment, of which four burnt out, leaving the unit only three operational tanks by the evening. The 122nd Independent Self-Propelled Artillery Battalion/84th Rifle Division lost one burnt out SU–76M during these battles, which was most likely destroyed by a *Panzerfaust*.[1093]

On the front of *2. Panzerarmee*, on the right flank of the assault group of *XXII. Gebirgskorps*, *Grenadier-Regiment 191/71. Infanterie-Division*, reinforced with a pioneer company, occupied Hosszúvíz 2 km northeast of Mesztegnyő after heavy fighting, and *Grenadier-Regiment 211*, similarly reinforced with a pioneer company, approached the railway station of Mesztegnyő from the northeast.[1094]

The previous evening and during the night of 18/19 March 1945, *16. SS-Panzergrenadier-Division* eliminated a number of Soviet incursions in the forested area north of the road leading from Mesztegnyő toward the east, and approached the road at a distance that they were able to close it off with gunfire.

SS-Hauptsturmführer Knobelspies, *Kommandeur* of *SS-Panzer-Abteilung 16*, was wounded by a mortar shell splinter while salvaging the bogged down assault guns at Gyótapuszta.

1090 NARA, T311, R162, F7214638.
1091 NARA, T311, R162, F7214644. In the afternoon of 18 March the German *6. Panzerarmee* still proposed to change to codenames to avoid mixing up the units in the new combat control system. Thus they proposed the following names, apart from the open denomination of the units: *SS-Kampfverband "Donau"* or *SS-Kampfgruppe "Frundsberg"* for *1. SS-Panzer-Division*, and *SS-Kampfverband "Kärten"* or *SS-Kampfgruppe "Götz von Berlichingen"* for *12. SS-Panzer-Division*. See NARA, T311, R163, F7214945.
1092 Central Archives of the Russian Defence Ministry (Podolsk), f. 243, op. 2928, gy. 131, li. 257.
1093 Central Archives of the Russian Defence Ministry (Podolsk), f. 243, op. 2928, gy. 131, li. 257.
1094 NARA, T311, R162, F7214647.

The command and control of all of the combat-ready assault guns of the *Abteilung* was then taken over by *SS-Obersturmführer* Heinz-Otto Rex.[1095]

In the Nagygyótai Forest, an approximately battalion-size Soviet force with two armoured fighting vehicles, most likely the 1st Guards Motorized Rifle Battalion/32nd Independent Guards Mechanized Brigade and part of one of the companies of the 249th Independent Tank Regiment, were still holding their positions southwest of the clearing 4 km east of Kelevíz late into the evening.[1096] The 249th Independent Tank Regiment lost two knocked out T-34 tanks on that day east of Hosszúvíz, in the sector of Hill 125.[1097]

The Soviet 864th Self-Propelled Artillery Regiment together with the 32nd Independent Guards Mechanized Brigade, held off further German attacks on the line of Szőkepuszta and Hill 146, northeast of Nyírespuszta. During the fighting, the Germans knocked out a SU–76M which burnt out.[1098]

The German *Eisenbahn-Panzerzug 78* was subordinated on that day to *1. Volks-Gebirgs-Division*.[1099]

On the front of the German *I. Kavallerie-Korps/6. Armee*[1100] on the night of 18/19 March 1945, the forces of *4. Kavallerie-Division* repulsed five battalion size attacks, against the German bridgehead.[1101] During the morning, the Soviets launched small scale attacks against the German bridgeheads east of Ádánd and at Simontornya. These were also repulsed by the defenders.[1102]

During the day, a plan was formulated that the corps staff and the two German cavalry divisions would be withdrawn from the frontline and reassembled in the sector of *6. Panzerarmee* and would be subordinated to the them.[1103] The *3. Kavallerie-Division* took over the frontline section held until then by *4. Kavallerie-Division*, and the Hungarian 25th Infantry Division was subordinated to the German *23. Panzer-Division*.[1104]

The Soviets concentrated the 5th Guards Cavalry Corps in the Siófok sector, with the 71th Tank Regiment, which had three operational T–34/85s, and its 1896th Self-Propelled Artillery Regiment, which had 16 SU–76Ms. The 2nd Guards Mechanized Brigade/1st Guards Mechanized Corps was also subordinated to the Corps, with 35 operational M4A2 tanks, but this unit was, for the time being, assembled in the Tamási sector. This Soviet group was to launch an attack later from Siófok towards Enying.[1105]

1095 Puntigam, Josef Paul: *Vom Plattensee bis zur Mur. Die Kämpfe 1945 im Dreiländereck*. Feldbach, without year of publication, [1993], p. 103.
1096 NARA, T311, R162, F7214647.
1097 Central Archives of the Russian Defence Ministry (Podolsk), f. 243, op. 2928, gy. 131, li. 257.
1098 Central Archives of the Russian Defence Ministry (Podolsk), f. 243, op. 2928, gy. 131, li. 257.
1099 NARA, T311, R163, F7215395.
1100 With the introduction of the new command and control system, at 1400 hours on 19 March 1945, *Armeegruppe "Balck,"* consisting of the German *6. Armee* and the Hungarian 3rd Army, ceased to exist. In theory, the Hungarian 3rd Army was subordinated to the German *6. Panzerarmee*, but this time there was no independent combat group formed from their strength.
1101 NARA, T311, R163, F7215388.
1102 NARA, T311, R162, F7214647.
1103 NARA, T311, R163, F7214967.
1104 NARA, T311, R163, F7215395.
1105 Central Archives of the Russian Defence Ministry (Podolsk), f. 243, op. 2928, gy. 131, li. 258.

Three T–34s of the 22nd Independent Tank Regiment were in firing positions at Balatonszabadi-fürdőtelep near the Zsófia children's sanitarium, and three other tanks and one SU–76M self-propelled gun were positioned at the western edge of Szabadhídvég.[1106]

The German *Panzergrenadier-Regiments 126* and *128/23. Panzer-Division* were holding off small scale Soviet attacks in the bridgehead at Simontornya. At 1300 hours, the Soviet armoured fighting vehicles and the rifle infantry were successfully advancing on the front of *Panzergrenadier-Regiment 126*. At 1600 hours, the *Panzergrenadier-Regiments* received a preliminary order to prepare for the retreat via the Sió Canal, which commenced at 2100 hours. The *Panzergrenadier-Bataillons* left their rearguard behind and crossed the canal on rubber boats. The rearguard followed them at 2200 hours. The Germans mounted cars, and concealed from Soviet eyes, retreated via Mezőszilas and established new positions in the Középbogárd–Ángyádpuszta–Ötvenkilencmajor sector. *Panzergruppe "Fischer"* was ordered to the western outskirts of Kishörcsökpuszta and was reinforced with five Jagdpanzer IV *Jagdpanzers* of *2. Kompanie/Panzerjäger-Abteilung 128* and *3. Kompanie/ Panzer-Pionier-Bataillon 51*.[1107]

The *9. SS-Panzer-Division/II. SS-Panzerkorps* and *44. Reichsgrenadier-Division* had withdrawn their forces to the new frontline, leaving forward troops in the former. The *2. SS-Panzer-Division* was withdrawn from the frontline and the majority of their forces reached the Szabadbattyán east–Nádasdladány sector during the night.[1108]

SS-Panzergrenadier-Regiment 3/2. SS-Panzer-Division, with the support of a few tanks, launched an attack from the northern outskirts of Várpalota towards the Vértes Mountains. However, the German armoured fighting vehicles became bogged down in the mud. Therefore the attack had to be continued by the infantry alone, and despite the circumstances, they proceeded at a good pace. North of the *SS-Regiment,* the Hungarian 1st Honvéd Hussars Division was in combat, but the majority of the troops were already retreating apart from a few stubbornly resisting combat groups. As a consequence of these combat actions *SS-Panzergrenadier-Regiment 3* reached the south-eastern outskirts of Győr, the new location of their deployment, a day later.

The majority of *2. SS-Panzer-Division* and the *Stab/II. SS-Panzerkorps,* were marching towards Kisbér. The *SS-Division* heading north, was to stop the Soviets pushing toward Komárom together with *6. Panzer-Division* of the *Wehrmacht* and *356. Infanterie-Division*. The *Division* was to launch a counterattack from Nagyigmánd toward the east. However, on the same night, the majority of *2. SS-Panzer-Division* was still marching in the eastern sector of Szabadbattyán–Nádasdladány. The armoured fighting vehicles were loaded onto trains at Herend, near Veszprém, and transported by rail to Győr.[1109]

The Panthers of *4. Kompanie/SS-Panzer-Regiment 2* were guarding the loading of *II. (Abteilung)/SS-Panzer-Regiment 2*. The *Kompanie* was running out of fuel and it also needed to get loaded onto trains. From the airport nearby, some fuel was acquired with

---

1106 Central Archives of the Russian Defence Ministry (Podolsk), f. 243, op. 2928, gy. 178, li. 88/2.
1107 Rebentisch, Ernst: *Zum Kaukasus und zu den Tauern. Die Geschichte der 23. Panzer-Division 1941–1945*. Esslingen, 1963. p. 492.
1108 NARA, T311, R162, F7214647.
1109 Weidinger, Otto: *Division Das Reich. Der Weg der 2. SS-Panzer-Division „Das Reich"*. Band V: 1943-1945. Osnabrück, without year of publication, pp. 462-463.

great difficulty, and then with 10 Panthers, they reported at the corps command post nearby, most likely *IV. SS-Panzerkorps*.[1110]

The *44. Reichsgrenadier-Division* was subordinated on this day to *III. Panzerkorps*.

In front of *III. Panzerkorps,* the Soviet 11th Guards Motorcycle Battalion/1st Guards Mechanized Corps and part of the 36th Guards Rifle Division southeast of Káloz, eliminated the German bridgehead east of Hatvanpuszta, then with a battalion-sized force crossed both canals of the Sárvíz, but a German counterattack to the east pushed them back beyond the Malom Canal. *SS-Panzer-Aufklärungs-Abteilung 1 and 2* of *SS-Kampfgruppe "Krag",* were withdrawn from the frontline on that day and sent after their parent division.[1111]

The battalion and regiment-size attacks of the Soviet 1st Guards Mechanized Corps and rifle forces from the south against Aba and along the Sárbogárd–Székesfehérvár railroad line resulted in two incursions, each one about 1 square km in size. Units of the 3rd Guards Mechanized Brigade occupied Heinrichmajor.

Units of the 206th Rifle Division, with the support of the armoured transport vehicles of the 1st Guards Mechanized Corps, crossed to the western bank of the Malom Canal in the sector of Nagyhörcsökpuszta.[1112]

In the evening, the 1st Guards Mechanized Corps had 9911 men, 85 operational M4A2 and T–34 tanks, 15 SU–100 self-propelled guns, 30 armoured cars, 30 armoured transport vehicles, 34 guns, 98 mortars, 18 anti-aircraft guns, 12 M17 self-propelled half-track 12.7 mm four-barrelled anti-aircraft heavy machine guns (lend-lease version of the M16 MGMC) and eight M–13 multiple rocket launchers and was waiting for the upcoming attack.[1113]

West of Sárosd and south of Seregélyes, the company and battalion-size Soviet assault attempts failed.

Between the Pusztaszabolcs–Seregélyes railroad line and Lake Velence, the Germans had withdrawn their frontline according to plan. Although *1. Panzer-Division* was chased by a considerable number of Soviet forces, they were unable to prevent the Germans from occupying their new positions. The German rearguard troops left at the earlier frontline, were forced back on a number of locations to the new positions under the pressure of armoured fighting vehicles. The battalion-sized attacks launched by the Soviets against the new positions were, however, repulsed by the Germans.

1110 Weidinger, Otto: *Division Das Reich. Der Weg der 2. SS-Panzer-Division „Das Reich".* Band V: 1943-1945. Osnabrück, without year of publication, pp. 463-464. The Panther-Kompanie launched a counterattack with one German armoured combat group, but this failed and they lost two Panthers during the retreat. After this the tanks of *4. Kompanie/SS-Panzer-Regiment 2* pushed themselves through the Soviet assault wedges, and reported to *SS-Panzer-Regiment 1*. Here, the *Regimentskommander, SS-Obersturmbannführer* Peiper, wanted to take the eight Panthers from Barkmann, saying that he only had 10 combat-ready tanks, but he has many more crews. In this case, Barkmann's unit would have had to cross toward their own troops on foot. At last the situation was resolved in a way when the Panthers of *SS-Panzer-Regiment 2* joined in combat with *SS-Panzer-Regiment 1* until 28 March, then they joined their own troops at Fertő Lake. The two Panthers, among them Barkmann's tank, knocked out during the fighting had to be blown up.
1111 NARA, T311, R163, F7214965.
1112 Central Archives of the Russian Defence Ministry (Podolsk), f. 243, op. 2928, gy. 131, li. 253.
1113 Summarized report of the 1st Guards Mechanized Corps of the combat actions during March – April 1945. Copy owned by the author. p. 20.

On the same day, the Soviet 23rd Tank Corps, upon the orders of the Staff of the 3rd Ukrainian Front, turned over its defensive positions to the 110th Tank Brigade/18th Tank Corps by 0400 hours, then proceeded to assemble its forces in the sector of Kápolnásnyék and Pettend.[1114] At the same time, the 110th Tank Brigade had turned over its own positions to the 9th Guards Tank Brigade/1st Guards Mechanized Corps.[1115]

The majority of the 18th Tank Corps however, remained in their original positions and were engaged on that day in combat with German forces. In the meantime, they reported to have knocked out a Tiger tank, but the Germans also knocked out a T–34/85.[1116]

During the evening, the Corps, with 47 operational T–34/85s, six ISU–152s, 10 ISU–122s and 13 SU–76Ms, together with two thirds of the subordinated 208th Self-Propelled Artillery Brigade with 27 operational SU–100s, upon the orders of the 27th Army, concentrated their forces in the Seregélyes south–Jakabszállás–Sárosd sector, to be able to further support the defence of the rifle infantry.[1117]

Between Lake Velence and Székesfehérvár, the Soviet troops launched regiment-size attacks with the support of a few armoured fighting vehicles, and the attackers managed to cross the Seregélyes–Székesfehérvár railroad line, but were halted on the line stretching from 5.5 km southeast of the train station of Székesfehérvár to three km south of there by the German *Panzer-Aufklärungs-Abteilung 6*.[1118]

The *Kommandeur* of *1. Panzer-Division*, *Generalmajor* Thunert, ordered the *Kommandeur* of *Panzer-Regiment 1*, *Oberst* Streith, to establish a new *Kampfgruppe*. This consisted of 12 Panthers and five Panzer IV tanks of *Panzer-Regiment 1*, a few pioneer-armoured personnel carriers and self-propelled 2 cm anti-aircraft guns, and one of the *Grenadier-Kompanies* of *Panzer-Feldersatz Bataillon 81*. By the late afternoon, the new *Kampfgruppe "Streith"*, together with part of *Panzer-Aufklärungs-Abteilung 1* and *Panzer-Pionier-Bataillon 37*, was able to occupy the Székesfehérvár south-eastern edge–Dinnyés sector as a strongpoint, and secured it by forwarding small armoured detachments. Afterwards the *Kampfgruppe* was relieved by the forces of *5. SS-Panzer-Division*.[1119]

On the night of 19/20 March 1945, *I. (Abteilung)/Panzer-Regiment 24* with 20 combat-ready Panther tanks was ordered to coordinate with *Kampfgruppe "Streith* to launch an assault from Székesfehérvár and retake Ráctemető southeast of the town.

The *4. Schwadron*, under *Oberleutnant* von Schlotheim with 10 Panthers, was to attack from the centre of the town towards the southeast, and then, together with the *Panzergrenadiers*, was to push forward from the west to break into the town. The tanks of *Leutnant* Jonas were to provide covering fire from the hills along the road, and were to cover their forces towards the northeast. The clear starry sky provided good visibility conditions as *4. Schwadron* occupied their point of departure on the edge of Székesfehérvár. When the *Panzergrenadiers* stepped out of the so-called "trumpet forest" 1 km west of the

---

1114 War log of the 23rd Tank Corps from March 1945. Copy owned by the author. p. 11.
1115 Central Archives of the Russian Defence Ministry (Podolsk), f. 243, op. 2928, gy. 131, li. 257.
1116 Central Archives of the Russian Defence Ministry (Podolsk), f. 243, op. 2928, gy. 131, li. 257, and War log of the 18th Tank Corps for March 1945. Copy owned by the author. p. 31.
1117 Central Archives of the Russian Defence Ministry (Podolsk), f. 243, op. 2928, gy. 131, li. 257.
1118 NARA, T311, R162, F7214648.
1119 Stoves, Rolf: Persönliches Kriegstagebuch Pz.Rgt. 1 (typewritten manuscript, a copy owned by the author), entry from 19 March 1945.

Ráctemető, a heavy Soviet barrage fired from the other side of the road around Hill 136 near Kuruchalom, greeted them. Thus the *Panzergrenadiers* and *4. Schwadron* were not able to join forces yet.[1120]

On the north-eastern edge of Székesfehérvár, at 0400 hours on 19 March, the assault group of the Soviet 122nd Guards Rifle Regiment/41th Guards Rifle Division reinforced by pioneers, attacked the Vadásztölténygyár ammunition factory site, from the northwest, supported by four SU–76M self-propelled guns and one T–34/85 tank of the 44th Guards Independent Self-Propelled Artillery Battalion. At the same time, other units of the Regiment assaulted the military factory from the north and north-east. By 1400 hours, effectively supported by the SU–76M self-propelled guns, the Soviets occupied the factory after heavy fighting, and pushed the units of *5. SS-Panzer-Division* into the centre of Székesfehérvár.[1121] The crews of the SU–76M self-propelled guns employed smoke grenades with great efficiency during these engagements, by which they were able to avoid incurring heavy losses.[1122]

The right flank of *5. SS-Panzer-Division* was pushed back by the assaults of the Soviet 126th Guards Rifle Regiment within the city to the sector of the railway station. The gap opened toward *III. Panzerkorps* was to be closed off by a night assault of the German *1. Panzer-Division* as well as retaking the original main line of combat.[1123]

The units of the Soviet 4th Guards Army in combat in the sector of Székesfehérvár, were still mostly supported by the independent self-propelled-artillery battalions of the divisions:

- the 75th Guards Independent Self-Propelled Artillery Battalion/69th Guards Rifle Division with 11 SU–76Ms at Pákozd;
- the 44th Guards Independent Self-Propelled Artillery Battalion/41st Guards Rifle Division with 12 SU–76Ms at Hóhérkút;
- the 85th Guards Independent Self-Propelled Artillery Battalion/80th Guards Rifle Division with 10 SU–76Ms at Máriamajor;
- the 13th Guards Independent Self-Propelled Artillery Battalion/5th Guards Airborne Division with two SU–76Ms in the north-western outskirts of Székesfehérvár, 1 km northwest of Imremajor;
- the 8th Guards Independent Self-Propelled Artillery Battalion/7th Guards Airborne Division with 12 SU–76Ms at Polgármalom;
- the 69th Guards Independent Self-Propelled Artillery Battalion/62nd Guards Rifle Division with 10 SU–76Ms at Point 122, 5 km southeast of Székesfehérvár.[1124]

The 366th Guards Heavy Self-Propelled Artillery Regiment was still stationed directly east of Székesfehérvár, securing the roads leading to Csala and Kisfalud. The unit reported that they knocked out a Tiger heavy tank and an armoured personnel carrier with their captured German armoured fighting vehicles. Their losses amounted to one knocked out

---

1120   Weidemann, Gert-Axel: *Unser Regiment. Reiter-Regiment 2 – Panzer-Regiment 24*. Groß-Umstadt, 1982. p. 277.
1121   Central Archives of the Russian Defence Ministry (Podolsk), f. 866, op. 1, gy. 65, li. 87.
1122   Central Archives of the Russian Defence Ministry (Podolsk), f. 243, op. 2900, gy. 1570, li. 204.
1123   NARA, T311, R162, F7214648.
1124   Central Archives of the Russian Defence Ministry (Podolsk), f. 243, op. 2928, gy. 131, li. 253.

and burnt German assault gun. By the evening, the unit had five *Hummel* self-propelled howitzers and three Panther tanks.[1125]

The 912th Self-Propelled Artillery Regiment/207th Self-Propelled Artillery Brigade, was three km southeast of Székesfehérvár at Point 134, and the 1004th Regiment was in defence at Point 122, 1.5 km southeast of there, with approximately 33 operational SU–100 self-propelled guns.[1126] The two self-propelled artillery regiments were supporting the 21th Guards Rifle Corps. Two batteries of the 1004th Self-Propelled Artillery Regiment were in defence 1 km north of Ráctemető along the railroad line, one battery was at the eastern edge of Székesfehérvár facing west, and these were defending the 62nd Guards Rifle Division against attacks of the German *1. Panzer-Division*. The Soviet 912th Self-Propelled Artillery Regiment was covering the road and railroad junction point 250 meters north-west of Point 122 in the section of the 69th Guards Rifle Division. During the day, one of the SU–100s had ran on an anti-tank mine and was damaged.[1127]

Around 1500 hours in the afternoon, the two Self-Propelled Artillery Regiments were supporting the attack of the two Guards Rifle Divisions. During the fighting, the 207th Self-Propelled Artillery Brigade reported to have destroyed two Tiger B heavy tanks.[1128]

On the same day, the 4th Guards Army received the 1922nd Self-Propelled Artillery Regiment/208th Self-Propelled Artillery Brigade as well, which established firing positions with 17 SU–100s on the western slopes of Hill 153 near Gombócsleő, four km north – northwest of Székesfehérvár.[1129]

In the front of the German *IV. SS-Panzerkorps/6. Panzerarmee*, the Soviet attempt to outflank Székesfehérvár had not been successful so far. However, later in the afternoon, the attackers managed to breach the German defence in-depth with armoured fighting vehicles from the north-west, and they reached the inner districts of the town.

Northwest of Székesfehérvár, the forces of the Soviet 6th Guards Tank Army commenced their final attempt to break through the tactical depth of the German–Hungarian defences. According to the original Soviet operational plan, the forces of the tank army were to outflank the forces of the German *6. Panzerarmee* and *6. Armee* in the east and north-eastern areas around Lake Balaton. However, three of the four *SS-Panzer-Divisions* of the German *6. Panzerarmee* were already in the process of being reassembled, and of these, two divisions were preparing for an attack at that time in subordination to *I. SS-Panzerkorps* in the area of the assaulting Soviet Tank Army.

The Soviets, attacking westwards with rifle forces supported by armoured fighting vehicles, occupied Isztimér and Bodajk.

The *III. (Bataillon)/SS-Panzergrenadier-Regiment 6/3. SS-Panzer-Division* and the remnants of *II. (Abteilung)/SS-Panzer-Regiment 3* were in combat east of Inota. Guttamási was defended until noon by *2. and 3. Batterie/SS-Panzer-Flak-Abteilung 3*, mostly in infantry combat. Three Panther tanks of *I. (Abteilung)/SS-Panzer-Regiment 3* were also deployed there.[1130]

1125 Central Archives of the Russian Defence Ministry (Podolsk), f. 243, op. 2928, gy. 131, li. 256.
1126 Central Archives of the Russian Defence Ministry (Podolsk), f. 243, op. 2928, gy. 131, li. 256.
1127 War log of the 207th Self-Propelled Artillery Brigade, 19 March 1945. Copy owned by the author.
1128 War log of the 207th Self-Propelled Artillery Brigade, 19 March 1945. Copy owned by the author.
1129 Central Archives of the Russian Defence Ministry (Podolsk), f. 243, op. 2928, gy. 131, li. 256.
1130 Wood, Ian Michael: *History of the Totenkopf's Panther-Abteilung*. Keszthely, 2015. p. 100.

The remaining four Jagdpanzer IV *Jagdpanzers* of *1. Kompanie/SS-Panzerjäger-Abteilung 3* encircled at Mór, had broken out around 1200 hours along the railroad line towards Aka, where they established new holding positions after reassembling their forces. En route, they reported to have knocked out three Soviet T–34 tanks.[1131]

The command post of the division was moved from Balinka to Dudar. The remnants of the battered *SS-Kampfgruppen* engaged around in the forested areas, attempted to establish a new frontline west of Balinka and Bakonykúti together with the forces of *SS-Panzergrenadier-Regiment 25/12. SS-Panzer-Division*.[1132]

Guards Captain Dmitry Fedorovich Loza, commander of the 1st Battalion/46th Guards Tank Brigade[1133], remembered this days combat around Bodajk:

"Around noon, the units of the 9th Guards Mechanized Corps approached Bodajk (a village south of Mór, and 60 km south-west of Budapest), which was the important centre of the enemy resistance on the road leading up to the Bakony Mountains. Immediately fierce fighting broke out.

Akulov drove his Sherman[1134] to the edge of the small gravel pit near the road. He remained there for a few minutes. He started to scan the terrain in front of them with his binoculars. The houses of Bodajk were clearly seen over the Mór River [the Móri Canal – the author]. The bridge was intact over the watercourse obstacle. But the enemy might have already prepared for the detonation of it. We thought that upon the first signs of our advancing troops heading the village, the enemy will blow the bridge up. The remaining tanks of the battalion fanned out on the left, and were firing salvos of two rounds each. The artillery was blanketing the enemy lines along the Mór River with explosions. Then the assault order arrived.

The tanks were rolling forward. The desantniks [escorting rifles– the author] were holding on the rails of the engine compartment covers. I ordered that up until I do not order otherwise, the commanders should keep them up on the tanks. The tanks without infantry – this is a well-known fact – could easily be destroyed by the enemy tank destroyers in a built-up environment.

The German anti-tank guns were silent until now; suddenly they have opened fire on the attacking tanks. The emcha[1135] of Junior Lieutenant Sergei Lodkov was hit; the crew resumed firing from the spot they were immobilized.

Akulov drove his own tank right toward the bridge, deep into the most dangerous section of defence. He was aware that in all probability the crossing point is heavily defended by fire. His driver, Guards Staff Sergeant Aleksandr Kliujev exploited the ground layout and quickly reduced the distance to the watercourse. Following the swift attack of Akulov's

---

1131 Mühlrath, Hans: Ungarn – Reise in die Vergangenheit. There were still no Soviet armoured fighting vehicles of that type in combat in the area. These were most likely the M4A2 tanks securing the flanks of the 9th Guards Mechanized Corps, however there is no evidence yet of this.
1132 Vopersal, Wolfgang: *Soldaten, Kämpfer, Kameraden. Marsch und Kämpfe der SS-Totenkopfdivision*. Band Vb. Bielefeld, 1991. p. 748.
1133 The 1st Battalion/46th Guards Tank Brigade had altogether 21 M4A2 tanks on 17 March 1945. Of these, 15 have freshly arrived to the unit.
1134 Guards Junior Lieutenant Viktor Akulov was the commander of the oldest and most worn out M4A2 tank of the battalion.
1135 The Soviet soldiers called the M4A2 tanks "em chitiri", or in short "emcha".

vehicle, the Shermans of Junior Lieutenants Vladimir Jurchenko and Nikolaj Kudryasov, were speeding after him. Two enemy anti-tank guns were sending shells in the direction of the first three brave tanks. One of the shells swept right next to the turret of Akulov's emcha. It had hit the armour and one of the splinters wounded one of the desantnik. Junior Lieutenant Jurchenko's tank had thrown off its shattered left track and turned around; at the same time, smoke grenades were thrown out of the turret, thus concealing it from the enemy. This had saved the tank from imminent destruction.

Approaching Bodajk, the enemy fire intensified, and was fired from all available types of artillery. Our advance was slowed down. The desantniks dropped off and advanced towards the river with the coverage provided by the tanks. The battle was raging meter by meter, but the assault itself seemed to be in danger. But we could not do anything else. It became apparent that the frontal attack against Bodajk would not be successful. The komkor, General Mikhail Volkov ordered the 46th Guards Tank Brigade to hold their current positions. The centre of the fighting against the enemy strongpoint was to be executed by the 3th Guards Mechanized Brigade, which was in action right with the troops.

By the evening of 19 March with the outflanking manoeuvre carried out by the subunits of the mechanized brigade and the frontal attack of the emchas of Lieutenant Colonel Mihno,[1136] we occupied Bodajk."[1137]

According to Soviet sources, units of the 9th Guards Mechanized Corps also knocked out six Panzer IV tanks of the Hungarian 2nd Armoured Division.[1138]

The *1. Batterie/SS-Panzer-Flak-Abteilung 3* with its last combat-ready 8.8 cm gun and with one 3.7 cm automatic cannon, established a new firing position west of Bodajk, in the front of a hill. One of the StuG. III assault guns of *SS-Panzerjäger-Abteilung 3* was also in combat here.[1139] In the morning at 0830 hours, the positions were raided by Fw 190 ground attack aircraft by mistake and they destroyed the towing vehicles of the anti-aircraft units. The number of battle casualties was high. According to the *Stab/3. SS-Panzer-Division,* this raid was carried out by Hungarian ground attack aircraft.[1140]

Around 0900 hours, units of the Soviet 9th Guards Mechanized Corps launched an attack from Bodajk towards Balinka. The 8.8 cm anti-tank gun of *1. Batterie/SS-Panzer-Flak-Abteilung 3,* knocked out two M4A2s before it was directly hit. The StuG. III assault gun in the meantime replenished its fuel supplies at one of the bridges by the mill. A member of the *Batterie, SS-Sturmmann* Batt, knocked out another tank with a *Panzerfaust*. Around 1000 hours, the Germans blew up all the bridges at the mill. At Balinka, *Festungs-Pak-Verband IX* was also in firing positions with 8.8 cm Pak 43 guns with which opened fire at the ten attacking Soviet tanks.

The first armoured assault against Balinka by the 46th Guards Tank Brigade and the 30th Guards Mechanized Brigade of the 9th Guards Mechanized Corps, was repulsed by

---

1136 Guards Lieutenant Colonel Nikolai Mihailovich Mihno was the commander of the 46th Guards Tank Brigade.
1137 Loza, Dmitriy: *Commanding the Red Army's Sherman Tanks*. Lincoln–London, 1996. pp. 77-78.
1138 Wood, Ian Michael: *History of the Totenkopf's Panther-Abteilung*. Keszthely, 2015. p. 100.
1139 The StuG. III assault gun was likely not from among those in combat at Söréd.
1140 Stöber, Hans: *Die Flugabwehrverbände der Waffen-SS. Aufstellung, Gliederung, Luftverteidigung und Einsätze an den Fronten*. Preussisch Oldendorf, 1984. p. 560.

the Germans who reported knocking out six Soviet tanks.[1141] At the church of Balinka, a Panzer IV tank, probably from *SS-Panzer-Regiment 3,* was in combat, however its gun had not been calibrated and there were only three shells left. Naturally, the counterattack carried out by the armoured fighting vehicle was unsuccessful. Around 1600 hours the Soviet units outflanked Balinka from the north. The units of *3. SS-* and *12. SS-Panzer-Division* abandoned the village through a gap a few hundred meters wide, and retreated towards Mecsér. Here they met the armoured personnel carriers of *12. SS-Panzer-Division,* which tried to strengthen the German frontline in the sector.[1142] In the meantime, the Soviets occupied Balinka.

The 18th Guards Mechanized Brigade/9th Guards Mechanized Corps and the 46th Guards Tank Brigade/9th Guards Mechanized Corps were engaged in combat at Hill 224, 2 km northwest of Bodajk.

At dawn, the 9th Guards Mechanized Corps set off with 173 M4A2s and 17 SU–76Ms, and by the evening 154 M4A2s and 16 SU–76Ms remained operational. The Corps lost 10 M4A2 tanks that were knocked out[1143]; five of which burnt out, and the others became bogged down in the mud.[1144].

Despite what is entered into the war log[1145] of *Heeresgruppe Süd,* Csór was not yet completely occupied by the Soviets on that day. This was because the commander of *I. (Abteilung)/SS-Panzer-Artillerie-Regiment 5/5. SS-Panzer-Division, SS-Hauptsturmführer* Günter Bernau, received an order from the division staff on the night of 20 March 1945 that as the commander of the village, he was to keep the Székesfehérvár–Várpalota road closed off as long as possible. To accomplish this, they only had their own two 10.5 cm field howitzer batteries, and 40-50 soldiers from *SS-Panzer-Aufklärungs-Abteilung 5,* which was under the command of *SS-Obersturmführer* Stichnot. However, the retreating soldiers were quickly caught up, organized into subunits and deployed in the perimeter defences at Csór. Reinforcements soon arrived in the evening, one platoon of the *Divisionsbegleitkompanie/5. SS-Panzer-Division,* one armoured personnel carrier company and five assault guns.[1146]. The armoured personnel carriers were supporting the infantry with their 2 cm automatic cannons and the assault guns were standing in reserve, ready for a counterattack.[1147]

The *1. SS-Panzer-Division/I. SS-Panzerkorps* formed a new defensive line from the western outskirts of Csór to the eastern edge of Bakonykúti, and *12. SS-Panzer-Division* did the same from Balinka towards the northwest.

In the morning, the forces of *12. SS-Panzer-Division* were attacked by Soviet ground attack aircraft. A few soldiers of the scattered *3. SS-Panzer-Division* reported at the

---

1141 NARA, T311, R162, F7214648.
1142 Stöber, Hans: *Die Flugabwehrverbände der Waffen-SS. Aufstellung, Gliederung, Luftverteidigung und Einsätze an den Fronten.* Preussisch Oldendorf, 1984. p. 561.
1143 Central Archives of the Russian Defence Ministry (Podolsk), f. 339, op. 5179, gy. 87, li. 11.
1144 Central Archives of the Russian Defence Ministry (Podolsk), f. 243, op. 2928, gy. 131, li. 255.
1145 NARA, T311, R162, F7214648.
1146 The unit of the assault guns is uncertain, perhaps they could have been the StuG. IV assault guns of *I. (Abteilung)/SS-Panzer-Regiment 5,* or the Jagdpanzer IV *Jagdpanzers* of *SS-Panzerjäger-Abteilung 5.* The armoured personnel carrier company was most likely part of *III. (Bataillon)/SS-Panzergrenadier-Regiment/1. SS-Panzer-Division* in combat at Inota.
1147 Bernau, Günter: Aus den letzten Kämpfen in Ungarn 1945. I. /SS-Panzer-Artillerie-Regiment 5. In: *Deutsches Soldatenjahrbuch 1975.* pp. 211-212.

forward divisional command post at Balinka. During the late afternoon, *II. (Bataillon)/ SS-Panzergrenadier Regiment 26* established defensive positions on the eastern edge of the village. The scattered soldiers of *3. SS-Panzer-Division* were assigned to the *Bataillon*. In the sector of Bodajk, *SS-Panzer-Aufklärungs-Abteilung 12* closed off the crossing points over Móri Creek.

In the afternoon, the divisional command post was relocated to Szápár, where *SS-Panzer-Flak-Abteilung 12* also established positions. *SS-Panzer-Regiment 12* was gathering at Bakonycsernye. *SS-Panzergrenadier-Regiment 25* and *SS-Panzerjäger-Abteilung 12* were, for unknown reasons, subordinated to *1. SS-Panzer-Division*.

With this, *I. SS-Panzerkorps* occupied its attack positions necessary for the assault to be launched on the following day. The *12. SS-Panzer-Division* was tasked with launching an attack at 0500 hours southeast of Bakonycsernye, to throw the Soviets out of Isztimér that was occupied by them on the same day.[1148]

During the afternoon, the Soviets executed a powerful assault between Csór and Bakonykúti and with this, they pushed the Germans on the western edge of the forest east of Inota and into the western outskirts of Bakonykúti. The German armoured fighting vehicles commenced retreat from Bakonykúti toward Inota around 1600 hours.[1149]

Some units of *1. SS-Panzergrenadier-Regiment/1. SS-Panzer-Division* supported by *SS-Panzer-Flak-Abteilung 1,* immediately went on the attack after arriving in the sector of Várpalota. The soldiers of *III. (gepanzert) (Bataillon)/SS-Panzergrenadier-Regiment 2*, commanded by *SS-Sturmbannführer* Diefenthal, dismounted from their armoured personnel carriers and took Inota back from the Soviets in heavy close quarters combat, and afterwards established positions east of the village. Beyond the holding line created by the armoured personnel carrier-battalion, the armoured group of the *Division* gathered around 1600 hours. In the evening, the Soviets launched a counterattack, but the forces of *1. SS-Panzer-Division* knocked out eight of their tanks.[1150]

Bakonykúti was attacked by the 20th Guards and 22nd Guards Tank Brigades/5th Guards Tank Corps/6th Guards Tank Army, supported by the 364th Guards Heavy Self-Propelled Artillery Regiment. During these battles, the Corps lost 11 knocked out T–34/85 tanks of which six were burnt out, and two knocked out ISU–122 self-propelled guns of which one was burnt out.

The SU-76M self-propelled guns of the 6th Guards Motorized Rifle Brigade and the 51st Guards Self-Propelled Artillery Brigade, tried to occupy the eastern edge of the forest 3 km east of Inota. Three SU–76Ms of the 1st Self-Propelled Artillery Battalion/51st Guards Self-Propelled Artillery Brigade were knocked out in the Csór sector, two of which burnt out.[1151] The 21st Guards Tank Brigade, in the corps commander's reserve, was on the march to Csór. On that day, the 5th Guards Tank Corps launched an assault with 120 T–34/85 tanks and 21 SU–76Ms, however by the evening, only 105 tanks

---

1148 Meyer, Hubert: *Kriegsgeschichte der 12. SS-Panzerdivision „Hitlerjugend".* Band II. Osnabrück, 1987. 2nd edition. p. 506.
1149 *Inter arma. Források a székesfehérvári egyházmegye történetéből II.* Edited, introduction written, annotated and references compiled by Gergely Mózessy. Székesfehérvár, 2004. p. 104.
1150 Tiemann, Ralf: *Die Leibstandarte.* Band IV/2. Osnabrück, 1987. pp. 299-301.
1151 War log of the 51st Guards Self-Propelled Artillery Brigade from the period of 20 January - 20 August 1945. Copy owned by the author. p. 5.

and 19 self-propelled guns remained operational. The 4th Guards Motorcycle Regiment, in the reserve of the commander of the 6th Guards Tank Army, stood at Gúttamási and had seven operational Mk–IX Valentine tanks and 76 motorcycles.[1152]

Thus the two corps of the 6th Guards Tank Army thrown into combat, met with considerable resistance, and their attack progressed slowly, therefore they were unable to quickly execute their attack and had not fully completely the task assigned to them. The slow pace of their attack was blamed on the forested terrain dotted with smaller hills, the heavy resistance of the SS-units, and the attitude of the 9th Guards Mechanized Corps that displayed "too much hesitation" and let itself get engaged in long, drawn out battles.[1153]

The 1513th Self-Propelled Artillery Regiment, supporting the rifle forces of the 9th Guards Army, lost an SU-76M in the sector of Csór. In the evening only nine operational self-propelled guns remained in the unit. The 1523rd Self-Propelled Artillery Regiment was engaged in combat throughout the day with 16 SU–76M self-propelled guns at Söréd. Around 1800 hours, the 1524th Self-Propelled Artillery Regiment was assembled at Borbálamajor in the reserves of the division commander, with 25 operational SU–76Ms in its possession.[1154]

Units of *1. SS-Panzer-Division* launched an attack at 2000 in the evening, aimed at retaking Csór[1155] and Bakonykúti.[1156] The *I. SS-Panzerkorps* reported to have knocked out 12 Soviet armoured fighting vehicles on that day.[1157]

On the frontline section of the 2nd Ukrainian Front

In the front of the Hungarian VIII Army Corps, the Soviets continued their attack from the Pusztavám–Dad sector toward the northwest; meanwhile they had taken Császár, Szák and Szend. The Soviet troops had not yet attacked Kisbér; instead they advanced in the direction of Ete, where they were held off.

Kampfgruppe "Wolf" with *Panzer-Aufklärungs-Abteilung 1* and *Sturmgeschütz-Brigade 325*, retreated from the Soviets to the Makkpuszta–Szend north-northwest four km sector, where it repelled a number of Soviet battalion-size attacks.[1158]

On the same day, the German *Kampfgruppe* was subordinated to *XXXXIII. Armeekorps* together with the arriving *356. Infanterie-Division*.

On the same day, *XXXXIII. Armeekorps* was preoccupied with establishing secure positions on the Nagyigmánd–Mocsa–Naszály–Füzítőpuszta line.[1159]

1152 Central Archives of the Russian Defence Ministry (Podolsk), f. 243, op. 2928, gy. 131, li. 255. According to the war log of the 5th Guards Tank Corps, the Germans knocked out only eight of their tanks, of which five were burnt out.
1153 Malakhov, M. M.: A Balatontól Bécsig (excerpt). In: *Fejezetek hazánk felszabadításának történetéből*. Budapest, 1960. p. 189.
1154 Central Archives of the Russian Defence Ministry (Podolsk), f. 243, op. 2928, gy. 131, li. 255-256.
1155 Csór – as seen above – was still in German hands, but the Soviets had cut off the supply lines of the troops in combat there towards Inota and Veszprém.
1156 NARA, T311, R162, F7214649.
1157 NARA, T311, R163, F7215400.
1158 NARA, T311, R162, F7214649.
1159 NARA, T311, R162, F7214649.

In the sector of the Hungarian 3rd Army, the Soviets continued their assault towards the north and north-east from the Dad sector, taking Kocs and breaking into Tata-Tóváros; subsequently, they advanced even further toward the north-west.

In this sector, the Soviet 2nd Guards Mechanized Corps were in combat. The 6th Guards Mechanized Brigade was attacking from the south, and occupied Kocs by 0940 hours. The Brigade was followed in the second echelon by the 37th Guards Tank Brigade. The 4th Guards Mechanized Brigade was advancing in the sector of Kömlőd and Tata and around 0940 hours, reached the road junction 4 km southeast of Kocs. The 5th Guards Mechanized Brigade followed this Brigade, so far without enemy contact, and by 0940 hours occupied Nagytagyospuszta, and Szentgyörgypuszta by 1100 hours.[1160]

After the occupation of Kocs, the 6th Guards Mechanized Brigade and the 37th Guards Tank Brigade turned to the northeast and after a short engagement, the armoured fighting vehicles occupied Tata around 1100 hours. Soon the 4th Guards Mechanized Brigade lined up also and attacked the Tóváros section of Tata, which they then occupied. The Soviets detected and identified the German *Sturmgeschütz-Brigade 325* south of Tata.[1161]

One of the tank platoon commanders of the 23rd Guards Tank Regiment/4th Guards Mechanized Brigade, Guards 1st Lieutenant Fyodor A. Timosenko, engaged six German assault guns in combat in the Tata sector and he knocked out three of them. Afterwards, he pursued the retreating German armoured fighting vehicles with his platoon and was the first Soviet to enter Tata.[1162]

On that day, the Soviet 991st Self-Propelled Artillery Regiment/46th Army was in temporary defence at the northern and north-western edge of Kocs with its 17 SU–76M self-propelled guns. Their three captured Panther tanks were being repaired in the Bicske sector.[1163]

Panzergrenadier-Brigade 92 (mot.) and *Kampfgruppe "Ameiser"/37. SS-Freiwilligen-Kavallerie-Division* retreated via Kecskéd and Környe to the southern edge of Nagy Lake at Tata, and to the southern perimeter of Bánhida, meanwhile remaining continuously engaged with the Soviets.[1164]

At 1200 hours, the Soviet 1505th Self-Propelled Artillery Regiment/46th Army, together with the forces of the 59th Guards Rifle Division, launched an assault in the direction of Környeimajor and Környe. The SU–76M self-propelled guns occupied firing positions 800 meters south of Környe while the rifles occupied the local road bridge. During the fighting for Kecskéd, the SU–76Ms knocked out one assault gun, five anti-tank guns and 17 fortified positions, according to their own reports.[1165]

One of the battalions of *356. Infanterie-Division* arrived south of Felsőgalla and joined the defensive battles at that location.[1166]

1160 Central Archives of the Russian Defence Ministry (Podolsk), f. 240, op. 2799, gy. 357, li. 10.
1161 Central Archives of the Russian Defence Ministry (Podolsk), f. 240, op. 2799, gy. 357, li. 10.
1162 HM HIM Hadtörténelmi Levéltár (Budapest), Szovjetunió Hőse kitüntetések gyűjteménye (*Collection of Hero of the Soviet Union awards*), 566.
1163 Central Archives of the Russian Defence Ministry (Podolsk), f. 240, op. 2799, gy. 342, li. 158.
1164 NARA, T311, R162, F7214649.
1165 Central Archives of the Russian Defence Ministry (Podolsk), f. 240, op. 2799, gy. 342, li. 113.
1166 NARA, T311, R162, F7214656.

The Soviet 1897th Self-Propelled Artillery Regiment/46th Army, at the orders of the commander of the 180th Rifle Division, established firing positions with two batteries at the railway station of Szár, and with one battery 800 meters from Újtelep, to close off the Felsőgalla–Nagynémetegyház road. Afterwards the commander of the tank and mechanized units of the 46th Army removed the Regiment from subordination to the 75th Rifle Corps, transferred them to the 18th Guards Rifle Corps and sent them to Dad.[1167]

The Hungarian 3rd Army was ordered to prepare their anti-tank guns to be ready for the appearance of Soviet gun boats on the Danube, which were expected from the direction of Budapest. *Panzerjäger-Abteilung 7/11. Infanterie-Division* was stationed in the Tát sector.[1168] It was at that exact location where the Soviets attempted to cross the river and land in the rear of the German-Hungarian forces with the 83rd Marine Infantry Brigade on the night of 19/20 March 1945.

The German *Luftflotte 4* supported their own troops on that day, flying 270 missions. The aircraft mainly targeted forward units, marching columns, the positions of the anti-tank and anti-aircraft guns in the sector of Tata, southwest of Bánhida, and at Székesfehérvár and northwest of there. The pilots reported to have destroyed 11 Soviet tanks and to have shot down 21 Soviet planes. On the night of 18/19 March 1945, the *Luftwaffe* carried out 80 night ground attack missions against Soviet troops moving in the direction of Csákvár–Bicske.[1169]

On the same day, the reconnaissance of the German *Heeresgruppe Süd* summarized what they knew about the assault that was launched by Soviet forces on 16 March 1945. According to this, the Soviet 4th Guards Army was to attack with the 23rd Tank Corps toward Lake Balaton aiming at the occupation of Székesfehérvár. Three rifle corps and a swiftly moving corps, assumed by the Germans to be either the 1st Guards Mechanized Corps, or the 7th Mechanized Corps of the 9th Guards Army, was to advance in the direction of Veszprém–Várpalota. They suspected the 2nd Guards Mechanized Corps, in subordination to the 46th Army, which was attacking through the Vértes Mountains towards Komárom, would then move towards Tata, in order to cut the Hungarian 3rd Army off from their main forces south of the Danube.[1170] At the same time, they still did not know anything about the 6th Guards Tank Army.[1171]

In this situation, it was assumed at the *Heeresgruppe* that it would be a realistic goal for the German *6. Panzerarmee* to prevent the Soviets from breaking through towards the west and northwest on the current frontline, and then eliminate and throw back the forces that had broken through on the Székesfehérvár–Vértes Mountains line toward the east.[1172] In connection with this, *I. SS-Panzerkorps* was to attack eastwards from the Bakonykúti west–Isztimér sector to be able to occupy the hills east of Csór, Fehérvárcsurgó and Bodajk, then to be able to turn southeast and reach the Székesfehérvár sector. The *2. SS-Panzer-Division*, *6. Panzer-Division* and *356. Infanterie-Division* were en route to prevent a Soviet

---

1167 Central Archives of the Russian Defence Ministry (Podolsk), f. 240, op. 2799, gy. 342, li. 115.
1168 NARA, T311, R163, F7215071.
1169 NARA, T311, R162, F7214650.
1170 NARA, T311, R162, F7214651.
1171 NARA, T311, R162, F7214652.
1172 NARA, T311, R162, F7214652.

breakthrough towards Komárom. Afterwards, *6. Panzer-Division* was to attack from the Kisbér sector and *2. SS-Panzer-Division* was to attack eastwards from Nagyigmánd, toward Dad and Kocs and to push the Soviets back beyond Által Creek.[1173] The German *Stab/6. Panzerarmee* requested to be able to withdraw *9. SS-Panzer-Division* from the frontline, in order to concentrate them south of the Székesfehérvár passage as part of the planned armoured attack. The *Heeresgruppe* supported this and ordered that during the night, the front of the *SS-Division* was to be taken over by *44. Reichsgrenadier-Division* and *3. Panzer-Division*.[1174] The sector between Kisbér and Nagyveleg was planned to be closed off by using *Panzer-Aufklärungs-Abteilung 6*.[1175] The *2. SS-Panzer-Division/II. SS-Panzerkorps* headed for Tárkány, and *6. Panzer-Division* headed for Kisbér. Both *Divisions* were directly subordinated to the German *6. Panzerarmee* on that day.[1176]

An attempt to secure the sector of Kisbér was made by *Generalleutnant* Walther Krause, commander of the *Korück* (*Kommandeur Rückwärtiges Armeegebiet*) of the German *6. Armee*, with hastily established rapid reaction units. The combat group of approximately 300 men, also consisted of, based on the *Generalleutnant's* statement, a heavy *Panzer-Abteilung* under establishment, with eight Tiger E heavy tanks.[1177]

Generalmajor Günther Pape, *Kommandeur* of the *Panzer-Division "Feldherrnhalle"* became the commander of the Komárom bridgehead by permission of the *OKH*; he was able to deploy units of his division in defence of the bridgehead in case the need arose. The forces in defence of the bridgehead remained in subordination to the German *8. Armee*. The request by the German *6. Panzerarmee* to transfer troops to their command was refused.[1178]

Because of the extremely dangerous operational situation, the *Kommandeur* of the *Heeresgruppe*, *General der Infanterie* Wöhler, requested that *Luftflotte 4* not only take part in close combat security tasks in the villages, but they should also form mobile tank destroyer units in the rear of the *Heeresgruppe* itself.[1179]

20 March 1945, Tuesday

(**WEATHER**: highest daytime temperature 9 Celsius, clear sky south of the Danube, correct visibility conditions. The roads continued to dry up.)

During the morning, in the front of *2. Panzerarmee*, a reinforced battalion of *Jäger-Regiment 750/118. Jäger-Division/LXVIII. Armeekorps* was in combat along the Böhönye–Mesztegnyő railroad line and reached the southern edge of Mesztegnyő.[1180]

1173 NARA, T311, R162, F7214653.
1174 NARA, T311, R162, F7214657 and T311, R162, F7214658.
1175 NARA, T311, R162, F7214658.
1176 NARA, T311, R163, F7215395.
1177 Krause, Walther: *Fighting in West Hungary and East Steiermark in the area of the Sixth Army from March 25 to May 8, 1945*, United States. Army, Europe. Historical Division. Foreign Military Studies Branch. 1946. p. 2. Unfortunately we have no further available data on the deployment of these Tiger E heavy tanks.
1178 NARA, T311, R162, F7214663.
1179 NARA, T311, R163, F7214970.
1180 NARA, T311, R162, F7214666.

At 0800 hours that morning, *71. Infanterie-Division/XXII. Gebirgskorps,* with armoured fighting vehicle support,[1181] continued the assault that was launched the previous day. At 0910 hours, *II. (Bataillon)/Grenadier-Regiment 211* occupied the railway station of Mesztegnyő and then around noon they occupied the village itself. The Soviet troops pushed out of the village retreated towards the south-east in the direction of the forest. The Germans were unable to stop and encircle the retreating Soviets, as the armoured fighting vehicles escorting the *Division* were not able to execute the necessary manoeuvres. This was due to the fact, that to accomplish this, they would have had to drive back to the west for a short distance, and their movement backwards was expressly prohibited by corps order.[1182] Units of *71. Infanterie-Division* advanced 2.5 km through the forested area south of the Mesztegnyő–Libickozma road to the east and south-east.[1183]

On the night of 19/20 March 1945, *16. SS-Panzergrenadier-Division* eliminated the Soviet penetration on its eastern flank 4.5 km south of Csömend, and with its own attack toward the south reached, the southern edge of a clearing in the forest 3 km east of the southern edge of Mesztegnyő. The Soviets launched a number of attacks from Kopárpuszta 2 km south-west of Libickozma toward the north-east, but the Germans repelled these attempts.[1184]

The *I. (Bataillon)/SS-Panzergrenadier-Regiment 36,* attacking from Gyótapuszta towards the south-south-east, was supported by four StuG. III assault guns of *Panzergruppe "Kriz"* of *3. Kompanie/SS-Panzer-Abteilung 16,* which knocked out three Soviet tanks. The Germans lost an assault gun that ran over a mine and was disabled, and another had its taper gear broken. German pioneers then opened a corridor through the minefield. Two assault guns pushed forward and, dragging the *SS-Panzergrenadiers* with them, occupied Point 140 south-west of Kopárpuszta and assisted with the occupation of the village itself.[1185]

Along the Libickozma road, *1. Volks-Gebirgs-Division* repelled a number of Soviet attacks facing north-east.[1186]

The 52nd Tank Regiment/32nd Independent Guards Mechanized Brigade with nine T–34 tanks, was withdrawn from Nikla and assembled in the sector of Szőkepuszta. The Brigade and the 864th Self-Propelled Artillery Regiment, with seven SU–76Ms, reported on that day that they knocked out three German armoured fighting vehicles, two armoured personnel carriers, four machine guns, plus six guns and mortars. One of the companies of the 249th Independent Tank Regiment, supporting the 2nd Guards Motorized Rifle Battalion/32nd Independent Guards Mechanized Brigade, knocked out one German armoured fighting vehicle and two armoured personnel carriers against the loss of one T–34. By the evening, the Regiment had only 10 operational tanks left.[1187]

1181   Units of *71. Infanterie-Division* were supported at that time by the assault guns of *Sturmgeschütz-Brigade 261.*
1182   *Die 71. Infanterie-Division im Zweiten Weltkrieg 1939–1945. Gefechts und Erlebnisberichte aus den Kämpfen der „Glückhaften Division" von Verdun bis Stalingrad, von Monte Cassino bis zum Plattensee.* Arbeitsgemeinschaft „Das Kleeblatt" (Hrsg.). Hildesheim, 1973. p. 415.
1183   NARA, T311, R162, F7214666.
1184   NARA, T311, R162, F7214666.
1185   Puntigam, Josef Paul: *Vom Plattensee bis zur Mur. Die Kämpfe 1945 im Dreiländereck.* Feldbach, without year of publication, [1993], p. 103.
1186   NARA, T311, R162, F7214666.
1187   Central Archives of the Russian Defence Ministry (Podolsk), f. 243, op. 2928, gy. 131, li. 260.

Upon orders from the Staff of the 3rd Ukrainian Front, the 53rd Motorcycle Regiment was detached from the 57th Army and was subordinated to the 23rd Tank Corps. The Regiment was en route to Szekszárd around 1600 hours, where they received 13 new T–34/85 tanks. Its remaining three old tanks were handed over to the 52nd Tank Regiment/32nd Independent Guards Mechanized Brigade.[1188]

In the front of the German *I. Kavallerie-Korps/6. Armee* the Soviets regrouped their forces, and from the bridgehead they held on the eastern outskirts of Siófok, they launched an attack with a significant number of rifle troops and a number of armoured fighting vehicles. The assault pushed back the units of the Hungarian 25th Infantry Division. The majority of the German *3. and 4. Kavallerie-Divisions*[1189], still being assembled, were forced to be deployed in a counterattack, with which they managed to repel the Soviet troops. In the end, the Soviet attack was contained on the Csárdamajor–Alsótekeres–Enying west and south edge line.

The 71st Tank Regiment and 1896th Self-Propelled Artillery Regiment/Soviet 5th Guards Cavalry Corps, with three T–34/85 tanks and 16 SU–76M self-propelled guns, was in combat at the end of the day 2 km north-east of Gamásza. The 2nd Guards Mechanized Brigade, subordinated to the Cavalry Corps, was in action in the southern outskirts of Balatonvilágos. The 19th Guards Tank Regiment of the Brigade lost 10 M4A2 armoured fighting vehicles during the day, three on mines and seven bogged down and sunken on the muddy ground. By the evening, the Regiment had 12 operational armoured fighting vehicles left.[1190] The 1952nd Self-Propelled Artillery Regiment/209th Self-Propelled Artillery Brigade was also fighting in subordination to the 2nd Guards Mechanized Brigade with 20 SU–100 self-propelled guns. At around 1700 hours, the Regiment was active in the south-western part of the Balatonvilágos sector.[1191]

The 22nd Independent Tank Regiment still had three T–34 tanks in firing position in the Balatonszabadi-fürdőtelep sector, and three other T–34s and one SU–85 had joined them from Szabadhídvég.[1192]

On the north-eastern shore of Lake Balaton, the Soviets now had approximately 58 mixed types of tanks and self-propelled guns by the evening, waiting for the continuation of the operation on the next day.

The majority of the Hungarian 25th Infantry Division was shattered by the Soviet attack and the remnants, in no larger than regiment-size units, were no longer in condition for any kind of deployment, based on German standards. The units of *3. Kavallerie-Division* opened fire with all available weapons on the retreating Hungarians troops, of which many surrendered to the Soviet troops.[1193]

1188 Central Archives of the Russian Defence Ministry (Podolsk), f. 243, op. 2928, gy. 131, li. 263.
1189 *Reiter-Regiment 32, Panzerjäger-Abteilung 69* and *schwere Kavallerie-Abteilung 3* were also deployed here. See Witte, Hans Joachim – Offermann, Peter: *Die Boeselagerschen Reiter. Das Kavallerie-Regiment Mitte und die aus ihm hervorgegangene 3. Kavallerie-Brigade/Division.* München, 1998. p. 410.
1190 Central Archives of the Russian Defence Ministry (Podolsk), f. 243, op. 2928, gy. 178, li. 91. At the end of the day,,12 M4A2 tanks of the 19th Guards Tank Regiment were waiting for recovery, either sunk in mud or due to mine damage.
1191 Central Archives of the Russian Defence Ministry (Podolsk), f. 243, op. 2928, gy. 178, li. 90/2.
1192 Central Archives of the Russian Defence Ministry (Podolsk), f. 243, op. 2928, gy. 178, li. 90/2.
1193 NARA, T311, R162, F7214676.

That evening, west of Balatonbozsok, the Soviets launched a battalion-size attack with the support of eight armoured fighting vehicles, which was stopped by the Germans with a small loss of ground.[1194]

The withdrawal of *I. Kavallerie-Korps* between Mezőkomárom and Hatvanpuszta on the night of 19/20 March 1945, was going on as planned. The Soviets followed the Germans very slowly and with small forces.[1195]

The 1951st Self-Propelled Artillery Regiment/209th Self-Propelled Artillery Brigade, in subordination to the Soviet 26th Army, was still standing in defence with 14 SU–100 self-propelled guns in the Cece, Ozora, Szabadhídvég and Pincehely sector. The 1953rd Self-Propelled Artillery Regiment, with 11 SU–100 self-propelled guns, had moved into the Balatonszabadi sector.[1196]

On the front of *III. Panzerkorps,* the Soviets crossed the two canals of the Sárvíz 2 km south of Káloz, with a division-size force, most likely with units of the 206th Rifle Division and the 1st Guards Mechanized Corps, and occupied Nagyhörcsökpuszta, Kishörcsökpuszta, and Káloz. The attack had thrown *SS-Panzer-Aufklärungs-Abteilung 2,* in defence here, back to the southern part of Belmajor.

Against the Soviets, who continued their attack towards the north-west, the *Stab/I. Kavallerie-Korps* deployed the armoured combat group, *Panzer-Aufklärungs-Abteilung 23* and *Panzer-Pionier-Bataillon 51* of *23. Panzer-Division* for a counterattack. These German forces attacked the Soviet left flank, retook Kishörcsökpuszta, and reached the Hatvanpuszta–Káloz road east of there.[1197]

Five Panther tanks of *Panzergruppe "Fischer"/23. Panzer-Division* and *3. Kompanie/ Panzer-Pionier-Bataillon 51,* launched an attack against Kishörcsökpuszta at 1115 hours. The armoured fighting vehicles moved in among the houses but were soon forced to retreat to the western edge of the cluster of houses, because they lacked the infantry support they needed for protection in an urban battle with unfavourable visibility conditions. The *Panzer-Pionier-Kompanie* was practically a heavy weapons company, with a 7.5 cm anti-tank gun section, one 2 cm anti-aircraft gun section, and an armoured personnel carrier section equipped with multiple rocket launchers.[1198]

At 1230 hours, *Panzergruppe "Fischer",* launched an attack with all of its forces against the Kishörcsökpuszta bridgehead held by the Soviets. The terrain was difficult and wet, and 600 meters from the bridge itself, the German attack became hopelessly bogged down. The Panther tanks with the *Panzer-Pionier-Kompanie* on their right flank, did not succeed in advancing into Kishörcsökpuszta. On the western bank of the Malom Canal, the Germans identified the locations of 10 Soviet armoured fighting vehicles and five anti-tank guns, to which another 13 armoured fighting vehicles[1199] gave fire support from the other bank. The engagement raged between the German and Soviet armoured fighting vehicles throughout

---

1194 NARA, T311, R163, F7215413.
1195 NARA, T311, R162, F7214667.
1196 Central Archives of the Russian Defence Ministry (Podolsk), f. 243, op. 2928, gy. 178, li. 90/2.
1197 NARA, T311, R162, F7214667.
1198 Rebentisch, Ernst: *Zum Kaukasus und zu den Tauern. Die Geschichte der 23. Panzer-Division 1941–1945*. Esslingen, 1963. p. 492.
1199 In the history of *23. Panzer-Division,* these were identified as IS–2 tanks, most likely due to the heavier fire than was expected, although they were in fact the SU-100 self-propelled guns of the 1st Guards Mechanized Corps.

the whole afternoon. The Germans irrecoverably lost a Panther, assuming it was hit by an anti-tank gun, and reported to have knocked out 13 Soviet armoured fighting vehicles. After nightfall set in, *Panzergruppe "Fischer"* was occupied recovering its sunken armoured fighting vehicles, which had put a considerable strain on their condition.[1200]

Panzergrenadier-Regiments 126 and *128* were only approached by the Soviets during the afternoon. Around noon, a new order came for preparations for the German retreat to begin to enable their withdrawal in the evening.

At 1830 hours, *23. Panzer-Division* commenced to retreat from its positions around Dég and, together with the 14th Infantry Regiment/Hungarian 20th Honvéd Infantry Division, established defensive positions in the south-western, southern and eastern outskirts of Kisláng, to be able to properly defend the Kisláng–Lobbmajor line. *Panzer-Aufklärungs-Abteilung 23* and *Panzergruppe "Fischer"*, with three Panthers, four Panzer IV tanks and two Panzer IV/70 *Jagdpanzers*, were standing in readiness at Jánosmajor, approximately in the middle of the frontline section of the *Division*. Three StuG. III assault guns of *1. Kompanie/Panzer-Regiment 23*, were supporting *Panzergrenadier-Regiment 128* at Lobbmajor. During the retreat of *Panzergruppe "Fischer"* from Kishörcsökpuszta, the Soviet armoured fighting vehicles followed them and engaged the Germans each time they tried to recover their bogged down vehicles. As a consequence of this, a Panther tank that had run over a mine and one that was damaged previously, had to be blown up.[1201]

At the end of the day, the 3rd Guards Mechanized Brigade/1st Guards Mechanized Corps and the 382nd Guards Self-Propelled Artillery Regiment/1st Guards Mechanized Corps, were engaged in combat at Kishörcsökpuszta and 2 km west of Nagyhörcsökpuszta, and the 1st Guards Mechanized Brigade and the 1821st Self-Propelled Artillery Regiment were engaged 2 km south of Nagyhörcsökpuszta. During the securing tasks around the crossing of the canal, one company commander of the 20th Guards Tank Regiment/3rd Guards Mechanized Brigade, Guards 1st Lieutenant Komarov, distinguished himself by engaging eight attacking German armoured fighting vehicles all alone and destroying one of them. However, he was also killed in action, after his tank was knocked out.[1202]

The 9th Guards Tank Brigade[1203] also crossed to the western bank of the Malom Canal directly opposite of Felsőtöbörzsök. In the evening the Corps had 89 operational M4A2s, three T–34 tanks and 14 SU–100 self-propelled guns.[1204] During the fighting that day, four M4A2s and one SU–100 were destroyed.[1205]

1200 Rebentisch, Ernst: *Zum Kaukasus und zu den Tauern. Die Geschichte der 23. Panzer-Division 1941–1945*. Esslingen, 1963. pp. 492-493.
1201 Rebentisch, Ernst: *Zum Kaukasus und zu den Tauern. Die Geschichte der 23. Panzer-Division 1941–1945*. Esslingen, 1963. p. 493.
1202 Summarized report of the 1st Guards Mechanized Corps of the combat actions during March – April 1945. Copy owned by the author.p. 21.
1203 The 9th Guards Tank Brigade received their new M4A2 tanks without trained crews. The assigned tank crews had not yet gotten used to working with each other, and some of the officers and non-commissioned officers were completely unfamiliar with the M4A2. All of this resulted in the exceptionally heavy losses that the 9th Guards Tank Brigade suffered in the following days. See Summarized report of the 1st Guards Mechanized Corps of the combat actions during March – April 1945. Copy owned by the author. p. 20.
1204 Central Archives of the Russian Defence Ministry (Podolsk), f. 243, op. 2928, gy. 131, li. 260. In this number, the operational armoured fighting vehicles of the 2nd Guards Mechanized Brigade subordinated to the 5th Guards Cavalry Corps, are not present.
1205 Central Archives of the Russian Defence Ministry (Podolsk), f. 243, op. 2928, gy. 178, li. 94.

The Soviets launched an attack against the two battalions of *9. SS-Panzer-Division* that still had not withdrawn, west and north-west of Sárosd with approximately 1200 soldiers and the armoured fighting vehicles of the 18th Tank Corps. The Germans reported to have knocked out 10 armoured fighting vehicles, but even with these achievements they were not able to prevent the Soviets breaking into their defences in three locations. One of the incursions was eliminated, but the other two were only sealed off by the defenders.[1206]

In the sector, by the end of the day, the 110th and 181st Tank Brigade, the 363rd Guards Heavy Self-Propelled Artillery Regiment and the 32nd Motorized Rifle Brigade of the 18th Tank Corps, were in combat on the Pálinkaházapuszta–Point 141 - Aba northeast four km – Aba southern edge line.[1207] They lost six knocked out T–34/85 tanks, of which four were burnt out. In the meantime, the 170th Tank Brigade, the 1438th Self-Propelled Artillery Regiment and the 1068th Self-Propelled Artillery Regiment/208th Self-Propelled Artillery Brigade,[1208] were assembled in the Sárosd sector as Corps reserve. In the evening, the Corps had 47 operational tanks, six ISU–152s and 13 SU–76M self-propelled guns.[1209]

The Soviets launched only small scale and unsuccessful attempts against the Seregélyes bridgehead. North-west of Seregélyes however, the Soviets attacked with considerable force and pushed *II. (Bataillon)/SS-Panzergrenadier-Regiment 10/5. SS-Panzer-Division* out of Börgönd.[1210]

Between Lake Velence and Székesfehérvár, the Soviets continued their attack with approximately 1200 soldiers and 23 armoured fighting vehicles. *Kampfgruppe "Bradel"/1. Panzer-Division,* launched a counterattack, together with *Panzergrenadier-Regiment 113*, supported by 16-20 Panther tanks, 10 pioneer-armoured personnel carriers and four self-propelled 2 cm anti-aircraft guns, and *I.* (self-propelled) *(Abteilung)/Panzer-Artillerie-Regiment 73.*[1211] They repelled the attack along the Aba–Székesfehérvár road and re-established contact among the German troops in defence of Székesfehérvár.

The *4. Schwadron* received an order at 0300 hours from *Kampfgruppe "Streith"*, relayed by the *Kommandeur* of *I. (Abteilung)/Panzer-Regiment 24,* that the unit was to reoccupy the Ráctemető (cemetery), even if the tanks were not able to make contact with the *Panzergrenadiers* who had been bogged down and halted 1 km west of the village the previous night. The Panther tanks took advantage of the darkness, and successfully broke into the Ráctemető from the north-west, and reported to have destroyed two T–34

[1206] NARA, T311, R162, F7214667.
[1207] Pálinkaházapuszta was occupied by the 110th Tank Brigade and the 363rd Guards Heavy Self-Propelled Artillery Regiment; Point 141 was occupied by the 181st Tank Brigade and the 1068th Self-Propelled Artillery Regiment.
[1208] The regiments of the 208th Self-Propelled Artillery Brigade reported the following achievements between 8-20 March 1945: the 1922nd Self-Propelled Artillery Regiment knocked out 23 German tanks and 11 armoured personnel carriers while losing three SU–10s of which one burnt out; the 1016th Self-Propelled Artillery Regiment knocked out seven German tanks and 14 armoured personnel carriers while losing three SU–100s; the 1068th Self-Propelled Artillery Regiment knocked out 11 German tanks including two Tiger Bs and three Panthers, plus 17 assault guns and *Jagdpanzers* at the expense of 11 knocked out or burnt out SU–100s. See Summarized report of the 208th Self-Propelled Artillery Brigade of the period between 6 March – 6 April 1945. Copy owned by the author. pp. 9-10. The German sources do not verify these numbers.
[1209] Central Archives of the Russian Defence Ministry (Podolsk), f. 243, op. 2928, gy. 131, li. 260.
[1210] NARA, T311, R162, F7214667.
[1211] Stoves, Rolf: Persönliches Kriegstagebuch Pz.Rgt. 1 (typewritten manuscript, a copy owned by the author), entry from 20 March 1945.

tanks, six anti-tank guns and three trucks on the main road of the village[1212]. However, the Soviets opened fire on *4. Schwadron* from the hills east of the village and knocked out two Panthers. The remaining eight German tanks would not be able to hold the village successfully without the *Panzergrenadiers*, therefore *Oberleutnant* Schlotheim was ordered to retreat to Székesfehérvár, using the dawn mist as cover.[1213]

The seven combat-ready Panther tanks of *I. (Abteilung)/Panzer-Regiment 24* subordinated to *1. Panzer-Division,* reported to have knocked out four T-34/85 tanks during the occupation of the Aba–Székesfehérvár road.[1214]

On the southern edge of Székesfehérvár, the armoured personnel carrier-group of *I. (Bataillon)/Panzergrenadier-Regiment 113,* attacked toward Úrhida and re-established contact with *Kampfgruppe "Streith",* in combat there. *Kampfgruppe "Elias"/Panzer-Regiment 1* with 15 Panther tanks and a few self-propelled 2 cm anti-aircraft guns, as well as *2. Kompanie/Panzer-Pionier-Bataillon 37* and eight Panthers of *I. (Abteilung)/Panzer-Regiment 24,* launched an attack from the sector of Fövenypuszta against the Soviet troops attacking from the direction of the Börgönd airfield toward the crossing points on the Nádor Canal. However, the German attack was bogged down in front of the airfield facing the Soviet anti-tank guns and mine obstacles. *Hauptmann* Hansjürg Elias, *Kommandeur* of *I (Abteilung)/Panzer-Regiment 1,* was fatally wounded during the fighting, when a Soviet anti-tank gun projectile hit the turret hatch of his tank. The officer died of his wounds the next day. The command of the *Abteilung* was taken over by *Hauptmann* Hagen, *Chef* of *4. Kompanie*. In the afternoon, following a regrouping, and supported by *I.* (self-propelled) *(Abteilung)/Panzer-Artillerie-Regiment 73* with approximately 20-25 Panther and Panzer IV tanks and StuG.III assault guns, the unit launched a new attack. This time the German armoured fighting vehicles managed to breach the anti-tank defence built up by the Soviets and reached Point 130, 2.5 km north-west of Belsőbáránd. With this accomplished, the Székesfehérvár–Aba road fell back into German hands again.[1215]

At 2000 hours, *Kampfgruppe "Bradel"/1. Panzer-Division,* was gradually withdrawn from Seregélyes to the sector of Falubattyán-Szabadbattyán, leaving *Kampfgruppe "Streith"* in defence southeast of Úrhida. On the left flank of the latter, *Kampfgruppe "Huppert"* was in combat together with *Panzergrenadier-Regiment 1*, with three Panzer IV tanks, a few *Marder* tank destroyers and self-propelled 2 cm anti-aircraft guns, plus 8.8 cm anti-aircraft guns and fire support from *II. (Abteilung)/Panzer-Artillerie-Regiment 73*. The *44. Reichsgrenadier-Division* was engaged in combat on the Falubattyán–Külső Fövenypuszta–Jánosfutás line together with *schwere Panzer-Abteilung 509* and the majority of *I. (Abteilung)/Panzer-Regiment 24*.[1216]

1212 At that time, in that sector, there were no Soviet T–34 or T–34/85 tanks in combat. In the sector of the Ráctemető, the Soviets deployed the 912th and 1004th Self-Propelled Artillery Regiments/207th Self-Propelled Artillery Brigade with SU–100 self-propelled guns. As these also had T-34 chassis, most likely the Germans mistakenly identified these tanks during the combat in the night.

1213 Weidemann, Gert-Axel: *Unser Regiment. Reiter-Regiment 2 – Panzer-Regiment 24*. Groß-Umstadt, 1982. p. 277.

1214 Senger und Etterlin, von F.M. jr.: *Die 24. Panzer-Division vormals 1. Kavallerie-Division 1939–1945*. Neckargemünd, 1962. p. 309.

1215 Stoves, Rolf: Persönliches Kriegstagebuch Pz.Rgt. 1 (typewritten manuscript, a copy owned by the author), entry from 20 March 1945.

1216 Stoves, Rolf: Persönliches Kriegstagebuch Pz.Rgt. 1 (typewritten manuscript, a copy owned by the author), entry from 20 March 1945.

A battalion-size Soviet attack, supported by a small number of armoured fighting vehicles, initiated from Csór, occupied Rétipuszta, then on the road leading to Nádasdladány, reached the Nádor Canal which was 2.5 km southeast of the occupied village. There the advance was halted in front of a blown bridge. *SS-Panzer-Aufklärungs-Abteilung 9* and *II. (Bataillon)/SS-Panzergrenadier-Regiment 19,* which were withdrawn from their positions south of Seregélyes on the night of 19/20 March 1945, established covering positions from the northern edge of Nádasdladány north-west to the vicinity north of the pump house, to the northern edge of Ősi and from there northwest to the Szigetpuszta forest, to be able to defend the left flank of *III. Panzerkorps.*[1217]

In the front of the German *IV. SS-Panzerkorps/6. Panzerarmee,* the Soviet attack concentrated against Székesfehérvár was repulsed by *5. SS-Panzer-Division* on the eastern edge of the town and along the railroad leading west of the town. A German counterattack had taken back Kiskecskemét. Heavy close quarters combat was raging among the streets in the town centre against the Soviet armoured fighting vehicles that had broken into the town the day before.

The *II. (Bataillon)/SS-Panzergrenadier-Regiment 10,* in a forward position at Börgönd, was cut off from the *Division* by the Soviets, who were pushing them back towards the south-west, following an attack launched by approximately 1200 infantry and 23 tanks between Székesfehérvár and Lake Velence.

During the day, *1. Panzer-Division/III. Panzerkorps,* managed to establish contact with the *SS*-units in combat in Székesfehérvár.[1218]

The 366th Guards Heavy Self-Propelled Artillery Regiment/4th Guards Army, was keeping the German positions under fire in the eastern outskirts of Székesfehérvár, with seven captured German self-propelled howitzers and three Panther tanks. During the fighting, the soldiers of *5. SS-Panzer-Division* knocked out a captured German self-propelled howitzer.[1219]

The 1004th Self-Propelled Artillery Regiment/207th Self-Propelled Artillery Brigade, was in combat 2 km south of Székesfehérvár, in the sector of Hill 136 near Kuruchalom, and the 912th Self-Propelled Artillery Regiment was fighting 2 km south-east of the town, at the Ráctemető.

The 1004th Self-Propelled Artillery Regiment was supporting the 62nd Guards Rifle Division, and occupied Hill 136 at 1030 hours. The 912th Self-Propelled Artillery Regiment, in cooperation with the 34th Guards Rifle Division, reached the southern slopes of Hill 136, then with two batteries marched to the Ráctemető by 1400 hours. During the second half of the day, the Germans tried to retake Hill 136, which was assaulted by a regiment-size infantry force supported by 20 armoured fighting vehicles. The SU–100 self-propelled guns reported to have knocked out six Tiger Bs, one T-34 that was captured, repainted and deployed by the Germans, one Churchill[1220] and one Panther tank.[1221] The 207th Self-

---

1217 NARA, T311, R162, F7214668.
1218 Tieke, Wilhelm: *Von Plattensee bis Österreich. Heeresgruppe Süd 1945.* Gummersbach, without year of publication, pp. 59-60.
1219 Central Archives of the Russian Defence Ministry (Podolsk), f. 243, op. 2928, gy. 178, li. 90.
1220 So far, the origins of this Churchill tank is not possible to verify from official sources. The Germans could have taken it from Hajmáskér, where the Hungarian troops kept and examined some of the armoured fighting vehicles captured at the Eastern Front.
1221 War log of the 207th Self-Propelled Artillery Brigade, 20 and 21 March 1945. Copy owned by the author.

Propelled Artillery Brigade lost four burnt out SU–100s on that day,[1222] and by the evening it had 36 operational SU–100s, one SU–57 self-propelled gun and two T–34 tanks.[1223]

On that day, the Soviet 23rd Tank Corps was subordinated to the 4th Guards Army and marched from the sector of Kápolnásnyék via Lovasberény to Mór. In the lead, was the 78th Motorcycle Battalion, then behind them the 39th Tank Brigade, the 56th Motorized Rifle Brigade, the 3rd Tank Brigade and the 1443rd Self-Propelled Artillery Regiment. By the evening, the Corps had 62 operational T–34 tanks, three IS–2 heavy tanks, eight ISU–122 and four ISU–152 self-propelled guns.[1224]

The units of *9. SS-Panzer-Division,* concentrated in the sector of Falubattyán and Nádasdladány, were subordinated to *IV. SS-Panzerkorps* and were deployed against the Soviet forces advancing from the western outskirts of Székesfehérvár toward the south-west.[1225] The *Division* was to retake, the essentially important, villages of Csór and Rétipuszta as soon as possible.[1226]

The *9. SS-Panzer-Division* had to launch a counteroffensive in the direction of Székesfehérvár to relieve *5. SS-Panzer-Division* defending the town, and to close the German-Hungarian frontline breached to the west of there.

Beyond the line established by *SS-Panzer-Aufklärungs-Abteilung 9* and *II. (Bataillon)/ SS-Panzergrenadier-Regiment 19, 9. SS-Panzer-Division* prepared for the attack on the Falubattyán–Nádasdladány–Ősi line.

On the left flank of the *Division,* on the Rétipuszta–Ősi line, *SS-Panzer-Flak-Abteilung 9* and *SS-Panzer-Aufklärungs-Abteilung 9,* were engaged in heavy fighting with the Soviet troops pushing toward the south-west, who closed up on the full length of the frontline of the *Division* by midnight. The majority of the *Division* was, at that time, in defence in the sector stretching from the Nádasdladány forest and the area 1 km north of Ősi against the Soviets attacking from Inota and Rétipuszta.

In this situation, it was out of question to even think of an ordered counteroffensive. Units of *SS-Panzergrenadier-Regiments 19* and *20* went over to the defence. The units of *SS-Panzer-Abteilung 9,* together with units of *1. SS-Panzer-Division,* temporarily halted the Soviets that had advanced almost to the railway station southeast of Várpalota.[1227]

Around midnight on 19 March 1945, *1. SS-Panzer-Division/I. SS-Panzerkorps,* repulsed a strong Soviet attack 4 km east of Inota, then at 0400 hours, launched its own attack against Hill 363 (Baglyas Hill) three km north-east of Inota. The German attack aimed at retaking the Hill, met the advance of the Soviet 5th Guards Tank Corps that was attacking in the direction of Várpalota, which resulted in a heavy armoured battle. In the fighting the Germans reported to have knocked out 31 Soviet armoured fighting vehicles.[1228]

1222 Central Archives of the Russian Defence Ministry (Podolsk), f. 243, op. 2928, gy. 178, li. 92. In the war log of the 207th Self-Propelled Artillery Brigade, only one burnt out SU-100 is recorded as a loss.
1223 Central Archives of the Russian Defence Ministry (Podolsk), f. 243, op. 2928, gy. 178, li. 90.
1224 Central Archives of the Russian Defence Ministry (Podolsk), f. 243, op. 2928, gy. 131, li. 260.
1225 NARA, T311, R162, F7214668.
1226 NARA, T311, R162, F7214673.
1227 Tieke, Wilhelm: *Im Feuersturm letzter Kriegsjahre. II. SS-Panzerkorps mit 9. und 10. SS-Division „Hohenstaufen" und „Frundsberg".* Osnabrück, without year of publication, [1975] pp. 505-506.
1228 NARA, T311, R162, F7214668 and T311, R162, F7214675.

The Soviet tanks were attacking along the Székesfehérvár–Veszprém route and pushed back the combat group of *SS-Panzergrenadier-Regiment 1* and the armoured group of the *Division* back to Inota, then outflanked and encircled the Germans from the south and from the north. As the Soviets had also broken into Inota around 1200 hours, the German situation became increasingly critical.

East of Inota, six Panzer IV tanks and two Tiger B heavy tanks of *7. Kompanie/SS-Panzer-Regiment 1,* were in defence of the road leading from Székesfehérvár toward Várpalota throughout the day. The *7. Kompanie/SS-Panzer-Regiment 1* reported to have knocked out 19 Soviet tanks.

SS-Obersturmführer Werner Wolff, *Kompaniechef* of *1. Kompanie/SS-Panzer-Regiment 1*, decorated with the Knight's Cross of the Iron Cross, was also severely wounded. He was heading for Várpalota from the east late in the afternoon with six Panther tanks, when they stopped approximately 2 km from the town, near Inota, so that he could pass instructions to the tank commanders. Afterwards, he was to signal for continuing the journey with his right hand, and was out of the tank from his waist up. It was at this moment when a Soviet mortar shell hit the right side of his Panther[1229]., wounding him in the head with a splinter.[1230]

At nightfall, *SS-Sturmbannführer* Poetschke decided to give up Inota and retreat towards Várpalota because of the attacking Soviet rifle forces.

Soviet tanks were moving west of Inota, so the *Divisionskommandeur, SS-Brigadeführer* Kumm, sent out a Tiger B heavy tank during the day, which found the Soviets and, according to its report, knocked out 15 of their armoured fighting vehicles. A hastily formed battalion combat group of *Panzergrenadier-Regiment 1* searched the forested area along the Várpalota–Székesfehérvár route and reported the destruction of another 15 Soviet tanks.

At the same time, the makeshift eastern frontline of the division, was attacked by Soviet tanks, rifle forces and artillery. By evening, their positions had to be drawn back to the eastern edge of Várpalota. Because of the retreat, *7. Kompanie/SS-Panzer-Regiment 1* was cut off from the main forces. On the night of 20/20 March 1945, its six Panzer IV tanks and the two subordinated Tiger B heavy tanks,, pushed through Soviet-occupied Inota to reach their own troops at Várpalota, while the Tiger B at the head of the column knocked out a number of T–34/85s.[1231]

The *Kommandeur* of *schwere Panzer-Abteilung 501* fighting within *SS-Panzer-Regiment 1, SS-Obersturmbannführer* Heinz von Westernhagen died[1232] was succeeded by *SS-Sturmbannführer* Heinz Kling.

1229 The officer was not in his own command Panther (tactical identification number "101"), because it had run over a mine while driving forward to Inota, and had to be sent for repair.
1230 Wolff died of his wounds on 30 March 1945 in the field hospital near Götzendorf. See Agte, Patrick: *Jochen Peiper. Kommandeur Panzerregiment Leibstandarte.* Berg am Starnberger See, 1998. p. 354.
1231 Tiemann, Ralf: *Die Leibstandarte.* Band IV/2. Osnabrück, 1987. pp. 303-306.
1232 According to the opinion of *Wolfgang Schneider (see: Tigers in Combat II. Mechanicsburg, 2005.* p. 218.), as the officer had been discharged on 19 March 1945 due to illness, he committed suicide the same day. According to the official version, which is incorporated into the majority of works on the topic, a splinter from a small bomb dropped by a harassing Soviet bomber killed him, and the incident was reportedly witnessed by none other than the *Divisionskommandeur, SS-Brigadeführer* Kumm. The circumstances of this official version are highly suspicious to the author, however unfortunately there is no possibility to further investigate this case in the scope of this work due to space limitations.

The scattered forces of *3. SS-Panzer-Division* were fighting alongside *1. SS* and *12. SS-Panzer-Division*. The *Panzergrenadiers* of *SS-Panzergrenadier-Regiment 6* and the soldiers of *IV. (Abteilung)/SS-Panzer-Artillerie-Regiment 3,* were in defence on the eastern edge of Várpalota. Another combat group of theirs, was in defence with the forces of *12 SS-Panzer-Division* at Mecsér.[1233] Here, at 0900 hours in the morning, the armoured fighting vehicles of the Soviet 9th Guards Mechanized Corps were already within 100 meters of the village when they opened fire. The majority of the German defenders gathered at the western exit of the village. Elements of *3. SS-Panzer-Division*, including the units of *SS-Panzer-Flak-Abteilung 3*, launched a counterattack at 1000 hours. The Germans knocked out two M4A2s with *Panzerfausts*, and a third was disabled. The Panther and Panzer IV tanks of *12. SS-Panzer-Division* arrived around noon and cleared the vicinity of Mecsér. The Germans took one of the captured M4A2 tanks into service with them.[1234]

By now, the Soviet armoured fighting vehicles not only threatened Várpalota, but also the most important German supply line and the oil refinery at Pétfürdő, which was the last one still in operation.[1235]

The German forces defending Csór were attacked by Soviet rifle forces around 0800 hours in the morning, however the 2 cm guns of the German armoured personnel carriers repelled the attempt and inflicted heavy losses on the Soviets. The defenders opened fire with only three or four armoured personnel carriers to prevent the whole unit from being exposed to the enemy. At 1100 hours in the morning, another Soviet attack commenced, which was supported by five armoured fighting vehicles. The Soviet rifles were bogged down by German artillery fire, and the two Soviet armoured fighting vehicles at the head were knocked out by the assault guns hiding in perfectly camouflaged firing positions. The other three tanks then retreated. The German combat group still had fuel supplies, but ammunition started to run low.[1236]

In the front of the 4th Guards Army, the 1922nd Self-Propelled Artillery Regiment/208th Self-Propelled Artillery Brigade, with 16 SU–100 armoured fighting vehicles, was directed to Csór from the north-western outskirts of Székesfehérvár at 1200 hours, and placed under subordination to the 9th Guards Army.[1237]

On the night of 19/20 March 1945, the Soviets continued their attacks against Várpalota from the direction of Csór and Bakonykúti. The Soviets broke into the town from the south-east and north-east, but the Germans immediately launched counterattacks and the enemy was pushed back to the Várpalota south railway-road junction–Inota west 1 km road fork–hill 500 meter northeast from the road fork–Várpalota north one km

---

1233 Vopersal, Wolfgang: *Soldaten, Kämpfer, Kameraden. Marsch und Kämpfe der SS-Totenkopfdivision*. Band Vb. Bielefeld, 1991. p. 759., furthermore Tieke, Wilhelm: *Von Plattensee bis Österreich. Heeresgruppe Süd 1945*. Gummersbach, without year of publication, p. 61.
1234 Stöber, Hans: *Die Flugabwehrverbände der Waffen-SS. Aufstellung, Gliederung, Luftverteidigung und Einsätze an den Fronten*. Preussisch Oldendorf, 1984. pp. 561-562.
1235 NARA, T311, R162, F7214674.
1236 Bernau, Günter: Aus den letzten Kämpfen in Ungarn 1945. I./SS-Panzer-Artillerie-Regiment 5. In: *Deutsches Soldatenjahrbuch 1975*. pp. 212-213.
1237 Central Archives of the Russian Defence Ministry (Podolsk), f. 243, op. 2928, gy. 178, li. 90, and Summarized report of the 208th Self-Propelled Artillery Brigade of the period between 6 March – 6 April 1945. Copy owned by the author. p. 12.

Hill 241 line. During the fighting, the Germans reported to have knocked out another eight Soviet armoured fighting vehicles.[1238]

At 0640 hours in the morning, the 6th Guards Motorized Rifle Brigade/5th Guards Tank Corps repulsed an attack of 16 German armoured fighting vehicles and 20 armoured personnel carriers as well as a regiment-size force of *Panzergrenadiers*, which was launched from the forested area 2 km east of Inota towards Bakonykúti. At 0800 hours in the morning, following a 10 minute artillery barrage, the Soviet 6th Guards Motorized Rifle Brigade launched an attack against Inota, supported by the 51th Guards Self-Propelled Artillery Brigade, then, after turning back a number of German counterattacks, occupied Inota at around 1800 hours. However, any further advance of the troops was halted east of Várpalota by the gunfire of the German defences.[1239] The 1st Self-Propelled Artillery Battalion/51th Guards Self-Propelled Artillery Brigade lost five burnt out SU-75Ms at the western edge of Inota.[1240]

The 20th Guards Tank Brigade, together with the 98th Guards Rifle Division/9th Guards Army, was bogged down 3 km southwest of Bakonykúti, in the sector of Hajágospuszta, around 0730 hours in the morning, while facing an attack of 30 German tanks. The Soviet Brigade flanked the settlement from the right and soon after 1000 hours, they occupied it.

The 20th Guards and 22nd Guards Tank Brigades/5th Guards Tank Corps, with the 364th Guards Heavy Self-Propelled Artillery Regiment/5th Guards Tank Corps, were in combat 1 km north and 1 km east of Várpalota, while the 6th Guards Motorized Rifle Brigade and the 51st Guards Self-Propelled Artillery Brigade was in combat 1 km west of Inota. The two Tank Brigades lost 27 knocked out T–34/85s, of which, 11 burnt out.[1241]

The 21st Guards Tank Brigade was the corps commander's reserve in the forest west of Bakonykúti. The 5th Guards Tank Corps was considerably weakened in the fighting of 19 and 20 March 1945, and it lost 41 knocked out T–34/85 tanks, of which 15 burnt out. In the evening, it had 80 operational tanks and 17 SU–76M self-propelled guns.[1242]

By the end of the day, the 364th Guards Heavy Self-Propelled Artillery Regiment had 20 ISU–122s while the 51st Guards Self-Propelled Artillery Brigade had 56 SU–76M self-propelled guns and three T–70 tanks. The 4th Guards Motorcycle Regiment, with seven Mk–IX Valentine tanks, stood at Gúttamási in army reserve.[1243]

The 1513th Self-Propelled Artillery Regiment, in support of the rifle forces of the 9th Guards Army, was fighting with nine SU–76Ms 800 meters southeast of Inota. The 17 SU–76M self-propelled guns of the 1523rd Self-Propelled Artillery Regiment, were in defence on the south-western edge of Söréd. The 1524th Self-Propelled Artillery Regiment was still stationed at Borbálamajor with 25 operational SU–76Ms.[1244]

1238 NARA, T311, R163, F7215412.
1239 War log of the 5th Guards Tank Corps for March 1945. Copy owned by the author. p. 13.
1240 War log of the 51st Guards Self-Propelled Artillery Brigade between 20 January - 20 August 1945. Copy owned by the author. p. 6.
1241 War log of the 5th Guards Tank Corps for March 1945. Copy owned by the author. p. 14.
1242 Central Archives of the Russian Defence Ministry (Podolsk), f. 243, op. 2928, gy. 131, li. 258.
1243 Central Archives of the Russian Defence Ministry (Podolsk), f. 243, op. 2928, gy. 131, li. 258.
1244 Central Archives of the Russian Defence Ministry (Podolsk), f. 243, op. 2928, gy. 178, li. 90.

The 1922nd Self-Propelled Artillery Regiment/208th Self-Propelled Artillery Brigade transferred over to the 9th Guards Army, was supporting the 114th Guards Rifle Division in the sector of Inota, then advanced further in the direction of Várpalota.[1245]

The Soviet troops continued their advance from Rétipuszta toward the west and northwest. The Germans still held their positions at Tés, where they were engaged in combat with the Soviets advancing westwards in the forested area north of Várpalota.[1246]

SS-Panzergrenadier-Regiment 26/12. SS-Panzer-Division, launched an attack at 0500 from the south-eastern outskirts of Bakonycsernye towards Isztimér. However the situation seemed to be the same here as with *1. SS-Panzer-Division*. The direction of the German attack crossed the route of the Soviet troops attacking westwards from the sector of Balinka with a number of armoured fighting vehicles, consequently the German attack did not unfold properly.

SS-Panzer-Regiment 12 was ordered to hold and contain the Soviets attacking Balinka and allow the *Panzergrenadiers* to retreat to their points of departure. *SS-Hauptsturmführer* Siegel, set off with four to five Panzer IV tanks, and soon noticed eight Soviet tanks east of Mecsér, the commanders of which were holding a briefing at the moment. The Germans immediately opened fire from a distance of 400 meters, and knocked out all of the Soviet tanks. One of the Soviet tank radios was still in working order, and they heard that there were two Soviet mechanized units approaching. These were the 30th Guards Mechanized Brigade and 46th Guards Tank Brigades/9th Guards Mechanized Corps, which the units of *12. SS-Panzer-Division* together with the subordinated forces of *3. SS-Panzer-Division* subsequently engaged in combat in the vicinity of Mecsér. On the left flank of *12. SS-Panzer-Division,* the Soviets attacked Nagyveleg and occupied it during the night.[1247]

During the evening, *SS-Panzerjäger-Abteilung 12* was fighting at Inota, and *SS-Panzergrenadier-Regiment 25* was fighting at Bakonykúti and Osküpuszta while subordinated to *1. SS-Panzer-Division*.[1248]

The 18th Guards Mechanized Brigade/9th Guards Mechanized Corps, was in combat 4 km west of Isztimér. The 31st Guards Mechanized Brigade was the corps commander's reserve in the sector of Bodajk, which was bombed three times by the Soviet air force by mistake.[1249] On that day, the corps lost 22 knocked out M4A2 tanks of which seven were burnt out[1250], and three were sunk in the mud. By the evening, 140 M4A2s and 17 SU–76Ms remained operational.[1251]

The commander of the 3rd Ukrainian Front again ordered the 6th Guards Tank Army, the 4th Guards and 9th Guards Army and the 27th Army, to speed up the pace of their attacks. The units were ordered to continue their attacks throughout the night as well.[1252]

1245 Summarized report of the 208th Self-Propelled Artillery Brigade of the period between 6 March – 6 April 1945. Copy owned by the author. p.. 12.
1246 NARA, T311, R162, F7214668.
1247 NARA, T311, R162, F7214669.
1248 Meyer, Hubert: *Kriegsgeschichte der 12. SS-Panzerdivision „Hitlerjugend"*. Band II. Osnabrück, 1987. 2nd edition. p. 507.
1249 Central Archives of the Russian Defence Ministry (Podolsk), f. 243, op. 2900, gy. 1570, li. 67.
1250 According to other sources the irrecoverable losses of that day consisted only of four M4A2s. See Central Archives of the Russian Defence Ministry (Podolsk), f. 243, op. 2928, gy. 178, li. 92.
1251 Central Archives of the Russian Defence Ministry (Podolsk), f. 243, op. 2928, gy. 131, li. 258.
1252 Malakhov, M. M.: A Balatontól Bécsig (excerpt). In: *Fejezetek hazánk felszabadításának történetéből*. Budapest, 1960. p. 191.

The *SS*-armoured units were not able to deal properly with the large numbers of Soviet rifle infantry, which took excellent advantage of the forests, settlements and terrain features and quickly outflanked any obstacles. The Germans assumed that the attack positions of the two *SS-Panzer-Division*s were attacked by freshly deployed Soviet tank and rifle forces, this time in groups consisting of 50 armoured fighting vehicles each, but they were still unable to identify which units were in place.[1253]

On the front of the 2nd Ukrainian Front

On the front of *II. SS-Panzerkorps*, the Hungarian *SS-Kampfgruppe "Ney"*, holding at Súr and Ácsteszér, reported that there were Soviets in Aka already. In the sector of *6. Panzer-Division*, subordinated that day to the *Panzerkorps*, the Soviets attacked with a force the size of three to four regiments between Hánta and Ete, although they were repulsed. Especially heavy fighting was going on for Point 216 located 3.5 km south-east of Kisbér, as well as Apátipuszta 4 km north-east of Kisbér. Ete was occupied by the Soviets. The German *6. Panzer-Division* launched a counterattack to retake the town.[1254]

At dawn, *2. SS-Panzer-Division* arrived to assist the forces at Nagyigmánd to stop Soviet advance there. For securing of the concentration point, a combat group was created from most of *SS-Panzer-Aufklärungs-Abteilung 2* and *SS-Panzer-Flak-Abteilung 2*, commanded by *SS-Hauptsturmführer* Dreike. Anti-aircraft duties were executed by the 3.7 cm anti-aircraft battery while the 8.8 cm guns were deployed against ground targets. The combat group reached the appointed area around 1200 hours, and established defensive positions between Kisbér and Nagyigmánd.

In the evening, *SS-Panzergrenadier-Regiment 4*, arrived on the Veszprém–Tét–Ménfőcsanak–Győr–Bábolnapuszta route to Csemerházimajor. On the next day at dawn, the *SS-Panzergrenadiers* prepared their makeshift positions. *SS-Panzergrenadier-Regiment 3* was delayed because of the battles around Várpalota.[1255]

On the night of 19/20 March 1945, in the early morning hours, *XXXXIII. Armeekorps* finished building up its fortifications in the Csép–Nagyigmánd–Mocsa–Naszály–Füzítőpuszta[1256] sector. During the morning, the Germans were still able to repel all Soviet attacks, however later on, the Soviets brought forward reinforcements, among them large numbers of armoured fighting vehicles. The subsequent Soviet attacks pushed back the German line and the Soviets advanced from Csép to Thalypuszta and the southern outskirts of Nagyigmánd.

The units of *356. Infanterie-Division* stopped the Soviet forces attacking along the Kocs–Mocsa road south of Mocsa.

1253 NARA, T311, R162, F7214672.
1254 NARA, T311, R162, F7214669, and Central Archives of the Russian Defence Ministry (Podolsk), f. 240, op. 2799, gy. 342, li. 115.
1255 Weidinger, Otto: *Division Das Reich. Der Weg der 2. SS-Panzer-Division „Das Reich"*. Band V: 1943-1945. Osnabrück, without year of publication, pp. 466-467.
1256 The oil refineries between Füzítőpuszta and Szőny, even if they were not operating at that time due to extensive damage suffered from air raids, were essential for the fuel supply of the German *Heeresgruppe Süd*. See NARA, T311, R162, F7214679.

Among others, the Soviet 991st Self-Propelled Artillery Regiment with the 429th Rifle Regiment/52nd Rifle Division, were also advancing in the direction of Mocsa. Their assault was launched at 0500 and it had, by 0800 hours in the morning, taken Tömördpuszta 2 km south-south-east of Mocsa, and launched an assault to capture Hill 193 (Öreg Hill) 500 meters northwest of there. The hill was taken, lost and retaken a number of times on that day, but by the evening it remained in Soviet hands. The Germans again launched two battalion-size attacks to recapture the hill, however the Soviets repulsed them.[1257]

According to Soviet reconnaissance data, the defence of Mocsa was secured by three 3.7 cm anti-aircraft gun batteries, two 7.5 cm gun batteries, most likely with Pak 40 anti-tank guns, three mortar batteries, five Panther tanks and 10 armoured personnel carriers.[1258]

The *6. Panzer-Division* training school was stationed at Kisigmánd under command of *Hauptmann* Tauber. The unit had approximately one company of infantry, five combat-ready Panther tanks and one Hungarian anti-aircraft battery with four 4 cm guns. The Soviets launched an attack against Kisigmánd with four armoured fighting vehicles and rifle infantry, but the defenders blocked the attempt and knocked out one of the armoured fighting vehicles. The Hungarian anti-aircraft guns were fighting bravely, but when their ammunition was completely used up, they had to retreat.[1259]

From the western outskirts of Tata-Tóváros, the Soviets occupied Naszály with 20 armoured fighting vehicles. Here, the 37th Guards Tank Brigade/2nd Guards Mechanized Corps were attacking, and by 0800 hours occupied Rétimalom. By that time, the 6th Guards Mechanized Brigade had taken Hill 134 (Nyúl Hill) two km south-west of Naszály. Afterwards, at 1400 hours, the 37th Guards Tank Brigade launched an attack from the south-east, and the 6th Guards Mechanized Brigade from the south-west against the village, pushing the defenders out by 1700 hours. In the sector of Naszály, the Soviets counted approximately 30 anti-aircraft guns and automatic cannon that were abandoned there. The 6th Guards Mechanized Brigade, together with one of the battalions of the 37th Guards Tank Brigade, cleared Pusztaalmás, which was defended by the Germans with five Panther tanks and anti-tank guns. The 37th Guards Tank Brigade in the meantime, minus one of its tank battalions, remained in reserve at Naszály.[1260]

On that day, the 5th Guards Mechanized Brigade crossed Által Creek in the north-western outskirts of Vértesszőlős, was in combat in the sector of Agostyán, then turned towards Tardos and Vértestolna, in an east-south-east direction.[1261]

The 4th Guards Mechanized Brigade with the 23rd Guards Tank Regiment was attacking northwards from the sector of Tata towards the Danube. At Ferencmajor however, the Soviets ran into the resistance of three German assault guns, plus field and anti-aircraft guns. One of the tank platoon commanders of the Tank Regiment, Guards 1st Lieutenant

---

1257 Central Archives of the Russian Defence Ministry (Podolsk), f. 240, op. 2799, gy. 342, li. 110.
1258 Central Archives of the Russian Defence Ministry (Podolsk), f. 240, op. 2799, gy. 342, li. 159.
1259 Paul, Wolfgang: *Brennpunkte. Die Geschichte der 6. Panzerdivision (1. leichte) 1937–1945*. Krefeld, 1977. p. 450.
1260 Central Archives of the Russian Defence Ministry (Podolsk), f. 240, op. 2799, gy. 357, li. 11, and the summarized report of the 2nd Guards Mechanized Corps of the combat actions during March and April 1945. Copy owned by the author. p. 121.
1261 Central Archives of the Russian Defence Ministry (Podolsk), f. 240, op. 2799, gy. 357, li. 11.

Fyodor Akimovich Tymoshenko, knocked out an assault gun and captured four anti-aircraft guns, and thus assured that his Brigade could continue their advance towards Dunaalmás. However, the 1st Lieutenant was also killed in the engagement and was posthumously awarded the Hero of the Soviet Union.[1262]

The Soviet 1505th Self-Propelled Artillery Regiment/46th Army was in a temporary defensive position around 1000 hours on that day, on the north-western edge of Tata, to be able to continue the attack towards Komárom with the 179th Guards Rifle Regiment/59th Guards Rifle Division. During this action the SU–76M self-propelled guns, according to their reports, knocked out one assault gun, three anti-tank guns and eight fortified positions. The 1505th Self-Propelled Artillery Regiment was subordinated on that day to the 52nd Rifle Division and was directed to Kocs.[1263]

The 112th Independent Self-Propelled Artillery Battalion/99th Rifle Division, with three self-propelled guns and one light tank, was gathered at 0600 hours in Környe.[1264]

During the afternoon, the Soviets increased their pressure on the eastern part of the German bridgehead at Komárom.[1265] The forces of *XXXXIII. Armeekorps* reported on that day to have knocked out 10 Soviet tanks and two self-propelled guns.[1266]

On the front of the Hungarian 3rd Army, the armoured fighting vehicles of the Soviet 4th Guards Mechanized Brigade, attacking north-east from Szomód, broke into Dunaszentmiklós, then reached Dunaalmás. Here, the Hungarian defenders knocked out seven Soviet armoured fighting vehicles, partly in close combat.[1267] The 4th Guards Mechanized Brigade had taken Szomód around 1200 hours, then reached the southern bank of the Danube in the western outskirts of Dunaalmás. The Brigade reported that they had occupied the village by 1800 hours.[1268] On the contrary, the heavy fighting continued at Dunaalmás.

The Soviet attacks, supported by a considerable amount artillery and ground attack aircraft, achieved a penetration in the Felsőgalla industrial area south of Baj and Vértesszőlős. The Soviets had even been able to widen the incursion northwards via Bánhida. In the industrial area,[1269] the German *96. Infanterie-Division* was in heavy and desperate close quarters combat and so far was holding its lines. The Germans were not able to decrease or eliminate the Soviet bridgehead at Tata despite the concentration of their forces. At the same time, the Soviets had also exerted considerable force against the bridgehead of the German–Hungarian troops at Bajna and Dorog. The Soviet marine infantry landed on the southern bank of the Danube with at least a battalion-size force and 70 boats seven km east of Nyergesújfalu at Tát, where they established a small bridgehead.[1270]

1262 HM HIM Hadtörténelmi Levéltár (Budapest), Szovjetunió Hőse kitüntetések gyűjteménye (*Collection of Hero of the Soviet Union awards*), 566.
1263 Central Archives of the Russian Defence Ministry (Podolsk), f. 240, op. 2799, gy. 342, li. 113.
1264 Central Archives of the Russian Defence Ministry (Podolsk), f. 961, op. 1, gy. 340, li. 159.
1265 NARA, T311, R162, F7214669.
1266 NARA, T311, R163, F7215424.
1267 NARA, T311, R162, F7214687.
1268 Central Archives of the Russian Defence Ministry (Podolsk), f. 240, op. 2799, gy. 357, li. 10.
1269 The coal extracted on the industrial area was essential for the railway system in operation in Hungarian, Slovakian and partly southeast-German areas. See NARA, T311, R162, F7214680.
1270 NARA, T311, R162, F7214670.

In the Komárom bridgehead of *8. Armee, Panzer-Kampfgruppe "Pape,"* established from units of *Panzerkorps "Feldherrnhalle",*[1271] repelled a company size attack along the Tata–Komárom road, in the sector of Boldogasszonypuszta. In the meantime, the *Panzer-Abteilung* of the *Kampfgruppe* reported the destruction of five Soviet tanks, then, following the fuel replenishment in the evening, they went into reserve at Szőny around midnight.[1272] East of Füzitőpuszta, 15 Soviet armoured fighting vehicles were in action, of which four were knocked out by the 8.8 cm guns of *II. (Abteilung)/Flak-Artillerie-Regiment 241.*[1273] The *Stab/8. Armee* planned to deploy *Panzer-Kampfgruppe "Pape"* in the afternoon to reoccupy Naszály, but the advance of the Soviet troops in the north-west direction made them abandon this plan.[1274]

South of Komárom, the Soviet Air Force raided the positions of the German anti-aircraft guns with approximately 30 bombers leaving three men dead and three wounded.[1275]

The German *Luftflotte 4* on that day, supported the defensive combat of the German *6. Panzerarmee,* flying 300 combat missions in the sector of Tata and the eastern outskirts of Várpalota. The pilots reported shooting down 23 Soviet planes and destroying a tank. On the night of 19/20 March 1945, a small German night ground attack aircraft formation raided Soviet unit movements in the Székesfehérvár–Bicske area.[1276]

The *Generalstabschef* of the *Heeresgruppe, Generalleutnant* von Grolman, had notified all units that day,, that they would not be able to obtain fuel supplies for an indefinite period of time due to the damage suffered by the oil refineries in Hungary. The troops would have to make the best use with the amount they currently had.[1277] Even with the strictest fuel conservation measures, this could only be a temporary solution. With this, effective deployment of the German armoured troops was extremely difficult.

21 March 1945, Wednesday

(**WEATHER**: highest daytime temperature 12 Celsius, partly clear skies, partly cloudy.)

In the front of *2. Panzerarmee, 71. Infanterie-Division/XXII. Gebirgskorps* set off from the south-eastern outskirts of the railway station at Mesztegnyő, broke through the

---

1271 The combat group consisted of the *Stab/Panzer-Division "Feldherrnhalle 1", I. (Abteilung)/Panzer-Regiment "Feldherrnhalle", I. and II. (Bataillon)/Panzergrenadier-Regiment "Feldherrnhalle", 3.* (armoured personnel carrier) *Kompanie/Panzer-Pionier-Bataillon "Feldherrnhalle", I. (Bataillon)/Panzergrenadier-Regiment 66* and *II.* (towed) *(Abteilung)/Panzer-Artillerie-Regiment 13.* The *I. Abteilung* of the *Panzer-Regiment "Feldherrnhalle"* was established from the formerly independent *Panzer-Abteilung 208.* Its *Kommandeur* was *Hauptmann* Mentor Loytved. The *Abteilungsstab* had two command Panzer IV tanks, *1. Kompanie* had nine Panther tanks and one Panzer IV/70 (A) *Jagdpanzer; 2.* and *3. Kompanies* each had nine Panzer IV tanks and one Panzer IV/70 (A) Jagdpanzers, and *4. Kompanie* had 10 Panther tanks. See Di Giusto, Stefano: *Panzer-Sicherungs-Kompanien und Panzer-Abteilung 208 - I. /Panzer-Regiment Feldherrnhalle. Italy 1943–1944. Hungary - Slovakia - Moravia 1944–1945.* Erlangen, 2010. pp. 158. and 185-187.
1272 Di Giusto, Stefano: *Panzer-Sicherungs-Kompanien und Panzer-Abteilung 208 - I. /Panzer-Regiment Feldherrnhalle. Italy 1943–1944. Hungary - Slovakia - Moravia 1944–1945.* Erlangen, 2010. p. 208.
1273 NARA, T311, R162, F7214670.
1274 NARA, T311, R162, F7214679.
1275 NARA, T311, R163, F7215407.
1276 NARA, T311, R162, F7214671.
1277 NARA, T311, R163, F7214985.

deeply echeloned Soviet defences, and advanced 1 km toward the east and south-east in the forested area east of the village.[1278]

The right flank of *16. SS-Panzergrenadier-Division* joined the attack of *71. Infanterie-Division* and gained minor ground. However, the left flank of the *Division* was halted by the Soviet defence.[1279]

The *I. (Bataillon)/SS-Panzergrenadier-Regiment 36* launched its attack at 0700 hours in the morning, but it was in need of armoured support. The commander of the *Kampfstaffel/ SS-Panzer-Abteilung 16*, *SS-Obersturmführer* Rex, wrote in his diary:

> *"0700 hours: […] The armoured group immediately joins the fight and by mistake, fires in front of SS-Panzer-Aufklärungs-Abteilung 16, which is attacking from Virágos toward the south-west, gains no ground and reaches the edge of the forest. At 1000 hours, the mistake was cleared at the command post of I. (Bataillon)/SS-Panzergrenadier-Regiment 36, where the time of the commencement of the south-east facing attack is set to 1020 hours. Rex refuses to attack in the given direction because the terrain is impossible to drive (swamp) and because of insufficient ammunition supply. Rex proposes the attack be commenced in the southern direction, with the deliberate delaying of the starting time. The battalion commander emphatically refuses this. The commander of the regiment, Maier gives clear orders: attack at 1045 hours. The five armoured fighting vehicles of the armoured group have 15 shells each (the full allowance is 90-98 shells which consists of 39 and 40 M fragmentation, smoke, incendiary and anti-tank shells). The direction of the attacks: 30-40 degree towards the forest, which was occupied by the enemy. Immediately at the launch of the attack, two armoured fighting vehicles sink into the mud and somewhat later another one, approximately 30 meters away from the enemy trenches. Rex, with the only remaining armoured fighting vehicle, takes over the task of closely guarding the one [assault gun – the author] that was sunken last, he clears the dangerous trench section with submachine guns and grenades and captures 16 soldiers. We just realize how well built the enemy trench system is. The Panzergrenadiers have serious losses. The joint attack is abandoned.*
>
> *1300 hours: New attack after the reorganization of the Grenadiers. Rex again refuses, as he only has two combat-ready armoured fighting vehicles left and altogether they have three fragmentation and two anti-tank shells.*
>
> *1500 hours: the attack is set off again, although the armoured fighting vehicles have not been replenished with ammunition. The armoured fighting vehicles are only there for psychological support for the Panzergrenadiers and they can only use their mounted machine guns. Strunz with his last shell destroys an anti-tank gun, and Rex an enemy tank. Heavy defensive fire from all barrels, the Panzergrenadiers are clinging in big bunches to the rear of our armoured fighting vehicles, to find shelter from the enemy fire. We leave the enemy trenches behind and approach the forest. The enemy behind us infiltrates the trench system again and attacks us from the rear, inflicting huge losses to the Infanterie. Approximately 100 meters in front of the forest the attack is called off and all units are recalled."*[1280]

1278 NARA, T311, R162, F7214684.
1279 NARA, T311, R162, F7214684.
1280 Puntigam, Josef Paul: *Vom Plattensee bis zur Mur. Die Kämpfe 1945 im Dreiländereck*. Feldbach, without year of publication, [1993], pp. 104-105.

The Soviet 32nd Independent Guards Mechanized Brigade/57th Army, with seven T–34 tanks, together with the 864th Self-Propelled Artillery Regiment with six SU–76Ms, and one of the companies of the 249th Independent Tank Regiment were in defence in the Kopárpuszta, east of the railway station in the Mesztegnyő–Libickozma–Szőkepuszta area.[1281]

On the front of the German *I. Kavallerie-Korps/6. Armee* the forces of *3.* and *4. Kavallerie-Divisions* stopped heavy Soviet attacks supported by armoured fighting vehicles on the night of 20/21 March 1945, and during the subsequent day on the Balatonfőkajár west 4.5 km–Balatonfőkajár–Mezőszentgyörgy north line.[1282]

On the night of 20/21 March 1945, the forces of the Soviet 27th Army swiftly followed the retreat of *23. Panzer-Division* and during the morning launched an attack from the Káloz sector and south-east of there, with rifle infantry and a large number of armoured fighting vehicles in the north-west. The Soviet 1202nd Self-Propelled Artillery Regiment with its SU–76Ms took part in the occupation of Káloz.[1283]

Around 0900 hours that morning, the units of the 1st Guards Mechanized Corps forced the units of the Hungarian 25th Infantry Division to flee from their positions south of Kisláng, and broke into the village from the south. The *I. (Bataillon)/SS-Panzergrenadier-Regiment 128/23. Panzer-Division* with the support of *Panzergruppe "Fischer"*, launched a counterattack and pushed the Soviets out of the village. After this, the Soviet troops returned with 42 tanks and self-propelled guns. The *I. (Bataillon)/SS-Panzergrenadier-Regiment 128* was scattered and they were only able to be reassembled around Jánosmajor.

The Soviets attacked with 10 tanks toward the farmstead. The Germans deployed the Panzer IV tanks of *Panzer-Regiment 23* and the three StuG. III assault guns that were taken from Lobbmajor north and east of Kisláng, in order to keep the road leading to Polgárdi open for their vehicle columns. The German tanks and assault guns reported destroying four M4A2 tanks. The remaining six armoured fighting vehicles broke into the lines of the retreating *Panzergrenadiers*, but after the Germans knocked out four more tanks, the remaining vehicles retreated. The majority of the 1st Guards Mechanized Corps were not engaged in combat with *23. Panzer-Division* but were advancing from Kisláng toward the north-west. The *23. Panzer-Division* established defensive positions on the line from Garasmajor to one km north-east, north-east to Point 147 near Alsótarnóca, from Alsótarnóca north-east one km to Point 155. The Panther tanks of *Panzer-Regiment 23* reported at 1300 hours that they knocked out two of the Soviet tanks advancing toward Alsótarnóca. Finally, at 1600 hours, *23. Panzer-Division* launched an attack towards Polgárdi to avoid encirclement. During the attack, a number of German armoured fighting vehicles and other vehicles were lost on the wet, muddy ground under fire of the Soviet artillery and tanks.[1284]

The Soviets, mainly the forces of the 1st Guards Mechanized Corps, who had been identified by German reconnaissance on that day,[1285] had torn open the lines of the German *I. Kavallerie-Korps* on a 12 km wide front and advancing further, occupied Enying, Lepsény

---

1281 Central Archives of the Russian Defence Ministry (Podolsk), f. 243, op. 2928, gy. 131, li. 263.
1282 NARA, T311, R162, F7214684.
1283 See Central Archives of the Russian Defence Ministry (Podolsk), f. 381, op. 8378, gy. 590, li. 61.
1284 Rebentisch, Ernst: *Zum Kaukasus und zu den Tauern. Die Geschichte der 23. Panzer-Division 1941–1945.* Esslingen, 1963. pp. 493-494.
1285 NARA, T311, R162, F7214692.

and Mezőszentgyörgy. The Soviet forward troops entered the Kölestelek forest area southeast of Füle. The German *6. Armee* deployed all available armoured forces, *1.* and *3. Panzer-Divisions*, *schwere Panzer-Abteilung 509* and *I. (Abteilung)/Panzer-Regiment 24*, here for a counteroffensive.[1286] The *I. Kavallerie-Korps* was assigned *Volks-Werfer-Brigade 19* on that day.

In the evening, the German *I. Kavallerie-Korps* with the forces of *3.* and *4. Kavallerie-Divisions* and *23. Panzer-Division*, stopped the Soviet advance on the Balatonfőkajár west three km–Balatonfőkajár–Lepsény north–Mezőszentgyörgy north–Polgárdi southeast general line. The *23. Panzer-Division* established holding positions on the Füle–Sándorka–forested area 1.5 km sector northeast of Polgárdi. In the forest, *Panzergrenadier-Regiment 126* and *Panzer-Pionier-Bataillon 51* established positions together with the armoured group of the *Division*. The same was executed in the sector of Füle by *Panzergrenadier-Regiment 128*, with the Jagdpanzer IV *Jagdpanzers* of *Panzerjäger-Abteilung 128* and the remnants of the Hungarian 25th Infantry Division, which arrived by flanking around Polgárdi from the south while the town was under attack by the Soviets. The two Panthers, two Panzer IVs and one assault gun of the armoured group, as well as two Jagdpanzer IV *Jagdpanzers* of *Panzerjäger-Abteilung 128,* were bogged down on the muddy ground. As the Germans had neither the towing capability, nor sufficient amount of fuel to recover them, they were blown up.[1287]

During the hours around noon, the German *I. (Abteilung)/Panzer-Regiment 24* was subordinated together with its few combat-ready Panther tanks to *23. Panzer-Division*, which were advancing toward the positions of *Panzergrenadier-Regiment 126*. Meanwhile, the armoured group of the *Division* was replenished with fuel and ammunition in Sándorka.[1288]

The *I. (Abteilung)/Panzer-Regiment 24* was ordered to march from the southern outskirts of Székesfehérvár to Polgárdi.

At nightfall, the Soviets launched a large-scale attack with a large number of armoured fighting vehicles from the sector of Lepsény toward the north-west and occupied Balatonfőkajár. At the same time, the units of the Soviet 1st Guards Mechanized Corps also broke into Polgárdi from the south-east.[1289]

As the *Kommandeur* of *I. (Abteilung)/Panzer-Regiment 24*, *Hauptmann* Weidemann, was approaching Polgárdi from the north-east to establish contact with *23 Panzer-Division*, he heard the roar of tank guns from Polgárdi. At the road junctions on the northern edge of the town, German vehicle columns were fleeing toward the west, and a few of the trucks had been hit and were already burning. At the northern edge of Polgárdi, the Germans placed damaged tanks on the roads so that they could close them off. *Hauptmann* Weidemann received an order from one of the *Stabsoffizier* of *23. Panzer-Division* to retake Polgárdi with his Panthers. The *Hauptmann* placed some of the tanks in a block position north of Polgárdi along the railroad, and with the remaining Panthers proceeded to attack the eastern part of the town. The western part should have been retaken by the Tiger B heavy tanks of *schwere Panzer-Abteilung 509*.[1290]

1286 NARA, T311, R162, F7214685.
1287 Rebentisch, Ernst: *Zum Kaukasus und zu den Tauern. Die Geschichte der 23. Panzer-Division 1941–1945.* Esslingen, 1963. p. 494.
1288 Rebentisch, Ernst: *Zum Kaukasus und zu den Tauern. Die Geschichte der 23. Panzer-Division 1941–1945.* Esslingen, 1963. p. 494.
1289 NARA, T311, R162, F7214705.
1290 Weidemann, Gert-Axel: *Unser Regiment. Reiter-Regiment 2 – Panzer-Regiment 24.* Groß-Umstadt, 1982. p. 278.

After nightfall, *schwere Panzer-Abteilung 509* had indeed set off from the direction of Falubattyán towards Polgárdi with five combat-ready Tiger Bs. They soon occupied Hill 228 near Kőhegy, from where there was a clear view toward both Polgárdi and Füle. The drive gear of the commanders tank was broken, therefore the vehicle had to be blown up. Afterwards, *Hauptmann* Dr. König took over command of another Tiger B.[1291]

In the meantime, the Panthers of *I. (Abteilung)/Panzer-Regiment 24*, occupied Bálintmajor on the eastern edge of Polgárdi with a swift assault. In the meantime, darkness had fallen. The *Abteilungskommandeur* received information from the medical officer, arriving from behind on the armoured personnel carrier bringing the wounded, that the Tiger B heavy tanks were holding in the rectangular shaped park of the Polgárdi mansion, although they were most likely at Hill 228 by then, and that there were a few "foreign" Panthers with them as well, likely from *23. Panzer-Division*. Because of this, *Hauptmann* Weidemann decided against the continuation of the attack, instead he would discuss it with the commander of the "foreign" Panthers, and he retreated westwards to be able to re-establish contact with the forces of *23. Panzer-Division*. Within an hour, the Panthers closed up to the *Division*, and reached the shore of Lake Balaton the next day..[1292]

In the front of the Soviet 26th Army on that day, the number of armoured fighting vehicles directly supporting the rifle forces were constantly growing. The 1953rd Self-Propelled Artillery Regiment/209th Self-Propelled Artillery Brigade was gathered on the northern side of Enying with nine SU–100 self-propelled guns, to escort the forces of the 66th Guards Rifle Division during their attack towards the north. Around 1600 hours, the 1952nd Self-Propelled Artillery Regiment was supporting the 2nd Guards Mechanized Brigade 4 km southwest of Lepsény at Hill 128, as well as west of the village, at Point 135. The Regiment lost two knocked out SU–100s on that day. The 1951st Self-Propelled Artillery Regiment was still stationed in the southern part of Simontornya with 15 SU–100s.[1293]

The 22nd Independent Tank Regiment, in cooperation with the forces of the 66th Guards Rifle Division, was fighting with six operational T-34s in the sector of Lepsény by the end of the day, during which they lost four burnt out vehicles.[1294]

The 71st Tank Regiment with three T–34/85s and the 1896th Self-Propelled Artillery Regiment with16 SU–76Ms of the 5th Guards Cavalry Corps, were in action four km southwest of Lepsény. The 54th Tank Regiment/Corps had received 10 replacement T–34/85s at the railway station at Szekszárd.[1295]

The 2nd Guards Mechanized Brigade, subordinated of the Soviet Cavalry Corps, and the 1952nd Self-Propelled Artillery Regiment/209th Self-Propelled Artillery Brigade, occupied the Balatonaliga railway station around 1700 hours, and Point 135 1 km northeast of there. During these actions, the 19th Guards Tank Regiment had lost six M4A2s with one

---

1291 *History of the schwere Panzer-Abteilung 509* (typewritten manuscript). Copy owned by the author. p. 57.
1292 Weidemann, Gert-Axel: *Unser Regiment. Reiter-Regiment 2 – Panzer-Regiment 24*. Groß-Umstadt, 1982. p. 279.
1293 Central Archives of the Russian Defence Ministry (Podolsk), f. 243, op. 2928, gy. 131, li. 262, and the summarized report of the 209th Self-Propelled Artillery Brigade of the combat actions between 10 March - 30 April 1945. Copy owned by the author. p. 4.
1294 Central Archives of the Russian Defence Ministry (Podolsk), f. 243, op. 2928, gy. 131, li. 262.
1295 Central Archives of the Russian Defence Ministry (Podolsk), f. 243, op. 2928, gy. 131, li. 263.

burnt out. By the evening, the Regiment had 21 operational tanks, whereas the 1952nd Self-Propelled Artillery Regiment had 16 operational SU–100s.[1296]

The Soviet 3rd Guards Mechanized Brigade/1st Guards Mechanized Corps reached the Alsótarnóca sector around 1400 hours. The armoured fighting vehicles of the 1st Guards Mechanized Brigade and the 1821st Self-Propelled Artillery Regiment occupied Mezőszentgyörgy around 1700 hours, then their forward troops reached the southern edges of Polgárdi. The 9th Guards Tank Brigade had followed the latter unit in the Corps commander's reserve.

During the battles on that day, the 1st Guards Mechanized Corps, according to Soviet archival data[1297], suffered considerably heavy losses, with 33 M4A2s knocked out by the Germans, of which, 12 burnt out, and another 28 tanks sunken on the muddy terrain. On that day, the Corps received 22 new M4A2s.[1298]

In the evening, *23. Panzer-Division* set off with units of the 25th Honvéd Infantry Division from 4 km southeast of Polgárdi and successfully reached the German frontline in the *Margarethen-Stellung*.[1299]

In the front of *44. Reichsgrenadier-Division/III. Panzerkorps*, the Soviets launched a number of holding attacks and managed to maintain two local incursions.

On the night of 20/21 March 1945, *3. Panzer-Division* was forced to give up the salient south of Seregélyes on their right flank. The Soviet troops launched three battalion and regiment-size attacks during the day, supported by 25 armoured fighting vehicles, and pushed back the right flank of the German frontline 2 km.[1300]

At dawn, a few kilometers west of Seregélyes, two Panzer IVs and one assault gun, commanded by *Zugführer* Grünhagen of *II. (Abteilung)/Panzer-Regiment 6/3. Panzer-Division*, was supporting one of the battalions of *Panzergrenadier-Regiment 394*. The gunner of the assault gun, *Zugführer* von Wietersheim, wrote in his diary:

"Suddenly at a distance of about 2 km, I saw impacts and smoke. These were our Panzergrenadiers, who had to retreat from the Soviet tanks. They reported eleven. We immediately set off with three vehicles, we establish our position behind a slope and we wait. All vehicles have a different designated area for checking. Through the gun sight I can see a line of trees, a plain open field and a small hill approximately 1000 meters away. The infantry in the meantime has marched past. Suddenly a turret appears on top of the hill. I aim and wait until I can see where the turret connects to the hull, and then I press [the gun's fire pedal]. Hit! The crew gets out. The hull is already in flames at the rear end. But the vehicle is still moving backwards. Another in there. Backdraft, it's the end of it! The whole turret is lifted out of its place and flies off next to the hull. Beside this one, another T-34 thrusts forward. The center of the gun sight is again at the spot where the turret joins the hull, and then –

1296 Central Archives of the Russian Defence Ministry (Podolsk), f. 243, op. 2928, gy. 178, li. 94.
1297 Central Archives of the Russian Defence Ministry (Podolsk), f. 243, op. 2928, gy. 131, li. 263.
1298 One other archival source at the same time states the total armoured fighting vehicle losses of that day consisted only of two M4A2 tanks. See Central Archives of the Russian Defence Ministry (Podolsk), f. 243, op. 2928, gy. 178, li. 96. Both referenced archival sources are from the documents of the commander of the tank and mechanized forces of the 3rd Ukrainian Front. The contradiction is unresolved at present.
1299 NARA, T311, R163, F7215425.
1300 NARA, T311, R162, F7214685.

fire! I got the second one too. In the meantime, heavy firing everywhere. Leutnant Schoch, the commander of one of the Panzer IVs, knocks out another T-34. The whole surrounding is dimmed with smoke. At the other side I have knocked out his comrade in an assault gun. On the extreme right, in a distance of about 1700 meters, stands a Stalin. Now this one is dangerous. All our vehicles are on it, but all hits just ricochet off it. Another three hits. Now it turns. We are relieved. The six hits must have made them think. Then a Panther comes to help from I. Abteilung, two Soviet T-34s are running at breakneck speed toward the vehicle of Leutnant Schoch. Schoch knocks the first out, and the other one knocks out the Panther. All this happened in just seconds.

On that day the small [armoured] group had to repel seven more Soviet infantry attacks, in which a 2 cm anti-aircraft gun was a great help. The Soviets are coming in just shirts, with combat helmets on their heads, rifles in hand. The political officers hurry the people forward again and again with spades, and all kinds of tools and weapons. Approximately 30 meters in front of us, in the maze of the trenches, they lie down and they fire at us like lunatics, and then of course the usual mortar fire. Suddenly a loud crash, bang, smoke in the vehicle, a hit on the rear armour. I can see via the rear window that we begin to burn. But a few cans of water tumbled over and this puts the fire out. Only our stuff is now garbled up totally.

After 1400 hours the Soviets come again. On their second advance, they reach us with a few men and they climb up onto our vehicle. I call the attention of my neighbour to this who immediately aims and sends the Soviets to heaven or who knows where with the machine gun. But this is really bothersome to us too. They ruined my gun sight. The order for retreat and to secure the other vehicles came at the best possible moment."[1301]

During these actions, the Soviet 110th Tank Brigade/18th Tank Corps and the 363rd Guards Heavy Self-Propelled Artillery Regiment/18th Tank Corps, reached the sector of the Hill 143 (Bolondvár) 2 km southwest of Seregélyes and Point 126 2 km east of Belsőbáránd. In the meantime, the Germans knocked out seven T–34/85s, six of which burnt out, and one ISU–152 self-propelled gun burnt out. The 181st Tank Brigade, with three T–34/85s and the 1016th Self-Propelled Artillery Regiment with 19 SU–100s, occupied Külsőkajtor around 1500 hours, where the self-propelled guns reported to have knocked out two German heavy tanks, one medium tank and eight armoured personnel carriers. The Soviets lost one burnt out T–34/85.[1302]

The 170th Tank Brigade[1303], together with the 1438th and 1068th Self-Propelled Artillery Regiments, was in the corps commanders' reserve at Sárosd. In the evening, the 18th Tank Corps had 42 operational tanks, 11 ISU–122s, six ISU–152s, 11 SU–76Ms and 27 SU–100s.[1304]

In the front of *1. Panzer-Division*, between Lake Velence and Székesfehérvár, three of the Soviet local attacks resulted in a penetration into the German defensive line. The

---

1301 *Geschichte der 3. Panzer-Division. Herausgegeben vom Traditionsverband der Division.* Berlin, 1967. p. 469.
1302 Summarized report of the 208th Self-Propelled Artillery Brigade of the period between 6 March – 6 April 1945. Copy owned by the author. pp. 11-12.
1303 The 170th Tank Brigade was being reorganized and replenished. On that day 20 new T-34/85 tanks arrived at the train station of Sárbogárd; these were assigned to the Brigade.
1304 Central Archives of the Russian Defence Ministry (Podolsk), f. 243, op. 2928, gy. 131, li. 263.

I. (Abteilung)/Panzer-Regiment 24 subordinated to the *Division,* was holding with 10 Panthers at Jánosfutás during the morning, where they reported knocking out a SU–100 self-propelled gun.[1305]

The units of the Soviet 99th Guards Rifle Division/9th Guards Army, with the support of a few armoured fighting vehicles, likely the SU–76M self-propelled guns of the 1513th Self-Propelled Artillery Regiment, occupied Ősi and pushed back units of *9. SS-Panzer-Division,* covering the flanks of *III. Panzerkorps,* toward the south. The Soviets continued their attack and reached the vineyards east of Berhida.[1306] On the northern and eastern edges of Berhida, *Reiter-Regiment 41/4. Kavallerie-Division* stood in defence, which at the moment was able to hold off the regiment size Soviet attacks coming in from the north and north-west direction.[1307]

On the front of the German *IV. SS-Panzerkorps/6. Panzerarmee,* the units of *5. SS-Panzer-Division* eliminated the deep Soviet penetrations in the northern and south-western parts of Székesfehérvár on the night of 20/21 March 1945. In the morning, the German frontline stood on the line of Székesfehérvár south, the western shore of Sós Lake, the area of the railway station, the western edge of the vineyards, the southern edge of Kiskecskemét and along the road leading to Mór up to the road junction north-west of Székesfehérvár.

On the night of 20/21 March 1945, the forces of *5. SS-Panzer-Division* in defence in Székesfehérvár, eliminated Soviet incursions in the north and south-west parts of the town. During the day, the Soviets concentrated their forces and launched another attack against the town. This time the Germans pushed them back to the area of the railway station and to the southern areas of Székesfehérvár.[1308]

Around noon, the severed contact with the command post of *IV. SS-Panzerkorps* at Vilonya, was restored after several days. After this, Hitler's orders were communicated to *SS-Standartenführer* Ullrich: Székesfehérvár is to be held at all costs. However, the *Divisionskommandeur* was well aware of the fact, that in the military sense, this was impossible, and would only result in the total annihilation of the already worn out *Division.* Therefore, opposing Hitler's order, he decided to execute a breakout attempt, to be carried out the next dawn in a west-south-west direction.[1309]

During the day, the Soviets launched another extensive attack against Székesfehérvár, and by the evening they occupied the majority of the town.[1310] At 2220 hours, *5. SS-Panzer-Division* reported via radio to the *Stab* of the German *6. Armee* that the railway station was already in the hands of the Soviets and their own forces had been confined to the south-western edge of Székesfehérvár.[1311] The *SS-Division* was subordinated to *III. Panzerkorps* on the same day.[1312]

1305 Senger und Etterlin, von F.M. jr.: *Die 24. Panzer-Division vormals 1. Kavallerie-Division 1939–1945.* Neckargemünd, 1962. p. 310. The source originally mentions SU–85 but there was no self-propelled gun of that type deployed in the sector. At that time, only one such self-propelled gun existed in the strength of the whole 3rd Ukrainian Front and that stayed along the Sió Canal.
1306 NARA, T311, R162, F7214685.
1307 NARA, T311, R162, F7214685.
1308 Tieke, Wilhelm: *Von Plattensee bis Österreich. Heeresgruppe Süd 1945.* Gummersbach, without year of publication, p. 64.
1309 Strassner, Peter: *Europäische Freiwillige. Die 5. SS-Panzerdivision Wiking.* Osnabrück, 1977. Third, revised edition. p. 341.
1310 NARA, T311, R162, F7214685.
1311 NARA, T311, R162, F7214700.
1312 NARA, T311, R163, F7215422.

A Soviet 366th Guards Heavy Self-Propelled Artillery Regiment/4th Guards Army kept the town under fire from the eastern outskirts of Székesfehérvár with eight captured self-propelled howitzers and three Panthers.[1313]

The 207th Self-Propelled Artillery Brigade was in combat in the Székesfehérvár sector with the units of the German *5. SS* and *1. Panzer-Divisions*, supported by their own rifle troops. The 1004th Self-Propelled Artillery Regiment with nine SU–100s, was in combat two km south of the town at the Hill 136 (Kuruchalom), the 912th Self-Propelled Artillery Regiment was in combat 5.5 km south of Székesfehérvár, at Point 129 north-east of Külső-Fövenypuszta, along the road leading to Sárkeresztúr. The 1004th Self-Propelled Artillery Regiment was still supporting the 62nd Guards Rifle Division, which was engaged by German armoured fighting vehicles. The Regiment reported knocking out 12 German heavy tanks on that day, while their own losses amounted to three knocked out SU–100s.[1314]

The 912th Self-Propelled Artillery Regiment, together with the forces of the 34th Guards Rifle Division, repulsed the attack of 14 German armoured fighting vehicles from the direction of Jánosfutás. In the course of this, they reported to have knocked out eight German tanks. Their losses amounted to six SU–100s, five of which burnt out.[1315]

By 1400 hours, the 1011th Self-Propelled Artillery Regiment handed over its four SU–100 self-propelled guns to the 912th Self-Propelled Artillery Regiment and went into reserve in the area of Ercsi. The 207th Self-Propelled Artillery Brigade had 27 SU–100s, two SU–57s and two operational T–34s in the evening.[1316]

The independent self-propelled-artillery battalions of the 4th Guards Army supported the Soviet rifle units assaulting Székesfehérvár with 62 SU–76Ms and five tanks.[1317]

The units of *9. SS-Panzer-Division* launched counterattacks, supported by some of their own armoured fighting vehicles, from the southern outskirts of Ősi toward the north, and from Öskü toward Várpalota. However the units of the *Division* abandoned Ősi after extremely heavy fighting. Afterwards, north of Berhida, the Soviets gradually pushed back the units of *SS-Panzergrenadier-Regiments 19* and *20*. During these actions *SS-Obersturmbannführer* Hofmann, *Kommandeur* of *SS-Panzergrenadier-Regiment 20*, was killed. After this, the still combat-ready units of the two *Panzergrenadier-Regiments* were concentrated under command of *SS-Obersturmbannführer* Seela.

On the left flank of the *Division*, at Pétfürdő and west of Berhida, units of *SS-Panzer-Flak-Abteilung 9* attempted to halt the Soviet armoured fighting vehicles, and they reported to have knocked out a large number of them.

Eight Jagdpanther *Jagdpanzers* of *4. Kompanie/SS-Panzer-Regiment 9*, were in well camouflaged ambush positions south of Ősi and according to their report, they knocked out 15 IS-2 heavy tanks in a short period of time[1318]. According to *SS-*

1313 Central Archives of the Russian Defence Ministry (Podolsk), f. 243, op. 2928, gy. 131, li. 262.
1314 War log of the 207th Self-Propelled Artillery Brigade, 21 March 1945. Copy owned by the author.
1315 War log of the 207th Self-Propelled Artillery Brigade, 21 March 1945. Copy owned by the author.
1316 Central Archives of the Russian Defence Ministry (Podolsk), f. 243, op. 2928, gy. 131, li. 262.
1317 Central Archives of the Russian Defence Ministry (Podolsk), f. 243, op. 2928, gy. 131, li. 262.
1318 There were no IS-2s in combat in this sector. These could perhaps be the ISU-122s of the 364th Guards Heavy Self-Propelled Artillery Regiment in combat at Várpalota on that evening; provided that these were deployed south-south-east of Várpalota. No further sources verifiy such a scale of armoured fighting vehicle loss of the Soviet regiment, as on that day three of its self-propelled guns were burnt out and at most, two could have suffered repairable damage.

Obersturmbannführer Telkamp, *SS-Panzer-Regiment 9* knocked out at least 70 Soviet armoured fighting vehicles on that day.[1319]

On the same morning, *SS-Panzer-Pionier-Bataillon 9* was still in action on the banks of the Malom Canal. The *SS-Pioniers,* marching towards Berhida ran into Soviet armoured fighting vehicles and mounted rifle units at Polgárdi, most likely the forces of the 1st Guards Mechanized Brigade. The *1. Kompanie/SS-Panzer-Pionier-Bataillon 9,* engaged them in combat in order to secure the route of the *Bataillon*. In close combat, the *SS-Pioniers* destroyed four Soviet armoured fighting vehicles. As a result, the other units of the *Bataillon* were able to reach Berhida via Küngös without any problems, and there they established defensive positions.[1320]

The 6th Guards Motorized Rifle Brigade/5th Guards Tank Corps with the 51st Guards Self-Propelled Artillery Brigade, the 301st Light Artillery Regiment, the 392nd Anti-Aircraft Artillery Regiment and one of the tank battalions of the 20th Guards Tank Brigade, renewed their attack at 0600 hours from the direction of Inota towards Várpalota. *SS-Kampfgruppe "Hansen",* based on *SS-Panzergrenadier-Regiment 1/1. SS-Panzer-Division* with the remaining Panther tanks of *SS-Panzer-Regiment 1,* temporarily stopped the attack of a Soviet force of approximately three rifle divisions, supported by tanks at Várpalota. During these actions the Germans reported to have knocked out 15 Soviet tanks. *SS-Obersturmführer* Hans Malkomes, *Chef* of one of the companies of *SS-Panzer-Regiment 1* equipped with Panther tanks, was killed when a Soviet snipers bullet hit him in the head while he was peering out of the turret cupola.[1321]

At 1520 hours, the 6th Guards Motorized Rifle Brigade, reinforced with tanks and self-propelled guns, broke into the south-western part of the village. Shortly before that, around 1400 hours, the reinforced Brigade had repulsed a German counterattack of nine tanks and a battalion of infantry, launched from the forest 2 km southwest of Várpalota.

The 20th Guards and 22nd Guards Tank Brigades, together with the 98th Guards and 99th Guards Rifle Divisions/9th Guards Army were attacking Várpalota from the northeast.

Units of *SS-Panzer-Regiment 1* destroyed seven Soviet armoured fighting vehicles at the southern edge of Várpalota with the loss of three of their own tanks. *SS-Untersturmführer* Konrad Heubeck, who took over command of the Panthers of *1. Kompanie/SS-Panzer-Regiment 1* after *SS-Obersturmführer* Werner Wolff was wounded, claimed to have knocked out seven Soviet ISU–122s[1322] at Várpalota. Counting these, Heubeck had knocked out 52 enemy armoured fighting vehicles during the war. For this deed, he was awarded the Knight's Cross of the Iron Cross on 17 April 1945.[1323]

1319 Tieke, Wilhelm: *Im Feuersturm letzter Kriegsjahre. II. SS-Panzerkorps mit 9. und 10. SS-Division „Hohenstaufen" und „Frundsberg".* Osnabrück, without year of publication, [1975] pp. 507-508. Soviet archival sources do not verify such scale of armoured fighting vehicle losses in this sector.
1320 Tieke, Wilhelm: *Im Feuersturm letzter Kriegsjahre. II. SS-Panzerkorps mit 9. und 10. SS-Division „Hohenstaufen" und „Frundsberg".* Osnabrück, without year of publication, [1975] p. 508.
1321 Tiemann, Ralf: *Chronik der 7. Panzerkompanie. An vorderster Front in der 1. SS-Panzerdivision „Leibstandarte SS Adolf Hitler".* Selent, 2015. p. 254.
1322 The German SS-officer reported to have knocked out IS–2 heavy tanks, however there were no such types of armoured fighting vehicles in combat at Várpalota. The German officer must have been engaged in combat with the ISU-122s of the 364th Guards Heavy Self-Propelled Artillery Regiment. The number of knocked out armoured fighting vehicles are only partially verified by Soviet archival sources.
1323 Agte, Patrick: *Jochen Peiper. Kommandeur Panzerregiment Leibstandarte.* Berg am Starnberger See, 1998. p. 355., and Krätschmer, Ernst-Günther: Die Ritterkreuzträger der Waffen-SS. Preussisch Oldendorf, 1982. p. 854.

Várpalota fell into Soviet hands around 1600 hours. During the intense close quarters combat, both sides suffered heavy losses. In the eight hours of fighting in the outskirts of the town and within the town perimeters, the Germans reported to have knocked out 46 Soviet armoured fighting vehicles.[1324]

The German defence also deployed two dug-in Panther tanks taken from the workshop company of *Panzer-Regiment 23* which were still under repair, however as they were not able to draw fire on the Soviet armoured fighting vehicles that were outflanking them, these Panthers were blown up.[1325]

Based on photographic evidence, units of *schwere Panzerjäger-Abteilung 560*, permanently subordinated to *12. SS-Panzer-Division*, were also taking part in the defence of Várpalota, because one Jagdpanther *Jagdpanzer* from *1. Kompanie* was certainly lost in the town, and one Panzer IV/70 (V) *Jagdpanzer* was lost on the road to Tés. It is also highly probable that many of the *Jagdpanzers* of *SS-Panzerjäger-Abteilung 12* were also fighting here, as they were subordinated to *1. SS-Panzer-Division* around this time.[1326]

The units of *1. SS-Panzer-Division* in combat east of Inota, and the armoured personnel carriers of *III. (Bataillon)/SS-Panzergrenadier-Regiment 2,* had broken through toward the west by the evening and re-joined their own troops. The combat group of *SS-Panzergrenadier-Regiment 2*, reinforced with the remaining combat-ready Panzer IV/70 *Jagdpanzers* of *SS-Panzerjäger-Abteilung 1* and part of *Panzer-Pionier-Bataillon 1*, were ordered to re-establish contact with the right flank of *12. SS-Panzer-Division*. However, the combat group was forced to fend off attacks from large numbers of rifle infantry west of Tés. In the meantime, contact with *9. SS-Panzer-Division* two km northeast of Ősi, was temporarily re-established.[1327]

The *1. SS-Panzer-Division/I. SS-Panzerkorps* together with units of *3. SS-Panzer-Division*,[1328] were in defence on the northern edge of the forest southwest of Várpalota against Soviet troops attacking with three divisions. *SS-Untersturmführer* Heubeck was ordered to secure the road leading towards Veszprém in the direction of Öskü and Hajmáskér with two Panthers and one Tiger B heavy tank of *3. Kompanie/schwere Panzer-Abteilung 501* commanded by *SS-Hauptsturmführer* Birnschein. Soon Soviet armoured fighting vehicles appeared, which were en route to Veszprém and the Germans knocked out 17 of them in a 2-hour engagement, according to their own report.[1329] According to the war log of *Heeresgruppe Süd,* the Germans reported knocking out 15 Soviet armoured fighting vehicles.[1330]

The forces of the 5th Guards Tank Corps repulsed a number of German attacks in the sector of Várpalota. At the end of the day, the 22nd Guards Tank Brigade established defensive positions on the northern edge of the town, the 20th Guards Tank Brigade, the 6th

---

1324 NARA, T311, R162, F7214686.
1325 Rebentisch, Ernst: *Zum Kaukasus und zu den Tauern. Die Geschichte der 23. Panzer-Division 1941–1945*. Esslingen, 1963. p. 497.
1326 See the photographs at the top of page 62 in Wydawnictwo Militaria 246 - Budapest Balaton 1945., and in the Appendix of this work!
1327 Tiemann, Ralf: *Die Leibstandarte*. Band IV/2. Osnabrück, 1987. pp. 309-310.
1328 On that day, *3. SS-Panzer-Division* together with *Volks-Artillerie-Korps 403* was subordinated to *I. SS-Panzerkorps*. See NARA, T311, R163, F7215422.
1329 Agte, Patrick: *Jochen Peiper. Kommandeur Panzerregiment Leibstandarte*. Berg am Starnberger See, 1998. p. 355.
1330 NARA, T311, R162, F7214686.

Guards Motorized Rifle Brigade and the 51st Guards Self-Propelled Artillery Brigade were in defence on the western edge of Várpalota, and the 21st Guards Tank Brigade and the 364th Guards Heavy Self-Propelled Artillery Regiment established positions on the south-eastern fringes of the town. The German armoured fighting vehicles and *Panzergrenadiers,* launched a number of counterattacks as late as 2000 hours, however they were not successful.[1331]

During the action around Várpalota that day, the 5th Guards Tank Corps lost 16 knocked out T–34/85 tanks and six SU–76M self-propelled guns[1332], and the 364th Guards Heavy Self-Propelled Artillery Regiment lost three burnt out ISU–122s.[1333]

In the evening, the 5th Guards Tank Corps had 59 operational tanks and assault guns of the subordinated 51st Guards Self-Propelled Artillery Brigade, and 15 ISU–122 self-propelled guns of the 364th Guards Heavy Self-Propelled Artillery Regiment.[1334]

The German mixed combat group defending Csór was still holding out. Around 0830 in the morning, the Soviets launched an attack against the village from the east and south-east with two battalions of infantry and eight armoured fighting vehicles. The Soviet rifle infantry was held back by the German artillery and machine gun fire and, German assault guns knocked out one Soviet armoured fighting vehicle. Afterwards, two of the Soviet tanks gave fire support to the other five, which succeeded in breaking into Csór and destroying a few armoured personnel carriers. However, the Germans succeeded in keeping the Soviet rifles away from the tanks in the village.[1335] The subsequent events were remembered by the German combat commander of Csór, *SS-Hauptsturmführer* Bernau:

"In the meantime the Russian tanks were moving around in the town, wildly firing everywhere. But a Rottenführer with a Panzerfaust is hiding behind one of the houses, waiting in absolute patience until the tank rushed past him again. Then the Panzerfaust hits and the shell burns through the hull. A meter-long backdraft and a detonation signals the end of the tank. It seems the curse has been lifted! The second tank sets an armoured personnel carrier on fire, but an assault gun soon gets it. The two Russian armoured fighting vehicles and our three to four armoured personnel carriers are burning like huge torches; they were well camouflaged from the south and south-east but were not hidden from the tanks arriving from the town. Now the third tank breached the firing position of the first battery, and crushed the gun mounts of a light field howitzer. But the outermost gun is turned by the crew and from a distance of 30 meters they immobilize the Russian. The remaining two enemy armoured fighting vehicles are now insecure, but our soldiers got over the shock quite quickly. Now strike upon strike. One of the assault guns rushed forward and with a direct hit, knocked out the fourth Russian; again detonation and backdraft, black smoke rises to the sky. The soldiers are shouting with joy. But then the fifth Russian hits the left tracks of the assault gun; in a matter of seconds however, a Panzerfaust immobilizes it. While we are carrying away

---

1331 Central Archives of the Russian Defence Ministry (Podolsk), f. 243, op. 2928, gy. 131, li. 261.
1332 Of these, five T–34/85s and four SU–76Ms were burnt out. See the war log of the 5th Guards Tank Corps for March 1945. Copy owned by the author. p. 15.
1333 Central Archives of the Russian Defence Ministry (Podolsk), f. 243, op. 2928, gy. 178, li. 95.
1334 Central Archives of the Russian Defence Ministry (Podolsk), f. 243, op. 2928, gy. 178, li. 95.
1335 Bernau, Günter: Aus den letzten Kämpfen in Ungarn 1945. I./SS-Panzer-Artillerie-Regiment 5. In: *Deutsches Soldatenjahrbuch 1975*. p. 213.

the killed and wounded, the interrogation of the captured Russian soldiers begin. They had the task of capturing Csór and then advancing toward Várpalota. They were told that there were no other German units in front of them."[1336]

By the evening, the soldiers of the German combat group defending Csór, found themselves in a situation impossible to hold. Ammunition supplies were so depleted that the four assault guns had only six shells each, the field howitzers had only 12 rounds left, and there was almost no infantry ammunition or 2 cm shells left. Therefore, *SS-Hauptsturmführer* Bernau decided to retreat to Inota on the night of 21/22 March 1945.[1337]

At dawn on 21 March 1945, in the defensive line of *12. SS-Panzer-Division,* the *Divisionsbegleitkompanie* marched to Bakonycsernye to secure the road leading to Zirc against the Soviets attacking from the east. At Kistéspuszta, *501. SS-Sicherungskompanie/I. SS-Panzerkorps* was in defence.

SS-Panzergrenadier-Regiment 26 and *SS-Panzer-Regiment 12* were defending Mecsér and the surrounding hills against the tanks of the Soviet 9th Guards Mechanized Corps and motorized rifle infantry. In the heavy fighting the Germans, according to their own reports, knocked out 19 Soviet armoured fighting vehicles, and captured two.[1338] Together with these, *I. SS-Panzerkorps* reported to have knocked out 66 Soviet armoured fighting vehicles during the fighting on the night of 20/21 March 1945.[1339]

Despite this, the Germans were not able to hold their positions here, The *II. (Bataillon)/SS-Panzergrenadier-Regiment 26* retreated via Sikátorpuszta to Bakonycsernye, and *I. (Bataillon)/SS-Panzergrenadier-Regiment 26* established new defences north of the village. The retreat was covered by the armoured fighting vehicles of *Panzer-Kampfgruppe "Siegel",* and afterwards, they marched to Bakonynána.

The armoured personnel carrier-battalion of the *Division* was also pushed back to Tés by the Soviet troops, then after they captured the village, the Germans fell back to take a stand on the hill west of there. With this move, the Soviets closed up to the area of the Veszprém–Zirc–Kisbér road. This was the reason why the Germans were determined to retake Tés whatever the cost.

In order to carry out this task, a combat group was created from four Jagdpanthers of *schwere Panzerjäger-Abteilung 560*, 10 armoured personnel carriers of *III. (Bataillon)/SS-Panzergrenadier-Regiment 26,* the *Divisionsbegleitkompanie, 501. SS-Sicherungskompanie* and a *Grenadier-Kompanie* whose identity is unknown. The attack that began around 1700 hours failed, as well as two renewed attempts at 1900 hours and 2030 hours, resulting in the loss of three Jagdpanthers. At last, the combat group established defensive positions on the hill 600 meters west of the village. In order to reinforce the infantry, a Jagdpanther and an armoured personnel carrier were left there.

1336 Bernau, Günter: Aus den letzten Kämpfen in Ungarn 1945. I./SS-Panzer-Artillerie-Regiment 5. In: *Deutsches Soldatenjahrbuch 1975.* pp. 213-214.
1337 Bernau, Günter: Aus den letzten Kämpfen in Ungarn 1945. I./SS-Panzer-Artillerie-Regiment 5. In: *Deutsches Soldatenjahrbuch 1975.* p. 214.
1338 Meyer, Hubert: *Kriegsgeschichte der 12. SS-Panzerdivision „Hitlerjugend".* Band II. Osnabrück, 1987. 2nd edition. p. 508.
1339 NARA, T311, R163, F7215412.

The retreating *SS-Panzergrenadier-Regiment 26* was pursued by the Soviets. On the left flank of the *Division* the withdrawing units of the Hungarian 2nd Armoured Division abandoned Csatka and with this, the northern flank of the Germans was opened up. The Soviet troops attacking from the northwest pushed out *I.* and *II Bataillons* of the *SS-Regiment* by the evening, and occupied Bakonycsernye.[1340]

From the north-eastern sector of Tés, the Soviets advanced towards the north-west and the Germans were only able to halt them temporarily on the eastern edge of Jásd, and at Points 259 and 263 north-east of Szápár.[1341]

At Jásd, defensive positions were established by *Panzer-Pionier-Bataillon 12*. The *Bataillon* was to retake Csőszpuszta with the help of some *Jagdpanzers*, but the armoured fighting vehicles did not arrive in time, and the Soviet troops launched another attack.[1342]

Northeast of Szápár, *I. (Bataillon)/SS-Panzergrenadier-Regiment 26* and *3. Panzer-Pionier-Bataillon,* established defences with the support of two Panzer IVs and one self-propelled 2 cm four barrelled anti-aircraft gun. The Soviet attacks, initiated from the south, were held back by the Germans. After the Soviets knocked out one of the Panzer IVs and the anti-aircraft gun, the German *SS-Kampfgruppe* broke through via Csetény to Dudar.[1343]

The guns of *SS-Panzer-Flak-Abteilung 12* were targeting the Soviet infantry. In the evening, the frontline of the *Division* stretched from the western sector of Tés via Szápár to six km east of Dudar. The *Division*'s command post was at Dudar.[1344]

The Soviet 9th Guards Mechanized Corps/6th Guards Tank Army occupied Szápár during this battle, with its 30th Guards Mechanized Brigade, and its 31st Guards Mechanized Brigade attacked Csetény by flanking Szápár from the south. The motorized infantry of the 18th Guards Mechanized Brigade was pushing forward 2 km north-east of Bakonynána. The 46th Guards Tank Brigade followed this Brigade and was marching 2 km southeast of Tés. In the evening, the Corps had 146 operational M4A2s and 18 operational SU–76M self-propelled guns.[1345] Between 18-21 March 1945, the Corps lost 22 knocked out tanks, seven of which burnt out.[1346]

The 1523rd Self-Propelled Artillery Regiment/9th Guards Army with 17 SU–76Ms, was stationed at Söréd, the 1513th Self-Propelled Artillery Regiment with four SU–76Ms, was at Szigetpuszta, 1 km north of Ősi, and four km south-east of Várpalota, and the 1524th Self-Propelled Artillery Regiment with 25 SU–76Ms was stationed at Isztimér.[1347]

The 1922nd Self-Propelled Artillery Regiment/208th Self-Propelled Artillery Brigade was supporting the 114th Guards Rifle Division in the sector of Várpalota, and around 1600 hours, was engaged in combat inside the town. The Regiment reported to have knocked out four German tanks and they lost one SU-100.[1348]

1340 Meyer, Hubert: *Kriegsgeschichte der 12. SS-Panzerdivision „Hitlerjugend"*. Band II. Osnabrück, 1987. 2nd edition. p. 509.
1341 NARA, T311, R162, F7214686.
1342 Vopersal, Wolfgang: *Soldaten, Kämpfer, Kameraden. Marsch und Kämpfe der SS-Totenkopfdivision*. Band Vb. Bielefeld, 1991.p. 785.
1343 Vopersal, Wolfgang: *Soldaten, Kämpfer, Kameraden. Marsch und Kämpfe der SS-Totenkopfdivision*. Band Vb. Bielefeld, 1991. p. 787.
1344 Meyer, Hubert: *Kriegsgeschichte der 12. SS-Panzerdivision „Hitlerjugend"*. Band II. Osnabrück, 1987. 2nd edition.p. 510.
1345 Central Archives of the Russian Defence Ministry (Podolsk), f. 243, op. 2928, gy. 131, li. 261.
1346 Central Archives of the Russian Defence Ministry (Podolsk), f. 339, op. 5179, gy. 87, li. 16.
1347 Central Archives of the Russian Defence Ministry (Podolsk), f. 243, op. 2928, gy. 178, li. 92.
1348 Summarized report of the 208th Self-Propelled Artillery Brigade of the period between 6 March – 6 April 1945. Copy owned by the author. p. 13.

On the same day, units of the Soviet 23rd Tank Corps launched an attack from the Mór sector toward the north-west. The 3rd Tank Brigade, in cooperation with the 1443rd Self-Propelled Artillery Regiment and the 1501st Anti-Tank Artillery Regiment, occupied Ácteszér at 1200 hours, and Súr by 1630 hours. The Hungarian *SS-Kampfgruppe "Ney"* in defence here, was pushed back to Point 261 (Bogánsánc) south of the village and Hill 318 southwest of there. The Hungarian forces holding at Ácteszér bypassed toward Csatka. In the evening, the Corps had 70 operational T–34/85s, four IS–2s, nine ISU–122 and three ISU–152 self-propelled guns. The 53rd Motorcycle Regiment, which was assembled at the southern edge of Mór with 13 T–34/85s, was also subordinated to them.[1349]

Units of *3. SS-Panzer-Division* launched a counterattack to reoccupy Ácteszér and Csatka.[1350]

It became evident by the evening on that day, that the main forces of the Soviet 3rd Ukrainian Front had not succeeded in carrying out one of their most important operational tasks, that is, the encirclement and elimination of the forces of the German *6. Panzerarmee* and *6. Armee* in the north-eastern area of Lake Balaton.[1351] The Germans were able to pull out most of their forces from the pocket that was forming, although they suffered heavy losses during the withdrawal.

On the frontline of the 2nd Ukrainian Front

On the front of *6. Panzer-Division/II. SS-Panzerkorps*, the Soviets concentrated reinforcements southeast of Kisbér. One to two company size Soviet attacks were launched from Hanta toward the north and north-east. The Soviets sent a number of reconnaissance patrols to Hill 235 (Öreg szőlőhegy, Old Vine Hill) 2.5 km southeast of Kisbér, which was a clear sign of impending attacks.

In the morning, the attack of *6. Panzer-Division* against Ete was repulsed by the Soviets with their own counterattack. However, around 1200 hours the Germans renewed their attempt from Kisbér and they successfully broke through the southern edge of Ete around 1410 hours with 13 tanks and assault guns, and *Panzergrenadier-Regiment 114*. One of the assault platoons of *3. SS-Panzer-Division* that happened to be in Kisbér also took part, together with one of the companies of *6. Panzer-Division* and two Tiger E heavy tanks.[1352]

The Soviets crossed the railroad line leading towards the northwest, from the sector of Csép, with a regiment-size force.[1353] The 1897th Self-Propelled Artillery Regiment, that was in subordination to the Soviet 18th Guards Rifle Corps, was supporting the

---

1349 Central Archives of the Russian Defence Ministry (Podolsk), f. 243, op. 2928, gy. 131, li. 263.
1350 NARA, T311, R162, F7214686.
1351 Malakhov, M. M.: A Balatontól Bécsig (excerpt). In: *Fejezetek hazánk felszabadításának történetéből*. Budapest, 1960. p. 192.
1352 Vopersal, Wolfgang: *Soldaten, Kämpfer, Kameraden. Marsch und Kämpfe der SS-Totenkopfdivision*. Band Vb. Bielefeld, 1991. p. 773. These two Tiger E heavy tanks could also have been the armoured fighting vehicles assigned to the rapid reaction unit *(Alarmtrupp)* of the *schwere SS-Panzer-Abteilung* that was being formed. According to Wolfgang Schneider the tanks were the armoured fighting vehicles detached from *SS-Panzer-Regiment 3*. See Schneider, Wolfgang: *Tiger der Division Totenkopf*. Uelzen, 2009. p. 255.
1353 NARA, T311, R162, F7214687.

761st and 606th Rifle Regiments of the 317th Rifle Division at Thalypuszta and north-west of Csép. When the German *6. Panzer-Division* reoccupied Ete at around noon, the 1897th Self-Propelled Artillery Regiment was ordered to seal off the direction leading to Makkpuszta, 1 km south of Bojszapuszta, before the Germans, with two batteries in coordination with the 606th Rifle Regiment. The SU–76Ms, together with the rifle troops, were already there in firing positions at 1300 hours. The other two batteries, with the 761st Rifle Regiment, continued their attack toward the north-north-west and reached Milkovics and Ghiczypuszta, north-east of Csép, where they established temporary defences. The 1897th Self-Propelled Artillery Regiment reported during the two days fighting in this sector, that they had knocked out three armoured personnel carriers and 13 machine guns, captured five anti-tank guns and 45 prisoners. Their own losses amounted to three burnt out SU–76Ms, six men killed, of which, two were self-propelled gun commanders, and three wounded.[1354]

The 1897th Self-Propelled Artillery Regiment, together with the 317th Rifle Division, reached the railroad lines 2 km east of Tárkány around 1500 hours. At this time, the Germans launched an attack from the sector of Csép with five tanks and 25 armoured personnel carriers in the direction of Makkpuszta and repulsed the Soviet rifle infantry. The SU–76Ms helped to suppress the German armoured fighting vehicles and by 1800 hours, the Soviets occupied Csép, Milkovicspuszta and Hill 160 south-west of there. At 1900 hours, the 1897th Self-Propelled Artillery Regiment occupied firing positions 1 km north-west of Makkpuszta.[1355]

The forces of *2. SS-Panzer-Division* closed up on the line of *Kampfgruppe "Dreike"* north of Kisbér. The 12 8.8 cm guns and nine 3.7 cm twin-barrelled anti-aircraft guns of *SS-Panzer-Flak-Abteilung 2,* were covered by the infantry of *SS-Panzer-Aufklärungs-Abteilung 2*, which also performed reconnaissance tasks in the meantime.

The *III. (Bataillon)/SS-Panzergrenadier-Regiment 4* occupied defensive positions east of Nagyigmánd. At the same time however, *II. (Bataillon)/SS-Panzer-Regiment 4* launched a limited objective attack against a farmstead north-east of Csép. The right flank combat group of *2. SS-Panzer-Division* occupied the houses south of Ghyczypuszta around 1700 hours, and with its left flank combat group, attacked towards Thalypuszta. The Germans also crossed the Ete–Kocs road towards the southeast.[1356]

Kisbér was assaulted by the Soviets the night before. *SS-Panzer-Aufklärungs-Abteilung 2* launched an assault to reoccupy the village. Fire support was provided by the guns of *SS-Panzer-Flak-Abteilung 2,* which set fire to many of Kisbér's outlying houses. Afterwards, *SS-Panzer-Aufklärungs-Abteilung 2* was able to reoccupy the village without any significant resistance.[1357]

On the front of *XXXXIII. Armeekorps,* between Nagyigmánd and Mocsa, the Soviets had drawn rifle and artillery troops forward. East of Nagyigmánd, *III. (Bataillon)/SS-Panzergrenadier-Regiment 4/2. SS-Panzer-Division* reported knocking out two Soviet tanks

---

[1354] Central Archives of the Russian Defence Ministry (Podolsk), f. 240, op. 2799, gy. 342, li. 115.
[1355] Central Archives of the Russian Defence Ministry (Podolsk), f. 240, op. 2799, gy. 342, li. 116.
[1356] NARA, T311, R162, F7214687.
[1357] Weidinger, Otto: *Division Das Reich. Der Weg der 2. SS-Panzer-Division „Das Reich".* Band V: 1943-1945. Osnabrück, without year of publication, p. 468.

in close combat, with anti-tank weapons. The attack of the Soviet rifle units collapsed in the fire of the attendants of the sniper-course of 6. *Panzer-Division*.[1358]

The Soviet 99th Rifle Division/68th Rifle Corps, with their own 112th Independent Self-Propelled Artillery Battalion with three SU–76Ms and one T–70, attacked from Kocs and reached the south-eastern outskirts of Kisigmánd.[1359]

There was heavy fighting going on with alternating results for occupation of Hill 193 (Öreg Hill) two km south of Mocsa. The Germans launched a counterattack for the reoccupation of the hill. The Soviet 429th Rifle Regiment and the 991st Self-Propelled Artillery Regiment defending the hill repulsed four German attempts on that day. During the fighting of 20 and 21 March 1945, the Soviets reported knocking out of three armoured personnel carriers, two guns and 10 machine guns. The losses of the 991st Self-Propelled Artillery Regiment amounted to four knocked out SU–76Ms three of which were repaired on the same day they were hit, one person was killed and three wounded.[1360] The Soviet self-propelled guns were knocked out by German anti-aircraft guns.[1361]

During the opposition of the Soviet armoured assault from Naszály towards Mocsa, the pioneer battalion of *356. Infanterie-Division* destroyed two Soviet armoured fighting vehicles in close combat.[1362]

The Soviet 1505th Self-Propelled Artillery Regiment, with the 439th Rifle Regiment/52nd Rifle Division, occupied firing positions 800 meters south-east of Kisigmánd at 0400 hours. The task of this group was to attack via Kisigmánd in the direction of Újmajor–Öregcsém–Komárom, and occupy Újmajor and Öregcsém. By 1200 hours, the SU-76M self-propelled guns of the Regiment reached the south-eastern edge of Kisigmánd, where at 1500 hours they repulsed the German counterattack, which was launched with a battalion-size infantry unit and six armoured personnel carriers. The Soviet self-propelled guns knocked out one armoured personnel carrier and three guns. Their own losses consisted of one burnt out SU–76M.[1363]

A company from the training school of the German 6. *Panzer-Division* in defence at Kisigmánd, held out against the Soviet assault carried out by approximately 300 rifle troops with artillery support. The success largely depended on the sharpshooting skills of the attendants of the sniper course of the school.[1364]

The torn and battered forces of the Hungarian 3rd Army, under constant pressure by the Soviet troops, created a makeshift and weak line on the night of 20/21 March 1945 east of Tata, near Hill 211 (Kalács Hill) 2.5 km south-west of Dunaszentmiklós–eastern edge of Agostyán–southern edge of Tardos–Point 268 2 km south-west of Vértestolna. An extremely fierce battle went on throughout the night of 20/21 March 1945, at the Felsőgalla industrial site. The Soviets occupied Bánhida and Felsőgalla in heavy close quarters fighting.

1358 Vopersal, Wolfgang: *Soldaten, Kämpfer, Kameraden. Marsch und Kämpfe der SS-Totenkopfdivision.* Band Vb. Bielefeld, 1991. p. 774.
1359 Central Archives of the Russian Defence Ministry (Podolsk), f. 1275, op. 1, gy. 35, li. 181.
1360 Central Archives of the Russian Defence Ministry (Podolsk), f. 240, op. 2799, gy. 342, li. 110.
1361 Central Archives of the Russian Defence Ministry (Podolsk), f. 240, op. 2799, gy. 342, li. 159.
1362 NARA, T311, R162, F7214687.
1363 Central Archives of the Russian Defence Ministry (Podolsk), f. 240, op. 2799, gy. 342, li. 113.
1364 Paul, Wolfgang: *Brennpunkte. Die Geschichte der 6. Panzerdivision (1. leichte) 1937–1945.* Krefeld, 1977. p. 450.

One of the soldiers of *Kampfgruppe "Ameiser"* of *37. SS-Freiwilligen-Kavallerie-Division* that was dispersed by the Soviets, had met a German tank between Felsőgalla and Tatabánya:

"Four of us have started off for Tatabánya. At least we thought so, seeing the many identical miner's houses. At one of the corners another six people joined up, so we were now ten going into the unknown. We arrived at a huge cemetery on the left, and at that moment a German Tiger tank[1365] was coming towards us. It stopped beside us, and the German officer jumped down from the turret of the tank and made us mount the vehicle. The tank brought us backwards [towards the frontline – the author]. Again, reaching the edge of the forest, the road took a turn towards Felsőgalla. Its tracks must have been hit, as the vehicle started to turn around and around, until the driver stopped the engine. There were soldiers who luckily fell off. I was grabbing at the turret and the soldier next to me grabbed me. His a** was outwards and he got a splinter in there. It was not bleeding much, but it hurt. If he wouldn't have been there, that splinter might have hit me. The tank was abandoned by the German soldiers as well."[1366]

Between Dunaalmás and Dunaszentmiklós, the armoured fighting vehicles of the Soviet 4th Guards Mechanized Brigade/2nd Guards Mechanized Corps reached the sector of Neszmély, despite heavy resistance from the Germans. Dunaalmás was encircled, but the defenders were still holding the town against Soviet assaults from the south and the east. The commander of the reconnaissance platoon of the 23rd Guards Tank Regiment of the Brigade, Guards Lieutenant Evgeny P. Tarasov, destroyed three field guns and one anti-tank gun with his T–34/85 tank between Dunaalmás and Dunaszentmiklós.[1367]

The 5th Guards Mechanized Brigade/2nd Guards Mechanized Corps, attacking from the direction of Baj and Vértesszőlős toward the north-east, occupied Tardos by 1700 hours.[1368]

The rifle forces attacking from Esztergom toward the east, pushed back the left flank of the German *711. Infanterie-Division* to the Körtvélyes Island 2 km east–Zsidópuszta line.[1369]

Because of the increasing and constant pressure of the Soviet troops, the southern frontline of the army was withdrawn on that day to the Alsógalla–Tarján south–Bajna south–Sárisáp section, in order to relieve the forces that would be redeployed in the defence westwards and eastwards. The Soviets further reinforced their bridgehead at Tát, although the German-Hungarian forces destroyed 3 of their 20 landing boats.[1370] One of the 1125 type BK–131 armoured gunboats of the Soviet Danube Flotilla was sunk by German artillery near Esztergom, most likely from the northern bank.[1371]

1365 It is probable that the young soldier had indeed met a Tiger E heavy tank, which might have been one of the Tigers of the *rapid reaction unit* formed in the sector of Kisbér, in the rear are of the German *6. Armee*.
1366 Memories of Lőrinc Nagy. Copy owned by the author. p. 11.
1367 HM HIM Hadtörténelmi Levéltár (Budapest), Szovjetunió Hőse kitüntetések gyűjteménye (*Collection of Hero of the Soviet Union awards*), 569.
1368 Central Archives of the Russian Defence Ministry (Podolsk), f. 240, op. 2799, gy. 357, li. 11.
1369 NARA, T311, R162, F7214687.
1370 NARA, T311, R162, F7214688.
1371 See http://www.navy.su/other/lost/dunai.htm (last accessed 29 September 2016.).

Panzer-Kampfgruppe "Pape"/8. Armee[1372] turned back an attack carried out by a battalion-size Soviet force along the Tata-Szőny road.

The 6th Guards Mechanized Brigade/2nd Guards Mechanized Corps, reinforced with one of the tank battalions of the 37th Guards Tank Brigade, occupied Pusztaalmás. Afterwards, the Soviet Brigade attempted a number of attacks with armoured support from the direction of the village toward the north-west and in the direction of Füzítőpuszta, but the Germans stopped all of them, knocking out nine Soviet tanks. Of these, seven were knocked out by *I. (Abteilung)/Panzer-Regiment "Feldherrnhalle"* between Pusztaalmás and Almásfüzítő.[1373] The Soviet tanks that were advancing from the east towards Füzítőpuszta, turned back as soon as the Germans opened fire at them.[1374]

In the evening, the 2nd Guards Mechanized Corps, had 35 operational T–34/85s, four ISU–122s, nine SU–85s and 14 SU–76M self-propelled guns.[1375]

On the same day, the German *Luftflotte 4* flew 270 missions in support of the troops in the sector of Várpalota, Csór, Környe and Mocsa. The airmen reported knocking out six armoured fighting vehicles and a number of trucks, as well as shooting down 10 Soviet planes, five of which were claimed by Hungarian pilots. On the night of 20/21 March 1945, German night ground attack aircraft flying 265 missions,[1376] raided Soviet artillery positions in the sector of Kisbér and Lake Velence.[1377]

In the morning, at 0940 hours, the *Heeresgruppe* received Hitler's orders, stating that the Soviet attacks must be stopped at all costs, and to then go over on the offensive and push them back. Afterwards, having reinforced the defences, and re-established contact with the Hungarian 3rd Army, a counteroffensive to the east is to be launched between Székesfehérvár and the Vértes Mountains, then, turning northwards on the eastern bank of the Váli-víz, encircle and eliminate the Soviet forces that have already crossed the Vértes.[1378] This completely unrealistic order did not even take into account that *Heeresgruppe Süd* had scarcely any fuel left, not to mention the essential supplies for the attack. According to *Generaloberst* Guderian, troops should have been transferred from *2. Panzerarmee*, such as *1. Volks-Gebirgs-Division*[1379].

On this day, German reconnaissance finally identified the Soviet 6th Guards Tank Army, which was, according to them, sent into combat only the day before in the direction of Székesfehérvár–Várpalota–Bakonycsernye. They suspected that the 5th Guards Tank Corps was situated on the southern flank of the Army, and that the 9th Guards Mechanized Corps was on the northern flank. They did not know where the 4th Guards Mechanized Corps could be.[1380]

1372 On that day, *I. Abteilung/Panzer-Regiment "Feldherrnhalle"* assigned to the armoured combat group, had 19 combat-ready tanks out of its 21 Panzer IVs, two of its three Panzer IV/70 *Jagdpanzers* were combat-ready, and 18 out of its 19 Panther tanks were combat-ready. See BAMA, RH 2 Ost 5491.
1373 Di Giusto, Stefano: *Panzer-Sicherungs-Kompanien and Panzer-Abteilung 208 - I./Panzer-Regiment Feldherrnhalle. Italy 1943–1944. Hungary – Slovakia – Moravia 1944–1945.* Erlangen, 2010. pp. 158. and 208.
1374 NARA, T311, R162, F7214688.
1375 Central Archives of the Russian Defence Ministry (Podolsk), f. 401, op. 9511, gy. 535, li. 109.
1376 NARA, T311, R163, F7215420.
1377 NARA, T311, R162, F7214689.
1378 NARA, T311, R162, F7214690.
1379 NARA, T311, R162, F7214695.
1380 NARA, T311, R162, F7214691.

General der Panzertruppe Balck, the *Kommandeur* of the German 6. *Armee*, had suggested to the *Heeresgruppe* on that day, the possibility of giving up Székesfehérvár in order to free up the German forces pinned down there, which in turn could be deployed elsewhere. The *Heeresgruppe* later raised this in a telephone conversation with the Chief of Staff of the German Army's General Staff, as well as the assumption that the main aim of the Soviet offensive might be Vienna.[1381] Hitler's decision arrived at the *Heeresgruppe* at 1640 hours: the right flank and the middle of the German 6. *Armee* may retreat, but Székesfehérvár must continue to be defended.[1382]

At 1800 hours, *General der Infanterie* Wöhler arrived to the headquarters of the German 6. *Panzerarmee* to point out that the attack of *I. SS-Panzerkorps* eastwards is essential for the situation of the whole *Heeresgruppe*.[1383]

22 March 1945, Thursday

(**WEATHER**: highest daytime temperature 12 Celsius, mostly sunny, clear sky. The roads and the terrain have mostly dried up.)

On this day, there were no significant combat actions carried out on the front of *2. Panzerarmee*, apart from Soviet combat reconnaissance missions.[1384] The German troops were regrouped in the south-eastern outskirts of Mesztegnyő and the north-western outskirts of Nagybajom to be able to launch a new assault the following day.[1385]

The *I. (Bataillon)/SS-Panzergrenadier-Regiment 36/16. SS-Panzergrenadier-Division*, with eight StuG.III assault guns of *Panzergruppe "Rex"/SS-Panzer-Abteilung 16*, carried out a reconnaissance mission south of Virágos. The task was initiated by the *Kommandeur* of the *Bataillon* and the *Panzergruppe* alone, on his own responsibility. The SS-unit was to establish whether the Soviets had reoccupied the positions they had lost earlier, and if the situation permitted, they also needed to reach the northern edge of the forest south of Virágos. The Germans had no luck, at the very beginning of the attack, they ran into a Soviet anti-tank position consisting of approximately 12 guns, which knocked out five of their assault guns. Of these, four were able to retreat on their own tracks, and later the fifth was also towed away. The StuG. IIIs knocked out eight guns and a few infantry firing positions. The *SS-Panzergrenadiers* advanced only about 100 meters, but suffered serious losses. Only three of the original eight assault guns remained combat-ready.[1386]

On the night of 21/22 March 1945, on the front of the German *I. Kavallerie-Korps/6. Armee,* the Germans cleared their frontline between Balatonfőkajár four km

---

[1381] NARA, T311, R162, F7214697.
[1382] NARA, T311, R162, F7214697.
[1383] NARA, T311, R162, F7214692.
[1384] NARA, T311, R162, F7214705.
[1385] NARA, T311, R162, F7214711.
[1386] Puntigam, Josef Paul: *Vom Plattensee bis zur Mur. Die Kämpfe 1945 im Dreiländereck*. Feldbach, without year of publication, [1993], p. 105.

west–Balatonfőkajár southern edge of the Soviet penetrations and also knocked out a Soviet tank.[1387]

The *Panzergruppe* of *23. Panzer-Division*, with two Panthers, two Panzer IVs and two assault guns, stood at Sándorka in readiness at 1100 hours. The village was raided by Soviet ground attack aircraft and the medical officer of *I. (Abteilung)/Panzer-Regiment 23* was killed in the raid.

In the meantime, the Soviet armoured fighting vehicles broke into Csajág on the front of *4. Kavallerie-Division*, and the armoured group of *23. Panzer-Division* was directed north-west of the village to stop them. Before the armoured group could arrive at the target area, one of the armoured reconnaissance detachments of *Panzer-Aufklärungs-Abteilung 23* reported that there were already 10 Soviet armoured fighting vehicles 10 km north-west of Csajág, at Istvánmajor, which either arrived from the south or the north. *Panzer-Regiment 23* sent two assault guns and one Panzer IV tank against them. The Panzer IV was knocked out by the Soviet tanks directly north of Csajág. After this, the two assault guns established holding positions north of Csajág with units of *Panzergrenadier-Regiment 126*.

As the situation unfolded, the *Kommandeur* of *23. Panzer-Division* informed the German *4. Kavallerie-Division*, *1. Panzer-Division* and *44. Reichsgrenadier-Division*, that their troops must withdraw from Csajág during the night in the direction of Manómajor, three km east of Balatonfűzfő. Only the armoured reconnaissance detachments were able to maintain contact with *4. Kavallerie-Division*, but there was absolutely no communication with *44. Reichsgrenadier-Division*.[1388]

The retreat was covered by the Jagdpanzer IV *Jagdpanzers* of *2. Kompanie/Panzerjäger-Abteilung 128*, which, together with units of *5. SS-Panzer-Division* carried out a relief attack against the Soviets that were following them, and destroyed five of their tanks.[1389]

During the day, Soviet troops launched more heavy attacks along the northern shore of Lake Balaton toward the north-west, supported by a significant number of armoured fighting vehicles. The Germans were only able to temporarily hold them up on the Balatonkenese south–Küngös south line. During these engagements, south-east of Balatonkenese, in the sector of Balatonakarattya, *Panzerjäger-Abteilung 69/3. Kavallerie-Division*, mainly *1. Kompanie*, commanded by *Oberleutnant* Kellinghusen, reported to have knocked out 22 Soviet armored fighting vehicles with assault guns and the *Panzerfausts* of the soldiers of the escort platoon.[1390] It's likely that 17 of them were M4A2s of the 2nd Guards Mechanized Brigade [1391], and the 1896th and 1952nd Self-Propelled Artillery Regiment.

On 21 and 22 March 1945, together with the above mentioned scores, *3. Kavallerie-Division* reported to have knocked out 34 Soviet armoured fighting vehicles[1392], with *I. Kavallerie-Korps* reporting to have knocked out 43 on a single day.[1393]

1387 NARA, T311, R163, F7215425.
1388 Rebentisch, Ernst: *Zum Kaukasus und zu den Tauern. Die Geschichte der 23. Panzer-Division 1941–1945*. Esslingen, 1963. p. 496.
1389 Rebentisch, Ernst: *Zum Kaukasus und zu den Tauern. Die Geschichte der 23. Panzer-Division 1941–1945*. Esslingen, 1963. p. 497.
1390 Witte, Hans Joachim – Offermann, Peter: *Die Boeselagerschen Reiter. Das Kavallerie-Regiment Mitte und die aus ihm hervorgegangene 3. Kavallerie-Brigade/Division*. München, 1998. pp. 414-415.
1391 Unfortunately there are no available data of the armoured fighting vehicle losses of the 2nd Guards Mechanized Brigade on that day. The data were estimated as the difference of the armoured fighting vehicles knocked out by the Germans and the known combined armoured fighting vehicle losses of the two Self-Propelled Artillery Regiments together.
1392 NARA, T311, R162, F7214705.
1393 NARA, T311, R162, F7214720.

The Soviet 1896th Self-Propelled Artillery Regiment/5th Guards Cavalry Corps, together with the 2nd Guards Mechanized Brigade, was in combat in the Balatonkenese sector on that day and lost two SU–76Ms, one of which burnt out. By the evening, only 14 of them remained operational. The 54th and the 71st Tank Regiment of the Corps received 10 new T–34/85s at Sárbogárd.[1394] The latter unit had been assembled in the evening on the north-eastern perimeter of Siófok with 13 operational tanks.[1395]

The Soviet 209th Self-Propelled Artillery Brigade/26th Army moved into the battle line in support of the rifle troops. At the end of the day, the 1951st Self-Propelled Artillery Regiment was fighting on the northeastern edge of Mezőszentgyörgy with 15 SU–100s. The 1952nd Self-Propelled Artillery Regiment was supporting the 2nd Guards Mechanized Brigade with 16 SU–100s in the fight to capture Balatonkenese, and reached the southern perimeter of the village at around 1700 hours. The Regiment lost three self-propelled guns knocked out on the same day.[1396] The 1953rd Self-Propelled Artillery Regiment was in firing positions on the northern edge of Lepsény with nine of their SU–100s.[1397]

The 22nd Independent Tank Regiment was withdrawn from the frontline on the same day. With its 15 remaining tanks and self-propelled guns, the crews returned to the ranks of the 22nd Training Tank Regiment stationed at Baja. During the battles of the Regiment in March 1945, it had lost, according to Soviet sources, five knocked out tanks, of which four burnt out, and two armoured fighting vehicles sunken into the mud.[1398] At the same time, based on the partial, and earlier mentioned archival data, the losses of the Regiment amounted to seven burnt out tanks.

During the morning, in the sector of *III. Panzerkorps,* the Soviets continued the attack with a significant number of troops and large numbers of armoured fighting vehicles, about 50 according to German information,[1399] via Polgárdi toward the north-east, occupied Falubattyán, then turned north and in so doing, destroyed the new frontline of the German *Panzerkorps* still under construction.[1400]

On the night of 21/22 March 1945, *5. SS-Panzer-Division* successfully withdrew its forces from the area of Székesfehérvár, and these units were then assembled around Úrhida. At dawn, these units, divided into two combat groups, launched their assault aimed at breaking out from the Székesfehérvár sector toward the northern shore of Lake Balaton. At Nádasdladány, *SS-Obersturmbannführer* Hack's *SS-Panzergrenadier-Regiment 10,* was guarding the south-western, north facing attack of the combat group created from the armoured units of the *Division*. The Soviets, who were attacking from the south, were not able to stop the *SS-Kampfgruppen*, which lost most of their tanks, assault guns, armoured personnel carriers and self-propelled howitzers during the breakout attempt. The remnants of *5. SS-Panzer-Division* were fighting their way out towards Lake Balaton deployed as infantry.[1401]

1394 Central Archives of the Russian Defence Ministry (Podolsk), f. 243, op. 2928, gy. 131, li. 266.
1395 Central Archives of the Russian Defence Ministry (Podolsk), f. 243, op. 2928, gy. 178, li. 96.
1396 Central Archives of the Russian Defence Ministry (Podolsk), f. 243, op. 2928, gy. 178, li. 98.
1397 Central Archives of the Russian Defence Ministry (Podolsk), f. 243, op. 2928, gy. 131, li. 265.
1398 Central Archives of the Russian Defence Ministry (Podolsk), f. 243, op. 2928, gy. 131, li. 265.
1399 NARA, T311, R162, F7214713.
1400 NARA, T311, R162, F7214705.
1401 Strassner, Peter: *Europäische Freiwillige. Die 5. SS-Panzerdivision Wiking*. Osnabrück, 1977. Third, revised edition. p. 341.

The successful breakout attempt of the *Division* was aided in great measure by the resistance of *9. SS-Panzer-Division* at the north-eastern edge of Lake Balaton, which kept the narrow passage open for the retreating troops.

SS-Standartenführer Ullrich and his *Stab*, had reported at the command post of *9. SS-Panzer-Division* established at Papkeszi, at around 1600 hours then, one hour later, he reported at *III. Panzerkorps* at Balatonfűzfő. In the evening, at 1800 hours, the worn out forces of *5. SS-Panzer-Division* were already assembled behind the German lines.[1402]

In the evening, *SS-Panzer-Regiment 5* only had one Panther and two Panzer IVs in combat-ready condition. The Panzer IV, with turret number 201, was knocked out by the Soviets west of Veszprém the following day.[1403]

The Soviet 1202nd Self-Propelled Artillery Regiment/27th Army with 20 SU–76Ms, was supporting the rifle troops in the vicinity of the railway station of Polgárdi. The 432nd Independent Self-Propelled Artillery Battalion/316th Rifle Division, with 12 operational SU–76Ms, was in firing positions on the western edge of Aba, but was not engaged in combat.[1404]

The 18th Tank Corps advanced through Fövenypuszta and Szabadbattyán, and crossed the Nádor and Malom Canals, to be able to continue hunting the retreating Germans. The 110th Tank Brigade and the 363rd Guards Heavy Self-Propelled Artillery Regiment attacked from Polgárdi, the 181st Tank Brigade with the 1438th Self-Propelled Artillery Regiment and units of the 32nd Motorized Rifle Brigade attacked toward the west from the railway station of Polgárdi, with the objective of establishing contact with the 5th Guards Tank Corps/6th Guards Tank Army. On the same day, the 18th Tank Corps lost only one T–34/85. In the evening, they had 76 operational tanks, 12 ISU–122s, five ISU–152s and 10 SU–76M self-propelled guns. The 170th Tank Brigade was stationed in Sárosd and was waiting for two rail shipments with 42 new T–34/85s, which arrived at Sárbogárd.[1405]

The 3rd Guards Mechanized Brigade/1st Guards Mechanized Corps reached Felsősomlyó by 1700 hours, the 1st Guards Mechanized Brigade reached Fácántelep, east of Sándorka, and the 9th Guards Tank Brigade reached Fodorpuszta and the northern edge of Küngös. The Corps lost nine burnt out M4A2s. In the evening, they had 98 operational M4A2s, three T–34s and 14 SU–100s.[1406]

Units of the German *1.* and *3. Panzer-Divisions*, and *44. Reichsgrenadier-Division* were in defence during the afternoon on the hills west of Falubattyán, against the Soviet rifle and armoured fighting vehicle attacks coming from the south, east and north-east.[1407]

Six Panther tanks of *1. Panzer-Division* and a few pioneer armoured personnel carriers, launched a counterattack in the Felsősomlyó–Polgárdi northeast sector and with this, successfully freed the units of *44. Reichsgrenadier-Division* from encirclement. The Panthers escorted the *Panzergrenadiers* back to the Felsősomlyó south-south-east–Jenő sector. A

1402 Strassner, Peter: *Europäische Freiwillige. Die 5. SS-Panzerdivision Wiking*. Osnabrück, 1977. Third, revised edition. p. 342.
1403 Klapdor, Ewald: *Mit dem Panzerregiment 5 Wiking im Osten*. Siek, 1981. p. 341.
1404 Central Archives of the Russian Defence Ministry (Podolsk), f. 243, op. 2928, gy. 131, li. 265.
1405 Central Archives of the Russian Defence Ministry (Podolsk), f. 243, op. 2928, gy. 131, li. 266.
1406 Central Archives of the Russian Defence Ministry (Podolsk), f. 243, op. 2928, gy. 131, li. 266. This data includes the 2nd Guards Mechanized Brigade which was deployed elsewhere.
1407 NARA, T311, R162, F7214706.

few of the M4A2s of the 1ˢᵗ Guards Mechanized Corps, while pursuing the units of *44. Reichsgrenadier-Division*, were knocked out from a distance of around 1000 meters by the Panthers of *1. Kompanie/Panzer-Regiment 1*.[1408]

Meanwhile, the Tiger B tanks of *schwere Panzer-Abteilung 509* were still in firing positions 2.5 km west-north-west of Polgárdi, on Hill 228 (Kőhegy), to keep the section between Polgárdi and Jenő open for the masses of their own troops coming from the east toward Lake Balaton.[1409]

Kampfgruppe "Huppert"/1. Panzer-Division, was in combat near Úrhida with the support of four Panther and four to five Panzer IVs. *Kampfgruppe "Hagen"/Panzer-Regiment 1*, with eight to ten Panthers, in the north-north-western outskirts of Felsősomlyó, was covering the rear of the units of *Panzergrenadier-Regiment 113* and *Panzer-Pionier-Bataillon 37*, as well as the four Panthers of *I. (Abteilung)/Panzer-Regiment 24* which were still holding at the Malom Canal. Meanwhile, the last damaged tanks of *Panzer-Regiment 1* were transported to Aszófő.

Another eight Panthers and a few pioneer armoured personnel carriers of *Panzer-Regiment 1*, together with the Panthers of *I. (Abteilung)/Panzer-Regiment 24* repulsed the penetrations of the Soviet T–34/85 and M4A2 tanks in the south-western outskirts of Felsősomlyó.

Around 1700 hours, the forward command post of *1. Panzer-Division* was relocated from Felsősomlyó to Jenő. *Generalleutnant* Rost, *Kommandeur* of *44. Reichsgrenadier-Division*, with a rifle battalion and eight Jagdpanzer 38(t) *Jagdpanzers* of his *Panzerjäger-Abteilung*, defended the hills south-east and south-west of Jenő. *Generalmajor* Thunert and *Generalleutnant* Rost agreed that at 1730 hours, all of their troops would be withdrawn to the sector of Jenő, including *Kampfgruppe "Bradel"*, which was still fighting between Falubattyán and Felsősomlyó. The *2. Kompanie/Panzer-Pionier-Bataillon 37* was an exception, which, with a few Panthers, Panzer IVs and self-propelled 2 cm anti-aircraft guns, was temporarily still in holding positions on their former frontline.

For the breakout attempt in the western direction, *1. Panzer-Division* established the following grouping:

- the spearhead group: *Panzergrenadier-Regiment 113/Kampfgruppe "Bradel"* reinforced by *I. (Abteilung)/Panzer-Regiment 1*;
- two covering groups:
- in the north, *Panzergrenadier-Regiment 1/Kampfgruppe "Huppert"*, six-to-eight tanks and a few pioneer armoured personnel carriers, as well as self-propelled 2 cm anti-aircraft guns of *Panzergruppe "Streith"*;
- in the south, the majority of *44. Reichsgrenadier-Division* with their own Jagdpanzer 38(t) *Jagdpanzers*;
- the rearguard group: *Panzer-Pionier-Bataillon 37* with six Panthers and Panzer IVs of *1. Kompanie/Panzer-Regiment 1*, and a few self-propelled 2 cm anti-aircraft guns; *I.* (self-propelled) and *II.* (towed) *(Abteilung)/Panzer-Artillerie-Regiment 37*.[1410]

[1408] Stoves, Rolf: Persönliches Kriegstagebuch Pz.Rgt. 1 (typewritten manuscript, a copy owned by the author), entry from 22 March 1945.
[1409] *History of schwere Panzer-Abteilung 509* (typewritten manuscript). Copy owned by the author. p. 57.
[1410] Stoves, Rolf: Persönliches Kriegstagebuch Pz.Rgt. 1 (typewritten manuscript, a copy owned by the author), entry from 22 March 1945.

The majority of schwere *Mörser-Bataillon 44/44. Reichsgrenadier-Division*, had already launched its own breakout attempt towards the west from the sector of Jenő at 1730 hours. According to the memories of one of the soldiers of the unit:

"The majority of the battalion is deployed as infantry, and it is in combat without any kind of heavy weapon support. Up to the first lines of the Soviets, three 'Hummel's and a few armoured personnel carriers equipped with machine guns, are also coming with us[1411]. However, these turn to the south soon afterwards. The mortar battalion is divided into three combat groups of 100 men in each, and thus these advance towards the west, the next lines of the Ivan.

The first combat group, commanded by the battalion's commander, Hauptmann Otto Rösch, shout loud hurrahs and launch an attack that eliminates four machine gun crews and makes the surprised Bolsheviks run. The successful breakthrough was executed as accurately as if we were on a field exercise, until Hauptmann Rösch, on the edge of one of the forested areas[1412] – in the meantime darkness has set in – discovers a T–34 which stood still until then. The commander covers the approximately 10 meters to the tank with a few large jumps. At the moment when the commander jumps up the tank from its side, the machine gun turns and opens fire. But it is very soon silenced, because Hauptmann Rösch deals a few very hard blows on the barrel and ensures it will be crooked to the extent it will be unusable. At this, the cover slowly opens and a head peeks out. At the same moment he falls back, as the German entrenching tool's contact that was delivered by Hauptmann Rösch to his head was not very gentle. Apart from this, submachine guns have also hit him, and the shells are now jumping around inside the tank. In the end, the Hauptmann also fires a tracer shot inside, and then jumps off. Ten seconds later, crackles can be heard: the tank blows up.

[…]

After approximately three kilometers of silent march, the combat group reached a railroad embankment[1413], parallel to which there is a road running along the embankment, a few meters away. Two enemy tanks were patrolling the road, a Sherman and a T–34. Hauptmann Rösch lies with his men for some time close by in the bushes of the embankment, and waits for the perfect moment when the two tanks, approaching each other, would meet and then the unit can cross the road with a few jumps. All goes well, and soon the combat group successfully reaches the German positions at Lake Balaton, first in our division, and without any losses incurred."[1414]

1411 These were most likely the vehicles of *3. Panzer-Division* (not only *Hummel*s, but also *Wespe* self-propelled howitzers could be among them), which turned southwards from the southern outskirts of Mariskamajor, towards Fácántelep. There they probably met the M4A2 tanks of the Soviet 1st Guards Mechanized Brigade, as according to another soldier of the *Mörser-Bataillon 44*: *"Soon after we have parted, we noticed heavy firing and detonations behind our backs, on the left in a distance of approximately one km. And I can still see this night fireworks display before my eyes. This must have been the vehicles that initially escorted us! I was happy not to be there."* Of this, see Agis, Hermann: *Das Ende am Plattensee. Die Hoch und Deutschmeister (44. I.D.) im Endkampf.* Nürnberg, 2006. pp. 214-215.
1412 This was most likely the northern edge of the woods west of Sándorka.
1413 This was most likely north-northwest of Küngös.
1414 Idézi Agis, Hermann: *Das Ende am Plattensee. Die Hoch- und Deutschmeister (44. I.D.) im Endkampf.* Nürnberg, 2006. pp. 210-211.

Mörser-Bataillon 44 had broken out successfully and, at 2100 hours, their soldiers, singing the German anthem at the top of their lungs, reached the tanks and armoured personnel carriers of *9. SS-Panzer-Division* at Istvánmajor, four km west-north-west of Küngös.[1415]

The majority of *1. Panzer-Division* and *44. Reichsgrenadier-Division* launched their breakout attempt, soon after 2000 hours, toward the west and Lake Balaton. The attack of the *Panzerkeil* that was launched without any artillery preparation, surprised the Soviets, allowing the Germans to break through their first anti-tank defensive position. The *Divisionsbegleitkompanie* was at the spearhead, followed by the armoured personnel carrier-group under *Oberleutnant* Fink, of *I. (Bataillon)/Panzergrenadier-Regiment 113*, and *Hauptmann* Hagen's six Panthers.[1416] During the breakout, the German tanks spent almost all of their high-explosive shells. They only had a few remaining armoured piercing rounds which were salvaged from their own damaged tanks that had been blown up and abandoned around Jenő.

The escaping units bypassed Dénesmajor from the south, but ran into another Soviet anti-tank block position before they could reach the Pétfürdő–Berhida–Küngös road. Here, *Hauptmann* Hagen's Panther used up his last shell. However, the arrival of the other Panthers and armoured personnel carriers successfully eliminated this blocking position as well.

The command staff of *Generalmajor* Thunert, and *Oberst* Bradel with a few armoured personnel carriers and Panzer IVs, were forced to break through another Soviet block position. *Generalleutnant* Rost, with other members of the *Stab* of *44. Reichsgrenadier-Division*, was travelling in one of the armoured personnel carriers of *Panzergrenadier-Regiment 113*, which bogged down approximately 4.5 km southeast of Berhida around 2100 hours. The driver of the armoured personnel carrier remembered this:

"As my secondary driver could hardly advance, I myself jumped off to see what was happening. The tank behind us had already started forward: it was a Panzer IV, but also could have been a Panther. It hardly got past me when one of the soldiers, most likely one of those persons I carried, made it stop to try and tow us away.
This was also in my mind, after I talked to the commander of the other tank. If, for example, they could push my armoured personnel carrier backwards and if we could place weight on only one side of the tracks, the securing pins would certainly twist, and this might cause the tracks to fall off. They were in bad shape already.
I called the attention of the other tank commander to the enemy tank that had moved forward on the left side in the meantime, probably lured here by the red glow from the exhaust pipe of my tank. However, the commander said he did not have more anti-tank shells; but the barrel of its gun was nevertheless turned toward the enemy. It fired the first shot at us from a distance of approximately 700 meters. The shell whistled through

---

1415 Agis, Hermann: *Das Ende am Plattensee. Die Hoch- und Deutschmeister (44. I.D.) im Endkampf.* Nürnberg, 2006. p. 216.
1416 Stoves, O. G. Rolf: *1. Panzer-Division 1935–1945. Chronik einer der drei Stamm-Division der deutschen Panzerwaffe.* Bad Nauheim, 1961. p. 763. The other tanks of *Panzer-Regiment 1*, in need of repair, had to be handed over to the German *6. Armee*.

between the tank and my armoured personnel carrier. I threw myself to the ground. The second shot from a distance of 300-400 meters was too short, as the shell impacted approximately 50 meters from us. The machine gun of the enemy tank was also firing. The third shot from approximately 200 meters hit the fuel tank of my armoured personnel carrier. The vehicle was on fire instantly! Before that, one person – but it's more probable that there were two of them if I remember correctly and if I am not mistaken – have already jumped out of the armoured personnel carrier. The burning vehicle perfectly lit up the whole surroundings. Approximately 10 minutes later the fire was out, as the tank had so little fuel left in it because of the scarce supplies.

The tank standing before my armoured personnel carrier was also directly hit by the enemy tank. This – which was almost certainly a T–34[1417] was at last knocked out by an armoured personnel carrier with its 7.5 cm short barrelled tank gun – was also burning. I remained lying down for about 15-20 minutes. I did not have any contact with either my two comrades in the armoured personnel carrier or those travelling with us in the compartment after I got out. With one of my comrades from the same division, whom I have found – most probably from the tank that was knocked out in front of us – at last followed the tracks of the vehicles."[1418]

The commander of *44. Reichsgrenadier-Division, Generalleutnant* von Rost, was pushed out of the knocked out armoured personnel carrier by the *Kommandeur* of *Grenadier-Regiment 132, Oberst* Heinz-Joachim Hoffmann, but the *Generalleutnant* unfortunately died almost instantly in the Soviet tank and machine gun fire.[1419]

Upon reaching the Küngös–Berhida road, the six Panthers detached from *I. (Abteilung)/Panzer-Regiment 1,* and under command of *Oberleutnant* Fink, were advancing toward the south. However the armoured fighting vehicles were soon stopped by order of *Oberst* Bradel sent via radio, according to which the Soviets have again closed off the salient at Point 172 1 km north of Küngös. Ludwig Guntz, a soldier of *Aufklärungs-Abteilung 44,* was here on a towed infantry gun:

"Approximately 300 meters before the road and railroad crossing, north of Küngös a number of Soviet anti-tank guns kept us under fire. Unbelievable panic spread like wildfire. Vehicles were burning, the wounded were howling, armoured personnel carriers were blowing up. Our towing vehicle got messed up with other vehicles and was seriously damaged. I had to go on foot afterwards. I also know that after the crossing point, on the left, there were couple of buildings visible, most likely Istvánmajor. In the vicinity, three or four armoured personnel carriers swept past me and went forward. Two of these were destroyed by anti-tank gun hits: one of them was blown up, and the other was burnt out."[1420]

1417 It is much more likely that this was one of the M4A2 tanks of the 1st Guards Mechanized Corps, as it attacked from the south.
1418 Idézi Agis, Hermann: *Das Ende am Plattensee. Die Hoch- und Deutschmeister (44. I.D.) im Endkampf.* Nürnberg, 2006. p. 311-313.
1419 Agis, Hermann: *Das Ende am Plattensee. Die Hoch- und Deutschmeister (44. I.D.) im Endkampf.* Nürnberg, 2006. p. 308.
1420 Quoted by Agis, Hermann: *Das Ende am Plattensee. Die Hoch- und Deutschmeister (44. I.D.) im Endkampf.* Nürnberg, 2006. p. 264.

The majority of the Germans were stranded there, and therefore the Panthers at the head had to turn back in order to open a gap from the west. At last, *Oberleutnant* Fink carried out the task successfully with two Panthers and an armoured personnel carrier-platoon.[1421] The German breakout could be resumed.

In the meantime, because of the combat noise, many German soldiers came forward whose units had been dispersed earlier around here and joined the majority of *1. Panzer-Division*. *Oberleutnant* Fink had, in the meantime, joined up with the Panthers that were fighting at the spearhead of the breakout group. *Hauptmann* Hagen used the short stop to obtain ammunition from the Panthers that were marching at the rear, and supplied them to the Panthers at the front.[1422]

The Soviets were attacking from the north, and on the night of 21/22 March 1945, occupied Ősi, Nádasdladány, where, according to *6. Panzerarmee,* the units of *9. SS-Panzer-Division* were fighting[1423], and Berhida. In the morning, they occupied the northern sections of Jenő and the wooded area north-east of there (Vadaskert). The SU–76Ms of the 1202nd Self-Propelled Artillery Regiment were also supporting the rifle forces of the 27th Army in occupying Jenő.[1424]

The German *3. Panzer-Division* and *5. SS-Panzer-Division,* that had broken out of Székesfehérvár, around noon were fighting their way through these units facing west-south-west and their spearheads successfully reached Balatonfűzfő.[1425]

General der Panzertruppe Breith, commander of *III. Panzerkorps* and his *Stab,* were withdrawn from command and control on that day, and with the centre at Keszthely,[1426] he was entrusted with organizing the supply units stationed west of Lake Balaton.[1427] The *1. Panzer-Division* was directly subordinated to the German *6. Armee* and was assembled in the sector of Szentkirályszabadja.[1428]

In connection with this, during the day, *9. SS-Panzer-Division,* the Hungarian "Szent László" Division and the remnants of *44. Reichsgrenadier-Division* were also subordinated to *I. Kavallerie-Korps* commanding *3.* and *4. Kavallerie-Divisions.*[1429]

In the front of *IV. SS-Panzerkorps,* the Soviet forces were attacking from the sector of Várpalota toward the south-west, and reached the Peremarton industrial site–Sóly-Kádárta–Gyulafirátót line. The Germans managed to contain the Soviet armoured wedges only 3 km east of Veszprém, where they reported to have knocked out three armoured fighting vehicles.[1430]

1421 Stoves, Rolf: Persönliches Kriegstagebuch Pz.Rgt. 1 (typewritten manuscript, a copy owned by the author), Entry from 22 March 1945. According to the history of *1. Panzer-Division*, *Oberleutnant* Fink attacked the Soviets in the rear at point 172, with the armoured personnel carrier-group of *I. (Bataillon)/Panzergrenadier-Regiment 113.*, while leaving behind three armoured personnel carriers and one self-propelled 2 cm anit-aircraft gun to guard the road. See Stoves, O. G. Rolf: *1. Panzer-Division 1935–1945. Chronik einer der drei Stamm-Division der deutschen Panzerwaffe.* Bad Nauheim, 1961. p. 766.
1422 Stoves, Rolf: Persönliches Kriegstagebuch Pz.Rgt. 1 (typewritten manuscript, a copy owned by the author), Entry from 22 March 1945.
1423 NARA, T311, R162, F7214714.
1424 See Central Archives of the Russian Defence Ministry (Podolsk), f. 381, op. 8378, gy. 590, li. 61.
1425 NARA, T311, R162, F7214706.
1426 BAMA, N 106/4, Diary of *General der Panzertruppe* Hermann Breith, 23 and 24 March 1945.
1427 NARA, T311, R163, F7215433.
1428 NARA, T311, R163, F7215433.
1429 NARA, T311, R163, F7215433.
1430 NARA, T311, R162, F7214706.

On the night of 21/22 March 1945, *9. SS-Panzer-Division*[1431] launched an attack toward the north to reoccupy Ősi, but the Soviets repelled the attempt. At 0730 hours that morning, the *SS-Division,* with the support of the *Luftwaffe,* launched a repeat attempt from the south-eastern outskirts of Berhida to recapture Ősi, but this was again unsuccessful.[1432]

After this, both units of *SS-Panzergrenadier-Regiment 19* and *20,* commanded by *SS-Obersturmbannführer* Seela, tried to slow down the pace of the Soviet attack south of Berhida.

The units of *9. SS-Panzer-Division* and *4. Kavallerie-Division* then established a covering line on the Berhida south–Papkeszi north–Vilonya north–Sóly north sector, and temporarily repelled the Soviet attacks that were also supported by armoured fighting vehicles.[1433] Soviet armoured fighting vehicles had broken into Berhida, which was defended by *Reiter-Regiment 41/4. Kavallerie-Division.*[1434] The majority of *9. SS-Panzer-Division* was in combat during the day between Papkeszi and Vilonya, and on that day they reported to have knocked out 17 Soviet armoured fighting vehicles.[1435]

The *Division* successfully established contact with *23. Panzer-Division* in combat north of Polgárdi.

South of Pétfürdő, the deployed *1. Batterie/SS-Panzer-Flak-Abteilung 9* had lost all but one of its guns and its remaining personnel continued to fight as infantry. The group of anti-aircraft artillery crews were surrounded, but on the night of 22/23 March 1945, they reached the German lines. The *2. Batterie/SS-Panzer-Flak-Abteilung 9* was in firing position southeast of Vilonya, and *4. Batterie/SS-Panzer-Flak-Abteilung 9* was, along with two 8.8 cm guns of the *Luftwaffe Flak-Regiment 25,* in firing positions along the Papkeszi–Berhida road. The latter were soon retreating towards Veszprém. The *SS*-anti-aircraft artillery crews repelled two heavy attacks that were supported by armoured fighting vehicles. The second attack was held up by the Germans with four 8.8 cm guns, three 3.7 cm automatic cannons and approximately 200 *Panzergrenadiers* of *SS-Panzergrenadier-Regiment 19.*[1436] A soldier of *2. Batterie/SS-Panzer-Flak-Abteilung 9, SS-Rottenführer* Helmut Semmler, remembers these combat actions:

> *"In the morning of 22 March, the 2. Batterie established firing positions in front of a village. When, during the morning, the infantry retreating in combat approached the position, the battery, upon battery commander Obersturmführer Gropp's own initiative, went into an anti-tank ambush position on the edge of the village [most probably Vilonya – the author]. Right from there, one of the 8.8 cm batteries of the Luftwaffe was in position. Soon a lonely T-34 appeared that was apparently rushed forward, and the*

1431 According to *General der Panzertruppe* Balck, *Kommandeur* of the German *6. Armee, 9. SS-Panzer-Division* had left its positions without being ordered to do so east of the Sárvíz and they had not handed over these positions to the units assigned to take over. This was why the Soviets were able to break into the German defence. See NARA, T311, R162, F7214719.
1432 NARA, T311, R163, F7215426.
1433 NARA, T311, R162, F7214706.
1434 NARA, T311, R162, F7214712.
1435 NARA, T311, R162, F7214720.
1436 Tieke, Wilhelm: *Im Feuersturm letzter Kriegsjahre. II. SS-Panzerkorps mit 9. und 10. SS-Division „Hohenstaufen" und „Frundsberg".* Osnabrück, without year of publication, [1975] pp. 509-510.

two batteries knocked it out with concentrated fire. The Luftwaffe battery then switched positions and retreated. The 2. Batterie with four guns held the village alone[1437] until the evening against the attacking enemy, and during this day, knocked out eight tanks, two armoured reconnaissance cars, and four trucks full of infantry. Unterscharführer Voss, from the light anti-aircraft detachments, knocked out two four-barrelled self-propelled anti-aircraft machine guns with Panzerfaust, and in the meantime, captured three enemy soldiers. The T–34s have set fire to two of our towing vehicles, therefore we had to blow up two of our guns as well... [...]
On the night of 22/23 March, Obersturmführer Gropp with guns 'Anton' and 'Emil',[1438] a 3.7 cm automatic cannon, and one of the 8.8 cm guns of the 1. Batterie went into the main combat line again as an anti-aircraft artillery unit. When the enemy noticed the more resolute resistance, they sent four T-34s to help their infantry. Our guns knocked out three of these while the fourth was damaged by Obersturmführer Gropp with Panzerfaust. Upon this, the crew abandoned the tank and left it rolling toward our guns; it stopped only at one of the gun mounts. Before dawn, we then retreated; using the captured and perfectly usable T-34 as a towing vehicle for one of the guns... "[1439]

General der Panzertruppe Balck, commander of *6. Armee*, appeared at the command post of *SS-Oberführer* Stadler, *Kommandeur* of *9. SS-Panzer-Division*, at Papkeszi and reprimanded the commander, shouting, "why are the personnel of *9. SS-Panzer-Division* fleeing from battle?" Stadler, who had arrived back around the same time from an inspection of the frontline, stated that his soldiers are in their positions, whatever happens. Balck stormed away upon hearing this. Stadler ordered the rumours to be investigated, and it turned out that the commander of *6. Armee* had met the supply units of *5. SS-Panzer-Division* who had just managed to break out from Székesfehérvár.[1440]

Around 1400 hours, the 1922nd Self-Propelled Artillery Regiment, subordinated to the 9th Guards Army, was in combat in the Vilonya sector and was supporting the 114th Guards Rifle Division with its SU-100s during the fighting for the village. The Regiment reported to have knocked out three German tanks, two armoured personnel carriers, one anti-tank gun and one mortar battery, with their own loss being one SU-100.[1441]

On the night of 21/22 March 1945, the 20th Guards Tank Brigade/5th Guards Tank Corps/6th Guards Tank Army, with the 1458th Self-Propelled Artillery Regiment, the 391st Guards Anti-Tank Artillery Regiment and the 21st Engineering Battalion, were attacking from Várpalota in the direction of Berhida. The grouping attacked Kispétipuszta at 0400 hours, then occupied it after a two-hour long battle. The reinforced 20th Guards Tank

---

[1437] Two Jagdpanthers were sent from *SS-Panzer-Regiment 9* in combat nearby to strengthen the battery, but these did not reached their destination due to the hardly trackable terrain. See Stöber, Hans: *Die Flugabwehrverbände der Waffen-SS. Aufstellung, Gliederung, Luftverteidigung und Einsätze an den Fronten*. Preussisch Oldendorf, 1984. p. 215.
[1438] At the German field and anti-aircraft artillery units, within the battery these were designated with names beginning with A, B, C in subsequent order.
[1439] Stöber, Hans: *Die Flugabwehrverbände der Waffen-SS. Aufstellung, Gliederung, Luftverteidigung und Einsätze an den Fronten*. Preussisch Oldendorf, 1984. pp.216-217.
[1440] Tieke, Wilhelm: *Von Plattensee bis Österreich. Heeresgruppe Süd 1945*. Gummersbach, without year of publication, p. 69.
[1441] Summarized report of the 208th Self-Propelled Artillery Brigade of the period between 6 March – 6 April 1945. Copy owned by the author. p. 13.

Brigade occupied the industrial site at Peremarton, 1.5 km west of Berhida, at 1100 hours after a short enemy engagement, and at the end of the day, was in combat for the occupation of Vilonya.

During the day, east of Berhida, the 22nd Guards Tank Brigade was not able to overcome the resistance of *III. (Bataillon)/SS-Panzergrenadier-Regiment 20* and *II. (Abteilung)/ SS-Panzer-Regiment 9*, therefore the commander of the Corps ordered them to move forward following the route of the 20th Guards Tank Brigade. The 22nd Guards Tank Brigade reached Alsódakapuszta around 1800 hours, only 3 km northeast of the shore of Lake Balaton. After this, they occupied the railway station of Papkeszi, then launched an assault to take over Papkeszi itself.

The 6th Guards Motorized Rifle Brigade and the 51st Guards Self-Propelled Artillery Brigade were covering the flanks of the Corps between the railway station of Papkeszi and Berhida. In the sector of the latter village, the 51st Guards Self-Propelled Artillery Brigade lost six knocked out SU–76Ms, of which four were burnt out.[1442]

The 21st Guards Tank Brigade was still in the Corps commander's reserve. During the fighting, the 5th Guards Tank Corps lost 10 T–34/85s and three SU–76Ms.[1443] In the evening, the Corps had 59 remaining operational T–34/85s and 13 SU–76Ms. The 51st Guards Self-Propelled Artillery Brigade on the other hand, had 52 remaining SU–76Ms, and the 364th Guards Heavy Self-Propelled Artillery Regiment had 15 ISU–122s in operational condition. The 4th Guards Motorcycle Regiment, with seven Mk–IX Valentine tanks and 76 motorcycles, was in army reserve at Várpalota.[1444]

On the same afternoon, *IV. SS-Panzerkorps* was subordinated to the German *6. Armee*[1445] after which, the *Stab/IV. SS-Panzerkorps* was in command of the remnants of *5. SS-Panzer-Division*, *3. SS-Panzer-Division*, and *3. Panzer-Division*.[1446]

At dawn, the *Stab/3. Panzer-Division* and the majority of the units retreated to Balatonkenese via Falubattyán, Polgárdi and Csajág. The Soviets knocked out a Tiger B of *schwere Panzer-Abteilung 509* that was in a holding position north of Polgárdi when the *Divisionsstab* was marching past. On the roads and in the fields, which were still wet and clogged in certain areas, fragments of German units, tanks, armoured personnel carriers, trucks and carts were rolling in great disarray towards the north-west. Soviet ground attack aircraft were continuously attacking the German columns, and on a number of occasions, the Soviets engaged them with artillery, mortar and machine gun fire.[1447]

The Soviet 366th Guards Heavy Self-Propelled Artillery Regiment/4th Guards Army, which occupied Székesfehérvár, was in firing positions on the western edge of the town with eight operational German self-propelled howitzers and three Panther tanks. In the independent self-propelled-artillery battalions of the Division, there were 59 SU–76Ms

---

1442 War log of the 51st Guards Self-Propelled Artillery Brigade between 20 January - 20 August 1945. Copy owned by the author. p. 6. Six persons (of these, one officer) was fallen, 10 soldiers (of these, four officers) were wounded.
1443 Central Archives of the Russian Defence Ministry (Podolsk), f. 243, op. 2928, gy. 178, li. 97. The war log of the 5th Guards Tank Corps describes five knocked out T-34/85 tanks, of which three were burnt out, for the day of 22 March 1945.
1444 Central Archives of the Russian Defence Ministry (Podolsk), f. 243, op. 2928, gy. 131, li. 264.
1445 NARA, T311, R163, F7215011.
1446 NARA, T311, R163, F7215433.
1447 *Geschichte der 3. Panzer-Division. Herausgegeben vom Traditionsverband der Division.* Berlin, 1967. p. 470.

and five tanks in operational condition by the evening, as they suffered the total loss of four SU–76Ms during the day.[1448]

The 912th Self-Propelled Artillery Regiment/207th Self-Propelled Artillery Brigade, fighting in subordination to the Army, had crossed the Malom Canal by 1400 hours and with two of its batteries of six SU–100s, reached Szabadbattyán, where they knocked out a Tiger B tank. One battery with four SU–100s, remained in the reserve of the brigade commander. The 1004th Self-Propelled Artillery Regiment with 11 SU–100s, crossed the Malom Canal as well, then met German resistance in the north-eastern outskirts of Úrhida, where one of its self-propelled guns was knocked out.[1449] After this, at the end of the day, two regiments of the 207th Self-Propelled Artillery Brigade, with 25 operational SU–100s, were gathered in the Gyulamajor– Hill 153 (Gombócleső)–city waterworks area.[1450]

The German *I. SS-Panzerkorps/6. Panzerarmee* was engaged in combat with the Soviet armoured fighting vehicles that were attacking from the sector of Ősi and Várpalota. The Soviet units bypassed the *SS*-troops fighting south and southwest of Várpalota, and advanced with 40 to 50 tanks via Hajmáskér towards Veszprém.

The *1. SS-Panzer-Division* was torn in three by the assault of the Soviet 9th Guards Mechanized Corps. An *SS-Kampfgruppe* of approximately regiment-size and which was reinforced by armoured fighting vehicles, tried to break through from the sector of Litér toward the north-west; the left flank of the *Division* was in combat in the sector of Hajmáskér, and a third combat group was encircled by the Soviets at Öskü.[1451]

On the southern flank of *1. SS-Panzer-Division,* the Várpalota-Veszprém road east of Öskü was closed off by the remaining combat-ready armoured and *Panzergrenadier* units of *SS-Panzergrenadier-Regiment 1* and *SS-Panzer-Regiment 1*. The units of *SS-Panzergrenadier-Regiment 2*, reinforced with the guns of *SS-Panzer-Flak-Abteilung 1* and the remaining combat-ready *Jagdpanzers* of *1. SS-Panzerjäger-Abteilung,* established defensive positions west of Tés. The Soviet attack encircled the southern combat group at Öskü, and the troops in combat in the north were thrown back towards Olaszfalu. By then, there was no radio contact anymore between the two groups.

The southern combat group, where the *Divisionskommandeur* himself was at the moment, sent *Panzergruppe "Poetschke"* forward, to clear the route toward Veszprém. The combat group consisted of 16 tanks and a few armoured personnel carriers and reached Litér around 1300 hours, still without enemy contact. After replenishing their fuel, the armoured fighting vehicles set off around 1430 hours toward the north-west, but soon ran into an ambush by some M4A2s of the Soviet 46th Guards Tank Brigade north-west of Litér at a road junction, and the Germans suffered heavy losses. Seven German tanks and a few armoured personnel carriers were destroyed, along with a significant loss of life as well. The *SS-Panzergruppe* retreated towards the south, then later they reached Veszprém with a bypass, this time without any combat engagements.[1452] *SS-Hauptsturmführer* Sternebeck remembered these events:

1448 Central Archives of the Russian Defence Ministry (Podolsk), f. 243, op. 2928, gy. 178, li. 97.
1449 War log of the 207th Self-Propelled Artillery Brigade, 22 March 1945. Copy owned by the author.
1450 Central Archives of the Russian Defence Ministry (Podolsk), f. 243, op. 2928, gy. 131, li. 264.
1451 NARA, T311, R162, F7214715.
1452 Tiemann, Ralf: *Die Leibstandarte*. Band IV/2. Osnabrück, 1987. pp. 317-318.

"The available space is quickly diminishing, we need to breathe. Two assault guns which are readily available, join the combat at the road junction, but they are so overwhelmed that they are not able to improve the situation.

We, the remnants of the armoured group of Sturmbannführer Poetschke, received the task to turn around on the road and immediately attack the enemy armoured fighting vehicles east of Veszprém.

We cannot get through the road junction straight ahead, as the enemy armoured fighting vehicles have such an advantageous position that we are not able to fan out. Therefore, we bypass southwards and attack, via Litér toward Veszprém. Directly north of Litér, we stumble into a defensive position of significant enemy forces by surprise. We are in a trap now, facing each other at a distance of not greater than 300-400 meters; a deadly armoured battle starts. In a short time we lost a number of Panzer IVs and Panthers[1453]; and the crews of the knocked out vehicles run around the battlefield like living torches. We don't have the slightest chance to destroy the enemy and occupy the road junction. We give up the fight and disengage from the enemy under cover of a thick smoke screen created by smoke candles."[1454]

On the night of 21/22 March 1945, in the sector of *12. SS-Panzer-Division*, *SS-Panzergrenadier-Regiment 26* and some units of *3. SS-Panzer-Division* joining its left flank, established new positions between Bakonycsernye and Szápár, as well as north-west of there. *Panzer-Pionier-Bataillon 12* was gathered at Jásd, as they had been withdrawn from the Simontornya bridgehead, together with *1. SS-Panzer-Division,* and had engaged the enemy again at Kisláng.

Early in the morning, the Soviet troops launched an attack against the line of *SS-Panzergrenadier-Regiment 26*. Although the Germans suffered significant losses, they were able to hold their positions.

The *1.* and *2. Kompanie/Panzer-Pionier-Bataillon 12,* spending the night around Tés in the mill, were surprised by the Soviets. The *2. Kompanie,* on the eastern bank of the Gaja Creek, was almost completely destroyed and 120 of its soldiers went missing. The *1. Kompanie*, equipped with armoured personnel carriers, was able to retreat to the western bank. The armoured pioneer units retreated during the day to the south-eastern edge of Dudar.

At dawn, west of Tés, the Soviets attacked the positions of *III. (gepanzert) (Bataillon)/Panzergrenadier-Regiment 26* and the *Divisionsbegleitkompanie* in the rear. From Tés, the Soviets attacked with more than 10 armoured fighting vehicles toward the north-west and repulsed the Germans. At 0800 hours, the Germans commenced to retreat. The command post of *III. (gepanzert) (Bataillon)/Panzergrenadier-Regiment 26* needed to be defended in hand-to-hand combat. Afterwards, the armoured personnel carriers retreated to Bakonynána and the *Divisionsbegleitkompanie* established new positions three km south of the village.

1453 According to the photographs, here the Germans lost two Tiger B heavy tanks and one *Wirbelwind* anti-aircraft armoured fighting vehicle as well, besides the seven knocked out armoured fighting vehicles. The *Luftwaffe's* liaison officer was travelling in one of the knocked out Panzer IVs; he flew out of the tank, engulfed in flames. See Agte, Patrick: *Jochen Peiper. Kommandeur Panzerregiment Leibstandarte*. Berg am Starnberger See, 1998. p. 356.

1454 Quoted by Tiemann, Ralf: *Chronik der 7. Panzerkompanie. An vorderster Front in der 1. SS-Panzerdivision „Leibstandarte SS Adolf Hitler"*. Selent, 2015. p. 256.

At 1000 hours that morning, the *SS*-armoured personnel carriers and the lone Jagdpanther, were withdrawn. Thus, the defence of Bakonynána remained to be carried out by the *Divisionsbegleitkompanie*, but they retreated at 1330, giving in to the pressure of the Soviet units towards Zirc. At dawn on the next morning, *I.* and *III. Zugs* of the *Kompanie* were covering the right flank of the *Division* at Lókút.

The *II. (Bataillon)/Panzergrenadier-Regiment 26*, broke through toward Dudar, as its flanks were left without coverage. The *I.* and *II. (Bataillons)/SS-Panzergrenadier-Regiment 26* established positions east of Dudar.

Around noon, the Soviet armoured fighting vehicles and rifle infantry, aided by ground attack aircraft, launched a new assault from the north in the sector of Dudar. The guns and automatic cannons of *SS-Panzer-Flak-Abteilung 12* opened fire effectively and, apart from a number of ground targets, they destroyed an Il−2 ground attack aircraft as well. During the afternoon, the remnants of *SS-Panzer-Flak-Abteilung 12* were ordered to Putrimajor, four km south-west of Zirc, to secure the village with the guns and the artillery forces in combat as infantry. The *2. Batterie* reported to have knocked out six Soviet armoured fighting vehicles, but in the meantime, lost two 8.8 cm guns and two 3.7 cm anti-aircraft guns.[1455]

In the evening, another attack was launched against Dudar, but this time from the north-west. Due to this, *SS-Panzergrenadier-Regiment 26* was ordered to retreat.

The units of *3. SS-Panzer-Division* were also in defence in the same sector. *Kampfgruppe "Barth"* repelled the Soviets north-west of Bakonycsernye, then prepared for defence at Szápár. At Dudar, together with the forces of *12. SS-Panzer-Division*, smaller fragments of *3. SS-Panzer-Division* were in defence.[1456] The units of *SS-Panzer-Flak-Abteilung 3*, and the remaining Panzer IVs of *SS-Panzer-Regiment 3*, established defensive positions in the north-eastern outskirts of Nagyesztergár and knocked out a number of Soviet tanks.[1457]

Between the southern flank of *12. SS-Panzer-Division* and *1. SS-Panzer-Division*, fighting in the south-western sector of Várpalota, a wide gap had been opened on the frontline. In order to be able to cover the open right flank, *SS-Panzergrenadier-Regiment 26*, without it's *III. Bataillon*, marched to Lókút. The soldiers of *II. (Bataillon)/Panzergrenadier-Regiment 26* were sent there via Zirc, mounted on armoured fighting vehicles, but due to the extreme congestion on the roads they didn't arrive until 0715 hours the next morning. The units of the *Divisionsbegleitkompanie* that were securing the village and the hills south-east of there, were subordinated to the battalion.

Szápár and Csetény fell into Soviet hands. On the left flank of the *Division*, the subordinated units of *3. SS-Panzer-Division* were pushed out of Koromlát, five km west of Súr, by the Soviets, but *SS-Panzer-Aufklärungs-Abteilung 12* reoccupied the cluster of houses with a counterattack launched at 0430 hours, from the south-east and south-west.[1458]

1455 Stöber, Hans: *Die Flugabwehrverbände der Waffen-SS. Aufstellung, Gliederung, Luftverteidigung und Einsätze an den Fronten.* Preussisch Oldendorf, 1984. p. 248.
1456 Vopersal, Wolfgang: *Soldaten, Kämpfer, Kameraden. Marsch und Kämpfe der SS-Totenkopfdivision.* Band Vb. Bielefeld, 1991. pp. 786-787.
1457 Vopersal, Wolfgang: *Soldaten, Kämpfer, Kameraden. Marsch und Kämpfe der SS-Totenkopfdivision.* Band Vb. Bielefeld, 1991. p. 788. The Soviet tanks knocked out at Nagyesztergár were identified as T-34s by one of the soldiers remembering the events, but most likely these were the M4A2s of the 9th Guards Mechanized Corps.
1458 NARA, T311, R162, F7214706.

By the evening, *12. SS-Panzer-Division* had reached the *Klara-Stellung* east of Zirc, together with the subordinated units of *3. SS-Panzer-Division*. The *Klara-Stellung* was already broken through by the Soviets south of the frontline of the *Division*. The combat group deployed at Lókút, *SS-Panzergrenadier-Regiment 25* and *SS-Panzerjäger-Abteilung 12* had not joined the *Division* yet.

The 30th Guards Mechanized Brigade/9th Guards Mechanized Corps of the Soviet 6th Guards Tank Army, occupied Csetény after performing a bypassing manoeuvre. The 31st Guards Mechanized Brigade took Bakonynána. The 18th Guards Mechanized Brigade and the 46th Guards Tank Brigade had taken Hajmáskér by surprise from the north, where they reported the destruction of 70 armoured fighting vehicles.[1459] The two brigades reached Veszprém together around 1700 hours, but there they met, according to Soviet sources, a counterattack of approximately 100 German armoured fighting vehicles. Therefore, the Soviets were forced to retreat and establish temporary defences 2 km north-east of Veszprém. The 9th Guards Mechanized Corps lost on that day seven burnt out M4A2s[1460] and in the evening still had 118 operational M4A2s and 12 SU–76Ms.[1461]

An officer of the 46th Guards Tank Brigade, Guards Captain Loza, remembers these events:

"In the evening of 22 March, the brigade received orders to march into the sector of Inota, 18 km west of Székesfehérvár, and by morning be prepared for action in the direction of Hajmáskér and Veszprém. At dawn, the units launched the attack toward the south-west, moving along the Várpalota–Veszprém railway line. The 1ˢᵗ Tank Battalion was at the head. Our reconnaissance unit consisted of two Shermans from the platoon of 2ⁿᵈ Lieutenant Sergey Krikun; one of them was Akulov's[1462]. Three km north of Öskü, a Tiger opened fire on the soldiers from an ambush position. An enemy shell hit the emcha of Akulov, which started to emit smoke. The commander ordered the crew to abandon vehicle. The most important obligation of all tankers is to save its "iron horse", whatever it costs, to put out fire with the fire extinguisher or sand or earth. The crew serving on the foreign vehicle violated this law. They retreated approximately 50 meters and lay down on the ground, but they kept their eyes on the abandoned Sherman. These must have been very tense moments. The "magic" tank was not smoking anymore. At this moment, Krikun's tanks were manoeuvring toward the left in order to get the Tiger in the flank.

In the unfolding situation, the crew of course, must have returned to the Sherman, but Akulov decided otherwise. He ordered the driver-mechanic, Senior Sergeant Kliujev, to go to the tank and get it into coverage. Aleksandr quickly sneaked to the tank, and jumped in. He started up the engine and slowly moved backwards. At that moment, the Tiger again fired at the Sherman and it went up in flames. The flames were spreading by the second. Kliujev was not to be seen anywhere. Two emcha-crew ran there to help their comrade.

1459 At Hajmáskér there were a number of armoured fighting vehicles within the strength of the various training units of the Royal Hungarian Army, and the repair workshop of *1. Panzer-Division* was also stationed here. Therefore the majority of the armoured fighting vehicles were most likely not knocked out in combat. The amount of 70 armoured fighting vehicles probably also includes the German armoured fighting vehicle losses suffered at the ambush positions at Litér.

1460 Central Archives of the Russian Defence Ministry (Podolsk), f. 243, op. 2928, gy. 131, li. 268.

1461 Central Archives of the Russian Defence Ministry (Podolsk), f. 243, op. 2928, gy. 131, li. 264.

1462 Guards Junior Lieutenant Viktor Akulov's tank was the oldest and most worn out M4A2 tank of the battalion.

They ran to the tank where they noticed Sasha as he was crawling out from under the tank. His left shoulder was stained with blood. The two comrades grabbed the third and ran back with him as fast as they could – the fire in the meantime encircled the whole hull and reached up to the turret. This time there was no doubt: the 'foreign' is over. For the second time, and now for real, it was deleted from the tables of equipment. This was a very sad event, an excellent tanker, Aleksandr Kliujev, was also lost.

[…]

The emcha crews and the tank mounted infantry, were working through the whole night. By dawn, with great effort, they cut a 12 km path [into the forest – the author]. The battalion arrived at the southern edge of the forest at Hill 235.5, just a stone's throw away from Hajmáskér. The morning mist enclosed the field and the roads leading toward the station in a shroud. This was both good and bad. The enemy did not see us but at the same time, we could also not see him from a great distance. In case of an engagement, we might have been fighting from a close distance or even in hand-to-hand combat, using our tracks. This would not be the first case.

The tanks formed into battle formation and rushed toward the railway station without even stopping. The crews of the right flank emchas, noticed the outlines of an enemy self-propelled gun among the trees of the small forested area right of the road. The words of warning were uttered in the radio, together with the description of the exact place of danger. No doubt, this was an ambush position. The Shermans of Guards Junior Lieutenant Pyotr Karamishev and Guards Lieutenant Mikhail Chezegov, opened fire at first on the self-propelled gun. The sudden blast of the tank guns in the morning silence signalled for the other armoured fighting vehicles too. Aimers Sergeant Petrosyan and Efreitor Kazakhov, have enflamed three camouflaged 'Ferdinands'[1463] with concentrated fire. Later we came to know from a captured German tanker that the crew of the self-propelled guns were sleeping. The German crews were not able to fire even one shot.

The post at Hajmáskér was alerted. Half-clothed Germans were running out of their sleeping quarters. Some of them were running toward the anti-tank guns which were still attached to the towing vehicles. But it was all too late. The Shermans were riding into the streets. They tore down fences, destroying equipment, crushing all with their tracks, and shooting down enemy soldiers and officers. The shots fired by the tank guns, the machine guns and the blattering of the submachine guns and the shrieking of the tank engines, altogether made a hellish thunder at the railway station. […]

A number of railway wagons were left idle on the tracks in front of us. The Shermans of the company of Guards 1st Lieutenant Aleksandr Ionov, were rushing to the railway crossing. The tankers have enflamed four Panthers still strapped onto railroad flat wagons, the submachine gunners captured 10 wagons of ammunition and a fuel supply depot not far from the station.

The battle was raging. The platoon of Guards Lieutenant Ivan Tuzikhov, which was sent out on a reconnaissance mission, reached the roads leading to Veszprém. They noticed a large enemy armoured column. "Enemy tanks are moving fast forward to engage you in

---

[1463] There were no Ferdinand heavy *Jagdpanzers* serving in Hungary. The name of the armoured fighting vehicle, which was introduced during Kursk, was used by the Soviets as a common name for the German assault guns and *Jagdpanzers*.

battle" – reported the platoon. The battalion had to leave Hajmáskér immediately, and had to fan out south of the railway station, where we could establish firing positions to wait for the approaching enemy. I ordered: "Without any delays, all go to the railroad crossing!" […]

In the meantime, the company of Danilchenko, appeared at the southern edge of Hajmáskér. An enemy vehicle column was approaching the station from the west along a dirt road. Wonderful target! At the given sign, Grigory Danilchenko's eight Shermans were firing parallel directed fire from their tank guns. These direct hits tore the trucks apart. The targeted infantry jumped off the trucks, and were fleeing in every direction. A hail of bullets were raining down on them… only a few could survive.

I ordered the company of Danilchenko to follow me. We drove across the tracks, past the railroad crossing, we advanced approximately 800 meters forward, and then established the battle formation. Fate was kind to us! We were very lucky in choosing our positions, as our battalion was now on an enemy artillery training ground. The whole place was full of positions made for different kinds of caliber guns and coverage for their towing vehicles..
[…]

For us, from the moment the Shermans occupied their positions, to the point when the German tank at the head appeared, it seemed like a whole eternity was spent. At last we noticed the head of the enemy column in the bend of the road[1464]. The tanks were moving with only a short distance between them. Very good. If they would need to stop suddenly, and soon this happened, the whole enemy column will immediately turned into a bottleneck. And then the aimers in the emchas could not miss the targets. In the meantime, our long-barrels[1465] were silent. I ordered not to shoot until my tank fires. At this sign, we will shoot concentrated fire, first targeting the Tigers and the Panthers.

I was eagerly waiting for the moment when the whole column would be in our sight. The aimer of my tank, Guards-Senior Sergeant Anatoly Romashkin, was always keeping the tank at the head in his crosshairs. The Shermans in Tuzinkhov's platoon targeted those tanks that followed the first. All the targets were divided among the Shermans..

This was my plan: the column will stop for a few seconds because of the destruction of the leading tank and those immediately after it, and this will be enough to decide the battle in our favour. The Sherman's swift-firing gun will not disappoint us.

'Just a little more, just a few more seconds!' – I said to myself. And at once, all enemy tanks became visible. I ordered: "Fire!" The air was torn by 17 shots sounded at the very same moment. The leading tank immediately burst in flames. The last tank of the column also froze on its spot. The column stopped, and this is what we needed. The Germans started to tumble in the surprise fire. A few tankers turned their vehicles on the road to show their thicker glacis plates towards us. This did not help them too much. Their occasional return fire was suppressed by the directed fire of the subunits of our battalion. The superiority of the emchas was apparent – fire directed from standing position. The road was covered in burning vehicles. Enemy tanks, trucks and fuel supply cars were burning. The sky was covered by smoke, and the air was hot.

1464 This was the armoured group *"Poetschke"/1. SS-Panzer-Division* approaching from the direction of Litér.
1465 The M4A2s equipped with 76 mm guns had longer gun barrels than those of the 75 mm guns.

This unusual battle did not last more than 15 minutes. We destroyed 21 enemy tanks and 12 armoured transport vehicles. One Sherman was immobilized, but its aimer, Guards-Sergeant Petrosyan and its driver-mechanic, Guards-Senior Sergeant Ruzhov survived. Both of them were constantly firing, thus preventing the enemy from attacking the battalion flank. [...]

Somewhat later, the subunits of the battalion approached Veszprém. What we saw on the roads leading to the town was absolutely astounding. Eight Panthers were standing on both sides of the road in carefully prepared positions. They were silent, and had not responded to our fire. We destroyed the Panthers from short distance, without any hesitation.

A prisoner who was captured somewhat later told us that the German soldiers had been dazed and distressed after they had seen their large tank column going up in flames in seconds. Therefore, when our subunits reached their well prepared positions in a cloud of smoke and dust, the crews of the Panthers left their vehicles and ran away in panic together with the infantry.

Veszprém was there in front of us, undefended. But we did not enter the town. There were only two to three shells left for each Sherman and approximately 100 machine gun bullets. In the 24 hour battle we depleted all of our supplies. Our fuel was also very low. The main forces of the 46th Guards Tank Brigade joined us an hour later. After we replenished our fuel and ammunition supplies, we set off and circled Veszprém toward the north. [...]

Thirty years later I visited Lake Balaton and this beautiful Hungarian city. I walked its narrow, winding streets. And I could see with my own eyes that I decided correctly on that old March morning in 1945, that we did not enter the town. The battalion was practically out of ammunition and we almost had no infantry. And the Shermans would have been easy targets for the enemy Panzerfausts in such an intricate web of streets and alleyways in the town."[1466]

Guards Captain Loza thus justified his decision on not entering Veszprém, not because of a counterattack by the German troops, but the fact that his M4A2s were low on fuel and ammunition supplies and their weak infantry support.

Between Veszprém and Szentkirályszabadja, seven Panthers of *23. Panzer-Division* were bogged down due to the lack of armoured recovery vehicles, and because of the close proximity of the Soviet armoured fighting vehicles, they blew these vehicles up.[1467] It is likely that the 1st Battalion/46th Guards Tank Brigade met these Panthers when they were pushing their way toward Veszprém from Hajmáskér.

The German *SS*-combat-group in defence of Csór, set off for Inota on the same day at 0100 hours. There were two armoured personnel carriers and two assault guns at the head of the column, and approximately 30 infantry soldiers behind them. They were followed by a towed artillery battery. Halfway towards Inota, before Point 148, in the bend of the road, the Germans were greeted by rifle, machine gun and mortar fire.

1466 Loza, Dmitriy: *Commanding the Red Army's Sherman Tanks.* Lincoln–London, 1996. pp. 79-87.
1467 Rebentisch, Ernst: *Zum Kaukasus und zu den Tauern. Die Geschichte der 23. Panzer-Division 1941–1945.* Esslingen, 1963. p. 497.

The two armoured personnel carriers with their 2 cm automatic cannons, targeted the identified Soviet artillery positions along the road and the assault guns fired one or two high-explosive shells. After this, the Soviet detachment retreated. At that time, the second artillery battery arrived, and the column was closed up by two armoured personnel carriers and two assault guns with the remainder of the infantry. The Germans soon reached Inota, where they established positions at dawn. The Germans observed from here, that around 0700 hours in the morning, eight Soviet ground attack aircraft attacked Csór with bombs and machine guns and set a number of houses on fire. The village, which was already abandoned by the Germans, was then raided by a rifle infantry of approximately regiment-size and 10 armoured fighting vehicles. The two *SS-Artillerie* batteries then opened fire and caused huge losses to the Soviet troops now in the village.[1468]

On the same day, the Soviet 9th Guards Army concentrated its armoured forces mainly around Várpalota. The Army received the complete 208th Self-Propelled Artillery Brigade with 43 operational SU–100s, three SU–76Ms and two T–34s. The 1922nd Self-Propelled Artillery Regiment of the latter, was in firing positions at Hill 191, 2 km south-west of Várpalota, and the 1068th and 1016th Self-Propelled Artillery Regiments were in Inota. The Brigade had lost a burnt out SU–100 on that day.[1469] The 9th Guards Army could not be content for too long about having the SU-100s, because around 1700 hours, the 208th Self-Propelled Artillery Brigade was subordinated to the 6th Guards Tank Army by the front command.[1470]

The 1513th Self-Propelled Artillery Regiment of the 9th Guards Army was also on Hill 191 with four SU–76Ms. The 1523rd Self-Propelled Artillery Regiment, with its 17 SU–76Ms, were assembled on the western edge of Balinka, and the 1524th Self-Propelled Artillery Regiment as army reserve was assembled seven km west of Isztimér.[1471]

On the same day, the Soviet 23rd Tank Corps was reassigned from the 3rd Ukrainian Front to the subordination of the 2nd Ukrainian Front. The 53rd Motorcycle Regiment that was subordinated to the Corps, was detached and was transferred to the 4th Guards Army.[1472] The Regiment was assembled with 10 T–34/85s and 133 motorcycles on the south-eastern edge of Mór.[1473]

At 1900 hours, the 23rd Tank Corps was assembled around Szák and Szend, with 59 operational T–34/85s, 14 IS-2 and ISU–122 armoured fighting vehicles, 890 combat troops, 17 76 mm guns, six 82 mm and 21 120 mm mortars, 16 37 mm anti-tank guns and eight M–13 multiple rocket launchers. The Corps was ordered to attack in the sector of Csép with the forces of the 18th Guards Rifle Corps, then cooperate with the 2nd Guards Mechanized Corps, to push towards Győr.[1474]

1468 Bernau, Günter: Aus den letzten Kämpfen in Ungarn 1945. I./SS-Panzer-Artillerie-Regiment 5. In: *Deutsches Soldatenjahrbuch 1975*. p. 214.
1469 Central Archives of the Russian Defence Ministry (Podolsk), f. 243, op. 2928, gy. 178, li. 97.
1470 War log of the 3rd Ukrainian Front from March 1945. Copy owned by the author. 22 March 1945. p. 6
1471 Central Archives of the Russian Defence Ministry (Podolsk), f. 243, op. 2928, gy. 131, li. 264.
1472 Central Archives of the Russian Defence Ministry (Podolsk), f. 243, op. 2928, gy. 131, li. 265.
1473 Central Archives of the Russian Defence Ministry (Podolsk), f. 243, op. 2928, gy. 178, li. 95.
1474 Central Archives of the Russian Defence Ministry (Podolsk), f. 240, op. 2799, gy. 357, li. 13.

On the front of the 2nd Ukrainian Front

The German *6. Panzer-Division/II. SS-Panzerkorps* was engaged in combat with the Soviet troops closing up in the small forested area between Ácsteszér and Hánta, and the leading Soviet troops had reached Réde and its south-western outskirts. *SS-Panzer-Aufklärungs-Abteilung 2,* subordinated to *6. Panzer-Division* was to close off the road between Románd and Bakonybánk.

1 km south and southeast of Kisbér, the Soviets temporarily breached the German frontline, but units of *6. Panzer-Division* launched an attack at 0600 hours that morning via Hill 246 (Csúcsos Hill), 2.5 km southeast of Bakonyszombathely, and Hill 235 (Öreg szőlőhegy), 2 km southeast of Kisbér, and they repulsed them. After the units of *2. SS-Panzer-Division* reoccupied Csép, the Soviet troops in combat in the north-eastern outskirts, a Soviet rifle unit of regiment-size, were dispersed with an assault initiated from the north-east. In the meantime, the frontline of *2. SS-Panzer-Division* faced continuous regimental size counterattacks from the south and from the east, which were supported by 25 armoured fighting vehicles. However the Germans repulsed these attempts.[1475]

At 2300 hours that evening, *SS-Panzergrenadier-Regiment 4* retreated to the Kisigmánd–Nagyigmánd line. The formerly absent *I. (Bataillon)/SS-Panzergrenadier-Regiment 4,* arrived there as well, and was deployed on the right flank of the *Regiment.*

Because of the reassignment of *SS-Panzer-Aufklärungs-Abteilung 2,* the right flank of the *Division* was secured by *SS-Panzer-Flak-Abteilung 2.* Soviet rifle forces of more than a regiment in size, launched an attack between Csép and Ete, but *SS-Panzer-Artillerie-Regiment 2* did not have any ammunition left. The assaulting Soviets, at last, were blanketed in fire by the *Flak-Abteilung,* their shells exploding 10 meters over the Soviet's heads. Their attack collapsed. The *Flak-Abteilung* shot down the last of its 251 enemy aircraft in the war.[1476]

SS-Panzergrenadier-Regiment 3 arrived at the south-eastern outskirts of Győr, where *I. Bataillon* of the *Regiment,* already replenished, was in position.[1477]

South-east of Csép, at Makkpuszta, the Soviet 1897th Self-Propelled Artillery Regiment was holding back German attacks throughout the day, during which they reported to have knocked out one Panzer IV tank, two assault guns, three armoured personnel carriers, one gun, one mortar battery and 11 fortified positions. Their own losses included one blown up SU–76M, two killed and three wounded soldiers. The task of the Regiment was to occupy Csép by the end of the day with the 606th and the 761st Rifle Regiment/317th Rifle Division.[1478]

In the front of the German *XXXXIII. Armeekorps,* the Soviets, with armoured support and two regiments of rifle infantry, pushed through between the defensive fortifications at Kisigmánd and Mocsa, which were still holding out. At Kisigmánd, the company of the training school of *6. Panzer-Division,* repelled the Soviet attack in hand-to-hand

---

1475 NARA, T311, R162, F7214707.
1476 Weidinger, Otto: *Division Das Reich. Der Weg der 2. SS-Panzer-Division „Das Reich".* Band V: 1943-1945. Osnabrück, without year of publication, p. 469.
1477 Weidinger, Otto: *Division Das Reich. Der Weg der 2. SS-Panzer-Division „Das Reich".* Band V: 1943-1945. Osnabrück, without year of publication, p. 470.
1478 Central Archives of the Russian Defence Ministry (Podolsk), f. 240, op. 2799, gy. 342, li. 116.

combat. There were three Panthers left in the village, but only one of them was completely combat-ready. This one towed the other two into different firing positions as was needed at the particular moment.[1479]

Driving through between Kisigmánd and Mocsa, the Soviets turned toward the north and broke into the German defence. The German defenders established defensive strongpoints along the Mocsa–Ács road and with these, sealed off further Soviet advances. The tanks and *Jagdpanzers* of *Panzer-Kampfgruppe "Pape"* and their armoured personnel carriers, also carried out a small scale attack in the direction of Mocsa, but they had not been engaged in any significant combat with the enemy. By the evening, the armoured fighting vehicles returned to the Komárom Fortress.[1480]

The Soviet 1505th Self-Propelled Artillery Regiment, in combat in the south-eastern outskirts of Kisigmánd, repulsed a German counterattack at 0500 hours, which was initiated west of Mocsa in the south-west direction with approximately 150 soldiers, three assault guns and 10 armoured personnel carriers. During these actions, the Soviet SU–76Ms reported to have knocked out two armoured personnel carriers and 13 fortified positions. At 1000 hours in the morning, the 1505th Self-Propelled Artillery Regiment, in support of the 439th Rifle Regiment/52nd Rifle Division, after a 30 minute preparatory artillery barrage, assaulted Point 137 west of Mocsa and Hill 140 south-east of there. In a one hour-long battle, the Soviet armoured fighting vehicles reached Hill 140, during which, they knocked out 10 guns and 13 fortified positions. At 1600 hours in the afternoon, the 1505th Self-Propelled Artillery Regiment was subordinated to the 99th Rifle Division, and around 1900 hours established firing positions four km northwest of Kocs.[1481]

At 0500 hours in the morning, the Germans launched a new attack aimed at the reoccupation of Hill 193 (Öreg-hill), two km south of Mocsa. This time they succeeded in pushing the Soviet 429th Rifle Regiment/52nd Rifle Division down off the hill. At that moment, the 991st Self-Propelled Artillery Regiment was needed to intervene, but was withdrawn to Kocs an hour earlier. The SU–76Ms launched an attack together with the 429th Rifle Regiment and, around 0700 hours, reoccupied the hill. The Germans, according to Soviet reports, lost one armoured personnel carrier, three guns, six machine guns and two radio transmitters. One of the SU–76Ms was hit by the Germans but was returned at the end of the day after being repaired. [1482]

At 1230 hours, the 991st Self-Propelled Artillery Regiment and the 429th Rifle Regiment were ordered to occupy Mocsa. At 1315 hours, the Soviets approached to within 500 meters of the village from the south. By then, the Germans had lost two guns and one armoured personnel carrier. At this moment, the Germans launched a counterattack with eight armoured fighting vehicles and supporting infantry, and the Soviet attack attempt collapsed within 20 minutes. The losses of the 991st Self-Propelled Artillery Regiment

---

1479 Paul, Wolfgang: *Brennpunkte. Die Geschichte der 6. Panzerdivision (1. leichte) 1937–1945*. Krefeld, 1977. p. 450.
1480 Di Giusto, Stefano: *Panzer-Sicherungs-Kompanien and Panzer-Abteilung 208 - I./Panzer-Regiment Feldherrnhalle. Italy 1943-1944. Hungary - Slovakia - Moravia 1944–1945*. Erlangen, 2010. p. 208.
1481 Central Archives of the Russian Defence Ministry (Podolsk), f. 240, op. 2799, gy. 342, li. 113. The subordination of the 1505th Self-Propelled Artillery Regiment to the 99th Rifle Division could have probably happened because the Division's own 112th Independent Self-Propelled Artillery Battalion with its three SU–76Ms and one T–70 tank was not considered to be a significant armoured support.
1482 Central Archives of the Russian Defence Ministry (Podolsk), f. 240, op. 2799, gy. 342, li. 160.

amounted to five knocked out SU-76Ms, of which, three burnt out, four dead and 12 wounded. The Self-Propelled Artillery Regiment was withdrawn from the fight at 1320 hours by the commander of the 68th Rifle Corps and was sent to Kocs, where they were subordinated to the 99th Rifle Division. The SU-76Ms, ordered into defensive positions six km north-west of Kocs, had the task to prevent the Germans from advancing towards Kocs from the direction of Nagyigmánd.[1483]

On the left flank of the German *XXXXIII. Armeekorps,* the Soviets launched a number of attacks of company size, also supported by armoured fighting vehicles, from the direction of Pusztaalmás toward the north, and along the Dunaalmás–Füzítőpuszta road. The defenders repulsed these attacks with the support of *Panzer-Kampfgruppe "Pape"* while reporting to have knocked out six Soviet tanks and two self-propelled guns.[1484]

According to the reconnaissance data of the 2nd Guards Mechanized Corps, the German–Hungarian defence had five tanks and assault guns at Füzítőpuszta, three tanks and 10 to 15 armoured personnel carriers at Bélapuszta, two assault guns to the eastern of Vértestolna, three assault guns and two armoured personnel carriers at Alsóbikol, and five to eight tanks and assault guns at Point 191.[1485] There were also infantry and tank destroyer units with *Panzerfausts* in position in all these villages.[1486]

On the front of the Hungarian 3rd Army, the Soviets still had Dunaalmás encircled. Their rifle forces, with the T–34/85s of the 4th Guards Mechanized Brigade and the support of ground attack aircraft, were vigorously attacking and pushed back the western side of the German–Hungarian bridgehead to the Neszmély one km east–road junction–Dunaszentmiklós three km north-east line. The rifle forces, supported by armoured fighting vehicles, had broken into the thin line of defence at a number of locations, and the defenders were barely able to maintain the line, but with considerable gaps. Neszmély and Dunaszentmiklós were occupied by the 4th Guards Mechanized Brigade. The Soviet forces, pushing relentlessly forward in the criss-crossed terrain and the hollow ravines, were attacking from the sector of Felsőgalla through Tarján and, at around 1030 hours, occupied Héreg. The village was assaulted successfully by the 5th Guards Mechanized Brigade/2nd Guards Mechanized Corps.[1487] The units of the Corps lost four burnt out tanks by 1100 hours.[1488]

The forces of the Soviet 2nd Guards Mechanized Corps fighting in this sector, had been withdrawn from the frontline in the second half of the day and, upon orders of the commander of the 2nd Ukrainian Front, they were assembled at Kocs at noon on the following day. The aim of the Corps was subsequently to break through the German defences on the Mocsa–Nagyigmánd line and to attack with its brigades towards Ács, then Győr afterwards.[1489]

1483 Central Archives of the Russian Defence Ministry (Podolsk), f. 240, op. 2799, gy. 342, li. 110.
1484 NARA, T311, R162, F7214707.
1485 The armoured fighting vehicles deployed on the frontline of the Hungarian 3rd Army were most likely Panzer II light tanks, StuG. IV assault guns and *Marder* tank destroyers of the German *96. Infanterie-Division*, the Jagdpanzer 38(t) *Jagdpanzers* of *711. Infanterie-Division*, furthermore the StuG.III assault guns, StuH.42 assault howitzers, Panzer II light tanks and armoured personnel carriers of *Sturmartillerie-Brigade 239.*
1486 Summarized report of he 2nd Guards Mechanized Corps of the combat actions during March - April 1945. Copy owned by the author. p. 122.
1487 Central Archives of the Russian Defence Ministry (Podolsk), f. 240, op. 2799, gy. 357, li. 11.
1488 Central Archives of the Russian Defence Ministry (Podolsk), f. 401, op. 9511, gy. 535, li. 112.
1489 Central Archives of the Russian Defence Ministry (Podolsk), f. 240, op. 2799, gy. 357, li. 12.

The Soviets, attacking from the sector of Szomor toward the north, bypassed Bajna and reached the southern outskirts of Nagysáp. The Soviets wanted to attack from the direction of Sárisáp toward the north-west and west and to establish contact with the marines in combat in the Tát bridgehead. In the area of the Soviet bridgehead, the Germans attacked from the west and reoccupied Szarkás. The Soviet troops also launched an attack toward Süttő from the sector of Dunaszentmiklós.[1490] The bridgehead that was still held by the German-Hungarian troops of the Hungarian 3rd Army, was subordinated to the German *8. Armee* as of 2100 hours on that day.[1491]

The fighter and ground attack aircraft of the German *Luftflotte 4* were mainly supporting troops north of Lake Balaton and in the southern outskirts of Komárom. However, their prospects were seriously limited by the fact that several of the air units had been relocated to different airfields.[1492]

According to *Heeresgruppe Süd*, the Soviets had two objectives: on the one hand, to cut off the German *6. Armee*'s route at the north-eastern edge of Lake Balaton, and on the other hand, to reach the Veszprém–Győr road before the Germans.[1493]

The German *6. Armee* was tasked with re-establishing contact, using every possible measure, with the southern flank of the German *6. Panzerarmee* towards the north, in the direction of Vilonya and Hajmáskér and, with a flanking attack, prevent the Soviet breakthrough towards Veszprém.[1494] The *Stab* of the German *6. Armee* had been searching for the bulk of *9. SS-Panzer-Division* since the previous day, but they had not located them as yet.[1495]

At the same time, the *Heeresgruppe* itself did not have enough reserves to close off the gap. Therefore it had again been suggested that units should be regrouped from the sector of *2. Panzerarmee* to the north of Lake Balaton, either *16. SS-Panzergrenadier-Division* or *1. Volks-Gebirgs-Division*. However this was dismissed by Hitler as well as the suggestion to abandon the bridgehead of the Hungarian 3rd Army south of the Danube. Instead of this, the following units were ordered to the frontline: the *232. Panzer-Division*, established from training units, to the sector of Győr and the *153. Infanterie-Division* north of the Danube.[1496]

On the same day, *Generaloberst* Guderian again questioned the commander of *Heeresgruppe Süd*, about why the Germans were unable to strengthen the operational situation, even with six *SS-Panzer-Divisions*? *General der Infanterie* Wöhler replied that the Soviet counteroffensive had not found the *Heeresgruppe* in solid defensive positions, but the assault hit the flanks of the German attack already launched on the front of *IV. SS-Panzerkorps*. Also, the relocation of the *Panzer-Divisions* toward the north was moving very slowly because only a single pair of railroad tracks were available.[1497]

Heeresgruppe Süd asked the *Luftwaffe* to establish anti-aircraft artillery detachments, to be used against armoured fighting vehicles, from the Hungarian anti-aircraft artillery

---

1490 NARA, T311, R162, F7214707.
1491 NARA, T311, R163, F7215016.
1492 NARA, T311, R162, F7214709.
1493 NARA, T311, R162, F7214709.
1494 NARA, T311, R162, F7214710.
1495 NARA, T311, R162, F7214713.
1496 NARA, T311, R162, F7214710.
1497 NARA, T311, R162, F7214721.

battalion under formation in Sopron. They could be used to close off the Rába River crossing at Marcaltő, on the *Zsuzsanna-Stellung*,[1498] as there were not enough anti-tank weapons at that position.[1499]

23 March 1945, Friday

(**WEATHER**: highest daytime temperature 12 Celsius, clear sky. The roads and the terrain have dried up everywhere.)

On the front of *2. Panzerarmee, Grenadier-Regiments 191* and *211/71. Infanterie-Division,* faced with constantly strengthening Soviet resistance, launched an attack from the north in the forested area south-east of Mesztegnyő, to be able to make contact with *118. Jäger-Division* that was advancing from the south, and together they would be able to eliminate the encircled Soviet forces.

The *71. Infanterie-Division* was supported by units of *Sturmartillerie-Brigade 261*. Although the assault guns were only able to move on the forest paths and in the clearings, they were able to effectively support the combat of the *Grenadiers*. Therefore, at 0915 hours, only two hours following the launch of the attack, *Grenadier-Regiment 191* occupied Soponyapuszta and continued to pursue the Soviet troops toward the south.[1500] Afterwards the Germans had to establish defences facing east.[1501]

The Soviet 32nd Independent Guards Mechanized Brigade/57th Army with 13 T–34s, the 864th Self-Propelled Artillery Regiment with five SU–76Ms and its 249th Independent Tank Regiment with 10 T–34s, were in defensive positions in the sector of Libickozma and Kopárpuszta. On 22 and 23 March 1945, the Self-Propelled Artillery Regiment lost three knocked out SU–76Ms, of which two burnt out.[1502]

The forces of *2. Panzerarmee* reported between 6 – 23 March 1945, to have knocked out or captured 45 Soviet tanks and self-propelled guns.[1503]

On the shredded front of the German *6. Armee,* the Soviets continued their relentless attacks during the night of 22/23 March 1945 and during the day as well. The Germans identified three main routes of attack in this section, the assault force of which was composed mainly of tank and mechanized forces:

1498 The *Zsuzsanna-Stellung* was a defensive belt built along the Rába River in the northwestern Transdanubia, in order to seal off the tactical route towards Vienna. It consisted of field fortifications to defend the river in the Győr–Rábaszentmihály–Mórichida–Rábaszentandrás–Sárvár–Rábahidvég–Körmend line. The villages and towns had been assigned as defensive fortifications to guard and defend the crossing points. The northern flank of the *Stellung* was connected to the Danube, and the southern flank was attached to the *Reichsschutzstellung*. The *Zsuzsanna-Stellung* was was built from the end of September 1944 mostly by Hungarian penal units, under German control, but the work had not been concluded.
1499 NARA, T311, R163, F7214998.
1500 *Die 71. Infanterie-Division im Zweiten Weltkrieg 1939–1945. Gefechts- und Erlebnisberichte aus den Kämpfen der „Glückhaften Division" von Verdun bis Stalingrad, von Monte Cassino bis zum Plattensee. Arbeitsgemeinschaft „Das Kleeblatt" (Hrsg.).* Hildesheim, 1973. p. 416.
1501 NARA, T311, R162, F7214725.
1502 Central Archives of the Russian Defence Ministry (Podolsk), f. 243, op. 2928, gy. 178, li. 98.
1503 NARA, T311, R163, F7215465.

- along the north-eastern shore of Lake Balaton with the support of approximately 70 armoured fighting vehicles
- with approximately 60 armoured fighting vehicles from the sector of Sóly and Vilonya towards the south-west;
- from the sector of Hajmáskér towards the west with approximately 50 armoured fighting vehicles.

The Soviet troops were also supported by significant artillery fire and continual ground attack aircraft missions. Due to the countless jammed vehicle columns and Soviet air raids, the resupply lift was faltering and fuel and ammunition shortages appeared among the German troops. The German and Hungarian troops suffered terrible losses, they were worn out and distressed, and were not able to hold their positions any longer.[1504]

On the night of 22/23 March 1945, in the section of *I. Kavallerie-Korps, 23. Panzer-Division* launched an attack from the northern outskirts of Balatonkenese towards the east and reached Küngös. During this action, the units of the *Division* reported to have knocked out 15 Soviet armoured fighting vehicles.[1505]

This way, *1.* and *3. Panzer-Divisions,* and units of *44. Reichsgrenadier-Division* that were encircled southwest of Falubattyán and were trying to break out towards the west, were now able to join forces with *23. Panzer-Division,* who opened the corridor for them.[1506]

In the early hours of dawn on 23 March 1945, the combat groups of *1. Panzer-Division* and *44. Reichsgrenadier-Division,* who were breaking out, turned toward the south-south-east of Berhida. At that moment, the Germans ran into new Soviet positions at Küngös, who were firing at them with anti-tank guns. *Hauptmann* Hagen's remaining four Panthers did not have any tank-gun ammunition, so *I. (Bataillon)/Panzergrenadier-Regiment 113* with Sd.Kfz. 251/9 armoured personnel carriers, mounting short barrelled 7.5 cm guns, simply rammed down the Soviet guns.[1507]

The majority of *1. Panzer-Division* turned west again at Küngös. North-west of Küngös and west of Hill 185, a Soviet blocking position held up the Germans. *Oberst* Bradel sent two 2 cm self-propelled four-barrelled anti-aircraft guns, which eliminated the Soviet position swiftly with their fire.[1508] On 23 March 1945, at around 0530 hours, *Panzer-Kampfgruppe "Fink"* with *Kampfgruppe "Bradel"* behind them, established contact with *4. Kavallerie-Division/I. Kavallerie-Korps* south of Papkeszi.[1509]

The rearguard troops of *1. Panzer-Division,* having broken out, set off from the sector of Jenő toward the west, around midnight the previous day. This force consisted of units of *Panzer-Pionier-Bataillon 37* and *Panzer-Nachrichten-Abteilung 37,* a few Panthers and

---

1504 NARA, T311, R162, F7214725.
1505 NARA, T311, R162, F7214725. The history of 23. *Panzer-Division* does not mention such an assault. See Rebentisch, Ernst: *Zum Kaukasus und zu den Tauern. Die Geschichte der 23. Panzer-Division 1941–1945.* Esslingen, 1963. pp. 496-497.
1506 NARA, T311, R162, F7214726.
1507 Stoves, O. G. Rolf: *1. Panzer-Division 1935–1945. Chronik einer der drei Stamm-Division der deutschen Panzerwaffe.* Bad Nauheim, 1961. p. 764.
1508 Stoves, O. G. Rolf: *1. Panzer-Division 1935–1945. Chronik einer der drei Stamm-Division der deutschen Panzerwaffe.* Bad Nauheim, 1961. p. 764.
1509 Stoves, Rolf: Persönliches Kriegstagebuch Pz.Rgt. 1 (typewritten manuscript, a copy owned by the author), entry from 23 March 145.

Panzer IVs of *Panzergruppe "Streith", I.* (self-propelled) and *II.* (towed) *Abteilung/Panzer-Artillerie-Regiment 73* and a few tank destroyers. The group reached the positions of *23. Panzer-Division* around 1000 hours in the morning between Litér and Balatonfűzfő. The *1. Panzer-Division* successfully completed the breakout manoeuvre and afterwards, was assembled in the sector of Balatonfüred, Vörösberény and Balatonalmádi.[1510] One of the soldiers of *Panzer-Nachrichten-Abteilung 37* noted the following in his diary:

> *"Exactly at 2400 hours, Major Behaim-Schwarz Bach's group began the attack. Besides the pioneers and the reinforced radio company of Panzer-Nachrichten-Abteilung 37, I. (Abteilung)/Panzer-Artillerie-Regiment 73 of Major Theilen prepared with their Hummels, also significant numbers of vehicles with high firepower, among them armoured fighting vehicles and guns.*
> *The attack began with a surprise artillery barrage. On the other side, only a few 2 cm guns stirred, left of us. These were held down by our 2 cm anti-aircraft guns while the assault group set off. To our great surprise we saw nothing and heard nothing of the enemy.*
> *After crossing the enemy blocking position, the group "Behaim" was again gathering, because at first, the route ahead was to be inspected. One of the tanks that started off northwards, against all warnings, had been knocked out by the enemy from a great distance. The column diverted toward the south, then again toward the west, and was going on continuously, only hindered by occasional mortar fire. By 1600 hours, they reached a farmstead on the Berhida–Küngös road, where they found two abandoned German Panzer Vs. From here, we started off on reconnaissance missions in different directions."*[1511]

After crossing the Berhida–Küngös road, the German group received tank gun and artillery fire from the left and right. A few of the *Hummel* self-propelled howitzers tried to break out towards the west at high speed. The column was protected against the Soviet rifle infantry attacking from the left by the machine gun fire of the signals armoured personnel carriers. The German group was moving toward the west very slowly while they were targeted by the Soviet mortars and anti-tank guns.[1512]

A soldier of *4. Batterie/Panzer-Artillerie-Regiment 37*, Heinz Engelhard, who was seriously wounded during the breakout attempt, noted down his memories three years later:

> *"Wherever I look, dead soldiers, staggering figures; these are anything but humans anymore. There – I am shivering at the sight – a tank rushes over three wounded soldiers lying on the ground. The night is as bright as the daylight and so full of noises that it swallows all screams for help. Vehicles crashed upon vehicles, guns and tanks everywhere; everybody wants to flee this chaos. Not even a hand would fit into the space between them in this grand chaos. Here a direct hit from an anti-tank gun, there a bomb, there again an*

1510   Stoves, Rolf: Persönliches Kriegstagebuch Pz.Rgt. 1 (typewritten manuscript, a copy owned by the author), entry from 23March 1945.
1511   Quoted by Stoves, O. G. Rolf: *1. Panzer-Division 1935–1945. Chronik einer der drei Stamm-Division der deutschen Panzerwaffe.* Bad Nauheim, 1961. p. 765.
1512   Stoves, O. G. Rolf: *1. Panzer-Division 1935–1945. Chronik einer der drei Stamm-Division der deutschen Panzerwaffe.* Bad Nauheim, 1961. p. 767.

armour-piercing shell – misery, destruction and complete devastation everywhere. What is now a man's life here? I feel miserable. There is no consolation or a word for us, those who lie about in the most wretched state; only one aim drives everyone – away from this hell. I close my eyes and grind my teeth – the tracks will reach me in seconds. A strong pull and the tank stops. I hear that they are calling my name, and I open my eyes, pushing myself towards 'Heinz'. He gets out of the escape hatch and picks me up; I could scream in pain, but at least he helps me. 'Thank you Heinz' – I mumble. The crew is cursing, they don't want to take me with them, and one even treads on my finger. This is the first moment in the war when I shed a tear. Are these comrades? Heartless people... I feel myself like a piece of meat that is kicked and tossed about.

The commander of the tank, a Leutnant, orders me to be picked up immediately, to avoid any further delays. They lay me on a pile of shells, directly beneath the breech of the gun. A strong pull and the tank is in motion again. I feel I am saved. I am thinking about Heinz – he is a real comrade. I met him at the Hannover tank driver school and later we camped together at Weimar. I only see the outlines of the armour and the blinding light. A swarm of parachuted trace lights above us. The Russian aircraft are constantly looking for new and better spots to shoot. The sound of the tank engine prevents me to hear the hellish noise of the outside combat. The explosive shells are ricocheting from the steel armour. The tracer machine gun rounds are alarmingly beautiful as they flew past us, to bring death to others.

The tank stops. The crew jump out in combat gear and submachine guns in hand. The engine is running still, as well as that tank in the coverage of which the team goes forward. A bright flash before my eyes, and my ears stuck in; I sense blood on my lips and I can feel around with my tongue to know where I was hit. A lukewarm thing also over my left eye; the shrapnel of a mortar shell. The crew crawls back, the tank turns over to direct firing, and the gun barrel over me slides left and right – It is terribly hot in there. At each shell that they pull out from under me, I could scream. I lose my consciousness again.

When I wake up, it's a whole new day. Over me it is clear sky, and peace all around; no firing, no tracer bullets, no bomber aircraft, no anti-tank guns, no tanks and machine guns. The calmness feels so good. The crew is sleeping, one of them asks for the time. '0830' says one, and he goes back to sleep instantly. Have I been sleeping as well? We drive for 10 more minutes. The tank stops, and a stretcher is put upon it. I again lose my consciousness."[1513]

The Soviet troops set off from the sector of Berhida and with a night attack, supported by armoured fighting vehicles, occupied Papkeszi and Vilonya. Thus, by the dawn of 23 March 1945, they arrived in the rear positions of *3.* and *4. Kavallerie-Divisions*, and also *23. Panzer-Division*, that were still being established.

In the morning, Soviet armoured fighting vehicles and rifle infantry bypassed the fortifications of *23. Panzer-Division,* established in the sector of Manómajor. The last three armoured fighting vehicles of *Panzer-Regiment 23* reported to have knocked out a T–34/85.

1513 Engelhard, Heinz: *24 Stunden an der Ost-Front in Ungarn.* Szerzői magákiadás. Darmstadt, 1948. pp. 10-12. The author mistakenly placed the date of the breakout for the night of 18/19 March 1945.

The last Panther was knocked out by the Soviets, and one of the two remaining assault guns was hit on its barrel, therefore it had to be sent back. The last remaining assault gun was sunken in, so it had to be blown up. Afterwards, the Soviets pushed the units of *23. Panzer-Division* back to the hills east of Balatonfűzfő.

The *3.* and *4. Kavallerie-Division* had given up the sector of Balatonkenese and, together with *I. (Abteilung)/Panzer-Regiment 24,* was in defence on the Vörösberény north–Szentkirályszabadja line. The armoured personnel carriers and anti-aircraft guns of *schwere Kavallerie-Abteilung 3* had repulsed the Soviet tanks and rifle infantry that were breaking in north of Vörösberény, and then established holding positions.[1514] Most likely this would have happened only after the six remaining combat-ready Panthers of *I. (Abteilung)/Panzer-Regiment 24,* subordinated to *3. Kavallerie-Division,* reported to have knocked out four T–34/85s and two SU–100 self-propelled guns north of Vörösberény.[1515]

The German columns retreating along Lake Balaton generated dense traffic which jammed the roads. On many occasions, chaos and desperation started to take over. All of this was made worse by the constant harassment of the Soviet ground attack aircraft and the ever increasing intensity of Soviet tank raids.[1516]

During the night, *I. Kavallerie-Korps* received almost nine tons of ammunition supplies, flown in by 10 Ju 52 aircraft.[1517]

During the day, the Soviets were continuing their attacks, with approximately 70 armoured fighting vehicles, along the northern shore of Lake Balaton, toward the northwest. At the same time, they were also advancing from the sector of Papkeszi toward the south-west with rifle forces that were supported by a number of armoured fighting vehicles. Following the constant strain of combat in the past few days, the German cavalry and *Panzergrenadier* units, were unable to repel these attacks anymore, and with this, the hastily established defence on the Balatonfűzfő–Királyszentistván line, collapsed. Afterwards, *I. Kavallerie-Korps* tried to retreat to the assigned area between Balatonalmádi and the south-western edge of Szentkirályszabadja, which was part of the *Klara-Stellung*.[1518]

On the night of 22/23 March 1945, on the front of *9. SS-Panzer-Division,* the Soviets increased the intensity of their attacks from the north and they occupied the sector of Sóly and Vilonya. In the center and on the right flank of the *Division,* combat was constantly raging where the Soviets had taken Papkeszi.

During these actions, *SS-Panzer-Regiment 9,* had again knocked out a significant number of Soviet armoured vehicles, but the Soviets also rendered many German tanks and assault guns unusable, and many had been blown up due to shortage of fuel.[1519]

On 22 and 23 March 1945, *9. SS-Panzer-Division* and *23. Panzer-Division* reported to have knocked out 102 Soviet armoured fighting vehicles.[1520] Of these, *23. Panzer-Division*

1514 Witte, Hans Joachim – Offermann, Peter: *Die Boeselagerschen Reiter. Das Kavallerie-Regiment Mitte und die aus ihm hervorgegangene 3. Kavallerie-Brigade/Division.* München, 1998. p. 415.
1515 Senger und Etterlin, von F.M. jr.: *Die 24. Panzer-Division vormals 1. Kavallerie-Division 1939–1945.* Neckargemünd, 1962. p. 310.
1516 Rebentisch, Ernst: *Zum Kaukasus und zu den Tauern. Die Geschichte der 23. Panzer-Division 1941–1945.* Esslingen, 1963. pp. 497-498.
1517 NARA, T311, R162, F7214729.
1518 NARA, T311, R162, F7214726.
1519 Tieke, Wilhelm: *Von Plattensee bis Österreich. Heeresgruppe Süd 1945.* Gummersbach, without year of publication, p. 73.
1520 Tieke, Wilhelm: *Von Plattensee bis Österreich. Heeresgruppe Süd 1945.* Gummersbach, without year of publication, p. 73.

knocked out six.[1521] Thus, 96 victories remain, which were reported by the troops of the *9. SS-Panzer-Division*. One of these was witnessed by a soldier of *Mörser-Bataillon 44*, *Obergefreiter* (Corporal) Hans Hacker, who was with his comrades sitting mounted on the armoured fighting vehicles of *SS-Panzer-Regiment 9* heading west from Istvánmajor, when, after covering a few kilometres, Soviet tanks attacked them. One of the German armoured fighting vehicles was hit and blown up. The armoured column created a smoke screen. *Obergefreiter* Hacker remembers:

> "*I was sitting on the tank before the last one in one of the columns. Suddenly a huge enemy tank appeared from the right, behind a hill. Because of its elevated position it might not have been able to directly target us. But the last tank had already stopped, turned its gun and with two shots knocked the Russian out.*"[1522]

A few, still combat-ready Tiger B heavy tanks and other armoured fighting vehicles of the German *schwere Panzer-Abteilung 509*, were retreating from Hill 228 (Kőhegy) to Sándorka on the night of 22/23 March 1945, then heading further toward the west. A soldier of the *Stab/Mörser-Bataillon 44*, Karl Masanec, was completely alone and wounded when he stumbled upon the armoured fighting vehicles in the dark:

> "*After a time – I was completely alone – I stumbled upon an armoured unit in a deeper section, which I joined. I heard from people talking, that a few hundred meters ahead of us, there is a farmstead[1523]. The road there was like an embankment, left and right of the road there was a swampy area. We could only proceed along this road, and the Soviets knew this as well. The enemy established a hedgehog position on the farmstead with three–four anti-tank guns. They set fire to the buildings, so the area in front of the farmstead was well lit. After a briefing of a few officers, the four armoured fighting vehicles, amongst us a Königstiger also, luckily, went into attack position: the Königstiger at the front and the smaller ones behind it. Other tracked vehicles were following. We - a few hundred soldiers – closed up.*
> *Upon orders, the attack has been launched. Our armoured fighting vehicles and the other vehicles were firing from their guns and machine guns and rushing towards the farmstead; we were following them, shouting. The Russians have also been firing at us madly. Their shells ricocheted off the Königstiger. The tracers were nice; this was like a fireworks, but sadly too stern for that. The tanks and the other vehicles made it through and crushed the positions of the enemy anti-tank guns. The Russians were fleeing. We infantrymen were gathering at the back of the farmstead and soon we marched away.*"[1524]

[1521] See Rebentisch, Ernst: *Zum Kaukasus und zu den Tauern. Die Geschichte der 23. Panzer-Division 1941-1945*. Stuttgart, 1982. p. 571. o.

[1522] Quoted by Agis, Hermann: *Das Ende am Plattensee. Die Hoch- und Deutschmeister (44. I.D.) im Endkampf*. Nürnberg, 2006. p. 219. Soon after this the soldiers dismounted the armoured fighting vehicles and went along on foot. They did not regret it though, because they all felt sick from the exhaust smoke.

[1523] This was most likely Fodorpuszta, northeast of Küngös.

[1524] Quoted by Agis, Hermann: *Das Ende am Plattensee. Die Hoch- und Deutschmeister (44. I.D.) im Endkampf*. Nürnberg, 2006. p. 229.

By dawn the Tiger Bs reached the hills between Manómajor and Istvánmajor, where they established perimeter defences. At dawn, the positions of *schwere Panzer-Abteilung 509* around Manómajor, were reached by another group of *Mörser-Bataillon 44* arriving from a different direction. The adjutant of the *Abteilung* remembered it this way:

"In the morning twilight, I saw a few Königstigers in front of us among the trees which believed us to be attacking Russians, and opened fire at us from all barrels. Although we have not sung the German anthem, we screamed and shouted all sorts of messages in German to our SS-colleagues[1525], until they realized their mistake and stopped firing. I have again learnt something: now I knew what it feels like lying in the cross hairs of a firing Königstiger and an MG42."[1526]

During the day the Tiger Bs attacked the Soviet tank forces advancing on Papkeszi via Küngös and knocked out a number of armoured fighting vehicles, most likely in the sector of the 18th Tank Corps, which slowed down the Soviet attack. On 22 and 23 March 1945, *schwere Panzer-Abteilung 509* reported to have knocked out eight T–34/85s and eight ISU–122 self-propelled guns. Their own losses amounted to three Tiger Bs, one of which was blown up by the Germans themselves.[1527]

Along the road south of Litér, a few repaired Panthers of *1. Panzer-Division* were standing guard from 0100 hours in order to keep the road open towards the west for those who had successfully broken out. Four hours later, they noticed the advance of 14 Soviet tanks, of which, according to the diary of one of the loaders, 13 were knocked out.[1528] These were most likely the T–34/85s of the 20th Guards Tank Brigade/5th Guards Tank Corps.[1529] Around 1500 hours, the German armoured fighting vehicles retreated to Balatonfüred because of the ever increasing Soviet pressure, together with the *Panzergrenadiers* who were withdrawing after having broken out of the salient.[1530]

The remnants of *5. SS-Panzer-Division* were fighting their way back toward Balatonfűzfő between Papkeszi and Balatonkenese. *Panzer-Feldersatz Bataillon 5* attempted to establish positions south of Litér.[1531]

By 1130 hours the 181st Tank Brigade/18th Tank Corps, together with the 1438th Self-Propelled Artillery Regiment, reached Rostáspuszta and Sáripuszta, two to three

---

[1525] The armoured fighting vehicles of *9. SS-Panzer-Division* were also in combat in the area, but *schwere Panzer-Abteilung 509* was of course not an *SS*-unit.
[1526] Quoted by Agis, Hermann: *Das Ende am Plattensee. Die Hoch- und Deutschmeister (44. I.D.) im Endkampf.* Nürnberg, 2006. p. 224.
[1527] *History of the schwere Panzer-Abteilung 509* (typewritten manuscript). Copy owned by the author. p. 57. The German unit history mentions IS–2 tanks, however, as there were no such tanks deployed in the area, these were most likely ISU–122 or ISU–152 armoured fighting vehicles of the 363rd Guards Heavy Self-Propelled Artillery Regiment/18th Tank Corps. At the same time, the 18th Tank Corps did not report any burnt out heavy self-propelled guns for these two days, therefore the Soviet armoured fighting vehicles could only have been damaged lightly. This is also highly likely because the repairable (or thought to be so) armoured fighting vehicle losses were not always reported by the Soviet troops, according to the experiences of the author.
[1528] See Krüger, Erich: Kriegstagebuch. Typewritten manuscript. Copy owned by the author. entry from 23 March 1945. The documents of the 18th Tank Corps has not verified such losses.
[1529] Central Archives of the Russian Defence Ministry (Podolsk), f. 3403, op. 1, gy. 69, li. 314.
[1530] See Krüger, Erich: Kriegstagebuch. Typewritten manuscript. Copy owned by the author. entry from 23 March 1945.
[1531] Tieke, Wilhelm: *Von Plattensee bis Österreich. Heeresgruppe Süd 1945.* Gummersbach, without year of publication, p. 73.

km east-north-east of Papkeszi, and at the end of the day they were engaged in combat on the western edge of Balatonfűzfő together with the 32nd Motorized Rifle Brigade. By the evening, the 181st Tank Brigade had six remaining operational T–34/85s, and the 1438th Self-Propelled Artillery Regiment had 10 SU–76Ms. 30 new tanks were en route to the 181st Tank Brigade.[1532]

The 110th Tank Brigade, together with the 363rd Guards Heavy Self-Propelled Artillery Regiment, were in combat at Papkeszi at the end of the day. During the day, the Germans knocked out four T–34/85s of the Brigade, one of which was burnt out.[1533] From the sector of Papkeszi they continued their advance together with the grouping of the 181st Tank Brigade toward the west, in the direction of Vilonya–Királyszentistván–Szentkirályszabadja–Veszprémfajsz–Tótvázsony. The 170th Tank Brigade was marching on the Cece–Tác route with 31 new T–34/85s, following the Corps in the direction of Polgárdi, then around 1800 hours they joined the attack of the 32nd Motorized Rifle Brigade, and then followed the 110th and 181st Tank Brigades.[1534]

On 22 and 23 March1945, the 18th Tank Corps destroyed 12 German tanks, 26 armoured personnel carriers, 13 guns, six mortars and 20 machine guns, plus captured two tanks, eight guns, 18 cars, 17 six-barrelled rocket-launchers (*Nebelwerfer*). In the evening, they had 53 operational T–34/85s with an additional 32 en route as a supplement, five ISU–152s, nine ISU–122s and 10 SU–76M self-propelled guns.[1535]

Around 1000 hours, the 1st Guards Mechanized Corps received orders in the sector of Papkeszi, to attack towards Alsódakapuszta, north-east of Balatonfűzfő, with its 3rd Guards Mechanized Brigade, and toward Balatonfűzfő with the 9th Guards Tank Brigade and the 1st Guards Mechanized Brigade arriving from Polgárdi. The units arrived in their sectors by 1600 hours. During the fighting that day, the Corps reported to have destroyed eight German armoured fighting vehicles, six armoured personnel carriers[1536], 50 cars and 12 guns. Their own losses amounted to six knocked out M4A2s, three of which were burnt out.

Around 2000 hours the 2nd Guards Mechanized Brigade was placed back under the command of its own Corps.

Around 2030 hours, the 1st Guards Mechanized Corps were withdrawn from the front with 98 operational M4A2s, two T–34s, and 14 SU–100 self-propelled guns, and were assembled at Nádasdladány and Jenő.[1537]

At 1500 hours, the 71st Tank Regiment/5th Guards Cavalry Corps with 13 T–34/85s, was supporting the cavalry troops 1.5 km southeast of Balatonfűzfő, and the 1896th Self-Propelled Artillery Regiment, with 14 SU–76Ms was supporting the units at the road

---

1532 Central Archives of the Russian Defence Ministry (Podolsk), f. 3415, op. 1, gy. 85, li. 21/2. On 21 and 22 March three train-loads, altogether 60 new T–34/85 tanks arrived at the train station of Sárbogárd. Of these, 30 were assigned to the 170th Tank Brigade, and 30 to the 181th Tank Brigade.
1533 War log of the 18th Tank Corps for March 1945. Copy owned by the author. p. 41.
1534 Central Archives of the Russian Defence Ministry (Podolsk), f. 3415, op. 1, gy. 85, li. 21/2.
1535 Central Archives of the Russian Defence Ministry (Podolsk), f. 243, op. 2928, gy. 131, li. 268.
1536 Among these was the armoured personnel carrier, in which the *Kommandeur* of the German *44. Reichsgrenadier-Division*, *Generalleutnant* Hans-Günther von Rost died in action.
1537 Central Archives of the Russian Defence Ministry (Podolsk), f. 243, op. 2928, gy. 131, li. 268.

crossing 1 km northeast of Fűzfő-gyártelep.[1538] The 54th Tank Regiment was assembled in Siófok, with 10 T–34/85s.[1539]

By 1900 hours that evening, the Soviet 209th Self-Propelled Artillery Brigade/26th Army, was supporting the rifle forces and the 1st Guards Mechanized Corps. The 1951st Self-Propelled Artillery Regiment was fighting with four SU–100s in the sector of Füle, and with 11 SU–100s at the north-western edge of Öregerdő north-west of there. The 1952nd Self-Propelled Artillery Regiment, with 12 SU–100s, together with the 2nd Guards Mechanized Brigade, reached Vilonya, and the 1953rd Self-Propelled Artillery Regiment, with 10 SU–100s, and together with the forces of the 66th Guards Rifle Division, reached Kiskovácsipuszta southeast of Berhida. In the evening, the Brigade had 36 operational SU–100s, two SU–57s and two T–34s. At 2200 hours, the unit, by orders of the 3rd Ukrainian Front, was subordinated to the 27th Army and was assembled in the sector of Vilonya.[1540]

Around 1300 hours, the 22nd Independent Tank Regiment that was withdrawn from combat the day before, set off from Enying to Baja. There were only four T–34s, one KV–1S and three SU–76s in its ranks.[1541]

The Soviet 1202nd Self-Propelled Artillery Regiment/27th Army, was in firing positions two km north-east of Polgárdi with 20 SU–76Ms.[1542] The Regiment took part in occupying Jenő on the same day.[1543]

On the night of 22/23 March 1945, in the front of *IV. SS-Panzerkorps,* the Soviet troops continued their offensive from the sector of Sóly toward the south-west with approximately 60 armoured fighting vehicles and rifle infantry. In the meantime, they occupied Litér and broke through the defences of *9. SS-Panzer-Division*, then reached the sector two km north-east of Szentkirályszabadja. South of Litér, the defence was manned by those units of *5. SS-Panzer-Division* that had successfully broken through together with the *Panzer-Feldersatz Bataillon* of the *Division*.[1544] The Soviet forces that were attacking from the direction of Hajmáskér, were advancing toward the west and south-west, and occupied Kádárta and Gyulafirátót.[1545]

A Soviet 18th Guards Mechanized Brigade and the 46th Guards Tank Brigade of the 9th Guards Mechanized Corps, bypassed Veszprém from the north, and approached to within three km of Márkó from the east, on the road leading to Városlőd. Here, the 8.8 cm guns of *I. (Abteilung)/Flak-Artillerie-Regiment 25* reported to have knocked out 20 Soviet armoured fighting vehicles.[1546]

The forces of the 5th Guards Tank Corps were attacking towards Veszprém. The 20th Guards Tank Brigade, arriving from Litér, bypassed the town from the north, and the 22nd Guards Tank Brigade, which turned north again from Fűzfő-gyártelep (industrial

---

1538 Central Archives of the Russian Defence Ministry (Podolsk), f. 243, op. 2928, gy. 178, li. 99.
1539 Central Archives of the Russian Defence Ministry (Podolsk), f. 243, op. 2928, gy. 131, li. 268.
1540 Central Archives of the Russian Defence Ministry (Podolsk), f. 243, op. 2928, gy. 131, li. 267.
1541 Central Archives of the Russian Defence Ministry (Podolsk), f. 243, op. 2928, gy. 131, li. 267. Based on these, the tank regiment arrived at the Sió Canal with 19 armoured fighting vehicles and during March of 1945, totally lost nine T–34s, one SU–76M, and one SU–85.
1542 Central Archives of the Russian Defence Ministry (Podolsk), f. 243, op. 2928, gy. 131, li. 267.
1543 See Central Archives of the Russian Defence Ministry (Podolsk), f. 381, op. 8378, gy. 590, li. 61.
1544 NARA, T311, R163, F7215436.
1545 NARA, T311, R162, F7214726.
1546 NARA, T311, R162, F7214726.

site), bypassed the town from the south-east. The 6th Guards Motorized Rifle Brigade and the 51st Guards Self-Propelled Artillery Brigade, in the meantime, was pushing through Veszprém in a six-hour long battle.[1547]

The town fell into Soviet hands around 1800 hours, after the weakened German *3. Panzer-Division*, which did not have any heavy armament in this sector,[1548] was not able to stop the units of the 5th Guards Tank Corps that were attacking from the north with approximately 50 armoured fighting vehicles. The Soviet 20th Guards Tank Brigade established defensive positions on the north-west edge of the town, the 6th Guards Motorized Rifle Brigade on the western, and the 22nd Guards Tank Brigade occupied defensive positions on the south-east edge of the town.[1549]

The Corps lost one T–34/85 on that day, and the 364th Guards Heavy Self-Propelled Artillery Brigade lost two ISU–122s[1550]. In the evening, the 5th Guards Tank Corps had 65 operational tanks and 14 SU–76Ms, the 51st Guards Self-Propelled Artillery Brigade had 49 SU–76Ms and four T–70s, and the 364th Guards Heavy Self-Propelled Artillery Regiment had 15 ISU–122s.[1551] The combat value of the Corps' own armoured forces had significantly decreased in the last few days:

- in the 20th Guards Tank Brigade there were 16 operational tanks, eight of them without a gun sight, and so far 24 armoured fighting vehicles had been destroyed and 11 needed repairs;
- the 21st Guards Tank Brigade with 17 combat-ready tanks was in reserve;
- the 22nd Guards Tank Brigade had 26 operational tanks;
- in the 1458th Self-Propelled Artillery Regiment there were 12 operational SU–76Ms.[1552]

The Germans did not launch a counterattack to reclaim the lost town. Instead, they started to establish new defensive positions on the Szentkirályszabadja south-west edge–Veszprém south-west–Márkó east general line.

The Soviet 208th Self-Propelled Artillery Brigade was subordinated to the 5th Guards Tank Corps. The 1016th and 1922nd Self-Propelled Artillery Regiments, with 18, and 15 operational SU–100 self-propelled guns respectively, together with the 20th Guards Tank Brigade, were attacking towards Veszprém and lost a burnt out SU–100. The 1068th Self-Propelled Artillery Regiment had seven operational SU–100s left.[1553]

The two 10.5 cm field howitzer batteries of *SS-Kampfgruppe "Bernau"*, occupying the eastern edge of Inota, were showering harassing fire on the Soviet supply columns moving around Csór and destroyed a number of trucks. When three Soviet tanks set off from Csór

---

1547 Central Archives of the Russian Defence Ministry (Podolsk), f. 243, op. 2928, gy. 131, li. 266.
1548 *Panzer-Regiment 6/3. Panzer-Division* had so few combat-ready tanks, *Jagdpanzers* and assault guns, that they were concentrated in one of the companies of each of *I.* and *II. Abteilungs*. The 53 crewmen that were without vehicles, were formed into an infantry armoured escort section.. See Munzel, Oskar: *Gekämpft – gesiegt – verloren. Geschichte des Panzerregiments 6 1740–1980*. Herford–Bonn, 1980. p. 182.
1549 Central Archives of the Russian Defence Ministry (Podolsk), f. 243, op. 2928, gy. 131, li. 266.
1550 The armoured fighting vehicle losses of the 20th Guards Tank Brigade at dawn on the outskirts of Litér are not included here. They might have deemed their T–34/85 tanks repairable.
1551 Central Archives of the Russian Defence Ministry (Podolsk), f. 243, op. 2928, gy. 178, li. 100.
1552 War log of the 5th Guards Tank Corps for March 1945. Copy owned by the author. pp. 16-17.
1553 Central Archives of the Russian Defence Ministry (Podolsk), f. 243, op. 2928, gy. 131, li. 97.

to Inota, the Germans knocked out one of them with a *Panzerfaust*. Finally, the German *Kampfgruppe* retreated to the sector of Veszprém.[1554]

In the front of *IV. SS-Panzerkorps*, imposing extremely strict disciplinary measures, the efforts of the dedicated generals and staff officers, were at last successful in assembling the scattered remnants of the leaderless units wandering about, and sending them back into the frontline.[1555]

General der Panzertruppe Balck reported to the *Heeresgruppe* on that morning, that the units of the German *6. Armee* were no longer fighting with the spirit expected of them. Many were saying that the war was practically lost and they did not want to be killed before the imminent end of hostilities. Everyone was afraid that the Soviets would encircle them, because nobody believed that their own troops could effectively relieve them anymore.[1556]

On the front of the German *I. SS-Panzerkorps/6. Panzerarmee*, the scattered units of *1. SS-Panzer-Division* continued their defensive battle without contact with each other. The units of *SS-Panzergrenadier-Regiment 2*, joining the forces of *12. SS-Panzer-Division*, were actively retreating to the line of the hills west of Lókút–Zirc. Units of *SS-Panzergrenadier-Regiment 1*, together with the remnants of *SS-Panzer-Regiment 1*, supported by *SS-Panzer-Flak-Abteilung 1* and units of *SS-Panzerjäger-Abteilung 1*, were in combat around Veszprém, but the town was still given up that afternoon.

As the southern combat group, commanded by the *Divisionskommandeur* reached the front of the German *6. Armee*, *General der Panzertruppe* Hermann Balck, the commander of the *Armee*, ordered Kumm's *Divisionskampfgruppe* into their direct subordination. Balck ordered them to disengage from the enemy north of Veszprém, toward Hajmáskér and Kádárta, and establish positions east of Márkó.

During the day, the commander of the armoured group in combat around Veszprém, *SS-Sturmbannführer* Poetschke, was in a briefing with other officers, when a mortar attack hit them. He was mortally wounded and died the following day.[1557] With this, *SS-Obersturmbannführer* Peiper had lost almost all of his experienced commanders in just three days, with whom he had been together since 1942.[1558]

Eight other tank commanders were also wounded. The combat group was left without a commander and with their nine remaining combat-ready armoured fighting vehicles, they tried to reach Márkó from the area of Veszprém.

In the aftermath of the battle around Veszprém, *1. SS-Panzer-Division* was nothing more than a loose group of small-scale combat units. It was not possible to talk about

---

1554 Bernau, Günter: Aus den letzten Kämpfen in Ungarn 1945. I./SS-Panzer-Artillerie-Regiment 5. In: *Deutsches Soldatenjahrbuch 1975*. p. 215.
1555 NARA, T311, R162, F7214727.
1556 NARA, T311, R162, F7214734.
1557 The lower part of *SS-Sturmbannführer* Poetschke's right leg was severely injured. The SS-clearing stations were at that time withdrawing from the approaching Soviets, therefore he was transported to a *Luftwaffe* clearing station with delays. He did not let the doctors amputate his leg. By the evening, his condition was turning for the worse, and he died by the morning, most likely his circulation had collapsed. According to the doctor of *I. (Abteilung)/SS-Panzer-Regiment 1*, amputation might have saved his life, but many knew that Poetschke was saying that if he could not get into a tank again, he would rather shoot himself in the head. See Agte, Patrick: *Jochen Peiper. Kommandeur Panzerregiment Leibstandarte*. Berg am Starnberger See, 1998. p. 357.
1558 Westemeier, Jens: *Joachim Peiper (1915–1976). SS-Standartenführer. Eine Biographie*. Osnabrück, 1996. p. 105. Peiper himself was more lucky. In 1945 his command tank had been hit a number of times within two days, but he did not suffer any serious injuries.

regiments or battalions anymore. The remaining Panzer IVs of *I. (Abteilung)/Panzer-Regiment 1* were commanded by *SS-Hauptsturmführer* Klingelhöfer, while the command of the remaining Tiger Bs and Panthers was taken over by *SS-Hauptsturmführer* Birnschein. The *Abteilungsstab* was removed from the chain of command and the only job left for them was the organization of supplies.[1559]

Various parts of *3. SS-Panzer-Division* were engaged in close quarters combat in Veszprém on the same day, and other units were in defence around Csesznek.[1560]

On the front of *12. SS-Panzer-Division*, the units of the *Divisionsbegleitkompanie* securing Olaszfalu from the east were withdrawn to Lókút sometime after 0300 hours.

During the day, the Soviets had taken Zirc, which was defended by the armoured personnel carriers of *III. (Bataillon)/SS-Panzergrenadier-Regiment 26*. Afterwards, the *Bataillon* retreated to Pénzeskút. Against the Soviet troops attacking towards Olaszfalu, *SS-Panzer-Flak-Abteilung 12* was defending Putrimajor until late in the night. The soldiers of *2. and 4. Batteries*, now fighting as infantry, were supported by the guns of *1. Batterie* switched over to an anti-tank role, which knocked out five Soviet armoured fighting vehicles. The *Flak-Abteilung* also retreated to Pénzeskút on the night of 23/24 March 1945.

At Lókút, the day was spent relatively calmly, with the Germans only knocking out a Soviet armoured reconnaissance vehicle. The positions of *SS-Panzergrenadier-Regiment 26* and *II. (Abteilung)/SS-Panzer-Regiment 12*, were hit by a significant Soviet attack from the east around 1930 hours. Covering fire of the German artillery repulsed the attack. At 2200 hours, the Soviets launched a new assault. The *SS-Panzergrenadiers* and the armoured fighting vehicles defended the village for some time, then at 0015 hours, they cleared Lókút and retreated toward Pénzeskút. During the fighting, according to their reports, they knocked out three Soviet tanks. The left flank of the division at Csesznek was covered by *SS-Panzer-Aufklärungs-Abteilung 12,* but despite this, the Soviets broke through them.

The worn out forces of *12. SS-Panzer-Division*, without *SS-Panzergrenadier-Regiment 25* and *SS-Panzerjäger-Abteilung 12*, but with units of *3. SS-Panzer-Division* in subordination, would have to hold a 16 km long frontline which lay across a forested area. Therefore, the defence could only be concentrated in the area of villages and roads, much like fortified points. The supply problems had been worsened due to the fact that, because of the Soviet advance, the *Division* had only one, not even fully usable supply line in the direction of Zirc–Pénzeskút–Bakonybél–Bakonykoppány–Pápa.[1561]

At Pénzeskút, *1. and 3. Batteries* of *SS-Panzer-Flak-Abteilung 12* were in defence on the night of 23/24 March 1945. The *1. Batterie* reported to have knocked out eight Soviet tanks, most likely from the Soviet 9th Guards Mechanized Corps.[1562]

The Soviets set off from the western outskirts of Gyulafirátót and crossed the Veszprém–Zirc railroad line. The rifle forces of the Soviet 9th Guards Army, attacking from Olaszfalu

---

1559 Tiemann, Ralf: *Die Leibstandarte*. Band IV/2. Osnabrück, 1987. pp. 322-325.
1560 Tieke, Wilhelm: *Von Plattensee bis Österreich. Heeresgruppe Süd 1945*. Gummersbach, without year of publication, p. 74.
1561 Meyer, Hubert: *Kriegsgeschichte der 12. SS-Panzerdivision „Hitlerjugend"*. Band II. Osnabrück, 1987. 2nd edition. p. 513.
1562 Stöber, Hans: *Die Flugabwehrverbände der Waffen-SS. Aufstellung, Gliederung, Luftverteidigung und Einsätze an den Fronten*. Preussisch Oldendorf, 1984. p. 248.

toward the west, had thrown the Germans back to Lókút and into the hills north of there. The Soviets also launched an armoured attack against Lókút from the south-east, but this attempt was held by the Germans. In the evening, the Soviets repeated the attempt with two battalions and the support of armoured fighting vehicles. The units of *3. SS* and *12. SS-Panzer-Division* tried to establish a secure line between Csesznek and Bakonyszentkirály, in the *Klara-Stellung*, but the Soviets quickly broke through this.[1563]

The 30th Guards and 31st Guards Mechanized Brigade/9th Guards Mechanized Corps/6th Guards Tank Army, occupied Zirc, then around 1700 hours, reached Pénzeskút. By the end of the day, the 30th Guards Mechanized Brigade had reached Bakonybél, where an extremely complex situation had been unfolding. A soldier of *SS-Panzer-Nachrichten-Abteilung 12*, Georg Jestadt, was an eyewitness to the events at Bakonybél:

"Hastily, a new defence line has been dug out in front of the village. In the background, two Panzer IVs were waiting for ammunition, which just has not arrived. On the two sides, hills and forests were surrounding us, which encircled the village quite closely on the southern side. Bakonybél was nestled in the bottom of a valley. The whole place was crowned by a 700 meter high, densely forested mountain wall. At the western end of the village, the road leads into a narrow and deep canyon which leads through a dense forest towards Bakonykoppány. In this cauldron, our columns were practically encircled from three sides. From the south, the assaulting Soviets were not able to break through. The mass of the troops on the road was impenetrable. Their command was lashing them: they were attacking here and there, but they were repulsed with huge losses. They were also coming with tanks where the terrain permitted, but these had been repulsed with Panzerfausts and Panzerschrecks. Nevertheless, they were there again after approximately two hours.
On the left, from the direction of Veszprém, there was an incoming road which was jammed just like the others due to the columns arriving on it. The masses of various carts on which the people fleeing were travelling, just worsened the situation. The road crossing was full – now nobody could go anywhere. On the right, there was a high wall and a monastery behind that. A Panther tank, which was still before the road crossing, turned its gun towards its rear armour, and rammed in the wall with full force. Through the hole and via the garden of the monastery, the traffic jam was slowly ebbing away. Then, in a low-altitude flight, a Soviet bomber formation was flying past. Now that's the end of us – many were thinking. But none of the bombs were dropped down on us. It would have been an immense catastrophe if they would have released their load here."[1564]

The 9th Guards Mechanized Corps lost during the day, 16 burnt out M4A2s[1565] and two SU–76Ms, and in the evening they had 85 tanks and 13 SU–76M self-propelled guns in operational condition.[1566]

1563 NARA, T311, R162, F7214727.
1564 Jestadt, Georg: *Ohne Siege und Hurra. Erlebnisse eines jungen Soldaten 1939–1945*. Norderstedt, 2005. p. 413.
1565 Central Archives of the Russian Defence Ministry (Podolsk), f. 243, op. 2928, gy. 178, li. 100.
1566 Central Archives of the Russian Defence Ministry (Podolsk), f. 243, op. 2928, gy. 131, li. 266.

The 1523rd Self-Propelled Artillery Regiment/9th Guards Army, was in firing position in Bakonycsernye with 17 SU–76Ms. The 1524th Self-Propelled Artillery Regiment, was fighting on the western edge of Olaszfalu with 25 SU–76Ms. The 1513th Self-Propelled Artillery Regiment's four SU–76Ms were in combat 1 km south of Litér.[1567]

The 4th Guards Army was concentrating its armoured forces in the sector of Bakonysárkány. West of the village 500 meters, at Györgymajor, the 366th Guards Heavy Self-Propelled Artillery Regiment was assembled, with six captured operational *Hummel* and one *Wespe* self-propelled howitzer, and three Panther tanks. Between Bakonysárkány and Hill 240 two km south of there, was the assembly area of the 207th Self-Propelled Artillery Brigade, but the unit, together with its 24 operational SU–100s, two SU–57s and two T–34s, set off from Gyulamajor north of Székesfehérvár only around 1300 hours. The independent self-propelled artillery battalions of the 4th Guards Army were supporting their divisions on that day, and lost four SU–76Ms. By the evening, these units had 54 operational self-propelled guns.[1568]

On the frontline of the 2nd Ukrainian Front

One of the combat groups of *6. Panzer-Division/II. SS-Panzerkorps* had broken into Réde, but the Soviets pushed them back with a counterattack. The *Kommandeur* of the German *II. (Bataillon)/Panzergrenadier-Regiment 114, Major* Gustav Reimar, was killed in this battle.[1569]

The Soviet units were attacking west and south-west of Réde, through the Bakony hills, with a battalion-size force. The Germans drew forward rapid reaction units, ad-hoc military units assembled for fast response, and with this, sealed off the area between Veszprémvarsány and Sikátor. Those Soviet forces who were attacking from the forest north of Ácsteszér at Bakonyszombathely, were pushed back by the Germans to the forest south of Bakonyszombathely. In the sector of Kisbér, the Germans had held off Soviet attacks of battalion-size forces.[1570]

The *2. SS-Panzer-Divisio,n* repulsed a Soviet attack that was launched between Ete and Csép, on a wide frontline with approximately division-size forces They also eliminated any penetrations and reported to have knocked out five Soviet armoured fighting vehicles.

South of Nagyigmánd, the right flank of *SS-Panzergrenadier-Regiment 4,* was hit by heavy Soviet attacks. The untrained *I. (Bataillon)/SS-Panzergrenadier-Regiment 4* suffered heavy losses.[1571]

The Soviets successfully widened one of their incursions on the north-eastern edge of Csép around nightfall, from the southern part of the village and to Point 158 west of there.

1567 Central Archives of the Russian Defence Ministry (Podolsk), f. 243, op. 2928, gy. 131, li. 267.
1568 Central Archives of the Russian Defence Ministry (Podolsk), f. 243, op. 2928, gy. 131, li. 267.
1569 Paul, Wolfgang: *Brennpunkte. Die Geschichte der 6. Panzerdivision (1. leichte) 1937–1945.* Krefeld, 1977. p. 450.
1570 NARA, T311, R162, F7214727.
1571 Tieke, Wilhelm: *Von Plattensee bis Österreich. Heeresgruppe Süd 1945.* Gummersbach, without year of publication, p. 75., furthermore Weidinger, Otto: *Division Das Reich. Der Weg der 2. SS-Panzer-Division „Das Reich".* Band V: 1943-1945. Osnabrück, without year of publication, p. 470.

The Soviet 56th Motorized Rifle Brigade/23rd Tank Corps was also engaged in combat here. The *SS*-troops launched a night counterattack.[1572]

Csép was attacked from the direction of Szend by the 3rd Tank Brigade and the 1501st Anti-Tank Artillery Regiment of the 23rd Tank Corps, while the 39th Tank Brigade with the 1443rd Self-Propelled Artillery Regiment, attacked from the direction of Szák. However, due to heavy German resistance, the Soviet tanks and self-propelled guns could only get as far as Csépi Creek, east of the village, by 1700 hours.[1573] As the bridges on the creek were blown up by the Germans, the Soviet armoured fighting vehicles set up concealed positions until the crossing was organized, meanwhile, firing at the German troops from these positions.[1574]

The German artillery destroyed the Soviet concentration of forces and armoured fighting vehicles that was detected at Thalypuszta.

The Soviet 1897th Self-Propelled Artillery Regiment, with the units of the 317th Rifle Division, was attacking towards Csép, and at 1200 hours, they reached Hill 132 which was 2.5 km north of the village, and Point 139, three km north-west of there. During these battles, the Soviet armoured fighting vehicles reported to have knocked out three captured 122 mm howitzers used by the Germans, plus three guns and four machine guns, and to have captured an operational German StuG. III assault gun. Their own losses included one burnt out SU–76M and one in need of major repairs, plus three men killed.[1575]

During the day, a part of *SS-Panzer-Aufklärungs-Abteilung 9* was subordinated to *II. SS-Panzerkorps*.[1576]

In the front of the German *XXXXIII. Armeekorps*, on the Kisigmánd–Mocsa line, the Soviets launched an attack on a wide frontline after a 15 minute long artillery barrage. The attack was launched against Nagyigmánd and Kisigmánd with battalion-size forces and 10 armoured fighting vehicles against each town, and against Mocsa with a force of two regiments. However the attackers were not able to break through toward Komárom on the Mocsa–Ács road, because the *Grenadiers of 356. Infanterie-Division* stopped them.[1577]

On the same day, the Soviet 991st Self-Propelled Artillery Regiment/46th Army, in subordination to the 99th Rifle Division, was supporting the rifle troops and launched multiple unsuccessful attacks to occupy Nagyigmánd, but in every single case they were held up by German tanks, assault guns, and infantry.[1578] In the 112th Independent Self-Propelled Artillery Battalion/99th Rifle Division, the commander of one of the SU–76M armoured fighting vehicles, 1st Lieutenant Fedorovsky, was killed on that day.[1579]

1572 NARA, T311, R162, F7214727.
1573 War log of the 23rd Tank Corps from March 1945. Copy owned by the author. p. 14.
1574 The main forces of the 23rd Tank Corps were not able to cross the creek on that day at Ete, because the Germans had blown up all of the bridges. Therefore the armoured fighting vehicles were gathering on the eastern bank of the creek. By 0600 hours in the morning on the next day, the 176th Engineering Pioneer Battalion had restored one of the bridges and thus the tanks and self-propelled guns were able to cross. See Central Archives of the Russian Defence Ministry (Podolsk), f. 240, op. 2799, gy. 357, li. 13.
1575 Central Archives of the Russian Defence Ministry (Podolsk), f. 240, op. 2799, gy. 342, li. 116.
1576 NARA, T311, R163, F7215443.
1577 NARA, T311, R162, F7214728.
1578 Central Archives of the Russian Defence Ministry (Podolsk), f. 240, op. 2799, gy. 342, li. 110.
1579 Central Archives of the Russian Defence Ministry (Podolsk), f. 961, op. 1, gy. 340, li. 163.

At dawn, the 1505th Self-Propelled Artillery Regiment was subordinated to the 52nd Rifle Division, and occupied firing positions two km north-west of Mocsa, on Hill 182 (Haraszti Hill).[1580]

Two kilometers north of Kisigmánd, at Újpuszta, the Soviets had broken into the German defences with 24 armoured fighting vehicles. At Kisigmánd, the worn and depleted company of the training school of *6. Panzer-Division*, was still holding their position, even when seven Soviet tanks got in their rear.[1581] From south-west and north-west, other forces of *6. Panzer-Division* launched a counterattack and reoccupied Újpuszta with armoured support. Against the Soviet forces that broke into the southern parts of Mocsa, another German counterattack was launched, which was still on going during the evening.[1582] In this area during the day, with permission granted from the *OKH*, the *Panzer-Abteilung* of *Panzer-Division "Feldherrnhalle"* and one of its *Panzergrenadier-Bataillons*, could have been deployed from the Komárom bridgehead, but the German *6. Panzerarmee* decided against it in the early afternoon.[1583]

The Staff of the Hungarian VIII Corps, together with the 2nd Honvéd Armoured Division, and with the remnants of the 1st Hussars Division moving beyond the frontline, were together assigned to secure the *Zsuzsanna-Stellung* in subordination to the *Befehlshaber des Rückwärtigen Heeresgebietes* (commander of the rear areas of the army) of *Heeresgruppe Süd*.[1584]

The Soviet 2nd Guards Mechanized Corps was at that moment, stationed in the vicinity of Kocs and was waiting to be deployed toward Győr. In the evening, the Corps had 47 operational T–34/85s, eight SU–85s, 17 SU–76Ms and three ISU–122 self-propelled guns.[1585]

In the bridgehead of the Hungarian 3rd Army, subordinated to the German *8. Armee*, the defenders repulsed a company-size attack east of Xavérmajor. Three kilometers south-south-west of Bajót, the Soviets occupied Hill 283, but the defenders soon reoccupied it. The Soviets had broken into the southern areas of Bajót, occupied Nagysáp, and established contact with the forces attacking from the Tát bridgehead southwards. With this move, the Soviets split the German–Hungarian bridgehead in two. Due to this, five battalions of the German *711. Infanterie-Division*, in combat in the Tokod sector and south-east of there, were ordered to attack westwards, and on the night of 23/24 March 1945, break through to the other side of the bridgehead.[1586] The abandonment of the bridgehead, and the retreat of the forces to the northern bank of the Danube was permitted by the *OKH* before the end of the day.[1587]

The German *Luftflotte 4* supported their own troops, mainly north of Lake Balaton, and with smaller scale forces between Kisbér and Nagyigmánd.[1588]

1580 Central Archives of the Russian Defence Ministry (Podolsk), f. 240, op. 2799, gy. 342, li. 113.
1581 Paul, Wolfgang: *Brennpunkte. Die Geschichte der 6. Panzerdivision (1. leichte) 1937–1945*. Krefeld, 1977. p. 450.
1582 NARA, T311, R162, F7214728.
1583 NARA, T311, R162, F7214739.
1584 NARA, T311, R163, F7215053.
1585 Central Archives of the Russian Defence Ministry (Podolsk), f. 240, op. 2799, gy. 357, li. 12.
1586 NARA, T311, R162, F7214728.
1587 NARA, T311, R162, F7214731.
1588 NARA, T311, R162, F7214729.

In order to be able to seal off the gap between Veszprém and Kisbér, and to reinforce *12. SS-Panzer-Division* that was holding there, at around 1000 hours, the German *6. Panzerarmee* demanded that the German *6. Armee* should reassign one combat group of *1. SS-Panzer-Division* to them, as well as *9. SS-Panzer-Division*, as soon as these units could possibly be withdrawn from the frontline.[1589] The *9. SS-Panzer-Division* had asked for this themselves, stating that their forces were completely worn out and destroyed.[1590] *General der Infanterie* Wöhler, commander of the *Heeresgruppe,* informed the *Divisionskommandeur, SS-Oberführer* Stadler in a telegram, that *General der Panzertruppe* Balck's orders were to be executed entirely and they should hold their positions until reinforcements arrived.[1591] Balck did not want the combat group of *1. SS-Panzer-Division* reassigned either, because there were no other units with which the Veszprém–Márkó road could have been held. According to his description, the unit simply marched out of Kádárta, thus endangering the defence of Veszprém.[1592] *General der Panzertruppe* Balck explained that if the units of *1. SS-Panzer-Division* were withdrawn from the sector of Márkó, a Soviet breakthrough would be unavoidable and in that case, he would rather be relieved as army commander.[1593]

On that day, Hitler at last permitted *1. Volks-Gebirgs-Division* to be reassembled from *2. Panzerarmee* to north of Lake Balaton in the Ajka–Pápa–Devecser sector. At first, *Gebirgs-Aufklärungs-Abteilung 54* and one of the companies[1594] of *Gebirgs-Panzerjäger-Abteilung 44*,[1595] were to be marched to the sector of Városlőd.[1596] However, as the defence of the Zala oil fields were still of essential importance to Hitler, in exchange for the reassembled units, the remnants of *44. Reichsgrenadier-Division, 14. SS-Grenadier-Division* from Karinthia and *297. Infanterie-Division* from the Balkans, were directed to *2. Panzerarmee*.[1597]

24 March 1945, Saturday

(**WEATHER**: highest daytime temperature 20 Celsius; cloudless, clear skies. the roads and the terrain are dry and trackable.)

At dawn on 24 March 1945, on the front of *2. Panzerarmee,* the German-Hungarian troops of *XXII. Gebirgskorps* established their defensive positions southeast of Mesztegnyő. During the day, no significant combat action had taken place.[1598] In the depth of the

---

1589 NARA, T311, R162, F7214732.
1590 NARA, T311, R162, F7214735.
1591 NARA, T311, R162, F7214735.
1592 NARA, T311, R162, F7214736, furthermore T311, R162, F7214738.
1593 NARA, T311, R162, F7214738.
1594 The *Kommandeur* of Gebirgs-Panzerjäger-Abteilung 44 was *Major* Josef Haselhorst.
1595 This was most likely *2. Kompanie* of *Panzerjäger-Abteilung* of the *Division*, which had towed 7.5 cm anti-tank guns. The *1. Kompanie* of the unit which was being equipped, received 10 Jagdpanzer 38(t) *Jagdpanzers* in Milowitz, Czechoslovakia on 18 March 1945, but they were not able to join the parent division then. Of the receipt of the vehicles, see NARA, T78, R621, F779.
1596 NARA, T311, R163, F7215037. the reinforced *Gebirgs-Aufklärungs-Abteilung* commenced their march at 0200 hours on 24 March 1945.
1597 NARA, T311, R162, F7214733.
1598 NARA, T311, R162, F7214745.

operational defence of *71. Infanterie-Division,* 10 assault guns of *Sturmartillerie-Brigade 261* stood in readiness in case the *Grenadiers* would need to launch a counterattack.[1599]

The *16. SS-Panzergrenadier-Division*[1600] was still engaged in small scale battles of local importance in the Mesztegnyő sector.

In the sector of the German *I. Kavallerie-Korps/6. Armee,* the Soviets launched an attack with rifle and tank forces against the newly established German defensive positions on the Vörösberény north-east–Szentkirályszabadja south-west section. North-east of Vörösberény, the regiment-size attacks of the Soviets were supported by six armoured fighting vehicles. The Soviets broke into the German positions, but the defenders launched a counterattack, with which they pushed the attackers back. South-west of Szentkirályszabadja, 15 Soviet armoured fighting vehicles and the escorting infantry broke into the German defences.[1601]

In the sector of Vörösberény, the 71st Tank Regiment, in support of the 5th Guards Cavalry Corps, was engaged in combat with 13 T–34/85s, and at Balatonalmádi, the 1896th Self-Propelled Artillery Regiment was in combat with 13 SU–76Ms. The 54th Tank Regiment, with nine T–34/85s marched to Balatonszabadi during the night.[1602]

During the day, the Soviets pushed the remnants of *3.* and *4. Kavallerie-Divisions,* and units of *23. Panzer-Division,*[1603] to the Balatonalmádi south one km–Felsőörs north one km–southern edge of Veszprém general line.[1604]

The 18th Tank Corps was at the centre of the Soviet attack. The 1st and 2nd Battalion/32nd Motorized Rifle Brigade, with the support of the 110th Tank Brigade, the 363rd Guards Heavy Self-Propelled Artillery Regiment, and the 1952nd and 1953rd Self-Propelled Artillery Regiments of the 209th Self-Propelled Artillery Brigade, attacked Tótvázsony unsuccessfully during a 4 hour long siege. Here, the Germans knocked out two T–34/85s, one of which burnt out, and one ISU–152.

Meanwhile, the 181st Tank Brigade, with the 1438th and the 1951st Self-Propelled Artillery Regiments, as well as the 3rd Battalion/32nd Motorized Rifle Brigade, occupied Felsőörs and, with its forward troops, launched an attack against Alsóörs. During the action, five T–34/85s and two SU–76Ms were burnt out.

During the day, the forces of the German *3. Panzer-Division* cleared out of Kövesgyűr, two km north of Tótvázsony, and retreated into Nemesleányfalu, one km south-west of Nagyvázsony.[1605]

1599 *Die 71. Infanterie-Division im Zweiten Weltkrieg 1939–1945. Gefechts- und Erlebnisberichte aus den Kämpfen der „Glückhaften Division" von Verdun bis Stalingrad, von Monte Cassino bis zum Plattensee.* Arbeitsgemeinschaft „Das Kleeblatt" (Hrsg.). Hildesheim, 1973. p. 416.

1600 The strength of *16. SS-Panzergrenadier-Division* was 9399 men, of which 3134 were combat-,ready for service as infantry. *SS-Panzer-Abteilung 16* had 12 assault guns in combat-ready condition. There were 16 7.5 cm heavy anti-tank guns. The combat strength of the *Panzergrenadiers* in six weak battalions was approximately 600 men. The artillery consisted of six light and three heavy batteries. The mobility of the *Division,* only suitable for defense was 40 percent. See Puntigam, Josef Paul: *Vom Plattensee bis zur Mur. Die Kämpfe 1945 im Dreiländereck.* Feldbach, without year of publication, [1993], p. 338.

1601 NARA, T311, R163, F7215446.

1602 Central Archives of the Russian Defence Ministry (Podolsk), f. 243, op. 2928, gy. 131, li. 271.

1603 On the same day *3.* and *4. Kavallerie-Divisions* had only two combat-ready assault guns each, and *23. Panzer-Division* had one assault gun and three Jagdpanzer IV *Jagdpanzers.* See NARA, T311, R163, F7215116.

1604 NARA, T311, R162, F7214745.

1605 *Geschichte der 3. Panzer-Division. Herausgegeben vom Traditionsverband der Division.* Berlin, 1967. p. 471.

The *I. (Abteilung)/Panzer-Regiment 24,* arriving at Tótvázsony, was able to salvage four command Panthers and 18 Panther tanks from the southern outskirts of Székesfehérvár. The two repair-recovery *Bergepanthers* and other prime movers of the *Abteilung,* towed back the damaged vehicles for about 130 km. In many of the Panthers, only 80 litres of fuel or less remained by that time. The *I. (Abteilung)/Panzer-Regiment 24* went into the direct subordination of *IV. SS-Panzerkorps,* and they were directly tasked by *SS-Obergruppenführer* Herbert-Otto Gille, to defend the road leading from Veszprém travelling through Tótvázsony, together with the remnants of *5. SS-Panzer-Division.* The weak combat groups of *5. SS-Panzer-Division* were collected by the remaining armoured personnel carriers along the Veszprém–Tapolca road, in order to establish fortifications to counter the advancing Soviet troops.

The 10 Panthers of *I. (Abteilung)/Panzer-Regiment 24,* were filled up with fuel, which was taken from other vehicles, and afterwards occupied positions for themselves under command of *Leutnant* Jonas at Kövesgyűr, northeast of Tótvázsony.[1606] Here the nine combat-ready Panther tanks of the unit reported to have knocked out three T–34/85s,[1607] most likely from the 170th Tank Brigade/18th Tank Corps. The German armoured fighting vehicles caught a glimpse of the rifle infantry and 30 armoured fighting vehicles, preparing for further attacks on the opposite hill. The *I. (Abteilung)/Panzer-Regiment 24,* did not have any infantry support, therefore they had to retreat to the next hill. The engine of one of the Panthers had mechanical problems, therefore it had to be abandoned and blown up. The Soviet rifle infantry, taking advantage of the darkness, approached the new positions of the German armoured fighting vehicles and exposed the targets for the following tanks and self-propelled guns, by shooting tracer rounds horizontally at them.[1608]

On both sides of the Veszprém–Nagyvázsony road, south-west of Nagyvázsony, *Kampfgruppe "Bradel",* concentrating the remaining forces of *1. Panzer-Division,* arrived in the afternoon with the task to defend and support the Hungarian troops retreating from the direction of Veszprém toward the south-west, as these troops had practically no heavy weapons. The *Divisionskommandeur*'s command post was established in Vigantpeterd.[1609] According to the daily report, the German *1. Panzer-Division* was in an alarmingly deplorable condition:

- *Panzer-Regiment 1* only had five combat-ready Panther tanks;
- *Panzergrenadier-Regiment 1* had three companies with 80 men, six light machine guns, one 2 cm anti-aircraft gun, two 7.5 cm anti-tank guns and five 8 cm mortars;
- *Panzergrenadier-Regiment 113,* again with three companies, had 80 men, 18 light machine guns, four 2 cm anti-aircraft guns, two 7.5 cm anti-tank guns, two light infantry guns and three 8 cm mortars, and a pioneer company with 30 men;
- *II.* and *III. (Abteilung)/Artillerie-Regiment 73* with eight 10.5 cm light and five 15 cm heavy field howitzers, and three 10 cm field guns;

1606 Weidemann, Gert-Axel: *Unser Regiment. Reiter-Regiment 2 – Panzer-Regiment 24*. Groß-Umstadt, 1982. p. 279.
1607 Senger und Etterlin, von F.M. jr.: *Die 24. Panzer-Division vormals 1. Kavallerie-Division 1939–1945*. Neckargemünd, 1962. p. 310.
1608 Weidemann, Gert-Axel: *Unser Regiment. Reiter-Regiment 2 – Panzer-Regiment 24*. Groß-Umstadt, 1982. pp. 279-280.
1609 Stoves, Rolf: Persönliches Kriegstagebuch Pz.Rgt. 1 (typewritten manuscript, a copy owned by the author), entry from 24 March 1945.

- *37. Panzer-Pionier-Kompanie* with a company and a Hungarian construction company; *Panzer-Nachrichten-Abteilung 37* with two combat-ready radio units.[1610]

The majority of the combat-ready armoured fighting vehicles of *Panzer-Regiment 1* and the self-propelled *Hummel* howitzers of *I. (self-propelled) (Abteilung)/Panzer-Artillerie-Regiment 73*, were missing from the reports. This was either due to the extreme losses inflicted on the Germans by the Soviets, or the reports of the *Division* were incomplete. The repair workshop platoons of *Panzer-Regiment 1* were working ceaselessly, and on that day at Bóde, south of Ajka, four repaired and combat-ready Panthers rolled out and another three to four were still under repair. However, their fuel tanks were only about 15 percent filled.[1611]

The Soviet 170th Tank Brigade was advancing from the direction of Szentkirályszabadja toward Veszprémfajsz, Nemesvámos and Tótvázsony. East of Nemesvámos, the Soviets had already encircled one of the combat groups of *9. SS-Panzer-Division*.[1612]

The company commander of the 1st Tank Battalion/170th Tank Brigade, 1st Lieutenant Brjukhov, saw the battle unfold that day as follows:

"The area of Nemesvámos was significantly reinforced. It was defended by approximately two infantry battalions, eight tanks and approximately four anti-tank batteries. We were pushing forward along the road, the 3rd battalion on the right side, the 2nd battalion on the left side, both reinforced by submachine gunners. The ground was very hard to drive on because it was not smooth, and this greatly hindered our tank manoeuvres. The poorly trained and inexperienced tank drivers were advancing very slowly, so the kombat had to ask them repeatedly to go forward the point of departure of the attack. After we had overcome these difficulties, the tanks of the forward troops and our own battalions advanced in heavy combat and occupied Nemesvámos. The enemy retreated and established new defensive positions along the hills that were quite close. The brigade was engaged in quite a long fight. Otroshenkov was searching for the way to move the Germans out of the dominating hills and to eliminate them. Sharkisyan was impatiently urging his tankers forward. The kombrig sent howitzers and self-propelled guns to the battalions as reinforcements. The enemy strongly repulsed our attacks and inflicted heavy losses upon us, three tanks burnt out in the 2nd battalion, and the 3rd battalion also lost three tanks. The rifle battalion also suffered serious losses. By the end of the day, we had destroyed the enemy and occupied the hills, but the brigade was not able to carry out its most important task.

1610 NARA, T311, R163, F7215078.
1611 Stoves, Rolf: Persönliches Kriegstagebuch Pz.Rgt. 1 (typewritten manuscript, a copy owned by the author), entry from 24 March 1945. Before the break out on 22 March 1945, 12-14 Panthers and one Panzer IV were blown up southwest of Székesfehérvár by *1. Panzer-Division*, which had damaged tracks or did not have sufficient fuel. The *Werkstatt-Kompanie/Panzer-Regiment 1* however managed to tow 35 damaged tanks, mainly Panthers, from the sector of Székesfehérvár via the Transdanubia to reach German territory, the sector of Fürstenfeld on 30 March. See Stoves, O. G. Rolf: *1. Panzer-Division 1935–1945. Chronik einer der drei Stamm-Division der deutschen Panzerwaffe*. Bad Nauheim, 1961. p. 779.
1612 Tieke, Wilhelm: *Von Plattensee bis Österreich. Heeresgruppe Süd 1945*. Gummersbach, without year of publication, p. 80. On the night of 24/25 March the combat group of *9. SS-Panzer-Division*, encircled at Nemesvámos broke out and reached the German lines at Hidegkút. During the fighting the Germans reported to have knocked out 23 Soviet armoured fighting vehicles.

Combat this day was extremely brutal, we had not suffered such losses for a long time. The cumbersome terrain of the mountains, the excellently organized and prepared enemy defence, our own weak reconnaissance and that the force of the enemy was unknown to us, has made us pay ultimately. Of course, the weak cohesion among our units, the lack of experience and the inadequate training of the newly arrived troops all contributed."[1613]

Around 1800 hours, the 170th Tank Brigade at last reached the western outskirts of Ágostonmajor, 3.5 km north of Tótvázsony, and the forest edge south-west of there. The Brigade reported to have knocked out five German tanks on that day, with 10 of their own T–34/85s knocked out, four of which were burnt out.[1614]

In the heavy armoured battles of that day, the 18th Tank Corps, lost 10 T–34/85s, one ISU–152 and two SU–76M self-propelled guns. Another seven damaged tanks needed repairs. In the evening, the units had 78 operational tanks, 10 ISU–122s, four ISU–152s and 10 SU–76M self-propelled guns. The 209th Self-Propelled Artillery Brigade also had 37 SU–100s, three SU–57s and two T–34s in operational condition.[1615]

On that day, the 1st Guards Mechanized Corps was ordered by the Staff of the 3rd Ukrainian Front to reassemble its forces via the sector of Hajmáskér to the sector of Bakonyszentkirály, Csesznek and Bakonyoszlop. The Corps that evening had 82 operational M4A2s, three T–34/85s, and 13 SU–100 self-propelled guns.[1616]

On the front of *IV. SS-Panzerkorps,* the Soviets also continued their attack in the western outskirts of Veszprém, and pushed the German troops in defence there, back to the Hidegkút eastern edge–Nemesvámos west four km sector. North of here, the armoured fighting vehicles of the Soviet 9th Guards Mechanized Corps, advanced via Márkó and Szentgál toward Úrkút, then continued their advance towards Pápa during the afternoon.[1617]

The forces of the Soviet 5th Guards Tank Corps pushed the German forces, the majority of *1. SS-Panzer-Division* and *Flak-Artillerie-Regiment 25* in defence in Márkó, out of the village, then crossing the road leading to Herend, the T-34/85s of the 22nd Guards Tank Brigade occupied Herend at 0400 hours, and Szentgál at 1800 hours. In the fighting, the Germans reported to have knocked out six Soviet armoured fighting vehicles.[1618] The combat group of *1. SS-Panzer-Division,* that was separated from the majority of the *Division,* was working in cooperation with *I. (Abteilung)/Flak-Artillerie-Regiment 25,* and tried to establish new defensive positions along the road in the western outskirts of Herend.[1619]

In this way, the combat group of *1. SS-Panzer-Division* ,that was subordinated to *6. Armee*, despite the reassignment order received the day before, was still in combat in the Herend sector.[1620]

1613   Bryukhov, Vasiliy: *Red Army Tank Commander. At War in a T–34 on the Eastern Front.* Barnsley, 2013. pp. 179-180.
1614   War log of the 18th Tank Corps for March 1945. Copy owned by the author. p. 44.
1615   Central Archives of the Russian Defence Ministry (Podolsk), f. 243, op. 2928, gy. 131, li. 270.
1616   Central Archives of the Russian Defence Ministry (Podolsk), f. 243, op. 2928, gy. 131, li. 271.
1617   NARA, T311, R162, F7214745.
1618   NARA, T311, R163, F7215446.
1619   NARA, T311, R163, F7215446.
1620   NARA, T311, R162, F7214753.

The 1016th and 1922nd Self-Propelled Artillery Regiments of the Soviet 208th Self-Propelled Artillery Brigade, together with units of the 20th Guards Tank Brigade/5th Guards Tank Corps, occupied Márkó during the morning, and the 22nd Guards Tank Brigade, together with the 1922nd Self-Propelled Artillery Regiment, occupied Bánd.[1621] When the latter two units launched an attack against Herend, the Germans launched a counterattack from the direction of Szentgál with 16 Tiger Bs and four *Jagdpanzers*. The SU–100 self-propelled guns there, reported knocking out nine heavy tanks.[1622]

By 1700 hours, the 5th Guards Tank Corps pushed forward to Városlőd. The 20th Guards and 22nd Guards Tank Brigade, and the 36th Guards Heavy Self-Propelled Artillery Regiment, targeted the northern edge of the village, while the 6th Guards Motorized Rifle Brigade and the 51st Guards Self-Propelled Artillery Brigade, attacked the south-eastern end. The 21st Guards Tank Brigade was standing at Márkó in reserve, but at the end of the day it relieved the 22nd Guards Tank Brigade, which went into reserve in Herend. The Corps reported for the day to have knocked out 10 German tanks, six assault guns and *Jagdpanzers*, plus nine armoured personnel carriers and their own losses amounted to 14 knocked out plus three burnt out tanks[1623]. In the evening, they had 45 operational T–34/85s and 12 SU–76M self-propelled guns.[1624]

On the night of 23/24 March 1945, in the front of the German *I. SS-Panzerkorps/6. Panzerarmee*, the Soviets advanced four km towards the west from the sector of Zirc.

During the day, the *Stab/1. SS-Panzer-Division*, defended Városlőd, then Kislőd, with a small combat group. In front of Kislőd, *SS-Panzergrenadier-Regiment 1* held up the advance of the Soviet armoured fighting vehicles with the help of tanks, *Jagdpanzers* and anti-aircraft guns. South of Kislőd, *III. (gepanzert) Bataillon/SS-Panzergrenadier-Regiment 2*, and on the eastern edge of Úrkút, the remnants of *SS-Panzer-Aufklärungs-Abteilung 1*, established defensive positions. The other combat group, which consisted of *SS-Panzergrenadier-Regiment 2* together with the *Kommandeursstab* of the *Division*, was in combat at Bakonyjákó during the late afternoon, then after the advance of the Soviet armoured fighting vehicles, retreated to the Kup–Pápakovácsi–Ugod line. With this, the gap between the northern and the southern combat groups was widened even more, through which the Soviet forces pushed forward, via Tapolcafő, toward Pápa.

As contact with *3. Panzer-Division* had been severed in the south as well, the combat group of *1. SS-Panzer-Division* in defence at Kislőd, was threatened with complete encirclement.[1625]

The scattered combat groups of *3. SS-Panzer-Division* were constantly retreating westwards in the forests of Bakony, all the while engaged in isolated skirmishes. In the evening, they were in combat on the Ugod–Pápateszér line with the support of a number of their armoured fighting vehicles – among these, two Tiger E heavy tanks.[1626]

1621 Summarized report of the 208th Self-Propelled Artillery Brigade of the period between 6 March – 6 April 1945. Copy owned by the author. p. 13.
1622 Summarized report of the 208th Self-Propelled Artillery Brigade of the period between 6 March – 6 April 1945. Copy owned by the author. p. 14.
1623 Central Archives of the Russian Defence Ministry (Podolsk), f. 339, op. 5179, gy. 87, li. 20.
1624 Central Archives of the Russian Defence Ministry (Podolsk), f. 243, op. 2928, gy. 131, li. 269.
1625 Tiemann, Ralf: *Die Leibstandarte*. Band IV/2. Osnabrück, 1987. pp. 327-328.
1626 Tieke, Wilhelm: *Von Plattensee bis Österreich. Heeresgruppe Süd 1945*. Gummersbach, without year of publication, p. 81., and Schneider, Wolfgang: *Tiger der Division Totenkopf*. Uelzen, 2009. p. 255.

At 1300 hours, the M4A2 armoured fighting vehicles of the Soviet 46th Guards Tank Brigade, advanced via Bakonyjákó to the west and north-west, and in the late afternoon the Germans were finally able to halt and contain them three km southeast of Tapolcafő. Between Tapolcafő and Ugod, the Germans created a makeshift holding line, against which a Soviet reconnaissance patrol had been sent at around 1900 hours, but the Germans repulsed this attempt.[1627]

In the sector of Tapolcafő, the 18th Guards Mechanized Brigade and the 46th Guards Tank Brigade/Soviet 9th Guards Mechanized Corps/6th Guards Tank Army were in combat. Guards Captain Loza, commander of the 1st Battalion of the Tank Brigade remembered:

"The brigade was targeted by strong air raids on a number of subsequent days. Thanks to the large-caliber anti-aircraft machine guns on the Shermans, we were able to fend off these attacks. The other problem however, became a real issue now. During the offensive of our forces against Vienna, the enemy widely used mines and the explosive engineer obstacles. During the last two days four tanks had blown up on enemy anti-tank mines. We had to conclude that this kind of conduct on enemy side was somewhat unexpected. We had never before met such a wide array of minefield usage. Our brigade did not have any minesweeping tools to search for mines and open corridors for the troops to pass. We did not have pioneers for each of the tanks. We had to search for other solutions."[1628]

Finally, as a solution to the problem, the 46th Guards Tank Brigade chose to use a specially fitted tank,[1629] which set off with a "flying start" and with the highest speed possible, rushed through the mined section. The mine blasts, happening seconds later, did not harm the tank, but in this way, a usable corridor was opened in the minefield. However, the corridor was not wide enough after one pass, so the act was repeated. After successfully solving the problem, the Soviet M4A2 tanks approached Tapolcafő.[1630] In the event there was an obstacle that was under observation by the defenders and also covered by fire, this type of solution would not have been successful.

The 30th Guards Mechanized Brigade/9th Guards Mechanized Corps was held up at Bakonybél by the German defences. The 31st Guards Mechanized Brigade was concentrated at Pénzeskút. The Corps lost on that day, only one burnt out M4A2 tank and in the evening, they had 76 operational tanks and nine SU–76M self-propelled guns.[1631]

Around 0320 hours, on the front of *12. SS-Panzer-Division,* the combat group of *SS-Panzergrenadier-Regiment 26* also arrived at Pénzeskút. The *Panzergrenadiers,* with the batteries of *SS-Panzer-Flak-Abteilung 12,* had to defend the village at least until the morning of the next day in order to provide enough time for the vehicle columns of the division to retreat on the poor roads.

1627 NARA, T311, R162, F7214745.
1628 Loza, Dmitriy: *Commanding the Red Army's Sherman Tanks.* Lincoln–London, 1996. p. 88.
1629 The spare fuel tanks were taken down from the appointed tanks, the ammunition were stored in the storage compartments of the turret instead of the floor of the combat compartment, and the gun and the anti-aircraft machine gun were fixed.
1630 Loza, Dmitriy: *Commanding the Red Army's Sherman Tanks.* Lincoln–London, 1996. pp. 89-90.
1631 Central Archives of the Russian Defence Ministry (Podolsk), f. 243, op. 2928, gy. 131, li. 269.

During the morning, at 1030 hours, the Soviets attacked the forward positions of the anti-aircraft artillery, but in the end they instead advanced through the forest. One hour later, the Soviet armoured fighting vehicles and rifles were already assaulting the German positions at Pénzeskút. A few immobilised German tanks opened fire and knocked out two Soviet tanks. On the right flank, a Flak-Panzer IV equipped with a 2 cm four-barrelled anti-aircraft gun, kept the Soviet infantry under fire and the Soviets withdrew.

At 1215 hours, the Soviets launched a new attack. In the heavy mortar fire, some of the *SS-Panzergrenadiers* panicked and retreated. The Soviets literally tore them apart with gunfire. The more battle-hardened Germans who were still fighting, also started to slowly retreat towards Somhegy. On the hills south of Pénzeskút, *II. (Bataillon)/SS-Panzergrenadier-Regiment 26* held its positions until the afternoon with the support of the 15 cm *Grille* heavy self-propelled infantry guns of *SS-Panzergrenadier-Regiment 26* and then retreated.[1632]

During the disengagement, the tank of *SS-Hauptsturmführer* Siegel was damaged and had to be blown up. Later, the *Kommandeur* of *II. (Abteilung)/SS-Panzer-Regiment 12*, acting as a rearguard, secured the retreat of the unit with two other Panzer IV tanks and a few *Panzergrenadiers,* and then in the evening, withdrew to Bakonybél.

Around 1600 hours in the afternoon, the *Divisionsbegleitkompanie* established positions 300 meters east of Somhegy. The remnants of *II. (Bataillon)/SS-Panzergrenadier-Regiment 26,* that had suffered serious losses, were reorganized as *Kampfgruppe "Ott",*[1633] with the SS-artillery crews and medical staff fighting as infantry. At 1810 hours in the evening, eight Soviet tanks and the escorting infantry, attacked Somhegy and blanketed the village with heavy fire. *Kampfgruppe "Ott"* retreated to Bakonybél in an hour, where they joined *Kampfgruppe "Hauschild",* which mainly consisted of inexperienced soldiers, new at the frontline.[1634] In the evening at around 2200 hours, the *Divisionsbegleitkompanie* also arrived.

The units of *12. SS-Panzer-Division* were not able to prevent the Soviets from breaking into Tapolcafő during the afternoon.[1635] The units of *12. SS-* and *3. SS-Panzer-Division,* kept their fortified defensive positions on the hills of Bakonybél south-east–Borzavár west four km sectors and on the eastern side of the Bakonykoppány–Szücs road against the Soviets attacking from Pénzeskút toward the north-west, and between Fenyőfő and Bakonyszentlászló toward the west. The German rapid reaction troops, from the pioneer and construction companies, equipped with anti-tank mines and *Panzerfausts,* started to build up a defensive line on the Járiföld–Ugod east–Szücs–Bakonyszentiván–Nagydém general line.

As the Soviet troops were already advancing on the north-western edge of Bakony towards Pápa on that day, the *Kommandeur* of *12. SS-Panzer-Division* ordered a retreat from Bakonybél to Bakonykoppány at 2130 hours. *Kampfgruppe "Ott"* was the first to set off with *Kampfgruppe "Hauschild"* providing the rearguard. The *Divisionsbegleitkompanie* remained as the last unit to disengage from the Soviets and carried out demolition duties with a few pioneers.[1636]

[1632] Vopersal, Wolfgang: *Soldaten, Kämpfer, Kameraden. Marsch und Kämpfe der SS-Totenkopfdivision.* Band Vb. Bielefeld, 1991. p. 808.
[1633] The *Kampfgruppe* was named after the *Bataillonskommandeur, SS-Hauptsturmführer* Alfons Ott.
[1634] The *Kampfgruppe* was organized around *I. (Bataillon)/SS-Panzergrenadier-Regiment 26.*
[1635] NARA, T311, R162, F7214761.
[1636] Meyer, Hubert: *Kriegsgeschichte der 12. SS-Panzerdivision „Hitlerjugend".* Band II. Osnabrück, 1987. 2nd edition. pp. 514-516.

The combat groups of *I. SS-Panzerkorps* reported to have knocked out 78 Soviet armoured fighting vehicles between 22- 24 March 1945.[1637]

On the southern flank of the German 6. *Panzerarmee,* between Bakonyjákó and Réde, there was an approximately 45 km wide gap in the frontline[1638], where only small German units drifted in the sea of Soviet troops pushing toward the west-north-west.

On the frontline of the 2nd Ukrainian Front

The weak defensive forces of *6. Panzer-Division/ II. SS-Panzerkorps*[1639], still in the sector of Bakonygyirót, were pushed towards the north by the Soviet forces advancing to the north-west from the sector of Bakonyszentlászló. The Germans at last reached the northern edge of the Csehi Forest south of Gic. In order to reinforce the right flank of the armoured corps, units of *SS-Panzer-Aufklärungs-Abteilung 9* were deployed between Bakonytamási and Gic.[1640]

The German troops holding between Bakonygyirót and Veszprémvarsány, held Sikátor and Vecsenytanya, two km north-east of there, against approximately battalion-size Soviet attacks. Between Réde and Kisbér, the Soviets only launched reconnaissance type missions.

The *2. SS-Panzer-Division*[1641] sealed off the attack of the Soviets that was launched with 10 armoured fighting vehicles north of Ete, and they held the positions against the renewed, regiment-size attacks as well. The Germans, in the meantime, proceeded to eliminate the incursion.

At 0700 hours in the morning, the Soviet 23rd Tank Corps joined the attack of the 18th Guards Rifle Corps against Csép and, at around 1400 hours, the village fell into Soviet hands. Although *II. (Bataillon)/SS-Panzergrenadier-Regiment 4,* that was deployed to recapture the village, had broken into the northern parts of the village, the Soviet counterattacks, supported by 10 armoured fighting vehicles, encircled the Germans around the church. The subsequent attacks launched to relieve the encircled battalion all failed. Later on however, some units of the battalion broke out successfully.[1642] On the north-western edge of Csép, defended by the Soviet 1897th Self-Propelled Artillery Regiment, reported to have repulsed 20 small scale German attacks.[1643]

The length of the frontline of the two *SS-Panzergrenadier-Regiment*s of *2. SS-Panzer-Division* was nearly 14 km, therefore all battalions needed to be deployed in the first line of defence. Around this time, new combat reinforcements arrived from the *Kriegsmarine*, however these new troops first needed to be trained in infantry combat.

1637 NARA, T311, R162, F7214746.
1638 NARA, T311, R162, F7214756.
1639 On the same day, *6. Panzer-Division* had 17 combat-ready Panthers and six Panzer IV tanks, plus five Jagdpanzer IV *Jagdpanzers*. See NARA, T311, R163, F7215117.
1640 NARA, T311, R162, F7214746.
1641 On the same day the *2. SS-Panzer-Division* had two combat-ready Panthers and five Panzer IV tanks, three StuG. III assault guns, two Panzer IV/70 (V)s and five Jagdpanther *Jagdpanzer*s. See NARA, T311, R163, F7215117.
1642 Tieke, Wilhelm: *Von Plattensee bis Österreich. Heeresgruppe Süd 1945*. Gummersbach, without year of publication, p. 81., furthermore Weidinger, Otto: *Division Das Reich. Der Weg der 2. SS-Panzer-Division „Das Reich"*. Band V: 1943-1945. Osnabrück, without year of publication, pp. 470-471.
1643 Central Archives of the Russian Defence Ministry (Podolsk), f. 240, op. 2799, gy. 342, li. 116.

The *Division* had 17 7.5 cm heavy anti-tank guns on that day. Its five average *Panzergrenadier-Bataillons* consisted of approximately 1000 men. One of the battalions of *Feldersatz-Brigade 102* and *Panzer-Aufklärungs-Abteilung/1. Panzer-Division,* were also subordinated to them. In its three *Artillerie-Abteilung,* there were 19 light and 21 heavy field howitzers and three guns. The mobility of the *Division* was at 60 percent, but it was suitable only for defensive duties now. According to the *Stab/II. SS-Panzerkorps* however, it was still suitable for limited scope attack missions.[1644]

The 3rd Tank Brigade/23rd Tank Corps, with two Battalions of the 5th Motorized Rifle Brigade, together with the 1501st Anti-Tank Artillery Regiment, was attacking from Csép toward the north, and at 1730 hours occupied Békavár and then assaulted Hill 132, 1 km north-west of there. At the same time, the 39th Tank Brigade, together with the 1443rd Self-Propelled Artillery Regiment and a Battalion of the 56th Motorized Rifle Brigade, was attacking Parraghpuszta south-west of Csép.[1645] During these battles, the 23rd Tank Corps lost five knocked out T–34/85s, of which four burnt out, and a burnt out ISU–122 self-propelled gun.[1646]

The 2nd Guards Mechanized Corps, which had been deployed north-east of Kisigmánd in the direction of Ács, on the previous afternoon, was almost unable to advance because of the counterattacks the Germans carried out with battalion-size infantry forces and 10-15 armoured fighting vehicles. By 1300 hours in the afternoon, the 4th Guards Mechanized Brigade occupied Bartusekpuszta and reached the railroad line. The commander of the reconnaissance platoon of the 23rd Guards Tank Regiment of the Brigade, Guards Lieutenant Tarasov, engaged six of the German armoured fighting vehicles which carried out the counterattack. The officer, with his T–34/85 tanks, knocked out three German armoured fighting vehicles, and the others retreated. However, on the same day, his own armoured fighting vehicle was hit as well, and he was killed in action. Posthumously, he was awarded the decoration Hero of the Soviet Union.[1647]

The 5th Guards Mechanized Brigade was in combat 800 meters north-east of Öregcsém at that time. The 6th Guards Mechanized Brigade with the 37th Guards Tank Brigade, in cooperation with the 32nd Rifle Regiment, occupied Kisigmánd in the early in the morning, then were attacking in the direction of Öregcsém.[1648] The units of the Corps however, were in combat on the Bartusekpuszta east 500–Csémi-Csárda line in the evening of 24 March 1945.[1649] The German counterattack aimed against the Soviet incursion north-east of Kisigmánd, ran into 500 Soviet soldiers and 20 armoured fighting vehicles, which turned back the Germans.[1650]

The assembly area of the Soviet armoured fighting vehicles was effectively kept under fire by German artillery. The Germans also organized an attack in the evening to reoccupy Kisigmánd.[1651]

1644 Tieke, Wilhelm: *Von Plattensee bis Österreich. Heeresgruppe Süd 1945.* Gummersbach, without year of publication, p. 92.
1645 Central Archives of the Russian Defence Ministry (Podolsk), f. 240, op. 2799, gy. 357, li. 14.
1646 War log of the 23rd Tank Corps for March 1945. Copy owned by the author. p. 15. o.
1647 HM HIM Hadtörténelmi Levéltár (Budapest), Szovjetunió Hőse kitüntetések gyűjteménye (*Collection of Hero of the Soviet Union awards*), 569.
1648 Central Archives of the Russian Defence Ministry (Podolsk), f. 401, op. 9511, gy. 535, li. 113.
1649 Central Archives of the Russian Defence Ministry (Podolsk), f. 240, op. 2799, gy. 357, li. 14.
1650 NARA, T311, R163, F7215446.
1651 NARA, T311, R162, F7214746.

The 2nd Guards Mechanized Corps, lost in combat that day, nine knocked out T–34/85s, of which, five burnt out. In the evening, they had 20 operational tanks, and two ISU–122, seven SU–85 and 12 SU–76M self-propelled guns.[1652]

The commander of the 46th Army reassembled the 23rd Tank Corps in the Mocsa sector, in order to be able to push into the breach created by the 68th Rifle Corps and to occupy Bőnyrétalap, then Győr on the following day, 25 March 1945. The Corps was already assembled at Mocsa on 25 March at 0500 hours.[1653]

The Soviet 991st Self-Propelled Artillery Regiment/46th Army, together with the forces of the 99th Rifle Division, continued their on going assault for the occupation of Nagyigmánd. Although, during the two days of fighting, the SU–76M self-propelled guns knocked out a German assault gun and one armoured personnel carrier, plus four guns and eight firing positions, they did not achieve any success. The losses of the 991st Self-Propelled Artillery Regiment during these days, amounted to two burnt out SU–76Ms and one of the captured Panther tanks, which was fatally hit 1 km east of Nagyigmánd. Three of the crew including two officers, one of which was the commander of the Panther, were killed, and one person was wounded.[1654]

On the front of *II. SS-Panzerkorps,* the Germans reported to have knocked out three Soviet tanks and four self-propelled guns.[1655]

In the front of *XXXXIII. Armeekorps,* the Soviets, after having fired a short artillery barrage, at 1600 hours launched a new attack with a force the size of two regiments with 30 armoured fighting vehicles, from the sector of Kisigmánd toward the west and north-west. The attempt was halted by the Germans after having knocked out eight Soviet armoured fighting vehicles and the Soviets were pushed back to the Öregcsém south-east 500 meters –Bartusekpuszta south (Csémi-Csárda) sector. With this, the Germans also reoccupied the road intersection four km north of Kisigmánd.

The Soviet 1505th Self-Propelled Artillery Regiment, together with the 439th Rifle Regiment/52nd Rifle Division, launched an attack at 0800 hours in the morning, in the direction of Bartusekpuszta and, by 1200 hours, they were in combat 800 meters north-west of Point 138, four km west-north-west of Mocsa. In the meantime, the armoured fighting vehicles reported to have knocked out seven anti-tank guns and 15 fortifications. At that moment, the Regiment received orders to attack further in the direction of Göbölkútpuszta, in support of the 439th Rifle Regiment.[1656]

At the same time, the Soviet armoured fighting vehicles occupied Mocsa, where the defenders reported knocking out three Soviet armoured fighting vehicles. The units of *356. Infanterie-Division*[1657] together with *Panzer-Kampfgruppe "Pape",* launched a counterattack, but their attempt proved unsuccessful. On the northern flank of the corps, the defenders repulsed two company-size attacks from the direction of Pusztaalmás.[1658]

1652 Central Archives of the Russian Defence Ministry (Podolsk), f. 401, op. 9511, gy. 535, li. 113/2.
1653 Central Archives of the Russian Defence Ministry (Podolsk), f. 240, op. 2799, gy. 357, li. 14.
1654 Central Archives of the Russian Defence Ministry (Podolsk), f. 240, op. 2799, gy. 342, li. 111.
1655 NARA, T311, R163, F7215454.
1656 Central Archives of the Russian Defence Ministry (Podolsk), f. 240, op. 2799, gy. 342, li. 113.
1657 The *356. Infanterie-Division* had on that day seven combat-ready Jagdpanzer 38(t) *Jagdpanzers.* See NARA, T311, R163, F7215117.
1658 NARA, T311, R162, F7214747.

In the front of *XXXXIII. Armeekorps*, between 20 – 24 March 1945, 25 Soviet armoured fighting vehicles were reported to have been knocked out. Of these, 11 were knocked out on 24 March. Another two armoured fighting vehicles were immobilized in the German gunfire.[1659]

In the Komárom bridgehead of *8. Armee,* units of *Panzer-Division "Feldherrnhalle"* and elements of *Panzer-Kampfgruppe "Pape",* halted the Soviet battalion-size attack launched from Bartusekpuszta supported by armoured fighting vehicles, while reporting to have knocked out three Soviet armoured fighting vehicles.[1660]

On the same day, the German *Luftflotte 4* was supporting their troops in the Veszprém area, flying approximately 140 fighter and ground-attack aircraft missions. The pilots reported to have destroyed four Soviet tanks. The Germans increased their air reconnaissance action on the whole frontline of *Heeresgruppe Süd.*[1661]

The reconnaissance of the German *Heeresgruppe,* stated that the forces of the Soviet 6th Guards Tank Army reached out of the Bakony at Bakonyjákó and approached Pápa. The *Panzergrenadiers* of *12. SS-Panzer-Division* were not able to stop and contain the Soviet breakthrough on the forested, almost impassable mountain roads.[1662]

The Soviet 27th Army, with the 18th Tank Corps and the 1st Guards Mechanized Corps, attacked the left flank of the German *6. Armee* in the flanks, then they tried to push them via Herend and Szentgál, to Lake Balaton and encircle them. The Germans wanted to counter this by creating a new makeshift frontline, but for this, contact between the left flank of *6. Armee* and the routed right flank of the German *6. Panzerarmee,* had to be re-established. Therefore, the first units of *1. Volks-Gebirgs-Division* to arrive, needed to be deployed along the Veszprém–Devecser road, west of Herend, and the combat group of *1. SS-Panzer-Division,* subordinated to the *6. Armee,* was to be deployed on the right flank of the German *6. Panzerarmee.*[1663]

By now, the Germans had anticipated that, besides the breakthrough and incursion attempts in the sector of Lake Balaton and Komárom, the main Soviet forces will continue their attacks via the sector of Celldömölk and Pápa toward the west and north-west, in the direction of Sopron.[1664]

The incoming *232. Panzer-Division*[1665] was ordered to assemble in the sector of Tét, between Győr and Pápa. Thus they were able to be deployed in a number of directions.[1666]

1659 NARA, T311, R163, F7215454.
1660 NARA, T311, R162, F7214747.
1661 NARA, T311, R162, F7214748.
1662 NARA, T311, R162, F7214748.
1663 NARA, T311, R162, F7214749.
1664 NARA, T311, R162, F7214749.
1665 According to data as of 15 March 1945, *232. Panzer-Division* had only one Panzer IV (L/48) tank, one Panzer 38(t) light tank, one short-barrelled (L/24) StuG.III assault gun, one *Marder* II and two *Nashorn* tank destroyers. All of the armoured fighting vehicles were combat-ready. See NARA, T78, R624, F000503, 000515, 000535. According to the report of the unit as of 23 March 1945., they had 2452 men, one Panzer IV tank, four tank destroyers, seven Sd.Kfz. 250s and six Sd.Kfz. 251 armoured personnel carriers, four armoured heavy reconnaissance cars, one 3.7 cm, five 7.5 cm and two 76 mm (captured) towed anti-tank guns, plus eight towed 7.5 cm infantry guns. See Nevenkin, Kamen: *Fire Brigades – The Panzer Divisions 1943–1945.* Winnipeg, 2008. p. 604. The four tank destroyers most likely meant the two *Nashorn*s, the *Marder* and the short-barrelled StuG. III assault gun.
1666 NARA, T311, R162, F7214754.

As ordered by Hitler, the *Heeresgruppe* ordered the two *SS-Panzerkorps* of the German *6. Panzerarmee* to send all of its capable combat forces, including the fresh troops with less than two weeks of training, into combat to be able to increase the combat force of the *Panzergrenadiers*. Soon a similar order was delivered to all of the *Armees* of the *Heeresgruppe*.[1667]

25 March 1945, Sunday

(**WEATHER**: highest daytime temperature 20 Celsius; sunny, warm day. The road conditions are favourable.)

The German *I. Kavallerie-Korps/6. Armee,* created a makeshift frontline on the night of 24/25 March 1945 on the Balatonfüred–Hidegkút general line. The *9. SS-Panzer-Division* broke through the Soviet troops to Hidegkút, during which they reported to have knocked out 23 Soviet armoured fighting vehicles.[1668]

On the front of *23. Panzer-Division,* the Soviets bypassed the German engineer blockades with four tanks and broke into Balatonfüred, where they dispersed *I. (Bataillon)/Panzergrenadier-Regiment 128*. The units of the German *Division* retreated to the eastern outskirts of Balatonudvari, where at 0200 hours on 26 March 1945, they established defensive positions together with the Jagdpanzer IV *Jagdpanzers* of *2. Kompanie/Panzerjäger-Abteilung 128*.[1669]

The fuel shortage became increasingly critical. Large numbers of armoured fighting and other types of vehicles had to be abandoned because of the lack of sufficient fuel. One of the armoured reconnaissance detachments of *Panzer-Aufklärungs-Abteilung 23* however, managed to secure some diesel fuel from one of the Hungarian refineries in southern Bakony, therefore it was still possible to secure the withdrawal of the troops.[1670]

The Soviets repeated their attack and occupied Hidegkút, and using the village as a jumping off point, they forced a deep penetration into the German defences. In the front of the *Korps,* the fuel shortage was so critical that all of the German heavy tanks had to be blown up.[1671] The German *Eisenbahn-Panzerzug 78* was subordinated to *I. Kavallerie-Korps*.[1672]

The remaining combat-ready Tiger B heavy tanks of *schwere Panzer-Abteilung 509,* were filled up with fuel and ammunition for the last time and they started their retreat along the northern shore of Lake Balaton past Balatonfüred, Tapolca and Körmend, toward Heiligenkreuz, where they crossed the border on 31 March 1945. The supply company and the workshop company of the *Abteilung* were towing the damaged heavy

---

1667   NARA, T311, R162, F7214752.
1668   NARA, T311, R163, F7215456.
1669   Rebentisch, Ernst: *Zum Kaukasus und zu den Tauern. Die Geschichte der 23. Panzer-Division 1941–1945*. Esslingen, 1963. p. 500.
1670   Rebentisch, Ernst: *Zum Kaukasus und zu den Tauern. Die Geschichte der 23. Panzer-Division 1941–1945*. Esslingen, 1963. p. 500.
1671   NARA, T311, R162, F7214760.
1672   NARA, T311, R163, F7215464.

tanks and they set off via the Veszprém–Herend–Jánosháza–Körmend route towards the German border. During the retreat, 14 Tiger B heavy tanks had to be blown up due to the shortage of fuel.[1673]

During the night of 24/25 March 1945, on the front of *IV. SS-Panzerkorps*, the units of *5. SS-Panzer-Division* repulsed the attack of the 18th Tank Corps supported by 17 armoured fighting vehicles at Tótvázsony, and reported to have knocked out seven of the assaulting armoured fighting vehicles. Afterwards, the Soviets deployed another 15 to 20 armoured fighting vehicles against which, the Germans launched a counterattack.[1674]

SS-Sturmbannführer Müller, who was leading *SS-Panzergrenadier-Regiment 9*, was seriously wounded. The command of the *Regiment* was assigned to *SS-Sturmbannführer* Karl Heinz Bühler, who earlier served as the *Kommandeur* of *II. (Abteilung)/SS-Panzer-Artillerie-Regiment 5*.

The recently resupplied *SS-Panzer-Aufklärungs-Abteilung 5*, the *Kommandeur* of which was then *SS-Sturmbannführer* Fritz Vogt, was the strongest unit in the *Division*.[1675]

The 170th Tank Brigade/18th Tank Corps, reinforced by two SU-100 regiments of the 209th Self-Propelled Artillery Brigade, repulsed a number of German counterattacks, which were launched with the support of seven to ten armoured fighting vehices from Kövesgyűr, from the northeast in the direction of Tótvázsony. Around 0630 in the morning, the reinforced Tank Brigade reached Csárdamajor, north of Tótvázsony, where they ran into the nine combat-ready Panther tanks and the artillery of *I. (Abteilung)/Panzer-Regiment 24*.

The *I. (Abteilung)/Panzer-Regiment 24,* in defence at Csárdamajor, had already identified 10 well camouflaged Soviet tanks in the valley laying in front of them. As soon as daylight appeared, the Germans opened fire and reported to have knocked out eight T–34/85s.[1676]

The ISU–122 and ISU–152 self-propelled guns of the Soviet 363rd Guards Heavy Self-Propelled Artillery Regiment/18th Tank Corps, opened fire on the German tanks from the forested Hill 375 and knocked out three Panthers. Afterwards, the Soviet troops launched an attack on wide front, and bypassed the Panther positions. The German armoured fighting vehicles were forced to cover the withdrawal of the *Panzergrenadiers* who arrived the night before. Three Panthers sunk in the mud during these actions, and due to the lack of prime movers, had to be blown up. *Leutnant* Jonas, with his remaining armoured fighting vehicles, reached the edge of the nearest hill, where he engaged the approaching tanks and self-propelled guns of which, the Panthers seriously damaged 10. Then the remaining combat-ready Panthers ran out of fuel, and needed to be blown up as well.[1677]

Hauptmann Weidemann, *Kommandeur* of *I. (Abteilung)/Panzer-Regiment 24* with six combat-ready Panthers, established firing positions in the sector of Vörös Lake. During the afternoon, the Soviet troops continued their attack from Tótvázsony. The last combat-

---

1673 *History of the schwere Panzer-Abteilung 509* (typewritten manuscript). Copy owned by the author. p. 58.
1674 NARA, T311, R163, F7215456.
1675 Strassner, Peter: *Europäische Freiwillige. Die 5. SS-Panzerdivision Wiking*. Osnabrück, 1977. Third, revised edition. pp. 342–343.
1676 Senger und Etterlin, von F.M. jr.: *Die 24. Panzer-Division vormals 1. Kavallerie-Division 1939–1945*. Neckargemünd, 1962. p. 310.
1677 Weidemann, Gert-Axel: *Unser Regiment. Reiter-Regiment 2 – Panzer-Regiment 24*. Groß-Umstadt, 1982. p. 280.

ready Panther tanks of *5. SS-Panzer-Division* then retreated from there and blew up their immobilised armoured fighting vehicles.[1678]

Soon after, Soviet tanks and self-propelled guns appeared, followed by the rifle infantry forces. The remaining Panthers of *I. (Abteilung)/Panzer-Regiment 24*, opened fire and knocked out three self-propelled guns. Soon after, the unit was ordered to disengage from the frontline and to retreat. East of Némerbarnag, at the supply strongpoint of the unit, five other Panthers had to be blown up due to extreme fuel shortage. The armoured recovery vehicles were only able to save two damaged tanks that they could tow away from the approaching Soviets.[1679]

Around 2000 hours, the Soviet 110th Tank Brigade joined in the ever lengthening combat. During the fighting, the reinforced 170th Tank Brigade, reported to have knocked out 12 German armoured fighting vehicles, nine armoured personnel carriers and seven guns, besides capturing six armoured fighting vehicles, 10 armoured personnel carriers and five guns. Their own losses included seven knocked out T–34/85s, of which five burnt out, and three knocked out SU–100s[1680], one of which burnt out. In the evening, the 170th Tank Brigade had 11 operational tanks of their own, besides the 26 subordinated SU–100s.[1681] An officer of the Brigade, 1st Lieutenant Bryukhov, saw the actions of the day:

> *"Early in the morning, we continued with the offensive. The 2nd battalion attacked from the north-east with a company of submachine gunners and a battery of SU–100s, the 3rd battalion arrived from the north with similar support. The brigade quickly broke into the north-eastern parts of Tótvázsony and close quarter combat ensued. The enemy launched a counterattack and the main assault was faced by the 2nd battalion. After the brigade lost three tanks, it could not hold its position and had retreated, but the price the enemy paid for their success was still there: altogether six burnt out tanks and assault guns, and four armoured transport vehicles.*
> *Observing the unfolding situation, Chunihin continuously assessed the situation and decided based on this. The company of 2nd Lieutenant Pilnikov, with a SU-100 battery, attacked from the north-west, 2nd Lieutenant Rogov, commander of the 2nd battalion, attacked with his company and a company of rifles from the north, manoeuvring exactly like they were ordered to. In the meantime, Otroshenkov encircled Tótvázsony 3 km in the north-western direction along the edge of the forest, and occupied Felsőcsepely; thus encircling the enemy from the rear."*[1682]

According to German records, during the day the Soviets attacked from the north-east and occupied Tótvázsony with approximately 2000 men and 11 armoured fighting vehicles,

---

[1678] Weidemann, Gert-Axel: *Unser Regiment. Reiter-Regiment 2 – Panzer-Regiment 24*. Groß-Umstadt, 1982. p. 280.
[1679] Weidemann, Gert-Axel: *Unser Regiment. Reiter-Regiment 2 – Panzer-Regiment 24*. Groß-Umstadt, 1982. p. 281.
[1680] These three SU–100s were most likely knocked out by the six combat-ready Panthers of the German *I. (Abteilung)/Panzer-Regiment 24* in the second half of the day near the Vöröstó two km south-east of Nagyvázsony. See Senger und Etterlin, von F.M. jr.: *Die 24. Panzer-Division vormals 1. Kavallerie-Division 1939–1945*. Neckargemünd, 1962. p. 310.
[1681] Central Archives of the Russian Defence Ministry (Podolsk), f. 243, op. 2928, gy. 131, li. 273.
[1682] Bryukhov, Vasiliy: *Red Army Tank Commander. At War in a T–34 on the Eastern Front*. Barnsley, 2013. p. 180. The 1st Lieutenant also states in his memoires that in the end the 170th Tank Brigade occupied Tótvázsony, but this is not verified by the archival documents detailing the actions of the 18th Tank Corps.

The village was occupied around 1300 hours by the Soviet 110th Tank Brigade, the 363rd Guards Heavy Self-Propelled Artillery Regiment and one of the battalions of the 32nd Motorized Rifle Brigade in heavy combat.

Units of *5. SS-Panzer-Division,* according to Soviet records, launched a counterattack with seven tanks and a company-size force of *Panzergrenadiers*, and temporarily reoccupied the village. The Germans reported to have knocked out four Soviet tanks. Afterwards, the Germans withdrew because of the increasing pressure of the Soviets on the Nagyvázsony–Akali section.[1683]

The reinforced 110th Tank Brigade reoccupied Tótvázsony, then continued its attack and, at around 1900 hours, reached Nagyvázsony. The reinforced 170th Tank Brigade joined them here, then they launched a joint attack against the village and captured it around 2000 hours. The 110th Tank Brigade reported that in the combat action of that day, they knocked out four German armoured fighting vehicles and four armoured personnel carriers. Their own losses included three knocked out T–34/85s, of which, two burnt out, and four knocked out ISU–122s, of which, two burnt out. The reinforced Brigade had 10 operational tanks, four ISU–152s and five ISU–122 self-propelled guns in the evening.[1684]

The 181st Tank Brigade, together with one of the SU-100 regiments of the 209th Self-Propelled Artillery Brigade and one of the battalions of the 32nd Motorized Rifle Brigade, marched from the sector of Felsőörs to Nagypécsely and, at 1900 hours, they were 1 km north of there. Here the Soviet troops ran into German resistance and during the fire fight, they reported to have knocked out one German armoured fighting vehicle and one armoured personnel carrier. Their own losses included one T–34/85 tank that ran over a mine. That evening, the reinforced 181st Tank Brigade had 18 operational tanks and eight SU–100s.[1685]

The 18th Tank Corps reported 32 knocked out or destroyed German tanks and three armoured personnel carriers including six Tiger Bs and 20 Panthers, one self-propelled anti-tank gun (tank destroyer) and four assault guns with Panzer IV chassis, assault or *Jagdpanzer*.[1686] The majority of these, as was mentioned before, were blown up by the Germans themselves. One of the armoured fighting vehicles was most likely one of the four Sturmpanzer IVs of *Sturmpanzer-Abteilung 219* in the Nagyvázsony sector. At 0100 hours on the same day, it received a direct hit during a Soviet night bomber attack, and blew up along with its crew.[1687]

The Soviet 1202nd Self-Propelled Artillery Regiment/27th Army, after being engaged in mopping up operations on that day,[1688] marched from the sector of Nemesvámos to the forest four km north of Nagyvázsony with their 20 operational SU–76M self-propelled guns. The 432nd Independent Self-Propelled Artillery Battalion/316th Rifle Division with 12 SU–76Ms, was assembled at Balatonfüred.[1689]

1683 NARA, T311, R162, F7214760.
1684 Central Archives of the Russian Defence Ministry (Podolsk), f. 243, op. 2928, gy. 131, li. 273.
1685 Central Archives of the Russian Defence Ministry (Podolsk), f. 243, op. 2928, gy. 131, li. 273.
1686 Central Archives of the Russian Defence Ministry (Podolsk), f. 381, op. 8378, gy. 516, li. 73.
1687 Bertram, Ludwig: Sturmpanzerabteilung 219. In: *Der Sturmartillerist*. Heft 101. 1991. p. 2338.
1688 See Central Archives of the Russian Defence Ministry (Podolsk), f. 381, op. 8378, gy. 590, li. 61.
1689 Central Archives of the Russian Defence Ministry (Podolsk), f. 243, op. 2928, gy. 131, li. 272.

A Soviet 2nd Guards Independent Self-Propelled Artillery Battalion/68th Guards Rifle Division/26th Army with its 10 SU–76Ms, was acting as anti-tank artillery reserve for the Division commander and was not engaged in any combat action on that day.[1690]

The 71st and 60th Tank Regiments/5th Guards Cavalry Corps, the former with 12 T–34/85s, and the latter without tanks, was gathered at Siófok, the 54th Tank Regiment with eight T–34/85s was gathered at Balatonszabadi, and the 1896th Self-Propelled Artillery Regiment with 15 SU–76Ms at Balatonakarattya.[1691]

The units of the Soviet 5th Guards Tank Corps that were attacking with a battalion-size force and 11 armoured fighting vehicles, were held up by the Germans at the Veszprém–Devecser road and reported to have knocked out two armoured fighting vehicles there. The Soviet 20th Guards Tank Brigade, attacking from Magyarpolány toward the south with 17 armoured fighting vehicles, were repulsed by units of *1. SS-Panzer-Division,* during which, they reported to have knocked out seven Soviet armoured fighting vehicles. While the units of *1. SS-Panzer-Division* were being relieved by the arriving *Gebirgs-Aufklärungs-Abteilung 54/1. Volks-Gebirgs-Division*[1692], the renewed Soviet attack had taken Városlőd and Kislőd with armoured support.

According to the report of the *Stab/6. Armee* to the *Heeresgruppe* in the morning, the subordinated troops of *1. SS-Panzer-Division* retreated to the eastern edge of Városlőd, as the *Divisionskommandeur, SS-Brigadeführer* Kumm, wanted to join up with *I. SS-Panzerkorps* in combat on their left with his remaining armoured fighting vehicles, without waiting for the arrival of *Gebirgs-Aufklärungs-Abteilung 54* that was assigned to relieve them.[1693]

Around 1200 hours, the 6th Guards Motorized Rifle Brigade and the 51st Guards Self-Propelled Artillery Brigade of the 5th Guards Tank Corps, encircled Kislőd and occupied the northern edges of the village. One of the SU-76Ms of the 51st Guards Self-Propelled Artillery Brigade was hit and burnt out.[1694] The village was covered from the east by units of the German *1. SS-Panzer-Division* with four tanks, two *Jagdpanzers*, three armoured personnel carriers and two companies of *Panzergrenadiers*.[1695] These forces retreated toward the west.

When the attack continued, the Soviet 22nd Guards Tank Brigade and the and 6th Guards Motorized Rifle Brigade of the 5th Guards Tank Corps, occupied Ajkarendek and Bakonygyepes around 1700 hours with a regiment-size force and 15 armoured fighting vehicles. The 6th Guards Motorized Rifle Brigade with the Tank Brigade, was in combat in the sector of Zalaszegvár at the end of the day.

On the eastern and southern edge of the forest west of Bakonygyepes, the reinforced German *Gebirgs-Aufklärungs-Abteilung 54* tried to establish defensive positions.[1696] The units of the Soviet 5th Guards Tank Corps, after bypassing the left flank of the German

---

1690 Central Archives of the Russian Defence Ministry (Podolsk), f. 243, op. 2928, gy. 131, li. 272.
1691 Central Archives of the Russian Defence Ministry (Podolsk), f. 243, op. 2928, gy. 131, li. 273.
1692 On that day, the German *Eisenbahn-Panzerzug 79* was subordinated to *1. Volks-Gebirgs-Division*. See NARA, T311, R163, F7215464.
1693 NARA, T311, R162, F7214767.
1694 War log of the 51st Guards Self-Propelled Artillery Brigade between 20 January - 20 August 1945. Copy owned by the author. p. 6.
1695 War log of the 5th Guards Tank Corps for March 1945. Copy owned by the author. p. 19.
1696 NARA, T311, R162, F7214760.

*Aufkl*ärungs-Abteilung north-west of Bakonygyepes, broke into Devecser at 2100 hours with a force consisting of T–34/85 tanks and SU–100 self-propelled guns, mounted rifle infantry and anti-aircraft artillery.[1697] After this, the dispersed German unit was to close off the road between Somlóvásárhely and Somló Hill.[1698]

The 21st Guards Tank Brigade was at first stationed in Kislőd, serving as the reserve of the commander of the Corps, then in the afternoon, followed the 22nd Guards Tank Brigade, and together with the 208th Self-Propelled Artillery Brigade, the 1458th Self-Propelled Artillery Regiment and an engineering company, launched an attack in the direction of Kisberzseny.[1699]

The 5th Guards Tank Corps lost four burnt out tanks on that day[1700] and in the evening had 36 operational T–34/85s and 10 SU–76M self-propelled guns. Within the 51st Guards Self-Propelled Artillery Brigade, there were 45 SU–76Ms, in the 208th Self-Propelled Artillery Brigade subordinated to the 5th Guards Tank Corps, there were 41 SU–100s, three SU–57s and two T–34s in operational condition.[1701]

SS-Panzer-Aufklärungs-Abteilung 1/1. SS-Panzer-Division was in defence in the sector of Úrkút.[1702]

The four SU–76M self-propelled guns of the 1513th Self-Propelled Artillery Regiment,[1703] supporting the rifle forces of the Soviet 9th Guards Army, were also in combat here, and reported on that day to have knocked out four German armoured fighting vehicles, three armoured personnel carriers and three guns. The 1523rd Self-Propelled Artillery Regiment stayed in Csesznek as the anti-tank artillery reserve of the Corps with 16 SU–76Ms. The 1524th Self-Propelled Artillery Regiment, with 25 operational SU–76M self-propelled guns, was stationed in Bakonybél, but was not engaged in combat on that day.[1704]

The *1. Volks-Gebirgs-Division* was to establish a bridgehead in the sector of Jánosháza, east of the Marcal Canal, where the Germans could at last re-establish contact between *6. Armee* and *6. Panzerarmee*.[1705] The southern combat group of *1. SS-Panzer-Division* that was withdrawn from combat during the afternoon, was assembled in the sector of Noszlop, north of Devecser, and on that day they were reassigned into the subordination of the German *6. Panzerarmee*.[1706]

1697 NARA, T311, R163, F7215467. Devecser was breached by the 20th Guards and 22nd Guards Tank Brigades, the 6th Guards Motorized Rifle Brigade, the 1458th Self-Propelled Artillery Regiment and 364th Guards Heavy Self-Propelled Artillery Regiment of the 5th Guards Tank Corps, and the 1016th and 1922nd Self-Propelled Artillery Regiments/208th Self-Propelled Artillery Brigade. The latter reported to have knocked out during the battle, seven heavy tanks, including, two Tiger Bs, three Panthers, three assault guns and 15 armoured personnel carriers. In addition, the regiments captured three operational Panthers. Their own losses amounted to three knocked out SU–100s, one of which was burnt out. See the summarized report of the 208th Self-Propelled Artillery Brigade of the 6 March – 6 April 1945. Copy owned by the author. p. 14.
1698 NARA, T311, R162, F7214771.
1699 War log of the 5th Guards Tank Corps for March 1945. Copy owned by the author. p. 19.
1700 War log of the 5th Guards Tank Corps for March 1945. Copy owned by the author. p. 19.
1701 Central Archives of the Russian Defence Ministry (Podolsk), f. 243, op. 2928, gy. 131, li. 271. The 5th Guards Tank Corps lost between 18-25 March 1945, 44 destroyed T–34/85s and eight SU–76M self-propelled guns. The 51st Guards Self-Propelled Artillery Brigade's total losses in the same period amounted to nine SU–76Ms.
1702 NARA, T311, R162, F7214761.
1703 The combat actions of the 1513th Self-Propelled Artillery Regiment between 16-24 March 1945 included the knocking out of, among others, 17 tanks and assault guns, 23 armoured personnel carriers, 21 wood-and-earth small fortifications, 27 anti-tank guns, and 68 machine guns. Their own losses amounted to 23 dead and 30 wounded soldiers and 21 SU–76M self-propelled guns. See Central Archives of the Russian Defence Ministry (Podolsk), f. 911, op. 1, gy. 165, li. 12-13.
1704 Central Archives of the Russian Defence Ministry (Podolsk), f. 243, op. 2928, gy. 131, li. 272.
1705 NARA, T311, R162, F7214765.
1706 NARA, T311, R162, F7214770.

In the evening, *General der Panzertruppe* Balck reported to the *Heeresgruppe,* that according to the reports of *IV. SS-Panzerkorps,* they were forced to blow up the heavy tanks due to the shortage of fuel and the imminent retreat.[1707]

In the front of the German *I. SS-Panzerkorps/6. Panzerarmee, 1. SS-Panzer-Division* was to defend the sector of Pápa.[1708] The training units of *232. Panzer-Division* were ordered to the northern outskirts of Pápa, in the Marcaltő bridgehead, in order to engage the Soviet troops which were advancing north-west from there, aiming towards Sopron.[1709]

Pápa was secured by the heavy and light anti-aircraft batteries of the German *20. Flak-Division* against the Soviet attacks, however the guns were relocated to the Marcaltő bridgehead. The German combat commander of the town was *Generalmajor* Bormann, who informed the *Stab/6. Panzerarmee* of this in a telegram at around 1700 hours.[1710]

By morning, the armoured fighting vehicles of the 18th Guards Mechanized Brigade and the 46th Guards Tank Brigade/9th Guards Mechanized Corps, and the supporting artillery, already arrived at the south-eastern outskirts of Pápa through Tapolcafő and began their bombardment of the town.

On the night of 24/25 March 1945, the units of *3. SS-Panzer-Division* were retreating in the direction of Koppány and then were holding the railroad line between Bakonyszentiván and Bakonytamási.[1711] Units of *SS-Panzer-Aufklärungs-Abteilung 3* and the *Divisionsbegleitkompanie* were defending Nagygyimót until the evening, where the command post of *SS-Brigadeführer* Becker was also situated.[1712]

The forces of the Soviet 31st Guards Mechanized Brigade, attacking from the Bakonykoppány–Pápateszér line, first occupied Szücs and Zsörki, and afterwards, broke through the line of fortifications between Ugodiújmajor and Bakonyszentiván, then occupied Csót. The Germans repulsed a Soviet attack launched with a battalion-size force in a north-west direction from Csót, on the southern edge of Vanyola and on Hill 189 and 190 south-west of there. South of Csót however, a regimental size Soviet force occupied Béb and advanced further towards Nagygyimót. In order to hold and contain the Soviets in the direction of Pápa and east of there, the right flank of *I. SS-Panzerkorps* had to be extended up to the Nagygyimót–Tótvázsony line.[1713]

Around 1800 hours, the forces of the 9th Guards Mechanized Corps reached Pápa from the east. The 31st Guards Mechanized Brigade was attacking the eastern edge of the town, the 18th Guards and 30th Guards Mechanized Brigade, and the 46th Guards Tank Brigade attacked the south-western edge of the town from the sector of Hill 172 (Öreghegy), three km southeast of Pápa. The Germans, however, launched a counterattack with approximately 40 armoured fighting vehicles. The forces of the 9th Guards Mechanized Corps reported on that day to have knocked out 12 German tanks and three assault guns.[1714]

1707 NARA, T311, R162, F7214770.
1708 NARA, T311, R162, F7214765.
1709 NARA, T311, R162, F7214765.
1710 NARA, T311, R163, F7215087.
1711 Tieke, Wilhelm: *Von Plattensee bis Österreich. Heeresgruppe Süd 1945.* Gummersbach, without year of publication, p. 84.
1712 Vopersal, Wolfgang: *Soldaten, Kämpfer, Kameraden. Marsch und Kämpfe der SS-Totenkopfdivision.* Band Vb. Bielefeld, 1991. p. 818.
1713 NARA, T311, R162, F7214761.
1714 Central Archives of the Russian Defence Ministry (Podolsk), f. 243, op. 2928, gy. 131, li. 271.

In the meantime, units of the 30th Guards Mechanized Brigade reached the northern edge of Ganna, 12 km southeast of Pápa, and Bakonypölöske. During the day, the Corps had lost seven knocked out tanks.[1715] In the evening, they had 76 operational M4A2s and nine SU–76M self-propelled guns. The 364th Guards Heavy Self-Propelled Artillery Regiment, subordinated to the Corps, had 15 operational ISU–122s.[1716]

At dawn, on the front of *12. SS-Panzer-Division*, the rearguard was covering the retreat operations at the bridge two km north of Gerenceipuszta. The Soviets followed the Germans with armoured cars and approximately 300 riflemen. As soon as the retreating German vehicles reached Bakonykoppány, the Soviets launched an attack against the village from the west. The *Kommandeur* of the *Division*, *SS-Brigadeführer* Kraas, launched a counterattack with units of *III. (Bataillon)/SS-Panzergrenadier-Regiment 26* and repulsed the attackers. *Kampfgruppe "Ott"* was positioned on the Bakonykoppány–Béb route. *Kampfgruppe "Hauschild"* was also expected to arrive there as well. As the last unit to retreat, the *Divisionsbegleitkompanie* retreated from Bakony towards Béb around 1000 hours. Around 1200 hours the command post of the *Division* was at Vanyola.

Kampfgruppe "Ott" and a heavy artillery *Abteilung*, repulsed a Soviet attack from west of Bakonykoppány sometime after 1100 hours, but in doing so, they spent all of their remaining ammunition. Around noon, the Soviets bypassed the left flank of the *Kampfgruppe*, occupied Bakonyszücs and later Csót. In the afternoon, they were already attacking Vanyola, where the command post of *SS-Brigadeführer* Kraas was situated. The Germans were only able to hold and contain them on the western edge of the town and in the south-western hills, partly among the artillery positions. The Soviets therefore turned toward the south and occupied Béb. With this, contact between *Kampfgruppe "Ott"* and the rest of the *Division* was severed, but they fought their way toward Nagygyimót, where they joined a combat group from *3. SS-Panzer-Division*. Early next morning, *Kampfgruppe "Ott"* and *"Hauschild"* reached the command post of the *Division*, relocated to Takácsi the day before. South of there, the *Divisionsbegleitkompanie* was securing positions at Antalházapuszta.

The *Divisionsbegleitkompanie* of *12. SS-Panzer-Division*, supported by a Jagdpanther *Jagdpanzer*, was given a special task to blow up the bridge on Gerence Creek, between Bakonykoppány and Bakonybél, two km north of Gerencepuszta. The *Kompanie*, under significant Soviet pressure, successfully executed the task and destroyed four bridges. The *SS-Kompanie* retreating towards Béb were dispersed after by Soviet troops however, and reassembled later in the sector of Vanyola.[1717]

Although *12. SS-Panzer-Division* was now again on relatively flat terrain, their armoured fighting vehicles and armoured personnel carriers were either knocked out by the Soviets, or they had to be blown up due to mechanical issues. Therefore, there was no armoured combat group available that could have been deployed against the Soviet penetrations into

---

1715 Central Archives of the Russian Defence Ministry (Podolsk), f. 339, op. 5179, gy. 87, li. 22.
1716 Central Archives of the Russian Defence Ministry (Podolsk), f. 243, op. 2928, gy. 131, li. 271. Between 18-25 March 1945, the 9th Guards Mechanized Corps irrecoverably lost 30 M4A2s and two SU–76Ms. During this period, the 364th Guards Heavy Self-Propelled Artillery Regiment lost six destroyed ISU–122s.
1717 War log of the *Divisionsbegleitkompanie/12. SS-Panzer-Division* (Copy owned by the author), 25 March 1945.

the villages among the fortifications defended by the *Panzergrenadiers*. Thus, active defence had become even more difficult.[1718]

The remnants of *3. SS-Panzer-Division* repulsed the majority of the Soviet troops in the sector of Bakonyszentiván, who were attacking toward the north and west from the direction of Pápateszér.[1719]

The *6. Panzer-Division/II. SS-Panzerkorps* was not successful the first time in stopping the Soviet attack launched with at least divisional strength in the Bakonyszentlászló–Réde sector and toward the northwest. Thus the Soviets have occupied Bakonygyirót and Sikátor. Afterwards, the Germans still managed to hold up the attackers on the Gic–Lázi–Bakonybánk sector southern edge, but when the sun went down, the Soviets broke into Bakonytamási, Bakonybánk and on both sides of Lázi, advanced up to the railroad line. The forces of *6. Panzer-Division,* with the help of their armoured fighting vehicles, launched a counterattack from Románd toward Lázi. Three km southeast of Lázi, a number of encircled German units were still fighting. In the sector of Kisbér, German fortifications were also ambushed by division-size Soviet troops with armoured support, but the Germans held out here for the time being.[1720] The hills west and north-west of Hánta, and those south and south-west of Kisbér, fell into Soviet hands. The Soviets were attacking the southern edge of the town with battalion-size forces from the forested area south of Kisbér.[1721]

The Soviet 366th Guards Heavy Self-Propelled Artillery Regiment/4th Guards Army, was in firing positions three km southeast of Kisbér, at Vérteskéthely, with nine operational captured German self-propelled howitzers and two Panther tanks. The independent self-propelled-artillery battalions of the Division were mostly serving as the anti-tank artillery reserves of their divisional commanders with 54 SU–76Ms and five tanks. The 207th Self-Propelled Artillery Brigade and the 53rd Motorcycle Regiment were subordinated to the 1st Guards Mechanized Corps upon orders from the commander of the Army, and they were assembled in the sector of Bakonyszentkirály.[1722]

On the same day, the 1st Guards Mechanized Corps was en route with all its units in the sector of the 4th Guards Army heading to their assigned assembly area. The units were battling with traffic congestion in the north-eastern edge of Lake Balaton and tried to replenish their fuel and ammunition supplies. During the reassembly, there was time to assess their combat value and the operational armoured fighting vehicles. According to the data from that day, the units possessed the following vehicles:

- the 1st Guards Mechanized Brigade: 20 M4A2 tanks, four BA–64 armoured cars, four armoured transport vehicles and six motorcycles;
- the 2nd Guards Mechanized Brigade: six M4A2 tanks, one BA–64 armoured car, four armoured transport vehicles and six motorcycles;

[1718] Meyer, Hubert: *Kriegsgeschichte der 12. SS-Panzerdivision „Hitlerjugend"*. Band II. Osnabrück, 1987. 2nd edition. pp. 516-517.
[1719] NARA, T311, R162, F7214761.
[1720] NARA, T311, R162, F7214761.
[1721] NARA, T311, R162, F7214762.
[1722] Central Archives of the Russian Defence Ministry (Podolsk), f. 243, op. 2928, gy. 131, li. 271-272.

- the 3rd Guards Mechanized Brigade: eight M4A2 tanks, eight BA–64 armoured cars, 11 armoured transport vehicles and six motorcycles;
- the 9th Guards Tank Brigade: 45 M4A2 tanks and one motorcycle;
- a 11th Guards Motorcycle Battalion: four M4A2 tanks, three BA–64 armoured cars, seven armoured transport vehicles and 90 motorcycles;
- the 78th Guards Signal Battalion: two tanks, three BA–64 armoured cars, seven armoured transport vehicles and seven motorcycles;
- the 382nd Guards Self-Propelled Artillery Regiment: eight SU–100s, one T–34 and one BA–64 armoured car;
- the 1821st Self-Propelled Artillery Regiment: five SU–100s and three motorcycles;
- the 1453rd Self-Propelled Artillery Regiment: six SU–100s and one BA–64 armoured car;
- the 1699th Anti-Aircraft Artillery Regiment: 12 M–17 four-barrelled self-propelled anti-aircraft heavy machine guns.[1723]

On the frontline section of the 2nd Ukrainian Front

In the front of *2. SS-Panzer-Division,* the Soviets were attacking with a division-size force from the northern outskirts of Ete and from Csép. The attack was also supported by a number of armoured groups. The Soviets managed to consolidate the areas of the smaller incursions, however the Germans stopped the attack east of the railroad line and inflicted heavy losses on the Soviets.

At 1100 hours in the morning, the 606th Rifle Regiment/317th Rifle Division, together with the 1897th Self-Propelled Artillery Regiment's SU–76Ms, were attacking from Csép in the west, toward Parraghpuszta nearby, to reach the railroad line. Two SU–76M batteries established firing positions on Point 170, 1.5 km southeast of Egyházpuszta and in the course of 48 hours, they knocked out 25 defensive fortifications.[1724]

The Soviet troops were also attacking in the sector of Kisigmánd with a regimental size force towards the west, but the Germans repulsed this attack. The Soviet assembly area, detected east of the village, was held under fire by the Germans.[1725]

On the front of *XXXXIII. Armeekorps,* the Soviets attacked between Kisigmánd and Mocsa toward the north-west and east, with approximately divisional-size forces and 40 armoured fighting vehicles. The Soviets only managed to create a temporary penetration at Bartusekpuszta, which was sealed off by the Germans with a counterattack at the railway line.[1726]

One of the tank battalions of the 39th Tank Brigade/23rd Tank Corps, was supporting the units of the 19th Rifle Division and occupied Öregcsém at 1030 hours. However, the Soviet rifle infantry did not reinforce the defences, and were not able to stop the German counterattack that was launched with a battalion of infantry and 10-15 armoured

---

1723 Central Archives of the Russian Defence Ministry (Podolsk), f. 243, op. 2928, gy. 131, li. 273.
1724 Central Archives of the Russian Defence Ministry (Podolsk), f. 240, op. 2799, gy. 342, li. 116.
1725 NARA, T311, R162, F7214762.
1726 NARA, T311, R162, F7214762.

fighting vehicles, ultimately reaching the tank battalion. The Germans knocked out four T–34/85s, three of which burnt out, and the battalion was pushed back to the eastern edge of Öregcsém.[1727]

The Soviet 991st Self-Propelled Artillery Regiment was also fighting in the sector, with their SU–76M armoured fighting vehicles, supporting the 315th Rifle Regiment/19th Rifle Division, in their attack launched in the direction of Öregcsém.[1728] At Újmajor, the Germans knocked out three SU–76Ms, one of which burnt out, one had to be sent for general repair, and the other for medium repair work. Around 1500 hours, the Self-Propelled Artillery Regiment gathering at Kocs had nine operational SU–76M self-propelled guns.[1729]

The 1505th Self-Propelled Artillery Regiment, together with the 439th Rifle Regiment/52nd Rifle Division, launched an attack at 0930 hours after a 30 minute artillery barrage, towards Göbölkútpuszta, but at 1500 hours they were still only 400 meters south of Bartusekpuszta. In the German artillery fire, the Soviet rifle infantry lay low to be able to search for coverage and the attack was halted. The Soviet armoured fighting vehicles continued to fight from a pinned down position with directed fire, and reported to have knocked out one German tank, two assault guns, three anti-tank guns and to have eliminated 11 fortifications. Their own losses amounted to a burnt out SU–76M and a captured German assault gun knocked out, besides one man killed and one wounded.[1730]

In the Komárom bridgehead of *Panzerkorps "Feldherrnhalle"/8. Armee*, north of Mocsa in the Bartusekpuszta–Boldogasszonypuszta sector, the Soviets had slightly pushed back the frontline of the Germans. The units of the 2nd Guards Mechanized Corps occupied Bartusekpuszta.[1731] The Germans repulsed the small scale attacks carried out against Füzitőpuszta and north-west of Pusztaalmás.[1732]

The forces of the 2nd Guards Mechanized Corps were in combat in the following sectors at the end of the day:

- the 4th Guards Mechanized Brigade with the 1509th Self-Propelled Artillery Regiment, the 565th Anti-Tank Artillery Regiment and the 2nd Battalion/524th Mortar Regiment west of Bartusekpuszta;
- the 5th Guards Mechanized Brigade with the 251st Guards Self-Propelled Artillery Regiment, the 462nd Anti-Tank Artillery Regiment and 1st Battalion/524th Mortar Regiment 500 meters west of the Csémi-csárda;
- the 6h Guards Mechanized Brigade with the 102nd Anti-Tank Artillery Regiment on the right flank of the 4th Guards Mechanized Brigade;
- the 37h Guards Tank Brigade, without its 10 T–34/85 tanks, which were reassigned to reinforce the 431st Rifle Regiment/52nd Rifle Division, stood ready to exploit the successes of the 5th Guards Mechanized Brigade.[1733]

1727 Central Archives of the Russian Defence Ministry (Podolsk), f. 240, op. 2799, gy. 357, li. 15.
1728 Central Archives of the Russian Defence Ministry (Podolsk), f. 240, op. 2799, gy. 342, li. 111.
1729 Central Archives of the Russian Defence Ministry (Podolsk), f. 240, op. 2799, gy. 342, li. 162. Another two SU–76Ms were in for major repairs and two captured Panther tanks were in for medium repair.
1730 Central Archives of the Russian Defence Ministry (Podolsk), f. 240, op. 2799, gy. 342, li. 114.
1731 Central Archives of the Russian Defence Ministry (Podolsk), f. 240, op. 2799, gy. 357, li. 15.
1732 NARA, T311, R162, F7214762.
1733 Central Archives of the Russian Defence Ministry (Podolsk), f. 3426, op. 1, gy. 79, li. 123-124.

On the night of 24/25 March 1945, in the Lábatlan bridgehead of the Hungarian 3rd Army, the Soviets broke into Nyergesújfalu, but a German counterattack pushed them back to the eastern edge of the village.[1734]

During the day, on the western frontline, the Soviets opened a gap with a battalion-size force, initiated from the south. The defenders created a fortified position two km south of Süttő, to counter this move. The smaller attacks against Bajót and Nyergesújfalu were repulsed by the Germans. German reconnaissance detected further troop movements with armoured support en route south-east of Bajót. The final abandonment of the German–Hungarian bridgehead was scheduled in the early morning hours of 27 March 1945.[1735] The *711. Infanterie-Division* had to be withdrawn as urgently as possible and reassembled into the Komárom bridgehead in order to let *Panzer-Kampfgruppe "Pape"*,[1736] in combat there, to be sent back to *Panzerkorps "Feldherrnhalle"* fighting north of the Danube. The reason for this, was that the main forces of the Soviet 2nd Ukrainian Front had launched their attack in the direction of Bratislava, on the Garam front of *8. Armee*.[1737]

The German *Luftflotte 4* supported their troops flying approximately 120 missions, mainly with ground attack aircraft, between Lake Balaton and Pápa and along the Garam river. The pilots reported to have destroyed five Soviet tanks. On the night of 24/25 March 1945, the German night ground attack aircraft flew 150 missions against the Soviet assembly areas and unit movements in the sector of Léva as well as the Vértes Mountains, west of Mór.[1738]

Generalleutnant von Gyldenfeldt had taken over as chief of staff of *Heeresgruppe Süd* from *Generalleutnant* von Grolman.[1739] Von Grolman became the *Kommandeur* of *4. Kavallerie-Division*.

General der Infanterie Wöhler reported on that day to *Generaloberst* Guderian, that according to the incoming reports, the German *6. Panzerarmee* and the German-Hungarian troops of the German *III. Panzerkorps/6. Armee* had knocked out 202 Soviet armoured fighting vehicles during the course of Operation *"Frühlingserwachen"*, and during the attack launched on 16 March, until 24 March, altogether 405 Soviet armoured fighting vehicles had been knocked out. Despite this, according to German estimations, the Soviets had at least 600 armoured fighting vehicles on that day in the Transdanubia, and at least 400-500 more north of the Danube.[1740]

1734 NARA, T311, R163, F7215456.
1735 NARA, T311, R162, F7214762.
1736 *I. (Abteilung)/Panzer-Regiment "Feldherrnhalle"* assigned to the armoured combat group had, on that day 19 combat ready Panzer IV tanks out of 21, one of the two Panzer IV/70 *Jagdpanzers*, and 12 of the 15 Panther tanks were combat-ready. See BAMA, RH 2 Ost 5512. Based on these, the *Panzer-Abteilung* had irrecoverably lost four Panther tanks and one Panzer IV/70 *Jagdpanzer* south of the Danube, in the sector of the Komárom bridgehead between 21-25 March 1945.
1737 NARA, T311, R162, F7214765.
1738 NARA, T311, R162, F7214764.
1739 NARA, T311, R162, F7214764.
1740 NARA, T311, R162, F7214773.

26 March, 1945. Monday

(**WEATHER**: highest daytime temperature 12 Celsius; thickening cloud base, visibility conditions are favourable. The road conditions are still favourable.)

On the night of 25/26 March 1945, the German *I. Kavallerie-Korps/6. Armee* established new defensive positions between Akali and Nagyvázsony. The Germans temporarily repulsed Soviet attacks in this sector. The Soviets tried to advance on the northern shore of Lake Balaton, as well as south and southwest of Tótvázsony with armoured fighting vehicles and rifle infantry, but the Germans held them up.[1741]

That evening, *23. Panzer-Division* retreated from Balatonudvari towards Tapolca. On the eastern edge of the town, on the night of 26/27 March, *Panzergrenadier-Regiment 126* and *128, Panzer-Pionier-Bataillon 51* and the remaining Jagdpanzer IV *Jagdpanzers* of *Panzerjäger-Abteilung 128* prepared for defensive action. The retreat was covered by the armoured personnel carriers of *Panzer-Aufklärungs-Abteilung 23,* which had withdrawn afterwards to Balatonederics via Káptalantóti and Nemestördemic.[1742]

The Soviet 1202nd Self-Propelled Artillery Regiment/27th Army supported the rifle infantry with 19 SU-76M armoured fighting vehicles in the sector of Vigántpetend.[1743] Although the 432nd Independent Self-Propelled Artillery Battalion/316th Rifle Division was not deployed on that day, one of its SU–76M armoured fighting vehicles was still burnt out.[1744] The reason for this might have been either an accident or a German air strike.

On the left flank of the German *I. Kavallerie-Korps,* the Soviets managed to break deep into the German lines. From the sector of Mencshely, a heavy Soviet attack was launched.[1745] During the day, a battalion-size combat group of *44. Reichsgrenadier-Division* was subordinated to the cavalry corps.[1746]

Panzerjäger-Abteilung 69 and *70* of *3.* and *4. Kavallerie-Divisions,* were each issued with four Panzer IV/70 (V) *Jagdpanzers* on that day.[1747]

In the front of *IV. SS-Panzerkorps,* the German defence was forced back from Nagyvázsony to the edge of the forest west of Nemesleányfalu.[1748] *SS-Panzer-Aufklärungs-Abteilung 5/5. SS-Panzer-Division* kept its guard position throughout the whole day at Nagyvázsony.[1749]

The majority of *3. Panzer-Division* retreated further south-west from the sector of Nemesleányfalu to Zalahaláp. *Panzergrenadier-Regiment 3,* which by that time had only four combat-ready armoured personnel carriers, secured Sümeg. The *Kommandeur* of

---

1741   NARA, T311, R163, F7215467.
1742   Rebentisch, Ernst: *Zum Kaukasus und zu den Tauern. Die Geschichte der 23. Panzer-Division 1941–1945*. Esslingen, 1963. p. 501.
1743   Central Archives of the Russian Defence Ministry (Podolsk), f. 243, op. 2928, gy. 131, li. 274.
1744   Central Archives of the Russian Defence Ministry (Podolsk), f. 243, op. 2928, gy. 178, li. 110.
1745   NARA, T311, R162, F7214774.
1746   NARA, T311, R163, F7215473. The majority of the remains of the *Division* were subordinated to *2. Panzerarmee.*
1747   NARA, T78, R621, F000768. The *Jagdpanzers* were set off on their route to the units on 21 March 1945.
1748   NARA, T311, R162, F7214774.
1749   Strassner, Peter: *Europäische Freiwillige. Die 5. SS-Panzerdivision Wiking*. Osnabrück, 1977. Third, revised edition. p. 343., furthermore Stoves p. 219.

I. (Bataillon)/ Panzergrenadier-Regiment 3, Hauptmann Gerhard Treppe, was killed that day by a hit from a Soviet anti-tank rifle.[1750]

The 170th Tank Brigade/18th Tank Corps, with two SU–100 regiments of the 209th Self-Propelled Artillery Brigade, advanced toward Ódörögd–Tapolca after occupying Nagyvázsony, but by the evening they had only reached and occupied Halimba. The Soviet attack that had been launched from Padrag towards Halimba with a battalion-size force, was at first repelled by the Germans.[1751]

In the sector of Halimba and Szőc, the remnants of the German *1. Panzer-Division* were in defence. The six combat-ready Panther tanks of *Oberleutnant* Stoves and the command Panther "R03", were placed into firing positions on the east and north-eastern edge of Szőc. They were supporting the battalion of *Panzergrenadier-Regiment 1* in *Kampfgruppe "Bradel"*. Around 1600 hours, the forces of the Soviet 18th Tank Corps launched an attack with 40-50 T–34/85 tanks, 15 ISU–122 and SU–100 self-propelled guns, and two-three motorized rifle battalions, supported by ground attack aircraft, and quickly bypassed the German defensive fortification at Szőc. A few Soviet tanks ran over German mines and the seven Panthers reported to have knocked out 10-15 Soviet armoured fighting vehicles, and the *Panzergrenadiers* reported knocking out two to three tanks with *Panzerfausts*. All of the Panthers were hit and burnt out or were immobilized and blown up by their own crews. The German defence was not able to hold on for a prolonged time because of the Soviet bypass manoeuvre, and therefore retreated towards Nyirád.[1752]

The 181st Tank Brigade, together with the 110th Tank Brigade, quickly occupied Szőc and were advancing toward Sáska and Zalahaláp. In the fighting that day, the units lost six burnt out T–34/85s and two ISU–122s. In the evening, the Corps had 51 operational T–34/85s, six ISU–122s, four ISU–152s and eight SU–76M self-propelled guns. The 209th Self-Propelled Artillery Brigade had 36 SU–100s, one SU–57 and two T–34s in operational condition.[1753]

On the front of *1. Volks-Gebirgs-Division*, the Soviet 21st Guards and 22nd Guards Tank Brigades/5th Guards Tank Corps, together with the SU-100 self-propelled guns of the 1016th Self-Propelled Artillery Regiment, assaulted Devecser on the night of 25/26 March 1945, and with artillery support, occupied the village by 0600 hours against the German rearguard troops.[1754]

The two Soviet Tank Brigades continued their advance through Devecser towards the west. They dispersed *Gebirgs-Aufkl*ärungs-Abteilung 54 and captured their anti-tank guns.[1755] The Germans were able to hold up the 22nd Guards Tank Brigade east of Jánosháza, after occupying Karakó, at the Marcal Canal, as they reported to have knocked out seven Soviet armoured fighting vehicles.

1750 *Geschichte der 3. Panzer-Division. Herausgegeben vom Traditionsverband der Division.* Berlin, 1967. p. 472. Interestingly, the internet database of the *Volksbund Deutsche Kriegsgräberfürsorge e.V.* assigns Jánosháza as the place where the *Hauptmann* died, which is 54 km away from Nemesleányfalu.
1751 NARA, T311, R162, F7214775.
1752 Stoves, Rolf: Persönliches Kriegstagebuch Pz.Rgt. 1 (typewritten manuscript, a copy owned by the author), entry from 26 March 1945., furthermore Stoves, O. G. Rolf: *1. Panzer-Division 1935–1945. Chronik einer der drei Stamm-Division der deutschen Panzerwaffe.* Bad Nauheim, 1961. p. 773.
1753 Central Archives of the Russian Defence Ministry (Podolsk), f. 243, op. 2928, gy. 131, li. 276.
1754 Central Archives of the Russian Defence Ministry (Podolsk), f. 243, op. 2928, gy. 131, li. 274.
1755 NARA, T311, R162, F7214779.

At dawn and throughout the day, in the fighting for Devecser and the Marcal Canal, the 22nd Guards Tank Brigade reported to have knocked out, among others, two German Tiger Bs, 12 Panther tanks, and five assault guns. Their own losses amounted to five knocked out T–34/85 tanks, two of which burnt out. The Brigade had only eight remaining operational tanks.[1756]

South of Jánosháza, in the sector of Zalaszegvár, the Soviet 6th Guards Motorized Rifle Brigade and the 51st Guards Self-Propelled Artillery Brigade, occupied a small bridgehead on the canal and the 21st Guards Tank Brigade occupied Nemeskeresztúr. The 51st Guards Self-Propelled Artillery Brigade lost two burnt out SU–76Ms at Karakó.[1757] On that day, the 20th Guards Tank Brigade stood in the sector of Tüskevár as reserve to the corps. The 208th Self-Propelled Artillery Brigade, subordinated to the Corps, was in combat in the sector of Karakó and Zalaszegvár with 41 operational SU–100s, three SU–76Ms and two T–34s. The 5th Guards Tank Corps lost 10 knocked out tanks, of which, six were burnt out.[1758] In the evening they had 47 operational T–34/85 tanks and 16 SU–76M self-propelled guns.[1759]

The Germans proceeded to build up defensive positions between Ukk and Celldömölk on the bank of the Marcal.[1760]

On the night of 25/26 March 1945, the *Stab/III. Panzerkorps* created an anti-tank position south-west of Devecser, on both sides of the road leading to Sümeg, made up of immobilised armoured fighting vehicles.[1761]

On the night of 25/26 March 1945, the weakened forces of *1. SS-Panzer-Division/I. SS-Panzerkorps/6. Panzerarmee* temporarily held up the Soviets on the Noszlop–Bakonypölöske west–Kup–Pápakovácsi line. The Soviet armoured fighting vehicles however, occupied Noszlop and Hill 183, 1.5 km north of there.[1762] Around noon at Noszlop, the Soviets bypassed units of the German defenders on the right flank and encircled them. Because of this, *SS-Panzergrenadier-Regiment 1* was forced to withdraw west to the Marcal. The other units of the *Division* retreated there as well. As the Soviets, by encircling the right flank forces, forced themselves into the gap between the German *6. Panzerarmee* and *6. Armee,* they were able to cross the Marcal undisturbed, and could enter Celldömölk.[1763]

At 0145 hours, units of the Soviet 9th Guards Army and the 9th Guards Mechanized Corps, broke into Pápa. The Germans tried to stop them west of the town,[1764] and in the morning, were still holding the south-eastern edge of the town.[1765]

The 1524th Self-Propelled Artillery Regiment/9th Guards Army took part in occupying the town and at the end of the day, they were standing 1.5 km south-west of Pápa with 23 SU–76M self-propelled guns. The 1513th Self-Propelled Artillery Regiment, with four self-propelled guns, was standing at Ajkarendek, as reserve to the commander of the 37th

---

1756 War log of the 5th Guards Tank Corps for March 1945. Copy owned by the author. p. 20.
1757 War log of the 51st Guards Self-Propelled Artillery Brigade between 20 January - 20 August 1945. Copy owned by the author. p. 7.
1758 Central Archives of the Russian Defence Ministry (Podolsk), f. 339, op. 5179, gy. 87, li. 24.
1759 Central Archives of the Russian Defence Ministry (Podolsk), f. 243, op. 2928, gy. 131, li. 274.
1760 NARA, T311, R162, F7214775.
1761 NARA, T311, R163, F7215467.
1762 NARA, T311, R162, F7214775.
1763 Tiemann, Ralf: *Die Leibstandarte*. Band IV/2. Osnabrück, 1987. pp. 332.
1764 NARA, T311, R162, F7214785.
1765 NARA, T311, R163, F7215467.

Guards Rifle Corps. During the day, the 1523rd Self-Propelled Artillery Regiment was en route to Pápa with 16 SU–76Ms.[1766]

On the front of *1. SS-Panzer-Division,* the forces of the Soviet 9th Guards Mechanized Corps crossed the Marcal Canal, broke into Celldömölk and advanced along the Nemesszalók–Mersevát road toward the Marcal Canal.[1767] The German *6. Armee* only had the Hungarian SS-Regiment "Ney" to deploy against the Soviets that had broken through at Celldömölk.[1768]

By 1900 hours, the Soviet 18th Guards Mechanized Brigade/9th Guards Mechanized Corps, occupied Belsővát, then crossed the Marcal Canal and broke into Mersevát at dawn the following day. The tanks of *SS-Panzer-Regiment 1* were defending the sector around the village.[1769]

The 30th Guards Mechanized Brigade occupied Adorjánháza on the same day, and with its motorized rifle infantry, crossed the Marcal Canal as well. The 14th Guards Motorcycle Battalion set off from Nemesszalók and occupied Vinyár, and with their units also crossed the Malom Canal at Szergény. In the evening, the 46th Guards Tank Brigade replenished their fuel and ammunition supplies in the sector of Dabrony. The 31st Guards Mechanized Brigade followed the 18th Guards Mechanized Brigade and reached Nemesszalók. On that day, the 9th Guards Mechanized Corps irrecoverably lost three burnt out M4A2s and two SU–76M self-propelled guns. In the evening, they had 76 tanks and 12 self-propelled guns in operational condition.[1770]

The German *232. Panzer-Division*[1771] was defending its positions around the bridgehead at Marcaltő. Around 1500 hours, four M4A2 tanks, most likely from the 1st Guards Mechanized Corps, were advancing from Csikvánd towards Újmalomsok, which was part of the bridgehead. The Germans opened fire with three anti-tank guns from the area of Újmalomsok and initially knocked out the third vehicle in the column, then the second one and at last, the first one. Due to the damage inflicted, all three M4A2s were burnt out.[1772]

North of there, on the western bank of the Marcal, the combat groups of *12. SS* and *3. SS-Panzer-Division* were in holding positions.[1773]

Panzer-Pionier-Bataillon 12 retreated beyond the Rába River, south-east of Szany. On the Pápa–Marcaltő–Szany road, the bridges on the Rába River and the Marcal were prepared to be blown up by the laborers of the *Organisation Todt.*

In the morning, on the right flank of the *Division,* the Soviets had broken through the positions of *SS-Panzergrenadier-Regiment 26.* A counterattack, which was launched with

---

1766 Central Archives of the Russian Defence Ministry (Podolsk), f. 243, op. 2928, gy. 131, li. 274.
1767 NARA, T311, R162, F7214775.
1768 NARA, T311, R162, F7214785.
1769 Agte, Patrick: *Jochen Peiper. Kommandeur Panzerregiment Leibstandarte.* Berg am Starnberger See, 1998. p. 360. The author placed this combat action on 28 March based on a *Soldbuch* of one of the soldiers of 6. *Kompanie/SS-Panzer-Regiment 1,* but this is most likely a typing mistake, as all units of *1. SS-Panzer-Division* were already in combat west of the Rába River on that day.
1770 Central Archives of the Russian Defence Ministry (Podolsk), f. 243, op. 2928, gy. 131, li. 274.
1771 The unit was only a division in name, but not in its strength, and it was subordinated to *I. SS-Panzerkorps*. On the same day, besides the *Divisionsstab,* the majority of *Panzergrenadier-Regiment 101* and *102* and one tank destroyer company, most likely equipped with self-propelled anti-tank guns. *I. (Bataillon)/Panzergrenadier-Regiment 101* was already deployed on the same day in the Marcaltő bridgehead. See NARA, T311, R163, F7215473.
1772 Written memories of Kálmán Polgár, a local resident and eyewittness. p. 52. Copy owned by the author.
1773 NARA, T311, R162, F7214775.

weak forces, was unsuccessful. Around noon, the Soviets also attacked Takácsi and in the afternoon, they broke into the village. The command post of *12. SS-Panzer-Division* was relocated to Marcaltő and Takácsi was abandoned.

Near the evening, the majority of the *Division* retreated via the Marcaltő bridgehead to the western bank of the Rába River and established positions north of the bridgehead. The *Divisionsbegleitkompanie*, a few pioneer assault troops, a tank in still combat-ready condition and an anti-aircraft gun, remained in the bridgehead as rear guards. The divisional command post was relocated to Szany. *SS-Panzer-Flak-Abteilung 12* was in position at Szil.[1774]

On the front of *II. SS-Panzerkorps,* on 25 March 1945 from around 2100 hours, the Soviet rifle troops had been attacking the German positions between Gic and Bakonyszombathely. The Soviets occupied Románd, Point 214 1 km north-west of there, Lázi, and the hills south-east of Bakonybánk. The German rapid response troops were engaged in combat on the southern edge of Bakonypéterd, on the hill south of the Lázi–Bakonybánk railroad line and on the southern edge of Bakonyszombathely.[1775]

During the day, the reinforced Soviet 1st Guards Mechanized Corps was advancing from the sector of Románd and Pápateszér in a north-west direction, and in the morning, the troops broke through the Szerecseny–Kajár area with armoured fighting vehicles and motorized rifle infantry, and arrived in the sector of Tét.[1776]

The 3rd Guards Mechanized Brigade, the 382nd Guards Self-Propelled Artillery Regiment and the 117th Anti-Tank Artillery Regiment/1st Guards Mechanized Corps, were preparing to attack in the eastern outskirts of Lázi. The 1st Guards Mechanized Brigade, with the 1821st Self-Propelled Artillery Brigade, set off from the sector of Hathalom and the 2nd Guards Mechanized Brigade, with the 912th Self-Propelled Artillery Regiment/207th Self-Propelled Artillery Brigade, set off west of Pápateszér. The 9th Guards Tank Brigade, the 1004th Self-Propelled Artillery Regiment/207th Self-Propelled Artillery Brigade and the 105th Guards Rifle Regiment/34th Guards Rifle Division, were following the 1st Guards Mechanized Brigade. The units of the Corps launched their attack at 0700 hours in the morning.[1777]

The 1st Guards Mechanized Brigade with the 9th Guards Tank Brigade, and the 1821st Self-Propelled Artillery Regiment, was in combat in the sector of Tét around 1500 hours, and the 2nd Guards Mechanized Brigade with two SU-100 regiments of the 207th Self-Propelled Artillery Brigade at Szerecseny. The 3rd Guards Mechanized Brigade with the 382nd Guards Self-Propelled Artillery Regiment and the 53rd Motorcycle Regiment, were attacking the southern edge of Tápszentmiklós.[1778]

By 1700 hours, the 912th Self-Propelled Artillery Regiment, escorting the 9th Guards Tank Brigade, reached Mórichida and occupied firing positions on the western edge of the village. The 1004th Self-Propelled Artillery Regiment was there already at 1400 hours and went into temporary defence on the southern part of Mórichida, as well as on the eastern outskirts of the forest 1 km east of there. The 207th Self-Propelled Artillery Brigade reported

---

[1774] Meyer, Hubert: *Kriegsgeschichte der 12. SS-Panzerdivision „Hitlerjugend".* Band II. Osnabrück, 1987. 2nd edition. p. 518.
[1775] NARA, T311, R163, F7215467.
[1776] NARA, T311, R162, F7214775.
[1777] Central Archives of the Russian Defence Ministry (Podolsk), f. 243, op. 2928, gy. 131, li. 275.
[1778] Central Archives of the Russian Defence Ministry (Podolsk), f. 243, op. 2928, gy. 178, li. 107.

on that day to have knocked out two German medium tanks, one armoured personnel carrier and two anti-tank guns.[1779]

In the German-Hungarian bridgehead held at Mórichida,[1780] the Hungarian 1st Honvéd Mountain Brigade repulsed the attack of the Soviet 9th Guards Tank Brigade on that day and reported to have knocked out one armoured fighting vehicle.

South-east of Rábaszentmihály, the Soviet armoured fighting vehicles were fighting their way to cross the Marcal, where the Germans launched a counterattack and reported to have knocked out six Soviet armoured fighting vehicles.[1781]

In the evening, the 1st Guards Mechanized Corps had 85 operational M4A2 and two T–34 tanks, plus 12 SU–100 self-propelled guns. The 207th Self-Propelled Artillery Brigade had 25 SU–100, three SU–57s and one T–34 tank in operational condition.[1782]

The Soviets increased their pressure on the German bridgehead at Koroncó, and on the bridgehead, held in the southern sector of Győr as well.

The Soviet troops attacking on the Románd–Kisbér south line, had thrown back the Germans beyond the railroad line. The Germans were not able to prevent the Soviets entering Kisbér either.[1783] Soviet pressure on the Ete–Csép sector was still very heavy.[1784]

The Soviet 366th Guards Heavy Self-Propelled Artillery Regiment/4th Guards Army was in firing positions 500 meters south of Kisbér, with six *Hummel* and two *Wespe* self-propelled howitzers and one Panther tank. The independent self-propelled artillery battalions of the divisions, were supporting their own rifle units with 54 SU–76M self-propelled guns and five tanks.[1785]

On the frontline of the 2nd Ukrainian Front

The German *6. Panzerarmee* notified the *Stab/Heeresgruppe* that they wanted to get back the units of *6. Panzer-Division* that were fighting in temporary subordination to other units:

- *Panzer-Feldersatz-Bataillon 76* assigned to Győrszentmárton from the Komárom bridgehead;
- *I. Bataillon/Panzergrenadier-Regiment 114* assigned to Győr from the *96. Infanterie-Division*;
- *Panzer-Aufklärungs-Abteilung 6* assigned to Győr from *III. Panzerkorps*.[1786]

1779 War log of the 207th Self-Propelled Artillery Brigade, 27 March 1945. Copy owned by the author.
1780 There were approximately 50 German soldiers and one mortar battery in the bridgehead. According to the original defense plans, the forces of the Hungarian 1st Mountain Brigade were to be stretched in the *Zsuzsanna-Stellung* along the Rába River between Rábaszentmihály and the Győr bridgehead. See NARA, T311, R163, F7215473. However in the assigned positions, there were no possible fields of fire toward the outskirts for infantry weapons, therefore the Hungarian unit withdrew the forces of their staff to the line of the Marcal. See HM HIM Hadtörténelmi Levéltár (Budapest), m. kir. Honvéd Vezérkar főnöke iratai, 86.718/vkf. eln. 1/a.–1945.
1781 NARA, T311, R162, F7214775.
1782 Central Archives of the Russian Defence Ministry (Podolsk), f. 243, op. 2928, gy. 131, li. 275.
1783 NARA, T311, R162, F7214775.
1784 NARA, T311, R162, F7214776.
1785 Central Archives of the Russian Defence Ministry (Podolsk), f. 243, op. 2928, gy. 131, li. 274.
1786 NARA, T311, R163, F7215089.

In the front of *XXXXIII. Armeekorps* on the night of 25/26 March 1945, Soviet armoured fighting vehicles were advancing in small groups toward Komárom in the north-western outskirts of Mocsa.[1787]

During this action, the Soviet 1505th Self-Propelled Artillery Regiment, together with the 439th Rifle Regiment/52nd Rifle Division, renewed its attack in the direction of Göbölkútpuszta at 0930 hours, after a 30 minute artillery bombardment, and at 1500 hours managed to occupy the village. During the fighting, the Soviet armoured fighting vehicles reported to have knocked out three anti-tank guns and 13 fortifications.[1788]

In the Komárom bridgehead of *8. Armee,* the Germans repulsed a Soviet armoured assault against Mocsa.[1789] The units of the German *15. Flak-Division* were assigned to secure the village against Soviet armoured fighting vehicles, but the anti-aircraft artillery units were withdrawn by the *Luftwaffe* without notifying the *Stab/XXXXIII. Armeekorps*. This caused significant tension between the air and ground forces, as it was not possible to subordinate the anti-aircraft units of the *Luftwaffe* to the ground forces, they could only be ordered to cooperate.[1790]

Luftflotte 4 attacked Soviet unit movements south of Pápa, and smaller Soviet forces north-east of Pápa and along the Garam.[1791]

On the same day, Hitler demanded that one of the armoured combat groups of *16. SS-Panzergrenadier-Division* was to be sent to the south-western edge of Lake Balaton to prevent the Soviets breaking through.[1792] The *Stab/2. Panzerarmee*, at the same time suggested that the decision on this should be delayed until the arrival of *297. Infanterie-Division*. One of the combat groups of *118. Jäger-Division,* reinforced with assault guns, was however already directed to the sector of Keszthely.[1793] During the day, under command of *Festungs-Regiments-Stab 35*, the following units were relocated into the sector of Kéthely: *Sturmgeschütz-Brigade 191, 11.* and *12. Kompanies/Festungs-Pak-Verband IX* with 8.8 cm anti-tank guns, a pioneer company of *16. SS-Panzergrenadier-Division* and the Hungarian 217th Fortress Machine-Gun Battalion.[1794]

This was not enough for Hitler however, and on 27 March 1945 at 0150 hours, he ordered *2. Panzerarmee* to direct a battalion of *16. SS-Panzergrenadier-Division,* reinforced with assault guns behind its left flank.[1795]

Because the Soviet troops crossed in the sector of Celldömölk, the *Heeresgruppe* decided to regroup *2. SS* and *6. Panzer-Divisions* in order to strengthen the southern flank of the German *6. Panzerarmee*, and prevent the Soviets gaining more ground in the north-west.[1796] The *Stab/6. Panzerarmee* informed them, that due to the fuel shortage and the constant Soviet attacks, it was not possible to withdraw the two armoured divisions.[1797]

1787 NARA, T311, R163, F7215468.
1788 Central Archives of the Russian Defence Ministry (Podolsk), f. 240, op. 2799, gy. 342, li. 114.
1789 NARA, T311, R162, F7214776.
1790 NARA, T311, R163, F7215092.
1791 NARA, T311, R162, F7214777.
1792 NARA, T311, R162, F7214784.
1793 NARA, T311, R162, F7214784.
1794 NARA, T311, R163, F7215473.
1795 NARA, T311, R162, F7214784.
1796 NARA, T311, R162, F7214787.
1797 NARA, T311, R163, F7215085.

At dawn on 27 March 1945, the second combat group of *37. SS-Kavallerie-Division* had been subordinated to *6. Panzerarmee,* but the unit was not yet available.[1798]

Generaloberst Guderian informed the *Stab/Heeresgruppe* on that day that Hitler was furious because of the low morale of the *SS-Panzer-Divisions* fighting in the Transdanubia. The *Führer* ordered *Reichsführer-SS* Heinrich Himmler, to investigate which units had carried out their duties and which had not. Chief of staff of *Heeresgruppe Süd*, *Generalleutnant* von Gyldenfeldt, suggested that the units were extremely worn out from facing the constant assaults of the enemy, the lack of fuel and almost all of their armoured fighting vehicles were destroyed.[1799]

27 March 1945, Tuesday

(**WEATHER**: highest daytime temperature: 16 Celsius; cloudy sky, occasional light showers. The roads are in good condition.)

On the front of the German *I. Kavallerie-Korps/6. Armee,* the Germans occupied their new positions when the Soviets, with 14 armoured fighting vehicles,[1800] advanced on the northern shore of Lake Balaton up to the Nemestördemic railway station.[1801] One of the *Jagdpanzer* platoons of the Hungarian 20th Assault Artillery Battalion engaged the Soviets in combat. According to the memories of 1st Lieutenant Tasziló Kárpáthy:

"The meeting point of the two roads[1802] is at the railway station of Balatonederics. A train carrying an anti-aircraft battery, was stranded there while its locomotive engine was being repaired. [...] Then we dug in the three guns[1803] up to their necks with the help of the anti-tank artillery unit, only their guns were sticking out. We also camouflaged them with boughs and branches. After waiting for 1.5 hours, 17 tanks and mounted troops appeared on the road to Szigliget, that is so well known from films. It was the time of the spring flooding, and both sides of the road were submerged and the road was completely soaked; therefore it was not possible to get along even with tracked vehicles. When the column approached within 200 meters, the most favourable distance for us[1804], we opened fire and knocked out the first and the last vehicle at the same time. The automatic cannon crews also joined the fight, bombarding the mounted infantry with high-explosive shells. The Soviet side was only able to respond with five-six shots. Everything was in flames on the road. In the meantime two Soviet combat aircraft

---

[1798] NARA, T311, R162, F7214788.
[1799] NARA, T311, R162, F7214787.
[1800] These were most likely the tanks of the 181st Tank Brigade/18th Tank Corps occupying Tapolca, although the log of the Corps did not mention that the Brigade had attacked in that direction. The cause of this might be that the Soviet armoured fighting vehicles did not succeed in their attack.
[1801] NARA, T311, R162, F7214791.
[1802] This means the two roads leading from Tapolca and Szigliget.
[1803] The three Jagdpanzer 38(t) *Jagdpanzers* of one of the sections of the 3rd Battery/20th Assault Artillery Battalion, under command of cadet dr. Ferenc Radványi.
[1804] The source mentions 2000 meters, but this is probably a typing error, as at this distance even the larger caliber and longer tank guns than that of the 7.5 cm gun of the Jagdpanzer 38(t) would have difficulty to achieve success.

appeared and attacked the assault guns in low-altitude raids and the train, but the violent gunfight has made them flee."[1805]

North of there, approximately 40 Soviet armoured fighting vehicles occupied Tapolca and Zalahaláp, and significant numbers of rifle infantry entered the forested area west of there. The units of the German corps were mixed up during the fighting to such an extent, that *General der Kavallerie* Harteneck had to personally intervene and restore order.[1806] In order to avoid the encirclement already taking shape, the Germans retreated to the Szigliget–Sümeg south general line. In the evening, the Soviets occupied Bazsi from the north. The Germans initiated a counterattack here.[1807]

The Soviet 181st Tank Brigade and the 1438th Self-Propelled Artillery Regiment/18th Tank Corps, the 1951st Self-Propelled Artillery Regiment/209th Self-Propelled Artillery Brigade and the 1st Battalion/2nd Motorized Rifle Brigade, reached Nyirád at 0100 hours, then they continued their attack from the north toward Tapolca. The two German *Panzergrenadier-Regiment*s of *23. Panzer-Division,* were not able to defend the village due to their weak anti-tank armament. After the Soviet air force attacked Tapolca around 0800 hours in two consecutive waves, the units of the 18th Tank Corps broke into the village at 1020 hours, with approximately 40 armoured fighting vehicles and, at around 1200 hours, occupied it with the help of the rifle forces of the 27th Army. After this, the forces of the Tank Corps established strong defences around the village then replenished their fuel and ammunition supplies. The reinforced 181st Tank Brigade lost on that day five knocked out T–34/85s, three of which burnt out, three knocked out SU–76Ms, two of which burnt out and one knocked out SU–100.[1808]

The *Panzergrenadier-Bataillons* of *23. Panzer-Division* retreated, then at 1330 hours they stopped and tried again to contain the Soviets west of Tapolca at the airfield, in order to provide enough time for their own vehicle columns crossing Lesence Creek towards the west. Around 1700 hours, the Germans blew up these bridges and withdrew their frontline with *Panzergrenadier-Regiment 126* establishing positions at Lesencetomaj, and *Panzergrenadier-Regiment 128* on the eastern edge of Lesenceistvánd.[1809]

Against the right flank of *IV. SS-Panzerkorps,* the Soviets launched battalion and regimental size attacks. In the morning hours, they were gathered at Padrag with the units of the 18th Tank Corps, with approximately 40 armoured fighting vehicles, then they launched an attack from the Nyírád–Káptalanfa general line toward Csabrendek.[1810]

The Soviet rifle infantry, supported by units of the 18th Tank Corps, and the 1952nd and 1953rd Self-Propelled Artillery Regiments of the 209th Self-Propelled Artillery Brigade, soon broke into Sümeg, then they encircled units of the German *3. Panzer-Division,* including units of *Panzergrenadier-Regiment 3.*

1805 Tasziló Kárpáthy: *A magyar királyi honvéd 20. rohamtüzérosztály története.* In: HM HIM Hadtörténelmi Levéltár (Budapest), Rohamtüzér-gyűjtemény, 14/7. gyűjtő. p. 21.
1806 NARA, T311, R162, F7214801.
1807 NARA, T311, R162, F7214792.
1808 War log of the 18th Tank Corps for March 1945. Copy owned by the author. p. 50.
1809 Rebentisch, Ernst: *Zum Kaukasus und zu den Tauern. Die Geschichte der 23. Panzer-Division 1941–1945.* Esslingen, 1963. p. 502.
1810 NARA, T311, R162, F7214800.

The 170th Tank Brigade, together with two SU-100 regiments of the 209th Self-Propelled Artillery Brigade, followed the 181st Tank Brigade, then turned west at Nyirád and via Deákipuszta and reached the road junction 4 km south-east of Sümeg. German armoured fighting vehicles were moving on the Sümeg–Ódörögd road. The Soviet armoured fighting vehicles repulsed them, and in heavy combat ,occupied Sümeg at 1310 hours[1811]. The reinforced 170th Tank Brigade reported to have knocked out six tanks, including four Tigers, and 12 armoured personnel carriers. Their own losses amounted to one knocked out T–34/85 and one SU–100.[1812]

1st Lieutenant Brjukhov, officer of the 170th Tank Brigade, remembers this day:

"The komkor was still very emphatic and again reprimanded Chunihin, demanding that he is to immediately occupy Sümeg. After he was cursing for a good while, he calmed down and listened to the reasons and questions of the kombrig. As a result of this, he ordered the 452nd Artillery Regiment and the 104th Artillery Regiment to reinforce the brigade. As soon as the artillery regiments have arrived, we continued our advance and approached Sümeg. This was quite a big town and an important traffic junction. The enemy had strengthened its defences considerably, placing their main forces on the eastern edge of the town and on the hills over the town. According to the report of Captain Gushak, Sümeg was defended by approximately a regiment-size infantry, ten entrenched Panther tanks, and approximately eight artillery batteries. The kombrig assessed the situation and decided that the 2nd battalion is to bypass the town on the forested area southwards, is to reach the Keszthely–Sümeg road and then attack the town from the south. This will surely split the enemy forces and then we can launch our attack from the south-east. He also ordered that all artillery should approach the town within such a distance that they can target the fortifications on the top of the hills, and if our main forces launch the attack, they can provide fire support.
Captain Sharkisyan successfully bypassed Sümeg and reached the road. When he broke into the southern part of the town, the fighting began. The enemy was surely not prepared for the attack of our armoured fighting vehicles from there, therefore they were forced to regroup some of their armoured fighting vehicles and artillery to repulse the attack of our 2nd battalion. This was what the kombrig planned. Now Otroshenkov's 3rd battalion, and Captain Dochenko's infantry battalion, went into attack. Our artillery on the hills eliminated the enemy firing positions with direct fire. The enemy suffered serious losses, started to waiver and retreated. Sümeg was soon occupied. The enemy lost six tanks and 18 vehicles; we captured freight trains, an armament depot and a military supply magazine.."[1813]

The Soviet armoured fighting vehicles acquired fuel and ammunition in the town after they occupied Sümeg.

One of the non-commissioned officers of *2. Kompanie/ Panzer-Aufklärungs-Abteilung 3*, Wilhelm Heinrichs, remembered this day:

1811 According to other Soviet sources the village only fell into Soviet hands at 1600 hours.
1812 War log of the 18th Tank Corps for March 1945. Copy owned by the author. p. 50.
1813 Bryukhov, Vasiliy: *Red Army Tank Commander. At War in a T–34 on the Eastern Front.* Barnsley, 2013. p. 182.

"In the evening we have been cut off again. The enemy armoured wedges stood at Sümeg. Only a few litres of fuel left in the tanks. No supplies are to come. We carry out a break-out action almost equal to fleeing, and in the course of this, we lose four or five tanks[1814] due to tank gun fire. Immediately a new blocking position is created. Major Medicus, with a few tank destroyers,[1815] stops the enemy."[1816]

However, parts of the 170th Tank Brigade were still after the retreating German troops on that day. With the words of 1st Lieutenant Brjukhov:

"As soon as the enemy retreated, the tank and rifle battalion went into pursuit. The platoon of 2nd Lieutenant Gerasjutyin was at the head, reinforced by a SU–100 battery. During the pursuit of the enemy, Gerasjutyin led his forward platoon up to Tótvármajor and occupied the village on the fly. Afterwards, the unit reached a creek [most likely Marcali Creek – the author] and engaged the forces defending the bridge in combat: a company sized infantry force, five tanks and two artillery batteries. Gerasjutyin ordered one self-propelled gun to provide short distance fire support, thereafter fanned out the platoon and attacked quickly, but the enemy managed to hit the first tank and also blow up the bridge. The tanks and self-propelled guns were in constant fire exchange on the banks of the creek, while the seriously wounded platoon commander was pulled out from his tank and sent back. The reconnaissance tried to find another crossing point while being in fire coverage, but they couldn't find any. The creek bed was soft and muddy, and the banks were swampy as well. The kombrig ordered Captain Kaluginto to build a bridge over the creek with the engineering troops and a rifle platoon; and by the morning it was ready."[1817]

The Soviet 110th Tank Brigade and the 363rd Guards Heavy Self-Propelled Artillery Regiment, with the 2nd Battalion/32nd Motorized Rifle Brigade, followed the 170th Tank Brigade, and around 1500 hours reached Deákipuszta. From here, the Brigade sent out a covering unit in the direction of Csabrendek.

In the evening, the 18th Tank Corps had 52 operational tanks, plus seven SU–76Ms, seven ISU–122s and four ISU–152 self-propelled guns. The 209th Self-Propelled Artillery Brigade, had 36 operational SU–100s, one SU–57 and two T–34 tanks.[1818]

The right flank of 5. SS-Panzer-Division, in combat on the middle of the front of IV. SS-Panzerkorps, held its positions north of Sümeg.[1819]

The Soviet 1202nd Self-Propelled Artillery Regiment/27th Army, supported the Soviet rifle troops assaulting Tapolca with 19 SU–76Ms and after the occupation of the town, took firing positions on the western edge of it. The 432nd Independent Self-Propelled Artillery

---

1814 The *2. Kompanie/Panzer-Aufklärungs-Abteilung 3* was equipped with Sd.Kfz. 250 armoured personnel carriers.
1815 *Major* Franz Medicus was the *Kommandeur* of *Panzerjäger-Abteilung 543/3. Panzer-Division*, who commanded Jagdpanzer IV Jagdpanzers.
1816 Heinrichs, Wilhelm: *5 Jahre und 25 Tage meines Lebens. Mein Tagebuch als Funker des Kradschützen-Bataillons 3 im Russlandkrieg von 1940–1945.* Bad Langensalza, 2014. p. 403.
1817 Bryukhov, Vasiliy: *Red Army Tank Commander. At War in a T–34 on the Eastern Front.* Barnsley, 2013. p. 183.
1818 Central Archives of the Russian Defence Ministry (Podolsk), f. 243, op. 2928, gy. 131, li. 278.
1819 Tieke, Wilhelm: *Von Plattensee bis Österreich. Heeresgruppe Süd 1945.* Gummersbach, without year of publication, p. 88.

Battalion/316th Rifle Division was assembled at Badacsonytomaj with 11 operational SU–76M self-propelled guns.[1820]

The 72nd Guards Independent Self-Propelled Artillery Battalion/68th Guards Rifle Division/26th Army, was assembled at Városlőd with its 10 operational SU–76M self-propelled guns.[1821]

At dawn on 27 March 1945, on the front of *1. Volks-Gebirgs-Division,* the Soviets cut through the Sümeg-Jánosháza road westwards at Nemeskeresztúr with the armoured fighting vehicles of the 5th Guards Tank Corps and with significant rifle infantry forces.[1822] During the day, the Soviet troops at Jánosháza crossed the Marcal Canal at first with rifle infantry forces, and afterwards with armoured fighting vehicles as well, and they reached the Bögöte–Kissomlyó sector. At Bögöte, the units of the German *Division* established new defensive positions.[1823] The Soviets occupied Jánosháza. The *1. Volks-Gebirgs-Division* received the remnants of *Festungs-Pak-Verband IX* equipped with 8.8 cm anti-tank guns.[1824]

On the night of 26/27 March 1945, in the sector of the German *I. SS-Panzerkorps/6. Panzerarmee,* the units of the Soviet 9th Guards Mechanized Corps broke into the southeastern side of Mersevát in the sector of *1. SS-Panzer-Division.* The Germans reported to have knocked out seven Soviet tanks, most likely M4A2 here.[1825]

The Soviets launched an attack on a wide front against the positions of *1. SS-Panzer-Division,* between Celldömölk and Kenyeri. The units of *SS-Panzergrenadier-Regiment 2* were in combat south of Kenyeri, and the units of *SS-Panzergrenadier-Regiment 1* were in combat northwest of Celldömölk. The worn out combat groups of the *Division* had to retreat to the line of the Rába River at noon, and establish new defensive positions on the western bank.

This was only partially successful, because they didn't have enough combat strength to carry out the task, and the Soviets had already crossed the Rába River even before the arrival of the *SS-Kampfgruppe*. At Sárvár, a smaller detachment of *SS-Panzergrenadier-Regiment 1*, reinforced by the remnants of *SS-Panzerjäger-Abteilung 1* and *SS-Panzer-Flak-Abteilung 1*, were holding a small bridgehead until the last remnants of the *Division* crossed the river. Around 1600 hours, the bridgehead itself was also eliminated by the Soviets.

SS-Obersturmbannführer Peiper, *Regimentskommandeur* of *SS-Panzer-Regiment 1,* was not commanding his units in combat on that day, but was attending the funerals of *SS-Sturmbannführer* Poetschke and *SS-Hauptsturmführer* Malkomes in Eisenstad (Kismarton).[1826] As the Soviets had also crossed the Rába River at Répcelak, in the afternoon the Germans created a combat group from the remaining armoured fighting vehicles of *SS-Panzer-Regiment 1* and the armoured personnel carriers of *III. (Bataillon)/SS-Panzergrenadier-Regiment 2*, after which, it was deployed between Hegyfalu and Jákfa.[1827]

1820 Central Archives of the Russian Defence Ministry (Podolsk), f. 243, op. 2928, gy. 131, li. 277.
1821 Central Archives of the Russian Defence Ministry (Podolsk), f. 243, op. 2928, gy. 131, li. 277.
1822 NARA, T311, R163, F7215477.
1823 NARA, T311, R162, F7214792.
1824 NARA, T311, R163, F7215484.
1825 NARA, T311, R163, F7215478.
1826 Agte, Patrick: *Jochen Peiper. Kommandeur Panzerregiment Leibstandarte*. Berg am Starnberger See, 1998. p. 359.
1827 Tiemann, Ralf: *Die Leibstandarte*. Band IV/2. Osnabrück, 1987. pp. 339-340.

From the bridgehead established at Szergény, the armoured fighting vehicles of the Soviet 14th Guards Motorcycle Battalion occupied Kemenesmagasi and Kemeneshőgyész[1828], then acting as a forward unit, occupied Pápoc and Rábakecskéd by the end of the day, thus reaching the Rába River.

In the early morning hours, the Soviet troops continued their attacks on the positions of *1. SS-Panzer-Division* on the Celldömölk west–Kenyeri sector, and at around noon, they pushed back the Germans to the line of the Rába River.

The 31st Guards Mechanized Brigade was in combat in the sector of Csönge. The 18th Guards Mechanized Brigade bypassed the village from the west and occupied the road junction 2.5 km west of there. The 30th Guards Mechanized Brigade occupied Hill 148 on the bank of the Rába River, four km south-west of Csönge. The 46th Guards Tank Brigade replenished their fuel and ammunition supplies in the Mihályfa part of the village of Sömjénmihályfa. On that day, the German *Eisenbahn-Panzerzug 79,* active on the Sárvár–Pápa railway line, was encircled and destroyed by Soviet troops west of Celldömölk.[1829] The Corps lost in the combat actions of the day, eight knocked out[1830] M4A2 tanks including six that were burnt out. In the evening, they had 67 operational tanks, 12 SU–76M and 14 ISU–122 self-propelled guns, the latter of which were fighting with the 364th Guards Heavy Self-Propelled Artillery Regiment in combat at Ostffyasszonyfa.[1831]

The 1523rd Self-Propelled Artillery Regiment/9th Guards Army stood at the western part of Pápa in reserve to the 38th Guards Rifle Corps with 18 operational SU–76Ms. The 1513th Self-Propelled Artillery Regiment was assembled at Ajkarendek with four SU–76M self-propelled guns. There were only 24 operational SU-76Ms in the 1524th Self-Propelled Artillery Regiment.[1832]

The Soviet 5th Guards Tank Corps continued its attack towards Sárvár and the Rába River. The 21st Guards Tank Brigade pushed through Nagysimonyi and reached the sector of Sárvár. The 22nd Guards Tank Brigade occupied the guard house one km east of there. From 1630 hours onwards, the Soviets were continuously attacking the bridgehead at Sárvár.[1833]

The 6th Guards Motorized Rifle Brigade and the 51st Guards Self-Propelled Artillery Brigade, pushed through Káld. The 20th Guards Tank Brigade and the 208th Self-Propelled Artillery Brigade was assembled at Jánosháza. The Corps lost, during the fighting that day, seven knocked out T–34/85 tanks, five of which burnt out. In the evening, they had 26 operational tanks[1834] and 15 SU–76M self-propelled guns. The 1016th Self-Propelled Artillery Regiment/208th Self-Propelled Artillery Brigade, reported to have knocked out two armoured personnel carriers along the Rába River, and the 1922nd Self-Propelled

---

1828 NARA, T311, R163, F7215478.
1829 Sawodny, Wolfgang: *Deutsche Panzerzüge*. Eggolsheim, without year of publication, p. 140.
1830 Central Archives of the Russian Defence Ministry (Podolsk), f. 339, op. 5179, gy. 87, li. 26.
1831 Central Archives of the Russian Defence Ministry (Podolsk), f. 243, op. 2928, gy. 131, li. 276.
1832 Central Archives of the Russian Defence Ministry (Podolsk), f. 243, op. 2928, gy. 131, li. 277.
1833 NARA, T311, R162, F7214792.
1834 Another six tanks of the Corps were under medium repair, and 16 were in major repair. See the war log of the 5th Guards Tank Corps for March 1945. Copy owned by the author. p. 21.

Artillery Regiment, reported to have knocked out two Tiger Bs.[1835] In the evening, the Brigade had 41 operational SU–100s.[1836]

On that day, the 252nd Amphibious Car Battalion, was reassigned from the ranks of the 57th Army, to the subordination to the 6th Guards Tank Army.[1837]

On the front of *12. SS* and *3. SS-Panzer-Division*, the Soviets also reached the Rába River everywhere.[1838]

In the morning, the units of *3. SS-Panzer-Division* were still defending the line of the Marcal at the bridgehead at Marcaltő, and then retreated at Várkeszö to positions established on the western bank between Beled and Szany. North of Marcaltő, the remnants of *3. SS-Panzerjäger-Abteilung 3* and *SS-Panzer-Regiment 3*, were deployed as infantry, and the same was also true for *SS-Panzergrenadier-Regiment 6*. However there were still shreds of units from *3. SS-Panzer-Division* wandering about deeply behind enemy lines.[1839]

On the night of 26/27 March 1945, the Soviets broke into the bridgehead at Marcaltő, but units of *Panzer-Pionier-Bataillon 12* repulsed them. *SS-Brigadeführer* Kraas was still in the bridgehead. In the morning, the *Division* created a combat group commanded by *Oberstleutnant i.G.* Waizenegger[1840], that was to support the Hungarian 1st Honvéd Mountain Brigade in combat in the Rába bridgehead at Mórichida. The combat group consisted, most likely of the *Stab/SS-Panzergrenadier-Regiment 26*, the companies, *I. (Bataillon)/SS-Panzergrenadier-Regiment 26*, the former *Kampfgruppe "Hauschild"*, and a few armoured fighting vehicles.

The *II. Bataillon/SS-Panzergrenadier-Regiment 26* was subordinated to *SS-Panzergrenadier-Regiment 25*, and established defensive positions south of Répcelak. The regiment arrived on the same day at the *Division* together with *SS-Panzerjäger-Abteilung 12*. On the right hand side of the *Panzergrenadier-Bataillon*, there was *SS-Panzer-Aufklärungs-Abteilung 12* in position, and on the left hand side, *SS-Panzergrenadier-Regiment 25*. The armoured reconnaissance soldiers established contact with *1. SS-Panzer-Division*. The right flank of the *Panzergrenadier-Regiment* joined *3. SS-Panzer-Division*.

During the afternoon, the Soviets crossed to the western bank of the Rába River at Nick. Here, *III. (Bataillon)/SS-Panzergrenadier-Regiment 2/1. SS-Panzer-Division* and a few tanks of *SS-Panzer-Regiment 1*, were engaged in combat with the Soviets.[1841] Due to the crossing of the Soviets, *II. (Bataillon)/SS-Panzergrenadier-Regiment 26/12. SS-Panzer-Division*, reinforced by a few Panzer IV tanks and two armoured personnel carriers, was deployed on the eastern and northern edge of Répcelak and its task was to cover the Germans crossing Répce Creek.[1842]

1835 Summarized report of the 208th Self-Propelled Artillery Brigade of the period between 6 March – 6 April 1945. Copy owned by the author. p. 14.
1836 Central Archives of the Russian Defence Ministry (Podolsk), f. 243, op. 2928, gy. 131, li. 276-277.
1837 Central Archives of the Russian Defence Ministry (Podolsk), f. 243, op. 2928, gy. 131, li. 277.
1838 NARA, T311, R162, F7214792.
1839 Vopersal, Wolfgang: *Soldaten, Kämpfer, Kameraden. Marsch und Kämpfe der SS-Totenkopfdivision*. Band Vb. Bielefeld, 1991. pp. 830-831.
1840 The officer of the *Heer* was assigned to the *Division* from the headquarters of Hitler. In certain sources, Waizenegger is mentioned as *SS-Obersturmbannführer* and the *Kommandeur* of *SS-Panzergrenadier-Regiment 25*.
1841 Agte, Patrick: *Jochen Peiper. Kommandeur Panzerregiment Leibstandarte*. Berg am Starnberger See, 1998. p. 359.
1842 Meyer, Hubert: *Kriegsgeschichte der 12. SS-Panzerdivision „Hitlerjugend"*. Band II. Osnabrück, 1987. 2nd edition. p. 519.

In the front of *232. Panzer-Division*, that morning, the Germans were still able to eliminate a Soviet penetration in the Marcaltő bridgehead at Emilháza, but later in the afternoon, the attackers occupied the bridgehead, and *I. (Bataillon)/Panzergrenadier-Regiment 101* was practically annihilated.[1843] Although the bridges over the Rába River and the Marcal were blown up by the Germans, the demolition charge had not went off on one bridge over the Rába River. Therefore, the *Kommandeur* of *12. SS-Panzer-Division* ordered *SS-Hauptsturmführer* Tauber, *Kommandeur* of *Panzer-Pionier-Bataillon 12*, to blow the bridge up:

"It is already getting dark. With Hauptscharführer Gauglitz, we immediately went to the bridge. The retreating soldiers of the 232. Panzer-Division are running toward us. I order a Major to immediately go into positions with its unit at the Rába River. Thereafter, everybody goes forward. Two meters above us, a four-barrelled anti-aircraft gun is constantly firing in the direction of the bridge on which there are already three T–34[1844] standing. With a torch we search for the break in the fuse, and luckily we find it very quickly. The fuse was simply torn; this seems to be sabotage for sure. Then we detonate the bridge over the Rába River, the three T-34s fell into the river. I report to the division commander that we have completed the task."[1845]

On the front of *II. SS-Panzerkorps*, the Hungarian 1st Mountain Brigade[1846] was not able to hold back the 2nd Guards Mechanized Brigade and 9th Guards Tank Brigades/1st Guards Mechanized Corps, which were attacking the bridgehead at Mórichida, as they had launched another attack with 15-20 armoured fighting vehicles, and run the defenders down. As the German troops did not blow up the Rába bridge at Árpás, because they suspected there might still be German forces east of there, the Soviet troops crossed the bridge with a few tanks and one company of rifle infantry and created a smaller bridgehead in the area of Árpás. After this, the Soviet armoured fighting vehicles completely occupied Árpás.[1847] The German–Hungarian forces launched a counterattack against the bridgehead established there, which was still on-going in the evening. But in the end, they were unable achieve any success in the raging close quarters combat due to the Soviet armoured fighting vehicles targeting them from the opposite bank, although at last the bridge was blown up.[1848]

The Hungarian mountain troops were also supported by their own five 7.5 cm anti-tank guns and a tank destroyer company, with 12 handheld anti-tank rocket launchers. According to the combat report of the 1st Mountain Brigade, in the last two days the Hungarian mountain troops had held and contained the attack of the Soviet armoured fighting vehicles, which were pursuing the retreating Germans on the line of the Marcal, except the crossing between Mórichida and Árpás, and during this time they, knocked out 13 of their tanks, mainly with close combat weapons.[1849]

1843 NARA, T311, R162, F7214792.
1844 These were most likely the M4A2 tanks of the Soviet 1st Guards Mechanized Corps and not T–34s.
1845 Quoted by Meyer, Hubert: *Kriegsgeschichte der 12. SS-Panzerdivision „Hitlerjugend"*. Band II. Osnabrück, 1987. 2nd edition. pp. 518-519.
1846 The Hungarian 1st Mountain Brigade was subordinated to the *II. SS-Panzerkorps* on that day.
1847 NARA, T311, R162, F7214792.
1848 HM HIM Hadtörténelmi Levéltár (Budapest), m. kir. Honvéd Vezérkar főnöke iratai, 86.718/vkf. eln. 1/a.–1945.
1849 HM HIM Hadtörténelmi Levéltár (Budapest), m. kir. Honvéd Vezérkar főnöke iratai, 86.718/vkf. eln. 1/a.–1945. According

The 1st Guards Mechanized Brigade/1st Guards Mechanized Corps, together with the 1821st and 1004th Self-Propelled Artillery Regiment, were in combat for the occupation of Tétlesvár and Hill 119 west of there, and its forward troops crossed the Marcal Canal and reached the eastern edge of Rábaszentmihály. The 3rd Guards Mechanized Brigade, with the units of the 382nd Guards Self-Propelled Artillery Regiment and the 117th Anti-Tank Artillery Regiment, were attacking towards Győrszemere. The 11th Guards Motorcycle Battalion, with 10 T-34/85s of the 53rd Motorcycle Regiment and units of the 382nd Guards Self-Propelled Artillery Regiment, occupied Koroncó at 1230 hours and by 1600 hours, they were already in combat in the sector of Kisbarát, three km east of Ménfőcsanak.[1850] The 912th Self-Propelled Artillery Regiment followed the 9th Guards Tank Brigade, and at the end of the day was assembled at Mórichida. In the evening, the 1st Guards Mechanized Corps had 87 operational M4A2 and two T–34 tanks, plus 12 SU–100s. The subordinated 207th Self-Propelled Artillery Brigade had 25 operational SU–100s, three SU–57s and two T–34 tanks.[1851]

On the night of 26/27 March 1945, the Soviet troops, exploiting their achievements north of Kerékteleki and in the Kisbér–Nagyigmánd sector, pushed back the front line of *6. Panzer-Division* and *2. SS-Panzer-Division* to the Ménfőcsanak–Nyúl–Győrszentmárton–Bőnyrétalap line.

The 366th Guards Heavy Self-Propelled Artillery Regiment/4th Guards Army, established firing positions on the north-eastern edge of Kisbér, but their eight captured German self-propelled howitzers and two Panther tanks were not engaged in combat with the enemy. The six independent self-propelled artillery battalions of the Army stood as anti-tank artillery reserves for their divisions, with 54 SU–76Ms and five tanks, but were not deployed either.[1852]

On the morning of 27 March 1945, the command of *6. Panzerarmee* received a telegram signed by *Reichsführer-SS* Heinrich Himmler, which ordered that the *SS-Divisions* that had not fully complied with their responsibilities and obligations, were to remove their armbands depicting the name of their elite unit. This was the infamous armband order (Ärmelstreifenbefehl), which was not passed on to the troops by *SS-General* Dietrich, even though everybody soon knew about it at the *Heeresgruppe*. The order, meant by Hitler to serve as a mark of disgrace, did not make any sense because the *SS*-units had already removed their armbands before coming to Hungary for security purposes, however it had devastating consequences on the morale of the otherwise, physically and mentally worn out troops.

On the frontline of the 2nd Ukrainian Front

During the day, the flanks of the German *6. Panzer-Division* were attacked multiple times by regiment-size forces. One of these attacks resulted in the occupation of Gyirmót, northwest of Ménfőcsanak. The Soviets had broken into Ménfőcsanak at two separate

---

to the after-action report of the Hungarian 1st Mountain Brigade, the 13 Soviet armoured fighting vehicles were knocked out in one single day, 26 March, but this is not highly likely based on the war log of the German *Heeresgruppe Süd*.
1850 Central Archives of the Russian Defence Ministry (Podolsk), f. 243, op. 2928, gy. 178, li. 110.
1851 Central Archives of the Russian Defence Ministry (Podolsk), f. 243, op. 2928, gy. 131, li. 278.
1852 Central Archives of the Russian Defence Ministry (Podolsk), f. 243, op. 2928, gy. 131, li. 277.

points, but the Germans eliminated these penetrations. The Soviet forces that broke into the southern parts of Écs were pushed out immediately with a single counterattack. Győrszentmárton was, however, occupied with rifle forces supported by armoured fighting vehicles.[1853]

The right flank of *2. SS-Panzer-Division* was attacked by battalion-size forces to contain the units, however the left flank was attacked by a considerable armoured force.

At 1300 hours in the afternoon, the forces of the 23rd Tank Corps assaulted Bőnyrétalap after an artillery barrage, but the tanks, assault guns and artillery of *2. SS-Panzer-Division* prevented them from succeeding. The Soviets lost one burnt out T–34/85 tank.[1854] The bridge of the Bakonyér was blown up by the Germans. The brigades of the Corps occupied the hills north of Bőnyrétalap at 1400 hours, and with this, achieved a four km deep salient. In the meantime, the 56th Motorized Rifle Brigade crossed the Bakonyér one km north-west of Bőnyrétalap, and at 2100 hours occupied the village.[1855]

In Pér, which was almost completely abandoned by the Germans the day before, only a few *SS*-armoured fighting vehicles were still engaged in delaying actions as rear guard in the Új street of the village, at Dörög and from the firing positions at the local inn against the Soviet forces attacking from Püspökalap and Pázmándfalu. Finally, the Soviets had taken Pér by surprise the next day at 0500 hours.[1856]

Pázmándfalu was occupied by the 12 self-propelled guns of the Soviet 1897th Self-Propelled Artillery Regiment and units of the 317th Rifle Division, where a SU–76M was hit and burnt out.[1857]

Between the Győr–Komárom railroad line and the Danube, approximately 40 armoured fighting vehicles, units of the 2nd Guards Mechanized Corps, were advancing and breaking into the eastern section of Győrszentiván. Here, *III. (Bataillon)/SS-Panzergrenadier-Regiment 4*, launched a counterattack with the support of its own armoured personnel carriers, which resulted in prolonged fighting that lasted well into the evening. The Germans reported on that day, that they knocked out nine Soviet armoured fighting vehicles.[1858] The wedge of the Soviets advancing toward Győr, was successfully stopped by *SS-Panzer-Flak-Abteilung 2* along the Danube.

Units of *2. SS-Panzer-Division* on that day, placed armoured fighting vehicles and heavy artillery in firing positions to the north and west of the village of Hegykő, to be able to secure the road leading toward Sopron.[1859]

In the southern sector of Győr, the *Division* received a replacement of approximately 2800 men, comprised mostly of 17 -18 year old youngsters, who were reassigned from the ranks of the *Kriegsmarine* into the *Waffen-SS*. It was more significant however, to

---

1853 NARA, T311, R162, F7214793.
1854 War log of the 23rd Tank Corps from March 1945. Copy owned by the author. p. 18.
1855 Central Archives of the Russian Defence Ministry (Podolsk), f. 240, op. 2799, gy. 357, li. 16.
1856 Written statement of parish priest József Vincze based on the Historia Domus at Pér. Published in the Lapozgató monthly magazine issued in Mezőörs.
1857 Central Archives of the Russian Defence Ministry (Podolsk), f. 240, op. 2799, gy. 342, li. 116.
1858 NARA, T311, R162, F7214793.
1859 Gyula Perger: „…*félelemmel and aggodalommal…*". *Plébániák jelentései a háborús károkról a Győri Egyházmegyéből, 1945*. Győr, 2005. pp. 73-74. The German artillery stationed here has opened fire in the morning of 28 March 1945 in the assault direction of the approaching Soviet troops and this was continued until 30 March 1945. At last, the village went into Soviet hands without combat in the morning of 31 March 1945 due to the Germans retreat.

receive 80 non-commissioned officers, though most were inexperienced, who arrived at the same time.[1860]

Panzer-Aufklärungs-Abteilung 1/1. Panzer-Division was fighting in the Győr bridgehead in subordination to *II. SS-Panzerkorps*. On that day, the *Heeresgruppe* wanted to reassign the unit to the Sárvár bridgehead, but the relocation process was going very slow.[1861]

In the front of *XXXXIII. Armeekorps,* the German forces fighting south of the Komárom bridgehead, were pushed back by the Soviets to the Gönyű south-east five km (Nagyszentjános train station)–Gönyü east two km - Duna line. The units of the Soviet 2nd Guards Mechanized Corps were in combat around 1200 hours in the sector of Kisszentjános, four km south-south-east of Gönyü. The forces of the 23rd Tank Corps occupied Bana around 0700 hours in the morning.[1862]

Units of the German *356. Infanterie-Division* and *Panzerjäger-Abteilung 662* were regrouped via Komárom to the northern bank of the Danube, to prepare for the possibility of the Soviets crossing the Danube between Komárom and Gönyü.[1863] The *Armeekorps* on that day was subordinated to *8. Armee.*[1864]

In the Komárom bridgehead of *8. Armee,* the Soviets managed to create a deep salient toward Komárom from the northern outskirts of Mocsa.[1865]

During the battle, the 991st Self-Propelled Artillery Regiment/46th Army, together with units of the 99th Rifle Division, occupied Öregcsém, the important road junction south of the Csémi-inn, and Újmajor. During the fighting, the Soviet SU–76M self-propelled guns knocked out five guns and 10 machine guns. The Soviet losses amounted to three knocked out SU–76M self-propelled guns, one of which burnt out, one killed and two wounded men. At 1500 hours, the regiment was withdrawn from the frontline and sent to Kocs by order of the commander of the 68th Rifle Corps.[1866]

On that day, the German *8. Armee* withdrew *Panzer-Kampfgruppe "Pape"*, consisting of units of *Panzerkorps "Feldherrnhalle",* from the Komárom bridgehead, and the frontline was moved back to the Komárom–Szőny–Füzítőpuszta line on the night of 27/28 March 1945.[1867] All of this had been done because Hitler still wanted to defend the oil refineries, which were bombed to ruins and had not been in operation for a long time already.[1868]

Due to the extreme shortage of fuel, the German *Luftflotte 4* only attacked the villages, marching columns and artillery positions on the inner flanks of *6. Armee* and *6. Panzerarmee.* The pilots reported shooting down four Soviet aircraft. During the night of 26/27 March 1945, approximately 50 night ground attack aircraft attacked the sector of Veszprém and Jánosháza, plus the western outskirts of Léva.[1869]

1860 Weidinger, Otto: *Division Das Reich. Der Weg der 2. SS-Panzer-Division „Das Reich".* Band V: 1943-1945. Osnabrück, without year of publication, p. 476.
1861 NARA, T311, R162, F7214802.
1862 Central Archives of the Russian Defence Ministry (Podolsk), f. 240, op. 2799, gy. 357, li. 15.
1863 NARA, T311, R162, F7214793.
1864 NARA, T311, R162, F7214802.
1865 NARA, T311, R162, F7214793.
1866 Central Archives of the Russian Defence Ministry (Podolsk), f. 240, op. 2799, gy. 342, li. 111.
1867 NARA, T311, R162, F7214804.
1868 NARA, T311, R162, F7214806.
1869 NARA, T311, R162, F7214794.

In the afternoon, Hitler permitted the German *6. Panzerarmee* to pull back it's frontline to the Győr bridgehead, which was considerably narrower, and deploy the surplus forces on its own right flank, against the Soviets troops that crossed the Rába River.[1870]

In the front of *2. Panzerarmee,* the Germans were alerted to the reassembly and preparations for attack on the Soviet side by the noise from the movement of the armoured fighting vehicles. The *Stab/Panzerarmee* requested the *Stab/Heeresgruppe* a number of times during the day, to transfer the forces of *I. Kavallerie-Korps,* then retreating north of Lake Balaton, to be able to cover its northern flank, and to be able to withdraw its forces to the *Margarethen-Stellung* built up between Lake Balaton and the Dráva River. The *Stab/Heeresgruppe* did not consider the former a useful idea, because *I. Kavallerie-Korps* and *IV. SS-Panzerkorps* had to be under joint command for the time being, to avoid the widening of the gap between them[1871], and only Hitler could have permitted a retreat to the *Margarethen-Stellung*[1872].

Generaloberst Guderian notified the *Heeresgruppe* late at night, that Himmler was to arrive in the Transdanubia the following afternoon, to personally inspect and assess the condition of the *SS-Panzer-Divisions*.[1873]

28 March 1945, Wednesday

(**WEATHER**: highest daytime temperature 16 Celsius; partially cloudy, partially clear skies, occasional showers. The road conditions are favourable.)

On the front of *2. Panzerarmee,* continuous Soviet and Bulgarian troop movements had been observed, and they also experienced the Soviet artillery practising target acquisition. The attack preparations went on in the largest measure around Háromfa, Nagykorpád and Csömend.[1874] Hitler categorically refused giving permission to the *Stab/Panzerarmee* to withdraw its forces to the *Margarethen-Stellung* and create reserves.[1875]

The Bulgarian 1st Independent Tank Battalion/1st Army was assembled that morning in the sector of Hencse with its Panzer IV tanks, repaired with Soviet help, plus the Hungarian Turán tank assigned to the reconnaissance company and two Italian self-propelled guns. The damaged tanks of the battalion waiting to be repaired, and the German assault guns and *Jagdpanzers* remained at Pellérd.[1876]

On the night of 27/28 March 1945, on the front of the German *I. Kavallerie-Korps/6. Armee,* the Germans launched a counterattack and eliminated the small Soviet incursions at Lesencefalu and Tapolca.[1877]

1870 NARA, T311, R162, F7214796.
1871 NARA, T311, R162, F7214798.
1872 NARA, T311, R162, F7214799.
1873 NARA, T311, R162, F7214806.
1874 NARA, T311, R162, F7214808.
1875 NARA, T311, R163, F7215126.
1876 Matev, Kaloyan: *The Armoured Forces of the Bulgarian Army 1936–45.* Solihull, 2015. p. 333. In the case of the Turan tank, there is no evidence that could confirm whether that was combat-ready at that time.
1877 NARA, T311, R163, F7215486.

The combat group of *9. SS-Panzer-Division* was in defence north-east of Lesencetomaj.[1878]

During the day, the Soviets launched battalion and regimental size attacks on wide fronts, supported by armoured fighting vehicles, at Sümeg. The Germans temporarily held up the Soviet attack and inflicted heavy losses on the enemy at the eastern and north-eastern edge of the forested area west of Balatonederics–Vindornyaszőlős–Zalaudvarnok south–western bank of the Zala River general line.[1879]

Panzergrenadier-Regiment 126/23. Panzer-Division, repulsed the Soviet attack south of Lesencetomaj in the morning. However, around 1100 hours, the two *Panzergrenadier-Regiments* of the *Division* were ordered to retreat and after occupying the middle ground, around 1900 hours, they reached the Zala River near Nemesbük via Balatonederics, Balatongyörök and Keszthely.[1880]

The significantly reduced combat strength of the Panzergrenadiers of *23. Panzer-Division,* was increased with men serving in the supply units, and from the soldiers of *Panzer-Regiment 23* who had no armoured fighting vehicles, two infantry armoured rifle companies were formed. In the evening, *I. (Bataillon)/Panzergrenadier-Regiment 128* established an eastern bridgehead on the Zala River around Kustány.[1881]

The Soviet 1202nd Self-Propelled Artillery Regiment/27th Army, marched on the same day from Sárvár to Zalaszántó, with its 19 operational SU–76M self-propelled guns. The 432nd Independent Self-Propelled Artillery Battalion/316th Rifle Division, with 10 SU–76Ms, was stationed in Szigliget, and the 72nd Guards Independent Self-Propelled Artillery Battalion/68th Guards Rifle Division/26th Army was in anti-tank artillery reserve in the sector of Tüskevár, 10 km northwest of Devecser.[1882]

The armoured forces of the 5th Guards Cavalry Corps were on the move. The 54th Tank Regiment, with nine operational T–34/85s, was at Nemesvámos, the 71st Tank Regiment, with 12 T–34/85s and the 1896th Self-Propelled Artillery Regiment, with 15 SU–76Ms, stood at Tótvázsony.[1883]

The *I. Kavallerie-Korps* was reinforced that day by *Sturmgeschütz-Brigade 191* from *2. Panzerarmee*, plus *Sperrgruppe "Steyrer"* with the following forces:

- *Festungs-Regiments 35* and *36*;
- combat group of *44. Reichsgrenadier-Division*;
- *Feldersatz Bataillon 79*;
- the assault guns of *SS-Panzer-Abteilung 16* and *SS-Panzer-Aufklärungs-Abteilung 16* combined in one armoured combat group;
- two fortress anti-tank gun companies with 8.8 cm guns;
  the Hungarian 213th and 217th Fortress Machine Gun Battalions.[1884]

1878 See Tieke, Wilhelm: *Im Feuersturm letzter Kriegsjahre. II. SS-Panzerkorps mit 9. und 10. SS-Division „Hohenstaufen" und „Frundsberg".* Osnabrück, without year of publication, [1975] map on p. 519.
1879 NARA, T311, R162, F7214809.
1880 Rebentisch, Ernst: *Zum Kaukasus und zu den Tauern. Die Geschichte der 23. Panzer-Division 1941–1945.* Esslingen, 1963. p. 501.
1881 Rebentisch, Ernst: *Zum Kaukasus und zu den Tauern. Die Geschichte der 23. Panzer-Division 1941–1945.* Esslingen, 1963. p. 502.
1882 Central Archives of the Russian Defence Ministry (Podolsk), f. 243, op. 2928, gy. 131, li. 279.
1883 Central Archives of the Russian Defence Ministry (Podolsk), f. 243, op. 2928, gy. 131, li. 281.
1884 NARA, T311, R163, F7215493.

On the front of *IV. SS-Panzerkorps,* the Soviet rifle forces and the armoured fighting vehicles, were attacking toward the west-south-west, and the Germans were only able to hold them up on the western bank of the Zala River, after knocking out seven Soviet armoured fighting vehicles.[1885]

The Soviet 18th Tank Corps was attacking in this direction, and experienced considerable difficulties when trying to cross the large number of creeks and canals. The water obstacles seriously limited the manoeuvring abilities of the armoured fighting vehicles as well. In addition to this, the Germans placed mine obstacles on the roads at different locations, and the bridges and culverts had been blown up.

In the morning, the 170th Tank Brigade together with the 1952nd and 1953rd Self-Propelled Artillery Regiment/209th Self-Propelled Artillery Brigade, crossed the military bridge built west of Tótvármajor, and after a short artillery barrage, went on the attack and occupied Mihályfa, then continued attacking toward the west, and soon occupied Batyk. En route, the Soviet armoured group eliminated the ambush positions of armoured fighting vehicles and repulsed counterattacks at Türje, Batyk and Pakod, and these villages were occupied as well.

The *5. SS-Panzer-Division,* together with the forces of *1. Panzer-Division,* were pushed back by the Soviets north of Zalaszentgrót to the Zalavég–Csipkerek line.[1886]

At Türje, the significantly intermingled *Panzergrenadier* units of *3. Panzer-Division* and *5. SS-Panzer-Division,* were also supported by one command Panther and three Panzer IV tanks of *Panzer-Regiment 1*, and two self-propelled 2 cm anti-aircraft guns commanded by *Oberleutnant* Stoves.[1887] Afterwards, the *Oberleutnant,* with his remaining three armoured fighting vehicles, met *II. (Abteilung)/Panzer-Artillerie-Regiment 73* at Zalaszentiván, then they marched together northwards, to Győrvár, and occupied firing positions in the eastern outskirts of the village.[1888]

The Soviet armoured grouping ran into a minefield near Zalabér, at the junction of the road and the railroad line. Engineers arrived to clear the area, but the Germans opened fire on them and the arriving forces of the brigade. The commander of the 170th Tank Brigade, Colonel Chunihin, ordered the subordinated artillery units to contain the German positions at Zalabér with suppressing fire. Thus, the engineers were finally able complete their tasks. When they finished clearing the mines from the area, the 3rd Tank Battalion stormed the German positions and the defenders were pushed out of Zalabér.[1889]

The reinforced 170th Tank Brigade reached Pókaszepetk at 1930 hours. However, they met resistance again, this time from the Hungarians. As we can read in the Historia Domus of the village:

1885 NARA, T311, R162, F7214809.
1886 Tieke, Wilhelm: *Von Plattensee bis Österreich. Heeresgruppe Süd 1945.* Gummersbach, without year of publication, p. 91.
1887 Stoves, Rolf: Persönliches Kriegstagebuch Pz.Rgt. 1 (typewritten manuscript, a copy owned by the author), entry from 28 March 1945.
1888 Stoves, O. G. Rolf: *1. Panzer-Division 1935–1945. Chronik einer der drei Stamm-Division der deutschen Panzerwaffe.* Bad Nauheim, 1961. p. 776.
1889 Bryukhov, Vasiliy: *Red Army Tank Commander. At War in a T–34 on the Eastern Front.* Barnsley, 2013. p. 183.

> *"At the northern edge of the village, 56-57 police officers[1890] tried to resist, knocking out three enemy tanks with Panzerfausts; but our whole village suffered a terrible retaliation. This was why the [church] tower was gunned down, two-thirds of the houses burnt down, and the people robbed and harassed more than the other villages."*[1891]

The reinforced 170th Tank Brigade reported to have knocked out seven German tanks while losing four knocked out T–34/85s, two of which burnt out, and one knocked out SU–100. Around midnight the Soviets occupied Pókaszepetk.[1892]

On the night of 27/28 March 1945, the 110th Tank Brigade, reinforced with the 1st Battalion/32nd Motorized Rifle Brigade, eliminated a number of German ambush positions and at 0500 hours, reached Zalaszentgrót, which they occupied after heavy fighting.

However, in the southern outskirts of Zalaszentgrót, the German *schwere Kavallerie-Abteilung 3/3. Kavallerie-Division* and the assault guns of *Sturmgeschütz-Brigade 191*,[1893] held up the Soviet armoured fighting vehicles just at the moment when they were to continue their attack south-wards and, but for this, they might have reached the rear of *3. Kavallerie-Division*.[1894] Therefore, around 1300 hours, the reinforced 110th Tank Brigade, instead, started off after the 170th Tank Brigade via Türje.

The 181st Tank Brigade, together with a Battalion of the 32nd Motorized Rifle Brigade reached the edge of Avaserdő, two km northwest of Nagytilaj, by 1930 hours, after they were engaged in combat with a German armoured combat group containing five tanks and six armoured personnel carriers.[1895] The Germans knocked out a T–34/85 and the Soviets reported that they knocked out three German armoured fighting vehicles. .[1896] The 1951st and 1952nd Self-Propelled Artillery Regiments/209th Self-Propelled Artillery Brigade, supporting the Tank Brigade, was in combat one km east of Nagytilaj, and the 1953rd Self-Propelled Artillery Regiment was en route to the railway station of Batyk.

The 18th Tank Corps reported to have knocked out, during the actions of that day, 14 German armoured fighting vehicles, nine armoured personnel carriers and two guns. Their own losses amounted to five knocked out T–34/85s, two of which burnt out,[1897] and one knocked out SU–100 self-propelled gun. During the battle on that day, the Head of the Operations Department of the Corps, Guards Lieutenant Colonel Nikita

---

1890 The Hungarian police forces were assigned to III Battalion/Hungarian "Dráva"- Regiment. This Battalion was formed from the strength of the Police Training Battalion at Szombathely, and it included a tank destroyer section as well. These arrived by train at Zalaszentiván on 25 March 1945. Its tank-destroyer section established a blocking position with weak forces at Zalaszentiván, and its three companies established another block position on a 15 km wide section, between Kemendollár and Pókaszepetk. The Bataillon did not have either heavy armament or artillery support. The police unit received more than 100 *Panzerfausts* from the retreating, worn out and disobedient forces of the German 5. *SS-Panzer-Division*,. See HM HIM Hadtörténelmi Levéltár (Budapest), *Tanulmányok és visszaemlékezések gyűjteménye*, issue 3148. (bequest of Pál Darnóy).
1891 Entry from 28 March 1945 in the Historia Domus of Pókaszepetk. Copy owned by the author.
1892 War log of the 18th Tank Corps for March 1945. Copy owned by the author. p. 53.
1893 *Sturmgeschütz-Brigade 191 (Kommandeur: Hauptmann* Karl-Erich Berg) consisted of *3.* and *4. Sturmgeschütz-Batteries* and one grenadier escort battery.
1894 Witte, Hans Joachim – Offermann, Peter: *Die Boeselagerschen Reiter. Das Kavallerie-Regiment Mitte und die aus ihm hervorgegangene 3. Kavallerie-Brigade/Division*. München, 1998. p. 419.
1895 Central Archives of the Russian Defence Ministry (Podolsk), f. 243, op. 2928, gy. 131, li. 281.
1896 War log of the 18th Tank Corps for March 1945. Copy owned by the author. p. 53.
1897 According to another archival source four T–34/85s were burnt out. See Central Archives of the Russian Defence Ministry (Podolsk), f. 243, op. 2928, gy. 178, li. 117.

N. Torgalo, was killed. In the evening there were 39 T–34/85s, four ISU–152s, six ISU–122s, seven SU–76Ms and 38 SU–100s in operational condition.[1898]

The German *1. Panzer-Division* occupied defensive positions between Mikosdpuszta, three km east of Mikosszéplak, and Csipkerek.[1899]

The attack of the Soviet forces threatened *1. Volks-Gebirgs-Division* with encirclement, despite their success in repulsing a number of Soviet attacks, supported by armoured fighting vehicles. Therefore the *Division* was forced to actively retreat to the Endrédpuszta–Potyrózsamajor–Csipkerek–Ökörhálás sector.[1900]

On the front of *III. Panzerkorps,* the Soviets crossed the Rába River from the east, occupied Ikervár, Megyehíd, and from the sector of Sárvár, mainly units of the 5th Guards Tank Corps, continued their attack toward the west and north-west. The counterattack of the German *II. (Bataillon)/Gebirgs-Jäger-Regiment 99,* was able to stop the Soviet attack south-east of Csénye. The Hungarian fortress battalions deployed in the sector of Sárvár, did not exert any resistance against the Soviets, who occupied Csénye and Csényeújmajor, and advanced until the Váti-erdő east of Vát.[1901]

The forces of *General der Panzertruppe* Breith were assembled on that day from various sources:

- seven Hungarian fortress battalions;
- combat-ready remnants of *Volks-Werfer-Brigade 17* and *19*;
- parts of the Hungarian SS-Regiment "Ney";
- *Sturmartillerie-Brigade 303*;
- *schwere Panzer-Abteilung 509*;
- *II. (Bataillon)/Gebirgs-Jäger-Regiment 99* from *1. Volks-Gebirgs-Division*;
- one field reserve battalion from each of *1.* and *3. Panzer-Divisions* (en route);
- *I. (Abteilung)/Artillerie-Regiment 77*.[1902]

The Soviet 5th Guards Tank Corps enlarged its bridgehead around Sárvár, and with its 21st Guards Tank Brigade, reached Rábabogyoszló north of there, and the 6th Guards Motorized Rifle Brigade reached the line between Lőrincmajor and Ölbő, five km north-west of Sárvár. The 20th Guards and 22nd Guards Tank Brigades, plus the 51st and 208th Self-Propelled Artillery Brigades were assembled in the area of Nagysimonyi, nine km west of Sárvár. In the evening, the Corps had 40 operational T–34/85 tanks and 16 SU–76M self-propelled guns. The 51st Guards Self-Propelled Artillery Brigade had 40 SU–76Ms, and the 209th Self-Propelled Artillery Brigade had the same number of SU–100s in operational condition.[1903]

The 252nd Amphibious Car Battalion was stationed at Ostffyasszonyfa with 99 American-manufactured DUKW amphibious trucks.[1904]

1898 Central Archives of the Russian Defence Ministry (Podolsk), f. 243, op. 2928, gy. 131, li. 281.
1899 NARA, T311, R162, F7214809.
1900 NARA, T311, R162, F7214809.
1901 NARA, T311, R162, F7214809.
1902 NARA, T311, R163, F7215493.
1903 Central Archives of the Russian Defence Ministry (Podolsk), f. 243, op. 2928, gy. 131, li. 279.
1904 Central Archives of the Russian Defence Ministry (Podolsk), f. 243, op. 2928, gy. 131, li. 279.

On the front of the German *I. SS-Panzerkorps/6. Panzerarmee, 1. SS-Panzer-Division* was unable to prevent the units of the Soviet 9th Guards Mechanized Corps continuing their attack west and in the direction of Zsédeny, from the bridgehead north of Sárvár, on the night of 27/28 March 1945.

The Soviet forces that crossed the Rába River, were continuing their attack and threatened the combat group on the right flank of *1. SS-Panzer-Division* with encirclement from the south. *SS-Panzergrenadier-Regiment 1* was forced to give up and abandon Jákfa, which they had developed into a fortified position. At the same time, *SS-Panzergrenadier-Regiment 2* was also attacked south of Nick, pushing the frontline of the *Division* back to the Hegyfalu–Vámoscsalád railroad line. *SS-Sturmbannführer* Jupp Diefenthal, the commander of *III. (Bataillon)/SS-Panzergrenadier-Regiment 2,* which was deployed in a counterattack at 1000 hours, was seriously wounded by a machine gun round. The *Divisionskommandeur*, *SS-Brigadeführer* Kumm, with his weak *Panzergrenadier* forces, consisting of five to six combat ready armoured fighting vehicles and short of artillery ammunition, could not even think of a long-term defence of the Rába River.[1905]

The Soviets occupied Jákfa in heavy combat, and with this, had deeply thrust in behind the rear of the right flank of *I. SS-Panzerkorps*. The Germans were forced to retreat, faced with the increasing pressure of the Soviets at the Ivánegerszeg–Vámoscsalád railroad line and to the southern edge of Nick.[1906]

As a result of these actions, by the end of the day, the Soviet 30th Guards Mechanized Brigade/9th Guards Mechanized Corps, advanced up to Szentivánfa, and the 31st Guards Mechanized Brigade advanced up to Ivánegerszeg. The battle was supported by the 364th Guards Heavy Self-Propelled Artillery Regiment with 14 ISU–122 self-propelled guns. The 18th Guards Mechanized Brigade was in combat in the sector of Pósfa. The 46th Guards Tank Brigade remained at Ostffyasszonyfa for the time being. In the evening, the Corps had 73 operational M4A2 tanks, 12 SU–76M and 14 ISU–122 self-propelled guns.[1907]

The combat groups of *12. SS* and *3. SS-Panzer-Divisions* were still holding the northern bank of the Rába River and eliminated the small incursions that were achieved the day before.[1908] The *12. SS-Panzer-Division* continued to defend their positions behind the Rába River and repulsed a number of Soviet attacks. The heaviest fighting was going on around Nick and Vág. The right flank of the *Division* was pushed back to the southern edge of Nick. The Soviets advanced to Csorna and were already threatening the rear of the *Division*.[1909]

The weak forces of *232. Panzer-Division* were hit in the side and in the rear and were partially dispersed by the Soviet armoured attack, most likely by the units of the 1st Guards Mechanized Corps.[1910] The *Divisionskommandeur*, *Generalmajor* Hans-Ulrich Back, was seriously wounded in a counterattack.[1911]

1905 Tiemann, Ralf: *Die Leibstandarte*. Band IV/2. Osnabrück, 1987. pp. 343.
1906 NARA, T311, R162, F7214809.
1907 Central Archives of the Russian Defence Ministry (Podolsk), f. 243, op. 2928, gy. 131, li. 279.
1908 NARA, T311, R162, F7214809.
1909 Meyer, Hubert: *Kriegsgeschichte der 12. SS-Panzerdivision „Hitlerjugend"*. Band II. Osnabrück, 1987. 2nd edition. p. 519.
1910 NARA, T311, R162, F7214809.
1911 NARA, T311, R162, F7214826.

The forces of *I. SS-Panzerkorps* reported that they knocked out 31 Soviet armoured fighting vehicles on that day.[1912]

The Soviet 1523rd Self-Propelled Artillery Regiment/9th Guards Army with its 18 operational SU–76M self-propelled guns, in cooperation with the 99th Guards Rifle Division, crossed the Rába River in the sector of Marcaltő and Várkesző. The 1524th Self-Propelled Artillery Regiment established firing positions four km east of Csönge, between Ragyogó and Augusztamajor, and supported the 114th Guards Rifle Division which was en route to cross the Rába River. The Regiment on that day, reported to have knocked out two German armoured personnel carriers and four guns. In the meantime, one of their SU–76Ms was burnt out, therefore they had 22 operational self-propelled guns by the evening. The 1513th Self-Propelled Artillery Regiment, with four SU–76Ms, was in reserve to the 37th Guards Rifle Corps.[1913]

In the front of *II. SS-Panzerkorps,* the Hungarian 1st Mountain Brigade launched a counterattack against the Soviet bridgehead at Árpás, and reached the northern and southern edges of the village, but then they were halted. The Soviet 1st Guards Mechanized Brigade/1st Guards Mechanized Corps, with the 18th Guards Tank Regiment and 20 M4A2 tanks, besides the SU–100 self-propelled guns of the 1821st Self-Propelled Artillery Regiment, at around 0700 hours, broke out of the bridgehead toward the west and the north-west, and around 1000 hours, they broke into Csorna. By 1100 hours the Soviets occupied almost the whole village, where they captured 460 Hungarian and German soldiers. Against this incursion, the armoured combat group of *2. SS-Panzer-Division* being withdrawn from the Győr bridgehead, was deployed from Kóny with 10 tanks. As the majority of the *SS-Division* was in combat on the Rábapatona–Kóny line, the *SS-Panzers* that had broken into Csorna were not able to hold the village on their own. The Soviets reported to have knocked out seven German armoured fighting vehicles, while their own losses amounted to two M4A2 tanks.[1914]

The 2nd Guards Mechanized Brigade/1st Guards Mechanized Corps, together with the 912th Self-Propelled Artillery Regiment, reached the eastern edge of Kistata, 2 km north-east of Szil, at 0400 hours, where they engaged the German–Hungarian troops in combat. The 9th Guards Tank Brigade, with the SU-100 self-propelled guns of the 1004th Self-Propelled Artillery Regiment, occupied Rábacsanak, and advanced to the eastern edge of Kistata. During the action on that day, the 207th Self-Propelled Artillery Brigade lost two knocked out SU–100s, one of which burnt out.[1915]

Considering the situation unfolding around Csorna, the *Stab/Heeresgruppe Süd,* left *Panzer-Aufklärungs-Abteilung 1* and the armoured combat group of *9. SS-Panzer-Division*[1916] with the German *6. Panzerarmee*, which they originally wanted to regroup at Vasvár, in the front of the German *6. Armee*.[1917]

1912 NARA, T311, R163, F7215504.
1913 Central Archives of the Russian Defence Ministry (Podolsk), f. 243, op. 2928, gy. 131, li. 279.
1914 Summarized report of the 1st Guards Mechanized Corps of the combat actions during March – April 1945. Copy owned by the author. p. 34.
1915 War log of the 207th Self-Propelled Artillery Brigade, 28 March 1945. Copy owned by the author.
1916 The *9. SS-Panzer-Division* did not have armoured (armoured personnel carrier) *Panzergrenadier-Bataillon*s, therefore the remaining forces of *SS-Panzer-Regiment 9* joined forces with the armoured personnel carriers and armoured reconnaissance cars of SS-*Panzer-Aufklärungs-Abteilung 9.*
1917 NARA, T311, R162, F7214818.

During the afternoon, the Soviets attacked between Egyed and Csorna and occupied Magyarkeresztúr, Potyond and Veszkény.[1918] The *2. SS-Panzer-Division* had, on that afternoon, vacated Szárföld without resistance, where they were forced to leave behind three armoured fighting vehicles and a few cars as it was impossible to have them towed away. They were soon knocked out by the Soviet armoured fighting vehicles.[1919]

The 9th Guards Tank Brigade/1st Guards Mechanized Corps and the SU-100 armoured fighting vehicles of the 912th Self-Propelled Artillery Regiment/207th Self-Propelled Artillery Brigade, occupied Farád, pushed through Szárfölde, and by 2000 hours, had also taken Babót. The forward detachment of the Brigade reached the outskirts of Kapuvár, which was occupied, based on their report, around 2200 hours that night.[1920] The 2nd Guards Mechanized Brigade, together with the units of the 1004th Self-Propelled Artillery Regiment/209th Self-Propelled Artillery Brigade, had taken Bogyoszló, and the 3rd Guards Mechanized Brigade with the other half of the SU–100 Regiment, were fighting to occupy Jobaháza, which lasted well into the evening.[1921]

The 1st Guards Mechanized Corps had, on 27 and 28 March 1945, lost five burnt out M4A2 tanks.[1922] The detailed combat strength of the troops on that evening was as follows:

- the 1st Guards Mechanized Brigade with 13 M4A2 tanks and five armoured transport vehicles;
- the 2nd Guards Mechanized Brigade with four M4A2 tanks and three armoured transport vehicles;
- the 3rd Guards Mechanized Brigade with eight M4A2 tanks and six armoured transport vehicles;
- the 9th Guards Tank Brigade with 34 M4A2 tanks and three armoured transport vehicles;
- the 11th Guards Motorcycle Battalion with four M4A2 tanks, nine armoured transport vehicles and 90 motorcycles;
- the 78th Guards Signal Battalion with three tanks and three armoured transport vehicles;
- the 382nd Guards Self-Propelled Artillery Regiment with three SU–100s and one T–34;
- the 1821st Self-Propelled Artillery Regiment with five SU–100s;
- the 1699th Anti-Aircraft Artillery Regiment with 11 M–17 four-barrelled anti-aircraft heavy machine guns.[1923]

The 207th Self-Propelled Artillery Brigade subordinated to the Corps, had that evening, 25 operational SU–100s, three SU–57s and two T–34s with which they were waiting for the continuation of the attack.[1924]

1918 NARA, T311, R162, F7214810.
1919 Gyula Perger: „...*félelemmel and aggodalommal...*". *Plébániák jelentései a háborús károkról a Győri Egyházmegyéből, 1945*. Győr, 2005. p. 107.
1920 Central Archives of the Russian Defence Ministry (Podolsk), f. 243, op. 2928, gy. 131, li. 280.
1921 Central Archives of the Russian Defence Ministry (Podolsk), f. 243, op. 2928, gy. 131, li. 280.
1922 Central Archives of the Russian Defence Ministry (Podolsk), f. 243, op. 2928, gy. 178, li. 115.
1923 Central Archives of the Russian Defence Ministry (Podolsk), f. 243, op. 2928, gy. 131, li. 280. In this case, the documents do not contain the data of the BA–64 armoured cars, the motorcycles and the 1453rd Self-Propelled Artillery Regiment. The latter most likely had no operational SU-100s.
1924 Central Archives of the Russian Defence Ministry (Podolsk), f. 243, op. 2928, gy. 131, li. 280.

The Soviet 5th Motorcycle Regiment was advancing from the sector of Kisbarát to the north, in the direction of Győr, and reaching the southern edge, they established contact with the forces of the 46th Army/2nd Ukrainian Front. The Regiment, attacking from the east, took part in the occupation of the town, which fell into Soviet hands at 1240 hours. The unit lost a burnt out T–34/85 tank, and another one was damaged. In the evening, eight operational tanks were withdrawn from the frontline and in subordination to the 1st Guards Mechanized Corps, they were sent to the sector of Tét.[1925]

The 366th Guards Heavy Self-Propelled Artillery Regiment/4th Guards Army, was en route to Barbacs on this day, where they were to establish firing positions on the western edge of the village with nine captured and operational *Hummels* and *Wespe* self-propelled howitzers, one German assault gun and one Panzer IV tank. The six independent self-propelled artillery battalions of the Army, with their 54 operational SU–76Ms and five tanks, were still being held as the anti-tank artillery reserves and were not yet deployed.[1926]

On the frontline of the 2nd Ukrainian Front

The Soviet 1897th Self-Propelled Artillery Regiment/46th Army, with the units of the 317th Rifle Division, reached the western outskirts of Ménfőcsanak by 1300 hours.[1927]

The German *6. Panzer-Division*, together with units of *2. SS-Panzer-Division*, engaged the Soviet forces which had started advancing at 0330 hours from Hecsepuszta, four km west of Győrszentiván, with 30-40 armoured fighting vehicles to the north-east, narrowing down the bridgehead at Győr, then pushed back the two *Panzer-Divisions* on the northern bank of the Rába River.

During the fighting, at 0200 hours, the forces of the Soviet 23rd Tank Corps with support from the 19th Rifle Division, launched an attack from the Kecskeméti-erdő north-west of Bőnyrétalap, toward Győr. The Soviet armoured fighting vehicles occupied Győrszabadhegy at 0830 hours, and breached the south-eastern part of the town.[1928]

The 6th Guards Mechanized Brigade/2nd Guards Mechanized Corps, was attacking on the road along the Kis-Duna and broke into the north-eastern part of Győr. The 37th Guards Tank Brigade and the 4th Guards Mechanized Brigade, were advancing along the Győr–Komárom railroad line, and broke into the eastern part of Győr. The 5th Guards Mechanized Brigade attacked the south-eastern part of the town. It's most probable that the 251st Guards Self-Propelled Artillery Regiment was supporting the latter Brigade, one SU–85 self-propelled gun of which, under command by Guards Lieutenant Aleksandr N. Yelagin, performed the following exceptional deed during combat:

"[…] In the heat of the battle for Győr, Guards Lieutenant Yelagin pulled in front of all the armoured fighting vehicles and the infantry, destroyed an enemy battery with direct

---

1925 Central Archives of the Russian Defence Ministry (Podolsk), f. 243, op. 2928, gy. 131, li. 280.
1926 Central Archives of the Russian Defence Ministry (Podolsk), f. 243, op. 2928, gy. 131, li. 279.
1927 Central Archives of the Russian Defence Ministry (Podolsk), f. 240, op. 2799, gy. 342, li. 116.
1928 Central Archives of the Russian Defence Ministry (Podolsk), f. 240, op. 2799, gy. 357, li. 16.

hits which were hindering the advance of the tanks and infantry. While he was hunting the enemy fleeing in panic, and was crushing them under the tank's tracks, Yelagin was separated from his own tanks and infantry. The enemy recovered themselves, and made a huge effort to capture the dauntless crew. Heavy tanks came out of their cover, self-propelled guns cut off the route back to his comrades, and they were crawling very close to his tank. Guards Lieutenant Yelagin took up the uneven challenge, destroyed two self-propelled guns, one armoured transport vehicle and a platoon of infantry; then Yelagin relieved the seriously wounded tank driver, and he himself drove the burning tank, which could have exploded at any moment, back out of the circle of the enemy, while he was soaked in blood, and also burned; thus he saved the crew and the self-propelled gun."[1929]

Guards Lieutenant Yelagin was later awarded the Hero of the Soviet Union.

According to Soviet reconnaissance, the German-Hungarian defensive forces established a number of small earth and wood fortifications, mine fields and barbed wire obstacles to defend the town. The roads were blocked. Reconnaissance of the 2nd Guards Mechanized Corps, determined the sector of Győr was defended by the German *2. SS-Panzer-Division, Sturmgeschütz-Brigade 325*, and the remnants of the Royal Hungarian 1st Hussars Division.[1930]

The 39th Tank Brigade/23rd Tank Corps, with the 1443rd Self-Propelled Artillery Regiment, and the 3rd Tank Brigade with the 56th Motorized Rifle Brigade, were attacking in the direction of Győr. At 0500 hours, in the sector of the railway station of Győrszentiván, the Soviet armoured fighting vehicles ran into an anti-tank ditch, over which the engineering troops opened a clear path by 0700 hours. Crossing through this corridor, the units continued their attack against the Nádorváros part of Győr and the factory sites.[1931]

The armoured fighting vehicles of the two Soviet corps repulsed a number of German counterattacks within the town, and in heavy close quarters combat occupied the eastern part of Győr up to the Rába River, by 1500 hours.

SS-Panzer-Flak-Abteilung 2 had also taken part in the defence of Győr on the southeastern edge of the town. The actively retreating *Abteilung* reported that they knocked out approximately a dozen Soviet armoured fighting vehicles, but in the meantime, they themselves suffered a 30 percent loss.[1932]

The retreating Germans demolished all of the bridges on the Rába River and the Kis-Duna in the vicinity of the town. The forces of the 23rd Tank Corps continued their attack during the night also, in order to be able to occupy a bridgehead on the western bank of the Rába River. At the same time, the forces of the 2nd Guards Mechanized Corps started off for the sector of Koroncó and Gáspárháza.[1933]

1929 See HM HIM Hadtörténelmi Levéltár (Budapest), Szovjetunió Hőse kitüntetések gyűjteménye (*Collection of Hero of the Soviet Union awards*), 594.
1930 Summarized report of the 2nd Guards Mechanized Corps of the combat actions during March and April 1945. Copy owned by the author. p. 129.
1931 War log of the 23rd Tank Corps from March 1945. Copy owned by the author. p. 19. o.
1932 Weidinger, Otto: *Division Das Reich. Der Weg der 2. SS-Panzer-Division „Das Reich".* Band V: 1943-1945. Osnabrück, without year of publication, p. 479.
1933 Central Archives of the Russian Defence Ministry (Podolsk), f. 240, op. 2799, gy. 357, li. 17.

During the fight for Győr, the 23rd Tank Corps reported to have knocked out, among others, 12 tanks, four assault guns, and 13 armoured personnel carriers. Their own losses were nine knocked out T–34/85 tanks, of which eight burnt out.[1934]

The Germans established holding positions between Győr and Vének, on the northern bank of the Kis-Duna.[1935]

Interestingly, the German *II. SS-Panzerkorps* reported that they knocked out only two Soviet armoured fighting vehicles on that day.[1936]

The *SS-Panzergrenadier-Regiments/2. SS-Panzer-Division,* were assembled west of Győr. *SS-Panzergrenadier-Regiment 4* marched via Csorna to Beled, where they established holding positions. During the afternoon, on the front of *II. (Bataillon)/SS-Panzergrenadier-Regiment 4,* the Soviets had broken through in the direction of Kapuvár. At 2300 hours, the *Regiment* retreated again.[1937]

The German *3. Kompanie/Sturmpanzer-Abteilung 219,* equipped with Sturmpanzer IV assault vehicles, was subordinated to *6. Panzerarmee,* but the *Heeresgruppe* called to the attention of the high command that they were not to be used in the role of a tank, but rather as self-propelled artillery.[1938]

In the Komárom bridgehead of *8. Armee,* on the night of 27/28 March 1945, the German–Hungarian troops retreated to the inner defensive line in the southern section of the town. The units of *XXXXIII. Armeekorps* were keeping the road along the southern bank of the Danube under fire from the northern bank, and reported to have knocked out five Soviet armoured fighting vehicles.[1939]

During the day, the Soviets, with significant artillery support, broke into the defences of the Hungarian troops. The bridges in the town on the Danube were blown up by the Germans.[1940] Therefore, part of the German–Hungarian forces, among them an anti-aircraft artillery battalion, were stuck on Erzsébet Island in the Danube, and continued to engage the enemy from there.[1941]

The Soviet 1505th Self-Propelled Artillery Regiment, together with the 439th Rifle Regiment/52nd Rifle Division, reached the southern outskirts of Komárom around 1400 hours, and were in combat around the cavalry barracks. During the two days of fighting for the town, the self-propelled guns reported to have knocked out one German assault gun, two armoured personnel carriers, six anti-tank guns and 17 fortifications. Their own loss was one burnt out SU–76M.[1942]

South-west of Komárom, the Soviet 991st Self-Propelled Artillery Regiment/46th Army, was drawn forward from Kocs to the eastern edge of Ács. The SU–76M self-propelled guns were in the reserve of the 252nd Rifle Division/23rd Rifle Corps.[1943]

1934 War log of the 23rd Tank Corps from March 1945. Copy owned by the author. p. 19.
1935 NARA, T311, R162, F7214810.
1936 NARA, T311, R163, F7215504.
1937 Weidinger, Otto: *Division Das Reich. Der Weg der 2. SS-Panzer-Division „Das Reich".* Band V: 1943-1945. Osnabrück, without year of publication, p. 479.
1938 NARA, T311, R163, F7215123.
1939 NARA, T311, R163, F7215486.
1940 NARA, T311, R162, F7214810.
1941 NARA, T311, R162, F7214820.
1942 Central Archives of the Russian Defence Ministry (Podolsk), f. 240, op. 2799, gy. 342, li. 114.
1943 Central Archives of the Russian Defence Ministry (Podolsk), f. 240, op. 2799, gy. 342, li. 111.

The German *Luftflotte 4* supported the German troops that were engaged in heavy combat, flying only about 100 missions, and the pilots reported knocking out one Soviet tank.[1944]

On the same day, *Heeresgruppe Süd* relocated its headquarters to Eisenstadt and with this, the *Stab* had left Hungarian territory. At last Himmler visited *General der Infanterie* Wöhler and *SS-Oberstgruppenführer und Generalmajor der Waffen-SS* Dietrich here. During their discussions, the question was raised as to why the *Wehrmacht* was not able to utilize the fuel supplies stored around Vienna?[1945] In connection with the *SS-Panzer-Divisions*, the participants agreed on the following:

- the infantry combat strength of the *SS*-troops was to be increased at all costs from the supply units and the combat-ready special crews without any heavy armament including the armoured fighting vehicles crews[1946];
- reports from the *SS*-troops were to be systematic and regular;
- the considerable lack of commanders is to be addressed;
- the troops are extremely worn out, to the very end;
- the soldiers dread encirclement;
- the younger soldiers were very much afraid of the artillery fire.[1947]

29 March 1945, Thursday

(**WEATHER**: highest daytime temperature 14 Celsius; mostly sunny, clear skies. The road conditions are favourable.)

On the front of *2. Panzerarmee,* the Soviet 57th and the Bulgarian 1st Army launched their assault, which had been anticipated by the Germans for days.

At 2200 hours on the previous evening, the following operational tank and self-propelled gun strength was available for the Soviet 57th Army:

- 52nd Tank Regiment/32nd Independent Guards Mechanized Brigade with 26 T–34s[1948];
- 249th Independent Tank Regiment with 11 T–34s;
- 3rd Guards Motorcycle Regiment with 10 T–34s;
- 864th Self-Propelled Artillery Regiment with nine SU–76Ms;
- 1201st Self-Propelled Artillery Regiment with 21 SU–76Ms and one T–34;
- 1891st Self-Propelled Artillery Regiment with 16 SU–76Ms;
- 122nd Independent Self-Propelled Artillery Battalion/84th Rifle Division with nine SU–76Ms.[1949]

1944 NARA, T311, R162, F7214811.
1945 NARA, T311, R162, F7214822.
1946 Concerning this the *Heeresgruppe* issued statements via an order towards the subordinated armies. See NARA, T311, R163, F7215128.
1947 NARA, T311, R162, F7214822.
1948 The 52nd Tank Regiment of the 32nd Independent Guards Mechanized Brigade received 12 repaired T-34s from the 3rd Mobile Tank Repair Workshop.
1949 Central Archives of the Russian Defence Ministry (Podolsk), f. 243, op. 2928, gy. 131, li. 282.

The 32nd Independent Guards Mechanized Brigade remained at Kaposfő, the 249th Independent Tank Regiment was at Szomajom, and the 3rd Guards Motorcycle Regiment remained at Juta as reserve to the commander of the 57th Army.

In the front of the German *LXVII. Armeekorps*, in the sector of Háromfa, battalion-size attacks were raging throughout the day. The penetrations achieved by the Soviets had to be eliminated in close combat. In the afternoon, the attacks were also targeting the positions of *71. Infanterie-Division*. The Soviets launched regimental size attacks, supported by armoured fighting vehicles, against Beleg and Kutas and occupied both villages. The incursion was sealed off by the Germans with the help of the last local reserves.[1950]

In the sector of Kutas, the 84th Rifle Division was supported by its own 122nd Independent Self-Propelled Artillery Battalion, which had nine operational SU–76Ms at the end of the day stationed 1.5 km north of the village. The 1201st Self-Propelled Artillery Regiment was also in combat here, supporting the 113th Rifle Division and at the end of the day, was in a firing position with 21 SU–76Ms, on the western slopes of Point 160, two km north-east of Kutas.[1951]

At Beleg, the 1891st Self-Propelled Artillery Regiment was supporting the 299th Rifle Division and at the end of the day, with its 16 SU–76Ms, was engaged in a firefight with German artillery between the southern edge of the village and Point 154, two km northeast of there.

On the front of *XXII. Gebirgskorps,* the Soviet forces south of Kisbajom broke through the positions of the Hungarian units and they were only stopped in-depth of the defence.[1952]

The Soviets had taken Nagybajom in the meantime, and launched battalion-size attacks to the north-west from there and south-east from Mesztegnyő. These attacks were repulsed by the German–Hungarian troops.

Nagybajom was occupied by the Soviet 73rd Guards Rifle Division/64th Rifle Corps, with the support of nine SU–76M self-propelled guns of the 864th Self-Propelled Artillery Regiment. During the fighting, the Regiment lost three burnt out self-propelled guns and at the end of the day, was in combat one km west of Nagybajom with six SU–76Ms.[1953]

In the sector of *16. SS-Panzergrenadier-Division,* a number of Soviet reconnaissance missions and battalion-size attacks were launched against Csömend.[1954] The *Division's* own *SS-Panzer-Aufklärungs-Abteilung 16,* reinforced with assault guns, was subordinated to the arriving *297. Infanterie-Division,* that was deployed south of Zalaegerszeg.[1955]

The German *I. Kavallerie-Korps/6. Armee* was compelled to take back its positions on the Keszthely–Kustány–Zalaudvarnok general line, in order to maintain the continuity of their frontline. At Keszthely, and south-west of Zalaszántó, the Germans left rear guards to

---

1950 NARA, T311, R162, F7214824.
1951 Central Archives of the Russian Defence Ministry (Podolsk), f. 243, op. 2928, gy. 131, li. 282.
1952 NARA, T311, R163, F7215495.
1953 Central Archives of the Russian Defence Ministry (Podolsk), f. 243, op. 2928, gy. 131, li. 282.
1954 NARA, T311, R162, F7214825.
1955 NARA, T311, R163, F7215502. *SS-Panzer-Aufklärungs-Abteilung 16* and *SS-Panzer-Abteilung 16* were withdrawn from the frontline as early as 27 March 1945 and they were subordinated to the German *297. Infanterie-Division* that was being transported by railway. Neither of the units returned to Hungarian territory to the rest of the *Division*. *SS-Panzer-Abteilung 16* became the reserve unit for *I. Kavallerie-Korps* until the end of the war. See Puntigam, Josef Paul: *Vom Plattensee bis zur Mur. Die Kämpfe 1945 im Dreiländereck*. Feldbach, without year of publication, [1993], p. 116.

cover the retreating units. The Soviets were following them with significant forces along the northern shore of Lake Balaton and from the sector of Zalaszentlászló. Keszthely temporarily fell into Soviet hands, but the Germans broke into the town again with a counterattack.[1956] In the evening, the Soviet armoured fighting vehicles[1957] attacked again, broke into the eastern parts of Keszthely and at dawn on the next day, occupied the town.[1958]

During the day, on the front of *23. Panzer-Division*, the Soviets broke into the defences of *I. (Bataillon)/Panzergrenadier-Regiment 126*, north of Egregy. At 2300 hours that night, the *Division* retreated to the Zalaapáti–Bókaháza line. The *I. (Bataillon)/Panzergrenadier-Regiment 128* established defensive positions at Gétye. The new frontline was only fully occupied on 30 March at 0500 hours.[1959]

The forces of *I. Kavallerie-Korps* reported between 20-29 March 1945, they had knocked out 222 Soviet armoured fighting vehicles and immobilized another seven.[1960]

During the day, the Soviet 1202nd Self-Propelled Artillery Regiment/27th Army with 19 SU–76Ms, was supporting the forces of the 35th Guards Rifle Corps in the sector of Alsónemesapáti, Padár and Almásháza. The 432nd Independent Self-Propelled Artillery Battalion/316th Rifle Division, with its 10 SU–76M self-propelled guns, was not deployed on this day, but was stationed at Rezi, because the engines had to be replaced in seven of their armoured fighting vehicles.[1961]

The armoured forces of the Soviet 5th Guards Cavalry Corps were en route on the same day, the 54thTank Regiment with nine operational T–34/85s stood at Kisgörbő, the 71st Tank Regiment with 11 T–34/85s at Szalapa, six km northeast of Zalaszentgrót, and the 1896th Self-Propelled Artillery Regiment with 16 SU–76Ms, stood at Ernye.[1962]

On the night of 28/29 March 1945, on the front of the German *IV. SS-Panzerkorps*, the Soviet 170th Tank Brigade/18th Tank Corps, the 1952nd and 1953rd Self-Propelled Artillery Regiments of the 209th Self-Propelled Artillery Brigade, plus two battalions of the 32nd Motorized Rifle Brigade, reached Zalaszentiván. The Soviets launched a three-hour long mortar barrage, and after this, assaulted the village with 30 tanks and self-propelled guns, and occupied it around 0930 hours. Here, the III Battalion/Hungarian "Dráva" Regiment, consisting of Hungarian gendarmerie forces, was in defence. The tank destroyer platoon of the unit reported to have destroyed seven Soviet armoured fighting vehicles and the three rifle companies reported to have destroyed another eight.[1963] The

---

1956 NARA, T311, R162, F7214825.
1957 Keszthely was occupied by the 108th Guards Rifle Division/37th Rifle Corps/27th Army and units of the 1st Guards Fortified Region on 28 March 1945, however neither of the units had their own armoured fighting vehicles, most likely the SU-76M self-propelled guns of the 432nd Independent Self-Propelled Artillery Battalion/316th Rifle Division of the army had been deployed in the fighting for the town.
1958 NARA, T311, R163, F7215506.
1959 Rebentisch, Ernst: *Zum Kaukasus und zu den Tauern. Die Geschichte der 23. Panzer-Division 1941–1945*. Esslingen, 1963. p. 502.
1960 NARA, T311, R163, F7215504.
1961 Central Archives of the Russian Defence Ministry (Podolsk), f. 243, op. 2928, gy. 131, li. 282.
1962 Central Archives of the Russian Defence Ministry (Podolsk), f. 243, op. 2928, gy. 131, li. 283.
1963 The casualty report of the 18th Tank Corps for the day does not support or verify the destruction of the 15 armoured fighting vehicles. At the same time it is true, that the reported strength of the operational armoured fighting vehicles of the Corps in the evening of 29 March was less than that of the previous evening's, with seven T–34/85 tanks, of which five were also contained in the casualty report of 29 March, five ISU–122s and two ISU–152 self-propelled guns, plus on that day, according to the casualty report, an SU–100 was also knocked out. This makes a total of 15 armoured fighting vehicles, the units of which were, in theory, driving through Zalaszentiván on their way to Zalaegerszeg. Most likely the majority of the Soviet armoured fighting vehicles knocked out by the Hungarian police force were immobilized therefore they have not been included in the casualty report.

Hungarian forces suffered approximately 50% losses during this action and retreated towards Zalaegerszeg.[1964]

During the day, the reinforced 170th Tank Brigade, together with the 3rd Guards Airborne Division/27th Army, launched an attack toward the south-west along the road leading towards Zalaegerszeg and at around 1600 hours, they occupied the town. The reinforced Tank Brigade lost two burnt out T–34/85s, three suffered mine damage; and one SU–100 was also knocked out on that day.[1965]

The 110th Tank Brigade, together with the 363rd Guards Heavy Self-Propelled Artillery Regiment, the 1953rd Self-Propelled Artillery Regiment/209th Self-Propelled Artillery Brigade and the 1st Battalion/32nd Motorized Rifle Brigade, with the 1000th Anti-Tank Artillery Regiment, exploited the successes of the reinforced 170th Tank Brigade and pushing after them, reached Nekeresdmajor, 1,5 km northeast of Zalaegerszeg, by the end of the day.

The 181st Tank Brigade together with the 1951st Self-Propelled Artillery Regiment/209th Self-Propelled Artillery Brigade, the 1438th Self-Propelled Artillery Regiment and the 452nd Light Artillery Regiment, set off from the sector of Batyk–Újmajor–Pakod, and by 1700 hours they reached Alsóbagod nine km north-west of Zalaegerszeg. The 18th Tank Corps reported on that day to have knocked out nine German tanks, eight armoured personnel carriers, and to have captured 350 soldiers. In the evening, the troops had 32 operational tanks, one ISU–122, two ISU–152s and eight SU–76M self-propelled guns, plus the 38 SU–100s, one SU–57 and two T–34s of the 209th Self-Propelled Artillery Brigade.[1966]

The Soviet troops launched battalion and regimental size forces, supported by armoured fighing vehicles, against the positions of *5. SS-Panzer-Division*. The front of *IV. SS-Panzerkorps*, after the fighting of that day, was stretched on the Gerse southern edge–Győrvár western edge–Olaszka western edge –Felsőoszkó eastern edge line.[1967] The remaining forces of *5. SS-Panzer-Division* were retreating to the Rába bridgehead at Vasvár.[1968]

Kampfgruppe "Bradel"/1. Panzer-Division, was retreating from the sector of Olaszka–Felsőoszkó towards Döbörhegy, in order to establish a bridgehead south of Körmend.[1969]

The personnel of *Sturmpanzer-Abteilung 219*, subordinated to *1. Panzer-Division*, were retreating towards Muraszombat on this day via Nova and Lenti, and on the following day, they reached Radkersburg. By then, all of the Sturmpanzer IVs were blown up due to the lack of fuel.[1970]

Because of the breakthrough the Soviets achieved in the sector of Zalaegerszeg, the German *Heeresgruppe Süd* subordinated *I. Kavallerie-Korps* on that day, as of 0600 hours, to *2. Panzerarmee*. At the same time, Hitler would still not permit the retreat of the German–Hungarian forces into the *Margarethen-Stellung*.[1971] The *IV. SS-Panzerkorps* was

---

1964 HM HIM Hadtörténelmi Levéltár (Budapest), *Tanulmányok és visszaemlékezések gyűjteménye*, issue 3148. (bequest of Pál Darnóy Pál).
1965 War log of the 18th Tank Corps for March 1945. Copy owned by the author. p. 56.
1966 Central Archives of the Russian Defence Ministry (Podolsk), f. 243, op. 2928, gy. 178, li. 117., furthermore f. 243, op. 2928, gy. 131, li. 283.
1967 NARA, T311, R162, F7214825.
1968 Strassner, Peter: *Europäische Freiwillige. Die 5. SS-Panzerdivision Wiking*. Osnabrück, 1977. Third, revised edition. p. 343.
1969 Stoves, Rolf: Persönliches Kriegstagebuch Pz.Rgt. 1 (typewritten manuscript, a copy owned by the author), entry from 29 March 1945.
1970 Bertram, Ludwig: Sturmpanzerabteilung 219. In: *Der Sturmartillerist*. Heft 101. 1991. 2338. o.
1971 NARA, T311, R162, F7214830.

ordered to maintain contact with *I. Kavallerie-Korps* and in order to achieve this, they were not to retreat towards the west.[1972]

In the section of *III. Panzerkorps,* the units of *1. Volks-Gebirgs-Division* deployed east of the Rába River, after repulsing a number of Soviet rifle infantry attacks, were forced to break through the Soviet troops which had outflanked them from the south, after which they reached the Csehi–Alsóújlak line.

At the end of the day, the Soviet 72nd Guards Independent Self-Propelled Artillery Battalion/68th Guards Rifle Division/26th Army, with nine SU-76M self-propelled guns, was fighting in Egervölgy, after losing a self-propelled gun to German gunfire during the day.[1973]

The Soviets continued the attack from the Sárvár bridgehead with large rifle and tank forces toward the west, pushed back the German rapid reaction troops and the Hungarian fortress battalions, and at around noon, occupied Szombathely.

The town was successfully assaulted by the rifle infantry of the 9th Guards Army[1974] in cooperation with the 5th Guards Tank Corps. At the end of the day, the 6th Guards Motorized Rifle Brigade, with the 51st and 208th Self-Propelled Artillery Brigades in support, were in combat on the western edge of the town, and the 20th Guards Tank Brigade was in combat two km west from there. The 22nd Guards Tank Brigade occupied Kámon, and the 21st Guards Tank Brigade occupied Perint. In the evening, the Corps had 40 operational T–34/85 tanks[1975] and 16 SU–76M self-propelled guns. The 51st Guards Self-Propelled Artillery Brigade had 40 operational SU–76Ms, and the 208th Self-Propelled Artillery Brigade had the same number of SU–100s.[1976]

The regimental combat group of the German *1. Volks-Gebirgs-Division,* was attacking in a north-north-west direction from the northern outskirts of Rum, had approached to within 2.5 km from the south of Ikervár, but had to abort its attack due to the dangerous situation unfolding at Szombathely. The *II. (Bataillon)/Gebirgs-Jäger-Regiment 98,* encircled at Kenéz, attempted to break out towards the south-west and to reach their own troops.[1977]

The Soviet 1523rd Self-Propelled Artillery Regiment/9th Guards Army with 18 SU–76M self-propelled guns, was supporting the rifle troops, one km north-west of Iván. The 1524th Self-Propelled Artillery Regiment, with 22 SU–76Ms, was in combat together with the rifle troops, one km south-west of Csepreg and four km south-west of there, at Nándormajor. The 1513th Self-Propelled Artillery Regiment acted as reserve of the 37th Guards Rifle Corps six km south-east of Sárvár with four SU–76M self-propelled guns.[1978]

The Soviet 31st Guards Mechanized Brigade/9th Guards Mechanized Corps and the 364th Guards Heavy Self-Propelled Artillery Regiment, were attacking towards Kőszeg and reached the north-western edge of the town and the 18th Guards Mechanized Brigade reached the

---

1972 NARA, T311, R162, F7214832.
1973 Central Archives of the Russian Defence Ministry (Podolsk), f. 243, op. 2928, gy. 131, li. 282.
1974 The Soviet 9th Guards Army paid a high price for the successes achieved by them during the period of 16-29 March 1945. The troops lost more than 21,000 soldiers with 4869 killed, and 16,242 wounded. See Central Archives of the Russian Defence Ministry (Podolsk), f. 243, op. 2900, gy. 1861, li. 66. The three Self-Propelled Artillery Regiments removed 31 destroyed SU–76Ms from their strength.
1975 Of these, the three Tank Brigades each had 11 operational T–34/85 tanks. See the war log of the 5th Guards Tank Corps for March 1945. Copy owned by the author. p. 21.
1976 Central Archives of the Russian Defence Ministry (Podolsk), f. 243, op. 2928, gy. 131, li. 281.
1977 NARA, T311, R162, F7214825.
1978 Central Archives of the Russian Defence Ministry (Podolsk), f. 243, op. 2928, d. 131, li. 282.

southern edge. The Soviet armoured fighting vehicles occupied Kőszeg, following a short engagement, then prepared for defence[1979], replenishing their fuel and ammunition supplies, and rested for the night. North of the town however, the 30th Guards Mechanized Brigade continued their attack, crossed the German border, and at 1105 hours launched an attack to occupy Kloster Marienberg (Borsmonostor).[1980] The 46th Guards Tank Brigade occupied Lukácsháza four km south-east of Kőszeg. In the evening, the Corps had 75 operational M4A2 tanks, 12 SU–76M and 14 ISU–122 self-propelled guns.[1981]

The Soviet 4th Guards Motorcycle Regiment/6th Guards Tank Army with seven operational Mk–IX Valentine tanks and 95 motorcycles, was still in the army commander's reserve on that day, eight km north-west of Sárvár, at Alsószeleste. The 252nd Amphibious Car Battalion with 99 DUKW amphibious trucks was stationed at Sárvár.[1982]

On the front of the German *I. SS-Panzerkorps/6. Panzerarmee,* the Germans repulsed a number of small scale Soviet attacks in the sector of Felsőság and Iván. The combat groups of the two *Panzergrenadier-Regiments* of *1. SS-Panzer-Division,* were trying to hold on to the positions around Lócs, but as the Soviets had again outflanked the *Division*'s units on the right, the Germans were compelled to retreat toward the west.[1983]

At 0300 hours on the front of *12. SS-Panzer-Division,* the *Divisionsbegleitkompanie* established the command post of *SS-Brigadeführer* Kraas at Csapod.

At 0645 hours in the morning, the Soviets launched an attack against the positions of *II. (Bataillon)/SS-Panzergrenadier-Regiment 26* at Répcelak. The first attack was repulsed by the Germans, but the second attack pushed them back to a distance of four km west of the village. At 0855 hours, the Soviets attacked again and knocked out an *SS* armoured personnel carrier. As a consequence of the fourth attack, the battalion needed to retreat to Iván. At 2010 hours that evening, the *SS-Panzergrenadiers* were ambushed here, but fire from the German artillery halted the Soviet advance. The repeated assault reached the battalion command post, therefore the Germans retreated another one km toward the west.

Units of *SS-Panzergrenadier-Regiment 25* were encircled by the Soviets at Dénesfa. That evening, the regimental command post was attacked at Csapod, and as result, was relocated to Pityérmajor. The *Divisionsbegleitkompanie* and *SS-Panzer-Aufklärungs-Abteilung 12* were also ordered there. As the Soviets had reached the sector of Kapuvár, the frontline of *SS-Panzergrenadier-Regiment 25* was withdrawn to the west of Csapod.[1984]

The units of the Soviet 4th Guards Army launched an attack between Felsőság and Mihályi with approximately division strength and the support of 14 armoured fighting vehicles. Following a prolonged battle, at last the forces of the Soviet 1st Guards Mechanized Corps entered Gyóró and Cirák from the south and north, during the afternoon. Gyóró was occupied by the 2nd Guards Mechanized Brigade, and Cirák by the 1st Guards Mechanized Brigade. The Germans in defence of Dénesfa were cut off from their own troops by this

---

1979 For example the 364th Guards Heavy Self-Propelled Artillery Regiment occupied firing positions on the western edge of Kőszeg with its ISU–122 self-propelled guns.
1980 NARA, T311, R162, F7214828.
1981 Central Archives of the Russian Defence Ministry (Podolsk), f. 243, op. 2928, d. 131, li. 281.
1982 Central Archives of the Russian Defence Ministry (Podolsk), f. 243, op. 2928, d. 131, li. 281.
1983 Tiemann, Ralf: *Die Leibstandarte.* Band IV/2. Osnabrück, 1987. p. 346.
1984 Meyer, Hubert: *Kriegsgeschichte der 12. SS-Panzerdivision „Hitlerjugend".* Band II. Osnabrück, 1987. 2nd edition. pp. 519-520.

surprise attack. Hill 137, three km west of Gyóró, fell into Soviet hands after a coordinated attack from the south and west at the same time. The ruins of the German *232. Panzer-Division,* approximately 60 men in a small combat group, continued to fight in the vicinity of Gyóró. South-east of Csapod, in the forested area (László Forest), the Soviets were attacking the Germans with a battalion-size forces and with a few armoured fighting vehicles.[1985]

The 9th Guards Tank Brigade/1st Guards Mechanized Corps, together with the 1004th Self-Propelled Artillery Regiment/207th Self-Propelled Artillery Brigade and the 4th Guards Rifle Division/4th Guards Army, occupied Kapuvár at 0300 hours in the morning, and on that day, until 1500 hours, rested their units and reorganized their troops. Afterwards, the reinforced 9th Guards Tank Brigade started off toward the south, in the direction of Gyóró. The 3rd Guards Mechanized Brigade was assembled with the 382nd Guards Self-Propelled Artillery Regiment at Beled. At 1000 hours, the 2nd Guards Mechanized Brigade, together with the 912th Self-Propelled Artillery Regiment/207th Self-Propelled Artillery Brigade, launched an attack from the sector of Magyarkeresztúr toward Mihályi, where they faced German resistance. Following this, they bypassed the village toward the north, in the direction of Kisfalud and Gyóró.[1986]

The 1st Guards Mechanized Corps lost 12 destroyed M4A2 tanks during the action that day.[1987] Its troops had 65 operational M4A2 tanks and eight SU–100s in the evening, and the 209th Self-Propelled Artillery Brigade had 26 SU–100 self-propelled guns. The 53rd Motorcycle Regiment was stationed at Csorna in the corps commander's reserve with eight operational T–34s and 107 motorcycles.[1988]

During the day, in the sector of Himod and Hövej, the Soviets launched battalion-size attacks, but these were temporarily repulsed by the forces of *2. SS-Panzer-Division.* The local priest at Hövej reported the following about the local engagements in the area:

> „[…] *In the afternoon new voices joined the crazy shooting. A German battle car [harcikocsi, sic!] entered my yard, and was firing ceaselessly. Around 5 o'clock Soviet aircraft attacked the village. Maybe they wanted to destroy the church because of the German observer, maybe they wanted to silence the German battle car [sic!] in my yard... […]*
> *The aircraft were buzzing ceaselessly overhead. The bombs were detonating, but farther from us. Around midnight, the battle was culminating. The phosphor guns[1989] [sic!] set fire to houses, barns, and haystacks. The village of Hövej was on the brink of destruction.*
> *[On March 30] at 0200 hours at dawn, the Germans ceased all resistance as the Soviet battle cars[1990] [sic!] were threatening them with encircling the forces from Himód [sic!]. Hövej was abandoned, but the village was targeted as late as in the morning hours from the direction of Csermajor. […]*"[1991]

1985 NARA, T311, R162, F7214826.
1986 War log of the 207th Self-Propelled Artillery Brigade, 29 March 1945. Copy owned by the author.
1987 Central Archives of the Russian Defence Ministry (Podolsk), f. 243, op. 2928, gy. 178, li. 117.
1988 Central Archives of the Russian Defence Ministry (Podolsk), f. 243, op. 2928, gy. 131, li. 283.
1989 Correctly: because of the phosphorus projectiles.
1990 Most likely parts of the 1st Guards Mechanized Corps.
1991 Gyula Perger: „…*félelemmel and aggodalommal…". Plébániák jelentései a háborús károkról a Győri Egyházmegyéből, 1945.* Győr, 2005. pp. 102-103.

The units of *3. SS-Panzer-Division* retreated to the Gyóró–Himod line, where they, together with the armoured personnel carrier-battalion of *2. SS-Panzer-Division,* repulsed a Soviet advance towards Himod.[1992]

In the south-western outskirts of Kapuvár, in the forested area south of Vitnyéd (Vitnyédi Forest), the Germans eliminated the Soviet incursion with a counterattack.[1993]

A 366th Guards Heavy Self-Propelled Artillery Regiment/4th Guards Army was en route to Szilsárkány with 11 operational German captured self-propelled howitzers, assault guns, and captured tanks. The six independent self-propelled-artillery battalions of the Army, supported their own rifle troops with 54 operational SU–76Ms and five tanks.[1994]

On the frontline of the 2nd Ukrainian Front

On the front of *II. SS-Panzerkorps* on the night of 28/29 March 1945, the Soviets launched an attack from the sector of Potyond and Bogyoszló, against *2. SS-Panzer-Division* in combat on the Magyarkeresztúr eastern edge–forest south of Babot sector.

The units of *2. SS-Panzer-Division* established blocking positions in the sector of Kapuvár against the Soviet troops advancing north and westwards. At Himod and Hövej, the Germans repulsed the Soviet attack. *SS-Panzergrenadier-Regiments 3* and *4* established holding positions between Himod and Vitnyéd.[1995]

On the front of the Hungarian 1st Mountain Brigade, the Soviets had broken into Kóny with rifle support, then 1 km north of Kóny and south of Enese, they wedged a gap into the defence of the Brigade. The Soviet 1897th Self-Propelled Artillery Regiment was also in combat here, which crossed the Marcal and then the Rába River in the sector of Koroncó, and together with the 761st Rifle Regiment/317th Rifle Division, occupied Kisbabot, Rábacsécsény, Kóny, Barbacs and Maglóca. During the day, one of the SU-76Ms of the 1897th Self-Propelled Artillery Regiment was damaged when it ran over a mine, and needed to undergo general repairs.[1996]

The *6. Panzer-Division* repulsed two Soviet attempts at crossing the Rába River. The Soviets had drawn forward military bridging columns, but the German artillery engaged them in fire.[1997]

During the day, the Hungarian 1st Mountain Brigade successfully defended Bősárkány from the small scale attacks of the Soviets, but around 1800 hours, the 761st Rifle Regiment/317th Rifle Division and the SU-76M self-propelled guns of the 1897th Self-Propelled Artillery Regiment occupied the village.[1998]

1992 Vopersal, Wolfgang: *Soldaten, Kämpfer, Kameraden. Marsch und Kämpfe der SS-Totenkopfdivision.* Band Vb. Bielefeld, 1991. p. 842.
1993 NARA, T311, R162, F7214826.
1994 Central Archives of the Russian Defence Ministry (Podolsk), f. 243, op. 2928, gy. 131, li. 282.
1995 Weidinger, Otto: *Division Das Reich. Der Weg der 2. SS-Panzer-Division „Das Reich".* Band V: 1943-1945. Osnabrück, without year of publication, p. 482.
1996 Central Archives of the Russian Defence Ministry (Podolsk), f. 240, op. 2799, gy. 342, li. 116.
1997 NARA, T311, R163, F7215496.
1998 Central Archives of the Russian Defence Ministry (Podolsk), f. 240, op. 2799, gy. 342, li. 116.

Enese and Rábapatona also fell into Soviet hands. From the bridgehead established at Rábapatona, the Soviet troops were attacking north-eastwards, and pushed the right flank of *6. Panzer-Division* back to the line of the railroad running north of Ikrény. After nightfall, the Soviets crossed the Rába River with a company size force at the south-western entrance of Győr. The Soviet regimental size attack between Alsóvámos and Nagybajcs, pushed back the German defenders. The bridge on the Danube that stood at Medve, was blown up by the Germans.[1999]

The German *Luftflotte 4* attacked the Soviet columns and tank assembly areas between Kapuvár and Csorna flying approximately 120 missions. The pilots reported the destruction of seven armoured fighting vehicles, 100 drawn vehicles and other vehicles, plus three anti-tank guns. The activity of the German–Hungarian aircraft units was seriously hindered by the fact that their ground crews were in retreat at the same time.[2000]

The reconnaissance of *Heeresgruppe Süd* assumed that the Soviet 6th Guards Tank Army, and the 4th Guards and 9th Guards Army, were to attack toward Vienna and Wiener Neustadt, via the sectors of Szombathely and Kőszeg, and as the Soviet 46th Army became free in the sector of Győr, it was to execute a frontal attack between Fertő Lake and the Danube, together with the 2nd Guards Mechanized Corps and the 23rd Tank Corps. Parallel to this, the units of the Soviet 27th Army were to advance from the sector of Zalaegerszeg toward the south-west with the 18th Tank Corps, in order to push the forces of the German *2. Panzerarmee* and *6. Armee* to the Mura River and to cut them off. According to the Germans, the occupation of the oilfields of Nagykanizsa was obviously a secondary target for the Soviets.[2001] Hitler was quite the opposite, who might have chosen rather to give up *Reich* territory temporarily just to keep the oil fields.[2002]

On that night, the "Father of German armoured forces", *Generaloberst* Guderian, made a phone call and said good bye to the *Stab* of the *Heeresgruppe*, as he was going on a six week leave "because of medical reasons". His successor as the chief of staff of the *Heer,* became *General der Infanterie* Hans Krebs.[2003]

30 March 1945, Friday

(**WEATHER**: highest daytime temperature 16 Celsius; partly sunny and clear skies, partly cloudy. Random showers. The road conditions are still favourable.)

The forces of *2. Panzerarmee* set off to retreat into the *Margarethen-Stellung*. On the front of *LXVII. Armeekorps,* at dawn on the night of 29/30 March 1945, the Soviets widened their salient between Beleg and Kutas and broke through the German defensive positions. The Germans were able to hold up the Soviet armoured and motorized rifle forces only in the sector of Inke.[2004]

1999 NARA, T311, R162, F7214826.
2000 NARA, T311, R162, F7214828.
2001 NARA, T311, R162, F7214828-7214829.
2002 NARA, T311, R162, F7214840.
2003 NARA, T311, R162, F7214840.
2004 NARA, T311, R162, F7214841.

The majority of the Soviet 57th Army was in combat here, the 32nd Independent Guards Mechanized Brigade with 24 T–34s, the 249th Independent Tank Regiment with 11 T–34s and the 3rd Guards Motorcycle Regiment with 10 T–34/85 tanks.[2005] The 16 SU–76M self-propelled guns of the 1891st Self-Propelled Artillery Regiment were supporting the 299th Rifle Division and were engaged in combat one km south-west of Inke at the end of the day. Meanwhile, 3.5 km north-east of the village, at Point 185, the 122nd Independent Self-Propelled Artillery Battalion/84th Rifle Division was in combat with nine SU–76Ms.[2006]

The 1201st Self-Propelled Artillery Regiment, with 21 SU–76Ms and one T–34, together with the 113rd Rifle Division, occupied Nemesdéd by the end of the day.[2007]

The 864th Self-Propelled Artillery Regiment, together with the forces of the 73rd Guards Rifle Division, reached Irmapuszta 16 km north-west of Böhönye, but one of its SU-76M self-propelled guns was burnt out. In the evening, they had five operational self-propelled guns.[2008]

In the front of *XXII. Gebirgskorps,* the rear guards of the retreating Germans were pushed back by the Soviets with attacks supported by armoured fighting vehicles. Through the gap they opened along the southern shore of Lake Balaton, the Soviets broke into Sármellék.[2009]

On the front of *I. Kavallerie-Korps,* the Soviets launched a series of regimental size assaults during the day. On the German right flank, these attacks were repulsed, except for the western outskirts of Alsópáhok, where the Soviets succeeded in breaking into the defences. Here, the Germans sealed off the breach.[2010]

The *3. Kavallerie-Division* launched an attack from the sector of Pacsa against the Soviets, but the Soviet rifle forces pushed them back to the Nemesrádó–Bebespuszta–four km from there general line. The Soviets, with armoured support, broke through the weak line of the Germans, and occupied the vineyards and forest north of Zalaszentmihály.[2011]

At 2200 hours in the evening, *23. Panzer-Division* retreated again and established defensive positions in the hills 2.5 km east of Pacsa. The *I. (Bataillon)/Panzergrenadier-Regiment 128* stood in ready reserve behind the frontline.[2012]

The Soviet 1202nd Self-Propelled Artillery Regiment/27th Army, supported the rifle troops in these battles and at the end of the day, was engaged in combat in the sector of Nagykapornak with 18 SU–76Ms. The 432nd Independent Self-Propelled Artillery Battalion/316th Rifle Division was in firing position at Egregy, four km northwest of Keszthely, with one of its batteries, but seven of its ten SU–76M self-propelled guns, comprising two batteries, were still waiting for an engine replacement.[2013]

The units of *297. Infanterie-Division* temporarily stopped the Soviet troops that were attacking from Zalaegerszeg toward the south and south-west.

2005 Central Archives of the Russian Defence Ministry (Podolsk), f. 243, op. 2928, gy. 131, li. 285.
2006 Central Archives of the Russian Defence Ministry (Podolsk), f. 243, op. 2928, gy. 131, li. 285.
2007 Central Archives of the Russian Defence Ministry (Podolsk), f. 243, op. 2928, gy. 131, li. 285.
2008 Central Archives of the Russian Defence Ministry (Podolsk), f. 243, op. 2928, gy. 131, li. 285.
2009 NARA, T311, R162, F7214842.
2010 NARA, T311, R162, F7214842.
2011 NARA, T311, R162, F7214842.
2012 Rebentisch, Ernst: *Zum Kaukasus und zu den Tauern. Die Geschichte der 23. Panzer-Division 1941–1945.* Esslingen, 1963. p. 502.
2013 Central Archives of the Russian Defence Ministry (Podolsk), f. 243, op. 2928, gy. 131, li. 284.

Between the flanks of *I. Kavallerie-Korps* and *IV. SS-Panzerkorps,* there was already a 25 km wide gap. Going through this, the Soviet armoured fighting vehicles occupied Zalalövő during the night of 29/30 March 1945, then advancing south and west, pushed back the assault battalion of *2. Panzerarmee* to Point 266 (Nagy Hill), five km south of Zalalövő.[2014] In order to close the gap near Szentgotthárd, the *Kommandeur* of *2. Panzerarmee, General der Artillerie* de Angelis, planned to withdraw 20 assault guns and three battalions from the eastern frontline of the *Armee*. These were most likely detached forces from *16. SS-Panzer-Division*, which were being assembled behind the *Margarathen-Stellung*.[2015]

The forces of the Soviet 18th Tank Corps continued their attack from the sector of Zalaegerszeg toward the west and north-west. The 181st Tank Brigade, together with a SU-100 regiment of the 209th Self-Propelled Artillery Brigade, occupied Zalalövő. The 110th and 170th Tank Brigade with the 363rd Guards Heavy Self-Propelled Artillery Regiment, the 1438th Self-Propelled Artillery Regiment and the 209th Self-Propelled Artillery Brigade with its two SU–100 regiments reached, and occupied Katafa and Nádasd, five km south of Körmend, by 1130 hours. One of the tank commanders of the Tank Brigade remembered this day:

"On 30 March 1945, we occupied a village and a mechanized column within: there were captives, vehicles, armoured vehicles, guns, but no tanks there. We stopped, replenished our ammunition supplies and refuelled. The enemy retreated three km. Everything was ready for us to continue our advance. The kombat said: "You are going to be in the forward unit". I ordered my tank to come forward. I sat up to the right of the driver at the ball-joint of the machine gun, my aimer and my radio operator were sitting on the turret, their legs were dangling inside the escape hatch, and at the back there were approximately ten desant soldiers. The first tank set off, ours followed, but the road was muddy from the melted snow, and the first armoured fighting vehicle left a deep track mark in the mud. Our driver kept left a little to avoid sinking us there, and then all of a sudden, a blast! The tank was blown up by an aircraft bomb dug in the ground[2016]*. The turret flew at least 20 meters away, together with the aimer and the radio operator – both survived, but were maimed for life on their legs. I was flung up to a rooftop, from where I fell down into a yard. I had fallen relatively well, I did not break any of my bones. I tore the gate open and jumped to the street. The tank was enflamed, the grenades and the other ammunition all blown up. I saw the commissar of the battalion four meters away from the tank – he was covered in fuel and was burning. I jumped on him, quenched the fire and dragged him to the other end of the gateway. My loader and my driver, who were in the tank, were dead, and almost all of the desant soldiers as well. Only I have come out almost unharmed – only my eardrums were cracked."*[2017]

The German *I. (Bataillon)/Panzergrenadier-Regiment 3*/*3. Panzer-Division* was temporarily defending the mansion on the south-eastern side of Körmend and the nearby Rába bridge.

2014 NARA, T311, R162, F7214842.
2015 NARA, T311, R162, F7214850.
2016 The aerial bomb was most probably planted by German pioneers as a explosive trap.
2017 Drabkin, Artem – Sheremet, Oleg: *T–34 in action. Soviet Tank Troops in WWII*. Mechanicsburg, 2008. p. 124.

However, the first units of the retreating *Division* had, in the meantime, already set foot on *Reich* territory at Heiligenkreuz (Rábakeresztúr).[2018]

Kampfgruppe "Huppert"/1. Panzer-Division, was in combat in the western outskirts of Kám on that day, and the reinforced *1. Kompanie/Panzergrenadier-Regiment 113* was in the bridgehead at Körmend. West of Körmend, in the northern outskirts of Vasalja, the road junction was planned to be defended by the damaged, but still combat-ready armament of the Panther and Panzer IV tanks of *Panzer-Regiment 1*. However, this came to nothing, because the armoured fighting vehicles had been towed away, and sent off on flatbed loaders toward Fürstenfeld.[2019]

The command post of *5. SS-Panzer-Division* was set up on the southern side of the bridgehead at Vasvár, near the bridge. Later, the *SS*-troops were ordered to assemble in the sector of Fürstenfeld. The still combat-ready soldiers and heavy armament were to be employed in the *Reichsschutzstellung* (South-east wall).[2020]

On the right flank of the German *IV. SS-Panzerkorps/6. Armee,* the units of the Soviet 18th Tank Corps reached the Rába River line between Nagycsákány and Nagymizdó, through the gap torn in the frontline toward *2. Panzerarmee*; then they crossed it with two armoured fighting vehicles and 200 soldiers at Csákánydoroszló.

Without delay, these forces continued their attack towards the west. The 110th Tank Brigade with the 363rd Guards Heavy Self-Propelled Artillery Regiment, the 1st Battalion/451st Light Artillery Regiment, the 1694th Anti-Aircraft Artillery Battalion and one of the SU-100 regiments of the 209th Self-Propelled Artillery Brigade, supported by an engineering company, eliminated the German mine obstacles and road blockades, and around 2000 hours, occupied Csörötnek, nine km east of Szentgotthárd.

The 170th Tank Brigade, with one of the SU-100 regiments of the 209th Self-Propelled Artillery Brigade, the 1st Battalion/32nd Motorized Rifle Brigade, and with the support of one mortar and two light artillery battalions, reached and occupied Kondorfa from Zalacséb to Viszák.

The forces of the corps reported to have knocked out six guns and two armoured personnel carriers, plus the capture of approximately 2500, mainly Hungarian, soldiers. In the evening, the units had 42 operational T–34/85 tanks, three ISU–152s, three ISU–122s, plus seven SU–76M self-propelled guns. The 209th Self-Propelled Artillery Brigade had 37 operational SU–100 self-propelled guns.[2021]

The 5th Guards Cavalry Corps assembled the 71st Tank Regiment with 11 T–34/85s west of Zalaegerszeg, in the sector of Zalalövő at Budafa. The 54th Tank Regiment's 10 T–34/85 tanks were stationed north-east of there, at Zalaszentgyörgy. However, the 1896th Self-Propelled Artillery Regiment with 15 SU–76Ms, was carrying out a combat mission three km north-west of Szőce, which was five km north-west of Zalalövő.[2022]

2018 *Geschichte der 3. Panzer-Division. Herausgegeben vom Traditionsverband der Division.* Berlin, 1967. p. 473.
2019 Stoves, Rolf: Persönliches Kriegstagebuch Pz.Rgt. 1 (typewritten manuscript, a copy owned by the author), entry from 30 March 1945.
2020 Strassner, Peter: *Europäische Freiwillige. Die 5. SS-Panzerdivision Wiking.* Osnabrück, 1977. Third, revised edition. p. 344.
2021 Central Archives of the Russian Defence Ministry (Podolsk), f. 243, op. 2928, gy. 131, li. 285.
2022 Central Archives of the Russian Defence Ministry (Podolsk), f. 243, op. 2928, gy. 131, li. 286.

The right flank of the bridgehead at Vasvár was narrowed down to Döröske by the Soviets, after the occupation of Gerse. The Soviet troops assaulting the left flank of the bridgehead from the sector of Oszkó, entered Vasvár, but a German counterattack pushed them out of the village. The Soviets repeated the attack and this time they were successful in occupying the village. The Germans set off to clear the bridgehead.[2023] The last three combat-ready tanks of *1. Panzer-Division,* commanded by *Oberleutnant* Stoves, had just reached Rábahídvég via Vasvár, before the pioneers of *5. SS-Panzer-Division* demolished the bridge on the Rába River. With fuel given to them by the SS-troops, the three armoured fighting vehicles reached their own troops in the western outskirts of Körmend.[2024]

The combat-readiness of *IV. SS-Panzerkorps* was practically shattered to pieces. The number of combat-ready armoured fighting vehicles and the amount of fuel available was extremely low. Artillery ammunition was almost completely used up, and the *Panzergrenadiers* seemed rather like makeshift, thrown together units.[2025]

In the front of *III. Panzerkorps,* which was mostly engaged in combat beyond the border by then, the Soviets had taken Bucsu, then advancing from there, for a second attempt, took Rechnitz (Rohonc), also situated on German *Reich* territory.[2026]

The Soviet 72nd Guards Independent Self-Propelled Artillery Battalion/68th Guards Rifle Division/26th Army, was in firing positions five km south-west of Szombathely, in the sector of Nárai, with eight SU–76M self-propelled guns. During the action that day, the Germans destroyed three self-propelled guns, so by the evening the regiment only had five remaining operational SU–76Ms.[2027]

The forces of the Soviet 5th Guards Tank Corps started off from the sector of Szombathely and crossed the German–Hungarian border, and attacking to the north, the 21st Guards and 22nd Guards Tank Brigade were in combat at the end of the day in the sector of Horitschon (Harácsony). With this, the Corps had concluded the unit's combat operations in Hungarian territory.[2028] The 364th Guards Heavy Self-Propelled Artillery Regiment was stationed on that day in Kőszeg, with 12 operational ISU–122 self-propelled guns. The 252nd Amphibious Car Battalion and the 4th Guards Motorcycle Regiment, with seven Mk–IX Valentine tanks and 97 motorcycles, were assembled in Csepreg in reserve of the army commander.[2029]

2023 NARA, T311, R162, F7214842.
2024 Stoves, O. G. Rolf: *1. Panzer-Division 1935–1945. Chronik einer der drei Stamm-Division der deutschen Panzerwaffe*. Bad Nauheim, 1961. p. 777.
2025 NARA, T311, R162, F7214852.
2026 NARA, T311, R162, F7214843.
2027 Central Archives of the Russian Defence Ministry (Podolsk), f. 243, op. 2928, gy. 131, li. 284.
2028 The 5th Guards Tank Corps had irrecoverably lost 69 T–34/85s and 10 SU–76Ms between 18 – 30 March 1945. The 51st Guards Self-Propelled Artillery Brigade had lost wihin the same period, 14 SU–76Ms, and the 364th Guards Heavy Self-Propelled Artillery Regiment lost six ISU–122s. See Central Archives of the Russian Defence Ministry (Podolsk), f. 243, op. 2928, gy. 178, li. 116. Of these losses – together with the nine burnt out T-34/85s lost already on Austrian territory on 31 March, the 20th Guards Tank Brigade had 67 knocked out including 37 burnt out, armoured fighting vehicles, 65 dead including 19 officers and 209 wounded including 28 officers. 55 tanks from the 22nd Guards Tank Brigade were knocked out, 36 of these burnt out. 88 men, including 18 officers, died, 162 men including 27 officers, were wounded. The 21st Guards Tank Brigade lost eight tanks including five that were burnt out with six dead including one officer and 35 wounded including eight officers. See the war log of the 5th Guards Tank Corps of March 1945. Copy owned by the author. Appendix following p. 25.
2029 Central Archives of the Russian Defence Ministry (Podolsk), f. 243, op. 2928, gy. 131, li. 284.

The 9th Guards Mechanized Corps was advancing from the sector of Kőszeg toward the north-west and crossed the border. The 31st Guards Mechanized Brigade occupied Landsee (Lánzsér), and the 83rd Guards Tank Regiment/18th Guards Mechanized Brigade with rifle desant, the village of Weinberg (Borosd). The 3rd Guards Mechanized Brigade was en route to Kaisersdorf (Császárfalu), and the 46th Guards Tank Brigade[2030] was following. The Corps lost on that day, five burnt out M4A2 tanks, most likely already on German territory.[2031]

The 1524th Self-Propelled Artillery Regiment/9th Guards Army, with the rifle troops mounted on its 22 SU–76Ms, occupied Salamonfa and Zsira, then by 1500 hours, established an anti-tank position at Naplopótanya, two km east of Gyalóka. Afterwards, they were regrouped and upon crossing the border, at the end of the day, were in combat with its units three km north-west of Kőszeg and two km west of Rattersdorf (Rőtfalva). The 1513th Self-Propelled Artillery Regiment with four self-propelled guns, stood first at Vát, then at Kőszegfalva in reserve of the 37th Guards Rifle Corps. The 1523rd Self-Propelled Artillery Regiment was assembled at Sajtoskál with 18 operational SU–76Ms.[2032]

The Soviet troops attacking the left flank of *1. SS-Panzer-Division/I. SS-Panzerkorps,* were only able to be temporarily halted by *SS-Panzergrenadier-Regiment 1,* already on Austrian territory of the Third Reich, in the sector of Nikitsch. The fortifications of *SS-Panzergrenadier-Regiment 2* at Lövő, first repulsed all Soviet attempts, but later the regiment was compelled to retreat to Sopronkövesd. The non-combat units of the *Division* had already retreated behind the South-east Wall (*Reichsschutzstellung*). They were soon followed by the command post of the *Division*, after they crossed the border at Deutschkreutz (Sopronkeresztúr).[2033]

On the right flank of *1. SS-Panzer-Division,* the Soviet 9th Guards Tank Brigade/1st Guards Mechanized Corps with the 1004th Self-Propelled Artillery Regiment/207th Self-Propelled Artillery Brigade, reached Csapod around 1300 hours, where they met resistance from German armoured fighting vehicles and artillery. The 2nd Guards Mechanized Brigade, with the 912th Self-Propelled Artillery Regiment/207th Self-Propelled Artillery Brigade, followed the reinforced 9th Guards Tank Brigade, crossed the Berek-patak east of Csapod at around 1300 hours, and at Csapod these forces also faced German resistance. The SU–100 self-propelled guns reported to have knocked out two Tiger B heavy tanks and three anti-tank guns.[2034]

The Soviets continued their attack toward the west and north-west from the direction of Csapod, with 26 armoured fighting vehicles.. With this, the Germans had been pushed

---

2030 The commander of the 46th Guards Tank Brigade, Guards Lieutenant Colonel Nikolai M. Mikhno, in reward for the combat actions of his unit between 18-30 March, especially for the Hajmáskér ambush and taking Veszprém, was awarded the Hero of the Soviet Union on 28 April 1945. See HM HIM Hadtörténelmi Levéltár (Budapest), Szovjetunió Hőse kitüntetések gyűjteménye (*Collection of Hero of the Soviet Union awards*), 548-550.
2031 Central Archives of the Russian Defence Ministry (Podolsk), f. 243, op. 2928, gy. 131, li. 283. The 9th Guards Mechanized Corps has irrecoverably lost 52 M4A2 tanks and four SU–76Ms between 18-30 March 1945. See Central Archives of the Russian Defence Ministry (Podolsk), f. 243, op. 2928, gy. 178, li. 116. Interestingly, altogether 45 M4A2 tanks were knocked out from the strength of the 46th Guards Tank Brigade in the period of 18 – 30 March 1945, but only 15 of these were burnt out. See Central Archives of the Russian Defence Ministry (Podolsk), f. 3139, op. 1, gy. 3, li. 227.
2032 Central Archives of the Russian Defence Ministry (Podolsk), f. 243, op. 2928, gy. 131, li. 284.
2033 Tiemann, Ralf: *Die Leibstandarte*. Band IV/2. Osnabrück, 1987. pp. 348-349.
2034 War log of the 207th Self-Propelled Artillery Brigade, 30 March 1945. Copy owned by the author.

back to the Kislédec–Lövő–Röjtökmuzsaj area. Here, the *SS*-troops temporarily repulsed further assault attempts.[2035]

In the morning, on the front of *12. SS-Panzer-Division*, the positions of *SS-Panzergrenadier-Regiment 25* were running eight km east of Lövő. To the right, *SS-Panzergrenadier-Regiment 26* was in defence. On the right flank of the *Division*, *II. (Bataillon)/SS-Panzergrenadier-Regiment 26* was in combat directly south of Lövő. The *Division* had no tactical contact with the neighbouring units on its right and left, *3. SS* and *1. SS-Panzer-Divisions*.

The *Divisionsstab*, the *Divisionsbegleitkompanie* and *SS-Panzer-Aufklärungs-Abteilung 12*, retreated from the Soviets at first to Lövő, then during the course of the morning, to Sopronkövesd.

For the *SS-Panzergrenadier-Bataillons*, replacements arrived at Lövő during the morning, mostly reassigned personnel from the coastal artillery of the *Kriegsmarine*, who neither had the necessary infantry combat training nor sufficient combat experience. The fresh soldiers assigned to the battalions stood almost no chance against the battle-hardened Soviets.

In the afternoon, at 1415 hours, the positions of *II. (Bataillon)/SS-Panzergrenadier-Regiment 26* on the southern edge of Lövő, were assaulted by the armoured fighting vehicles and motorized rifle units of the Soviet 1st Guards Mechanized Brigade. The fresh soldiers panicked, which spread to the whole battalion. Four Soviet tanks ran down the fleeing *SS-Panzergrenadiers*, who were only able to be stopped and forced back into position again by their commanders, three km north-west of the village.

The *4. Batterie/SS-Panzer-Flak-Abteilung 12* at Lövő, knocked out two M4A2 tanks and one SU–100 self-propelled gun, and destroyed a third tank in close combat, after which the German unit retreated to Sopronkövesd.[2036]

SS-Panzergrenadier-Regiment 25 was assaulted by the Soviets at Pusztacsalád, which escalated into hand-to-hand combat. The Germans were withdrawing to the north-west.

The positions of *II. (Bataillon)/SS-Panzergrenadier-Regiment 26* were penetrated by the Soviets during the afternoon and the *Bataillon* was forced to retreat to Sopronkövesd. When the Soviet armoured fighting vehicles broke into that village as well, the divisional command post was relocated to Nagycenk. The *II. (Bataillon)/SS-Panzergrenadier-Regiment 26* retreated to here as well.

The combat group containing the units of the *Divisionsbegleitkompanie*, the guard unit of the division staff, two 8.8 cm anti-tank guns and eight 8.8 cm anti-aircraft guns was tasked with securing the Nagycenk–Sopron route. The detachment established its positions around midnight at the northern and southern exits of Harka.[2037]

By morning, the units of the Soviet 21st Guards Rifle Corps pushed back the remnants of *3. SS-Panzer-Division* to the Csapod–Göbösmajor line.[2038]

West of Csapod, the line of the, to some degree, still combat-ready forces of *Panzer-Pionier-Bataillon 3*, was broken through by 40 Soviet armoured fighting vehicles early

---

2035 NARA, T311, R162, F7214843.
2036 Vopersal, Wolfgang: *Soldaten, Kämpfer, Kameraden. Marsch und Kämpfe der SS-Totenkopfdivision*. Band Vb. Bielefeld, 1991. p. 849.
2037 Meyer, Hubert: *Kriegsgeschichte der 12. SS-Panzerdivision „Hitlerjugend"*. Band II. Osnabrück, 1987. 2nd edition. pp. 520-521.
2038 Vopersal, Wolfgang: *Soldaten, Kämpfer, Kameraden. Marsch und Kämpfe der SS-Totenkopfdivision*. Band Vb. Bielefeld, 1991. p.849.

in the afternoon. In the front of *3. SS-Panzer-Division,* the M4A2 tanks of the Soviet 2nd Guards Mechanized Brigade and 9th Guards Tank Brigade, breached Röjtökmuzsaj in heavy combat where they encircled the soldiers of *SS-Panzerjäger-Abteilung 3* in combat on foot, however, they later successfully broke out of the encirclement.[2039] The Soviets were attacking further toward the north-west and north-east and occupied the southern part of Fertőszentmiklós and the Haraszti Forest east of Pinnye. The German artillery, employing direct fire, reported to have knocked out three Soviet armoured fighting vehicles.[2040]

By the end of the day, the 1st Guards Mechanized Brigade occupied Lövő after a short engagement, and dispatched a reconnaissance unit toward Sopronkövesd. The 3rd Guards Mechanized Brigade took Völcsej. At the end of the day, the 207th Self-Propelled Artillery Brigade with its 912th Self-Propelled Artillery Regiment, was in combat one km south-east of Röjtökmuzsaj, and was engaged with its 1004th Self-Propelled Artillery Regiment at Lövő. In the evening, the Corps had 46 operational M4A2 and four T–34 tanks, plus 13 of its own SU–100 self-propelled guns. The 207th Self-Propelled Artillery Brigade had 26 SU–100s, three SU–57s and two T–34 tanks in operational condition.[2041]

The 53rd Motorcycle Regiment, with eight operational T–34/85 tanks and 100 motorcycles, in subordination to the Corps, had occupied Petőháza. Their own and subordinated troops of the 1st Guards Mechanized Corps, reported on that day to have knocked out six German tanks, one assault gun, nine guns, 12 machine guns, and to have captured 31 guns, 10 mortars and approximately 100 cars, besides 468 prisoners.[2042]

The Soviets reached Peresztey at dawn. The local priest described the events:

"The Soviet soldiers, tanks, armoured reconnaissance, and infantry came into the village at 0400 hours on 30 March. The tanks were in the parish garden, turned toward Füles and Németkeresztúr and were firing at the retreating Germans; the other tanks in the churchyard were rolling toward Nagyczenk on the area beyond the river. The very loud battle noises lasted approximately half an hour. There were not too many dead. Approximately 20 at the forest and one or two along the southern railroad, all Germans."[2043]

The Soviet 366th Guards Heavy Self-Propelled Artillery Regiment/4th Guards Army, was not engaged in combat on this day, but was en route and, from 1500 hours, was assembled at Rábacsanak with five operational *Hummel* and two *Wespe* self-propelled howitzers, one captured German assault gun and a Panther tank. The independent self-propelled artillery battalions of the Army made up the anti-tank artillery reserves of their own divisions with the following units:

2039 Vopersal, Wolfgang: *Soldaten, Kämpfer, Kameraden. Marsch und Kämpfe der SS-Totenkopfdivision.* Band Vb. Bielefeld, 1991. p. 850.
2040 NARA, T311, R162, F7214843.
2041 Central Archives of the Russian Defence Ministry (Podolsk), f. 243, op. 2928, gy. 131, li. 285.
2042 Central Archives of the Russian Defence Ministry (Podolsk), f. 243, op. 2928, gy. 131, li. 285.
2043 Gyula Perger: „*...félelemmel and aggodalommal...". Plébániák jelentései a háborús károkról a Győri Egyházmegyéből, 1945.* Győr, 2005. p. 81.

- the 75th Guards Independent Self-Propelled Artillery Battalion/69th Guards Rifle Division with 10 SU–76Ms;
- the 44th Guards Independent Self-Propelled Artillery Battalion/41st Guards Rifle Division with seven SU–76Ms;
- the 85th Guards Independent Self-Propelled Artillery Battalion/80th Guards Rifle Division with seven SU–76Ms, one SU–85s and one T–70;
- the 13th Guards Independent Self-Propelled Artillery Battalion/5th Guards Airborne Division with 12 SU–76Ms;
- the 8th Guards Independent Self-Propelled Artillery Battalion/7th Guards Airborne Division with 10 SU–76Ms;
- the 69th Guards Independent Self-Propelled Artillery Battalion/62nd Guards Rifle Division with six SU–76Ms.[2044]

On the frontline of the 2nd Ukrainian Front

The armoured fighting vehicles of the Soviet 2nd Guards Mechanized Corps were assembled in the sector of Mórichida, because the bridge located there was intact and they could cross the Rába River this way. The units were assigned the following tasks:

- the 6th Guards Mechanized Brigade was to cross the Rába River at Hugotpuszta, was to occupy Mosonszentmiklós and the north-eastern part of Lébény;
- the 5th Guards Mechanized Brigade was to cross the Rábca south of Lébény, occupy the village and reach Barátföld with its forward troops;
- the 4th Guards Mechanized Brigade with the 37th Guards Tank Brigade, the 251st Guards Self-Propelled Artillery Regiment and the 1509th Self-Propelled Artillery Regiment, after the crossing the Rába River, were to asssemble in the sector of Fehértó, then at Bősárkány capture the two bridges on the Rábca and the Hanság Canal with its motorized rifles, and then advance towards Mosonszentpéter.[2045]

At the end of the day, the 6th Guards Mechanized Brigade/2nd Guards Mechanized Corps, was in combat one km north of the Rábca, the 5th Guards Mechanized Brigade was in the process of crossing near Arankamajor, and the motorized rifles of the 4th Guards Mechanized Brigade, were in combat for the two railroad bridges north-west of Bősárkány.

By 1300 hours on that day, the Corps had irrecoverably lost two T–34/85 tanks, four BA–64 armoured cars, and one Universal Carrier armoured transport vehicle. Its operational vehicles included 23 T–34/85 tanks, three ISU–122s, five SU–85s, 15 SU–76Ms, 34 BA–64s, 13 Universal Carriers, eight M3A1 wheeled armoured transport vehicles, and 12 M17 half-tracked self-propelled 12.7 mm four-barrelled anti-aircraft heavy machine guns.[2046]

[2044] Central Archives of the Russian Defence Ministry (Podolsk), f. 243, op. 2928, gy. 131, li. 284.
[2045] Central Archives of the Russian Defence Ministry (Podolsk), f. 240, op. 2799, gy. 357, li. 18-19.
[2046] Central Archives of the Russian Defence Ministry (Podolsk), f. 401, op. 9511, gy. 535, li. 272.

On the front of *II. SS-Panzerkorps,* the Soviet armoured fighting vehicles launched an attack on the road leading toward the west and in the direction of Fertőendréd, but the forces of *2. SS-Panzer-Division* repulsed them and reported to have knocked out nine armoured fighting vehicles. The Soviets occupied a bridgehead east of Süttör on the Ikva Canal, but the Germans impeded their crossing attemps on the Rábca at Tárnokréti and Győrsövényház. However, west of Tárnokréti, the Soviets managed to establish a small bridgehead. The fact that the Soviet 1897th Self-Propelled Artillery Regiment north-west of Bősárkány, found an intact road bridge probably had a major role in the success.[2047]

At Vitnyéd, *2. Kompanie/SS-Panzer-Aufklärungs-Abteilung 2* and an 8.8 cm anti-aircraft gun closed off the road. The Soviet tanks, attacking at high speed, quickly destroyed the gun and shot the *SS*-soldiers who surrendered.[2048]

The units of *2. SS-Panzer-Division* were in combat north of the Kapuvár–Sopron road, but by the evening the Soviets pushed them back to Sarród. Afterwards, the *Division* retreated toward Eszterháza. Around 2300 hours, the *SS*-troops arrived in the eastern outskirts of Fertó Lake. On the same day, contact was established with *I. SS-Panzerkorps* in combat south of the *Division.*[2049]

The Soviets repulsed the German forces into the fortified position established around Abda. The Soviets forces that had broken into the Szigetköz at Jánosmajor, east of Zsejke and Ásványráró, were pushed out of the villages by German counterattacks.[2050]

According to the report of the German *6. Panzerarmee* at noon, approximately 100 Soviet armoured fighting vehicles were identified in the sector of Kapuvár, and more than 40 at Csapod.[2051] On the same day, the *Armee* was ordered by the *Heeresgruppe* to launch an attack toward the south and close the gap on the left flank of the German *6. Armee.* The *SS-Panzer-Divisions* however, no longer had the strength to carry out these orders. The commander in chief of the *Heeresgruppe, Generalleutnant* Gyldenfeldt, hoped that a large number of armoured fighting vehicles could be obtained from the area of *Wehrkreis XVII,* which he wanted to deliver to those units of *2. Panzerarmee* which were able to use them.[2052]

31 March 1945, Saturday

(**WEATHER**: highest daytime temperature 18 Celsius; generally warm and sunny day. The road conditions are unchanged and are favourable.)

In the sector of *XXII. Gebirgskorps/2. Panzerarmee* on the night of 30/31 March 1945, the Soviets attacking from the southern outskirts of Keszthely, occupied Sármellék.

2047 Central Archives of the Russian Defence Ministry (Podolsk), f. 240, op. 2799, gy. 342, li. 116.
2048 Vopersal, Wolfgang: *Soldaten, Kämpfer, Kameraden. Marsch und Kämpfe der SS-Totenkopfdivision.* Band Vb. Bielefeld, 1991. p. 851.
2049 Weidinger, Otto: *Division Das Reich. Der Weg der 2. SS-Panzer-Division „Das Reich".* Band V: 1943-1945. Osnabrück, without year of publication, p. 485.
2050 NARA, T311, R162, F7214843.
2051 NARA, T311, R162, F7214853.
2052 NARA, T311, R162, F7214855.

The boundary of the mountain corps to *I. Kavallerie-Korps* was pushed back by the Soviets to the western bank of the Zala, between Balatonhídvégpuszta and the western outskirts of Zalaapáti.[2053]

In the section of *I. Kavallerie-Korps*, the frontline of *9. SS-Panzer-Division* was stretched from Sármellék to an area two km west of Alsópáhok. In the meantime, according to literature detailing the divisional history, Soviet T-34 tanks arrived at Sármellék, with mounted rifle infantry. The eight Panther tanks of *SS-Panzer-Regiment 9*, the rear guard of the *Division*, and the armoured personnel carriers of *III. (Bataillon)/SS-Panzergrenadier-Regiment 20*, launched an attack against Sármellék. The close quarters battle between the armoured fighting vehicles lasted an hour, and the Germans had again taken the village, losing two Panthers but knocking out 12 T–34s according to their own reports. The Soviets then retreated northwards.[2054] This event has not been verfied by Soviet sources.

At the same time, *SS-Panzer-Pionier-Bataillon 9*, established a defensive position at the three-way road junction at Sármellék. The retreating German columns were followed by Soviet armoured fighting vehicles, and the *SS-Pioniers* knocked out at least two with *Panzerfausts*. The *SS-Panzer-Pioniers* of *SS-Sturmbannführer* Möllers, defended Sármellék and the road junction until 1500 hours, then crossed the Zala bridges towards Zalaapáti, then blew them up.[2055]

The Soviet attack towards Zalaszentmihály was halted by the Germans north of the village, at the Zalaapáti north–Zalaszentmihály northern edge–Pölöske north general line.

The Germans also repulsed the Soviet attacks launched south of Zalalövő and reported to have knocked out two attacking armoured fighting vehicles.[2056] Around 1700 hours, the 71st Tank Regiment/5th Guards Cavalry Corps was assembled at Kálócfa with six remaining T–34/85 tanks, after they had been supporting the forces of the 11th Guards Cavalry Division. Four km south of Zalalövő, the German *Sturmbrigade "Rudno"* and units of *16. SS-Panzergrenadier-Division*, knocked out two of their T–34/85s, one of which burnt out, and another three were blown up on mines. The 54th Tank Regiment was engaged in combat at Csesztreg with 10 operational T–34/85s, and the 1896th Self-Propelled Artillery Regiment was supporting the 12th Guards Cavalry Division, the unit that had taken Nova, with 14 SU–76M self-propelled guns.[2057]

The units of the German *16. SS-Panzergrenadier-Division*, one artillery *Abteilung* and *I. (Bataillon)/SS-Panzergrenadier-Regiment 36*, were in defence at Csesztreg. According to the recollections of *SS-Unterscharführer* Engelbert Meier, serving in *II. (Abteilung)/SS-Artillerie-Regiment 16*:

"There were two positions between Csesztreg and Lenti. For Easter, we have been encircled for a while, and the vehicles did not have any fuel anymore. I was able to

---

2053 NARA, T311, R163, F7215517.
2054 Tieke, Wilhelm: *Im Feuersturm letzter Kriegsjahre. II. SS-Panzerkorps mit 9. und 10. SS-Division „Hohenstaufen" und „Frundsberg"*. Osnabrück, without year of publication, [1975] p. 521.
2055 Tieke, Wilhelm: *Im Feuersturm letzter Kriegsjahre. II. SS-Panzerkorps mit 9. und 10. SS-Division „Hohenstaufen" und „Frundsberg"*. Osnabrück, without year of publication, [1975] p. 521.
2056 NARA, T311, R163, F7215517.
2057 Central Archives of the Russian Defence Ministry (Podolsk), f. 243, op. 2928, gy. 131, li. 288.

stop the infantry and armoured assault of the Soviets with approximately 20 grenades, and the armoured fighting vehicles of the supporting Heer set two tanks aflame with their hits. When we broke out, we were fired at from both sides of the road leading to Alsólendva. A German armoured fighting vehicle was burning and its ammunition detonated."[2058]

Subsequently, the forces of the Soviet 5th Guards Cavalry Corps approached the Lenti-Bak railroad line west of Zalaegerrszeg via Nova, a distance of seven km. *Heeresgruppe Süd* ordered *2. Panzerarmee* to attack from the sector of Bak with the forces of *23. Panzer-Division* and *4. Kavallerie-Division*, and with *SS-Panzer-Aufklärungs-Abteilung 16* towards Lenti, attack the flanks of the Soviet 5th Guards Cavalry Corps and close off their route.[2059] This order was due to the fact that the Soviets, with their attack on that day, approached the oilfields around Lispe from the north to within 15 km.[2060] Defensive combat was made more difficult by the Hungarian troops, who were surrendering in ever increasing numbers, and the artillery ammunition supplies were rapidly diminishing.[2061]

For the first time since 23 March, *23. Panzer-Division* had combat-ready armoured fighting vehicles on that day. The *Panzergruppe* of *Panzer-Regiment 23* was commanded by *Major* Fischer. The workshop company of the regiment had repaired five Panther and four Panzer IV tanks, two Panzer IV/70 *Jagdpanzers* and one assault gun. However, at first the armoured group was subordinated to *3. Kavallerie-Division*, and on the night of 31 March/1 April, marched to Gutorfölde via Söjtör, Hahót and Tófej, to attack the Soviet 5th Guards Cavalry Corps at Csömödér. The *Panzergrenadier*-battalions of *23. Panzer-Division* also travelled by car from Pacsa to Gutorfölde.[2062]

During the day, along the front of the German *2. Panzerarmee*, the Soviet troops launched battalion and regimental size attacks. The German–Hungarian troops repulsed a large number of these with counterattacks. However, the Soviets succeeded in breaking into the defence at Csicsópuszta with significant armoured support, and they reached Sand and Miháld from the northern outskirts of Inke.

The Soviet 864th Self-Propelled Artillery Regiment/57th Army in cooperation with the 214th Guards Rifle Regiment, occupied Somogysimonyi, three km west of Nemesvid, by the end of the day. During combat, two SU–76Ms were burnt out. In the evening, four km south-east of Kiskomárom, the Regiment had three self-propelled guns and one T–34 tank in operational condition.[2063]

The 1201th Self-Propelled Artillery Regiment was in combat together with the 113th Rifle Division and at the end of the day, had 18 SU–76Ms and one T–34 tank two km north-west of Nemesvid and they were in firing positions at the edge of the Nagyerdő.

2058 Puntigam, Josef Paul: *Vom Plattensee bis zur Mur. Die Kämpfe 1945 im Dreiländereck*. Feldbach, without year of publication, [1993], p. 123.
2059 NARA, T311, R162, F7214866.
2060 NARA, T311, R162, F7214867.
2061 NARA, T311, R162, F7214857.
2062 Rebentisch, Ernst: *Zum Kaukasus und zu den Tauern. Die Geschichte der 23. Panzer-Division 1941–1945*. Esslingen, 1963. pp. 502-503.
2063 Central Archives of the Russian Defence Ministry (Podolsk), f. 243, op. 2928, gy. 131, li. 287.

Miháld was occupied by the 84th Rifle Division with the support of nine SU-76Ms of its own 122nd Independent Self-Propelled Artillery Battalion.[2064]

The 249th Independent Tank Regiment was assigned to the forward troops of the 32nd Independent Guards Mechanized Brigade, and with its seven T–34 tanks, reached Iharosberény. The Brigade itself, despite having 24 operational T–34 tanks, had been halted at the end of the day two km west of Inke by German resistance. The 3rd Guards Motorcycle Regiment, with eight operational T–34/85 tanks and 164 motorcycles, together with the main forces of the 32nd Independent Guards Mechanized Brigade, were also in combat at Inke. The 1891st Self-Propelled Artillery Regiment with 15 SU–76Ms, in cooperation with the main forces of the 299th Rifle Division, was assembled at Inke around 1500 hours, to be able to continue their attack toward Nagyrécse.[2065]

South of Zalaegerszeg, the rifle infantry of the Soviet 27th Army were in attack. The 1202nd Self-Propelled Artillery Regiment was supporting the infantry of the 35th Guards Rifle Corps, with 18 SU–76M self-propelled guns, seven km south-east at Csatár. The other armoured unit of the Army, namely the 432nd Independent Self-Propelled Artillery Battalion/316th Rifle Division, with 10 operational SU–76Ms, was still stationed at Egregy, north-west of Keszthely.

In the front of the German *IV. SS-Panzerkorps/6. Armee*, the German–Hungarian troops cleared the Sárvár bridgehead on the night of 30/31 March 1945. The withdrawal of the divisions into the South-East Wall (*Reichsschutzstellung*), only partially built up along the German–Hungarian border, was going slowly due to severe traffic congestion on the roads. From the east, the Soviet troops assaulted the weak forces guarding the Szentgotthárd bridgehead with armoured support, and according to German reconnaissance, with units of the 18th Tank Corps[2066], and with the SU-100 self-propelled guns of the 1953rd Self-Propelled Artillery Regiment/209th Self-Propelled Artillery Brigade, occupied Szentgotthárd by 0530 hours in the morning.[2067]

North of Szentgotthárd, the Soviet rifle troops reached the *Reichsschutzstellung* with 15 armoured fighting vehicles east of Heiligenkreuz (Rábakeresztúr), but there the Germans were able to hold them up temporarily. From the Csákánydoroszló bridgehead, the Soviet troops attacked westwards and occupied the villages along the road leading to Heiligenkreuz; Gasztony, Rátót, Vasszentmihály, Alsórönök, Jakabháza and Rábafüzes.

The forces of the 18th Tank Corps were after the retreating Germans. At 1600 hours in the afternoon, the 110th Tank Brigade and two battalions of the 32nd Motorized Rifle Brigade were already advancing on German territory and reached Neumarkt (Farkasdifalva).

The 181st Tank Brigade with the 1438th Self-Propelled Artillery Regiment and one of the SU-100 regiments of the 209th Self-Propelled Artillery Brigade, reached even farther, to Bonisdorf (Bónisfalva), approximately 27 km south-west of Szentgotthárd.

2064 Central Archives of the Russian Defence Ministry (Podolsk), f. 243, op. 2928, gy. 131, li. 287.
2065 Central Archives of the Russian Defence Ministry (Podolsk), f. 243, op. 2928, gy. 131, li. 287.
2066 NARA, T311, R162, F7214869.
2067 The summarized report of the 209th Self-Propelled Artillery Brigade of the combat actions between 10 March - 30 April 1945. Copy owned by the author. p. 6.

The 170th Tank Brigade with two battalions of the 32nd Motorized Rifle Brigade and with the 1952nd Self-Propelled Artillery Regiment/209th Self-Propelled Artillery Brigade,[2068] was advancing from the sector of Csörötnek along the border toward the south-west and for the time being, remained on Hungarian territory. By 1600 hours, they reached Kuzma via Farkasfa and Szentmátyás, after which they crossed the border and left the territory of Hungary. The command post of the Corps Command was, however, still in Kondorfa on that evening. On the same day, the 18th Tank Corps lost only one burnt out T–34/85 tank, probably already on German territory.[2069]

One of the combat groups of the German *1. Panzer-Division,* set off from the sector of Inzenhof (Borosgödör) on the other side of the border, toward the south to cut off the Csákánydoroszló–Rábafüzes road behind the Soviet troops. The *3. Panzer-Division* launched an attack in a south-south-east direction against the Csákánydoroszló bridgehead, and although they reoccupied the Rábadoroszló part of the village, the attack soon lost its momentum.[2070]

On the front of *III. Panzerkorps* that was still in Hungarian territory, between Egyházasrádóc and Ják, units of the Hungarian army surrendered to the Soviets. What is more, according to the war log of *Heeresgruppe Süd,* they had even joined the Soviet attack against the gap in the line left by their surrender. The Soviets occupied Egyházasrádóc and advanced up to the forest east of Szentpéterfa, still on the Hungaran side of the border, where units of the German *Gebirgs-Jäger-Regiment 99* were able to stop them. Because of the deep salient, the right flank and the troops in the middle of the frontline of *III. Panzerkorps* were withdrawn into the *Reichsschutzstellung*.[2071]

The Soviet 72nd Guards Independent Self-Propelled Artillery Battalion/68th Guards Rifle Division/26th Army was still supporting the infantry with five operational SU–76M self-propelled guns on the western side of Nárai.[2072]

Of the three armoured units of the Soviet 9th Guards Army, only the 1513th Self-Propelled Artillery Regiment was stationed in Hungarian territory. Its four operational SU–76M self-propelled guns were standing in reserve of the 37th Guards Rifle Corps at the northwestern edge of Kőszeg.[2073]

2068 The three regiments of the 209th Self-Propelled Artillery Brigade reported between 10 March – 1 April 1945 during the combat actions in Hungary, to have knocked out 92 German tanks, 40 assault guns or *Jagdpanzers* and 39 armoured personnel carriers. See the after-action report of the 209th Self-Propelled Artillery Brigade of the period between 10 March – 30 April 1945. Copy owned by the author. p. 6.
2069 Central Archives of the Russian Defence Ministry (Podolsk), f. 243, op. 2928, gy. 131, li. 288. Between 1 – 31 March 1945, the 18th Tank Corps lost, on Hungarian territory, 91 T–34/85 tanks, six ISU–122s, two ISU–152s, and 17 SU–76M self-propelled guns as total losses. 191 soldiers were killed, of which, 25 were officers, 633 were wounded, of which, 56 were officers. At the same time, the forces of the Corps within this period reported to have knocked out, 262 German tanks and 217 armoured personnel carriers. See the war log of the 18th Tank Corps for March 1945. Copy owned by the author. p. 60. Of the above numbers, the Corps irrecoverably lost during the Hungarian phase of the Vienna Offensive, between 18 – 31 March 1945, 49 T–34/85 tanks, two ISU–122s, two ISU–152s, and one SU–76M self-propelled gun. See Central Archives of the Russian Defence Ministry (Podolsk), f. 243, op. 2928, gy. 178, li. 119.
2070 NARA, T311, R162, F7214858.
2071 NARA, T311, R162, F7214858.
2072 Central Archives of the Russian Defence Ministry (Podolsk), f. 243, op. 2928, gy. 131, li. 287.
2073 Central Archives of the Russian Defence Ministry (Podolsk), f. 243, op. 2928, gy. 131, li. 286.

On the night of 30/31 March 1945, the forces of the German *I. SS-Panzerkorps/6. Panzerarmee* between Pinnye and Nikitsch (Füles), were withdrawn into the *Reichsschutzstellung*.[2074]

In the sector of Sopron, the remnants of *1. SS, 12. SS* and *3. SS-Panzer-Divisions* repulsed a number of Soviet attacks supported by armoured fighting vehicles on the Deutschkreutz (Sopronkeresztúr)–Nagycenk–Fertőboz section, but the Soviets in the end managed to break through the left flank of the Germans and advance toward Sopron. At Fertőboz, the Germans counted approximately 60 Soviet armoured fighting vehicles.[2075]

SS-Panzergrenadier-Regiment 2/1. SS-Panzer-Division, fighting at Sopronkövesd, was also withdrawn to German *Reich* territory. The majority of the remnants of *Panzergruppe "Peiper"* crossed the border as well north-west of Sopron. The three Tiger B heavy tanks of *2. Kompanie/schwere SS-Panzer-Abteilung 501* subordinated to *SS-Panzer-Regiment 1,* left Hungary at Deutschkreutz.[2076]

At around 0600 hours in the morning, on the front of *12. SS-Panzer-Division,* 16 Soviet tanks were advancing from Hidegség toward Nagycenk. The armoured fighting vehicles first thrust forward to the command post of *Panzer-Pionier-Bataillon 12,* securing the southern and south-eastern edge of the village with 150 soldiers, and they destroyed the battalion commander's armoured personnel carrier as well. Afterwards, they turned against the command post of *12. SS-Panzer-Division*. At the *Stab*, one Russian auxiliary soldier had a *Panzerfaust*, and knocked out one of the tanks. With this, the *Stab* gained some time to flee on foot to Deutschkreutz (Sopronkeresztúr) four km west, already on German *Reich* territory. Here, the units of *SS-Panzergrenadier-Regiment 25* had already established defensive positions. Of the 16 Soviet tanks that broke into Nagycenk, the armoured fighting vehicles of *12. SS-Panzer-Division* knocked out 15, according to their reports.

During the morning the Soviets occupied Deutschkreutz. Therefore, the new command post of the *Division* was established in the forest south of Sopron, as they had returned to Hungarian territory via Harka.

At 0915 hours in the morning, *II. (Bataillon)/SS-Panzer-Regiment 26* was attacked by the Soviets five km south of Harka, in the *Reichsschutzstellung* on the Austrian side of the border, and then retreated to Harka and went into defence on the southern edge of the village, back on Hungarian territory. In the afternoon, at 1530 hours, the battalion was again ambushed by the Soviets from the west and east. At last the Soviets broke into the village at 1830 hours, forcing *II. (Bataillon)/SS-Panzer-Regiment 26* to retreat toward Sopron.

The units of *SS-Panzergrenadier-Regiment 25* in combat at Deutschkreutz and *Panzer-Pionier-Bataillon 12* were encircled, but they later broke out of the encirclement towards Sopron.

The worn out combat groups of the two *Panzergrenadier-Regiments* of *12. SS-Panzer-Division* and a few armoured fighting vehicles, managed to get through the Soviet lines towards Sopron. The command and control staff of the *Division* was dispersed and were

---

2074 NARA, T311, R162, F7214859.
2075 NARA, T311, R162, F7214859.
2076 Agte, Patrick: *Jochen Peiper. Kommandeur Panzerregiment Leibstandarte*. Berg am Starnberger See, 1998. p. 360.

able to reassemble the next day on Austrian soil, as they had crossed the border around midnight on the night of 30 March/1 April at Sopron.[2077]

On the front of *3. SS-Panzer-Division*, *I. and III. Bataillons/SS-Panzergrenadier-Regiment 5*, plus the infantry combat group of *SS-Panzerjäger-Abteilung 3*, were deployed between Fertőboz and the Kapuvár–Sopron railroad line, and the other detachments of the *Division* were deployed north-east of Nagycenk. During the day, the Soviet 1st Guards Mechanized Corps broke through these positions, therefore *SS-Brigadeführer* Becker, on his own initiative, ordered a retreat into the *Reichsschutzstellung*. Some units of *3. SS-Panzer-Division* were pushed backwards in the direction of Sopron by the Soviet troops.[2078]

The Soviet 2nd Guards Mechanized Brigade/1st Guards Mechanized Corps and the 912th Self-Propelled Artillery Regiment/207th Self-Propelled Artillery Brigade, reached Kópháza at 1415 hours. The 9th Guards Tank Regiment, together with the 1004th Self-Propelled Artillery Regiment, were in combat around 1400 hours at Mária-kápolna, 500 meters south-east of Kópháza.[2079] The 53rd Motorcycle Regiment, with eight T–34/85 tanks, reached Balf, and with their forward troops, reached Hill 212 one km north-west of there, around 1700 hours. During the fighting, four T-34/85 tanks of the 53rd Motorcycle Regiment were burnt out.[2080]

The 1st Guards Mechanized Brigade and the 9th Guards Tank Brigade were in combat 2.5 km south-east of Sopron around 1700 hours. By then, the 3rd Guards Mechanized Brigade was already on German territory and occupied Deutschkreuz (Sopronkeresztúr).[2081]

The forces of the Corps broke into Sopron at 1830 hours, and in a battle that lasted around one hour, they occupied the city. Afterwards, the Soviet troops established temporary defences, acquired fuel and ammunition and had a rest for the soldiers. The Corps reported to have knocked out during the combat for the city, 31 German armoured fighting vehicles, 17 armoured personnel carriers, 42 various field guns, 16 anti-aircraft guns and automatic cannons, 30 machine guns, plus they reported the destruction of 55 aircraft on the ground, the capture of eight mortars, eight *Nebelwerfers* and 17 various guns, and the capture of 3298, mainly Hungarian soldiers. Its own loss accumulated in the combat against the German armoured fighting vehicles and the artillery amounted to 10 burnt out M4A2 tanks and three SU–100s[2082]. In the evening it had 49 operational M4A2s, four T–34 tanks, and 13 of its own SU–100 self-propelled guns.[2083]

The 1004th Self-Propelled Artillery Regiment/207th Self-Propelled Artillery Regiment, was supporting the combat of the 1st Guards Mechanized Corps at Deutschkreuz, and with its 912th Self-Propelled Artillery Regiment at Sopron, then its 23 SU–100s, three SU–57s and two T–34 armoured fighting vehicles established firing positions on the western edge of Sopron.[2084]

2077 Meyer, Hubert: *Kriegsgeschichte der 12. SS-Panzerdivision „Hitlerjugend"*. Band II. Osnabrück, 1987. 2nd edition. pp. 522-523.
2078 Vopersal, Wolfgang: *Soldaten, Kämpfer, Kameraden. Marsch und Kämpfe der SS-Totenkopfdivision*. Band Vb. Bielefeld, 1991. pp. 859-861.
2079 War log of the 207th Self-Propelled Artillery Brigade, 31 March 1945. Copy owned by the author.
2080 Central Archives of the Russian Defence Ministry (Podolsk), f. 243, op. 2928, gy. 178, li. 121.
2081 Central Archives of the Russian Defence Ministry (Podolsk), f. 243, op. 2928, gy. 178, li. 119.
2082 War log of the 207th Self-Propelled Artillery Brigade, 31 March 1945. Copy owned by the author.
2083 Central Archives of the Russian Defence Ministry (Podolsk), f. 243, op. 2928, gy. 131, li. 287.
2084 Central Archives of the Russian Defence Ministry (Podolsk), f. 243, op. 2928, gy. 131, li. 288.

The 366th Guards Heavy Self-Propelled Artillery Regiment/4th Guards Army, was supporting these rifle troops and by the end of the day, one of its batteries stood in firing positions four km east of Kapuvár, on the north-western edge of Veszkény, and the other battery was at the north-western edge of Osli. By the end of the day, the Regiment had four *Hummels* and one *Wespe* self-propelled howitzer, plus one captured German assault gun in operational condition. The independent self-propelled artillery battalions of the six divisions of the Army had 52 operational SU–76Ms and five tanks that were fighting in the battle line with the rifle troops.[2085]

On the frontline section of the 2nd Ukrainian Front

In the front of *II. SS-Panzerkorps,* the Soviet troops occupied Fertőszentmiklós and Eszterháza on the night of 30/31 March 1945.

On that day, the rearguard of *SS-Panzergrenadier-Regiment 3/2. SS-Panzer-Division,* also left the southern sector of Eszterháza. The command post of the regiment was relocated to Wallern, on Austrian *Reich* territory. The mansion at Eszterháza remained intact. The bailiff of the duke allegedly expressed their gratitude to the Germans for not ransacking the mansion by presenting a bottle of Tokaji to *SS-Obersturmbannführer* Wisliceny.[2086]

Afterwards, the Germans established makeshift defensive lines on the Pinnye–Sarród general line and closed off the roads coming from Fertőszenmiklós toward the south and the north.[2087]

North of Bősárkány, the Soviet troops crossed the Hansági Canal with a battalion-size force on the night of 30/31 March 1945. The 2nd Battery/1897th Self-Propelled Artillery Regiment covering the manoeuvre, lost two knocked out SU–76Ms, one of which burnt out. The commander of the burnt out self-propelled gun was killed.[2088]

The German–Hungarian troops left stronger rear-guards in the sector of Öttevény and Kunsziget and withdrew the left flank to the Lébény–Mosonszentmiklós–Sándorházamajor line. From the Soviet bridgehead, where the Germans counted 25 armoured fighting vehicles of the 2nd Guards Mechanized Corps and the 23rd Tank Corps north of the Hansági Canal, battalion and regimental size attacks were initiated. The Soviet troops that advanced as far as Lébény were repulsed by the defenders and they blew up the bridge over the Herceg Canal, south of the village.[2089]

The 6th Guards Mechanized Brigade/2nd Guards Mechanized Corps was in combat in the southern outskirts of Mosonszentmiklós in the morning at 0800 hours. The 5th Guards

---

2085 Central Archives of the Russian Defence Ministry (Podolsk), f. 243, op. 2928, gy. 131, li. 286.
2086 Weidinger, Otto: *Division Das Reich. Der Weg der 2. SS-Panzer-Division „Das Reich".* Band V: 1943-1945. Osnabrück, without year of publication, p. 486.
2087 NARA, T311, R162, F7214859.
2088 Central Archives of the Russian Defence Ministry (Podolsk), f. 240, op. 2799, gy. 342, li. 140. Between 16 – 31 March 1945, the 1897. Self-Propelled Artillery Regiment lost nine knocked out SU–76Ms, of which seven were burnt out, 13 killed including four self-propelled gun-commander officers and nine wounded. During the combat actions of the Regiment during March, they fired 1850 high-explosive shells, 300 tank destroyer shells, 40 sub-caliber tank-destroyer projectiles, plus 120 F–1 hand grenades hurled out of the SU–76M armoured fighting vehicles. See Central Archives of the Russian Defence Ministry (Podolsk), f. 240, op. 2799, gy. 342, li. 141.
2089 NARA, T311, R162, F7214859.

Mechanized Brigade reached the southern edge of Lébény where they met a German counterattack, so they bypassed the village on the right. The 4th Guards Mechanized Brigade was in combat north of the Hansági Canal for Hills 117 and 121, four to six km north-west of Bősárkány. By 1700 hours in the afternoon, the 37th Guards Tank Brigade, plus the 251st Guards Self-Propelled Artillery Regiment and the armoured fighting vehicles of the 1509th Self-Propelled Artillery Regiment, all crossed the Hansági Canal. By 1300 hours in the afternoon, the Corps had lost one SU–76M self-propelled gun and one BA–64 armoured car that burnt out. At that time, they had 23 T–34/85 tanks, plus three ISU–122s, four SU–85s and 14 SU–76M self-propelled guns in operational condition.[2090]

At midnight on 30 March 1945, the 23rd Tank Corps was assembled in the sector of Rábcakapi, Bősárkány, Maglóca and Cakóháza, then launched an attack towards Mosonszentpéter.[2091] This was stopped by the Germans, most likely by units of *2. SS-Panzer-Division,* directly south-east of Mosonszentpéter, and reported to have knocked out 21 Soviet armoured fighting vehicles in the area.

The Soviet 1505th Self-Propelled Artillery Regiment/46th Army was assembled in the sector of Fehértó on the same day. It had five operational SU–76Ms, six German medium assault guns under repair, and one *Wespe* self-propelled howitzer.[2092]

The night ground attack aircraft of the German *Luftflotte 4* on the night of 30/31 March, raided the sector of Szombathely and Csorna.[2093]

During the day, *2. Panzerarmee* and the German *6. Armee,* received orders that the gap between them was to be closed off with an attack toward each other for both units to meet.[2094]

1 April 1945, Sunday

In the front of the Soviet 57th Army, the 864th Self-Propelled Artillery Regiment, in support of the 73rd Guards Rifle Division, reached Kiskomárom. Another two SU–76M self-propelled guns were destroyed during the battle. In the evening the regiment had four operational SU–76Ms and one T–34 tank.[2095]

The 1201st Self-Propelled Artillery Regiment, together with units of the 113th Rifle Division, was in combat at the end of the day at Nagyrécse, four km north-east of Nagykanizsa, with 19 operational SU–76Ms and one T–34 tank.[2096]

The 1891st Self-Propelled Artillery Regiment was supporting the troops of the 122nd Rifle Division during the engagements on the grounds of Nagykanizsa. The SU–76M self-propelled guns reached the western edge of the town, however during the fighting,

---

2090 Central Archives of the Russian Defence Ministry (Podolsk), f. 401, op. 9511, gy. 535, li. 286.
2091 Central Archives of the Russian Defence Ministry (Podolsk), f. 240, op. 2799, gy. 357, li. 19.
2092 Central Archives of the Russian Defence Ministry (Podolsk), f. 240, op. 2799, gy. 342, li. 114. As on 16 March 1945 the 1505th Self-Propelled Artillery Regiment only had five captured German assault guns, it is likely that they had either captured or acquired another further armoured fighting vehicle in the second half of March.
2093 NARA, T311, R162, F7214860.
2094 NARA, T311, R162, F7214868.
2095 Central Archives of the Russian Defence Ministry (Podolsk), f. 243, op. 2928, gy. 131, li. 303. Between 17 March – 1 April 1945, the 864th Self-Propelled Artillery Regiment had irrecoverably lost four self-propelled guns.
2096 Central Archives of the Russian Defence Ministry (Podolsk), f. 243, op. 2928, gy. 131, li. 303. Between 17 March – 1 April 1945, the 1201st Self-Propelled Artillery Regiment had lost two destroyed SU–76Ms.

the Germans[2097] destroyed two self-propelled guns, and another two were destroyed by mines. The self-propelled artillery regiment reported on that day to have knocked out three German tanks[2098] and the same number of assault guns. In the evening they had 13 operational SU–76Ms.[2099]

The 84th Rifle Division and its 122nd Independent Self-Propelled Artillery Battalion also attacked Nagykanizsa. The regiment established firing positions 500 meters south-west of the town and in the evening, had nine operational SU–76M self-propelled guns.[2100]

The 32nd Independent Guards Mechanized Brigade, with the 249th Independent Tank Regiment in subordination, reached Pogányszentpéter, four km north-west of Iharosberény, by the end of the day. The task of the reinforced Brigade was to continue its attack towards Becsehely and Letenye. On that day, the three Motorized Rifle Battalions were only supported by the 249th Independent Tank Regiment, which lost a burnt out T–34 during the battle. In the evening they had eight tanks in operational condition. The 52nd Tank Regiment, with 24 operational T–34s, remained in reserve of the brigade commander at Iharosberény.

The 3rd Guards Motorcycle Regiment was withdrawn from the ranks of the 57th Army on that day, were reassigned to the 27th Army and set off on their march to Keszthely with eight operational T–34/85 tanks and 163 motorcycles.[2101]

On the same day, the units of the Bulgarian 1st Army captured a German Panzer IV/70 *Jagdpanzer* still in combat-ready condition, which had no fuel or ammunition. The vehicle was assigned to the 1st Independent Tank Battalion. The Tank Battalion lost 11 damaged Panzer IV tanks during the breach of the *Margarethen-Stellung* and in pursuing the fleeing German–Hungarian troops.[2102]

The Soviet 1202nd Self-Propelled Artillery Regiment/27th Army set off from the sector of Csatár, seven km south of Zalaegerszeg, and in the afternoon marched to Apátistvánfalva 6 km south of Szentgotthárd, arriving around 1800 hours. They had at that time, 19 operational SU–76M self-propelled guns. The 432nd Independent Self-Propelled Artillery Battalion/316th Rifle Division was assembled at Keszthely with 10 operational SU–76Ms.[2103]

The German *3. Kavallerie-Division/I. Kavallerie-Korps* and units of *4. Kavallerie-Division*, launched an attack in the morning from the sector of Gutorfölde via Cserta Creek toward Nova. The Soviets soon launched counterattacks supported by armoured fighting vehicles and they pushed *Reiter-Regiment 41* back to the eastern bank of the creek. *Reiter-Regiment 31*, on the right of *Reiter-Regiment 41*, managed to push forward, and after knocking out four Soviet armoured fighting vehicles, got hold on the western bank of the creek. Afterwards, *Reiter-Regiment 32* was also drawn forward and, together with *Reiter-Regiment 41* attacking again, they pushed back the units of the Soviet 5th Guards Cavalry Corps to

---

2097 During the close quarters combat on the streets of Nagykanizsa, the independent *Füsilier-Bataillon* of the German *71. Infanterie-Division* excelled. See *Die 71. Infanterie-Division im Zweiten Weltkrieg 1939–1945. Gefechts- und Erlebnisberichte aus den Kämpfen der „Glückhaften Division" von Verdun bis Stalingrad, von Monte Cassino bis zum Plattensee*. Arbeitsgemeinschaft „Das Kleeblatt" (Hrsg.). Hildesheim, 1973. p. 420.
2098 They were probably the captured tanks of the German *118. Jäger-Division* in combat nearby.
2099 Central Archives of the Russian Defence Ministry (Podolsk), f. 243, op. 2928, gy. 131, li. 303.
2100 Central Archives of the Russian Defence Ministry (Podolsk), f. 243, op. 2928, gy. 131, li. 303.
2101 Central Archives of the Russian Defence Ministry (Podolsk), f. 243, op. 2928, gy. 131, li. 303.
2102 Matev, Kaloyan: *The Armoured Forces of the Bulgarian Army 1936–45*. Solihull, 2015. p. 334. On 13 April 1945, the Bulgarians received a few (not more than six) captured Panther tanks from the Soviets in the sector of Szombathely.
2103 Central Archives of the Russian Defence Ministry (Podolsk), f. 243, op. 2928, gy. 131, li. 302.

Nova. The German cavalry units were not supported by their own armoured units, because they were not able to cross Cserta Creek. The last three combat-ready assault guns of *Panzerjäger-Abteilung 69* were sunken in the muddy ground on the banks of the creek.[2104]

The armoured group of the German *23. Panzer-Division*, launched an attack at 0800 hours that morning, from Gutorfölde towards Csömödér. After passing Ortaháza, the two 76 mm divisional guns placed by the Soviets at Kissziget, opened fire on the right flank of the German armoured fighting vehicles, hitting one Panther. The Panzer IV tanks and the Panzer IV/70 *Jagdpanzers*, plus one assault gun at the head, kept advancing but the Panthers turned and returned fire and knocked out the Soviet guns. At Páka, the commander of the vanguard unit, *Oberleutnant* Quintel, was informed by a Hungarian command staff member, that there were Hungarian troops in Csömödér. However, when two German armoured fighting vehicles, one Panzer IV and one assault gun, approached the village from Páka, approximately 300 meters before they reached the bridge over Berek Creek, a small caliber Soviet anti-tank gun opened fire at them. There were Soviet troops already at Csömödér, who, after their initial surprise, engaged the Germans in combat. The two German tanks knocked out the anti-tank gun, but they alone were not able to take the village. They kept the Soviets down with high-explosive shells and machine gun fire until a *Leutnant* arrived with seven soldiers. Together with them, the two armoured fighting vehicles launched an attack over a newly built wooden bridge. The anti-tank guns and the Soviet infantry, without tank support,[2105] retreated toward the north.

Around 1600 hours in the afternoon, *Panzergrenadier-Regiment 128* followed the armoured fighting vehicles which were pushing after the Soviets. Around 1800 hours, the Germans broke in to Hernyék, eight km north of Csömödér, and after they occupied the village, they went over to defence. In the meantime, *Panzergrenadier-Regiment 126*, together with the Jagdpanzer IV *Jagdpanzers* of *Panzerjäger-Abteilung 128*, were advancing northwards, east of *Panzergrenadier-Regiment 128*.[2106]

The 1896th Self-Propelled Artillery Regiment/5th Guards Cavalry Corps with 14 SU–76Ms, was in combat at Nemesnép, the 71st Tank Regiment in support of the forces of the 11th Guards Cavalry Division was in combat with six T–34/85s at Lentikápolna, four km north of Lenti, and the 54th Tank Regiment with the 12th Guards Cavalry Division with 10 T–34/85 tanks, was at Hernyék, five km southwest of Nova.[2107]

At Zalatárnok, the German *297. Infanterie-Division* and *Sturmgeschütz-Brigade 191*, plus the retreating forces of *Reiter-Regiment 5/Kavallerie-Brigade 4*, were engaged in combat. At 0800 hours in the morning, the Soviet 759th Rifle Regiment/163rd Rifle Division/27th Army, attacking from the north-east, from the direction of Gellénháza, reached the eastern and southern edges of Zalatárnok, then occupied the village. The Germans continued their resistance on the Habártanya–Szentkozmadombja–Hill 230 (Durgó) line, but the Soviet 759th Rifle Regiment had also breached Szentkozmadombja around 1100 hours. The Germans launched a counterattack with a battalion-size force

---

[2104] Witte, Hans Joachim – Offermann, Peter: *Die Boeselagerschen Reiter. Das Kavallerie-Regiment Mitte und die aus ihm hervorgegangene 3. Kavallerie-Brigade/Division*. München, 1998. p. 423.
[2105] These were most likely the dismounted cavalry soldiers of the Soviet 12th Guards Cavalry Division.
[2106] Rebentisch, Ernst: *Zum Kaukasus und zu den Tauern. Die Geschichte der 23. Panzer-Division 1941–1945*. Esslingen, 1963. p. 503.
[2107] Central Archives of the Russian Defence Ministry (Podolsk), f. 243, op. 2928, gy. 131, li. 304.

and 10 assault guns around 1200 hours, and they pushed back the Soviets to the sector 700 meters south of Zalatárnok.[2108]

At 1630 hours, south-west of Zalatárnok, the Soviet 458th Rifle Regiment/78th Rifle Division/27th Army met with a counterattack of 150-200 German soldiers, five armoured fighting vehicles, likely assault guns, and four armoured personnel carriers. The Soviet Rifle Regiment only lost two wounded soldiers and by 2200 hours that night, they repulsed the German attempt and also knocked out one armoured personnel carrier.[2109]

Units of *SS-Panzer-Abteilung 16*, subordinated to *I. Kavallerie-Korps*, were securing the road at Söjtör leading south from Hahót, in the section of the *297. Infanterie-Division*. At 1200 hours, the Soviet 163rd Rifle Division launched an attack from Bak toward Söjtör with eight armoured fighting vehicles, most likely with the SU–76M self-propelled guns[2110] of the Soviet 1202nd Self-Propelled Artillery Regiment. The *Grenadiers* of *297. Infanterie-Division* were fleeing the village in panic. *Panzergruppe "Rex"* of the *SS-Panzer-Abteilung*, managed to stop at least some of them at the edge of the village, by threatening them with execution. German artillery was targeting the village that was already thought to be lost, together with the *SS-Panzergruppe* still there. Around 1500 hours, the Soviet troops launched another attack from the north-east against the northern edge of Söjtör. The *SS*-assault guns in defensive positions here, stopped them with a counterattack and knocked out a Soviet tank.[2111] The majority of *16. SS-Panzergrenadier-Division* moved over to the *Dorottya-Stellung*, established on the western bank of the Principális Canal, in the sector of Magyarszerdahely.[2112]

The Hungarian 20th Assault Artillery Battalion, subordinated to the German *I. Kavallerie-Korps*, was constantly fighting rear guard battles, and at the beginning of April 1945, crossed the present day Hungarian border west of Lenti. Afterwards, those *Jagdpanzers*[2113] of the Hungarian Assault Artillery unit that did not have any fuel or ammunition left anymore, as well as their anti-tank guns and towing vehicles, were handed over in a German assembly centre. According to the memories of 1st Lieutenant Taszіló Kárpáthy Taszіló:

"I do not wish for anyone, not even my enemies, to experience these feelings. And not only I felt this way, I am sure my comrades felt the same. Some of us had tears in our eyes when we secretly caressed our trusty weapons. We could only keep that number of vehicles that were needed for the soldiers to be transported."[2114]

2108 Central Archives of the Russian Defence Ministry (Podolsk), f. 1400, op. 1, gy. 157, li. 118-119.
2109 Central Archives of the Russian Defence Ministry (Podolsk), f. 1224, op. 1, gy. 26, li. 1.
2110 According to the Germans T–34 tanks were attacking. It is not impossible however, that on the contrary, the T-34/85 tanks of the 3rd Guards Motorcycle Regiment were deployed here. The unit had been reassigned from the 57th Army to the 27th Army and was en route to Keszthely. The Soviet unit however did not report any losses on that day.
2111 Puntigam, Josef Paul: *Vom Plattensee bis zur Mur. Die Kämpfe 1945 im Dreiländereck*. Feldbach, without year of publication, [1993], p. 121.
2112 Puntigam, Josef Paul: *Vom Plattensee bis zur Mur. Die Kämpfe 1945 im Dreiländereck*. Feldbach, without year of publication, [1993], p. 117.
2113 According to the memories of Taszіló Kárpáthy, approximately 13 Jagdpanzer 38(t) Jagdpanzers were handed over to the Germans. Of these, see the interview of András Palásthy with Taszіló Kárpáthy on 20 October 1999 in Budapest (transcribed copy owned by the author). Interestingly, in the first half of April at the German 3. Kavallerie-Division subordinated to I. Kavallerie-Korps, at least five such Jagdpanzers had appeared, without central authorization, and seven of these armoured fighting vehicles at 9. SS-Panzer-Division. Based on this, it cannot be excluded that the armoured fighting vehicles of the Hungarian assault artillery battalion had been assigned to the two German divisions.
2114 Taszіló Kárpáthy: *A magyar királyi honvéd 20. rohamtüzérosztály története*. In: HM HIM Hadtörténelmi Levéltár (Budapest), Rohamtüzér-gyűjtemény, 14/7. collection. p. 22.

The German *3. Panzer-Division/IV. SS-Panzerkorps,* with the forces of *Panzer-Kampfgruppe "Medicus,"*[2115] renewed its attack that day from Csákánydoroszló toward Vasszentmihály. The German armoured fighting vehicles occupied the village in the Rába River valley at 1030 hours. However, as every drop of fuel counted, the German *Kampfgruppe* retreated in the evening to the north, to the German side of the border. With this attack the Germans had effectively diverted the supply lines of the Soviets who were pushing through the *Reichsschutzstellung.*[2116]

A Soviet 72nd Guards Independent Self-Propelled Artillery Battalion/68th Guards Rifle Division/26th Army, was supporting the rifle troops with five operational SU–76Ms at the end of the day at the western edge of Pornóapáti, 12 km west of Szombathely.[2117]

The forces of the 1st Guards Mechanized Corps, with the SU–100 self-propelled guns of the 207th Self-Propelled Artillery Brigade in subordination, continued the attack on that day from Sopron, toward the north, and left the territory of Hungary. The 53rd Motorcycle Regiment however, subordinated to the Corps, was still stationed in Hungary in reserve to the Corps commander two km north of Sopron with four operational T–34/85 tanks.[2118]

The Soviet 366th Guards Heavy Self-Propelled Artillery Regiment/4th Guards Army, in subordination to the 20th Guards Rifle Corps, supported the rifles to begin with, from the western edge of Nagycenk with four operational *Hummel*s and one *Wespe* self-propelled howitzer, plus one captured German assault gun. Subsequently, it established firing positions on the eastern slopes of the hills north of Sopron. By the end of the day, it was withdrawn to Veszkény. In the evening, they had six operational captured German self-propelled guns and assault guns, plus eight under repair in their possession. The unit also had four German tanks under repair.[2119]

The independent self-propelled artillery battalions of the 4th Guards Army, compised the anti-tank artillery reserves of their own divisions, with the following combat strength:

- the 75th Guards Independent Self-Propelled Artillery Battalion/69th Guards Rifle Division with 10 SU–76Ms in the sector of Nagycenk and Peresteg;
- the 44th Guards Independent Self-Propelled Artillery Battalion/41st Guards Rifle Division with seven SU–76Ms in the sector of Osli and Földszigetmajor, six km northwest of Csorna;
- the 85th Guards Independent Self-Propelled Artillery Battalion/80th Guards Rifle Division with seven SU–76Ms in the sector of Osli, then Fertőszéplak;
- the 13th Guards Independent Self-Propelled Artillery Battalion/5th Guards Airborne Division with 12 SU–76Ms in the sector of Balf;

2115 The combat group consisted of the last six combat-ready tanks and six *Jagdpanzer*s of the *Division*, plus a few self-propelled guns and armoured personnel carriers under command of *Major* Medicus, *Kommandeur* of *Panzerjäger-Abteilung 543.*
2116 *Geschichte der 3. Panzer-Division. Herausgegeben vom Traditionsverband der Division.* Berlin, 1967. p. 474.
2117 Central Archives of the Russian Defence Ministry (Podolsk), f. 243, op. 2928, gy. 131, li. 302. Between 17 March – 1 April, the 72nd Guards Independent Sef-Propelled Artillery Battalion lost three destroyed SU–76M self-propelled guns.
2118 Central Archives of the Russian Defence Ministry (Podolsk), f. 243, op. 2928, gy. 131, li. 303.
2119 Central Archives of the Russian Defence Ministry (Podolsk), f. 243, op. 2928, gy. 131, li. 302., furthermore f. 243, op. 2928, gy. 178, li. 120. The unit left the territory of Hungary on the following day.

- the 8th Guards Independent Self-Propelled Artillery Battalion/7th Guards Airborne Division with 10 SU–76Ms in the sector of Kópháza;
- the 69th Guards Independent Self-Propelled Artillery Battalion/62nd Guards Rifle Division with six SU–76Ms en route.[2120]

On the frontline of the 2nd Ukrainian Front

The units of the German *2. SS-Panzer-Division,* with their artillery and armoured fighting vehicles, cleared the village of Levél between 1600 hours and 1800 hours in the afternoon, and driving away many horses, pigs and cows, retreated towards Hegyeshalom.[2121]

The Soviet 3rd Tank Brigade/23rd Tank Corps, in cooperation with the 37th Guards Tank Brigade/2nd Guards Mechanized Corps, occupied Mosonszentjános at 0200 hours, and at 0600 hours in the morning they occupied Mosonszentpéter.[2122]

The 23rd Tank Corps continued their attack in the direction of Pandorf. The 3rd Tank Brigade and the 1443rd Self-Propelled Artillery Regiment assaulted Jessemajor and Újszajdamajor from the south-east, the 39th Tank Brigade with the 1501st Anti-Tank Artillery Regiment and the 56th Motorized Rifle Brigade, attacked from the north-east. The two villages were occupied by Soviet armoured fighting vehicles around 1200 hours. Here, they assaulted the staff and various units of the Royal Hungarian 1st Honvéd Mountain Brigade. The Corps captured 4000 Hungarian and German soldiers on that day and acquired a significant amount of military materiel, including 4000 rifles and submachine guns, plus 100 cars and 1850 horses. The 3rd Tank Brigade and the 1443rd Self-Propelled Artillery Regiment, reached Albertkázmérpuszta near the border at 1900 hours, where they were halted because the Germans were firing at them from the direction of Halbturn (Féltorony).[2123]

At the same time, the 39th Tank Brigade with the 1501st Anti-Tank Artillery Regiment and the 56th Motorized Rifle Brigade, crossed the border and reached Friedrichshof (Frigyesmajor). Upon receiving orders from the corps commander, the 3rd Tank Brigade and the 1443rd Self-Propelled Artillery Regiment changed their destination to this area, and with this they left the territory of Hungary.[2124] In the fighting of that day, the 23rd Tank Corps reported to have knocked out five German tanks and 10 armoured personnel carriers. Their own losses amounted to 10 knocked out T–34/85 tanks, of which six were burnt out.[2125]

2120 Central Archives of the Russian Defence Ministry (Podolsk), f. 243, op. 2928, gy. 131, li. 302, and the war log of the 3rd Ukrainian Front, 1 April 1945. The independent self-propelled artillery battalions of the 4th Guards Army crossed the German-Hungarian border on the next day, on 2 April, while supporting the combat of their own units.
2121 Gyula Perger: „...*félelemmel and aggodalommal...*". *Plébániák jelentései a háborús károkról a Győri Egyházmegyéből, 1945.* Győr, 2005. p. 91.
2122 Today, both villages are part of Jánossomorja.
2123 Central Archives of the Russian Defence Ministry (Podolsk), f. 240, op. 2799, gy. 357, li. Central Archives of the Russian Defence Ministry (Podolsk), f. 240, op. 2799, gy. 357, li. 22.
2124 Central Archives of the Russian Defence Ministry (Podolsk), f. 240, op. 2799, gy. 357, li. 23.
2125 War log of the 23rd Tank Corps from April 1945. Copy owned by the author. p. 2.

The 6th Guards Mechanized Brigade/2nd Guards Mechanized Corps, cleared the sector of Barátfölde and Horvátkimle of German obstacles, and around 1000 hours, was engaged in a fire fight on the south-eastern edge of Mosonmagyaróvár. The 5th Guards Mechanized Brigade followed the 6th Guards Mechanized Brigade, but three km west of Horvátkimle, at Hill 118, they ran into a counterattack with a battalion of German infantry and five tanks. The 6th Guards Mechanized Brigade left a covering unit at the south-eastern edge of Mosonmagyaróvár and then bypassed the town from the south-west.[2126]

The 4th Guards Mechanized Brigade and the 37th Guards Tank Brigade pushed the Germans out of Császárrét and from Hill 119 one km north of there, and afterwards continued their attack toward Mosonszolnok.[2127]

In the sector of Mosonszolnok, a heavy armoured battle was forming. In these battles, the units of the Hungarian 1st Mountain Brigade also took part and after nightfall, they knocked out a number of Soviet armoured fighting vehicles. As reported by the local priest:

"The battle for Mosonszolnok began on 1 April of the current year, that is, on Easter Sunday at 0300 hours. It lasted from 0300 hours at dawn until 1800 hours in the evening which proves its utter violence without doubt. The Soviets had come through the Hanság at Lébény, but they also attacked on the Mosonszentjános-Moson road, along the Mosonszentjános-Hegyeshalom railroad line, and from the direction of the Mosonszentjános-Pünkösdvásár road as well. Since the end of the battle, 10 German and seven Russian tanks are lying deserted on different roads. Around noon, the Russian aircraft have also intervened, and dumped blockbuster bombs and incendiary bombs on the village, and this has sparked fires at six different locations."[2128]

The 4th Guards Mechanized Brigade and the 37th Guards Tank Brigade occupied Újudvar by the end of the day. They reported to have knocked out 16 German tanks.[2129] By 1330 hours in the afternoon, the 2nd Guards Mechanized Corps lost four T–34/85 tanks and one SU–76M self-propelled gun. At that time, they only had 17 T–34/85 tanks, plus three ISU–122s, four SU–85s and 11 SU–76M self-propelled guns that were in operational condition.[2130]

2 April 1945, Monday

The Soviet 1201st Self-Propelled Artillery Regiment/57th Army, in support of the forces of the 113th Rifle Division, was in combat with 19 operational SU–76Ms in the sector of Bocska, 12 km north-west of Nagykanizsa.

2126 Central Archives of the Russian Defence Ministry (Podolsk), f. 240, op. 2799, gy. 357, li. 22.
2127 Central Archives of the Russian Defence Ministry (Podolsk), f. 240, op. 2799, gy. 357, li. 22.
2128 Gyula Perger: *"...félelemmel and aggodalommal...". Plébániák jelentései a háborús károkról a Győri Egyházmegyéből, 1945.* Győr, 2005. p. 96.
2129 Central Archives of the Russian Defence Ministry (Podolsk), f. 240, op. 2799, gy. 357, li. 22.
2130 Central Archives of the Russian Defence Ministry (Podolsk), f. 401, op. 9511, gy. 535, li. 287.

The 1891st Self-Propelled Artillery Regiment was stationed at Szepetnek in reserve of the corps commander, with 10 operational SU–76M self-propelled guns. Similarly, the 864th Self-Propelled Artillery Regiment was stationed in Kiskomárom with three SU–76Ms.

The 32nd Independent Guards Mechanized Brigade and the 249th Independent Tank Regiment, continued their attacks and reached Rigyác, seven km west of Nagykanizsa, where they replenished their fuel and ammunition supplies and the units rested. In the evening, the 52nd Tank Regiment had 22 operational armoured fighting vehicles and the 249th Independent Tank Regiment had five T–34 tanks.[2131]

The 84th Rifle Division and its 122nd Independent Self-Propelled Artillery Battalion were in combat one km north of Borsfa, 17 km north-west of Nagykanizsa.[2132]

The Soviet 1202nd Self-Propelled Artillery Regiment/27th Army, was assembled 12 km south of Zalaegerszeg, in the sector of Bak with 19 operational SU–76M self-propelled guns. The 432nd Independent Self-Propelled Artillery Battalion/316th Rifle Division, was still stationed in Keszthely with 10 operational SU–76Ms. The 3rd Guards Motorcycle Regiment was at Kálócfa, 10 km north-west of Nova, with eight operational T–34/85 tanks and 160 motorcycles.[2133]

East of Pusztamagyaród, *Panzergruppe "Rex"/SS-Panzer-Abteilung 16,* carried out combat reconnaissance with *1. Kompanie/Panzer-Pionier-Bataillon 16* around 1600 hours on a narrow road, where they ran into Soviet armoured fighting vehicles and mounted rifle infantry. These were most likely the forward troops of the Soviet 113th Rifle Division and the SU–76M self-propelled guns of the 1201st Self-Propelled Artillery Regiment, pushing from the sector of Bocska. The *SS*-pioneers knocked out one Soviet armoured fighting vehicle with a *Panzerfaust* and the Soviets retreated. The *SS-Kampfgruppe* followed them for three km, then stopped and established defensive positions until the next day.[2134]

In the sector of the German *I. Kavallerie-Korps,* a reconnaissance detachment of *3. Kompanie/Panzergrenadier-Regiment 128/23. Panzer-Division,* reached Nova on the night of 1/2 April 1945, but the forces of the Soviet 12th Guards Cavalry Division held them. The German *Division* was ordered to occupy Nova and cut off the supply lines of the 5th Guards Cavalry Corps.

At 0300 hours, *Panzergrenadier-Regiment 128,* with two foreign field replacement battalions (*Feldersatzbataillon*) and an alpine light infantry (*Gebirgsjäger*) battalion, launched an attack against Nova. The Germans occupied Újhelyipuszta 1.5 km south of Nova, but afterwards their attack was bogged down against the Soviet defensive lines established between Points 235 and 238. The Soviets also repulsed one of the field replacement battalions.

At 1150 hours, *I. (Bataillon)/Panzergrenadier-Regiment 128,* occupied the bend in the road two km south-west of Nova, but they were not able to take Point 235 as that was defended by Soviet tanks. Point 238 also remained in Soviet hands. The armoured group of *23. Panzer-Division,* with its five remaining armoured fighting vehicles, was supporting *I. (Bataillon)/Panzergrenadier-Regiment 128,* but they were not able to push beyond

---

2131 Central Archives of the Russian Defence Ministry (Podolsk), f. 243, op. 2928, gy. 131, li. 306.
2132 Central Archives of the Russian Defence Ministry (Podolsk), f. 243, op. 2928, gy. 131, li. 306.
2133 Central Archives of the Russian Defence Ministry (Podolsk), f. 243, op. 2928, gy. 131, li. 306.
2134 Puntigam, Josef Paul: *Vom Plattensee bis zur Mur. Die Kämpfe 1945 im Dreiländereck.* Feldbach, without year of publication, [1993], p. 121.

Újhelyipuszta in the north due to intensive firing from the Soviet armoured fighting vehicles and anti-tank guns. As soon as the Germans reached their designated area, they went into defence and they held the area against the Soviets attacks on that afternoon. However, during the evening the units of *23. Panzer-Division* retreated into the sector of Iklódbördöce. *Panzer-Pionier-Bataillon 51* built engineering obstacles and mine fields around the area. The armoured group of the *Division* and the Jagdpanzer IV *Jagdpanzers* of *Panzerjäger-Abteilung 128* stayed behind the frontline in readiness.[2135]

The units of *16. SS-Panzergrenadier-Division* were retreating through Lenti towards the west. According to the recollections of a former *SS-Panzergrenadier*:

"We left Lenti again toward the west. After a course of five-six km, we went past a new Königstiger tank. This was the first and only occasion throughout the war when I had seen such a vehicle. The crew was preparing the tank for demolition, as all its fuel was already used up."[2136]

The 54th Tank Regiment/5th Guards Cavalry Corps was in combat in the sector of Nova and lost a burnt out T-34/85, and by the end of the day had nine operational armoured fighting vehicles. The 71st Tank Regiment was attacking Lenti, but the Germans destroyed one of their tanks. In the evening they had four operational T-34/85 tanks. The 1896th Self-Propelled Artillery Regiment, was in firing positions in the sectors of Lendvajakabfa and Baglad and lost two burnt out SU–76Ms on that day. In the evening they had 11 operational self-propelled guns. Together, the three regiments reported to have knocked out one German assault gun, two armoured personnel carriers, seven machine gun nests and two mortars, plus they had taken 30 prisoners.[2137]

During the afternoon, the German *3. Panzer-Division/IV. SS-Panzerkorps*, together with *Panzergrenadier-Regiment 3*, *1. Kompanie/Panzergrenadier-Regiment 394* and the forces of *Panzer-Aufklärungs-Abteilung 3*, executed another ambush in the valley of the Rába River. The German armoured personnel carriers rushed down the other side of the border from the north and fell upon the Soviet truck and car columns travelling on the road from the east toward the west. The Soviet supply troops started to flee. The German armoured personnel carriers captured Vasszentmihály again, as well as Gasztony, Rátót and Alsórönök. A large number of Soviet trucks and mortars were captured by the Germans. The Germans freed 50 women and girls from a cellar who were to be transported away that evening. The German armoured group went into a hedgehog defence at Vasszentmihály for the night.[2138]

Due to the German armoured forces in their rear, the Soviet 202nd Rifle Division, turned its 645th Rifle Regiment back from German territory. Around 1700 hours in the afternoon, the Regiment was fighting on the south-western edge of Felsőrönök and on

---

2135 Rebentisch, Ernst: *Zum Kaukasus und zu den Tauern. Die Geschichte der 23. Panzer-Division 1941–1945*. Esslingen, 1963. p. 504.
2136 Puntigam, Josef Paul: *Vom Plattensee bis zur Mur. Die Kämpfe 1945 im Dreiländereck*. Feldbach, without year of publication, [1993], p. 129.
2137 Central Archives of the Russian Defence Ministry (Podolsk), f. 243, op. 2928, gy. 131, li. 307.
2138 *Geschichte der 3. Panzer-Division. Herausgegeben vom Traditionsverband der Division*. Berlin, 1967. p. 475.

the line of Point 312 one km west-north-west of there, then after the Germans retreated back to Vasszentmihály, the Soviets reoccupied the village.[2139]

The Soviet 72nd Guards Independent Self-Propelled Artillery Battalion/68th Guards Rifle Division/26th Army, was in firing positions with seven operational SU-76Ms in the sector north of Kisnarda, 12 km west of Szombathely, on Hill 302 right on the border.[2140]

On the frontline section of the 2nd Ukrainian Front

The units of the Soviet 2nd Guards Mechanized Corps bypassed the village from the south, and repulsed the German rearguard in the sector of Hegyeshalom. At 0900 hours in the morning, the brigades were in combat in the following sectors:

- the 5th Guards Mechanized Brigade at the north-western edge of Zurndorf (Zurány);
- the 4th Guards Mechanized Brigade and the 37th Guards Tank Brigade occupied the vineyards 1.5 km south-west of there;
- the 6th Guards Mechanized Brigade was assembled at the south-eastern edge of Zurndorf.[2141]

With this, the forces of the 2nd Guards Mechanized Corps crossed the border and left Hungarian territory.

3 April 1945, Tuesday

The Soviet 864th Self-Propelled Artillery Regiment/57th Army with the 73rd Guards Rifle Division, was fighting for the occupation of Bánokszentgyörgy around 2000 hours with three SU–76Ms and one T–34 tank.[2142]

The German *Panzergruppe "Rex"/SS-Panzer-Abteilung 16*, retreated that day at around 0600 hours, via Bánokszentgyörgy toward Bázakerettye and around 1000 hours, established defensive positions west of there along the road. The Soviet troops, attacking with armoured support, were temporarily held up by the StuG. III assault guns which reported to have knocked out two armoured fighting vehicles. *Panzergruppe "Rex"* destroyed many of the Soviet oil machinery tools and devices that fell into their hands, then they disengaged from the Soviets and retreated.[2143]

During the day, the forces of the Soviet 299th Rifle Division crushed the resistance of the Hungarian "Bakony" Regiment retreating toward the Mura River and they

---

2139 Central Archives of the Russian Defence Ministry (Podolsk), f. 899, op. 1, gy. 219, li. 397.
2140 Central Archives of the Russian Defence Ministry (Podolsk), f. 243, op. 2928, gy. 131, li. 306. On the following day, the unit left the territory of Hungary.
2141 Central Archives of the Russian Defence Ministry (Podolsk), f. 240, op. 2799, gy. 357, li. 23.
2142 Central Archives of the Russian Defence Ministry (Podolsk), f. 243, op. 2928, gy. 131, li. 309.
2143 Puntigam, Josef Paul: *Vom Plattensee bis zur Mur. Die Kämpfe 1945 im Dreiländereck*. Feldbach, without year of publication, [1993], p. 121.

occupied Murarátka. The 956th and 960th Rifle Regiments of the division, then reached the eastern edge of Alsószemenye, but the 958th Rifle Regiment remained at Murarátka on that day.[2144]

The Soviet 1891st Self-Propelled Artillery Regiment was supporting the forces of the 122nd Rifle Division, and at the end of the day established firing positions on the western edge of Murarátka with its 13 SU–76M self-propelled guns. In the fighting that day, the Regiment reported to have knocked out four German assault guns, six mortars, three guns and 13 machine guns.[2145]

The 32nd Independent Guards Mechanized Brigade, together with the 1201st Self-Propelled Artillery Regiment and the 249th Independent Tank Regiment, occupied the Lendvaújfalu area of Tornyiszentmiklós six km north of the Mura River with their forward unit,, then they sent a reconnaissance party towards Dobri. During the combat actions on that day, the Soviets reported to have knocked out 24 machine guns and three anti-tank guns. The losses of the 249th Independent Tank Regiment consisted of two burnt out T–34 tanks. In the evening the 52nd Tank Regiment/32nd Independent Guards Mechanized Brigade had 23 operational tanks, and the 249th Independent Tank Regiment had five operational T–34s; plus, the 1201st Self-Propelled Artillery Regiment had 17 operational SU–76Ms and one T–34 tank.[2146]

The 122nd Independent Self-Propelled Artillery Battalion/84th Rifle Division stood in the reserve of the army commander, and was stationed in Borsfa with nine operational SU–76M self-propelled guns.[2147]

The German *I. (Bataillon)/Panzergrenadier-Regiment 128/23. Panzer-Division* was pushed out of Iklódbördöce by the Soviets during the morning. At 1400 hours, the division retreated to the hills directly east of the previous Hungarian–Yugoslav border.[2148]

Around 1700 hours, the 71st Tank Regiment/5th Guards Cavalry Corps, was in combat at Lentiszombathely, two km east of Lenti, with four T–34/85s, and the 54th Tank Regiment was at Kissziget, 10 km east of there. The latter unit lost a burnt out T–34/85, so by the evening they only had six tanks in operational condition. The 1896th Self-Propelled Artillery Regiment and the 3rd Guards Motorcycle Regiment, in subordination of the Cavalry Corps, was in combat with 12 SU–76Ms and eight T–34/85 tanks for the occupation of Lendvavásárhely, 13 km north-west of Lendva.[2149]

The Soviet 1202nd Self-Propelled Artillery Regiment/27th Army was subordinated to the 33rd Rifle Corps as ordered the day before, and on the night of 2/3 April 1945, they marched from the sector of Bak via Zalaegerszeg and Zalalövő. At around 1500 hours, it arrived at Csörötnek, seven km east of Szentgotthárd, where it established firing positions with its 19 SU–76Ms and cooperated in repulsing a German counterattack.[2150]

2144 Central Archives of the Russian Defence Ministry (Podolsk), f. 1604, op. 1, gy. 38, li. 167.
2145 Central Archives of the Russian Defence Ministry (Podolsk), f. 243, op. 2928, gy. 131, li. 309.
2146 Central Archives of the Russian Defence Ministry (Podolsk), f. 243, op. 2928, gy. 131, li. 309.
2147 Central Archives of the Russian Defence Ministry (Podolsk), f. 243, op. 2928, gy. 131, li. 309.
2148 Rebentisch, Ernst: *Zum Kaukasus und zu den Tauern. Die Geschichte der 23. Panzer-Division 1941–1945*. Esslingen, 1963. p. 504.
2149 Central Archives of the Russian Defence Ministry (Podolsk), f. 243, op. 2928, gy. 131, li. 310.
2150 Central Archives of the Russian Defence Ministry (Podolsk), f. 243, op. 2928, gy. 131, li. 309.

The 432nd Independent Self-Propelled Artillery Battalion/316th Rifle Division, with 10 operational SU–76M self-propelled guns, was still stationed at the western edge of Keszthely.[2151]

The armoured personnel carriers of *Panzergrenadier-Regiment 3* and *Panzer-Aufklärungs-Abteilung 3/3. Panzer-Division/IV. SS-Panzerkorps,* were camouflaged at the entrance of Vasszentmihály, waiting for the Soviet supply lifts to come. When the machine gun rounds hit the first truck, it exploded with a huge blast because, as it turned out, it was carrying mines. A number of civilian houses were also destroyed in the blast and the other trucks turned and fled. The Germans acquired a number of fuel drums, with which they could replenish their armoured personnel carriers.[2152]

4 April 1945, Wednesday

The Soviet 864th Self-Propelled Artillery Regiment/57th Army with the 73rd Guards Rifle Division, was in combat at Szécsisziget. At the end of the day, the Regiment was assigned to army reserves and were withdrawn to Nagykanizsa. Three of its SU–76Ms were handed over to the 1891st Self-Propelled Artillery Regiment, and one T–34 tank was handed over to the 32nd Independent Guards Mechanized Brigade.[2153]

The German *Panzergruppe "Rex"/SS-Panzer-Abteilung 16,* was retreating via Szécsisziget towards Kútfej. En route, they saw the trucks, guns and other vehicles of the German and Hungarian troops who were fleeing encirclement, as they struggled to keep moving west on the heavy, wet ground. The majority of the wounded and the heavy equipment were left behind. The *SS-Kampfgruppe* lost three StuG. IIIs to taper gear failures from trying to tow other vehicles and were immobilized. Around 1900 hours, another assault gun had to be blown up for the same reason, but the last remaining assault gun at last reached Csentevölgy. The crew of the blown up StuG. III discovered an assault gun of *Sturmartillerie-Brigade 261* abandoned during retreat, which they used to reach Alsólendva, before the German pioneers blew the bridges there.[2154]

The 1891st Self-Propelled Artillery Regiment was supporting the forces of the 133rd Rifle Corps and by 1200 hours, reached the eastern edge of the Lukói Forest north of Pince with 13 SU–76Ms.[2155] The regiment had irrecoverably lost a SU–76M.[2156]

The 32nd Independent Guards Mechanized Brigade, reinforced by the 1201st Self-Propelled Artillery Regiment and the 249th Independent Tank Regiment, was in combat 800 meters north-west of Pince. During a German counterattack, two T–34 tanks of the 52nd Tank Regiment were destroyed. In the evening the Regiment had 23 operational tanks, the 1201st Self-Propelled Artillery Regiment had 17 SU–76Ms and one T–34, and the 249th

---

2151 Central Archives of the Russian Defence Ministry (Podolsk), f. 243, op. 2928, gy. 131, li. 309.
2152 *Geschichte der 3. Panzer-Division. Herausgegeben vom Traditionsverband der Division.* Berlin, 1967. p. 475.
2153 Central Archives of the Russian Defence Ministry (Podolsk), f. 243, op. 2928, gy. 131, li. 312.
2154 Puntigam, Josef Paul: *Vom Plattensee bis zur Mur. Die Kämpfe 1945 im Dreiländereck.* Feldbach, without year of publication, [1993], pp. 121-122.
2155 Central Archives of the Russian Defence Ministry (Podolsk), f. 243, op. 2928, gy. 131, li. 312.
2156 Central Archives of the Russian Defence Ministry (Podolsk), f. 243, op. 2928, gy. 178, li. 130th

Independent Tank Regiment had five operational tanks.[2157] The units were assembled at Völgyifalu in the evening.[2158]

The 122nd Independent Self-Propelled Artillery Battalion/84th Rifle Division, with nine SU–76M self-propelled guns, were in combat at Kútfej, 1.5 km north-west of Lovászi.[2159]

The 1896th Self-Propelled Artillery Regiment and the 3rd Guards Motorcycle Regiment of the 5th Guards Cavalry Corps, were in combat for the occupation of Lendvahosszúfalu, west of Rédics, with 12 SU–76Ms and eight T–34/85 tanks. During the fighting, one SU–76M was burnt out.[2160] At around 1500 hours, the 54th Tank Regiment was supporting the Cavalry Divisions at Kerkaszentkirály with T–34/85s, and the 71st Tank Regiment was supporting them at Pince with four T–34/85 tanks.[2161]

The units of the German *16. SS-Panzergrenadier-Division* crossed the Mura north-west of Letenye, and had now left the territory of Hungary.[2162]

The German *23. Panzer-Division* continued falling back that day, and occupied a bridgehead 10 km north-north-west of Muraszerdahely, from where they were able to cover the German troops and civilians who were fleeing west and crossing the Lendva and Mura. After everyone was on the other bank, all of the bridges in the sector were blown up by the soldiers of *Panzer-Pionier-Bataillon 51* at around 1930 hours. The *Panzergrenadiers* established defensive positions on the Muraszerdahely east–Lapány area by 0300 hours on 5 April 1945.[2163]

The German *71. Infanterie-Division* established temporary defensive positions east of Csáktornya from which they could cover the rear of the units retreating into the *Reichsschutzstellung*. The rearguard consisted of *II. (Bataillon)/Grenadier-Regiment 211*, the cavalry platoon of the *Regiment*, six *Jagdpanzers* of *Panzerjäger-Abteilung 171*, half of the infantry guns of the *Regiment*, a pioneer platoon and the *Eisenbahn-Panzerzug 64*. After the *Pioniers* placed their obstacles, the German rearguard received permission to retreat to the *Reichsschutzstellung* and this was executed unnoticed by Soviet reconnaisance.[2164]

The German *3. Panzer-Division/IV. SS-Panzerkorps,* ordered its armoured personnel carrier-group, which had been assaulting the Soviet supply lifts for days around Vasszentmihály, to retreat behind the German border. On the same day, *Major* Franz Medicis, *Kommandeur* of *Panzerjäger-Abteilung 543,* was killed in a Soviet ground attack aircraft raid. Since the unit no longer had any combat-ready *Jagdpanzers* it was disbanded.[2165]

2157 Central Archives of the Russian Defence Ministry (Podolsk), f. 243, op. 2928, gy. 131, li. 312.
2158 Central Archives of the Russian Defence Ministry (Podolsk), f. 243, op. 2928, gy. 178, li. 128.
2159 Central Archives of the Russian Defence Ministry (Podolsk), f. 243, op. 2928, gy. 131, li. 312.
2160 Central Archives of the Russian Defence Ministry (Podolsk), f. 243, op. 2928, gy. 178, li. 130th
2161 Central Archives of the Russian Defence Ministry (Podolsk), f. 243, op. 2928, gy. 131, li. 312.
2162 See the draft on p. 126 in Puntigam, Josef Paul: *Vom Plattensee bis zur Mur. Die Kämpfe 1945 im Dreiländereck.* Feldbach, without year of publication, [1993].
2163 Rebentisch, Ernst: *Zum Kaukasus bis zu den Tauern. Die Geschichte der 23. Panzer-Division 1941–1945.* Esslingen, 1963. p. 505.
2164 *Die 71. Infanterie-Division im Zweiten Weltkrieg 1939–1945. Gefechts- und Erlebnisberichte aus den Kämpfen der „Glückhaften Division" von Verdun bis Stalingrad, von Monte Cassino bis zum Plattensee.* Arbeitsgemeinschaft „Das Kleeblatt" (Hrsg.). Hildesheim, 1973. p. 421.
2165 *Geschichte der 3. Panzer-Division. Herausgegeben vom Traditionsverband der Division.* Berlin, 1967.p. 475.

The Soviet 1202nd Self-Propelled Artillery Regiment/27th Army, with 19 operational SU–76M self-propelled guns, was in combat during the night on the northern edge of Rábafüzes, two km north of Szentgotthárd. The 432nd Independent Self-Propelled Artillery Battalion/316th Rifle Division was assembled at Gesztenyés, 22 km south-west of Szentgotthárd with nine operational SU–76Ms.[2166]

On the same day, the 18th Tank Corps in combat on German territory, received a replenishment of 21 new T–34/85 tanks and 30 British Universal Carrier armoured transport vehicles, that were delivered to the Celldömölk railway station.[2167]

5 April 1945, Thursday

The Soviet 432nd Independent Self-Propelled Artillery Battalion/316th Rifle Division/27th Army was assembled on that day at Gesztenyés, 16 km south-west of Szentgotthárd, with 10 operational SU–76Ms.

The 1891st Self-Propelled Artillery Regiment, with 15 operational SU–76M self-propelled guns, was assigned to the Army and was waiting for orders in the sector of Dobri.[2168]

The 71st Tank Regiment/5th Guards Cavalry Corps, with six T–34/85 tanks, was assembled at Kerkaszentkirály, and the 54th Tank Regiment, with six T–34/85s, was assembled at Pince. The 1896th Self-Propelled Artillery Regiment, with 11 SU–76M self-propelled guns, was waiting at Völgyifalu.[2169]

The forces of the German *23. Panzer-Division*, among them an armoured group and units of *Panzer-Artillerie-Regiment 128*, cleared the positions held at Muraszerdahely and they crossed the border over to German *Reich* territory. The *Panzergrenadiers* set off for Luttenberg via Muraszentmárton.[2170]

The Soviet 84th Rifle Division/57th Army and its 122nd Independent Self-Propelled Artillery Battalion were in combat in the sector of Pince on that day with seven SU–76Ms.[2171]

The 32nd Independent Guards Mechanized Brigade, with 22 T–34s, the 1201st Self-Propelled Artillery Regiment, with 17 SU–76Ms and one T–34, plus the 249th Independent Tank Regiment with five T–34s, were marching on that day from the sector of Völgyifalu towards Radkersburg and left the territory of Hungary.[2172]

The 3rd Guards Motorcycle Regiment stood in army reserve in the sector of Lendvahosszúfalu with eight T–34/85 tanks.[2173]

[2166] Central Archives of the Russian Defence Ministry (Podolsk), f. 243, op. 2928, gy. 131, li. 312.
[2167] Central Archives of the Russian Defence Ministry (Podolsk), f. 243, op. 2928, gy. 178, li. 128. On 9 April 1945, 20 new T–34/85s arrived at Celldömölk by train assigned to the 5th Guards Tank Corps.
[2168] Central Archives of the Russian Defence Ministry (Podolsk), f. 243, op. 2928, gy. 131, li. 315.
[2169] Central Archives of the Russian Defence Ministry (Podolsk), f. 243, op. 2928, gy. 131, li. 315.
[2170] Rebentisch, Ernst: *Zum Kaukasus und zu den Tauern. Die Geschichte der 23. Panzer-Division 1941–1945*. Esslingen, 1963. p. 505.
[2171] Central Archives of the Russian Defence Ministry (Podolsk), f. 243, op. 2928, gy. 131, li. 315.
[2172] Central Archives of the Russian Defence Ministry (Podolsk), f. 243, op. 2928, gy. 131, li. 315.
[2173] Central Archives of the Russian Defence Ministry (Podolsk), f. 243, op. 2928, gy. 131, li. 315.

6 April 1945, Friday

The Soviet 432nd Independent Self-Propelled Artillery Battalion/316th Rifle Division/27th Army was marching from Gesztenyés with 10 operational SU–76M self-propelled guns towards Neumarkt (Farkasdifalva) and with this, crossed the Hungarian border into Austria.[2174]

At around 1600 hours, the 1891st Self-Propelled Artillery Regiment arrived at Kondorfa with 12 operational SU–76M self-propelled guns.[2175]

The 71st Tank Regiment/5th Guards Cavalry Corps, with six T–34/85 tanks, was still active at Kerkaszentkirály, and the 54th Tank Regiment, also with six T-34/85s, was active in the sector of Pince. The 1896th Self-Propelled Artillery Regiment, with 11 operational SU–76Ms, was directed to Rédics.[2176]

The 122nd Independent Self-Propelled Artillery Battalion/84th Rifle Division/57th Army, was assembled in the sector of Pince with seven operational SU–76Ms, while the 3rd Guards Motorcycle Regiment, with eight T–34/85 tanks and 140 motorcycles, was assembled at Lendvahosszúfalu.[2177]

7 April 1945, Saturday

The Soviet 1891st Self-Propelled Artillery Regiment/27th Army with 14 operational SU–76M self-propelled guns was ordered from Kondorfa to Csörötnek early that day, where they were deployed. Later on, they were sent to the western edge of Heiligenkreuz im Lafnitztal (Rábakeresztúr) four km north of Szentgotthárd, where they were engaged in a firefight with the Germans.[2178] With this, the unit had temporarily left the territory of Hungary.[2179]

The 71st Tank Regiment/5th Guards Cavalry Corps with five T–34/85 tanks, was still stationed at Kerkaszentkirály, and the 54th Tank Regiment with six T-34/85s were stationed at the sector of Pince. The 1896th Self-Propelled Artillery Regiment, with seven operational SU–76Ms, was assembled at Bárszentmihályfa.[2180]

A Soviet 3rd Guards Motorcycle Regiment/57th Army with eight T–34/85 tanks was directed to Lendvanemesd, in subordination to the 32nd Independent Guards Mechanized Brigade. The latter unit, together with the 249th Independent Tank Regiment and the

---

2174 Central Archives of the Russian Defence Ministry (Podolsk), f. 243, op. 2928, gy. 131, li. 318.
2175 Central Archives of the Russian Defence Ministry (Podolsk), f. 243, op. 2928, gy. 131, li. 318.
2176 Central Archives of the Russian Defence Ministry (Podolsk), f. 243, op. 2928, gy. 131, li. 319.
2177 Central Archives of the Russian Defence Ministry (Podolsk), f. 243, op. 2928, gy. 131, li. 318.
2178 Central Archives of the Russian Defence Ministry (Podolsk), f. 243, op. 2928, gy. 131, li. 321.
2179 The 1891st Self-Propelled Artillery Regiment was in combat in Hungary, at Szentgotthárd, on 10 April 1945. See Central Archives of the Russian Defence Ministry (Podolsk), f. 381, op. 8378, gy. 590, li. 61.
2180 Central Archives of the Russian Defence Ministry (Podolsk), f. 243, op. 2928, gy. 131, li. 322. The armoured units of the 5th Guards Cavalry Corps were regrouped to the sector of Körmend on 9 April 1945, from where the 54th and 71st Tank Regiments had been drawn forward on 11 April to the sector of Oberwart (Felsőőr). The 1896th Self-Propelled Artillery Regiment with seven operational SU–76Ms was still stationed in the sector of Körmend in the middle of April 1945. Thus the tank and self-propelled artillery units of the 5th Guards Cavalry Corps, which stepped on Hungarian territory as the first Soviet units on 26 September 1944, left as the last units toward the west from Hungary.

1201ˢᵗ Self-Propelled Artillery Regiment, returned from the sector of Ratkersburg to the Hungarian side of the border and was assembled in the sector of Szécsényfa. The 52ⁿᵈ Tank Regiment/32ⁿᵈ Independent Guards Mechanized Brigade that evening, had 19 operational T–34s, the 249ᵗʰ Independent Tank Regiment had three T–34s, and the 1201ˢᵗ Self-Propelled Artillery Regiment had 16 SU–76Ms and one T–34 tank.[2181]

The 122ⁿᵈ Independent Self-Propelled Artillery Battalion/84ᵗʰ Rifle Division, was supporting the actions of the rifle troops with seven SU–76Ms in the sector of Szécsénykút.[2182]

Summary of further events during the course of the Vienna Offensive

The German troops of *Heeresgruppe Süd*, after they were unable to hold the ground in the Transdanubia any longer, retreated to the Southeast Wall (*Reichsschutzstellung*). The fortified area on the south-eastern borders of Germany, in the foreground of the *Alpenfestung*, which still existed only on paper, was originally planned to include three successive defensive lines, one behind the other. The first line, which started on Slovakian territory, west of Trenčín, ran along the Austro-Hungarian border, on a smaller scale on Hungarian territory depending on the terrain conditions, then onwards to the south along to Varasd and Zagreb. Its construction had begun in September 1944, supervised by the *Volkssturm*, and the work was carried out by workers from many different countries, prisoners of war, approximately 38,000 Hungarian Jews on labour service, the Austrian members of the *Hitlerjugend*, and by local civilians, men not serving in the military, women, and children who were not yet of military service age. Due to the inhuman conditions, the weather and the insufficient amount of food provided, many of the labour service workers and the Jews, forcibly relocated from the Eastern parts of the *Reich*, died. At the end of March, the Jews who were unable to walk, were exterminated, and the others were carried away to the Mauthausen concentration camp. Despite this, the *Reichsschutzstellung* had not been properly completed. Although the positions were better built up at some places, and were reinforced by concrete bunkers, the flamboyant name generally meant more or less dug out makeshift infantry trenches and tank obstacles. The armoured blockades on the roads were easy to bypass.

On 30 March 1945, the swiftly moving corps of the 3ʳᵈ Ukrainian Front, supported by the 17ᵗʰ Air Army, breached the *Reichsschutzstellung* and entered the territory of *Ostmark* (Austria) south of Sopron, on a 20 km wide front.

As a result, the fighting on Hungarian soil was nearing its end. However, based on research conducted by István Ravasz, it is known that the fighting had not ceased completely by 4 April in Hungary. The frontline reached the Pinkamindszent–Körmend–Szentgotthárd sector

---

2181 Central Archives of the Russian Defence Ministry (Podolsk), f. 243, op. 2928, gy. 131, li. 321. The 32ⁿᵈ Independent Guards Mechanized Brigade and the subordinated armoured fighting vehicle units were still stationed in the sector until the middle of April 1945, but they have not been engaged in significant combat actions.

2182 Central Archives of the Russian Defence Ministry (Podolsk), f. 243, op. 2928, gy. 131, li. 321. The 122ⁿᵈ Independent Self-Propelled Artillery Battalion was, within the strength of its division, deployed between 7 – 9 April 1945 six km southwest of Muraszerdahely, in the sector of Göröghegy with seven SU–76Ms, the unit was also deployed between 10 – 15 April at Ligetfalva, 12 km west of Muraszerdahely.

on 30 March 1945. The Soviet 93rd Rifle Division/104th Rifle Corps/26th Army, plus the 202nd and 337th Rifle Divisions of the 33rd Rifle Corps/27th Army, were bogged down on the Güssing (Németújvár) defensive line in the *Steiermark* sector of the *Reichsschutzstellung*. Ten days of inactivity ensued, which ended on 10 April by the assault of the 108th Guards, 316th and 320th Rifle Divisions/37th Soviet Rifle Corps/27th Army at Heiligenkreuz (Rábakeresztúr). The above mentioned Soviet forces joined this assault on 11 and 12 April, after *General der Panzertruppe* Balck, commander of the German *6. Armee* issued a retreat order for the defenders on 11 April 1945. The positions were mostly built up on Hungarian territory still, on the top of hills in the line of Rábafüzes and Nemesmedves–Pinkamindszent, and were defended by the German *1. and 3. Panzer-Divisions/IV. SS-Panzerkorps/6. Armee*. Behind the frontline, there were still a number of Hungarian villages, but on 12 April 1945, after capturing Dénes, then Kapuy-major belonging to Pinkamindszent, all combat actions ceased on Hungarian territory.

On 1 April 1945, the Headquarters of the Main Command of the Armed Forces of the USSR (Stavka), ordered the 3rd Ukrainian Front to direct the 9th Guards and 4th Guards Armies, plus the 6th Guards Tank Army to occupy Vienna, and by 15 April at the latest, should reach the Tulln–Sankt Pölten–Lilienfeld sector. The combined 26th, 27th and 57th armies, in cooperation with the Bulgarian 1st Army, were to occupy the cities of Gloggnitz, Bruck, Graz and Maribor, then were to reinforce their frontline along the Mürz, the Mura and the Dráva rivers. The 46th Army/2nd Ukrainian Front, with 57 armoured fighting vehicles of the 2nd Guards Mechanized Corps, and the 32 operational armoured fighting vehicles of the 23rd Tank Corps, received orders to attack in the general direction of Bruck–Vienna, and cooperate with the 3rd Ukrainian Front to occupy Vienna together. In the meantime, the 4th Guards Army was regrouped on the right flank of the 9th Guards Army in order to enable them to continue their attack via Sopron in the direction of Vienna.

On 1 April 1945, the German *2. Panzerarmee* commenced their retreat to the Austrian border. At that time, the *Panzerarmee* consisted of the following units: the *LXVIII. Feld-*, the *XXII. Gebirgs-* and the *I. Kavallerie-Armeekorps*, with the following units in subordination: the German *71.* and *297. Infanterie-*, the *44. Reichsgrenadier-*, the *23. Panzer-*, the *3.* and *4. Kavallerie-*, the *117.* and *118. Jäger-*, the *9. SS-Panzer-*, the *16. SS-Panzergrenadier-*, the *13. Waffen-Gebirgs-Division der SS*, and the *14. SS-Grenadierdivisions*, three battalions of the *Polizei-Regiment 6*, the *Festungs-Bataillons 1011 and 1100*, the *Eisenbahn-Panzerzug 19*, a few blocking and fortress anti-tank gun detachments, plus the Hungarian Szent László Division, the 25th Infantry Division, two battalions of the 20th Infantry Division, the 20th Assault Artillery Battalion, the Bakony-Regiment, the 211st, 212nd, 213rd and 214th Fortress Battalions, the 215th, 216th and 218th Fortress Machine-Gun Battalions and one police battalion. The northern flank of *2. Panzerarmee* was constantly threatened by the swift moving divisions of the Soviet 5th Guards Cavalry Corps.

On 7 April 1945, the first units of the German *2. Panzerarmee* reached the line of the *Reichsschutzstellung* at Radkersburg near the Mura. The Soviet 18th Tank Corps entered the lower valley of the Rába River, to continue their advance towards Marburg and Graz. With this, the Soviet troops were threatening the rear of *2. Panzerarmee* and *Heeresgruppe "E"*. However, on 6 April the Soviet Tank Corps was withdrawn to support the attack facing Vienna, and the forces of the Soviet 26th, 27th and 57th Army were turned north as well. The attack on Styria (Steiermark) was only conducted by the Bulgarian 1st Army and the units of the People's Liberation Army of Yugoslavia (NOVJ). Against these, the German forces reinforced their defences and at many locations reoccupied the territories in the *Reichsschutzstellung* that had been lost earlier. The forces on the right flank of the 3rd Ukrainian Front were quickly closing up on Vienna. The units of the 9th Guards Army and the 9th Guards Mechanized Corps/6th Guards Tank Army, took Wiener Neustadt on 2 April 1945. The 4th Guards Army was ordered to advance to Florisdorf, north-east of the city, through the center of Vienna. The 6th Guards Tank Army was reinforced by the 18th Tank Corps and the 12th Engineering Brigade, then they were ordered to enter the south-western part of Vienna with the forces of the 5th Guards Tank Corps, and encircle the city from the west with the 9th Guards Mechanized Corps. The 39th Guards Rifle Corps/9th Guards Army was to follow the 5th Guards Tank Corps to support the armoured fighting vehicles in taking the south-western part of Vienna. The Army's 38th Guards Rifle Corps, at the same time, was to close up on the Vienna–Linz road, and with two of its rifle divisions, they were to support the attack on Vienna from the west. The task of the 37th Guards Rifle Corps was to cover the open left flank of the assault force.

The outskirts of Vienna were defended by *I. SS- and II. SS-Panzerkorps/(SS-) 6. Panzerarmee*, with the combat groups of *1. SS-, 3. SS-,* and *12. SS-Panzer-Divisions* in their ranks, the remnants of the *356. Infanterie-Division*, the combat group of *232. (Feldausbildungs-) Panzer-Division, I. (Bataillon)/SS-Panzergrenadier-Regiment 24 "Danmark"*, the students of the military academy for non-commissioned officers at Wiener Neustadt, one regimental combat group of *37. SS-Kavallerie-Division*, the guns of *Volks-Artillerie-Korps 403* and *Heeres-Artillerie-Brigade 959*, the forces of *2. SS-* and the *6. Panzer-Divisions*, the *Panzer-Aufklärungs-Abteilungs* of *1. Panzer-* and *9. SS-Panzer-Divisions*, seven independent battalions, two close combat companies, two tank destroyer battalions, two artillery training *Abteilungen*, an anti-aircraft artillery *Abteilung*; and, from Hungarian side, the remnants of the 2nd Armoured Division, a battalion of the 20th Infantry Division, the remnants of the 1st Mountain Brigade, and a battalion of SS-Regiment Ney. The staff of the Hungarian 1st Army and the the ruins of the 1st Hussars Division as well, were under direct subordination of the *Armee*.

At the beginning of April, between *2. Panzerarmee* and *6. Panzerarmee*, from Szentgotthárd to Kirchschla, the weak forces of *6. Armee* were in defence. The *Armee* had, in subordination to *IV. SS-* and *III. Panzerkorps, 1.* and *3. Panzer-Divisions*, plus the combat groups of *5. SS-Panzer-Division, 1. Volks-Gebirgs-Division, I. (Bataillon)/SS-Panzergrenadier-Regiment 23 "Norge"*, four weak, brigade size combat groups, *Festungs-Pak-Verband IX, Volks-Werfer Brigades 17* and *19, Sturmartillerie-Brigade 303, Artillerie-Abteilung 171, schwere Panzer-Abteilung 509, I. (Panther) (Abteilung)/Panzer-Regiment 24*[2183], *Sturmpanzer-Abteilung 219, Flammpanzer-Kompanie 351* and the remnants of seven Hungarian battalions.

2183 *I. (Abteilung)/Panzer-Regiment 24* managed to reach German territory at the end of March 1945 from Hungary by filling the fuel tanks of the remaining 10 Panthers with oil mixed in aircraft fuel. At the beginning of April 1945 all of the remaining Panthers were reassigned to *1. Schwadron*, plus they received as replenishment, five captured Soviet T–34/85 tanks as well. See Weidemann, Gert-Axel: *Unser Regiment. Reiter-Regiment 2 – Panzer-Regiment 24*. Groß-Umstadt, 1982. pp. 290-291.

Athough Hitler, similarly to Budapest, officially named Vienna as a fortress, the civilians did not take part in any significant measure in the fortification works, not even upon orders from *Gauleiter* Baldur von Schirach. The Austrian resistance movement was preparing plans to counter the Germans in defending the city until the very end, and to contact the Soviet forces.

On 5 April 1945, Marshal Tolbukhin ordered the 4th Guards Army to occupy the eastern and south-eastern parts of Vienna. The 9th Guards Army was to launch its attack from the south, and was to encircle the city toward the west. The 6th Guards Tank Army was tasked with advancing toward the north, thus cutting off the roads from Vienna toward the west and north, and afterwards, together with the 9th Guards Army, enter the city from the west. The 46th Army/2nd Ukrainian Front was to encircle Vienna from the north by advancing along the eastern bank of the Danube.

On 5 April 1945, *General der Infanterie* Wöhler, commander of *Heeresgruppe Süd*, was dismissed. His successor was *Generaloberst* Lothar Rendulic.

On the morning of 6 April 1945 at 0730 hours, the direct attack on Vienna by the Soviets has launched. The 20th Guards and 21st Guards Rifle Corps/4th Guards Army, reinforced by the 1st Guards Mechanized Corps, and in cooperation with the 39th Guards Rifle Corps/9th Guards Army, soon entered the western and southern suburbs of Vienna. The extremely heavy close quarters combat had begun, which was fought on the streets, along the canals and in the industrial districts. The 21st Guards Tank Brigade/5th Guards Tank Corps reached Tulln on that day, and with this accomplished, Vienna was completely encircled from the west. The 9th Guards Mechanized Corps launched its attack from the west against the city. However, the delaying actions of the German combat groups at the end of March and at the beginning of April, significantly decreased the combat strength of the Soviet forces. Certain brigades of the Soviet 6th Guards Tank Army had less than ten tanks. For example, the 46th Guards Tank Brigade/9th Guards Mechanized Corps had 13 tanks and the 364th Guards Heavy Self-Propelled Artillery Regiment had four-to-five SU–152 self-propelled guns when launching the attack in the western suburbs.

Inside Vienna, in subordination to *II. SS-Panzerkorps*, *2. SS-* and *3. SS-Panzer-Divisions*, *6. Panzer-Division*, and the newly assigned *Führer-Grenadier-Division*, plus a few fragmented units and rapid reaction units, were in defence. The Germans did not want to defend the Austrian capital to the end, therefore they were retreating gradually, and Vienna was cleared during the delaying actions.

Up to 8 April 1945, the Soviet troops were approaching closer and closer to the inner districts of the city, they occupied the Arsenal, plus the Südbahnhof and the Westbahnhof. The 5th Guards Tank Corps regrouped its forces into the northern suburbs, and continued its attack toward the south-east, to be able to establish contact with the 4th Guards Army and the 1st Guards Mechanized Corps arriving from the south.

The Germans were not successful in building up substantial defences in the western parts of Vienna, because on many occasions, the Austrian resistance had led the Soviet armoured fighting vehicles into their rear, and on other occasions, they were directly shooting at the German troops. Not even the public hangings organized by the *Gestapo* and the *SS* eliminated these activities.

The German *Panzergrenadier*-infantry exerted significant resistance along the Ringstrasse to cover the retreat of the tanks and assault guns over the Danube canals and then over the Danube. The Soviet rifle infantry had hauled their anti-tank guns to the upper levels of multi-story houses to provide fire support for the assault troops. In many areas, the grenades and shells of the Soviet artillery caused significant and large-scale damage. The 20th Guards Rifle Corps was progressing slowly against 6. *Panzer-Division* , because they were trying to cover the only possible route for retreat, over the bridges on the Danube.

On the night of 10/11 April 1945, the 4th Guards Army crossed the Danube Canal, and continued pushing back the German troops, which were gradually retreating to the northern bank of the Danube.

In the early afternoon of 13 April 1945, the Soviet troops completely occupied Vienna and the surrounding area. Approximately 18,000 Soviet soldiers were killed in the battle for the city and approximately 5000 German soldiers were buried after the battle was over.

The armies of the 3rd Ukrainian Front, attacking in the middle and on the left flank, reached the Eastern Alps by the middle of April, but their attack was bogged down there against the German *6. Armee* and *2. Panzerarmee*, and they did not gain much more ground toward the west until the German capitulation. The Bulgarian 1st Army was attacking along the Dráva River, and on 8 April, it reached the north-western outskirts of Varasd, however they were forced to establish defensive position because of the strong resistance of the German troops. On 15 April, 52 of the 276 armoured fighting vehicles of *2. Panzerarmee* were operational, and of the 60 tanks and assault guns of *6. Armee,* only 44 were in operational condition.

On 13 April 1945, the Headquarters of the Main Command of the Armed Forces of the USSR (Stavka), issued an order to the 3rd Ukrainian Front according to which, it was to reach the Treusen River with its right flank, to occupy Sankt Pölten and to keep the area occupied. Following this, the 9th Guards Army was to be withdrawn and reassembled west of Vienna. The 104th Guards Rifle Division/38th Guards Rifle Corps/9th Guards Army and the forces of the 18th Tank Corps, reinforced with the 209th Self-Propelled Artillery Brigade, took Sankt Pölten on 15 April, with large-scale artillery and aircraft support. The *6. Panzerarmee* still had 249 tanks and assault guns on that day, of which, 124 were combat-ready.

After this, the operation aimed at Vienna was practically over. The 3rd Ukrainian Front and the units of the 2nd Ukrainian Front, during the 31 days of the Vienna Offensive, lost 167, 940 soldiers, of these 38,661 dead and missing, 603 tanks and self-propelled guns, 764 guns and mortars, plus 614 aircraft. The Bulgarian 1st Army had lost 9805 soldiers, and of these, 2698 were dead and missing.

Between 11 and 20 April 1945, the German *Heeresgruppe Süd* reported 3295 dead, 15,547 wounded and 6120 men missing in action. Summarized German battle casualty reports from this period are not available anymore. According to Soviet sources, between 16 March and 15 April, the Red Army captured 130,000 German soldiers, and knocked out or captured 1345 armoured fighting vehicles and 2250 guns.

On 5 March 1945, *Heeresgruppe Süd* still had 1676 combat-ready armoured fighting vehicles[2184], then on 10 April, together with the replenishments received of approximately 106 armoured fighting vehicles, they only had 874 remaining armoured fighting vehicles.[2185] Based on this data, between 5 March and 10 April, at least 900 tanks, assault guns, *Jagdpanzers* and tank destroyers were deleted from the combat strength of the German *Heeresgruppe*.

Assessment of the performance of the opposing forces of the Vienna Offensive

The 3rd Ukrainian Front, together with the left flank of the 2nd Ukrainian Front, successfully concluded the Vienna Offensive, but one of the main tasks in the original plan, namely, the encirclement and destruction of *6. Panzerarmee* advanced to the Sió Canal, was not possible to achieve.

Between 16 and 25 March 1945, the Soviet forces successfully broke through the frontline of the forces of *Heeresgruppe Süd* in combat between Lake Balaton and the Danube, and on 26 March they began the pursuit of the retreating forces. Although the forces of the 3rd Ukrainian Front managed to break into the gap between the German *6. Panzerarmee* and *6. Armee* both engaged in delaying actions, they were not able to encircle these units.

It is not coincidental, that the combat actions of the Soviet 6th Guards Tank Army during the Hungarian part of the Vienna Offensive, were criticised by their superiors. As it was voiced by Colonel M. M. Malakhov:

"I have to admit that the 6th Guards Tank Army did not manage to advance quickly during the pursuit of the enemy and they did not manage to disengage from the combined army units. The cause of the slow assault of the army has to be explained by the enemy's staunch resistance on a terrain extremely hardly trackable by tracked vehicles, and they have perused the previously prepared anti-tank strongpoints as well.
During retreat, the Germans have destroyed bridges, established obstacles and strongly defended their positions along the way. All this has decreased the pace of the advance of the 6th Guards Tank Army and on the other hand, required extremely hard work from our engineering units.
Despite all these mentioned factors, the actions of the 6th Guards Tank Army was not definite and organized enough. Our infantry regularly reached the tank units by the evening, which, instead of bypassing the strong enemy fortifications, got engaged in lengthy combat actions in order to occupy these enemy fortifications."[2186]

During the Hungarian part of the Vienna Offensive, combat engagement between the German and the Soviet armoured troops happened only once, in the Várpalota sector

---
2184 BAMA, RH 2 Ost 5455.
2185 NARA, T78, R621, F000483-000487.
2186 Malakhov, M. M.: A Balatontól Bécsig (excerpt). In: *Fejezetek hazánk felszabadításának történetéből*. Budapest, 1960. p. 198.

between 20 and 22 March 1945. Interestingly, this engagement reached its peak on 21 March with a close quarters battle between armoured fighting vehicles.

It is important to note that on 21 March, that is, on the sixth day of the Vienna Offensive, the *1. SS-, 2. SS-, 9. SS-* and *12. SS-Panzer-Divisions/6. Panzerarmee* deployed in Operation *"Frühlingserwachen"*, still had 408 armoured fighting vehicles, but only 108 of these were in combat-ready condition.[2187]

From 25 March, the fuel supply system of *Heeresgruppe Süd* practically collapsed. As a result, not only the armoured fighting vehicles in combat were immobilized in constantly increasing numbers, but the recovery vehicles had less and less fuel as well. The crews always tried to destroy their abandoned vehicles, but this was not always possible because of the swift approach of the Soviet troops.

The "mass extinction" of the German armoured fighting vehicles had begun in the Transdanubia. Thus, when the retreating German armoured divisions left the Transdanubian Mountains (Dunántúli-középhegység) in their course of retreat towards the west, they did not have either enough fuel to organize a mobile defence, or enough armoured fighting vehicles and armoured personnel carriers.

Due to this, after 25 March, the Germans were only able to deploy small armoured groups of 10-20 armoured fighting vehicles, in order to support their *Grenadier* or *Panzergrenadier*-infantry, using the villages as fortifications in delaying battles, or to repulse the Soviets who breached the defences with counterattacks.

According to *SS-Hauptsturmführer* Hans Siegel, *Kommandeur* of *II. (mixed) Panzer-Abteilung/SS-Panzer-Regiment 12*, their tanks and subordinated *Jagdpanzers* for example, strived to achieve the shortest range to have the most effective and accurate firing possible. Therefore, the guns opened fire at a distance of 800 meters in attack, and from 500 meters in defence, while strictly observing fire discipline, that is, the armoured fighting vehicles could only start firing after confirmation arrived from the commander of the unit via radio. Infantry targets were fired upon mostly from the turret machine gun and the coaxial machine gun. Tracer rounds were used mostly in attacks and counterattacks, which also helped correcting the fire of the main guns.[2188] The other German armoured regiments and tank destroyer battalions probably followed the same practice.

Regarding the tank and mechanized corps of the 3rd Ukrainian Front, the Soviets managed to replenish their ever mounting losses with a simple method, the subordination of the 207th, 208th and 209th Self-Propelled Artillery Brigades equipped with SU–100 self-propelled guns. This however, meant that the self-propelled guns needed to fulfil the combat role of the tank as well. For example, according to the experience report of the Soviet 208th Self-Propelled Artillery Brigade, the armoured fighting vehicles of the SU-100 regiments subordinated to the 5th Guards Tank Corps, were attacking either in the battle line of the tanks or behind them at a distance of 150-200 meters. However it had also occurred that the self-propelled guns had to attack in front of the tanks in the tank brigades that had an insufficient number of tanks.[2189]

2187 The detailed data regarding the armoured fighting vehicle strength of the German *6. Panzerarmee*, *6. Armee* and *2. Panzerarmee* as of 21 March 1945. is contained in the Appendix.
2188 The written statement of Hans Siegel from 1998, in response to the author's questionnaire.
2189 Central Archives of the Russian Defence Ministry (Podolsk), f. 339, op. 5179, gy. 69, li. 235.

Assessment of the inflicted and suffered armoured losses of the opposing forces during the combat actions in the Transdanubia in the spring of 1945

The various committees of the 3rd Ukrainian Front had, by 10 April 1945, counted 968 enemy tanks, assault guns, *Jagdpanzers* and self-propelled guns, plus 446 armoured personnel carriers and armoured cars in the Transdanubia.[2190] This is a realistic number also based on German archive sources.[2191]

Between 24 March and 20 April, the committee of the Soviet 17th Air Army travelled around the route and locations of the battles between December 1944 and end of March 1945, and from the number mentioned above, investigated 430 German and Hungarian armoured fighting vehicles.[2192] According to the findings of the Soviet committee, of the armoured fighting vehicles investigated on the field, 99 (23 percent) were destroyed by gun fire, 26 (six percent) were destroyed by the tank destroyer units of the Soviet rifle infantry[2193], 239 (55.7 percent) were destroyed by the Germans themselves, and 66 (15.3 percent) were destroyed by the aircraft of the Soviet air force. The latter consisted of 53 armoured fighting vehicles which were destroyed by the aircraft alone, and 13 vehicles were knocked out by a joint effort with the artillery.

If we project this percentage to the 968 German and Hungarian armoured fighting vehicles found in the Transdanubia, then at least 539 armoured fighting vehicles were abandoned by their own crews or blown up by them, and the remaining number (429) were lost directly due to Soviet or Bulgarian action.

The majority of the *Jagdpanzers* of the German *schwere Panzerjäger-Abteilung 560* were blown up by the Germans themselves in the second half of March 1945. The causes of this were closely investigated by *Oberleutnant* Bock, working in the office of the *Inspekteur der Panzertruppen*. His report records interesting details of the "mass extinction" of the German armoured fighting vehicles in the Transdanubia, therefore the full text is provided here:

"My task was to acquire the strength report of the armoured divisions of the 6. Panzerarmee and the 8. Armee and to determine what was the cause of the high numbers of Jagdpanzers that were blown up by the schwere Panzerjäger-Abteilung 560 during the retreat?
The consultation with the commander of the schwere Panzerjäger-Abteilung 560, at present subordinated to the 12. SS-Panzer-Division 'Hitlerjugend', regarding the Jagdpanther explosions especially frequent on the Hungarian–German borders, resulted in the following:

2190 M. Svirin – O. Baronov – M. Kolomiets – D. Nedogonov: *Boj u ozera Balaton*. Moscow, 1999. p. 70.
2191 At least 663 armoured fighting vehicles are missing from the strength of *6. Panzerarmee* and *6. Armee* based on the strength report of 5 March and of that at the beginning of April. The details are contained in the Appendix.
2192 Archer, Lee–Nevenkin, Kamen: *Panzerwrecks Nr. 20. Ostfront 3*. Sussex. 2016. p. 5. Of the 430 fighting vehicles, seven Panzer IIIs, 56 Panzer IVs, 110 Panthers, two Tiger Es and 39 Tiger B tanks, 27 Jagdpanzer 38(t)s and 12 Jagdpanther *Jagdpanzers*, 63 armoured fighting vehicles with Panzer IV chassis (Panzer IV/70s and Jagdpanzer IV *Jagdpanzers* and StuG.IV assault guns, 25 StuG.III assault guns and StuH.42 assault howitzers, 23 *Wespe* and *Hummel* self-propelled howitzers, 13 *Marder* tank destroyers, 12 anti-aircraft armoured fighting vehicles, 17 Bergepanther armoured recovery vehicles, plus 24 Hungarian-manufactured tanks (and most likely Nimród armoured automatic cannons as well).
2193 Most likely those armoured fighting vehicles are included which were not destroyed by blowing them up, but by *Panzerfaust* (for example at Söréd), as it was not possible to discern whether a German or a Soviet soldier had targeted the armoured fighting vehicle.

The Abteilung was subordinated to the 12. SS-Panzer-Division 'Hitlerjugend' and was deployed as the third Abteilung of the armoured regiment. The supply company of the Abteilung was grouped together with the supply troops of the armoured regiment into a so-called supply group. The towing unit of the Abteilung was equally merged in by the regiment, in order to be able to centrally control the towing and workshop units. Because of this, the commander of the Abteilung did not have any control over the supply or the workshop-units anymore. As the orderly officer of the Abteilung had to be reassigned to the regiment, there was nobody left who could be employed with these kinds of things. During the retreat from the forests of the Bakony toward Sopron, the Abteilung did not have any fuel supplies allocated. The fact that the remaining nine Panzerjäger IVs and three Panzerjäger Vs[2194] were saved, was only made possible by ruthlessly requisitioning the fuel from other units.

The majority of the armoured fighting vehicle-explosions can be seen as a result of the insufficient method with which the regiment had centrally organized the towing tasks. Towing was first carried out for the regiment's own vehicles, and the towing of the Jagdpanzers of schwere Panzerjäger-Abteilung 560, were always left for the last.

In the majority of the cases, it was already too late at that time for towing, because the weak resistance of our infantry let the Soviets bypass our positions; even if the Jagdpanzers were only sunken or had small mechanical problems. For example the towing away of a Jagdpanzer that was sunken on 8 March 1945 was only attempted on 21 March 1945. The continuous demands of the commander of the Abteilung and the pressing requests toward the regiment and the division regarding allocation of towing vehicles, remained mostly ineffective, or they were dealt with the note that there are not any sufficient towing vehicles available, thus they should blow up their vehicles, if the need arises. The Jagdpanzers were fully under control of the armoured regiment and the repaired Jagdpanzers were allocated to different units in a way that the Abteilung was not notified beforehand. This way the commander of the Abteilung did not know how many Jagdpanzers they actually had, and where the available vehicles were.

A further cause of the loss of the significant amount of Jagdpanzers, was the tactically incorrect deployment. The Jagdpanzers were deployed almost exclusively as assault guns; in the available cases together with the infantry, as a rearguard left in front of the enemy. For a vehicle that can only fire to the front, this is clearly not advantageous, for as each position shifts they at first need to turn. In some of the combat situations it was ordered that the damaged Jagdpanzers should be dug in; for a vehicle that is effective only in forward position, this is an impossible way to be used. The result was the loss of these vehicles, which were blown up, in order to avoid their capture by the enemy.

Due to the fact that the armoured regiment kept the supply, the towing, the repairing and the tactical use of the vehicles in their capacity, we can absolutely not deem the Abteilungskommandeur's work as responsible leadership. In a way, the commander of the Abteilung was only a company commander within the armoured regiment."[2195]

[2194] This concerns the Panzer IV/70 and the Jagdpanther *Jagdpanzers*.
[2195] Közli Spielberger, Walter J. – Doyle, Hilary L. – Jentz, Thomas L.: *Schwere Jagdpanzer. Entwicklung – Fertigung – Einsatz.* Stuttgart, 1993. p. 55.

Between 16 March and 2 April 1945, the forces of the 3rd Ukrainian Front irrecoverably lost 346 tanks and self-propelled guns on Hungarian territory.[2196] The German-Hungarian troops of course, knocked out more armoured fighting vehicles than the number that was destroyed. For example, the Soviet 18th Tank Corps lost the following armoured fighting vehicles during the Vienna Offensive between 21 March – 4 April 1945:

- gunfire knocked out 86 T–34 and T–34/85 tanks, of which 42 were damaged beyond repair;
- of other causes another 13 tanks were temporarily disabled;
- gunfire knocked out 12 ISU–122 self-propelled guns, of which two were damaged beyond repair;
- of other causes, another four ISU–122 self-propelled guns were temporarily disabled;
- gunfire knocked out three ISU–152 self-propelled guns, of which one was damaged beyond repair;
- of other causes, another two ISU–152s were temporarily disabled;
- gunfire knocked out 15 SU–76M self-propelled guns, of which five were damaged beyond repair;
- of other causes, another three SU–76M self-propelled guns were temporarily disabled.[2197]

The total armoured losses of the 6th Guards Tank Army/3rd Ukrainian Front during the Vienna Offensive amounted to the following[2198]:

Unit	Losses in Hungary	Losses in Austria	Total losses during the offensive
5th Guards Tank Corps	69 T–34/85s 10 SU–76Ms	16 T–34/85s 5 SU–76Ms	85 T–34/85s 15 SU–76Ms
9th Guards Mechanized Corps	52 M4A2s 4 SU–76Ms	16 M4A2s 1 Mk–IX6 SU–76Ms	68 M4A2s 1 Mk–IX10 SU–76Ms
51st Self-Propelled Artillery Brigade	14 SU–76Ms	6 SU–76Ms 2 T–70s	20 SU–76Ms 2 T–70s
364th Guards Heavy Self-Propelled Artillery Regiment	6 ISU–122s	3 ISU–122s	9 ISU–122s
Total	155 armoured fighting vehicles	55 armoured fighting vehicles	210 armoured fighting vehicles

---

2196 The total armoured fighting vehicle losses of the 3rd Ukrainian Front from 16 March to 2 April 1945 are detailed in the Appendix in two tables.
2197 Central Archives of the Russian Defence Ministry (Podolsk), f. 3415, op. 1, gy. 77, li. 139/2.
2198 Central Archives of the Russian Defence Ministry (Podolsk), f. 339, op. 5179, gy. 87, li. 66.

Based on the above data, the 6th Guards Tank Army had lost almost three quarters of its armoured fighting vehicles on Hungarian territory during the Vienna Offensive.

The forces of the 2nd Ukrainian Front, the 46th Army, the 2nd Guards Mechanized Corps and the 23rd Tank Corps, attacking south of the Danube lost 90 tanks and self-propelled guns irrecoverably during the Vienna Offensive on Hungarian territory.[2199]

On 5 March 1945, the combat forces of the 3rd Ukrainian Front had 407 armoured fighting vehicles. If this number is added to the armoured replenishment they received during the month of 590 armoured fighting vehicles, and the 425 tanks and self-propelled guns of the freshly arrived 6th Guards Tank Army, plus the 75 self-propelled guns of the 9th Guards Army, and the ranks of the makeshift 22nd Independent Tank Regiment, we will see that during March, 1516 armoured fighting vehicles were available for the forces of the Front. From this, we have to deduct the 83 armoured fighting vehicles of the 23rd Tank Corps that were handed over to the 2nd Ukrainian Front, and the eight remaining armoured fighting vehicles of the 22nd Independent Tank Regiment, returned to the ranks of the 22nd Training Tank Regiment. The remaining 1425 armoured fighting vehicles are to be compared to the 836 tanks and self-propelled guns that were operational and under minor repair in the ranks of the Ukrainian Front on 31 March. The difference amounts to 589 armoured fighting vehicles and this is the number that is missing permanently from the ranks.

Based on the daily reports of the commanders of the tank and mechanized units within the 3rd Ukrainian Front, there is evidence and data for 500 destroyed armoured fighting vehicles for the month of March 1945. Where can the cause for the difference of 89 armoured fighting vehicles be found? Based on the author's opinion, this was the number of the tanks and self-propelled guns in for extensive repairs on 31 March 1945. Some of the armoured fighting vehicles on major repair were soon deemed irrecoverable, but the actual number is not able to be found in the available data anymore.

During the Hungarian phase of the Vienna Offensive, based on the Soviet daily combat loss reports, the 2nd and 3rd Ukrainian Front lost 436 Soviet armoured fighting vehicles in the Transdanubia. At the end of Operation *"Frühlingserwachen"*, the 3rd Ukrainian Front had 154 lost tanks and self-propelled guns. With this number, the Soviet troops occupied the Transdanubia at a cost of 590 armoured fighting vehicles, not counting the 1215 Soviet tanks and self-propelled guns that were destroyed in the region between November 1944 – February 1945.

Performance of the air force units against the armoured fighting vehicles in the Transdanubia in March 1945

The Soviet pilots claimed the largest number of victories against armoured fighting vehicles during daytime ground attack aircraft and bomber missions. The troops of the Soviet 17th Air Army, based on the war log entries of the 3rd Ukrainian Front, reported between 6 – 15 March 1945 to have destroyed 178 tanks and assault guns, plus 54

[2199] The Appendix contains the detailed data of the total armoured fighting vehicle losses of the forces of the 2nd Ukrainian Front in combat south of the Danube.

armoured personnel carriers, and between 16 – 31 March, another 174 tanks and assault guns, plus 53 armoured personnel carriers.

The Soviet high command themselves did not even believe this number as there were 88 armoured fighting vehicles and 43 armoured personnel carriers confirmed to be destroyed or damaged by the Soviet air units in support of the 3rd Ukrainian Front between 6 – 15 March, according to the combat action reports and machine gun cameras.[2200] A large number of over claimed kills is still suspected, because the Soviets themselves later found much less armoured fighting vehicle wreckage on the ground that were proved to be destroyed by aircraft. In case these confirmed kills do not only contain the destroyed but the damaged armoured fighting vehicles as well, that is, also those that suffered still repairable damages, then this amount, according to the author, might be closer to the actual truth.

It is unknown where the Soviets classified their armoured fighting vehicles knocked out by their own aircraft. Because, as it was previously mentioned, there were at least two cases when it was confirmed that the Soviet pilots had attacked their own armoured and mechanized troops, on 14 March 1945 at Seregélyes the 170th Tank Brigade was raided, and on 20 March at Bodajk, the 31st Guards Mechanized Brigade was assaulted.

Of the 66 German and Hungarian armoured fighting vehicles destroyed from the air as confirmed by the committee of the 17th Air Army, 26 were destroyed by fragmentation bombs, 23 by high explosive anti-tank shells, nine by the 23 mm or 37 mm rounds from the on board automatic cannons, and eight by unguided rockets.[2201]

However, even the very detailed committee report, supplemented with photographs, has a few flaws as a source.

The first is that in the areas affected by the battles, a number of offensives and attacks were executed in rapid succession, and because the committee conducted its investigation somewhat later, the losses of the different offensives are sometimes completely impossible to tell apart.

The second problem is the number of German armoured fighting vehicles clearly destroyed by Soviet land weapons as if they would have been destroyed by Soviet aircraft as well. A Tiger B heavy tank of *schwere Panzer-Abteilung 503* is a good example for the latter, which burnt out in December 1944 in Polgárdi due to a hit from a Soviet anti-tank gun. The committee investigated the case (case number 196) and they found damage inflicted by a PTAB high explosive anti-tank shell.[2202]

At the same time, the report contains German armoured fighting vehicles that were clearly not destroyed by Soviet units. One of the Jagdpanzer IV *Jagdpanzers* of the German *23. Panzer-Division* is a clear example, which the committee identified three km north-east of Simontornya (case number 48).[2203] This armoured fighting vehicle was knocked out by

---

2200 Central Archives of the Russian Defence Ministry (Podolsk), f. 243, op. 2900, gy. 2047, li. 123.
2201 Archer, Lee–Nevenkin, Kamen: *Panzerwrecks Nr. 20. Ostfront 3*. Sussex. 2016. p. 5. Detailed data are contained in the Appendix. *SS-Hauptsturmführer* Hans Siegel, the officer commanding the combat-ready armoured fighting vehicles of *SS-Panzer-Regiment 12* responded to the questionnaire of the author in writing, and stated in 1998 that he himself observed few Soviet ground attack aircraft raids during their combat actions in Hungary; and these were only bombing raids.
2202 Archer, Lee–Nevenkin, Kamen: *Panzerwrecks Nr. 20. Ostfront 3*. Sussex. 2016. p. 57.
2203 Archer, Lee–Nevenkin, Kamen: *Panzerwrecks Nr. 20. Ostfront 3*. Sussex. 2016. p. 26.

the forces of the *SS-Panzer-Division* by mistake. [2204]. The combat damage on this vehicle by Soviet weapons was inflicted "post mortem". The same is the case with one of the Panther tanks of *23. Panzer-Division*, turret number 524, which was investigated near Várpalota with case number 85.[2205] This tank, in need of repair, was used as a dug-in fortification on 21 March at Várpalota, but the ever changing combat situation forced them to abandon the vehicle and blow it up.

According to the above, it can not be fully excluded that the Soviet aircraft also attacked armoured fighting vehicles that were abandoned or blown up by the German forces, and they also attacked those armoured fighting vehicles that were earlier knocked out by the land forces already. Here the pilots did not need to be aware of the German unit anti-aircraft defences, and they were able to fly their "death rounds", releasing their high explosive anti-tank shells. However, it should also be considered that many hundreds of meters above the ground, traveling at a few hundred km/h, it is very difficult to discern the still active armoured fighting vehicles from the already disabled ones. When the investigation committees came, these armoured fighting vehicles looked just like any other armoured fighting vehicle knocked out from the air (without the dead crew inside). The over claims during Operation *"Frühlingserwachen"* however, cannot be explained by just one such practice.

According to their own data, the Soviet 17th Air Army had irrecoverably lost 44 aircraft between 6 and 15 March 1945:

- four Il–2 ground attack, four Yak–9 fighter and three B–3 bombers were shot down by German or Hungarian fighter aircraft;
- eight Il–2 ground attack, one La–5 fighter and four B–3 bombers were shot down by German or Hungarian anti-aircraft artillery;
- 14 Il–2 ground attack, four Yak–9 and two La–5 fighter aircraft had not returned from a mission from causes unknown.[2206]

During the course of the Vienna Offensive, between 16 March – 13 April 1945, the 17th Air Army reported a further 140 total aircraft losses during combat:

- 28 Il–2 ground attack, nine La–5 and two Yak–9 fighter ,plus five B–3 bombers were shot down by German or Hungarian fighter aircraft;
- 60 Il–2 ground attack, 10 La–5 and eight Yak–9 fighter, plus four B–3 bombers were shot down by German or Hungarian anti-aircraft artillery;
- four Il–2 ground attack, five Yak–9 and three La–5 fighter, plus two Pe–2 bombers had not returned from a mission from causes unknown.[2207]

[2204] Between 6 – 20 March 1945, *23. Panzer-Division* lost as irrecoverable only three Jagdpanzer IVs, and all three were destroyed by "friendly fire" in the sector of Zichyángyád, which is farther from the location given by the Soviet committee, however still in the vicinity of Simontornya. On the other hand, no other unit had this type of armoured fighting vehicle in their strength in the Simontornya.

[2205] See Archer, Lee–Nevenkin, Kamen: *Panzerwrecks Nr. 20. Ostfront 3*. Sussex. 2016. p. 39. In this publication, the tank is, in the author's opinion, mistakenly identified by the authors as an armoured fighting vehicle of *5. SS-Panzer-Division*.

[2206] Central Archives of the Russian Defence Ministry (Podolsk), f. 236, op. 2673, gy. 338, li. 99.

[2207] Central Archives of the Russian Defence Ministry (Podolsk), f. 236, op. 2673, gy. 338, li. 103.

During the course of the Vienna Offensive the Soviet 5th and 17th Air Armies lost 614 aircraft.[2208]

The Soviets also tried to harass the German–Hungarian troops with night bombing raids to prevent them being able to rest at night or to regroup. These aircrafts were obsolete, usually biplanes and the bomb release was effected manually, throwing 2 kg fragmentation grenades, mortar grenades, pressure-plate mines with impact fuses, but it was not infrequent either to throw down railroad rail parts. Georg Jestadt, who served in *Nachrichten-Abteilung/12. SS-Panzer-Division,* also experienced at the end of February 1945, near Tatabánya, T-34 rollers being thrown down at them from planes mocked as "sewing machines".[2209]

Luftflotte 4. reported 38 direct hits on armoured fighting vehicles by aircraft in March 1945, in the following order:

- On 13 March one in 280 missions,
- On 17 March two in 180 missions,
- On 19 March 11 in 270 missions,
- On 20 March one in 300 missions,
- On 21 March six in 270 missions,
- On 24 March four in 140 missions,
- On 25 March five in 120 missions,
- On 28 March one in 100 missions,
- On 29 March seven in 120 missions.

The largest reported number coincides with the deployment of the 6th Guards Tank Army. The German and Hungarian air units, battling with crippling fuel shortages, were probably concentrating their scarce supplies on deploying fighter aircraft, to be able to defend their own troops against the constantly attacking Soviet ground attack aircraft.

One of the most peculiar missions of the German tank destroyer aircraft was executed on 9 April 1945 near Vienna, when the Hs 129 tank destroyer aircraft of *10.Staffel/ Schlachtgeschwader 9* with fighter cover, were deployed on a mission to destroy the immense fuel storage tanks near the city to prevent these falling into the hands of the enemy. A few storage tanks were successfully set on fire, while a heavy dogfight was going on over the territory with American and Soviet fighter aircraft. According to some opinions, the fuel supply storage tanks around Vienna were not opened earlier for *Heeresgruppe Süd* battling catastrophic fuel shortages because of sabotage by a member of the Austrian resistance, *Major* Carl Szokoll, *Quartiermeister* of *Wehrkreis XVII*.[2210]

2208   Hooton, E. R.: War over the Steppes. The Air Campaigns on the Eastern Front 1941–45. New York, 2016. p. 232. The German *Luftflotte 4.* had, by 9 April 1945, 430 of their 850 aircraft of which 60 were Hungarian. The cause of the significant decrease, in the author's opinion, is not only due to combat losses and air accidents, but the reassignment of different units to other frontline sections, and also the ground losses due to shortage of fuel caused by low-altitude enemy air raids and destruction by their own forces.
2209   Jestadt, Georg: *Ohne Siege und Hurra. Erlebnisse eines jungen Soldaten 1939–1945.* Norderstedt, 2005. pp. 389-390.
2210   See erre Georg, Friedrich: *Verrat an der Ostfront. Vergebliche Verteidigung Europas 1943–45.* Tübingen, 2014. p. 235.

TABLES

Table 1.: Armoured fighting vehicle strength of the German 2. Panzerarmee on 5 March 1945[1]

Unit	StuG. III	StuH. 42	Jagdpanzer 38(t)	Total
16. SS-Panzergrenadier-Division	33/15			33/15
Sturmartillerie-Brigade 261	21/20	9/9		30/29
1222. Panzerjäger-Kompanie			7/7	7/7
Sturmartillerie-Brigade 191	13/10	2/2		15/12
118. Jäger-Division	8/7			8/7
Total	75/52	11/11	7/7	93/70

Source: BAMA RH 2 Ost 5455.

---

[1] The table does not contain the assault guns of Italian origin.

Table 2.: Armoured fighting vehicle strength of the German 6. *Panzerarmee* on 5 March 1945[1]

Unit	Pz. II and Pz. III	Pz. IV	Panther	Tiger	StuG. III	StuH. 42	Pz. IV/70	Jg.Pz. IV	Jg.Pz. 38(t)	Jagdpanther	Artillery observer tank	Anti-aircraft armoured fighting vehicle	Total
1. SS-Panzer-Division		30/21	28/25		3/2		20/17				4/1	3/0	88/66
schwere SS-Panzer-Abteilung 501				33/9 B								8/7	41/16
12. SS-Panzer-Division		30/12	30/9				31/13				4/3	8/5	103/42
schwere Panzerjäger-Abteilung 560							22/6			16/8		8/8	46/22
2. SS-Panzer-Division		28/19	29/12		29/23		21/16			10/9		8/2	125/81
9. SS-Panzer-Division		23/19	40/24		26/14		24/18			10/10	4/3	4/4	131/92
44. Reichsgrenadier-Division								11/6	10/5				22/17
3. Kavallerie-Division					7/7	4/4							10/5
4. Kavallerie-Division	5/4[2]				12/8			4/2					21/14
20th Assault Artillery Battalion (Hun)									36/22				36/22
23. Panzer-Division	2/2	18/16	38/16		9/6		7/4	15/12					89/56
Total	7/6	129/87	165/86	33/9	86/60	4/4	125/74	30/20	46/27	36/27	12/7	39/26	712/433

Explanation: numerator shows the number of available armoured fighting vehicles, and denominator shows the combat-ready armoured fighting vehicles thereof.
Source: Material of BAMA RH 2 Ost 5455 and RH 10.

1   The table does not contain the *Marder* tank destroyers and prime mover armoured fighting vehicles.
2   Panzer II and Luchs light tanks.

Table 3.: Armoured fighting vehicle strength of the German-Hungarian *Armeegruppe Balck* on 5 March 1945[1]

Unit	Pz. III	Pz. IV	Panther	Tiger	StuG. III	StuH. 42	Pz. IV/70	Jg.Pz. IV	Jg.Pz. 38(t)	Nashorn	Artillery observer tank	Anti-aircraft armoured fighting vehicle	Sturmpz. IV	Total
3. Panzer-Division	21/7[2]	14/9	29/22		7/4		11/5	10/7			4/1			96/55
1. Panzer-Division	1/0	15/8	59/24		2/0					4/1				81/33
Sturmpanzer-Abteilung 219													20/9	20/9
Flammpanzer-Kompanie 351	11/8													11/8
356. Infanteriedivision									14/12					14/12
schwere Panzer-Abteilung 509				35/26 B								8/6		43/32
I. (Abteilung)/Panzer-Regiment 24			38/36											38/36
5. SS- Panzer-Division	2/1	4/3	18/9		5/1 (IV)			10/6						39/20
3. SS- Panzer-Division	1/0	19/17	16/9	9/7 E	17/12			7/5						69/50
Hungarian 2nd Armoured Division		24/18	2/0											26/18
6. Panzer-Division		22/16	68/32					18/14			4/1	5/3		117/66
96. Infanteriedivision					9/7									9/7
711. Infanteriedivision									13/12					13/12
Sturmartillerie-Brigade 239					14/11	13/11								27/22
Sturmartillerie-Brigade 303					15/13	5/3								20/16
Total	**36/16**	**98/71**	**230/132**	**44/33**	**69/48**	**18/14**	**11/5**	**45/32**	**27/24**	**4/1**	**8/2**	**13/9**	**20/9**	**623/396**

Explanation: numerator shows the number of available armoured fighting vehicles, and denominator shows the combat-ready armoured fighting vehicles thereof. The grey lines contain data of the units deployed in the Operation "*Frühlingserwachen*".
Source: Material of BAMA RH 2 Ost 5455 and RH 10.

1 The table does not contain the Panzer II light tanks, the *Marder* tank destroyers and prime mover armoured fighting vehicles.
2 Aufklärer auf Fahrgestell Panzer 38(t) reconnaissance armoured fighting vehicles.

Table 4: Irrecoverable armoured fighting vehicle losses of the 3rd Ukrainian Front in January 1945

Unit	Available armoured strength on 1 January 1945 Tank	Self-propelled gun	Total	Replenishment in January 1945 Tank	Self-propelled gun	Total	Available and replenishment total Tank	Self-propelled gun	Total	Available armoured fighting vehicle strength on 1 February 1945 Tank	Self-propelled gun	Total	Difference (total losses) Tank	Self-propelled gun	Total
18th Tank Corps	134 T-34s	37 T-34s and ISU-122s	171	119 T-34s	38 SU-76Ms, 1 SU-85s, 21 ISU-122s, 18 ISU-152s	197	253	115	368	68 T-34s	18 SU-76Ms, 6 SU-85s, 18 ISU-122s, 5 ISU-152s	115	185	68	253
7th Mechanized Corps	23 IS-2s, 75 T-34s	29 SU-76Ms and SU-85s	127	10 M3 Lees, 10 M3 Stuarts	10 SU-76Ms	30	118	39	157	7 T-34s, 3 M3 Stuarts	8 SU-76Ms, 1 SU-85	19	108	30	138
2nd Guards Mechanized Corps	9 IS-2, 45 T-34	13 SU-85s	67	45 T-34	20 SU-76Ms	65	99	33	132	64 T-34s	20 SU-76Ms, 15 SU-85s	35	–	35	35
5th Guards Cavalry Corps	27 T-34s, 14 foreign	8 SU-76Ms	49	5 T-34s, 10 M3 Lees, 7 M3 Stuarts	11 SU-76Ms	33	63	19	82	7 T-34s, 18 foreign	11 SU-76Ms	36	38	8	46
1st Guards Mechanized Corps	189 M4A2s	63 SU-100s	252	–	–	–	189	63	252	78 M4A2s	28 SU-100s	106	111	35	146
23rd Tank Corps	153 T-34s	21 ISU-122s	174	–	21	21	153	21	174	72 T-34s	20 ISU-122s	92	81	1	82
32nd Guards Mechanized Brigade	21 T-34s	–	21	9 T-34s	–	9	30	–	30	26 T-34s	–	26	4	–	4
249th Tank Regiment	16 T-34s	–	16	–	–	–	16	–	16	14 T-34s	–	14	2	–	2
3rd Guards Motorcycle Regiment	6 T-34s	–	6	–	–	–	6	–	6	5 T-34s	–	5	1	–	1
366th Guards Heavy Self-Propelled Artillery Regiment	–	19 ISU-122s and ISU-152s	19	2 IS-2s	2	2	2 IS-2s	19	21	2 IS-2s	1 ISU-122s, 6 ISU-152s	9	–	12	12
991st Self-Propelled Artillery Regiment	–	2 SU-76Ms	2	–	20 SU-76Ms	20	–	22	22	–	20 SU-76Ms	20	–	2	2
1201st Self-Propelled Artillery Regiment	12 T-34s	–	12	9 T-34s	–	9	21	–	21	17 T-34s	–	17	4	–	4
1202nd Self-Propelled Artillery Regiment	–	–	–	–	40 SU-76Ms	40	–	40	40	–	17 SU-76Ms	17	–	23	23
1505th Self-Propelled Artillery Regiment	–	17 SU-76Ms	17	–	–	–	–	17	17	–	16 SU-76Ms	16	–	1	1
1891st Self-Propelled Artillery Regiment	–	6 SU-76Ms	6	–	20 SU-76Ms	20	–	26	26	–	12 SU-76Ms	12	–	14	14
1. Total armoured self-propelled artillery battalions of the 4th Guards Army	7 T-70s	79 SU-76Ms	86	–	–	–	7	79	86	6 T-70s	39 SU-76Ms	45	1	40	41
Total armoured fighting vehicle losses of the 3rd Ukrainian Front in January 1945													570	234	804

Table 5.: Artillery of the 3rd Ukrainian Front on 6 March 1945[1]

Artillery pieces	4th Guards Army	26th Army	27th Army	57th Army	Front HQ units	Total
82 mm mortar	409	285	280	451	192	1617
107 mm mortar	–	–	24	–	–	24
120 mm mortar	229	226	117	191	120	883
160 mm mortar	–	–	–	–	32	32
Mortars total	**638**	**511**	**421**	**642**	**344**	**2556**
45 mm anti-tank gun M1937, M1942	143	93	143	102	35	516
57 mm anti-tank gun ZiS-2	63	34	–	–	32	129
76 mm regimental gun M1927, M1943	48	44	46	65	29	232
76 mm divisional gun M1936, M1939, ZiS-3	308	305	225	205	134	1177
7,5 cm PaK 40 captured anti-tank gun	–	16	–	–	–	16
8,8 cm PaK 43 captured anti-tank gun	5	–	–	–	–	5
10,5 cm lFH 18 captured field howitzer	–	3	–	–	–	3
122 mm howitzer M1910/30, M-30	172	144	94	87	101	598
122 mm gun A-19	–	36	12	–	–	48
152 mm gun-howitzer ML-20	109	41	24	42	32	248
204 mm howitzer B-4	4	4	–	–	22	30
Guns total	**852**	**720**	**544**	**501**	**385**	**3002**
37 mm anti-aircraft automatic cannon M1939	91	112	16	55	240	514
85 mm anti-aircraft gun M1939	48	22	–	–	28	98
Anti-aircraft guns total	**139**	**134**	**16**	**55**	**268**	**612**
Multiple rocket launchers BM-8, BM-13, BM-31-12	60	88	22	24	99	293
Artillery pieces total	**1689**	**1453**	**1003**	**1222**	**1096**	**6463**

Source: Central Archives of the Russian Defence Ministry (Podolsk), f. 243, op. 2900, gy. 2047, lt. 51-53., also Isaev, Aleksei–Kolomiets, Maksim: *Tomb of the Panzerwaffe. The Defeat of the 6th SS Panzer Army in Hungary 1945.* Solihull, 2014. p. 131.

1 Without the armament of the subordinated Bulgarian 1st Army and the Yugoslavian troops.

Table 6: Total armoured fighting vehicle losses of the 3rd Ukrainian Front in February 1945

Unit	T–34 and T–34/85	IS–2	M4A2	ISU–122	SU–100	SU–85	SU–76M	Total
23rd Tank Corps	40	–	–	9	–	–	–	49
18th Tank Corps	18	–	–	2	–	–	2	22
1st Guards Mechanized Corps	–	–	36	–	6	–	–	42
7th Mechanized Corps	1	–	–	–	–	2	–	3
2nd Guards Mechanized Corps	–	1	–	–	–	2	–	3
5th Guards Cavalry Corps	10	–	–	–	–	–	–	10
32nd Independent Guards Mechanized Brigade	5	–	–	–	–	–	–	5
991st Self-Propelled Artillery Regiment	–	–	–	–	–	–	4	4
1891st Self-Propelled Artillery Regiment	–	–	–	–	–	–	5	5
self-propelled artillery battalions of the 4th Guards Army	–	–	–	–	–	–	20	20
Total	74	1	36	11	6	4	31	163

Source: Central Archives of the Russian Defence Ministry (Podolsk), f. 243, op. 2900, gy. 1979, li. 69.

Table 7: Tank and mechanized units of the 3rd Ukrainian Front on the evening of 5 March 1945

Unit	T-34 T-34/85	IS-2	M4A2	T-70	Other	SU-76	SU-100	ISU-122	ISU-152	Total
18th Tank Corps	42				12			16	5/1	75/1
208th Self-Propelled Artillery Brigade	2				3	63				68
1st Guards Mechanized Corps	3		47/1				15/2			65/3
23rd Tank Corps	20/1	1						7/1		28/2
366th Guards Heavy Self-Propelled Artillery Regiment		3							4	7
71st Tank Regiment	7									7
54th Tank Regiment					1					1
60th Tank Regiment					2					2
1896th Self-Propelled Artillery Regiment						8				8
5th Guards Cavalry Corps total	7				3	8				18
Front HQ units total	*74/1*	*4*	*47/1*	*0*	*3*	*23*	*78/2*	*23/1*	*9/1*	*261/6*
1891st Self-Propelled Artillery Regiment						2				2
independent self-propelled artillery battalions						26				26
4th Guards Army total	*0*	*0*	*0*	*0*	*0*	*28*	*0*	*0*	*0*	*28*
432nd Independent Self-Propelled Artillery Battalion				1		7				8
27th Army total	*0*	*0*	*0*	*1*	*0*	*7*	*0*	*0*	*0*	*8*
1202nd Self-Propelled Artillery Regiment						14				14
72nd Independent Self-Propelled Artillery Battalion						2				2
26th Army total	*0*	*0*	*0*	*0*	*0*	*16*	*0*	*0*	*0*	*16*
32nd Guards Mechanized Brigade	19/2									19/2
249th Tank Regiment	10/1									10/1
1201st Self-Propelled Artillery Regiment	14									14
864th Self-Propelled Artillery Regiment	1					21				22
3rd Guards Motorcycle Regiment	10									10
53rd Motorcycle Regiment	10									10
57th Army total	*64/3*	*0*	*0*	*0*	*0*	*21*	*0*	*0*	*0*	*85/3*
All total	**138/4**	**4**	**47/1**	**1**	**3**	**95**	**78/2**	**23/1**	**9/1**	**398/9**

Explanation: numerator shows the number of operational armoured fighting vehicles, and denominator shows the armoured fighting vehicles under repair.
Source: Central Archives of the Russian Defence Ministry (Podolsk), f. 243, op. 2928, gy. 131, li. 289.

Table 8.: Armoured fighting vehicle strength of the German 6. *Panzerarmee* on 15 March 1945

Unit	Pz. III	Pz. IV	Panther	Tiger	StuG. III	StuH. 42	Pz. IV/70	Jg.Pz. IV	Jg.Pz. 38(t)	Jagd-panther	Artillery observer tank	Anti-aircraft armoured fighting vehicle	Total
1. SS-Panzer-Division	2/0[1]	29/14	32/18		3/0		20/2				4/1	6/3	96/38
schwere SS-Panzer-Abteilung 501				32/8 (B)								8/1	40/9
12. SS-Panzer-Division		23/10	24/9				30/10			4/2	4/2	8/2	89/33
schwere Panzerjäger-Abteilung 560							20/5			13/7		8/4	41/16
2. SS-Panzer-Division	2/1[2]	22/14	27/17		26/7		18/7			10/10	3/2	8/4	116/62
9. SS-Panzer-Division		18/10	35/12		25/11		22/10			10/6	4/2	5/3	119/54
44. Reichsgrenadier-Division								8/2	10/5 + 10/5[3]				20/10
3. Kavallerie-Division					7/4[4]	4/0							19/6
4. Kavallerie-Division	5/3[5] 4/0[6]				12/2			3/0					24/5
Hungarian 20th Assault Artillery Battalion													no data available
23. Panzer-Division	3/2[7]	15/5	33/7		9/7	1/0	8/0	12/7	1/1[8]		5/4	1/0	88/33
Total	**16/6**	**107/53**	**151/63**	**32/8**	**82/31**	**5/0**	**118/34**	**23/9**	**21/11**	**33/23**	**20/11**	**44/17**	**652/266**

Explanation: numerator shows the number of available armoured fighting vehicles, and denominator shows the combat-ready armoured fighting vehicles thereof.
Source: NARA T-78, Roll 624, F000502-000528.

1. Two Panzer 38(t) light tanks under repair.
2. Commander Panzer III tanks.
3. Marder III tank destroyers.
4. Of this, one was a StuG. IV, which was under 4/0 repair.
5. Luchs light reconnaissance tanks.
6. Panzer II light tanks.
7. Of the two commander Panzer III tanks one was combat-ready, and one further commander Panzer IV tank was combat-ready.
8. Marder III tank destroyer.

Table 9.: Armoured fighting vehicle strength of the 6. *Panzerarmee* on 15 March 1945

Unit	Tanks Combat-ready	Tanks Repairable within 14 days	Tanks Repairable in more than 14 days	Tanks Total loss (06–15 March)	Assault guns and Jagdpanzers Combat-ready	Assault guns and Jagdpanzers Repairable within 14 days	Assault guns and Jagdpanzers Repairable in more than 14 days	Assault guns and Jagdpanzers Total loss (06–15 March)	Armoured personnel carriers and armoured cars Combat-ready	Armoured personnel carriers and armoured cars Repairable within 14 days	Armoured personnel carriers and armoured cars Repairable in more than 14 days	Armoured personnel carriers and armoured cars Total loss (06–15 March)
12. SS-Panzer-Division	16	25	13	5	28	21	20	2	96	54	44	–
1. SS-Panzer-Division	34	33	19	12	12	10	–	1	152	17	29	–
9. SS-Panzer-Division	25	31	–	4	29	28	–	–	141	41	38	–
2. SS-Panzer-Division	14	37	–	4	18	38	–	5	126	97	–	–
23. Panzer-Division	10	20	24	5	6	12	11	3	70	14	14	1
44. Reichsgrenadier-Division	–	–	–	–	4	6	–	–	–	–	–	–
3. Kavallerie-Division	–	–	–	–	4	18	–	–	1	7	–	–
4. Kavallerie-Division	–	4	–	–	4	12	–	–	8	4	–	–
Total	99	150	56	30	105	145	31	11	594	234	125	1

Source: NARA, T311, R163, F7214982.
Total: 1581 tanks, assault guns, *Jagdpanzers*, armoured personnel carriers and armoured cars.
Of these, combat-ready: 798 tanks, assault guns, *Jagdpanzers*, armoured personnel carriers and armoured cars.
Total armoured loss ratio at the *I*. and *II*. SS-*Panzerkorps*
12. SS-Panzer-Division: Of 59 tanks, 5 (8.5%) were destroyed, furthermore, of 71 *Jagdpanzers*, 2 (2.8%) were destroyed.
1. SS-Panzer-Division: Of 98 tanks, 12 (12.2%) were destroyed, furthermore, of 23 *Jagdpanzers* and assault guns, 1 (4.3%) was destroyed.
9. SS-Panzer-Division: Of 60 tanks, 4 (6.6%) were destroyed, furthermore, of 57 *Jagdpanzers* and assault guns, 0 (0%) was destroyed.
2. SS-Panzer-Division: Of 55 tanks, 4 (7.3%) were destroyed, furthermore, of 61 *Jagdpanzers* and assault guns, 5 (8.2%) were destroyed.
Average total loss ratio: of 272 tanks, 25 (9.2%) were destroyed, furthermore, of 212 *Jagdpanzers* and assault guns, 8 (3.8%) were destroyed.
Summarized total loss ratio at the four SS-*Panzer-Divisionen*: of 484 tanks, 33 (6.8%) were destroyed.

Table 10.: Armoured fighting vehicle strength of the German-Hungarian *Armeegruppe Balck* on 15 March 1945

Unit	Pz. III	Pz. IV	Panther	Tiger	StuG. III	StuH. 42	Pz. IV/70	Jg.Pz. IV	Jg.Pz. 38(t)	Nashorn	Artillery observer tank	Anti-aircraft armoured fighting vehicle	Sturmpz. IV	Total
3. Panzer-Division	21/12[1]	14/4	39/13		6/1	1/1	11/2	8/2			4/2			104/37
1. Panzer-Division	2/2[2]	4/1	59/10		2/1			14/9[3]	1/0[4]	4/0	11/6			97/29
Sturmpanzer-Abteilung 219													20/5	20/5
Flammpanzer-Kompanie 351	no data available													no data available
356. Infanteriedivision									14/10					14/10
schwere Panzer-Abteilung 509				35/8 (B)								8/2		43/10
I. (Abteilung)/Panzer-Regiment 24		4/3	32/3											32/3
5. SS- Panzer-Division		18/12	18/12		5/4[5]			10/6			3/3			40/28
3. SS- Panzer-Division		17/16	17/8	9/7 (E)	17/13			7/5	4/3[6]		3/2			74/54
6. Panzer-Division		24/16	68/19		9/7[9]		18/13				4/2	5/3		117/41
Hungarian 2nd Armoured Division	2/1[7]	20/3	2/0						8/7[10]					26/16
96. Panzer-Division									13/13					13/13
71. Infanteriedivision					15/14	12/12			4/3[12]					35/32
Sturmartillerie-Brigade 239	4/3[11]				15/4	5/3								20/7
Sturmartillerie-Brigade 303									19/15					19/15
Total	**31/19**	**83/43**	**235/65**	**44/15**	**69/44**	**18/16**	**11/2**	**57/35**	**44/36**	**4/0**	**25/15**	**13/5**	**20/5**	**654/300**

Explanation: numerator shows the number of available armoured fighting vehicles, and denominator shows the combat-ready armoured fighting vehicles thereof. The grey lines contain data of the units deployed in Operation "*Frühlingserwachen*".
Source: NARA T-78, Roll 624, F000502-000527.

1 Aufklärer auf Fahrgestell Panzer 38(t) reconnaissance armoured fighting vehicles.
2 One commander Panzer III and one commander Panzer IV tank.
3 Of the 12 Marder II tank destroyers, nine were in combat-ready condition, and a further two Marder IIIs were under repair.
4 Panzer 38(t) light tank under repair.
5 StuG. IV assault guns.
6 Two Marder IIIs and one Marder II were in combat-ready condition, one further Marder II was under repair.
7 Commander Panzer IV tanks.
8 Panzer II light tanks.
9 StuG. IV assault guns.
10 Marder III tank destroyers.
11 Panzer II light tanks.
12 Most probably the Jagdpanzer 38(t) Jagdpanzers taken over from the 2. Kompanie/SS-Panzerjäger-Abteilung 8

403

Table 11.: Armoured fighting vehicle strength of the German 2. *Panzerarmee* on 15 March 1945

Unit	StuG. III	StuH. 42	Jagdpanzer 38(t)	Italian assault gun with 47 mm gun	Total
16. SS-Panzergrenadier-Division	35/28				35/28
Sturmartillerie-Brigade 261	18/15	9/7			27/22
1222. Panzerjäger-Kompanie			no data available		no data available
Sturmartillerie-Brigade 191	11/7	2/2			13/9
118. Jäger-Division	8/7				8/7
Panzerjäger-Kompanie/LXVIII. Armeekorps				3/3	3/3
Total	72/57	11/9	no data available	3/3	86/69

Source: NARA T-78, Roll 624, F000514-000515.

Table 12.: Field artillery and infantry self-propelled gun strength of the *Heeresgruppe Süd* on 15 March 1945

Unit	10.5 cm Wespe (on Pz. II chassis)	15 cm Hummel (on Pz. IV chassis)	15 cm Grille (on Pz. 38[t] chassis)	Total
1. SS-Panzer-Division	1/0	12/10	5/3	18/13
2. SS-Panzer-Division	–	6/3	2/0[1]	8/3
9. SS-Panzer-Division	3/3	8/5	–	11/8
12. SS-Panzer-Division	2/2	–	5/3	7/5
23. Panzer-Division	13/9	6/3	5/5	24/17
3. Panzer-Division	9/7	5/3	–	14/10
1. Panzer-Division	–	17/11	5/3	22/14
5. SS-Panzer-Division	11/11	4/4	5/2	20/17
3. SS-Panzer-Division	5/4	9/9	7/4	21/17
6. Panzer-Division	4/2	10/7	6/5	20/14
Total	**48/38**	**77/55**	**40/25**	**165/118**

Explanation: numerator shows the number of available armoured fighting vehicles, and denominator shows the combat-ready armoured fighting vehicles thereof.
Source: NARA T-78, Roll 624, F000502-000527.

1 In the period between 6 and 15 March 1945 the 2. *SS-Panzer-Division* has suffered the total loss of one infantry heavy self-propelled gun.

Table 13: Irrecoverable armoured fighting vehicle losses of the 3rd Ukrainian Front between 6 – 15 March

Unit	6 March	7 March	8 March	9 March	10 March	11 March	12 March	13 March	14 March	15 March	Total
1201st Self-Propelled Artillery Regiment	1 T-34	9 T-34s									10
72nd Independent Self-Propelled Artillery Battalion		2 SU-76s									2
864th Self-Propelled Artillery Regiment		1 SU-76	2 SU-76s		1 SU-76						5
18th Tank Corps		1 ISU-122	6 T-34s, 2 ISU-122s	2 T-34s	3 T-34s, 1 SU-76	5 T-34s	4 T-34s	12 T-34s	4 T-34s 5 SU-76s	1 T-34 3 SU-76s	49
208th Self-Propelled Artillery Brigade			2 SU-100s	6 SU-100s	7 SU-100s				1 SU-100		16
1202nd Self-Propelled Artillery Regiment			1 SU-76								1
209th Self-Propelled Artillery Brigade					4 SU-100s	4 SU-100s	3 SU-100s		3 SU-100s		14
1896th Self-Propelled Artillery Regiment					1 SU-76					2 SU-76s	3
1st Guards Mechanized Corps						2 M4A2s	3 M4A2s	4 M4A2s 1 SU-100	1 M4A2		11
23rd Tank Corps							2 M4A2s 19 SU-100s	4 T-34s 1 SU-100			6
207th Self-Propelled Artillery Brigade											20
71st Tank Regiment							3 T-34s		2 T-34s		5
22nd Independent Tank Regiment									5 T-34s 1 SU-85		6
1889th Self-Propelled Artillery Regiment								1 SU-76	1 SU-76	2 SU-76s	4
32nd Guards Mechanized Brigade										2 T-34s	2
Total	1	13	13	8	10	19	31	26	22	11	154

Source: Central Archives of the Russian Defence Ministry (Podolsk), f. 243, op. 2928, gy. 178, li. 66-85.

Table 14: Tank and mechanized units of the 3rd Ukrainian Front in the evening of 16 March 1945

Unit	T-34 T-34/85	IS-2	M4A2	T-70	Other	SU-76	SU-100	ISU-122	ISU-152	Total
18th Tank Corps	48/4					16	27/2	12	6	82/4
majority of 208th Self-Propelled Artillery Brigade	2		60/1			3	13/3			32/2
1st Guards Mechanized Corps	3							8		76/4
23rd Tank Corps	34/1	4					20/1			46/1
majority of 207th Self-Propelled Artillery Brigade	2				3 SU-57s					25/1
71st Tank Regiment	2									2
54th Tank Regiment					1					1
60th Tank Regiment						16/2				16/2
1896th Self-Propelled Artillery Regiment					2					20/2
5th Guards Cavalry Corps total										1
Front HQ units total	91/5	4	60/1	0	5	35/2	60/6	20	6	281/14
1513th Self-Propelled Artillery Regiment						24/1				24/1
1523rd Self-Propelled Artillery Regiment						25				25
1524th Self-Propelled Artillery Regiment						25				25
9th Guards Army total	0	0	0	0	0	74/1	0	0	0	74/1
366th Guards Heavy Self-Propelled Artillery Regiment					13/2 heavy self-propelled guns, 2 Panther tanks					15/2
1004th Self-Propelled Artillery Regiment /207th Self-Propelled Artillery Brigade						20	20/1			20/1
independent self-propelled artillery battalions	1			5		78				84
4th Guards Army total	1	0	0	5	15/2	78	20/1	0	0	119/3
1202nd Self-Propelled Artillery Regiment						20				20
1922nd Self-Propelled Artillery Regiment /208th Self-Propelled Artillery Brigade							16/1			16/1
independent self-propelled artillery battalions						22				22
27th Army total	0	0	0	0	0	42	16/1	0	0	58/1
209th Self-Propelled Artillery Brigade	2				2/1 SU-57s		46/2			50/3
22nd Tank Regiment	6/6				0/1 SU-85	2/1				8/8
26th Army total	8/6	0	0	0	2/2	2/1	46/2	0	0	58/11
32nd Guards Mechanized Brigade	8/1									8/1
249th Tank Regiment	13/1									13/1
1201st Self-Propelled Artillery Regiment	2					21				23
864th Self-Propelled Artillery Regiment	1					10/1				11/1
3rd Guards Motorcycle Regiment	10									10
1891st Self-Propelled Artillery Regiment						16				16
53rd Motorcycle Regiment	10									10
57th Army total	44/2	0	0	0	0	47/1	0	0	0	91/3
All total	144/13	4	60/1	5	22/4	278/5	142/10	20	6	681/33

Explanation: numerator shows the number of operational armoured fighting vehicles, and denominator shows the armoured fighting vehicles under repair.
Source: Central Archives of the Russian Defence Ministry (Podolsk), f. 243, op. 2928, gy. 131, li. 290–291.

Table 15.: Armoured fighting vehicle strength of the 2nd Ukrainian Front south of the Danube, on 17 March 1945[1]

Unit	T-34/85	IS-2	T-70	SU-76M	SU-85	ISU-122	ISU-152	Panther	StuG. III	Wespe	Total
2nd Guards Mechanized Corps	63			19	9	5					96
23rd Tank Corps[2]	56/9	2				6/5	2/3				66/17
991st Self-Propelled Artillery Regiment				18				0/3			18/3
1505th Self-Propelled Artillery Regiment				15/1					5	1	21/1
1897th Self-Propelled Artillery Regiment				21							21
112th Independent Self-Propelled Artillery Battalion			1	3			0/3				4
Total	119/9	2	1	76/1	9	11/5	2/3	0/3	5	1	226/21

Explanation: numerator shows the number of operational armoured fighting vehicles, and denominator shows the armoured fighting vehicles under repair.

---

1 **Source:** Central Archives of the Russian Defence Ministry (Podolsk), f. 240, op. 2799, gy. 357, li. 37.
2 The 23rd Tank Corps has been assigned to the strength of the 3rd Ukrainian Front only on 22 March 1945. The data of the armoured fighting vehicle strength show the status in the morning of 23 March 1945.

Table 15/a.: Armoured strength of the 2nd Ukrainian Front south of the Danube, on 25 March 1945[1]

Unit	T-34/85	IS-2	T-70	SU-76M	SU-85	ISU-122	ISU-152	Panther	StuG. III	Wespe	Total
2nd Guards Mechanized Corps	22/10			10/6	5/4	2/2					39/22
23rd Tank Corps	59/3	2				8/3	2/3				71/9
991st Self-Propelled Artillery Regiment				12/2				0/2			12/4
1505th Self-Propelled Artillery Regiment				7/4					0/5	0/1	7/10
1897th Self-Propelled Artillery Regiment				14/2							14/2
112th Independent Self-Propelled Artillery Battalion			1	4							5
Total	81/13	2	1	47/14	5/4	10/5	2/3	0/2	0/5	0/1	148/47

Explanation: numerator shows the number of operational armoured fighting vehicles, and denominator shows the armoured fighting vehicles under repair. Total loss between 17–25 March: in the 2nd Guards Mechanized Corps: 31 T-34/85s, three SU-76Ms, one ISU-122; in the 23rd Tank Corps: three T-34/85s; in the 991st Self-Propelled Artillery Regiment: four SU-76Ms, one Panther; in the 1505th Self-Propelled Artillery Regiment: five SU-76Ms; in the 1897th Self-Propelled Artillery Regiment: five SU-76Ms, in total 53 tanks and self-propelled guns.

Table 16.: Armoured strength of the German 2. *Panzerarmee* on 21 March 1945[1]

Unit	StuG. III	StuH. 42	Jagdpanzer 38(t)	Total
16. SS-Panzergrenadier-Division	28/13			28/13
Sturmartillerie-Brigade 261	17/12	9/6		26/18
1222. Panzerjäger-Kompanie			14/11	14/11
Sturmartillerie-Brigade 191	8/7	3/0		11/7
118. Jäger-Division[2]	8/5			8/5
Total	61/37	12/6	14/11	87/54

Source: BAMA RH 2 Ost 5491 and 5512.

1 The table does not contain the assault guns of Italian origin.
2 Data as of 25 March 1945.

Table 17.: Armoured fighting vehicle strength of the German 6. *Armee* on 21 March 1945[1]

Unit	Pz. III	Pz. IV	Panther	Tiger	StuG. III	StuH. 42	Pz. IV/70	Jg.Pz. IV	Jg.Pz. 38(t)	Nashorn	Artillery observer tank	Anti-aircraft armoured fighting vehicle	Sturmpz. IV	Total
3. Panzer-Division		8/0												8/0
1. Panzer-Division	1/1	15/3	?/22		?					4/?				min. 42/26
Sturmpanzer-Abteilung 219													20/3	20/3
Flammpanzer-Kompanie 351	11/9													11/9
schwere Panzer-Abteilung 509				35/5 B								8/2		43/7
1. (Abteilung)/Panzer-Regiment 24			32/22											32/22
Sturmartillerie-Brigade 303					15/6	5/3								20/9
23. Panzer-Division		16/10	34/10		11/4		8/0	12/8	10/4		3/1			84/33
44. Reichsgrenadier-Division					7/4	4/2			10/4					10/4
3. Kavallerie-Division								11/5						22/11
4. Kavallerie-Division					12/3			4/0						16/3
Total	12/10	39/13	min. 88/54	35/5	45/17	9/5	8/0	27/13	10/4	4/?	3/1	8/2	20/3	**min. 308/127**

Explanation: numerator shows the number of available armoured fighting vehicles, and denominator shows the combat-ready armoured fighting vehicles thereof.
Source: material of BAMA RH 2 Ost 5512 and RH 10.

---

[1] The table does not contain the Panzer II light tanks, the *Marder* tank destroyers and prime mover armoured fighting vehicles.

Table 18.: Armoured fighting vehicle strength of the German 6. *Panzerarmee* on 21 March 1945[1]

Unit	Pz. IV	Panther	Tiger	StuG. III	StuH. 42	Pz. IV/70	Jg.Pz. IV	Jg.Pz. 38(t)	Jagdpanther	Artillery observer tank	Anti-aircraft armoured fighting vehicle	Total
1. SS-Panzer-Division	18/11	19/10		3/1		22/11				1/1	4/3	67/37
schwere SS-Panzer-Abteilung 501			26/9								6/1	32/10
12. SS-Panzer-Division	18/9	20/6			2/2	18/7				4/3	6/4	68/31
schwere Panzerjäger-Abteilung 560						13/8			6/3		6/6	25/17
2. SS-Panzer-Division	24/10	17/11		23/2		19/6			10/7	4/0	8/4	105/40
9. SS-Panzer-Division	20/10	33/11		23/10		20/9			9/6	1/0	5/4	111/50
Sturmartillerie-Brigade 239				11/11								11/11
Sturmgeschütz-Brigade 325				14/14								14/14
356. Infanteriedivision								13/8				13/8
711. Infanteriedivision								?/9				min. 9/9
6. Panzer-Division	?/2	?/16					?/7					min. 25/25
3. SS-Panzer-Division	?/8	?/4	?/4	?/9								min. 25/25
5. SS-Panzer-Division	?/8	?/5		?/6								min. 19/19
Total	min. 98/58	min. 114/63	min. 30/13	min. 89/53	2/2	92/41	min. 7/7	min. 22/17	25/16	10/4	35/22	min. 524/296

Explanation: numerator shows the number of available armoured fighting vehicles, and denominator shows the combat-ready armoured fighting vehicles thereof.
Source: Material of BAMA RH 2 Ost 5512 and RH 10

1 The table does not contain the Panzer II light tanks, the *Marder* tank destroyers and prime mover armoured fighting vehicles. The Hungarian 2nd Armoured Division and the German 96. *Infanteriedivision* have not prepared a report.

Table 19.: Irrecoverable armoured fighting vehicles losses of the 3rd Ukrainian Front between 16 – 24 March

Unit	16 March	17 March	18 March	19 March	20 March	21 March	22 March	23 March	24 March	Total
864th Self-Propelled Artillery Regiment	2 SU-76s				1 SU-76			2 SU-76s		5
18th Tank Corps		4 T-34s		4 T-34s	4 T-34s	7 T-34s 1 ISU-152	1 T-34			17
5th Guards Tank Corps				6 T-34s	5 T-34s 1 SU-76	16 T-34s 6 SU-76s	10 T-34s	1 T-34	3 T-34s	48
9th Guards Mechanized Corps			2 M4A2s	4 M4A2s	4 M4A2s	7 M4A2s	16 M4A2s		1 M4A2	30
51st Self-Propelled Artillery Brigade				2 SU-76s	5 SU-76s	4 SU-76s				11
364th Self-Propelled Artillery Regiment				1 ISU-122		3 ISU-122s		2 ISU-122s		6
1523rd Self-Propelled Artillery Regiment	7 SU-76s		3 SU-76s							10
1513rd Self-Propelled Artillery Regiment	14 SU-76s		5 SU-76s	1 SU-76						20
366th Guards Self-Propelled Artillery Regiment			1 captured self-propelled gun		1 captured self-propelled gun					2
4th Guards Army independent self-propelled artillery battalions	1 tank	1 T-34	3 SU-76s 1 tank				4 SU-76s	1 SU-100		10
208th Self-Propelled Artillery Brigade								1 SU-100		2
1st Guards Mechanized Corps			2 M4A2s		4 M4A2s 1 SU-100 4 SU-100s	3 M4A2s	9 M4A2s			19
207th Self-Propelled Artillery Brigade										4
22nd Independent Tank Regiment		3 T-34s		2 T-34s	1 T-34					3
249th Tank Regiment					3 T-34s			1 T-34		4
53rd Independent Motorcycle Regiment										3
1891st Self-Propelled Artillery Regiment		1 SU-76	1 SU-76							2
32nd Guards Mechanized Brigade	10 T-34s				1 T-34					11
Total	**34**	**9**	**18**	**12**	**35**	**36**	**36**	**23**	**4**	**207**

Source: Central Archives of the Russian Defence Ministry (Podolsk), f. 243, op. 2928, gy. 178, li. 81-102, also f. 243, op. 2928, gy. 131, li. 247-271.

Table 20.: Total losses of armoured fighting vehicles of the German 6. *Panzerarmee* and the 6. *Armee* based on the *available strength*, 1 March – 1 April 1945.

Unit	05 March 1945	1 April 1945	Difference	Total
1. *Panzer-Division*	2 BefIIIs, 10 IVs, 59 Vs, 2 StuGs, 4 *Nashorns*, 13 *Marders*, 3 ArtPzIIIs, 8 ArtPzIVs, 17 *Hummels*	1 BefIIIs, 3 IVs, 42 Vs, 4 *Nashorns*, 9 *Marders*, 2 ArtPzIIIs, 4 ArtPzIVs, 9 *Hummels*, + 9 Soviet captures	1 BefIII, 7 IV, 17 V, 4 *Marder*, 1 ArtPzIII, 4 ArtPz IV, 8 *Hummel*	42
3. *Panzer-Division* (min.)	4 IIIs, 14 IVs, 11 IV/70s, 29 Vs, 7 StuGs, 10 JgPz IVs	2 IIIs, 3 IVs, 8 Vs, 15 IV/70s and JgPz IVs, 2 StuGs	2 IIIs, 11 IVs, 21 Vs, 5 StuGs, 6 IV/70s and JgPz IVs	45
6. *Panzer-Division*	22 IVs, 68 Vs, 18 JgPz IVs	22 IVs, 58 Vs, 20 JgPz IVs	10 Vs, ? JgPz IVs	min. 10
1. SS-*Panzer-Division* (15 April)	30 IVs, 28 Vs, 20 IV/70s, 3 StuGs, 3 FlakPzs	18 IVs, 5 Vs, 13 IV/70s, 10 StuGs, 6 ArtPzs	12 IVs, 23 Vs, 7 IV/70s, 3 FlakPz,s	min. 45
2. SS-*Panzer-Division*	28 IVs, 21 IV/70s, 29 Vs, 29 StuGs, 10 JgPz Vs, 8 FlakPzs	22 IVs, 18 IV/70s, 27 Vs, 17 StuGs, 10 JgPz Vs, 8 FlakPzs	6 IVs, 3 IV/70s, 2 Vs, 12 StuGs	23
23. *Panzer-Division*	2 IIIBefs, 18 IVs, 38 IV/70s, 7 IV/70s, 9 StuGs, 15 JgPz IVs	1 IIIBef, 7 IVs, 5 IV/70s, 10 Vs, 2 StuGs, 8 JgPz IVs, 1 JgPz 38	1 BefIII, 11 IVs, 28 Vs, 7 StuG, 7 JgPz IVs	54
3. SS-*Panzer-Division* (04 March/15 April)	17 IVs, 16 Vs, 9 VIs, 17 StuGs, 7 JgPz IVs, 1 ArtPz III, 2 ArtPz IVs, 5 *Wespes*, 9 *Hummels*	3 IVs, 1 V, 3 VIs, 1 StuG.	14 IVs, 15 Vs, 6 VIs, 16 StuGs, 7 JgPz IVs	58
5. SS-*Panzer-Division*	4 IVs, 18 Vs, 5 StuGs, 10 JgPz IVs, 3 ArtPzIII, 11 *Wespes*, 4 *Hummels*	2 IVs, 7 Vs, 2 StuGs, 3 JgPz IVs	2 IVs, 11 Vs, 3 StuGs, 7 JgPz IVs, 3 ArtPzIIIs, 11 *Wespes*, 4 *Hummels*	41
9. SS-*Panzer-Division* (10 April)	23 IVs, 24 IV/70s, 40 Vs, 26 StuG, 10 JgPz Vs, 4 FlakPzs	8 IVs, 15 Vs, 7 JgPz 38s, 1 JgPz V, 1 FlakPz	15 IVs, 24 IV/70s, 25 Vs, 26 StuGs, 9 JgPz Vs, 3 FlakPzs	102
12. SS-*Panzer-Division*	30 IVs, 31 IV/70s, 30 Vs, 8 FlakPzs	10 IVs, 16 IV/70s, 12 Vs, 4 FlakPzs	20 IVs, 15 IV/70s, 18 Vs, 4 FlakPzs	57
schuere Panzerjäger-Abteilung 560	22 IV/70s, 16 JgPz Vs, 8 FlakPzs	6 IV/70s, 4 JgPz Vs, 8 FlakPzs	16 IV/70s, 12 JgPz Vs	28
I. (*Abteilung*)/*Panzer-Regiment* 24	38 Vs	10 Vs	28 Vs	28
Flammpanzer-Kompanie 351	11 IIIFlamms	8 IIIFlamms	3 IIIFlamms	3
Sturmpanzer-Abteilung 219	20 StuPz IVs	7 StuPz IVs (new equipment)	20 StuPz IVs	20
schuere Panzer-Abteilung 509	35 VIB, 8 FlakPzs	13 VIBs	22 VIBs, 8 FlakPzs	30
Sturmgeschütz-Brigade 325	34 StuG + StuHs	10 StuGs + StuHs	24 StuGs. + StuHs	24
Sturmartillerie-Brigade 303	15 StuG, 5 StuH.	5 StuGs, 3 StuHs.	10 StuGs, 2 StuHs.	12
Sturmartillerie-Brigade 239 (25 March)	14 StuG, 13 StuH.	6 StuGs, 8 StuHs.	8 StuGs, 5 StuHs.	13
1. *Volks-Gebirgs-Division*				
schuere SS-*Panzer-Abteilung* 501	33 VIBs	5 VIBs	28 VIBs	28

All totals a minimum of 663 armoured fighting vehicles

The armoured fighting vehicle losses of the *Bergepanzers*, the 232. *Panzer-Division*, the 3. and 4. *Kavallerie-Divisions*, the German infantry divisions and the Hungarian units are not included there; neither are included the self-propelled howitzers (*Hummel* and *Wespe*), the self-propelled infantry guns (*Grille*), the armoured personnel carriers (Sd.Kfz. 250 and 251), and the armoured reconnaissance vehicles, in the case of most of the German armoured divisions.

Table 21.: Tank and mechanized units of the 3rd Ukrainian Front on the evening of 31 March 1945

Unit	T-34 T-34/85	IS-2	M4A2	T-70	Other	SU-76	SU-100	ISU-122	ISU-152	Total
5th Guards Tank Corps	44/1				11					55/1
51st Guards Self-Propelled Artillery Brigade				4		40/3				44/3
208th Self-Propelled Artillery Brigade	2					3	39/5			44/5
9th Guards Mechanized Corps						10/2				89/20
364th Guards Heavy Self-Propelled Artillery Regiment							14/2			14/2
4th Guards Motorcycle Regiment					7 MK-9s					7
6th Guards Tank Army total	**46/1**	**0**	**79/18**	**4**	**7**	**64/5**	**39/5**	**14/2**	**0**	**253/31**
18th Tank Corps	45/17				8		4/1		3/2	60/20
200th Self-Propelled Artillery Brigade	2				1/2 SU-57s	38/5				41/7
1st Guards Mechanized Corps	4		46/28			13/1				63/29
20th Self-Propelled Artillery Brigade	2				3 SU-57s		23/7			28/7
53rd Motorcycle Regiment	4									4
71st Tank Regiment	6/3									6/3
54th Tank Regiment	10									10
1896th Self-Propelled Artillery Regiment						14/1				14/1
5th Guards Cavalry Corps total	16/3					14/1				30/4
Front HQ units total	**73/20**	**0**	**46/28**	**0**	**4/2**	**22/1**	**74/13**	**4/1**	**3/2**	**226/67**
1513th Self-Propelled Artillery Regiment						4/1				4/1
1523rd Self-Propelled Artillery Regiment						17				17
1524th Self-Propelled Artillery Regiment						20/4				20/4
9th Guards Army total	**0**	**0**	**0**	**0**	**0**	**41/5**	**0**	**0**	**0**	**41/5**
366th Guards Heavy Self-Propelled Artillery Regiment					6/4 heavy self-propelled guns, 0/2 Panthers					6/6
independent self-propelled artillery battalions	0	0	0	5		52/10	0	0	0	57/10
4th Guards Army total	**0**	**0**	**0**	**5**	**6/6**	**19/1**	**0**	**0**	**0**	**63/16**
1202nd Self-Propelled Artillery Regiment						19/1				19/1
432nd Independent Self-Propelled Artillery Battalion						10/2				10/2
27th Army total	**0**	**0**	**0**	**0**	**0**	**29/3**	**0**	**0**	**0**	**29/3**
72nd Guards Independent Self-Propelled Artillery Battalion						5/2				5/2
26th Army total	0	0	0	0	0	5/2	0	0	0	5/2
32nd Guards Mechanized Brigade	24/2									24/2
249th Tank Regiment	7/1									7/1
1201st Self-Propelled Artillery Regiment			1			18/1				19/1
86th Self-Propelled Artillery Regiment						3/1				4/1
3rd Guards Motorcycle Regiment	8/2									8/2
1891st Self-Propelled Artillery Regiment						15/1				15/1
122nd Independent Self-Propelled Artillery Battalion						9/1				9/1
57th Army total	**41/5**	**0**	**0**	**0**	**17/8**	**45/4**	**0**	**0**	**0**	**86/9**
All total	**160/26**	**0**	**125/46**	**9**	**17/8**	**258/30**	**113/18**	**18/3**	**3/2**	**703/133**

Explanation: numerator shows the number of operational armoured fighting vehicles, and denominator shows the armoured fighting vehicles under repair.
Source: Central Archives of the Russian Defence Ministry (Podolsk), f. 243, op. 2928, gy. 131, li. 292–293.

Table 22: Irrecoverable losses of armoured fighting vehicles of the 3rd Ukrainian Front between 25 March – 2 April 1945

Unit	25 March	26 March	27 March	28 March	29 March	30 March	31 March	1 April	2 April	Total
864th Self-Propelled Artillery Regiment							2 SU-76s			2
18th Tank Corps	8 T-34s 2 ISU-122s	6 T-34s 1 ISU-152 1 SU-76	4 T-34s	4 T-34s	11 T-34s		1 T-34			38
5th Guards Tank Corps	3 T-34s 1 SU-76		5 T-34s		20 T-34s 2 SU-76s					31
9th Guards Mechanized Corps	2 SU-76s	3 M4A2s 2 SU-76s	6 M4A2s		13 M4A2s					26
51st Self-Propelled Artillery Brigade				3 SU-76s						3
364th Self-Propelled Artillery Regiment										0
1524th Self-Propelled Artillery Regiment						1 SU-76				1
1896th Self-Propelled Artillery Regiment									2 SU-76s	2
432nd Independent Self-Propelled Artillery Battalion		1 SU-76								1
71st Tank Regiment							2 T-34s		1 T-34	3
209th Self-Propelled Artillery Brigade	1 SU-100									1
1st Guards Mechanized Corps			5 M4A2s		12 M4A2s	10 M4A2s				27
207th Self-Propelled Artillery Brigade				1 SU-100						1
1201st Self-Propelled Artillery Regiment							2 SU-76s			2
249th Tank Regiment							1 T-34			1
Total	17	14	15	9	12	57	12	0	3	139

Source: Central Archives of the Russian Defence Ministry (Podolsk), f. 243, op. 2928, gy. 178, li. 103-124, furthermore f. 243, op. 2928, gy. 131, li. 271-307.

Table 23.: Irrecoverable losses of armoured fighting vehicles of the 2nd Ukrainian Front south of the Danube, 17 March – 1 April 1945

Unit	17 March	18 March	19 March	20 March	21 March	22 March	23 March	24 March	25 March	26 March	27 March	28 March	29 March	30 March	31 March	01 April	Total
2nd Guards Mechanized Corps			7 on 21 March, 4 on 22 March, 5 on 24 March, total: 31 tanks, 3 self-propelled guns							2 self-propelled guns on 30 March, 1 on 31 March, 3+1 self-propelled guns on 1 April total: 8 tanks, 2 self-propelled guns						44
23rd Tank Corps									3		1	8				6	23
991st Self-Propelled Artillery Regiment		1				3	2 +1 Panther	4 tanks, 1 self-propelled gun	1								7+1
1505th Self-Propelled Artillery Regiment		4			1	1					1		1	1			8
1897th Self-Propelled Artillery Regiment		5	?	?	3	1	1		1		1		1	1	?		7
	?	5	?	?	4	4		9	39	?	2	9	1	1	?	16	90

417

Table 24.: Knocked out armoured fighting vehicles reported by the Soviet 17th Air Army in March 1945

Date	Number of deployments	Knocked out armoured fighting vehicles
6 Marc 1945	358	4 tanks and assault guns
7 March 1945	270	–
8 March 1945	887	–
9 March 1945	874	18 tanks and assault guns, 9 armoured personnel carriers
10 March 1945	177	14 tanks and assault guns, 10 armoured personnel carriers
11 March 1945	990	36 tanks and assault guns, 10 armoured personnel carriers
12 March 1945	714	13 tanks and assault guns, 4 armoured personnel carriers
13 March 1945	796	51 tanks and assault guns, 7 armoured personnel carriers
14 March 1945	727	35 tanks and assault guns, 10 armoured personnel carriers
15 March 1945	173	7 tanks and assault guns, 4 armoured personnel carriers
Total between 6 – 15 March 1945		*178 tanks and assault guns, 54 armoured personnel carriers*
16 March 1945	536	13 tanks and assault guns, 5 armoured personnel carriers
17 March 1945	642	9 tanks and assault guns, 2 armoured personnel carriers
18 March 1945	1148	34 tanks and assault guns, 7 armoured personnel carriers
19 March 1945	1091	13 tanks and assault guns
20 March 1945	1124	21 tanks and assault guns, 11 armoured personnel carriers
21 March 1945	1136	17 tanks and assault guns, 7 armoured personnel carriers
22 March 1945	896	14 tanks and assault guns, 13 armoured personnel carriers
23 March 1945	990	20 tanks and assault guns
24 March 1945	731	8 tanks and assault guns, 1 armoured personnel carrier
25 March 1945	733	4 tanks and assault guns, 5 armoured personnel carriers
26 March 1945	806	7 tanks and assault guns, 2 armoured personnel carriers
27 March 1945	no data available	no data available
28 March 1945	404	no data available
29 March 1945	564	5 tanks and assault guns
30 March 1945	759	4 tanks and assault guns
31 March 1945	990	5 tanks and assault guns
Total between 16 – 31 March 1945		*174 tanks and assault guns, 53 armoured personnel carriers*
All total		**352 tanks and assault guns, 107 armoured personnel carriers**

Source: War log of the Soviet 3rd Ukrainian Front

Table 25.: Detailed data of the German armoured fighting vehicles destroyed by the Soviet 17th Air Army

Deployed armament	Destroyed armoured fighting vehicles per type	Number of total destroyed armoured fighting vehicles
50, 100 and 250 kg fragmentation bomb	two Panzer IVs, nine Panthers, one StuG. III, eight Jagdpanzer IVs or Panzer IV/70s, three *Wespes* or *Hummels*, three Jagdpanzer 38(t)s	26
PTAB cumulative anti-tank bomb	one Panzer III, three Panzer IVs, five Panthers, three Tiger Bs, six StuG. IIIs, two Jagdpanzer IVs or Panzer IV/70s, one *Wespe* or *Hummel*, two Jagdpanzer 38(t)s	23
23 or 37 mm automatic cannon	two Panthers, four Jagdpanzer IVs or Panzer IV/70s, one *Wespe* or *Hummel*, two Jagdpanzer 38(t)s	9
ROFS-132 unguided rocket	one Panther, one StuG. III, three Jagdpanzer IVs or Panzer IV/70s, two *Wespes* or *Hummels*, one Jagdpanzer 38(t)	8

Source: Archer, Lee–Nevenkin, Kamen: *Panzerwrecks Nr. 20. Ostfront 3.* Sussex, 2016. p. 5.

Tank and mechanized forces of the 3rd Ukrainian Front (16 March 1945)

1st Guards Mechanized Corps (Lieutenant-General Ivan Nikitich Russiyanov):

- 1st Guards Mechanized Brigade (Guards Colonel Stepan Paramonovich Zatulej)
- within: 18th Guards Tank Regiment (Guards Lieutenant Colonel Ivan Uljanovich Lesenko, M4A2)
- 2nd Guards Mechanized Brigade (Guards Lieutenant Colonel Sergey Aleksejevich Ivanov)
- within: 19th Guards Tank Regiment (Guards Major Grigory Nikolayevich Fokin, M4A2)
- 3rd Guards Mechanized Brigade (Guards Lieutenant Colonel Kuzma Jolevich Vyaznikov until his death on 21 March 1945; thereafter Lieutenant Colonel Stepan Ivanovich Privalov)
- within: 20th Guards Tank Regiment (Colonel Andrey Afanasyevich Verba, M4A2)
- 9th Guards Tank Brigade (Lieutenant Colonel Josif Fyodorovich Saligin, M4A2)
- 382nd Guards Self-Propelled Artillery Regiment (Guards Major Jefim Mikhailovich Mihejev, SU–100)
- 1453rd Self-Propelled Artillery Regiment (Guards Lieutenant Colonel Aleksandr Maksimovich Saydulin, SzU–100)
- 1821st Self-Propelled Artillery Regiment (Lieutenant Colonel Dmitry Pavlovich Gromov, SU–100)
- 267th Mortar Regiment
- 407th Guards Mortar (rocket launcher-) Artillery Battalion
- 1699th Anti-Aircraft Artillery Regiment (37 mm)
- 11th Guards Motorcycle Battalion

18th Tank Corps (Major General Pyotr Dmitryevich Govorunyenko):

- 110th Tank Brigade (Lieutenant Colonel Nikolai Vasilyevich Jezhelov, T–34/85)
- 170th Tank Brigade (Colonel Nikolai Petrovich Chunihin, T–34, T–34/85)
- 181st Tank Brigade (Lieutenant Colonel Anatoly Mihajlovich Indejkin, T–34, T–34/85)
- 32nd Motorized Rifle Brigade (Colonel Boris Ivanovich Gorchinsky)
- 363rd Guards Heavy Self-Propelled Artillery Regiment (Guards Lieutenant Colonel Andrey Efimovich Savkin, ISU–122)
- 1438th Self-Propelled Artillery Regiment (Guards Lieutenant Colonel Mejer Moskovich Estrah, SU–76M)
- 452nd Light Artillery Regiment (76 mm)
- 1000th Independent Anti-Tank Artillery Regiment (76 mm)
- 292nd Mortar Regiment
- 106th Guards Mortar (rocket launcher-) Artillery Battalion
- 1694th Anti-Aircraft Artillery Regiment (37 mm)
- 78th Motorcycle Battalion

23rd Tank Corps (Lieutenant-General Aleksey Osipovich Ahmanov):

- 3rd Tank Brigade (Lieutenant Colonel Ivan Dmitryevich Ivliev, T–34/85)
- 39th Tank Brigade (Lieutenant Colonel Kirill Ignatyevich Vorona, T–34/85)
- 135th Tank Brigade (Colonel Andrey Semenovich Sevcov, T–34/85)
- 56th Motorized Rifle Brigade (Lieutenant Colonel Filipp Feofanovich Stanko)
- 1443rd Self-Propelled Artillery Regiment (Guards Lieutenant Colonel Vasily Ivanovich Grebenik)
- 1669th Light Artillery Regiment
- 1501st Anti-Tank Artillery Regiment
- 457th Mortar Regiment
- 442nd Guards Mortar (multiple rocket launcher-) Artillery Battalion
- 1697th Anti-Aircraft Artillery Regiment
- 82nd Motorcycle Battalion

5th Guards Cavalry Corps (Lieutenant-General Sergey Iljich Gorskov):

- 11th Guards Cavalry Division
- 37th, 39th, 41st Guards Cavalry Regiment
- 71st Tank Regiment (T–34/85)
- 182nd Guards Artillery Mortar Regiment
- 12th Guards Cavalry Division
- 43rd, 45th, 47th Guards Cavalry Regiment
- 54th Tank Regiment (T–34/85)
- 184th Guards Artillery Mortar Regiment
- 63rd Cavalry Division
- 214th, 220th, 223rd Cavalry Regiment
- 60th Tank Regiment (not replenished)
- one artillery mortar regiment
- 1896th Self-Propelled Artillery Regiment (Colonel Dmitry Vasiljevich Zajcev, SU–76M)
- 150th Guards Independent Anti-Tank Artillery Regiment (76 mm)
- 5th Guards Independent Anti-Tank Artillery Battalion
- 72nd Guards Mortar (rocket launcher-) Artillery Battalion
- 9th Guards Mortar Regiment
- 585th Anti-Aircraft Artillery Battalion (37 mm)
- 32nd Independent Guards Mechanized Brigade (Colonel Mikhail Emelianovich Hvatov, T–34, T–34/85)
- 207th Self-Propelled Artillery Brigade (Colonel Nikolai Mihajlovich Ivanov, SU–100)
- 912nd Self-Propelled Artillery Regiment (Major Lev Ivanovich Lopatnikov)
- 1004th Self-Propelled Artillery Regiment (Guards Lieutenant Colonel Fyodor Fedosejevich Kravchenko)
- 1011st Self-Propelled Artillery Regiment (Guards Major Kuzma Petrovich Jermin until he was wounded on 17 March 1945; thereafter Captain Boris Andreyevich Moskovcev)

- 208th Self-Propelled Artillery Brigade (Colonel Georgy Ivanovich Saharov, SU–100)
- 1016th Self-Propelled Artillery Regiment (Colonel Pavel Viktorovich Makacyuba)
- 1068th Self-Propelled Artillery Regiment (Major Ivan Petrovich Nikolaiev)
- 1922nd Self-Propelled Artillery Regiment (Major Aleksey Stepanovich Korolev)
- 209th Self-Propelled Artillery Brigade (Colonel Aleksandr Nikolaievich Lukyanov)
- 1951st Self-Propelled Artillery Regiment (Guards Major Vasily Nikotovich Vagner)
- 1952nd Self-Propelled Artillery Regiment (Major Nikolai Ivanovich Mironov)
- 1953rd Self-Propelled Artillery Regiment (Major Georgy Ivanovich Nikolaiev until 15 March 1945; thereafter Captain N. Rakov until 30 March 1945)
- 249th Independent Tank Regiment (T–34)
- 22nd Training Tank Regiment (Colonel Aleksey Illarionovich Selyavkin, IS–2, KV–1, T–34, T–34/85, T–60, T–70, Mk–2, Mk–3, SU–76M, SU–85, SU–152)
- 366th Guards Heavy Self-Propelled Artillery Regiment (Guards Lieutenant Colonel Viktor Semenovich Gajevsky, captured armoured fighting vehicles)
- 864th Self-Propelled Artillery Regiment (Guards Lieutenant Colonel Aleksey Nikolaievich Kartasev, SU–76M)
- 1201st Self-Propelled Artillery Regiment (Colonel Vasily Safonovich Muhin, SU–76M)
- 1202nd Self-Propelled Artillery Regiment (Guards Lieutenant Colonel Jakov Aronovich Dvorkin, SU–76M)
- 1891st Self-Propelled Artillery Regiment (Guards Major Aleksandr Grigoryevich Katilov, SU–76M)
- 3rd Guards Motorcycle Regiment (T–34/85)
- 53rd Motorcycle Regiment (T–34/85)
- 252nd Amphibious Car Battalion
- 67th Motorcycle Battalion

6th Guards Tank Army (Lieutenant-General Andrey Grigoryevich Kravchenko):

- army staff
- 5th Guards Tank Corps (see below in detail)
- 9th Guards Mechanized Corps (see below in detail)
- 51st Guards Self-Propelled Artillery Brigade (Guards Colonel Nikolai Aleksandrovich Obdalenkov, SU–76M)
- 49th Guards Heavy Tank Regiment (not replenished)
- 364th Guards Heavy Self-Propelled Artillery Regiment (Guards Lieutenant Colonel Ivan Afanasyevich Gorlach, ISU–122)
- 4th Guards Motorcycle Regiment (Guards Lieutenant Colonel Vasily Fyodorovich Savelyev, Mk–9)
- 202nd Light Artillery Brigade
- 301st Guards Anti-Tank Artillery Regiment
- 22nd Motorized Engineer Brigade

5th Guards Tank Corps (Major General Mikhail Ivanovich Savelyev):

- 20th Guards Tank Brigade (Colonel Fyodor Andreyevich Zhilin, T–34/85)
- 21st Guards Tank Brigade (Colonel Ivan Dmitryevich Beloglazov, T–34/85)
- 22nd Guards Tank Brigade (Colonel Ivan Kirillovich Ostapenko, T–34/85)
- 6th Guards Motorized Rifle Brigade (Colonel Pyotr Ivanovich Gribov until his death on 22 March 1945; thereafter Lieutenant Colonel Mikhail Korneyevich Sorochinsky)
- 390th Guards Self-Propelled Artillery Regiment (not replenished)
- 1458th Self-Propelled Artillery Regiment (Guards Major Aleksandr Vasiljevich Barysnikov, SU–76M)
- 391st Guards Anti-Tank Artillery Regiment
- 454th Mortar Regiment
- 127th Guards Mortar (multiple rocket launcher-) Artillery Battalion
- 392nd Guards Anti-Aircraft Artillery Regiment
- 15th Guards Motorcycle Battalion

9th Guards Mechanized Corps (Lieutenant-General Mikhail Vasiljevich Volkov):

- 18th Guards Mechanized Brigade (Guards Lieutenant Colonel Aleksandr Mihailovich Ovcharov)
- within: 83rd Guards Tank Regiment(M4A2)
- 30th Guards Mechanized Brigade (Guards Colonel Ivan Jakovlevich Voronov)
- within: 84th Guards Tank Regiment (Guards Major Pavel Dmitryevich Bistrov, M4A2)
- 31st Guards Mechanized Brigade (Colonel Pavel Ivanovich Goryachev)
- within: 85th Guards Tank Regiment (Guards Lieutenant Colonel Nikolai Petrovich Belov, M4A2)
- 46th Guards Tank Brigade (Lieutenant Colonel Nikolai Mihailovich Mikhno, M4A2)
- 389th Guards Self-Propelled Artillery Regiment (not replenished)
- 697th Self-Propelled Artillery Regiment (Major Pyotr Petrovich Uskov, SU–76M)
- 458th Guards Mortar Regiment
- 35th Guards Mortar (multiple rocket launcher-) Artillery Battalion
- 388th Guards Anti-Aircraft Artillery Regiment
- 14th Guards Motorcycle Battalion

Tank and mechanized forces of the 2nd Ukrainian Front south of the Danube (17 March 1945)

2nd Guards Mechanized Corps (Lieutenant-General Karp Vasiljevich Sviridov):

- 4th Guards Mechanized Brigade (Colonel Mikhail Ivanovich Lyasenko)
- benne a 23rd Guards Tank Regiment (T–34/85)
- 5th Guards Mechanized Brigade (Guards Colonel Jakov Ivanovich Trochenko until his death on 27 March 1945; thereafter Guards Lieutenant Colonel Ivan Dmitryevich Malisev)
- within: 24th Guards Tank Regiment(T–34/85)
- 6th Guards Mechanized Brigade (Guards Colonel Nurtin Safiulich Safiulin)
- within: 25th Guards Tank Regiment (Guards Lieutenant Colonel Pyotr Petrovich Chernenko, T–34/85)
- 37th Guards Tank Brigade (Colonel Nikolai Aleksandrovich Ognev, T–34/85)
- 30th Guards Heavy Tank Regiment (not replenished)
- 251st Guards Self-Propelled Artillery Regiment (SU–85)
- 1509th Self-Propelled Artillery Regiment (SU–76M)
- 524th Mortar Regiment
- 408th Guards Mortar (rocket launcher-) Artillery Battalion
- 159th Anti-Aircraft Artillery Regiment (37 mm)
- 99th Guards Motorcycle Battalion

- 991st Self-Propelled Artillery Regiment (Lieutenant Colonel Vasily Ivanovich Gergeyev, SU–76M, captured armoured fighting vehicles)
- 1505th Self-Propelled Artillery Regiment (Lieutenant Colonel Ilya Fyodorovich Rogachev, SU–76M, captured armoured fighting vehicles)
- 1897th Self-Propelled Artillery Regiment (Colonel Mikhail Filippovich Rizhanov, SU–76M)
- 112th Independent Self-Propelled Artillery Battalion (SU–76M)

PHOTOGRAPHS

Jagdpanzer 38(t) Hetzer of the Hungarian 20th Assault Artillery Battalion, 700 meters east of Balatonszabadi-fürdőtelep. According to Soviet sources, the armoured fighting vehicle was destroyed by high explosive anti-tank rounds. It is more likely however, that this was one of those Hungarian armoured fighting vehicles that were knocked out by a T-34 tank of the Soviet 22nd Independent Tank Regiment on 11 March 1945.

Destroyed German Flak-Panzer IV "Möbelwagen" anti-aircraft armoured fighting vehicle near Balatonakarattya. According to Soviet sources, it was destroyed by an unguided rocket fired by an Il-2 ground-attack aircraft.

Panther Ausf.G tank of 2. Kompanie/SS-Panzer-Regiment 1/1. SS-Panzer-Division at the train station of Balatonkenese. According to Soviet sources, it was destroyed by an Il-2 ground-attack aircraft with 37 mm automatic cannon fire. It is more likely however that the tank had been knocked out farther away during combat, and was towed here to be loaded for train transportation, and the air attack struck at that time.

German Panzer IV Ausf.J tank, most likely from 23. Panzer-Division near the road leading to Cece, 2 km northeast of Simontornya. According to Soviet sources, the armoured fighting vehicle was destroyed by high explosive anti-tank rounds, presumably on 13 March 1945.

German Panzer IV/70 (V) Jagdpanzer, most likely from SS-Panzerjäger-Abteilung 12 in the vicinity of Várpalota on the road currently known as Nr. 8 main. According to Soviet sources, it was destroyed by an unguided rocket fired by an Il-2 ground-attack aircraft and the armoured fighting vehicle burnt out. The penetration on the left side of the glacis plate originates however, from an artillery projectile which might have caused an internal explosion.

Panther Ausf.A tank from 5. Kompanie/Panzer-Regiment 23/23. Panzer-Division at Várpalota. According to Soviet sources, it was set aflame by the 37 mm automatic cannon fire of an Il-2 ground-attack aircraft. Based on German sources, we are aware that the immobile, partially dug-in tank was blown up by the Germans on 21 March 1945; the Soviet hit marks originate from a later date.

Hungarian Jagdpanzer 38(t) Hetzer of the 3rd Battery/20th Assault Artillery Battalion, 1 km north of Balatonfűzfő. According to Soviet sources, it was hit by an aerial bomb

German StuH.42 assault howitzer, most likely from Panzerjäger-Abteilung 69/3. Kavallerie-Division 3.5 km south of Berhida. According to Soviet sources it was destroyed by an unguided rocket fired by an Il-2 ground-attack aircraft.

German Panzer IV/70 (V) Jagdpanzer, most likely from SS-Panzer-Regiment 9/9. SS-Panzer-Division, 2 km south-southeast of Berhida, in the vicinity of Hill 173. According to Soviet sources, it was destroyed by the combined effect of a bomb impact and the 37 mm automatic cannon fire of an Il-2 ground-attack aircraft.

German StuG. III Ausf.G assault gun of 7. Kompanie/SS-Panzer-Regiment 9/9. SS-Panzer-Division 4 km south of Berhida. According to Soviet sources, it was destroyed by the combined effect of a bomb impact and the 37 mm automatic cannon fire of an Il-2 ground-attack aircraft.

German StuG. III Ausf.G assault gun, most likely from II. (Abteilung)/SS-Panzer-Regiment 9/9. SS-Panzer-Division 4 km south of Berhida. According to Soviet sources the armoured fighting vehicle was destroyed by high explosive anti-tank rounds. Behind the assault gun, a Panzer IV tank can be seen, most likely also from II. (Abteilung)/SS-Panzer-Regiment 9.

German artillery observation Panzer IV "Panzerbeobachtungswagen IV" tank at the northern perimeter of Seregélyes, most likely from the 3 Panzer-Division. According to Soviet sources, it was destroyed by an aerial bomb hit.

German Panther Ausf.G tank from 2. Kompanie/SS-Panzer-Regiment 1/1. SS-Panzer-Division between Balatonfűzfő and Balatonkenese. According to Soviet sources, the armoured fighting vehicle was destroyed by high explosive anti-tank rounds. The disabled tank was probably towed here to be loaded for train transportation, and the Soviet air attack struck at that time.

German "Hummel" self-propelled howitzer southeast of Berhida, most likely from I. (Abteilung)/Panzer-Artillerie-Regiment 73/1. SS-Panzer-Division in the vicinity of Kiskovácsipuszta. According to Soviet sources, it was destroyed by an unguided rocket fired by an Il-2 ground-attack aircraft.

German "Hummel" self-propelled howitzer, most likely from I. (Abteilung)/Panzer-Artillerie-Regiment 73/1. SS-Panzer-Division at the southern edge of Jenő. According to Soviet sources, it was destroyed by an aerial bomb hit.

German "Wespe" self-propelled howitzer, most likely from 5. Batterie/Panzer-Artillerie-Regiment 75/3 SS-Panzer-Division, north of Sándorka. The armoured fighting vehicle must have been destroyed in the evening of 22 March 1945. According to Soviet sources it was destroyed by high explosive anti-tank rounds, but it is more likely that it was knocked out while engaged in combat with the M4A2 tanks of the 1st Guards Mechanized Corps.

German StuG. III Ausf.G assault gun from SS-Panzerjäger-Abteilung 3/3. SS-Panzer-Division northwest of Söréd. According to Soviet sources, the armoured fighting vehicles here were mostly destroyed by high explosive anti-tank rounds. More likely however, prior to this, the Germans themselves blew them up during the breakout from Söréd, on 18 March 1945.

More destroyed StuG. III Ausf.G assault guns of SS-Panzerjäger-Abteilung 3, 100 meters southwest of Söréd.

German Panzer IV/70 (V) Jagdpanzer, most likely from 2. or 3. Kompanie/schwere Panzerjäger-Abteilung 560 in the sector of Várpalota, at the cemetery at the beginning of the road leading towards Tés. According to Soviet sources, the armoured fighting vehicle was destroyed by high explosive anti-tank rounds.

German artillery observer Panzer III tank, "Panzerbeobachtungswagen III", most likely from 5. SS-Panzer-Division on the road between Nádasdladány and Sárszentmihály. According to Soviet sources, the armoured fighting vehicle was destroyed by high explosive anti-tank rounds.

In the foreground, a Bergepanther Ausf.D armoured recovery vehicle from 5. SS-Panzer-Division, and behind it, a Panther Ausf.G tank from II. (Abteilung)/SS-Panzer-Regiment 9/9. SS-Panzer-Division, presumably in the sector of Balatonfőkajár. The destroyed armoured fighting vehicles were most likely blown up by the Germans themselves on 22 or 23 March 1945.

German Jagdpanzer IV from Panzerjäger-Abteilung 128/23. Panzer-Division, north of Simontornya. According to Soviet sources, it was destroyed by the combined effect of artillery fire and an aerial bomb hit. According to German sources, the armoured fighting vehicle had been knocked out by mistake by the armoured fighting vehicles of the 12. SS-Panzer-Division on 10 March 1945.

MAPS AND ORGANISATIONAL CHARTS

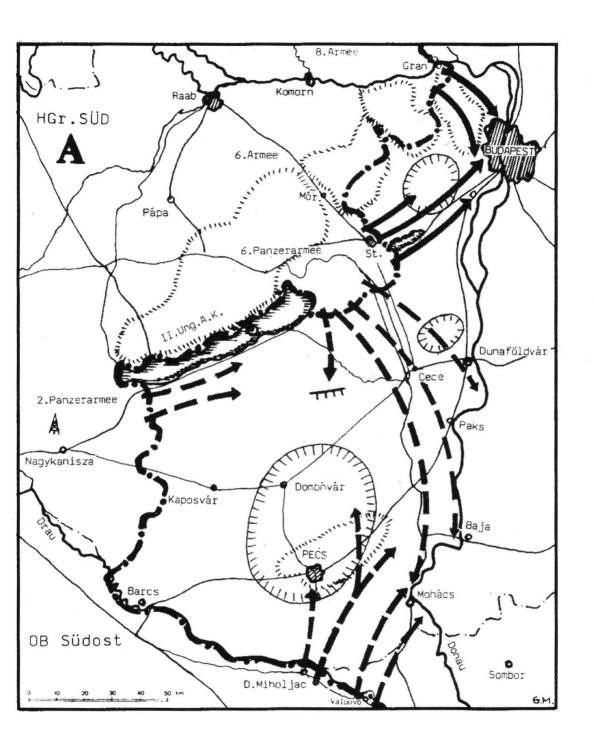

German plan "Lösung A"

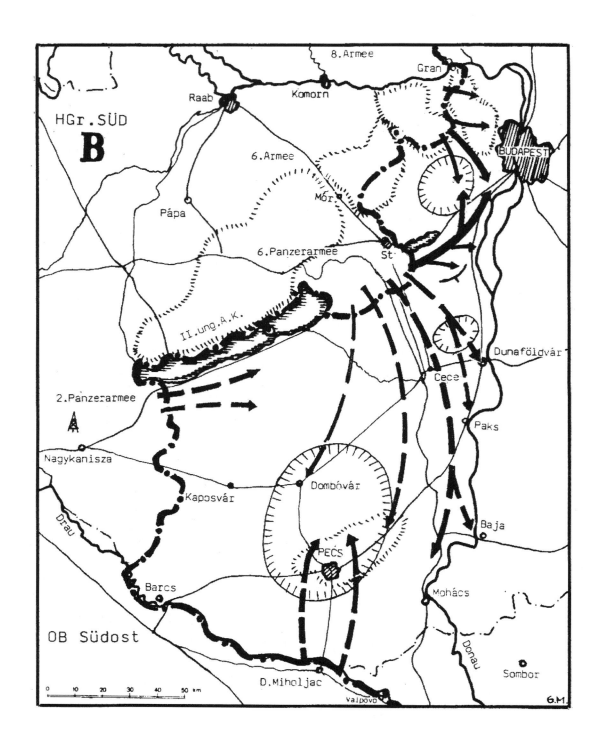

German plan "Lösung B"

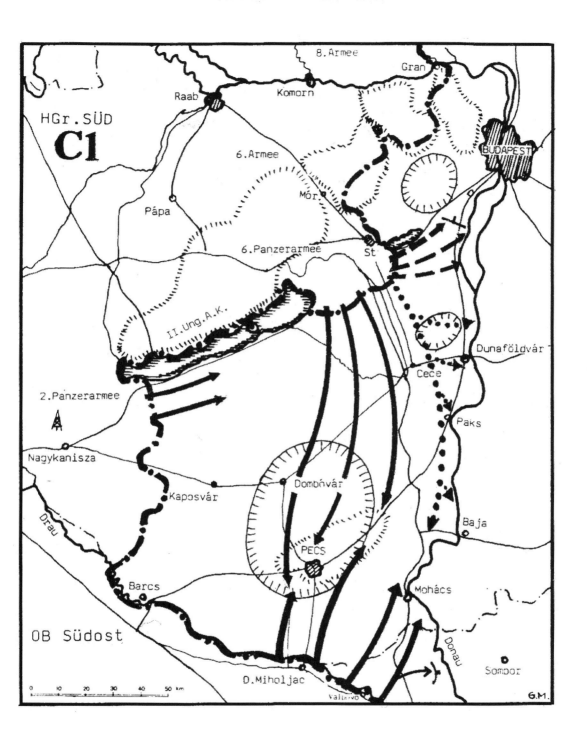

German plan "Lösung C1"

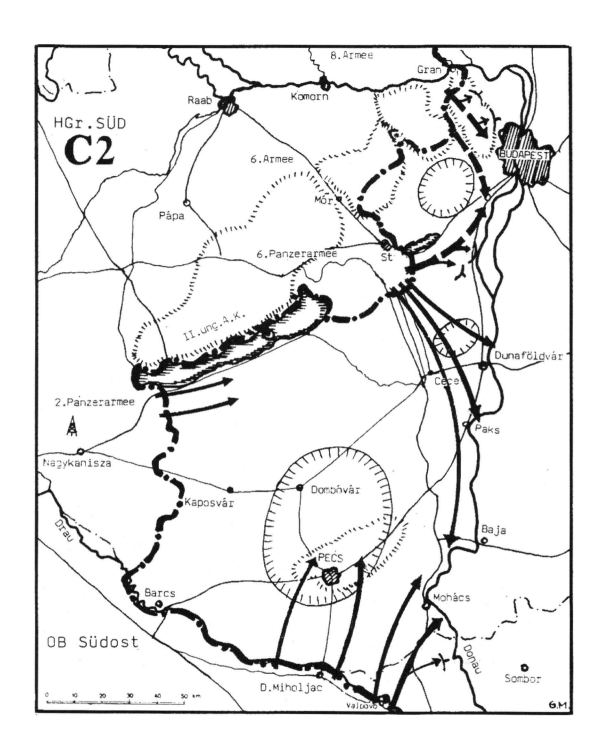

German plan "Lösung C2"

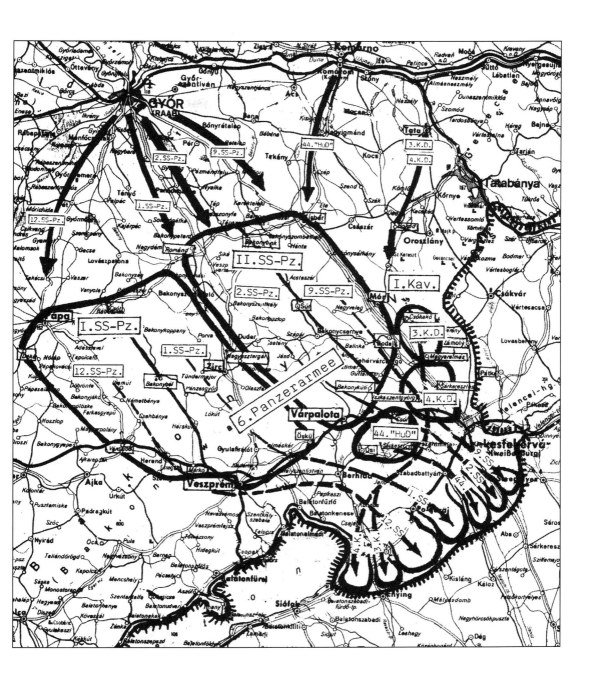

The German 6. Panzerarmee drawn forward between Lake Balaton and Lake Velence at the beginning of March 1945

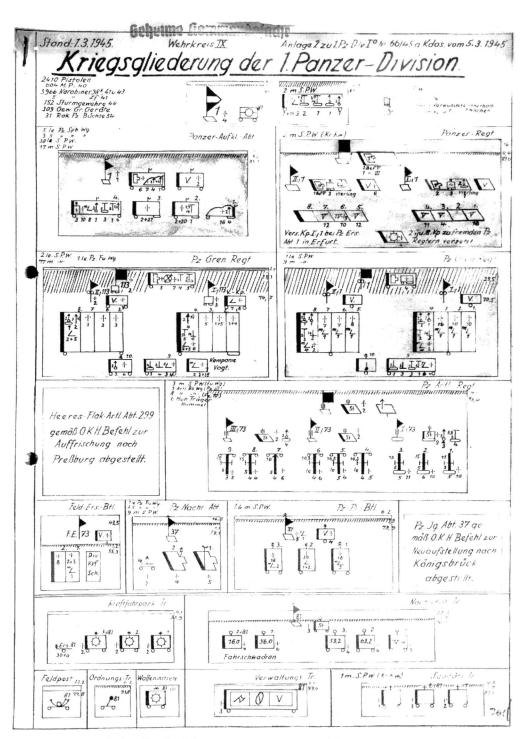

Order of battle of the German 1. Panzer-Division on 1 March 1945

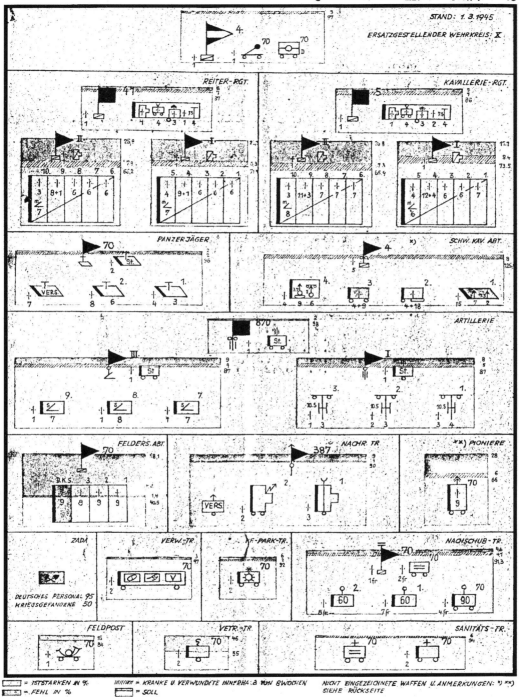

Order of battle of the German 4. Kavallerie-Division on 1 March 1945

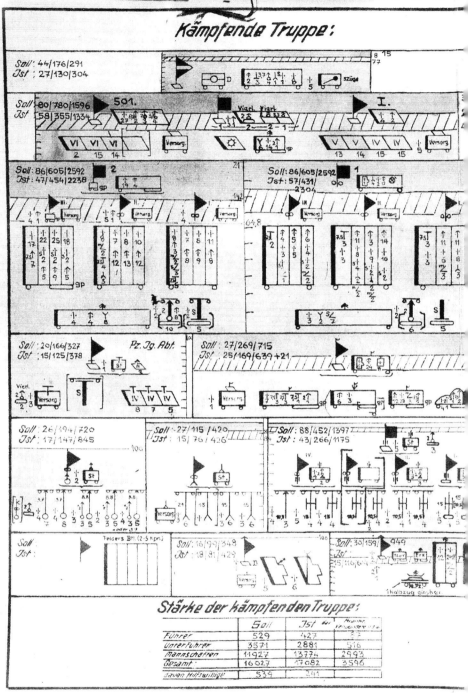

Order of battle of the German 1. SS-Panzer-Division on 1 March 1945

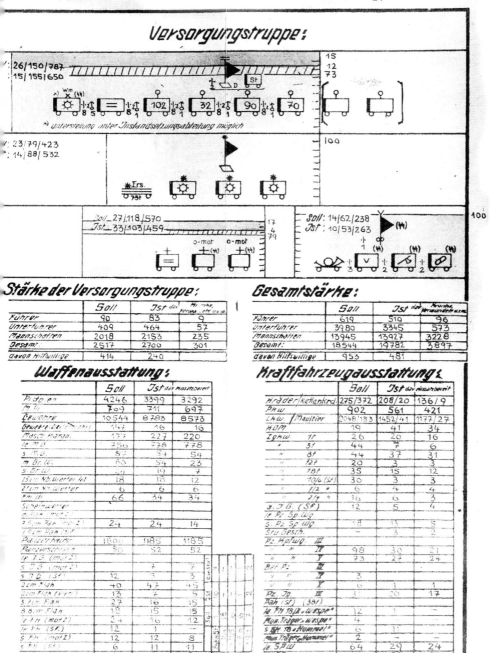

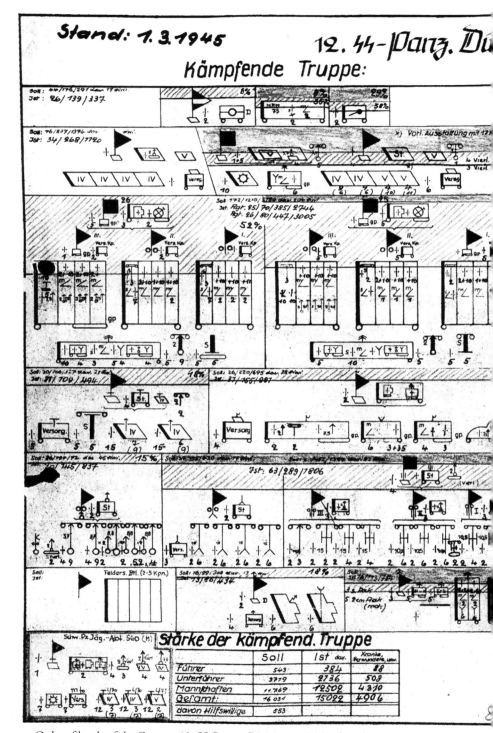

Order of battle of the German 12. SS-Panzer-Division on 1 March 1945

"Hitlerjugend"

Versorgungstruppe:

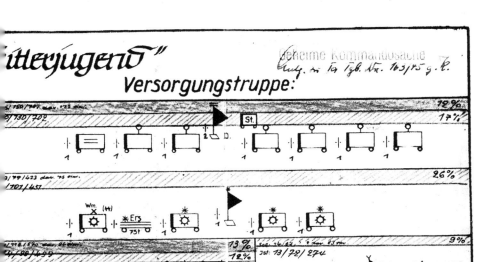

Stärke der Versorgungstr.	Soll	Ist dav.	Kranke, Verwundete
Führer	90	73	8
Unterführer	409	402	56
Mannschaften	2078	1926	334
Gesamt:	2577	2407	398
davon Hilfswillige		314	

Gesamtstärke	Soll	Ist dav.	Kranke, Verwundete
Führer	633	457	96
Unterführer	4128	2538	564
Mannschaften	13787	14428	4644
Gesamt:	18548	17423	5304
davon Hilfswillige		967	

Waffenausstattung

	Soll	Ist	davon einsatzbereit
Pistolen	4172	2764	2764
M.Pi.	2250	727	727
Gewehre	11266	8322	8322
Gewehre(Zieffernr.)	747	26	26
Karabiner 43	777	231	231
le.M.G.	857	669	669
s.M.G.	99	30	30
m.Gr.W.	66	29	29
s.Gr.W.	26	20	20
15cm Nb.Wrf 41	78	24	24
21cm Nb.Wrf	6	–	–
Fm.W.	68	28	28
Scheinwerfer	4	–	–
m.Pak (mot Z)	–	–	–
7,5cm Pak (mot Z)	25	28	27 davon 5 i.SpW
7,5cm Pak (Sf)	–	–	–
Panzerfaust	1800	2600	2600
Panzerschreck	80	60	60
le.I.G.(mot Z)	–	–	–
s.I.G.(mot Z)	–	5	5
s.I.G.(Sf)	72	5	5
2cm Flak x)	41	17	17
2cm Flak (Vierl.)	73	16	16
3,7cm Flak	27	29	29
8,8cm Flak	78	9	9
le.F.H.(mot Z)	25	34	30
le.F.H.(Sf)	12	2	2
s.F.H.(mot Z)	12	10	9
s.F.H.(Sf)	6	–	–
10,5cm Kan.	4	3	2
Feldküchen(kl.gr.)	/6	/6	/6
Feldkochherde(kl.gr)	27/107	20/115	20/115
Sturmgewehre		473	473

Kraftfahrzeugausstattung

	Soll	Ist	davon einsatzbereit
Kräder	675	170	99
PKW	856	435	236
Lkw (Maultier)	1937	1355	986
KDM	17	17	14
Zgkw. 1to	19	23	17
" 3to u.5to.	44	16	9
" 8to	44	36	18
" 12to	20	10	7
" 18to	23	9	6
" 10/4 (Sf)	30	–	–
" 7,2 "	6	4	3
" 9,1 "	13	2	2
s.I.G.(Sf)	72	5	4
le.Pz.Sp.Wg.	4	9	–
s.Pz.Sp.Wg.	16	7	7
Stu.Gesch.	–	–	–
Pz.Kpfwg. III	–	–	–
" IV	98	30	18
" V	73	29	8
Bef.Pz. III	–	–	–
" IV	5	4	3
" V	6	1	1
Pz.Jg. IV	31	31	13
Pak (Sf) (38to)	–	–	–
le.F.H.18/2 "Wespe"	12	–	–
Mun.Träger "Wespe"	4	–	–
s.F.H.18 "Hummel"	6	–	–
Mun.Träger "Hummel"	2	–	–
le.SPW.	64	40	24
m.SPW.	100	137	83
Flak Pz.IV(3,7cm)	8	8	5
Nebelwerfer - Kw	24	–	–
Anhänger	438	81	78

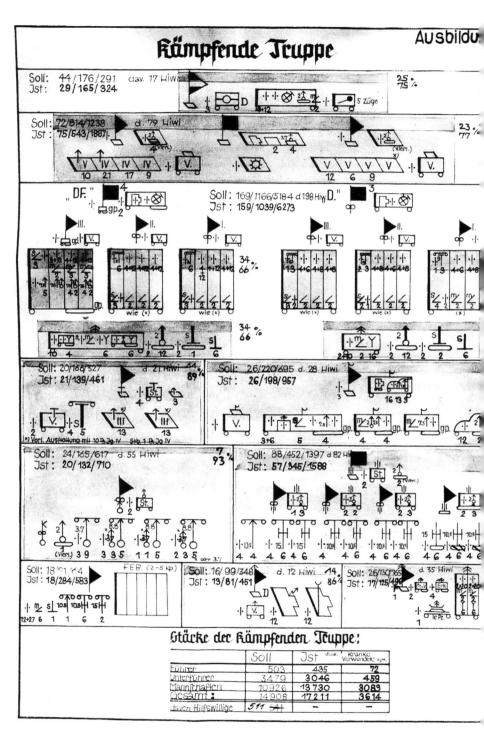

Order of battle of the German 2. SS-Panzer-Division on 1 March 1945

SS-Ausb.Stab Süd
Ia Tgb.Nr.285/45 g.Kdos.

Versorgungstruppe

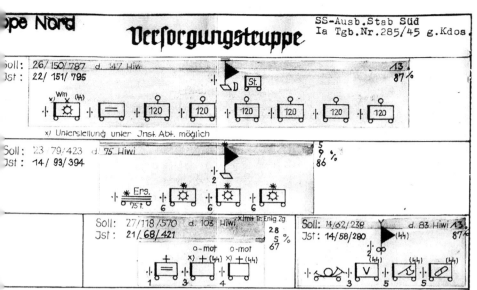

Stärke der Versorgungstruppe:

	Soll	Jst	dav. Kranke verwundete usw.
Führer	90	71	13
Unterführer	409	370	38
Mannschaften	2018	1890	204
Gesamt:	2517	2331	355
davon Hilfswillige	414 ~~408~~	-	-

Gesamtstärke:

	Soll	Jst	dav. Kranke verwundete usw.
Führer	593	506	85
Unterführer	3888	3416	497
Mannschaften	12944	15620	3287
Gesamt:	17425	19542	3869
davon Hilfswillige	925 ~~949~~		

Waffenausstattung:

	Soll	Jst	dav. einsatzbereit
Karabiner 98k	9859	10129	10129
Karabiner m. Zf.	111	34	34
Karabiner 43	177	132	132
Pistolen	3418 919	4521	4521
M.Pi.	433 ~~815~~	427	427
M.Pi. im gep. Kfz.	-	-	-
Gew. Gr. Gerät	41	281	281
Panzerfaust	1000	-	-
Panzerschreck	80	-	-
le.M.G.42	639 816 x)	508	490
s.M.G.42	86 ~~98~~	98	78
M.G. im gep. Kfz.	-	-	-
8 cm Gr.W.34	56 ~~62~~	58	52
12 cm Gr.W.42	24 26	23	21
Fm.W.41	54 ~~50~~	56	51
7,5 cm Pak 40	27 28	26	22
s.J.G. 33 (Sf.)	12	3	2
2 cm Flak	41	35	32
2 cm Flak (Vierl.)	13	7	5
3.7 cm Flak	18	16	15
8.8 cm Flak	18	15	13
le.F.H.18 (Kzg)	24 ~~25~~	36	34
le.F.H.18 (Sf)	12	-	-
s.F.H.18 (Kzg)	12	14	10
s.F.H.18 (Sf)	6	6	6
s.10 cm Kan.18	4	5	4
s.J.G. (Kzg)	-	13	12
Sturmgewehr	400	1391	1391
Feldküchen (kl./gr.)	6 ~~124~~	} 116	116
Feldkochherde (kl./gr.)	118		

x) (o.gep.)

Kraftfahrzeugausstattung:

	Soll	Jst	dav. einsatzbereit
Kräder	600	244	156
Pkw.	832	712	577
Lkw. (Maultier)	1985	1260	1049
Kom.	17	20	18
Zgkw. 1 to	19	17	9
" 3 to	38	18	9
" 5 to	1	9	4
" 8 to	38	27	14
" 12 to	20	7	3
" 18 to	11	11	5
" 35 to	4	-	-
Flak-Sf 10/4	3 30	6	4
Flak-Sf 7/2 9/1	3	2	2
Flak-Sf 7/1	13	2	2
Anhänger	-	-	-
le.Pz.Sp.Wg.	} 16 ~~4~~	1	-
s.Pz.Sp.Wg.	~~16~~	15	6
Panzer IV	28 ~~30~~	26	24
Panzer V+3g.V	42 ~~40~~	37	14
Bef.Wg. IV	2 8	2	2
Bef.Wg. V	3 4	2	-
Stu.Gesch.	28	29	23
Flak-Panzer IV	8	8	2
Jagdpanzer IV	21 ~~24~~	21	13
s.J.G. (Sf)	12	3	2
le.F.H. (Sf)	12	-	-
Mun.Träger (le.F.H)	4	-	-
s.F.H. (Sf)	6	6	6
Mun.Träger (s.F.H)	2	-	-
Beob.Pz. III od. IV	35 499	} 209	150
le.SPW.	135 ~~388~~		
m. SPW.			

x) LKW. m. Sd.-Aufbau u. Sd.-Kfz. 3, Maultier eingerechnet

KARTENSTELLE Ia. 132

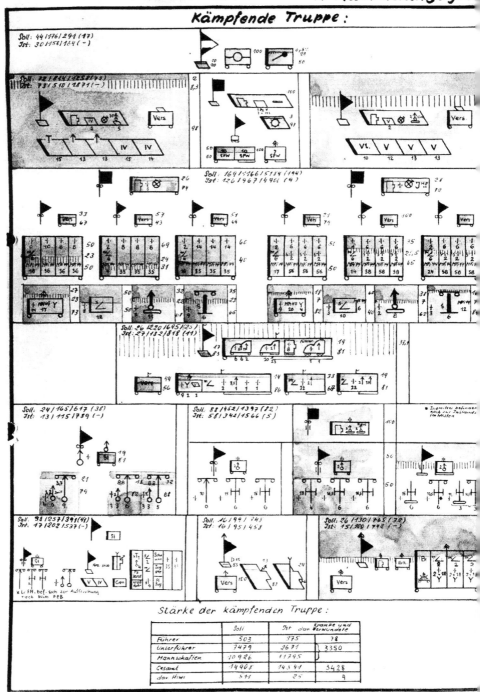

Order of battle of the German 9. SS-Panzer-Division on 1 March 1945

Anlage ... zu Tagebuch Nr. **193** 45 g.Kdos.
Stand vom 1.III.45

Versorgungstruppe:

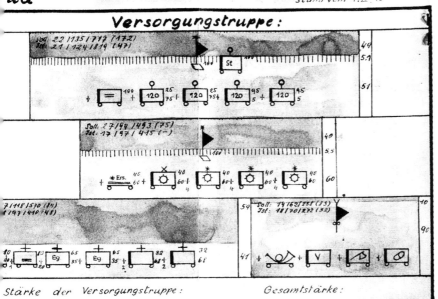

Stärke der Versorgungstruppe:

	Soll	Ist dav.	Kranke und Verwundete
Führer	90	84	7
Unterführer	409	388	114
Mannschaften	2018	1916	
Gesamt	2517	2488	121
davon Hiwi	414	113	1

Gesamtstärke:

	Soll	Ist dav.	Kranke und Verwundete
Führer	593	459	85
Unterführer	3888	3059	3464
Mannschaften	12944	13701	
Gesamt	17425	17279	3549
davon Hiwi	925	138	5

Waffenausstattung:

	Soll	Ist	dav. einsatzber.
Pistolen	3413	3136	3136
M.Pi.	433	425	425
Gewehre	9859	8818	3818
" Zielfernrohr	111	17	17
Masch. Karabiner	177	85	85
le.M.G.	639	615	615
s.M.G.	80	59	59
m.Gr.W.	50	54	54
s.Gr.W.	24	24	24
Fm.W.	54	34	34
m.Pak (mot.Z)			
7,5 Pak ( )	27	17	12
7,5 Pak			
Panzerfaust	1000	538	538
Panzerschreck	80	29	29
le.J.G. (mot.Z)			
s.J.G. ( )		12	9
s.J.G. (SF)	12		
2 cm Flak	44	55	51
2 cm Flak (Vierl.)	13	4	3
3,7 cm Flak	18	21	21
8,8 cm Flak	18	14	11
le.F.H. (mot.Z)	24	28	26
le.F.H. (SF)	12	5	5
s.F.H. (mot.Z)	12	13	4
s.F.H. (ES)	6	9	6
10 cm Kanonen	4	4	4
Feldküchen (kl.gr)	6		
Feldkochherde	118	118	118

Kraftfahrzeugausstattung:

	Soll	Ist	dav. einsatzber.
Kräder	600	160	141
PKW	832	581	346
LKW	1985	648	276
kom.	17	25	22
Zgk.W. 1t	19		
" 3t	38	40	21
" 5t	1		
" 8t	38		
" 12t	20	37	17
" 18t	11		
" 10/4 (SF)	30	21	9
" 9/1	3	-	-
" 7/2	3	-	-
" 5/1	13	4	2
" 35t	4	-	-
" 38t			
s.J.G. (SF)	12	-	-
le.Pz.Sp.Wg	46	44	8
s.Pz.Sp.Wg			
Stu.Gesch.	28	26	15
Pz.Kpfw.IV	28	21	17
" V	42	38	12
Bef.Pz.IV	2	2	2
" V	3		
Pz.Jg.IV	1	40(V)34(IV)	N(V)19(IV)
le.F.H.18/8 "Wespe"	12	3	3
Mu.Träger	4	1	1
s.F.H.18 "Hummel"	6	8	5
le.SPW	55	48	40
m.SPW	135	163	114
Flak Pz.IV (3,7cm)	8	4	4
Berge Pz.III		2	1
Berge Pz.V		9	5

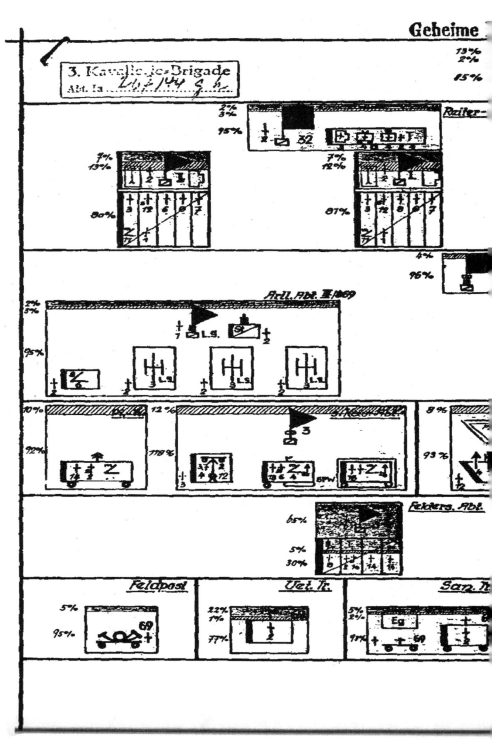

Order of battle of the German 3. Kavallerie-Division on 1 March 1945

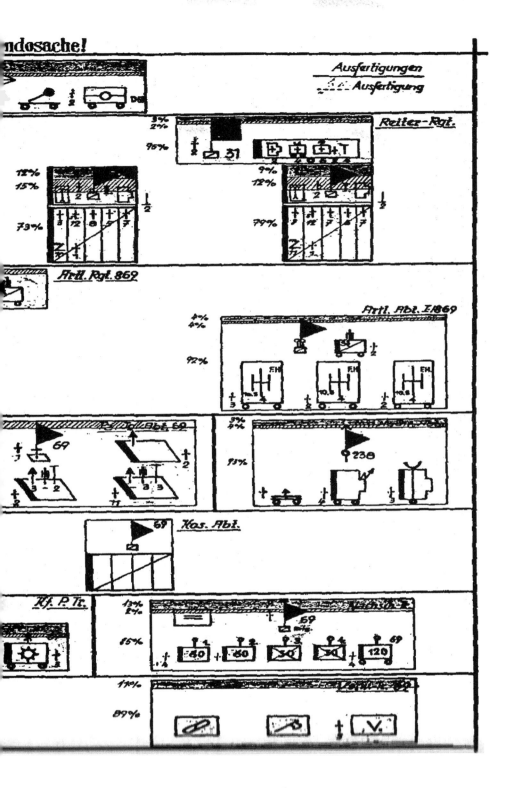

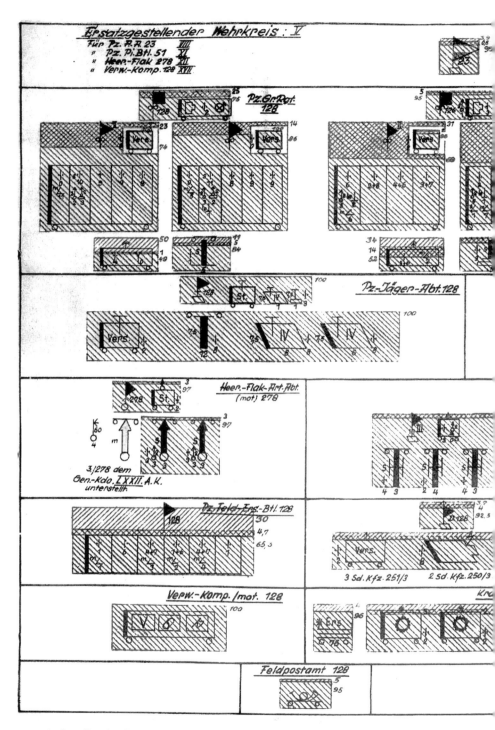

Order of battle of the German 23. Panzer-Division on 1 March 1945

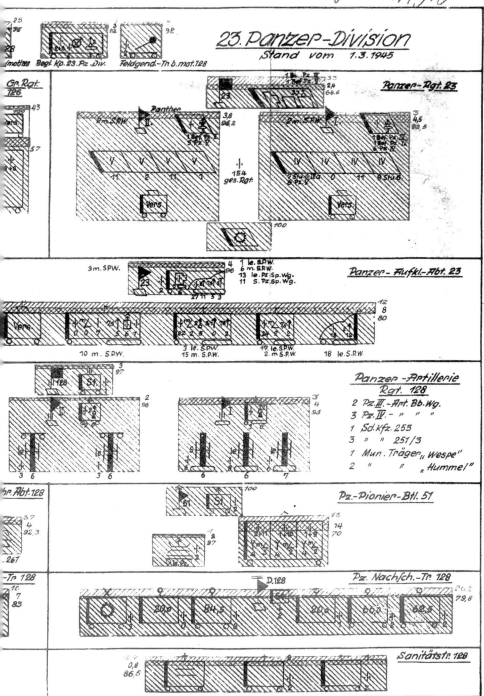

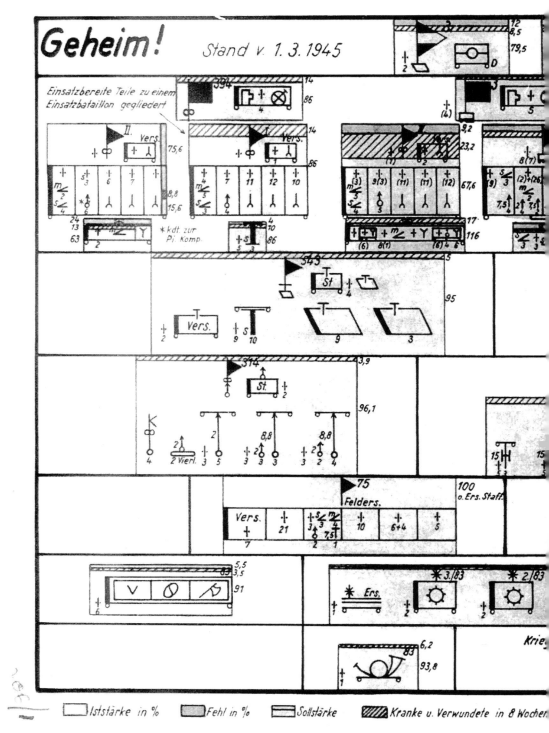

Order of battle of the German 3. Panzer-Division on 1 March 1945

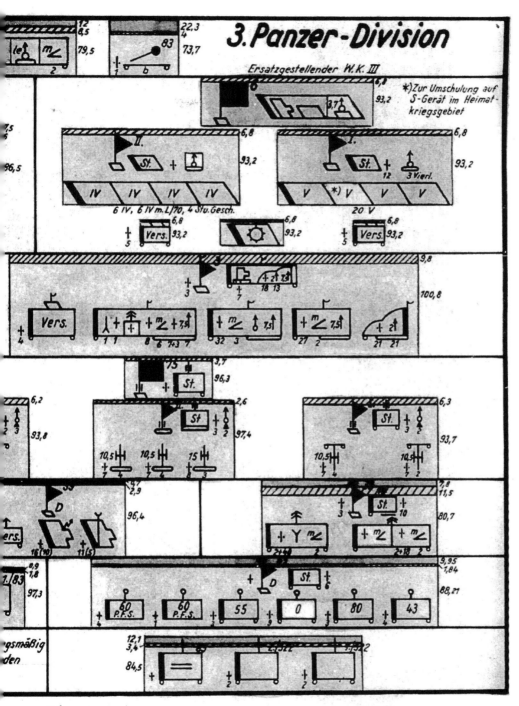

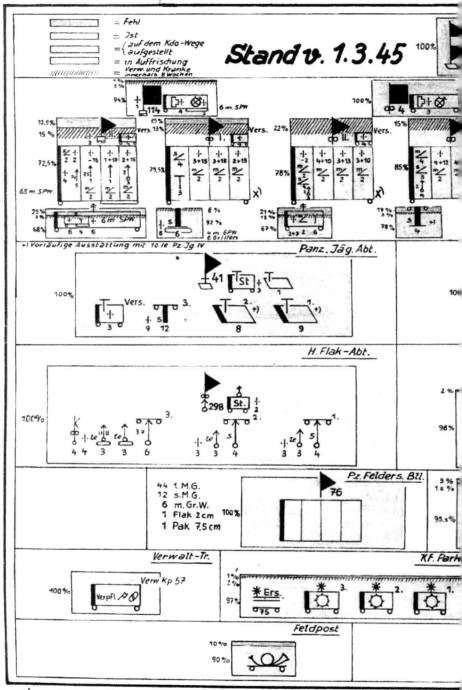

Order of battle of the German 6. Panzer-Division on 1 March 1945

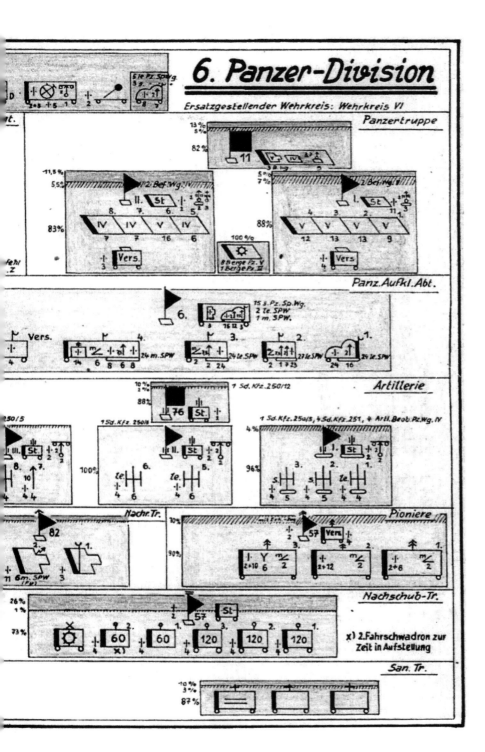

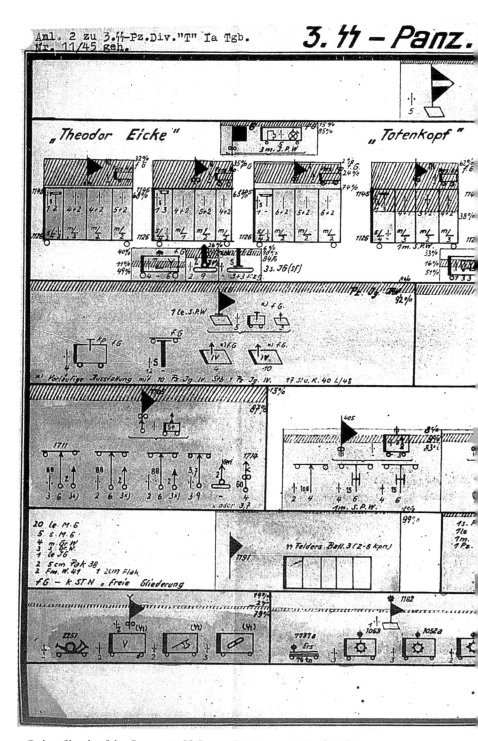

Order of battle of the German 3. SS-Panzer-Division on 1 March 1945

"Totenkopf" Vorläufige Gliederung Stand: 1.1.1945

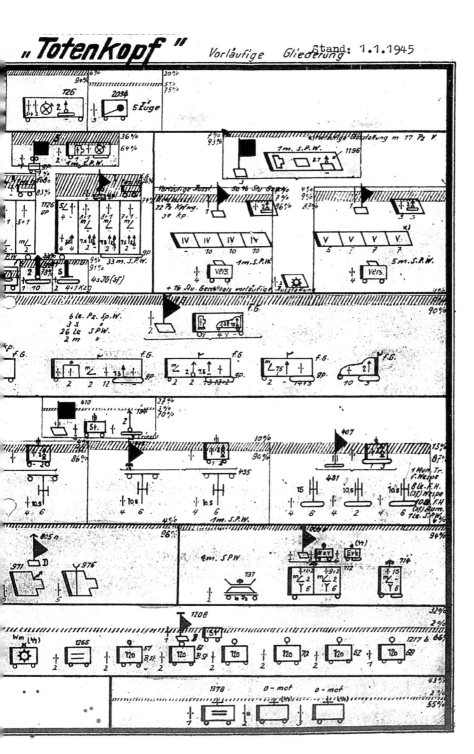

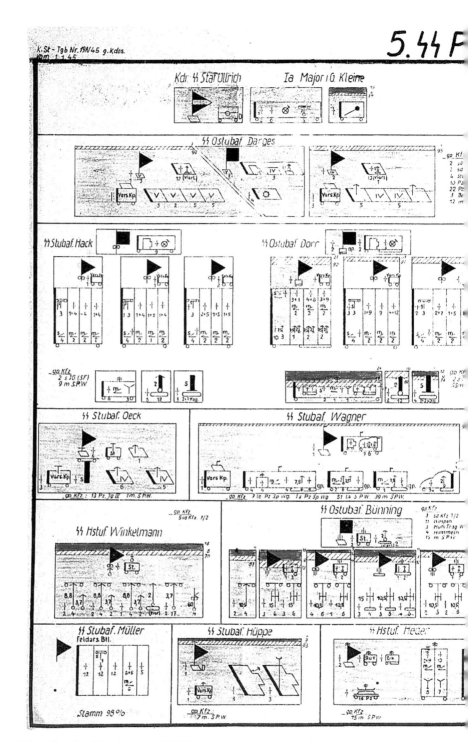

Order of battle of the German 5. SS-Panzer-Division on 1 March 1945

v. Wiking Geheime Kommandosache   84 Ausfertigungen
                                    80 Ausfertigung

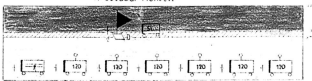

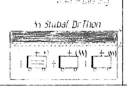

Nicht eingezeichneter Waffenbestand

```
Seitengewehr 84/98     7 900    Gew Gr Gerät            518
Karabiner 98 k        10 058    Leuchtpistolen          464
Karabiner Zf.                   5 cm Pak 38               1
Karabiner 43/41          239    le J G 18                15
Pistolen               5 573    Wurfgestell 41           15
M P 38/40                333    Ofenrohr                 69
M P 44                    45    Faustpatrone          2 873
M P 739 (i)              217    M G in gep.Soll:363      82
```

Beutewaffen

```
Gewehre          -        M G. (r)             126
M P (a)         56        8,2 cm Gr. W. (r)      9
M G (a)          3        12 cm Gr. W. (r)       2
```

465

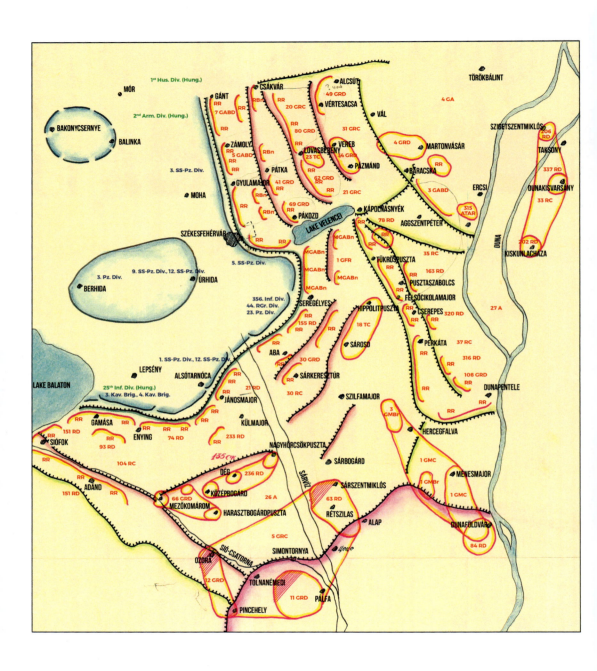

Defences of the 3rd Ukrainian Front between Lake Balaton and the Danube on 6 March 1945

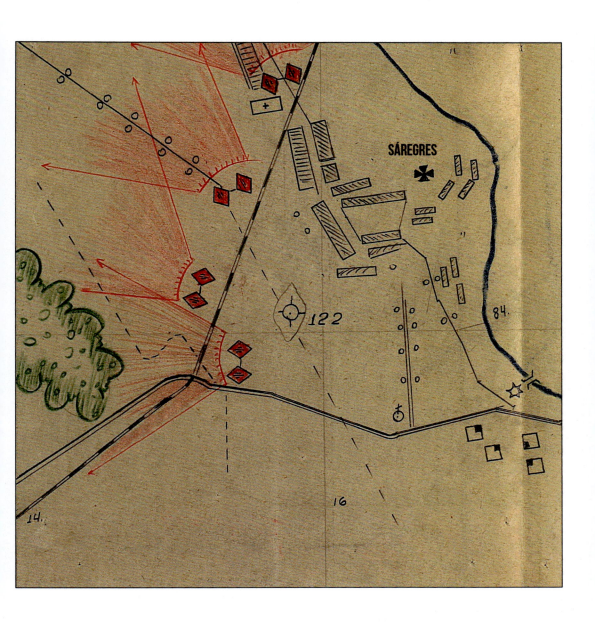

Defences of the Soviet 1951st Self-Propelled Artillery Regiment in the Sáregres sector on 10 March 1945

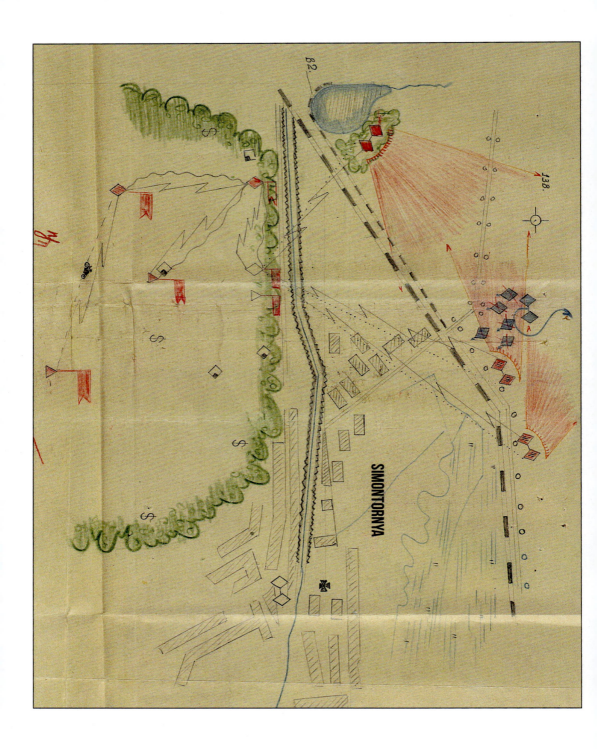

Defences and signalling system of the Soviet 1953rd Self-Propelled Artillery Regiment in the vicinity of Simontornya between 10 – 13 March 1945

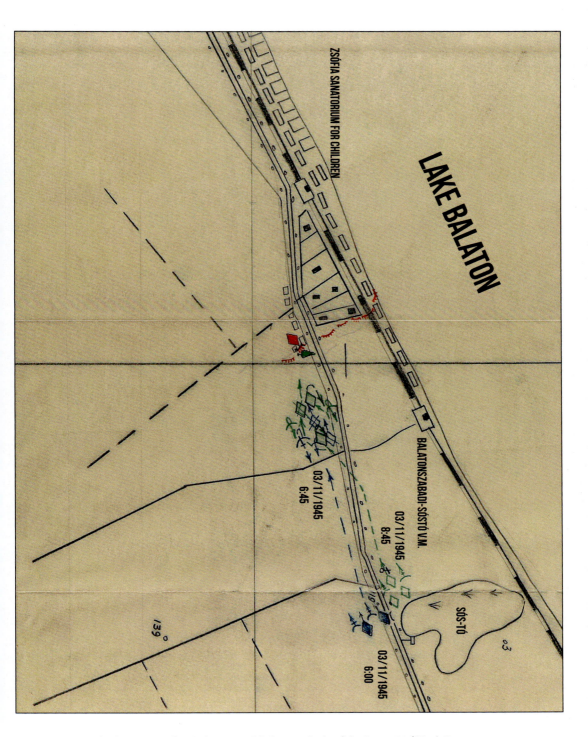

Ambush position of a T-34 armoured fighting vehicle of the Soviet 22nd Tank Regiment at Balatonszabadi-fürdőtelep on 11 March 1945

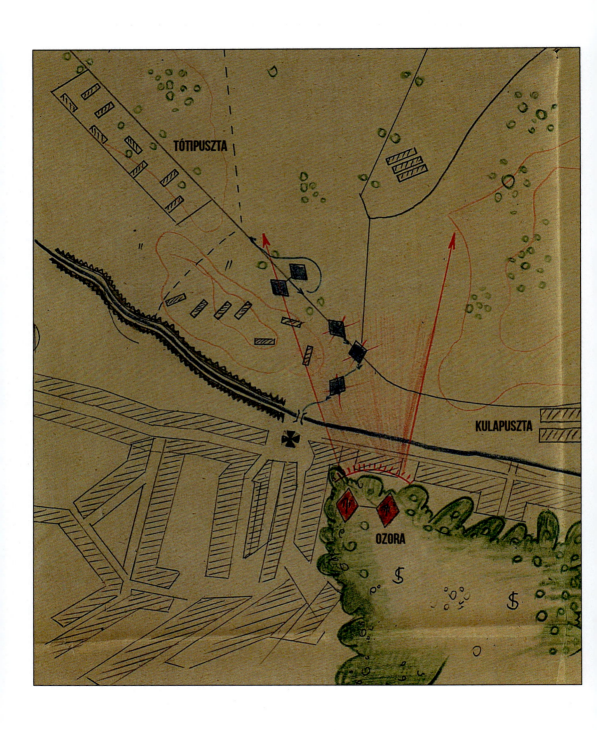

Ambush position of the Soviet 1st Battery/1952nd Self-Propelled Artillery Regiment at Ozora on 11 March 1945

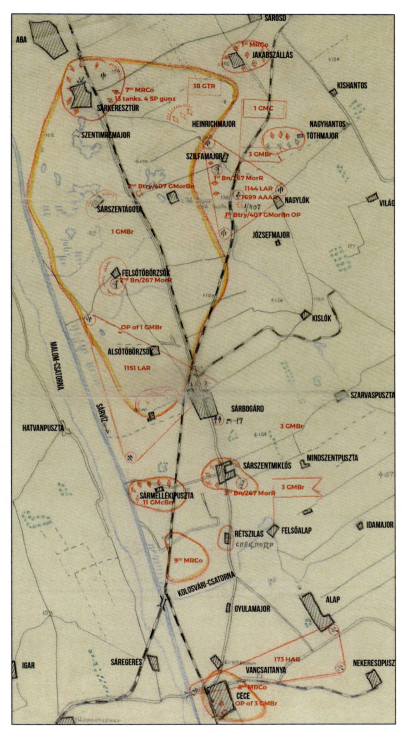

Defences of the Soviet 1st Guards Mechanized Corps on 11 March 1945

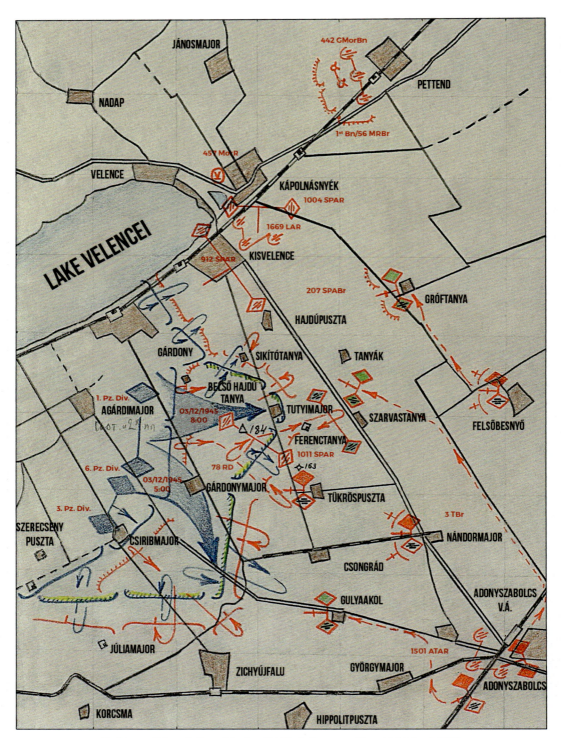

Defences of the reinforced Soviet 23rd Tank Corps on 11 and 12 March 1945

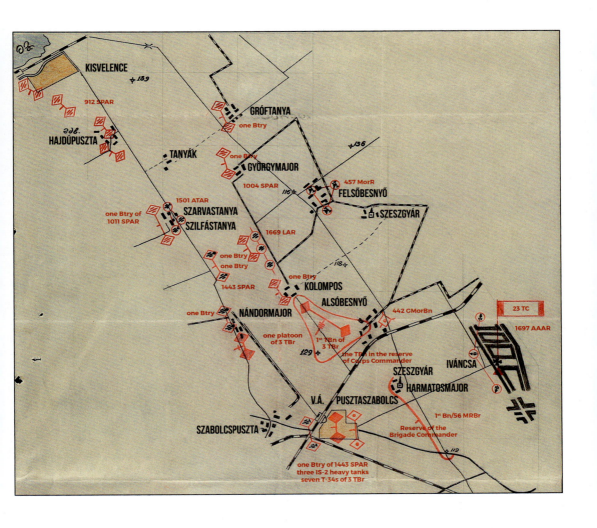

Defences of the Soviet 23rd Tank Corps on 14 March 1945

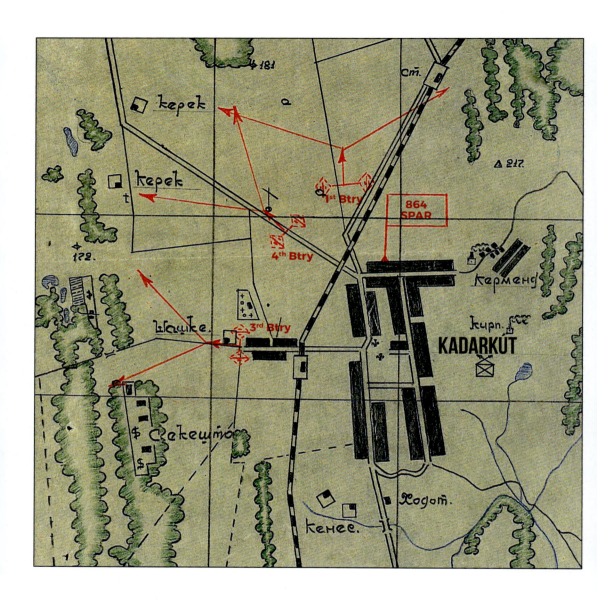

Firing positions of the Soviet 864th Self-Propelled Artillery Regiment/57th Army in the Kadarkút sector around 14 March 1945

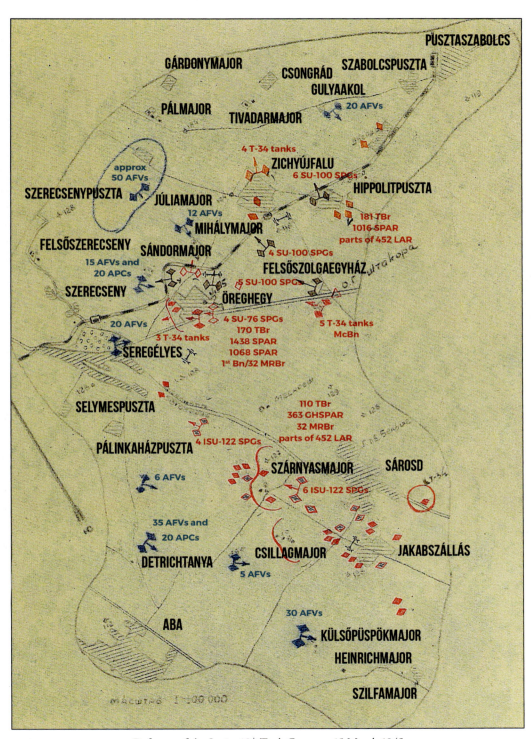

Defences of the Soviet 18th Tank Corps on 15 March 1945

475

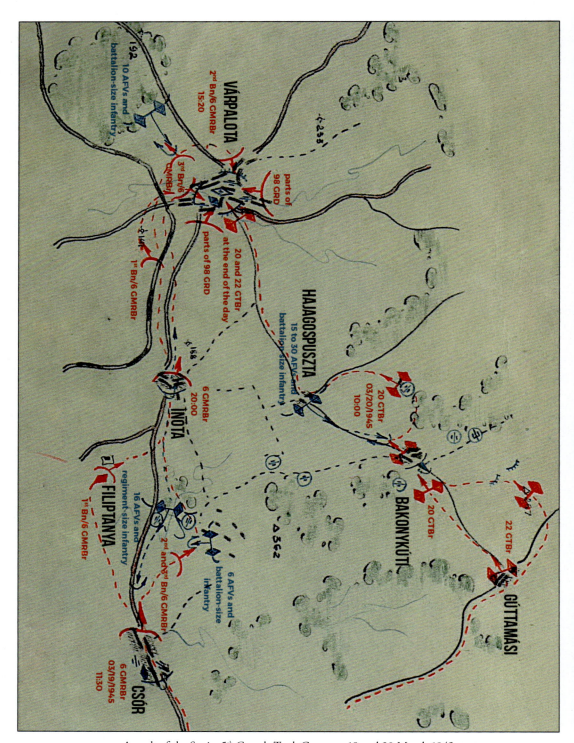

Assault of the Soviet 5th Guards Tank Corps on 19 and 20 March 1945

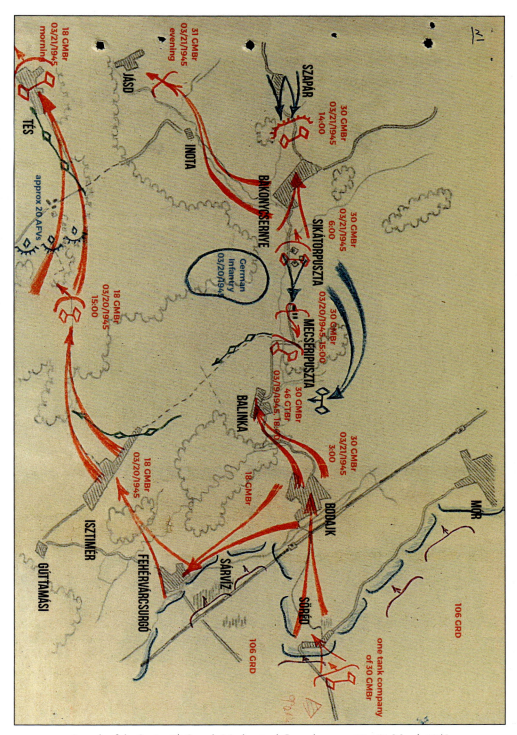

Assault of the Soviet 9th Guards Mechanized Corps between 19 – 21 March 1945

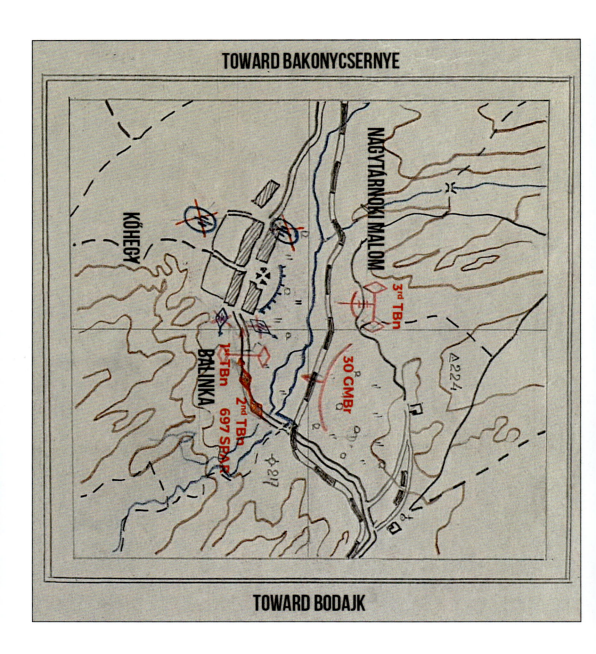

Battles of the Soviet 46th Guards Tank Brigade in the Balinka sector on 19 March 1945

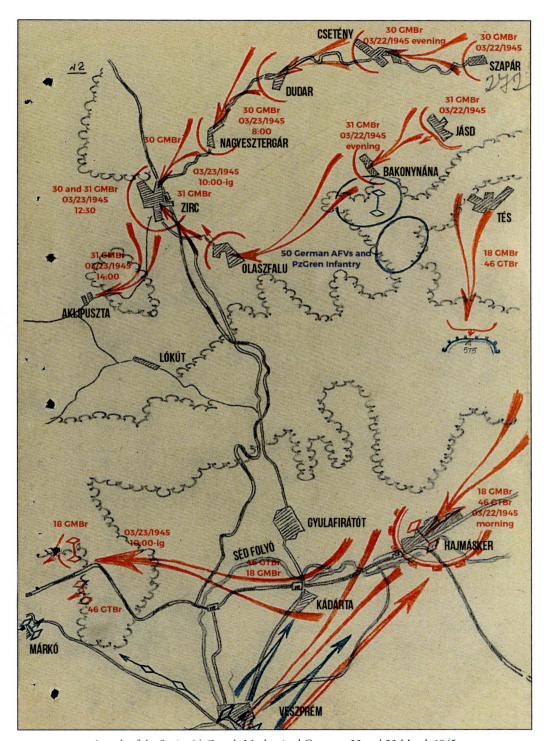

Assault of the Soviet 9th Guards Mechanized Corps on 22 and 23 March 1945

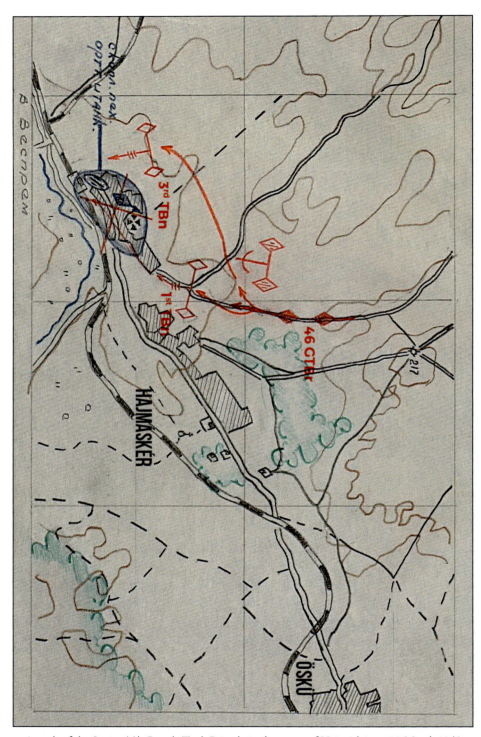

Assault of the Soviet 46th Guards Tank Brigade in the sector of Hajmáskér on 22 March 1945

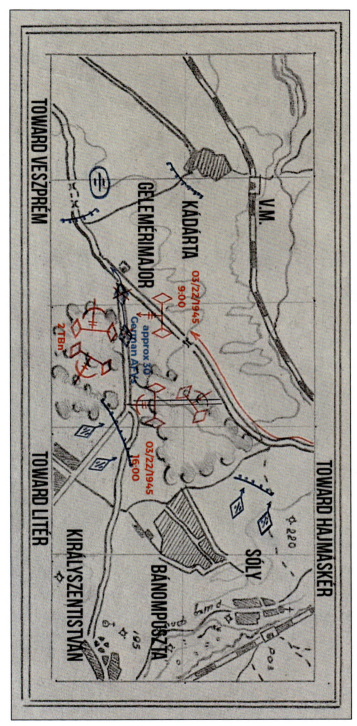

Ambush position of the 46th Guards Tank Brigade between Litér and Gelemérimajor on 22 March 1945

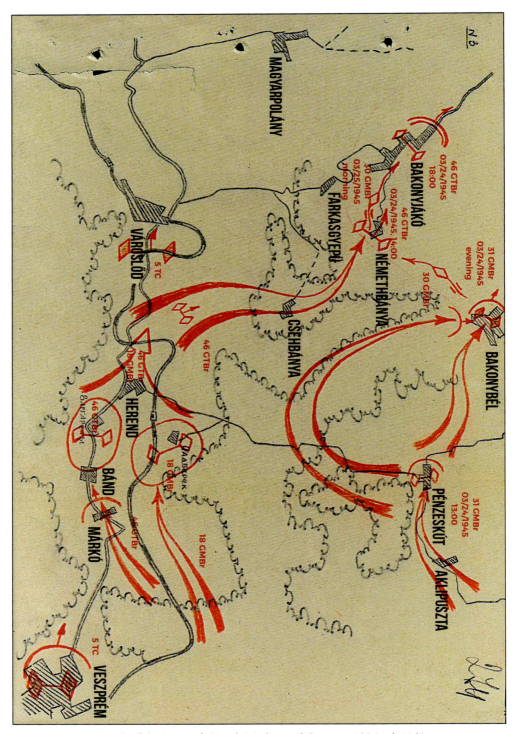

Assault of the Soviet 9th Guards Mechanized Corps on 24 March 1945

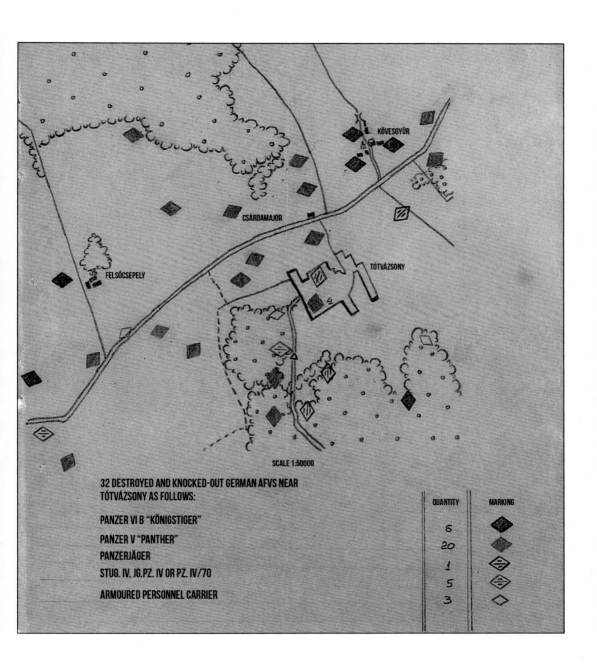

Wrecks of German armoured fighting vehicles in the sector of Tótvázsony, reported by the Soviet 18th Tank Corps on 25 March 1945

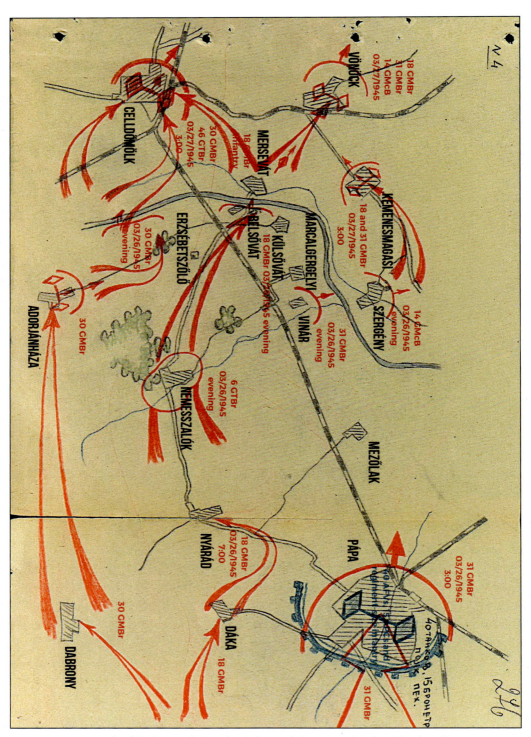

Assault of the Soviet 9th Guards Mechanized Corps on 26 and 27 March 1945

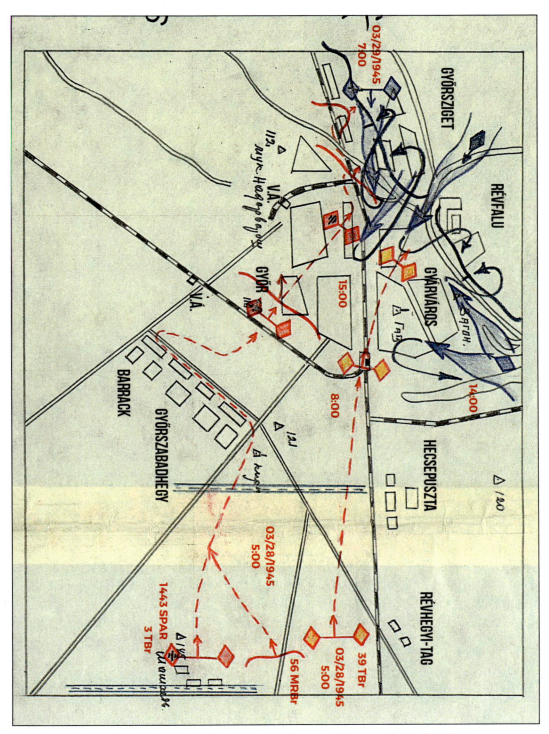

Battles of the Soviet 23rd Tank Corps in the sector of Győr on 28 March 1945

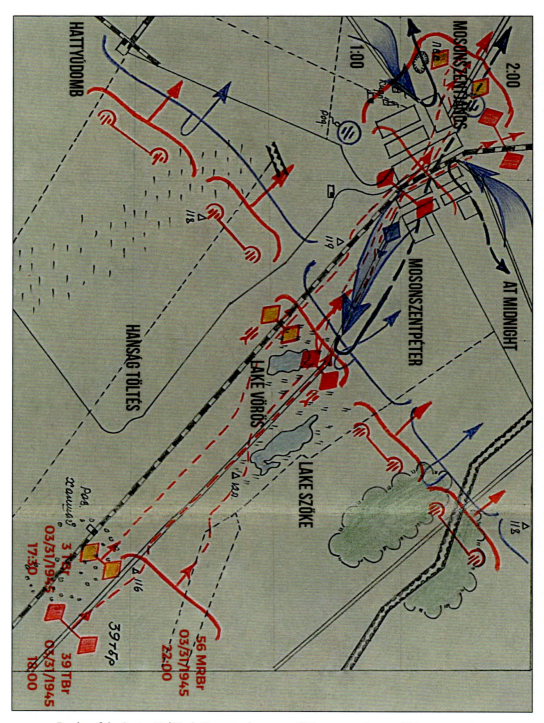

Battles of the Soviet 23rd Tank Corps in the sector of Mosonszentjános and Mosonszentpéter on 31 March and 1 April 1945

LIST OF ABBREVIATIONS

AAAR = Anti-Aircraft Artillery Regiment
AD = Advance Detachment
AFV = Armoured Fighting Vehicle
APC = Armoured Personnel Carrier
Arm. = Armoured
ATAR = Anti-Tank Artillery Regiment
Btry. = Battery
CD = Cavalry Division
Div. = Division
GA = Guards Army
GABD = Guards Airborne Division
GAMR = Guards Artillery Mortar Regiment
GCC = Guards Cavalry Corps
GCD = Guards Cavalry Division
GCR = Guards Cavalry Regiment
GFR = Guards Fortified Region
GHSPAR = Guards Heavy Self-Propelled Artillery Regiment
GMC = Guards Mechanized Corps
GMcBn = Guards Motorcycle Battalion
GMorBn = Guards Mortar Battalion
GMRBn = Guards Motorized Rifle Battalion
GMRBr = Guards Motorized Rifle Brigade
GRC = Guards Rifle Corps
GRD = Guards Rifle Division
GTA = Guards Tank Army
GTBr = Guards Tank Brigade
GTR = Guards Tank Regiment
GTBn = Guards Tank Battalion
HAR = Howitzer Artillery Regiment
Hus. = Hussar (Hungarian)
Inf. = Infantry (Hungarian and German)
Kav. = Cavalry (German)
LAR = Light Artillery Regiment
McBn = Motorcycle Battalion
MGABn = Machine gun Artillery Battalion
MIBr = Marine Infantry Brigade
MorR = Mortar Regiment
MRBr = Motorized Rifle Brigade
MRBn = Motorized Rifle Battalion
MRCo = Motorized Rifle Company
OP = Observation post
Pz. = Panzer (German)
RBn = Rifle Battalion
RCoy = Rifle Company
RC = Rifle Corps
RD = Rifle Division
RGr. = Reichsgrenadier
RR = Rifle Regiment
SPABr = Self-Propelled Artillery Brigade
SPAR = Self-Propelled Artillery Regiment
SPG = Self-Propelled Gun
TBn = Tank Battalion
TBr = Tank Brigade
TC = Tank Corps